Frances Donaldson, daughter of the famous playwright Frederick Lonsdale and wife of Lord Donaldson, the Labour Peer, is the author of *The Marconi Scandal* and books on the great actor managers and Evelyn Waugh. She spent four years working on her major study of *Edward VIII*, some early chapters of which appeared in 1973 in the *Sunday Telegraph*.

D1136633

Frances Donaldson

Edward VIII

Futura Publications Limited
An Omega Book

An Omega Book

First published in Great Britain in 1974
by Weidenfeld & Nicolson Limited

First Omega edition published in 1976
by Futura Publications Limited

ISBN 0 8600 7735 7
Printed in Great Britain by
Hazell Watson & Viney Ltd
Aylesbury, Bucks

Futura Publications Limited
Warner Road, London SE5

ILLUSTRATIONS

*Cover photograph reproduced by kind permission
of the Leeds Art Galleries.*

CONTENTS

INTRODUCTION

Towards the end of 1969 Robin Denniston asked me whether I would write a full-scale biography of HRH the Duke of Windsor. The Duke was then in his seventy-sixth year, and Mr Denniston pointed out that, since his contemporaries were subject to the same laws as the rest of us, they were already becoming a little thin on the ground. If anyone was to get the benefit of the knowledge and understanding of people who had known King Edward VIII, this would not wait forever.

I at first refused because I felt the task too difficult. However, Mr Denniston was very persistent, as publishers have to be, and presently I found myself beginning in a desultory way to read existing literature about the ex-King. Once I allowed myself to do that I was doomed; condemned to struggle for four years for some understanding of this strange man and for words in which to express it.

I did not escape the unaccountable appeal to the emotions, the spur to the curiosity which, if we are honest, the royal presence exerts on most of us, but I realized almost at once that the task was one for a biographer rather than a historian, the reconstruction of a personality, not a period. The life of a king is usually the life of his times, and, although the best official biographers make every attempt to present the person and even some of the warts, it is the place of the man in the political and social history of his reign which gives these volumes their solid importance. The history of Edward VIII is the history of an abdication.

The facts of the Abdication have been told again and again from every point of view and in the greatest possible detail. It is unlikely that a great deal will ever now be added or much fresh light thrown on a story which by constant repetition has been rammed into immutable shape. It seemed to me when I first thought about these things that what no one had yet attempted was a serious explanation of what happened, how these things came to be. How did the beautiful, eager English boy turn into the sad-faced man living between Paris and New York; the most popular Prince of Wales in history into the Duke of Windsor?

It is obvious that there is no easy answer. Only by learning as much as one could of the developing character, by adding detail to detail until one had the man, or something of the man, could one get anywhere near it. This is the task of the biographer – not ignoring the field of the psychologist but not usurping it – to seek out and represent as faithfully as possible the human being behind the history. A desperate enterprise at the best of times, it is a hundred times worse when the subject is a member of the Royal Family.

At about this point in my musings I became aware that it was true that the recollections of the people who actually knew the man were the most valuable and least durable evidence we should ever have. In the years to come there may be an official history of Edward VIII, and then the documents in the case will be revealed. But these will be more in the nature of the private papers of an individual than documents of history: and no matter when the official life is written they will still be there, while only now can the sources of personal recollection be tapped.

The present volume is evidence that I succumbed to this argument and to the fascination of the task. I cannot claim to have completely understood the character of this man who, whatever one may think about it, performed an act unique in the history of kings, nor to have presented a picture finished in detail. Far from it. I claim only to have rescued a great deal that would otherwise be lost, to have thought for four years about it, and to have strewn the ground with clues for others to pick up. I have tried to be impartial in presenting the evidence, but books are not written without emotion and I cannot claim not to have formed my likes and dislikes. I have not tried very hard to disguise these prejudices, but, as far as possible, to show the evidence which might be cited in support of views different from my own.

I had not previously written a book which required a study of the history of the immediate past. One of the first things that struck me when I began to read was how often, when one came upon new or interesting information, it was innocent of any attribution or any indication as to its source. This applied to the most scholarly books, one might say above all to the most scholarly books, where the care with which other sources had been given made these provoking exceptions all the more glaring. My own book will not be an exception to the rule.

The friends and contemporaries of Edward VIII do not wish to go into print. Sometimes this is for reasons which can be easily understood, at others merely from preference. One of them said to me: 'Having avoided publication all my life, I don't want to begin now.' This is a matter of absolutely no importance to the general reader, who would not recognize new material woven into the text as new or old, but even the general reader will wish to have some proof of good faith. I cannot give one of those long lists which are customary thanking people for every sort of service from acknowledging a letter to the loan of private documents, so I have had to devise a method which may do instead. I have marked one copy of the manuscript of the book in my own handwriting with the source of every piece of information or any opinion which cannot be fully documented, and this will be available to historians ten years after the death of the last person whose name occurs in this way. Secondly, I have observed the following rules: (1) I have not stated anything as a fact unless the source for it is unimpeachable or independently corroborated; (2) Where I use 'it is said' or other phrases of that sort, it means that I believe it and have evidence for it, but have been unable to get corroboration.

Since I cannot thank everyone who has helped me I have decided to thank only those who are actually quoted in the text. I have already observed that there are not nowadays so many people living who had access to information about the subject of this biography and, if I mention the names of those who would not object to my doing so, it would greatly narrow the field for speculation about the rest.

However, it is obvious from the text that I owe a very great debt to Mrs Dudley Ward; to Lady Alexandra Metcalfe for permission to quote from Major Metcalfe's letters to her and from her own diaries; and to Miss Monica Baldwin for permission to quote from the notes she made under the title *An Unpublished Page of History* of an account of the abdication given her by her uncle, Stanley Baldwin, when he visited her in a convent in Bruges in the autumn of 1937. I must also thank the following people who have been good enough to give me information either in conversation or by letter or by allowing me to see papers and who are quoted in the text: Earl Mountbatten of Burma, Earl Baldwin of Bewdley, Sir John Balfour, Lady Diana Cooper, Helen, Lady Hardinge of Penshurst, Sir Etienne Dupuch, Sir George Haynes, Sir Martin Lindsay of Dowhill, Professor Rushbrook Williams, Mrs Ronald Tree, Mr Ian Scott, Mr David Shelley Nicholls, Mr Daniel Burlingham, the late Rev. Philip Clayton, the late Mr Ralph Jarvis, the late Mr Sylvester Gates and the late Major Gray Phillips.

I must acknowledge my debt to professional historians and writers. I have experienced the most kind help wherever I have sought it and wish particularly to record my gratitude to: Mr Keith Middlemas and Mr John Barnes, Professor Donald Watt, Mr Brian Inglis, Mr H. Montgomery Hyde, Mr Ladislas Farago and Mr David Irving. I must also acknowledge a particular indebtedness to *Abdication* by Brian Inglis, *Baldwin* by Middlemas & Barnes, and *Baldwin: The Unexpected Prime Minister* by H. Montgomery Hyde. I have to thank the executors of the late Lord Monckton and Sir Edward Peacock for permission to quote from their notes made at the time of the Abdication and afterwards. And finally I have to thank the Foreign Office, the India Office, the Public Record Office and Queen's University Archives, Kingston, Ontario, for permission to quote from the official documents, which are identified in the list of sources. Many thanks also to the librarians in all these libraries and last but never least the librarians at the London Library.

I want to thank Mrs Eileen Crisp for typing and re-typing the manuscript and also for her kindness in inventing methods for keeping my papers in order.

Finally I want to thank the following for kind permission to reproduce extracts from their works: Randolph Churchill and William Heinemann, *Lord Derby – King of Lancashire*; Lord Monckton and Allen & Overy, *The Monckton Papers*; James Pope-Hennessy and Allen & Unwin, *Queen Mary*; John Wheeler-Bennett and Macmillan, *King George VI*; Michael Joseph, *The Heart Has Its Reasons*; Baring Brothers for permission to reproduce extracts from Sir Edward Peacock's Notes; and Paul Channon for permission to reproduce extracts from Sir Henry Channon's diaries, *Chips*.

PART 1
PRINCE OF WALES

I

CHILDHOOD

King George v had been married for seventeen years when he came to the throne, and, because of this and because he and Queen Mary were so well suited to each other, their life together has come to be regarded in twentieth-century terms. Wars and revolutions have swept crowned heads from their thrones and reduced the number of marriageable princes and princesses, and the effect has been to widen the choice of the Royal Family, so that the arranged marriage, between two princelings who may have hardly met, has become a thing of the past. But in 1891 Queen Victoria surveyed the eligible princesses with an expert eye and chose Princess May of Teck as the one most suitable to be Queen.* Prince Albert Victor (Prince Eddy), the Queen's grandson and, in succession to his father, her heir, thereupon proposed marriage to Princess May and was joyfully accepted. Soon after he died of pneumonia – his sad and terrible death watched over by his young fiancée as well as his family – and a wife had then to be chosen for his brother. Rather to the embarrassment of the Royal Family, it quickly became apparent that Princess May was still unrivalled as a candidate for the hand of the heir to the throne.† It was a matter of chance, though a happy one, that the Duke of York was, by character and temperament, the more suitable both for the crown and to the tastes and affections of his future wife.

Princess May was a girl of serious and purposeful character. Mr Pope-Hennessy says of her:

---

* It would not be correct to suggest that the sons of the Prince of Wales had hardly met Princess May. They had known her since childhood.

† Queen Alexandra seems to have been the person who minded it most but there was an exact precedent in her own family, her sister Dagmar having been engaged to the Grand Duke Nicholas of Russia, the heir to the throne, and on his death having married his brother, the Grand Duke Alexander.

Her withdrawn, reserved manner, her cool, even temperament, made it unlikely that Princess May would ever inspire a violent emotion. Nor was she herself an emotional person. It seemed most probable that any marriage she might make would be predominantly a reasonable one: not in the exact French sense of a marriage of reason, but rather a reasonable marriage to a reasonable man of reasonable rank and fortune, which would offer her remarkable character a field for reasonable activity.[1]

He tells us several times that when she was young she was high spirited and gay, although he is rather pushed to illustrate these qualities; and from photographs one can see that her looks were charming, if not exactly beautiful. In any case, it was not for her looks or high spirits that Queen Victoria chose her, but because, naturally of a good and reliable disposition, she was steeped in the history and traditions of the British Royal Family and trained from her earliest days to revere them. She was cut out to be Queen.

The Duke of York, having modestly announced that he believed he could love someone who returned his love, found no difficulty in falling in love with Princess May. 'I adore you, sweet May,'[2] he wrote to her quite early in their married life, while she, more self-contained, wrote to her old governess, Madame Bricka, 'Georgie is a dear ... he adores me which is touching,' and added, 'I feel as if I had been married for years and quite settled down.'[3]

When this couple had been married for a few years there is no doubt that their relationship to each other was neither less close nor more prosaic than that of most happily married couples, and while this may be partly attributed to the fact that, through birth, inclination and training, they both found it natural and wholly satisfying to devote their lives to the exalted roles they had to play, it owed a great deal to the exceptional domesticity of the males of this family.

It was nevertheless remarkable, not least because, having been married by arrangement, the young couple unquestioningly accepted arrangements which could have seemed tolerable only in the circumstances of the old arranged marriages. They were so seldom alone. Immediately after her wedding the Duchess of York had to appoint a lady-in-waiting, and Lady Eva Greville came to join the Duke's equerry, Colonel Derek Keppel, in constant attendance on them. Presently other ladies and gentlemen were appointed, and from the first those in attendance were present in the dining-room at all meals and in the drawing-room at tea-time and after dinner. The lack of privacy was completed by the small rooms and narrow passages of the house in which the Duke and Duchess of York (after Queen Victoria's death in 1901 the Prince and Princess of Wales) spent most of their time for the seventeen years before he became King. 'Until you have seen York Cottage, you will never understand my father,'[4] the Duke of Windsor told Harold Nicolson when the latter was at work on his biography of George V; and in turn each royal biographer has expressed the sense of astonishment which York Cottage, Sandringham, invariably provokes.

It was originally built for the male guests of King Edward VII, then Prince of Wales, because the vast new house at Sandringham could not contain them, and it was called 'The Bachelors' Cottage'. Re-naming it and adding on to it, the Prince of Wales gave it to his son as a wedding present. The young family who were presently born to the Duke and Duchess of York moved with their parents to other royal residences in London, Windsor and Scotland at certain times of the year, but York Cottage was their home. Sir Harold Nicolson, who has called it 'this most undesirable residence', has given a general description of it.

It was, and remains, a glum little villa, encompassed by thickets of laurel and rhododendron, shadowed by huge Wellingtonias and separated by an abrupt rim of lawn from a pond, at the edge of which a leaden pelican gazes in dejection upon the water lilies and bamboos. The local brown stone in which the house was constructed is concealed by rough-cast which in its turn is enlivened by very imitation Tudor beams. The rooms inside, with their fumed oak surrounds, their white overmantels framing oval mirrors, their Doulton tiles and stained glass fanlights, are indistinguishable from those of any Surbiton or Upper Norwood home.[5]

At the time of the Duke's marriage the plumbing was primitive, the bedrooms like cubicles, while the lady-in-waiting slept in a cell above the pantry 'separated from it by the thinnest of flooring through which every sound penetrated'.[6] As for the servants, the Duke of York himself said he supposed they slept in the trees. When his family increased he constantly added on to the house until outside it was 'all gables and hexagonal turrets and beams and tiny balconies', while inside it 'became a rabbit-warren of tiny rooms connected by narrow passages, in which royal pages and tall footmen would sit or stand, blocking the way'. The bathrooms were insufficient and before meals 'the whole house reeked of food'.[7]

The Duke was responsible for the decoration. He knew so little of his future bride that he thought to save her trouble by preparing everything for her coming, and both here and at York House, which they were given for their use in London, he spent hours with someone he called 'the Maples man'. His own sitting-room was darkened by shrubberies outside the windows and the walls were covered by a red cloth originally designed for the trousers of the French army. Strangest of all when one considers the wealth and possessions of the Royal Family, the pictures were reproductions of some of the more popular acquisitions of the Chantrey bequest. Too large and too full of footmen to be unremarkable in Surbiton or Upper Norwood, York Cottage is in its own context a monument to the eccentricity of the family who lived there.

In the course of time the Duke and Duchess of York, with their public and ceremonial private life and their restricted human responses, their inescapable sense of vocation, gave birth to five sons and a daughter – children born to an especial load of sorrow. Five of them were born at York Cottage, but the eldest was born at White Lodge, in Richmond Park, today occupied by the Royal Ballet School, but at that time the home of the Duke and Duchess of Teck. (The younger children were born at York Cottage for the endearingly human reason that the Duke of York could not a second time stand the long association with his mother-in-law. 'I am very fond of dear Maria,' he wrote to his wife, 'but I assure you I wouldn't go through the six weeks I spent at White Lodge again for anything.')[8]

With the birth of their eldest son, the Duke and Duchess of York immediately became involved in a covert struggle with Queen Victoria as to the name he should bear. It was the Queen's wish that her own son should be known as Albert Edward when he became King and that all his male descendants should bear the name Albert to the end of time, forming a Coburg line as formerly there had been Tudor, Stuart and Brunswick lines. In turn each of her children can be seen determined to avert the name Albert. On this occasion the Duke of York expressed to his grandmother his wish to name his son Edward, after his dead brother, Prince Eddy, to which the Queen replied that the real name of 'dear Eddy' had been not Edward but Albert Victor. There is therefore a fine inconsequence in the fact that, although the baby was finally christened Edward Albert Christian George Andrew Patrick David (the last four after the patron saints of England, Scotland, Ireland and Wales), he was always known to his family as David.

To mark his birth telegrams were received from all the royal families of Europe and every public body in England, while a marquee was erected at White Lodge where hundreds of people signed the book. Crowds lined the roads from the station when Queen Victoria travelled to Richmond to see her great-grandson, and at Sandringham the Prince of Wales gave a party in celebration. *The Times* remarked that never before in the history of these islands had the sovereign seen three male descendants in the direct line of inheritance, and went on to say:*

The young Prince is heir to a noble inheritance, not only to a station of unequalled dignity, but more than all to the affection of a loyal people, which it will be his office to keep and to make his own. Our heartfelt prayer is that he may prove worthy of so great a trust.[9]

And in the House of Commons, speaking on a motion 'that a humble

---

* During the early pages of this book it is a little difficult to indicate by such titles as 'Prince of Wales' exactly which of these heirs is being spoken of. It may help to remember that Prince Edward was six in 1901 when Queen Victoria died and that soon after this his father, the Duke of York, became Prince of Wales in succession to his father King Edward VII; and he was almost sixteen in 1910 when King Edward died, soon after which he became Prince of Wales himself.

address be presented to Her Majesty to congratulate Her Majesty on the birth of a son to His Royal Highness the Duke of York and Her Royal Highness the Duchess of York', Mr Keir Hardie made a speech which is so eminently quotable that it is unlikely anyone will ever write about this prince without reference to it. Having remarked that the Motion sought to 'elevate to an importance it does not deserve an event of every day occurrence', he said:

From his childhood onward this boy will be surrounded by sycophants and flatterers by the score and will be taught to believe himself as of a superior creation. A line will be drawn between him and the people he is to be called upon some day to reign over. In due course, following the precedent which has already been set he will be sent on a tour round the world, and probably rumours of a morganatic alliance will follow (loud cries of Oh! Oh! and Order!) and the end of it all will be the country will be called upon to pay the bill.[10]

During the early years of their married life the Duke and Duchess of York were not called upon to perform many public duties and until 1901 when, after the death of Queen Victoria, they went on tour in Australia, they lived, except in ways that have already been described, lives that were not immensely different from those of a country squire and his wife. The upbringing of their young children might have been expected to be much the same and certainly not less propitious than that of hundreds of other upper-class children of the day.

At York Cottage nurseries had been added on the unambitious scale of the rest of the house and, although these would always be waited on by footmen, they consisted of only two rooms. When the family had been increased by the addition of another boy and then a girl, the three children and their nurse shared one small room by day and slept together in the other at night – a circumstance which was not particularly unusual then, although it might be thought inadequate by most middle-class mothers of today. All upper-class children were reared in isolation from their parents whom in many families they saw once, at the most twice, a day when they had been specially dressed and prepared to meet them, and it was quite common for their parents to be uneducated in child care and subject to the conventions of the time. The only obvious difference between the routine arrangements for the royal children and those for hundreds of others throughout the land was that, when they were dressed and taken to the drawing-room to meet their mother, she was normally attended by a lady-in-waiting. There were, however, other differences and these were for the most part unlucky.

At this time there reigned in the nurseries of England, in complete charge of the children and in respectful control of the parents as far as anything affecting these was concerned, that historical character, the English nanny. The nanny at her best had a vocation – a generous vocation to give her charges the mother-love which is all important to the early years of the human child, to ensure them a stable and secure background, a nursery fire and an aproned lap; to teach them a moral sense and a satisfying, if sometimes oddly conceived, sense of right and wrong; to read to them and tell them stories; to supply in fact all the things that are necessary to children but which through the conventions of the day were often withheld by their parents. Because the arrangement was a bad one, the nanny herself has fallen into some disrepute, but she was often a woman of strong maternal instincts who, having failed to marry, loved the children she cared for as though they were her own. She was an absolutely necessary part of the system and only she could prevent her charges becoming what in modern sociological language is called 'deprived'.

The nurse who had charge of the children at York Cottage drew attention to herself after she had been with the family three years by having a nervous breakdown, when it was discovered among other things that she had not had a day off during all this time. This nurse, who was 'sadistic and incompetent' was totally unfitted for her job.[11] She adored Prince Edward and, when she took him to the drawing-room to see his parents, she indulged a strangely perverted love for him by pinching him or twisting his arm, so that he bawled and screamed on entering the room and was speedily returned to her. Her feeling for him, although distorted by her insane possessiveness was, nevertheless, one of love. Prince Albert she ignored and neglected, and fed so badly that he developed a chronic stomach trouble. No one has attempted to explain how these things could have happened in this over-filled house with its ladies-in-waiting and its thinly partitioned walls, nor how such an unsuitable nurse came to enter the service of the Duke and Duchess of York in the first place.

There is no doubt that King George v and Queen Mary failed in their relationships with their children and were for different reasons temperamentally unsuited to parenthood. It is more common for parents to be lacking in deep affection for young children than is sometimes believed and it is noticeable that in societies where married couples hand their babies over to the care of servants they tend to check the development of their own parental love. In addition the King and Queen suffered the handicap of majesty, which was bound to increase both the awe in which it was proper for their sons to hold them and their own mortification in face of an inability to predict or control the behaviour of very young children. The King particularly was afflicted with that kind of irrational pride which causes people to see themselves in a permanently superior relationship to their children and this affliction would, as Prince Edward and Prince Albert grew to maturity, become very pronounced and in a large measure be responsible for the breakdown in trust and affection which occurred between himself and his elder son.

Yet the King was affectionate and fond of children and when his own children were born he was unaffectedly happy as a family man, bathing the babies and playing with them. He was by nature a disciplinarian and a martinet. In his youth he had embraced a naval career with enthusiasm and he was tidy, punctual and hard working. He was also very excitable. 'Since he was impetuous by nature,' Mr John Gore says, 'he gave vent to his feelings instantly and without reserve.'[12] And Sir John Wheeler-Bennett adds that the Queen found it difficult 'to stand between them [the children] and the sudden gusts of their father's wrath'.[13] These two sentences alone make it plain that in moments of stress the King, like his father before him, exercised little restraint with his Household or with his children.* But whereas his servants and courtiers understood him and were equipped to deal with him, his children were not.

Yet it is asserted that he was wonderfully good and disarming with other people's children. He loved to joke and chaff with the young, and, when he stayed with his friends for shooting parties, he was 'the jolliest and least formal of guests'.[15] His young friends had most probably been taught how to behave in his presence, however, because the King, like Colonel Blimp, the famous character of the Low cartoons, was a stickler for tradition. He believed that the customs and fashions of his youth were immutable and he attached a moral significance to such things as dress or speech. A new kind of hair cut or the wrong pair of shoes were quite strong evidence of going downhill, and might earn the final condemnation, a cad. 'I am devoted to children and good with them,' he said once, 'but they grow up, and you can only watch them going their own way and can do nothing to stop them. Nowadays young people don't seem to care what they do or what people think.'[16] There is nothing very unusual in such views, which can be heard in every generation, but people who hold them with too great complacency usually cause their children to suffer embarrassment or fear, or a mixture of both.

The King's temperamental qualities were distorted in his relations with his own children by anxiety, and this was particularly so in his dealings with his eldest son. Here he found himself in the uncharted realm of the education proper to the heir to the throne. Prince Albert and Queen Victoria had once attempted to devise the ideal upbringing for the future sovereign and had reduced Edward VII as a child to a physical and nervous exhaustion which used to bring on screaming fits. King Edward in his turn had been determined that his own children should never suffer anything of the sort and he and Queen Alexandra were by nature affectionate and indulgent parents. They had, perhaps, been lucky in Canon Dalton, and also in the fact that the Naval career decided upon for their second son

* Speaking of King Edward VII, Sir Philip Magnus writes: 'His habitual generosity and thoughtfulness, his natural kindness and heartfelt desire to see everyone around him happy and smiling inspired deep affection; but Frederick Ponsonby recorded that "even his most intimate friends were all terrified of him" and Ponsonby's daughter, Loelia (Duchess of Westminster) added that "his angry bellow, once heard, could never be forgotten".'[14]

had been so well suited to the tastes and character of the future King. Far less tolerant by nature than his father, George V was oppressed by the necessity to inculcate in his children good character and seriousness of purpose, and there were some branches of their education in which he would have liked to see them excel. What in another man might have been a rather low desire for self-glorification through his children, must be credited in him as a very real understanding of the importance to the monarchy of the qualities he tried to instil.

Consequently, he was too often harsh and fault-finding, while his anxiety spoiled even his most genial characteristics. The jolly chaff became in his own family that rather frightening kind of banter in which parents indulge who are distrustful of their children. We have not been given examples but this nervous bantering is quite common and goes something like this. 'Where have you been? Cutting up the paths with your bicycles, I suppose.' The children were nearly always uneasy in his presence and sometimes reduced to what Harold Nicolson has described in words that have clearly been very carefully chosen as 'nervous trepidation'.[17]

Yet all who knew him are agreed that he was kind and humane and he is vehemently defended against charges of jealousy and the insane hostility the earlier Georges felt towards their heirs, as also against any streak of sadistic cruelty. This defence has become necessary in later years because of the work of two much-quoted authors. The first of these is Randolph Churchill who, in his life of the seventeenth Earl of Derby, gives the following account of a conversation for which he says he is indebted to Harold Nicolson.

Derby was distressed by the way King George bullied his children, and he ventured one day at Knowsley, when they were walking up and down the terrace, to raise the subject, justifying his remarks on the ground that he was the King's oldest friend. He said what delightful companions his own children had become for him when they grew up, and begged the King to realize that the royal children were on the verge of manhood and that he was missing very much in life by frightening them and continuing to treat them as if they were naughty schoolboys. Lord Derby told me that the King remained silent for some four minutes after this and then said: 'My father was frightened of his mother; I was frightened of my father, and I am damned well going to see to it that my children are frightened of me.'[18]

This story has the two qualities of being irresistibly quotable and rather disagreeable if taken at its face value, since it suggests that the King was deliberately cruel or at the best an unpleasant bully. It will be argued here that it should not be taken at its face value, although it is so strong in its attributions. In the first place, if it were accurate in detail, one would still have to allow for the fact that the King was quite unused to being spoken to in this way even by his greatest friends, and would almost certainly have reacted strongly and in anger. In the second, to people who knew the two men the story seems wrong in almost every particular.

Lord Derby was an exceedingly upright, generous and benevolent man, but his desire to please and his lack of confidence in his own judgment earned him the name 'Genial Judas', although he was not treacherous, only weak. Haig once wrote of him: 'Like a feather pillow, he bears the mark of the last person who sat on him.'[19] He is really not the man for this story, although he might well have spoken to the King in some more tentative way, saying perhaps how much pleasure he found in the company of his own sons.

An air of unreality is then given to the whole episode by the statement that there was a silence of nearly four minutes after Lord Derby had made his remarks. The picture of these two men, walking up and down the terrace with Lord Derby refraining, in the appalling quiet, from any kind of backtracking, or, in the phrase Lloyd George once used about him, 'looping the loop', is too much to swallow.

Finally, and most importantly, the King was not really frightened of his father, nor Edward VII of his mother. There is a shade of distinction here which should be most accurately expressed. There is no doubt that both men stood in great awe of their parents – as who did not? – and this was not only on account of their majesty, but also because of their personal characteristics. Edward VII suffered hideously as a child from his parents' endeavours to make him the ideal prince and he was under his mother's authority until he was an old man, but he was courageous by nature and he did not give the impression of being seriously frightened of her. He always stood up to her and sometimes defied her in matters relating to his own family, and he wrote to her with humour about the 'jobations' she sent him. And the strongest emotion King Edward felt for his own family was his adoration of his second son. Late in his life it was a torment for him when they were separated, and Sir Philip Magnus speaks of his being 'utterly devoted' to his son and of their 'ideal relationship'. 'We are more like brothers,' he wrote to him once, 'than like father and son.'[20]

If there was room within this happy relationship for a feeling of overwhelming awe on the part of the son, this is not unusual in children, nor was King George alone in thinking it desirable. But this is not the kind of construction which has been put on the King's alleged remarks to Lord Derby. In his subsequently published *Diaries and Letters* Harold Nicolson gives a different source for the story and one which suggests (what is true) that it had achieved a wide circulation long before it reached print.

At dinner I sit next to Cromer. He makes interesting points about George v. (1) He believed that Princes ought to be brought up in fear of their father: 'I was always frightened of my father; they must be frightened of me.'[21]

This version is less portentous and more plausible.

The other writer who might be read as suggesting that the King was unnaturally lacking in affection, at least for his eldest son, and severe to his children, is the Duke of Windsor himself. On the first page of his autobiography he tells us that his father recorded his birth with the words 'A sweet little boy was born'[22] and he comments rather wryly that he thinks it unlikely his father was ever inspired to use such words about him again. Later, speaking of his childhood, he tells us that nothing would ever be so 'disconcerting to the spirit'[23] as a message delivered by a footman that the King wished to see him in the library.

The Duke of Windsor wrote altogether three books, all with the help of what is known as a 'ghost'. On all three he managed to stamp evidence of a personal style, in spite of the ghostly collaborator, and the faintly ironical tone of these sentences is very typical of it. It is difficult to be certain how much allowance to make for this kind of almost self-deprecating irony, but without it there would be nothing in his account of his childhood to suggest that he suffered anything more positively cruel than sternness, stupidity and impatience. His description of what followed at the interviews in the library is no worse or more frightening than was probably normal in any Victorian library and in fact comes as an anti-climax. Sometimes his father merely wished to show him something, although usually he wished to scold him for being dirty or late or making too much noise, or to deliver one of the vast number of 'don'ts' which were an intrinsic part of the educational system of the time. The truth seems to be that the King was unimaginative and very opinionated, had a rather tiresome sense of humour, was over-anxious and maintained an attitude of hectoring disciplinarianism to his sons long after it ceased to be appropriate. But people who knew him are genuinely horrified at the suggestion that he was deliberately cruel or threatening to his children in any way which might by itself induce 'nervous trepidation'. These charges are too crude an explanation of the far more ordinary and at the same time more subtly tragic situation caused by the almost total inability of this family to communicate with one another. Both the King and the Queen wrote charming letters to each other and to their children but the King as well as the Queen was almost completely inhibited from any more personal expression of affection or any intimate exchange of ideas. Harold Nicolson has made it plain how much the King depended on his wife, how important their relationship was to him. Nevertheless, he almost never put any of his feelings into words. In addition it seems probable that the distance and hostility that grew between himself and his eldest son was due in part, as family hostility so often is, as much to the qualities they shared as to those in which they differed. As his children grew to manhood the King's desire to dominate them and to hold them captive to his authority certainly became excessive and had undoubtedly damaging effects, but it seems likely that in their childhood his shortcomings were not so very different from, or so much greater than, those of many another

Victorian papa. In households where there is some warm and stable influence that supports them, children become acclimatized to grumbling and hectoring, irritability and jokes they cannot understand, just as they do to the east wind and having their hair combed.

Without it, they are a prey to fear. In childhood the princes surely suffered less from the failings of their father than from their almost total estrangement from their mother, the coldness with which she rejected them. After all the curious story of the possessive, pinching nursemaid rests on the assumption by everyone concerned that if, over a period of time, her eldest son, not yet three, screamed with pain in her presence, he would instantly be removed from it.

The earliest years are the most formative and during these years the most necessary part of a child's environment is his mother's love. Given the security of mother-love, the child will gradually and naturally be weaned from his dependence on it, whereas denied it, he may seek it in one form or another for the rest of his life. Queen Mary's exceptionally reserved and undemonstrative temperament made it impossible for her to give her children the love and affection which is taken for granted in happier homes. From the first she disliked the period of pregnancy and the physical aspects of childbirth and held herself aloof from the demonstrations of intimacy and affection these were apt to provoke. The Empress Frederick described her as 'very cold and stiff and very unmaternal'[24] while someone who knew her in later life summed up what dozens of people bear witness to by saying: 'Queen Mary had nothing of the mother at all.'

The Queen's inability to communicate with other people was extended to almost all human relationships. Thus she could not deal with her own staff or correct or dismiss the people who served her, so that if the arrangements for the children were unsatisfactory it was the King who altered them. With her children she reminds one of a very shy person in an enforced contact with someone else's. Speaking of her first child she wrote to his father in terms in which the note of humour does not disguise a genuine difficulty. 'I really believe he begins to like me at last, he is most civil to me.'[25] And, although as her family grew up she began to feel more at ease with them and to perform many of the normal maternal functions such as reading aloud or teaching them little things, she never had the slightest doubt where her first duty lay. 'I have always to remember,' she said of her children, 'that their father is also their King.'[26]

When Prince Edward was three years old and his nurse's mental instability was discovered, her place was taken by the under-nurse Mrs Bill, who came to be known to the family as 'Lala'. For a few years she seems to have provided a stable presence and the Duke of Windsor attributes to her, as he does to his mother, all the conventional virtues. Yet there is no evidence to suggest that she had the exceptional character that would have been necessary to replace all that was lacking in this nursery. Certainly the

Prince of Wales was aware of the coldness of the climate in which he was nurtured. As a young man he was very much devoted to the two little daughters of Mrs Dudley Ward and one day, scolding one of them, for some reckless act, he said: 'You see, you are so much loved you are spoilt. You have no idea of the lives of many children.' And he told her that in his own childhood he had never known love. There were servants, he explained, who seemed to love him, but he could never forget that this might be because he was heir to the throne.

However, above all it should not be overlooked that with his three eldest sons the King was dealing with children of a highly nervous temperament. Children vary very much in their response to their parents even in the same family. The King's fourth son, Prince George, was of a totally different temperament and neither as a child nor apparently as a young man – the age at which his brothers suffered so much from their father's domination – was he easily perturbed. In illustration of this, a story is told of a game he invented to while away the time at the magnificent luncheon parties which took place on shooting days. Unlike the rest of his family he did not care for this sport and he therefore imposed a fine on anyone who failed to avoid the word 'shoot' during the course of the meal. This became progressively more difficult to avoid the nearer one sat to the King, who is said to have noted his son's activities, while continuing to talk as he chose. And Howlett, the King's valet, speaking of the two elder sons, once remarked to a member of his Household: 'These boys are so silly with the King. There never was a kinder man.'

Prince Albert stammered from an early age and gave other signs of a nervous disposition; but the half-controlled physical indications that the heir to the throne was at least equally highly strung have attracted less attention. People find it so difficult to believe in the vulnerability of princes that the constant tie-pulling and cigarette-smoking of the Prince of Wales as he grew to manhood passed as an extra charm, an unexpected and delightful human modesty, instead of being understood for what they were, the outward signs of an extreme inner tension.

When they were children Prince Edward and Prince Albert were also terrified in the presence of their great-grandmother, although it is not certain whether their terror was caused by the Queen herself or by her Indian servants. In any case, they would frequently burst into tears in her presence for no very obvious reason which 'both saddened and annoyed the Queen, who would ask, with the petulance of old age, what she had done wrong now. It also mortified the children's parents.'[27] In the then state of knowledge, it is not surprising that this mortification led the anxious parents to believe that what was needed was more 'character-building', rather than less. Prince Albert also suffered nervous rages, not unlike those his grandfather and his 'impetuous' father had suffered before him. 'You must really give up losing your temper when you make a mistake in a sum,' King

George wrote to him once. 'We all make mistakes sometimes, remember now you are nearly twelve years old and ought no longer to behave like a little child of six.'[28] And he wrote to the boy's tutor to be strict with him. Yet so different is the world from how it is represented to a boy of twelve that at about the same time we find King George (then Prince of Wales) writing to his secretary, Sir Arthur Bigge, in the following unpretentiously repentant terms: 'I fear sometimes I have lost my temper with you and often been very rude, but I am sure you know me well enough by now to know that I did not mean it.'[29]

However, much has been made of the mishandling of these boys in their childhood, and it should never be forgotten that in their family environment they had the benefit of noble ideals and a strong sense of purpose, and that their parents and grandparents were all people of a very high and, in the circumstances, surprising degree of natural goodness. And, if their parents were excessively strict, and had temperamental difficulties in communication, their grandparents suffered no such constraints, but adored them openly and spoiled them considerably. There are several charming stories of Prince Edward as a child, and of these the following is both amusing and revealing. It is said that a tailor's assistant had called at York House with a suit for Prince Edward to try on and was waiting in the passage outside the nursery when the little Prince rushed out to her. 'Come in,' he said, 'there's nobody here.' She replied that she thought she had better wait, the time might not be convenient. 'There's nobody here,' he persisted. 'Nobody that matters, only grandpapa!'[30]

As soon as the children were old enough to start lessons their nurse, Mrs Bill, was joined by Madame Bricka, their mother's old governess. Then, when Prince Edward was seven, he and Prince Albert were handed over to the care of a valet, Frederick Finch, who stayed with them in one capacity or another until he finally became Prince Edward's butler. In 1901, when the Duke and Duchess of York were on tour in Australia after the death of Queen Victoria, King Edward and Queen Alexandra took charge of their grandchildren and their whole entourage, and took them with them wherever the court went. They liked children to be 'romps' and their own boys had been very wild as children. Now they had their grandchildren constantly with them, and encouraged them to run about and show off even in the dining-room, and mix freely with the guests. On one occasion 'Grandpapa' dodged the disciplinary presence of Madame Bricka for two whole weeks at Sandringham by the simple expedient of leaving her in London. One little anecdote from this time shows Prince Edward acting as mouthpiece for his grandfather's jokes. Sir Felix Semon, the King's doctor and a specialist in throat diseases, shot by mistake an underweight stag and became the butt of King Edward's humour. A few days later at the shooting luncheon the little Prince was sent up to Sir Felix to ask 'Have you killed a little staggie today, Sir Felix?' 'Who set you on to this Prince Eddie?' Semon asked, and the child replied triumphantly: 'Grandpapa.'[31]

So strongly did the Duchess of York feel about this spoiling of her children that she, who had obediently accepted the complete authority of her parents-in-law, even on such matters as the planting of her own garden at Sandringham, wrote in complaint and Queen Alexandra was forced to protest:

> You ask me about Bricka and his french – well all I can say is that she has been giving him lessons & had *him to herself all the time here* & *at Windsor* – since you left excepting our two visits to Sandringham – The reason we did not take her there was that [Doctor] Laking particularly asked that he might be left more with his brothers and sisters – for *a little while* – as *we all* noticed *how* precautious [sic] & *old-fashioned* he was getting – & quite the *ways* of '*a single child*'! which wld make him ultimately a 'tiresome child' – laying down the law & thinking himself far superior to the younger ones ... In *that short* time his Education was *not* neglected.[32]

One of the strangest aspects of these children's lives is that they were so seldom in the company of other children. When Prince Edward was nearly nine his mother decided that while they were at York House in London, her children should learn dancing and she gathered together a class consisting of twenty to thirty children of people she knew. A lady at the piano provided the music and a fat lady named Miss Walsh taught the steps. The Duke of Windsor, writing of these classes, tells us that, although they had none of the spontaneity of a children's party, they did mean something to himself and his brother and sister, taking them out of their 'walled-in'[33] lives and introducing them to the company of other children.

The little walled-in family grew very close together, sharing jokes, family conventions, punishments, treats; and in this closed society the eldest child established a dominance over the others which seems to have owed as much to his own qualities as to their awareness of his unique and exalted destiny. Psychologists and sociologists have lately cast doubt on the long-held belief that a large family is of itself a good thing but these children owed most of their happiness to the companionship of one another. And, if they were 'walled-in', they were walled into unusually splendid places. When King Edward moved to Buckingham Palace after his mother died, he gave his son Marlborough House in London, Frogmore House in Windsor Home Park and the little castle of Abergeldie in Scotland. From this time, although the children still spent most of the year at York Cottage, they were in London in the spring, from where their mother often took them to Frogmore, and they spent August at Abergeldie.

Sandringham estate had been chosen by King Edward in preference to several places with historical and beautiful houses and here he had built a house in the style of late Victorian or Edwardian Tudor. Most Englishmen, shown a photograph of it, would guess it to be an hotel at a seaside town like Cromer or possibly at one of the later spas. But the house is surrounded by beautiful gardens and farmland and vast sums were spent improving the agricultural property and turning it into one of the best shooting estates in England. Successive generations of the Royal Family have loved it, and to this generation of children it offered a variety of opportunity. When they were young they spent much of their time on bicycles and they were allowed to bicycle to the nearby village of Dersingham to buy sweets or to the station at Wolferton to watch the trains. They were all physically courageous and, crouched over their handlebars, they would race about, the eldest in front, his brother and sister tearing along behind.

Frogmore House at Windsor lies between the Long Walk on its west and a private road running from the castle to some buildings of the Home Park Estate on its east. The house was built by James Wyatt and finished in about 1809. In the garden great lawns are broken by a lake and by belts of trees and shrubs, underplanted with bulbs, much of it planted by Queen Mary who found the place neglected and overgrown when she first went there. Wide drives are cut through the lawns and up to bridges crossing the lake, and, strictly from a bicyclist's point of view, to find oneself at Frogmore would be like being put down on an airport with instructions to use the runways. As usual, strangely indifferent to comfort, the Royal Family installed one bathroom at Frogmore on the ground floor, and the nurseries under the roof in this house were so hot in summer that water was sprayed on to it to cool them off.

The little castle of Abergeldie was 'in the matter of creature comforts', no improvement but here there were in the early days picnics with their mother in the wild Highland country, and later, when they were old enough, grouse-shooting and deer-shooting.

Yet if the family life of the princes was in some ways more propitious than it is often represented to be, the same cannot be said for their early education. At York Cottage the cultural environment was no richer, the vitality of the intellectual life no greater than in the villas of Upper Norwood and Surbiton.

I fear that I am getting a down on George v – his biographer would complain to his diary many years later. He is all right as a gay young midshipman. He may be all right as a wise old King. But the intervening period when he was Duke of York, just shooting at Sandringham, is hard to swallow. For seventeen years he did nothing at all but kill animals and stick in stamps.[34]

George v was quite without what Henry James has termed 'the deeper sense', and his children were conditioned to disregard, if not to disapprove of, the things of the intellect or the spirit, which one suspects, like many another Englishman, he believed prejudicial to the development of the character and a moral sense, as well as boring to himself. Sticking in his stamps he managed to indulge the instincts of the collector and remain absolutely pure of any trace of aestheticism. Queen Mary, on the other hand, was to acquire a reputation as a collector of furniture and *objets d'art*. Her biographer makes it plain however that this hobby was developed late in her life, primarily as a result of her interest in the history of the British Royal Family. And he says:

It is relevant to note that she first saw Hamlet given on the stage when she was seventy-seven, and that she was first enthralled by the novels of Tolstoy and Dostoevsky when she was eighty years of age.[35]

In these circumstances it is hardly a surprise to find that when Mr Hansell was engaged as tutor to the boys the choice fell on him not for his intellectual attainments but for his keenness as a yachtsman and a golfer. According to Sir John Wheeler-Bennett Mr Hansell was fully conscious of his inadequacy for his task and often said that the princes would be far better off at a good preparatory school. Since this suggestion was always vetoed out of hand, he tried to do his best.

In his own strange way Mr Hansell endeavoured to create at York Cottage as much of this school atmosphere as possible. He fitted up a classroom with two standard desks, a blackboard, bookshelves, etc., in a corner room of the first floor; here from 7.30 till 8.15 the boys would do their preparation before breakfast; and from 9 till 1 and between tea and supper they did their lessons. On some occasions ... Mr Hansell would organize immature football matches in pick-up sides in which the Princes joined with the boys of the village school, but it is doubtful whether these games gave very much enjoyment to anyone.[36]

The trouble was that, having easily achieved the dull and ugly appearance of an Edwardian school and the dreary routine that went with it, Mr Hansell was unable to supply even the uninspired but technically competent education which should have accompanied them. He starved his pupils of any stimulus to the imagination and blunted such intellectual curiosity as they might have had. He had no idiosyncrasy of his own to illuminate some unusual subject and it was left to the Sandringham village schoolmaster, a self-taught naturalist who used to take the boys on long rambles in the woods, to introduce them to the only genuine enthusiasm for knowledge they met. Extra tutors were brought in to teach French and German and, when King George discovered that his two eldest sons, aged about twelve and ten, could not strike the average weight of the stags he had shot at Abergeldie from the game record, a master was engaged to teach mathematics. Unless one counts the performance of a pipe major from the Scots Guards or the childish singing of folk songs, no attempt seems to have been made to teach music or any appreciation of the arts. The princes were not taken to concerts, nor, until they were nearly grown up, to the theatre, and none of the people who surrounded them seriously attempted to interest them in the arts.

In the palaces of the sovereigns of England these children were brought up with their backs to one of the finest collections of pictures in the world, with their ears attuned only to the bagpipes and in almost total ignorance of the vast inheritance of English literature. If this feat seems almost incredible, one can only say that it was easily achieved by others of the heirs to the great builders and collectors. There was a great deal of philistinism in the British upper class at the time and the children who grew up to a background of genuine culture were correspondingly rare.

What is nevertheless surprising is that the princes were not taught, or at any rate not well taught the things that the King was himself interested in. He personally taught them to handle a gun safely and with skill, but Prince Edward, who, as Prince of Wales, was later to be a brave and enthusiastic rider, was never a very good one. Horsemanship is something that is best learned young, when some degree of proficiency can usually be acquired by someone with the Prince's physical courage and co-ordination. Then he tells us that he was sometimes allowed to caddy for his father when the golf professional, Ben Sayers, was staying at Windsor (where King Edward had laid out a nine-hole golf course), but, when Sayers suggested to King George that the children might have some lessons too, he refused to allow it on the grounds that they might hack up the fairway. The King mistrusted excellence and had no desire for his sons to acquire it.

What qualities can one begin to discern in the little boy who would one day be King of England? From the time when his nurse carried him into the room where his mother sat with her lady-in-waiting, he had learned that he and his family were the objects of homage from the rest of mankind. As soon as they could walk, he and his brothers went first behind their parents or grandparents as they entered a room and the subservience of the courtiers and the reality of the power was unquestioned. Both his grandfather and his father bawled at their courtiers if crossed, and their lightest words brought the noblest in the land scurrying to attention. Prince Edward seems to have understood at a very early date that on him devolved both great honour and some special responsibility. While still a child, he instructed his brother to 'Smile'[37] while listening to a dull story, and, when told at a children's party to thank his hostess for the sword she had given him, he mounted a chair and said: 'Thank you for giving me such a beautiful sword. I shall always keep it and remember this night.'[38] For many years of his life the Prince would be the object of a close and affectionate regard from Lord Esher and the fact that the latter took an almost entirely favourable view of his character does not diminish the revelatory nature of some of his earliest comments. Of these, one of the most remarkable is the first. On 25 May 1904, staying at Windsor Castle, he wrote:

I have been walked off my legs, and pulled off them by the children. The youngest is the most riotous. The eldest, a sort of head nurse. It was queer looking through a weekly paper, and coming to a picture of the eldest with the label 'our future King'. Prince Albert at once drew attention to it – but the elder hastily brushed his brother's finger away and turned the page.[39]

On 23 January 1906, again at Windsor Castle, he noted:

The kids were in high spirits, and Prince Edward as composed and clever as ever. He had thought of a riddle in bed, and it was really quite witty for a child. He grows more like the *old* family every day. He has the mouth and expression of old Queen Charlotte.[40]

And on the following day:

Prince Edward develops every day fresh qualities, and is a most charming boy; very direct, dignified and clever. His memory is remarkable – a family tradition; but the look of *Weltschmers* in his eyes I cannot trace to any ancestor of the House of Hanover.[41]

From all of which one must assume that Prince Edward was alert and clever and, most remarkable of all, that even at this early age some element of embarrassment entered into his feelings about his exalted position. We know that he was shy, frightened of his father and kept at a distance by his mother, but that he was not lacking in physical courage. From what Lord Esher tells us, although he had the fairest looks, he quite early acquired an air of wistfulness, as though something in the view from his elevated position had permanently blighted his hopes.

In contrast to the simple life of York Cottage, at the Big House at Sandringham the little princes found themselves at the very apex of Edwardian splendour, extravagance and gaiety, and in a world which, purely for the number of people who waited on other people and the enormous resources which were put to the pursuit of pleasure, has become difficult even to imagine. Edward VII, who spent the greater part of his life deprived by his position and his mother of any serious occupation, suffered intensely from boredom, and a vast fortune and a whole society were used to keep this at bay. He was a lavish and a genial host and his wife, Queen Alexandra, had a spontaneous delight in society as great as his own.

Sandringham had been built as a country home where he and his family could relax from official cares, and his entertaining here, although it soon became as constant and generous as at his official residences, was less formal. Much of it was of a purely local kind. For the King and all the male members of his family and entourage, the greatest attraction of Sandringham was the shoot, which soon equalled its most famous neighbours, and, at a time when the 'battue', the method of driving birds on to the guns, was first coming into fashion, excited some criticism. The King and the shooting party, who were quite few in number on any one day and chosen for their skill, conducted a slaughter of the birds, and at the end of a big day it was not uncommon for some two thousand pheasants to lie on the ground bedraggled and bloody. There were countrymen even then who did not approve of this holocaust and the King (then Prince of Wales) found himself unpopular with some of his neighbours. It became politic as well as pleasant to entertain the local society and he built a ballroom at Sandringham and began to give parties and balls to which he invited the farmers and their wives and daughters, his own tenants and the county families. Even the most radical and humanitarian of his critics seem to have succumbed to this treatment, unable to withstand the charm of his hospitality and friendliness and the radiant beauty of the princess.

After his mother's death, King Edward came less to Sandringham but he was still there for the shooting and again at Christmas time. Some days before he was expected, the watching children at York Cottage would see an army of servants arrive, who lit the fires, arranged the flowers, received and prepared enormous quantities of food. Then a few days later the lights of the great house would go on and the wheels of carriage after carriage would be heard on the drive as the King and Queen arrived with their Household and twenty or thirty guests with their personal servants.

The interior of Sandringham House was as new and as obviously late Victorian in style as the exterior, the furniture being almost entirely contemporary and the house cluttered with trophies from the King's travels and objects both valuable and valueless collected by the Queen. Georgina Battiscombe has remarked that the King liked to think of himself as an old-fashioned Norfolk squire but that his home was the typical home of a nineteenth-century industrial magnate.[42] Much of the entertaining took place in the great hall the family called the Saloon. In the evening after the day's shooting many of the guests would sit in conversation here, while in the drawing-room next door others played cards. One generation after another of the Royal Family have found background music easeful and Gottlieb's German Orchestra was brought down from London to provide this. The company that assembled has often enough been described. It included representatives of the arts and professions, as well as bankers, statesmen, diplomats and the leaders of international society; beauty, wit and the power to entertain the King, rather than noble birth, were the passport to it. It is disappointing how little came out of these brilliant gatherings to illustrate the wit and wisdom which were undoubtedly there. For all his desire for entertainment, the presence of the King, while heightening the glamour and excitement, inhibited the flow of conversation, and even at Sandringham, where the atmosphere was less ceremonial than at Buckingham Palace or Windsor, Gottlieb fulfilled a necessary function.

The two little boys from York Cottage used to run up after tea to visit this splendid scene and on Sundays they would accompany their grandparents on the tour of Sandringham which the King and Queen made regularly with their guests; visiting the stables, the kennels, Queen Alexandra's model farm and last the stud farm where two Derby winners stood at stud. To the children these visits to the Big House were excursions into a different world and it was with excitement that they approached its gaily lighted windows.

Edwardian society had its own social and moral code which was founded both on a lack of knowledge of birth control and the consequent need for an outward appearance of complete discretion. Sexual appetite and basic attitudes to sexual satisfaction vary less from generation to generation than it is customary to suggest. What alters is the code of manners to which society must conform if the family life on which in the western world it is based can continue to exist. In Edwardian society the truth could never be spoken and much compromise was necessary between the parties to any social contract. Sir Philip Magnus has put it extremely well:

> The nineteenth century social code made allowance for frailty in high places by licensing fusion between husband, wife and lover, on condition that no confusion was permitted to occur. Everyone intimately concerned had to be consenting parties, and all who possessed the freedom of *Vanity Fair* were required to behave with the utmost decorum in order to prevent the innumerable irregular liaisons, which beguiled the tedium of excessive leisure and about which they loved to gossip privately, from becoming publicly known. Any indiscretion which impaired Society's prestige invited a sentence of social death which was ruthlessly executed.[43]

In these circumstances what became known as a 'cuckoo in the nest' was widely condoned, and it even happened that an heir to one of the noble families carried none of the blood of his predecessors.

When the little princes ran up after tea to their grandparents' house, among the brilliant and varied society they met must often have been Mrs Keppel. Mrs Keppel was one of the two women the King loved best in his lifetime, the other being Queen Alexandra, and she shared many qualities with the Queen. Both were beauties, although Alexandra was infinitely the more beautiful; both were so candid, courageous, spontaneous and un-affected in their manner and personality that they inspired genuine affection and admiration wherever they went. Both were generous, kind and without malice. Queen Alexandra, who was idolized by the British public, was completely captivating even to Queen Victoria who, while seriously criti-cizing her for her frivolity and love of society, could never resist the 'sunny warmth of the princess's actual presence'.[44] But she early became terribly handicapped by deafness and a stiff leg. She was never in any sense of the word an intellectual and such intellectual appreciation as she might have had was thwarted and stunted by not being able to hear what was said. Mrs Keppel, who was also adored – by doctors and bank managers and children, as well as by the King and his friends – was on the other hand a very clever woman and one who, in spite of being straightforward and outspoken, had the rare quality of complete discretion. Lord Hardinge of Penshurst wrote the following note in his private file after the death of King Edward:

I take this opportunity to allude to a delicate matter upon which I am in a position to speak with authority. Everybody knew of the friendship that existed between King Edward and Mrs George Keppel, which was intelligible in view of the lady's good looks, vivacity and cleverness. I used to see a great deal of Mrs Keppel at that time, and I was aware that she had knowledge of what was going on in the political world.

I would like here to pay a tribute to her wonderful discretion, and to the excellent influence which she always exercised upon the King. She never utilized her knowledge to her own advantage, or to that of her friends; and I never heard her repeat an unkind word of anybody. There were one or two occasions when the King was in disagreement with the Foreign Office, and I was able, through her, to advise the King with a view to the policy of the Government being accepted. She was very loyal to the King, and patriotic at the same time.

It would have been difficult to find any other lady who would have filled the part of friend to King Edward with the same loyalty and discretion.[45]

Sir Philip Magnus also tells us that the King could seldom be persuaded to give formal audiences to his ministers, with the exception of the Prime Minister and the Foreign Secretary, but devised instead a 'characteristic means of bringing his influence to bear'. He formed a circle of seven trusted friends who performed collectively the kind of services the Prince Consort had performed for Queen Victoria. Six of these were Sir Ernest Cassel, Lord Esher, Sir John Fisher, Sir Charles Hardinge, Lord Knollys, and the Marquis de Soveral; the seventh was Mrs Keppel.*

'The special position of Mrs George Keppel,' Sir Philip Magnus writes, 'was accepted and welcomed by ministers. She was ready at all times to smooth their paths while behaving with exemplary discretion, and her Liberal political views were particularly helpful after the Liberal Party had achieved power in December 1905.'[46]

All this Mrs Keppel managed without any break in her family life, and she was passionately adored by her children.

When the King first met Mrs Keppel, the Queen welcomed her as a great improvement on Lady Warwick who had caused public scandal and she received her at Windsor as well as at Sandringham. She became at ease

* Cassel, Sir Ernest, King Edward's financial adviser and friend. Esher, 2nd Viscount, very close to the King who once remarked: 'Although you are not exactly a public servant, yet I always think you are the most valuable public servant I have.' Fisher, Sir John, Admiral of the Fleet and First Sea Lord, later Lord Fisher of Kilverstone. Hardinge, Sir Charles, later 1st Baron Hardinge of Penshurst; travelled with the King and wrote many of his speeches, Ambassador in St Petersburg and Permanent Head of the Foreign Office, Viceroy of India. Knollys, 1st Viscount, King Edward's private secretary. Soveral, Marquis de, Portuguese Minister in London, the King's friend and a much loved member of Society.

with her and sometimes made use of her to keep the King happy. Because of this, and because of the Edwardian code of behaviour, the absurd fiction has grown up that Queen Alexandra liked and approved of Mrs Keppel, and that the three lived happily together with Mrs Keppel as 'a second wife'. In fact the Queen believed jealousy to be an ignoble quality, 'the bottom of all mischief and misfortune in this world'[47] and she would not allow her relationship with her loved and loving husband – 'my Bertie' as she endearingly referred to him – to be undermined by so unworthy an emotion. But she was not inhuman and the idea that her feeling for Mrs Keppel was one of total forbearance or even affection is a false one. When, towards the end of his life, King Edward began to see less and less of his wife and more and more of Mrs Keppel, such liking as the Queen had for her rival must have been under great strain. Long before that, while Queen Victoria was still alive, we find the Duchess of York, who was a bad sailor, writing to the Duke of York, on board the Prince of Wales's yacht one Cowes week, to ask: 'How are things going in general? I mean, does peace reign or have you had a difficult time?' And the Duke replying: 'Alas, Mrs K. arrives tomorrow and stops here in a yacht, I am afraid that peace and quiet will not remain.' On which the Duchess commented: 'What a pity Mrs G.K. is again to the fore! How annoyed Mama will be!'[48]

The Duchess's eldest son, Prince Edward, was only four when King Edward first met Mrs Keppel but he was nearly sixteen when the King died and in the meantime he must have seen a great deal of her. It is not likely that in his home in the company of the gentlemen and ladies-in-waiting much discussion of the matter ever took place in front of him, but he was alert and sensitive. It seems probable that, whether he was conscious of it or not, the strongest impression left on his mind of this exceptional woman was of the dislike and disapproval felt for her by his parents and his grandmother.

2

NAVY

He was well aware that his education as a sailor had ill fitted him for many of his new responsibilities. It had been only during his father's reign, nine swiftly moving years, that under the influence of Sir Arthur Bigge he had done something to repair the gaps in his knowledge of English and Constitutional History and to attain to the normal educational standard of the average public-schoolboy at the leaving age. These gaps had not yet been repaired, that standard not reached when he came to the Throne. . . . He was still methodically plodding on with his education when his reign was half over.[1]

These words were written about King George v by his official biographer, who, in case he had left any doubt in our minds about the state of the King's education, returned to the matter in the following passage:

At the risk of a charge of repetition, the point must be stressed here. His planned education ended just where and when it should seriously have begun. He was (until he had painfully taken his own education in hand late in life) below the educational and perhaps intellectual standard of the ordinary public school-educated country squire.[2]

One would have been grateful in the circumstances for some explanation of why, at the time when the King was engaged in repairing the deficiencies of his own education, he should have chosen for his two eldest sons the very schooling which had made his task necessary. Few people would care to dogmatize on the proper education for the heir to the throne, but on the surface it seems fairly obvious that some knowledge of languages (almost every crowned head in Europe was a close relation of the Prince's at the time), of history and of the classics was more suitable for the future King of England than the specialized training of a naval officer. And, if the King was intent on character-building, one would have thought that the rigours of an English public school would have been great enough for two little boys who had never been away from home and scarcely ever met other children of their own age.

The King himself and his elder brother Prince Albert Victor had both been sent to the Navy but this was because Canon Dalton had so urgently pleaded that, because of the inadequacies in the elder boy's character, it would be fatal to part him from his brother. And when this plan had first been presented to Queen Victoria she had protested against it for the heir to the throne in the following words:

> The very rough sort of life to which boys are exposed on board ship is the very thing not calculated to make a refined and amiable Prince, who in after years (if God spares him) is to ascend the throne. It would give him a very one-sided view of life which is not desirable ...[3]

King George is always presented as extraordinarily attached to tradition but also as a sensible man who made up for his intellectual and educational deficiencies by a kind of modest shrewdness. Yet all we have been told of his decision to repeat for his eldest son the education which had so conspicuously failed in his own case is that, when suggestions were made to him about the Prince's education, he was always quite confident that the navy could teach him all he needed to know, a fact which, in view of Mr Gore's revelations, is incomprehensible.

He was never neglectful of his sons' interests or happiness in the upper-class way exemplified by Lord and Lady Randolph Churchill's treatment of their son, Winston, and, when the Prince went to Osborne for the first time, his father accompanied him, travelling from Portsmouth to Cowes in the Admiralty yacht. Before leaving his son the King told him that he must always remember that he was his best friend, advice the Prince would always find impossible to follow, although it was sincerely meant. King George visited his children at school when he was able to and had a normal father's pride in their accomplishments and pleasure in their company. 'Dear David,' he recorded in his diary, while staying at Goodwood, 'looking thinner but wonderfully well, came from Osborne, his holidays having just begun.'[4] And on a different occasion: 'Darling May's birthday ... children all recited their poems. David did it quite extraordinarily well. He said Wolsley's farewell (Sheakespeare) without a mistake.' [sic][5]

King Edward VII had been educated by private tutors and, although King George and his elder brother, Prince Albert Victor, had been sent to the *Britannia* they had been accompanied by their tutor Canon Dalton. Prince Edward and Prince Albert were the first generation of the Royal Family to be sent to school alone. Mr Hansell's incompetent and uninspired regime had ensured that in turn each of the boys would find it hard to keep up with his class. In the specialized curriculum of the Naval Colleges, priority was given to mathematics, navigation, science and engineering. A great deal of time was spent in learning how to tie knots, splice rope, sail a cutter, read and make signals, box the compass and master all the intricacies of seamanship. Prince Albert once achieved the feat of being 68th out of 68 and Prince Edward wrote of being 46 in the order, or 32nd, which, he said bravely, he thought quite good for him. At the end of each term at Osborne every boy was given an envelope to take home. Prince Edward's first report passed without comment but his second produced the dreaded summons to the library. Mathematics 'in all its hideous aspects' had been his undoing and his report, which his father gave him to read, seemed curt and cruel and bearing no resemblance to what he thought he had achieved. When, therefore, after his third term he was once more sent for to the library he burst into tears before the King had time to speak. Yet here again his father is shown as behaving not unkindly, and, after saying that this was no way for a naval cadet to behave, he added: 'Besides, you have quite a good report this time; and I am pleased with the progress you have made.'[6]

On another occasion the King wrote to the Prince: 'I am sorry that ... you ... lost several places in the last order, that is a pity & I am afraid you didn't pay as much attention as you ought to have done, but perhaps the questions were harder.'[7]

Both Mr Hector Bolitho and the Duke of Windsor himself have given us some account of the Prince's schooldays. The King's decision that his son should attend the Naval Colleges rather than one of the public schools, while ensuring that the Prince would grow up at least as ill-educated as himself, seems to have had two more immediate effects. The first is that the physical conditions he encountered were much harder and the impact unnecessarily cruel. It may be argued that in 1907 life at many of the public schools was fairly barbaric, particularly in that so little attempt was made to control the bullying of younger boys. The difference was that in the naval and army schools a harsh philosophy behind the strict discipline made a virtue of physical discomfort and led to an attitude which, if it did not exactly condone bullying, inevitably encouraged it. If the Prince had been sent, for instance, to Eton (Prince Henry, the King's third son, went to this school, for reasons equally unexplained) he would have had a room of his own. At Osborne, this boy, to whom a dancing class had hitherto presented an unusual opportunity to meet children of his own age, lived in a dormitory with thirty others. He was called by a bugle blowing reveille at 6 o'clock in summer and at 6.30 in winter and then, in answer to a series of gongs, he was expected to jump out of bed, say his prayers, brush his teeth and run to the end of the dormitory and plunge, shivering, into a green-tiled pool. This, like everything else at Osborne, had to be done at the double. All day long the boys were expected to run from pillar to post, a system that may have done less to stimulate the desired alertness than was believed. The food was so bad that the Prince was often hungry, and on one occasion was caught malingering, having pleaded sick in the hope of getting a square meal out of the friendly matron in the sick bay. He had no freedom to follow his own pursuits or to develop those personal tastes and preferences which are the reserves most people fall back upon in times of loneliness or trouble. Everywhere outside the college grounds was out of bounds, and every hour of every day, except Sunday afternoon, was filled.

When he first arrived at Osborne he was faced with the barrage of questions customarily fired at new boys. Here again, if one may once more make the comparison with Eton, in the relatively sophisticated atmosphere of that school he would have been merely one, even if the most exalted, of the sons of a great English family, and he would have found it easier to achieve that anonymity which is so essential to the happiness of the very young. Mr Bolitho tells us that at Osborne he replied: 'Just Edward,' to the question 'Edward what?' He was alone in never having been to school before, and he was embarrassed by questions about his father and his home.[8] For these and similar unorthodoxies he received, if we are to believe what we are told, punishments to fit the crime. On one occasion his head was thrust through a window, the sash was let down on his neck and he was left to reflect on the fate of Charles I and the treatment England gave to kings who did not please her, until someone heard his cries. On another occasion he had a bottle of red ink poured over his hair, down his neck and on to his shirt. Bravely he made the decision to wash and change and take the punishment he would receive for being late for evening prayers, rather than give away to the authorities what had happened.

However it is difficult to believe he had to submit to a great deal of individual bullying. There was much talk about his being treated the same as everyone else, but, right from the first when he appeared to take the entrance examination, we find the examiners eagerly reporting that this Hansell-taught child was the best candidate they had seen. It seems unlikely that his fellows were left completely unsupervised to treat him as they pleased; and even more unlikely that his unique position, although a real embarrassment in some ways, was entirely without advantage in his relationship with the other boys. He seems to have achieved a reasonable degree of popularity and the nickname 'Sardine'.*

Soon after he arrived at Osborne he witnessed, according to his own account, a particularly unpleasant example of naval discipline. The College was administered by a post-captain RN with a staff of twenty-seven officers to whom the teaching staff was subordinate. The head of the school, Captain Alexander-Sinclair, had a son called Mervyn who was in the same term as

---

* In his biography Hector Bolitho says that the Prince was thus nicknamed 'for no apparent reason'. But Compton Mackenzie remarked that: 'the origin ... so puzzling to his biographer Mr Bolitho, may be guessed without severely taxing the mind as a schoolboy antithesis to Wales. And the new cadet was not a massive boy.'[9]

the Prince. This boy was continually reported for petty misdemeanours and, for these trivial offences, his father presently sentenced him to 'six official cuts' with a bamboo cane. For this rare and extreme punishment, the Duke tells us, the boy was strapped to a gymnasium horse, and a naval doctor had to be present. The cuts were then administered by a physical training petty officer. What turned the scene of this punishment, horrible enough in itself, into one of organized cruelty was the presence of the other cadets drawn up in two lines to watch it. Every boy present must have noted with some degree of disturbance that it was the boy's father who inflicted this punishment on him and ordained that it should be watched. To the Prince, who was so nervous of his own father, the effect must surely have been traumatic.

In an atmosphere thus brutalized the routine mass bullying by the senior boys of whole groups of juniors would have been difficult to check. The Duke of Windsor tells us that when the boys were transferred from Osborne to Dartmouth the effect was to bring them back, after a period at the head of the lower school, under the authority of the seniors they had not met for two years, and whose skill at persecution had gained much from their extra experience. When Prince Edward was first at Dartmouth, the cadet captain in charge of his dormitory remarked to the boys one evening that they were 'an idle, lazy bunch of warts'[10] and ordered that in future the time allowed for undressing and putting on their pyjamas would be reduced from one minute to thirty seconds. As it was quite impossible to comply with this order, it was merely a method of selecting victims for the gong rope, while causing the maximum of fear and anxiety to the boys who escaped this fate.

When Prince Albert first went to Osborne, Prince Edward was in his last term and the rigid etiquette of the school forbade him to be seen in the company of a new boy, even that of his own brother. However, he soon became aware that his brother was in trouble, and arranged to meet him on the far side of the playing fields where the younger boy could tell him about it and he could do his best to advise him from his own superior experience.

One is continually surprised by the resilience and adaptability of children from every walk of life when confronted with situations alien to their whole experience, but one must, nevertheless, admire the fortitude of these two boys, wrenched from the regal splendour and isolation of their home lives and thrown into this world where the discipline, the austere physical conditions and the whole philosophy encouraged an insensibility in their school mates for which they were totally unprepared, but who, nevertheless, kept their troubles to themselves and even put on a brave show of enjoying the life.

The second effect of the Prince being sent to the Naval Colleges was that, since so many of his companions were to spend most of their lives at sea, he made few friends at school whom he would meet later in life. Writing when he was over fifty, he said that he had had very little association with any of his term since he left school and he added that in the most recent Navy List the names of only four of his term are recorded: one Admiral of the Fleet (himself): one Admiral (Sir Philip Vian): and two Vice Admirals (Sir Charles Daniel and Sir Reginald Portal). At first sight this appears a further major disadvantage to the Naval Colleges, but, as one speculates on these things, one begins to believe that here on the contrary might be one of the clues to the King's decision. Of an earlier generation Sir Philip Magnus wrote:

Excessive anxiety caused the Queen [Victoria] and her husband to draw an arbitrary distinction between companions and friends, and to hold that the latter were a luxury which princes were bound to deny themselves. They warned their children often that they were no better than other children, while hesitating even to admit companions to Buckingham Palace and Windsor Castle because they considered that ingenuous youth would seek inevitably to convert companionship into friendship, and friendship into an impermissible relationship of equality.[11]

And the Duke of Windsor tells us that much as he dreaded his father's summons to the library, he had reason to be grateful to him because he had always taught him not to think he was either different from or better than other people. To which the Duke adds the rider: 'To be sure by *other people* he meant the children of the well-born.'[12] These sentences are manifestations of more than one hidden attitude which if understood might throw light on the King's choice of school for his sons.

When the King told Prince Edward that he must never get the idea that he was different or better than other people, he clearly meant that the boy should not confuse his person with his position. But it was itself a confused and confusing statement to make to a child who must have noted every minute of every day that he and his family were treated as very different from and certainly superior to other people. The difference between a person and his position is a concept easily understood when applied to anyone but the sovereign and his heir, but in their case it ignores the most important aspect of modern monarchy – the metaphysical one. No longer the leader in the field, nor even the holder of much political power, the sovereign today owes his very existence to the desire of the people for a transcendent figure. There is a sense in which the King has got to be 'better than other people', and it is the difficulty of reconciling this with the Christian belief that all men are equal in the sight of God which gives royal utterances on the subject a naive, even disingenuous, air.

George v laboured under a further difficulty, which is implicit in the Duke of Windsor's statement that by other people he meant the well-born. The King paid lip service to Christian ideals by teaching them to his children but he did not entirely believe what he said himself. In the world over which he reigned he would have been very unusual if he had not made this division between the well-born and everyone else. One of the aspects of the aristocratic and hierarchical society which existed in England before the First World War, really until after the second, is that the nobility, upper and middle classes were alike in regarding the working population as a different and inferior type of human being. Concepts such as 'blue blood' and 'well-born' were understood to have a real meaning. Children were brought up emotionally so conditioned to this attitude that, even when people of the most devout Christian beliefs went among the working classes in an effort to improve their lot, they did so as anthropologists, benefactors or missionaries, visiting a tribe more primitive than themselves. In the same way, people were able to speak and behave with the greatest intimacy in front of other people providing these were servants; and the most remarkable thing about the history of domestic service is the opportunities for blackmail that were simply not used. If one proceeded upwards through the endless divisions and sub-divisions of the social classes, it would be found that the same belief in an actual superiority over others operated all the way, becoming gradually weaker in regard to those nearer in the social scale; so that expressions such as 'Not Like Us', which have appeared so much in recent literature on the subject of the class system, were only superficially-ironical.

George v's anxiety that his children should not make friends was probably no less than his grandmother's had been, and progress towards democracy made it all the more necessary for him to adopt a double standard when speaking to his children. It is probably not stretching the point too far to suggest that consciously or sub-consciously his choice of school was influenced by his belief in the dangers of friendship. Playing football with the Sandringham village children, let out once a week for a dancing class, the little princes were in no danger. Trotting about at the double with only Sunday afternoon free to get into harm, and meeting only men who looked forward to a career at sea, the risk at the naval colleges was not very great. Here one is brought up sharply against the fact that both George v and George vi did make life-long friends during their naval years. Yet this was chiefly with men of such stable and loyal character that they were picked out to become part of the King's Household. In service there is no real equality, although there may be mutual affection. The words 'the King's old friend' often precede the name of a gamekeeper, or valet or village schoolmaster, and, although they may describe a genuine relationship, it is not the one that is being discussed here.

If the princes had been sent to one of the leading public schools – Eton or Harrow – they would have met the children of the 'well-born' (for the King this meant the nobility), that class with whom the taboos were at their weakest. Some of these boys might have been the over-confident, rather raffish type often met among the well-born, who exert so much

charm over the minds of the very young. There are children of a phleg-
matic and unresponsive nature who might survive these dangers, but, for
the little, alert heir to the throne, far better to grow up unable to spell the
name of the national poet than run such risks as these.

Thus in his human situation the outlook for the little Prince must seem
to the ordinary observer rather grim – not at all a matter for pleasantries.
Nineteenth-century Europe held hosts of royal relations who could fill the
gap of friendship, and history is partly written in the letters that passed
between them. But, even as Prince Edward grew up, they were engulfed by
the disastrous history of the twentieth century, leaving the Crown of
England in an isolation that only total dedication could support.

The pretence that Prince Edward was or could be treated the same as other
boys was subjected to increasing strain. One day in the year of 1909
twenty-four battleships, sixteen armoured cruisers, forty-eight destroyers
and numerous other vessels sailed across the Solent to celebrate the arrival
of the Czar of Russia with his wife and children on board the Imperial
yacht *Standart*. The Czar was 'Uncle Nicky' to the Prince, who three days
later conducted the imperial party round the Naval Colleges and through
the rooms at Osborne, where the busts of his ancestors still stood in niches
in the corridors.

At home he began to be less in the background and the adjustment he
had to make as he travelled between one of the royal residences and
Dartmouth is unimaginable. His father began to take him with him on
'small' shooting days, and like other boys of his age he was allowed to stay
down to dinner. Sometimes he was taken to the theatre. The manner of all
these more or less ordinary occasions was very different, however, from
that experienced by other boys, even those from aristocratic families. On
27 April 1910, for instance, King Edward arrived late in the evening from
Biarritz and went to hear Tetrazzini sing in *Rigoletto* accompanied by his
son and daughter-in-law, the Duke of Connaught and his two elder grandsons. At this famous theatre at Covent Garden the royal box is the second
one from the stage on the right (viewed from the auditorium) and behind it
there is a small supper room. Immediately below it there is another small
room called the smoking-room which was made for King Edward as
Prince of Wales because his mother refused to allow smoking in the supper
room. This room was copied from King Edward's room on the Royal
yacht *Victoria and Albert*. (At one end there is a crimson upholstered bench
behind small decorated arches and on the two side walls there is a frieze
and swags between pilasters in plaster work, while the ceiling is cross-
beamed, or coffered, with mouldings in the bays.) We have been left a good
description of King Edward's supper parties on opera nights by his chef,
Gabriel Tschumi. Although all the food was taken to the Opera House in
hampers there was nothing to distinguish these supper parties from those

held at Buckingham Palace except that the food was cold. Six footmen would go down early in the afternoon with hampers packed with cloths, silver and gold plate. Later the chef himself went in a horse brake bearing the King's Arms with dozens of hampers of food. The food was served during an hour's interval between 8.30 and 9.30.

Sometimes there were nine or ten courses, all served cold, and sometimes up to a dozen; and as each guest had to be given a clean plate for each course, the footmen had a strenuous time of it carrying in the hampers which often contained three hundred and sixty or four hundred plates alone, to say nothing of all the other silver used during the meal. ... These supper menus always began with cold consommé, and ended with patisserie, usually *Petites patisseries Fondantes*, or *Patisserie Parisienne* and dessert. There would be lobster mayonnaise, cold trout, duck, lamb cutlets, plovers' eggs, chicken, tongue and ham jelly, mixed sandwiches, and a choice of three or four desserts made from strawberries or fresh fruit.[13]

The day after the visit to the opera, the strenuous and music-loving King took his grandsons with their parents to the Royal Academy and the following night he again visited the Opera House to hear *Siegfried*. This was the last time he would visit Covent Garden. The next morning he went to Sandringham and, although the weather was bad, he spent a long time supervising the planting of his gardens. For years he had suffered from a bronchial condition and when he returned to London on Monday 2 May it was soon realized that he was very ill. The following morning Queen Alexandra, who was on a cruise in the Mediterranean, was sent for. For four days the King persisted in what Virginia Cowles has called 'a strange and almost fanatical effort to carry on his daily life'.[14] On 5 May the Queen arrived back in London and a bulletin was issued saying that the King's condition was causing anxiety.

At Marlborough House Prince Edward and Prince Albert were preparing to return to Dartmouth and Osborne after the Easter holidays which, in the rather odd phrase of the Duke of Windsor, had been 'unmarred by a single melancholy note', when they were sent for by their father.

'I have wired your Captains that I want you both to remain with me here,' he told them. 'Your Grandpapa is very ill, and the end may not be far off.'[15]

On the evening of 6 May, while the two princes remained quietly at Marlborough House, at Buckingham Palace the noble and generous Queen gave orders for Mrs Keppel to be fetched, so that she might say good-bye to the King. At a little before midnight he died.

From the bedroom which they shared at Marlborough House, the princes could look across The Mall at Buckingham Palace. The next morning Prince Edward was awakened by his brother, Bertie, who told him that the Royal Standard was at half-mast. Later, as they were dressing, the man servant, Finch, came to tell them their father wished to see them both downstairs.

A curious scene followed. The new King was deadly tired and he wept as he told them that their grandfather was dead. (In his diary he had written the previous night: 'I have lost my best friend & the best of fathers. I never had a word with him in his life. I am heartbroken and overwhelmed with grief.')[16] Prince Edward replied that they had already seen the Royal Standard at half mast and understood what this meant. At first the King did not notice this remark, then he asked his son to repeat what he had said. When the boy did so he muttered that this was all wrong. 'The King is dead,' he said, 'Long live the King!' and he sent for an equerry and told him to see that a mast was rigged on the roof of Marlborough House.

For ten days King Edward's body lay in the throne room at Buckingham Palace, and for three days more at Westminster Hall, while the crowned heads of Europe, for so many of whom time was so fast running out, assembled to pay their last respects.* Then on 20 May the new King of England led the sovereigns of Germany, Spain, Denmark, Portugal, Norway, Belgium, Greece and Bulgaria, and the Archduke Franz Ferdinand representing the Emperor of Austria, the Grand Duke Michael Alexandro-vitch representing the Czar of Russia, and the Duke of Aosta representing the King of Italy, in a procession from Westminster Hall to Paddington Station. At Windsor the coffin was placed on a gun carriage and the procession continued on foot to St George's Chapel, the princes Edward and Albert marching behind their father in the uniforms of naval cadets.

With the accession of his father Prince Edward automatically became the Duke of Cornwall and inherited vast estates and properties in the West of England and at Kennington in London. This title and the properties that go with it were created in the fourteenth century to provide an income and establishment for the eldest son of the King, and it was from the revenues accumulated during his minority that Edward VII had bought and improved the estate at Sandringham. After the funeral of his grandfather the new Duke of Cornwall proceeded back to Dartmouth and continued to receive the pocket money of a naval cadet. He was conscious however of a subtle change in his fellow cadets' attitude towards him.

On 4 June 1910 Lord Esher wrote the following:

The King sent for me two days ago. He was as friendly and frank as ever. He spoke a great deal about his eldest son, whom he proposed to create Prince of Wales on his birthday, the 23rd June, when the boy will be sixteen. He does not wish him to lose any chance of improving his mind and realizes that the boy is young for his years. He would like to postpone his entry into public life for some years, but I told him I did not think he would manage to do this beyond the time when the boy was 'royally' of age.

* During the reign of King George V the world witnessed the disappearance of five Emperors, eight Kings and eighteen more dynasties.[17]

The boy is a mere child now, much of which is due to the limitations of his tutor, a man, however, in whom the King reposes great confidence.[18]

It was natural that all shortcomings of the young princes should be blamed on poor Mr Hansell, whose inadequacy was so unfortunately obvious, but there may have been hereditary reasons for their slow development. On many pages of Mr Gore's life of King George V there is a suggestion of concern about the immaturity of the King as a young man.

The title of Prince of Wales does not pass automatically and the King could, although it is unlikely that he would, withhold it from his son. On Prince Edward's sixteenth birthday King George carried out the intentions expressed to Lord Esher and, summoning his son to Windsor, conferred the title upon him.

The Royal Family now moved from Marlborough House to Buckingham Palace, from Frogmore to Windsor Castle and from Abergeldie to Balmoral. When at Sandringham they still lived at York Cottage, however, because, although this was inadequate for their expanded household and it was impossible for guests to be invited there, the King, insisting that his father had built the house for her, refused to ask Queen Alexandra to leave the Big House. And she stayed there until her death in 1925.

The year 1911 was one of great public ceremonies for the young Prince. While at Newquay, convalescing from an illness, he received a letter from his father telling him that, as he would play a prominent part in the coronation ceremonies, his time at Dartmouth must be cut short. It was the custom for cadets in their last term to embark on a final cruise before graduating as a midshipman, and the Prince who had inherited his father's and grandfather's real love of the sea regarded this cruise as the goal of his present ambition and was naturally very much disappointed. Before leaving Dartmouth he performed his first public ceremony by returning to the town a silver oar that had for long been in the office of the Duchy of Cornwall, a symbol of the rights of the Duke of Cornwall over the water of Dartmouth.

The Coronation of the new King took place on 22 June 1911. When Queen Elizabeth II was crowned in 1953 the magnificent ceremony was seen for the first time by people other than those taking part in it. Before the advent of television even the majority of the peers and peeresses in Westminster Abbey could see very little of what took place.* After the ceremony of the actual crowning the Archbishop puts the crown on the head of the King and all the peers put on their coronets and the Kings of Arms their crowns. Then there follows the Homage. The first to pay homage is the Archbishop for the Lords Spiritual, the second the Prince of Wales.

As Prince of Wales, Prince Edward took precedence over the peers of

* For a description of the ceremony see Harold Nicolson: *King George V.*

the realm and would, if he had been of age, have worn a peer's robe. Since this was not possible the King had earlier invested him with the Order of the Garter so that at the Coronation he might wear the robes of this ancient order of chivalry, over a costume of cloth-of-silver. Kneeling before his father he recited the words:

I, Edward Prince of Wales, do become your liege man of life and limb and of earthly worship; and faith and truth I will bear unto you, to live and die against all manner of folks. So help me God.

Then he kissed his father's cheek and the King kissed his. The Prince was followed by the Duke of Connaught and then by a representative of each order of the peerage, each of whom repeated the same oath.

That night in his diary the King recorded:

I nearly broke down when dear David came to do homage to me, as it reminded me so much of when I did the same thing to beloved Papa, he did it so well.[19]

And other observers spoke of the dignity with which the young Prince played his part, 'in his face the bashfulness of youth and the serious thought of a man called to a great destiny'.[20]

But the great ceremonial for the Prince of Wales was his own investiture at Caernarvon. Although legends tell of the investiture at Caernarvon Castle of Prince Charles (afterwards Charles I) in 1616, there existed no authentic record of an English prince having been formally invested in Wales, previous investitures having taken place at Westminster and at various English towns. It was Lloyd George, the famous enemy of inherited privilege, who conceived the idea of transforming the ceremony into a Welsh pageant. The site chosen for the ceremony was a ruined castle at Caernarvon and part of this was restored for the purpose with stone presented by Lord Anglesey from the quarries from which the original stone had been taken six centuries before, and with massive beams of Canadian oak.

For the ceremony the Prince of Wales wore white satin breeches and a mantle and surcoat of purple velvet edged with ermine. When he first saw this costume, which he later called 'fantastic', there ensued what he has described as a 'family blow-up'. He complained that whereas the costume of the Garter was historical this 'preposterous rig' would make him a laughing stock to his friends in the Navy. His mother persuaded him that his friends would understand, however, and so on a sweltering summer day he appeared in this costume at Caernarvon Castle where, after Winston Churchill, as Home Secretary, had proclaimed his titles, he was invested by his father as Prince of Wales. The King put a coronet cap on his head as a token of principality, into his hand the gold verge of government and the ring of responsibility on to his middle finger. Leading him by the hand through an archway to one of the towers of the battlements, he presented him to the people of Wales. Then the young Prince who had been coached by Lloyd George spoke some sentences in Welsh. 'Diolch fy nghalon i Hen wlad fy nhadau.' (Thanks from the bottom of my heart to the old land of my fathers.) And 'Mor o gan yw Cymru i gyd.' (All Wales is a sea of song.) Today the only thing that seems remarkable in all of this is that since the fifteenth century it had never before been deemed necessary to pay these courtesies to the principality of Wales.

That night the King wrote in his diary: 'The dear boy did it all remarkably well and looked so nice.'[21] But the Prince tells us that when the commotion was over he made a discovery about himself; and in one of those long analytical passages in which he recollects the emotions of his youth he says that, whereas he was willing to play his role in the pomp and ceremony, he recoiled from personal homage, and he realized that even the association he had been allowed with the village boys at Sandringham and the Naval cadets had made him 'desperately anxious to be treated exactly like any other boy of my age'.[22]

His father's immediate reaction to the commotion was to arrange for his son to go to sea on a short voyage. In August therefore the Prince joined the battleship *Hindustan* and served three months aboard her as a midshipman.

3

OXFORD

When the Prince left the *Hindustan* he went to York Cottage to see his father. There in the library the King explained to him that the time had come for him to leave the Navy, which was too 'specialized', and that he had therefore decided to send him to Oxford. This decision was very surprising to the Prince who knew that basically his father distrusted scholarship and, like many other Englishmen, regarded intellectual capacity and attainments almost as a handicap to sound judgment. However, we have been told of the difficulties the King struggled with himself and, although it is said that it was Mr Hansell's idea to send the Prince to Oxford, he probably did not need much persuasion that a year or so spent on languages, history and political economy might benefit his son. The Prince however was upset and angry. He told the King he had no interest in learning – and that if he was sent to Oxford his years there would be wasted; and he told Mr Hansell what he thought about it in very much stronger terms. He was slightly mollified by being told that his vacations would be spent in educational trips to France and Germany to learn the languages.

When Edward VII went to Oxford as Prince of Wales (and, following a short period there, to Cambridge) he was accompanied by his Household. At Oxford he lived at Frewin Hall, specially rented for himself and his establishment. Here selected professors delivered lectures to him and six other undergraduates, who were specially chosen to be his companions. Occasionally he attended lectures in the ordinary way, but he was then dressed in the gown and tufted cap of the nobleman, and, when he entered the room, everyone rose and remained standing until after he had sat down.

When the arrangements were made for the Prince of Wales to go up to Oxford it was decided that he should be sent to Magdalen College as an ordinary undergraduate. He was to be spared the entrance examinations, for which he was so ill-equipped, and to be accompanied by Mr Hansell and an equerry. Great trouble was taken in the choice of the equerry. On 12 July 1912 Lord Esher recorded a long talk with the Queen on this subject.

The Queen wants an equerry for the boy. But how difficult is the selection. Several people have been mentioned to her. I think them all unsuitable. It is difficult to find a man who will be watchful but not seem to be so; instructive and not a bore; moral and not a prig; high spirited and not reckless. It would be an interesting task for a young man with imagination.[1]

The choice for this post finally fell on Major the Hon. William Cadogan, who attended the Prince on all occasions which were not academic.

The King also attempted to find suitable companions for his son, although in a manner more discreet than had been thought necessary in the case of Edward VII. We find Lord Derby writing to him.

Mr Hansell has been to see me and tells me Your Majesty would like my eldest boy to go to the same college as H.R.H. The Prince of Wales. I cannot say how pleased and honoured I am and how gladly I will consent to his going to whatever college is chosen.

There appear to be three in the running – Christ Church, New and Magdalen. New College I should not like as according to the Archbishop of York there is much trouble there and his is a judgment I would implicitly rely on. Christ Church is a large college apparently where all the *nouveaux riches* go and where the sole object seems to be to spend money and prove themselves men instead of being what they are – boys. Magdalen would appear to have none of these disadvantages, and if Your Majesty choose this college I can only most humbly say I should be very content. I had a long talk with Mr Hansell on various subjects and never have I found a man who understood boys better. Absolutely straight, but very broad-minded. I can imagine no man better able to guide rather than drive a boy, and moreover well able to put him on the right path at Magdalen where apparently he was. Of course when a boy goes to Oxford, he ceases to be a schoolboy and I can imagine nobody better than Mr Hansell to look after him, see that he goes straight and yet not make him think he is still in leading strings. We also talked over tutors in France and Germany, but doubtless he will have written Your Majesty on the subject. May I again say how honoured I am by Your Majesty's wish and how much I hope that Edward may be as devoted to the Prince of Wales as I am to Your Majesty.[2]

To this letter the King replied from HMS *Medina* at sea, on his way to India.

I am so glad you had a satisfactory talk with Hansell and thought him sensible and broad-minded. I always think his judgment is good. He has also written to me on the subject of your conversation.

Although I do not propose to settle anything until my return home, I should think that Magdalen College without a doubt is the one I shall choose as it appears to have all the advantages and none of the disadvantages of the other two. Both the Queen and I are delighted that you are willing and ready for your son to go to the same college as ours and I hope that my boy will get on with and be as fond of your boy as I am of you.[3]

However, in the autumn of 1911, when the Prince first heard of this project, the time had not yet come for him to go up to Oxford, and while his parents were away in India he spent the winter at Sandringham studying the subjects he would take. His youngest brother Prince George was also at Sandringham that winter and it was at this time that the two discovered a special affinity of tastes and a real affection for each other. They formed a friendship then based on more than the fact they were brothers which was to endure closely for many years. As young men, the two Princes were often to be seen in each other's company.

A letter the Prince of Wales wrote to the King at this time is an example of the immaturity Lord Esher had remarked upon and also evidence of a desire to propitiate his father at least as great as normal for his age. He begins by saying that he loves shooting and thanking his father for allowing him to shoot at Sandringham. Then he goes on: 'I have had some splendid practice, & feel that my shooting has very much improved. It is the small days that give one far more practice than the big ones. One can take one's time and shoot much better.'[4]

From HMS *Medina* on his way back from India 'waiving his customary prefix of 'My dearest David', the King replied in curmudgeonly style:

Judging from your letters and from the number of days you have been shooting, there can't be much game left at Sandringham, I should think. It also seems a mistake to shoot the coverts three times over, I never do that unless a few more cocks have to be killed. I can't understand Bland wishing you to do so. You seem to be having too much shooting and not enough riding or hunting. I can't understand why you didn't hunt when Sir C. Fitzwilliam came expressly for that, and Bertie and Harry went out, what on earth were you doing?* You must learn to ride and hunt properly and you have had such good chances this winter at Sandringham. I must say I am disappointed.[5]

The Duke of Windsor tells us that the desire that he should ride became at this time a recurrent theme in the King's letters.

In your position [he wrote once] it is absolutely necessary that you should ride well as you will continually have to do so at parades, reviews, etc., and so the sooner you make up your mind to it the better. The English people like riding and it would make you very unpopular if you couldn't do so. If you can't ride, you know, I am afraid people will call you a duffer.[6]

In the spring of 1912 the Prince of Wales, travelling incognito, went to Paris to stay with the Marquis of Breteuil, who had been a friend of his grandfather's. His visit naturally had no political implication but the fact

---

* The name Harry refers to the King's third son, later the Duke of Gloucester, born 31 March 1900.

that his first foreign visit was paid to France was, in the troubled state of the world, seen as a token of friendship between the two countries. In a house on the Avenue du Bois de Boulogne he was given a suite of rooms far more beautiful than anything he had known at home and here he met all that was most brilliant in French society. He was a shy boy with no particular facility for the language, and the distinguished people whom he met often passed on after paying him formal courtesies as they might have passed on from any other tongue-tied youth. But they must often have turned to look at him as they stood talking to one another across the room. His presence would never again go unremarked, partly because of the Royal aura which now that he was grown up had settled upon his shoulders, but also because of his developing looks. He was very small and immature but his bright head of yellow hair and his fair wistful face were immediately noticeable. Describing him at the time, Compton Mackenzie wrote:

If there had been any left alive in France with long enough memories the likeness between the young Prince of Wales and his grandfather when he was a young Prince of Wales could not have failed to strike them. They would have recognized the same shyness, the same hint of sadness, and the same charm of *feerie*.[7]

Writing himself of this period in France, the Duke of Windsor tells us that there were two figures who stood out with special clarity from all those he met at the time: Sir Francis Bertie, the British Ambassador, whose duty it was to keep an eye on him, because of the awe he inspired as the representative of the King, and a French painter called Edouard Detaille, because to his surprise this gentleman was wearing the trousers of the Black Watch. The Prince's interest in this matter was so great that he summoned up courage to ask him how he came by his trousers. M. Detaille replied that they had been given him as an honorary member of the officers' mess when he was staying as a guest of the 42 Royal Highlanders in order to paint some pictures of British Army life and that he always wore them on special occasions. And he invited the Prince to his studio to see his military paintings.

Prince Edward spent five months in France accompanied by Mr Hansell and a French tutor, M. Maurice Escoffier, and sometimes by the two sons of the Marquis de Breteuil. He rode in the Bois, played golf, tennis and attended the races. He motored in France with his tutors, accompanying Mr Hansell while he indulged his passion for churches and cathedrals, he made a short cruise with the Mediterranean Fleet off the Côte d'Azur and he visited the armament works at Le Creusot. Then in the autumn he returned to England, where, at Balmoral, Lord Esher again recorded his impression of him. In a letter written on 19 September, he wrote:

I have had two walks alone with the Prince of Wales. He is a most captivating, strange, intelligent boy, with a remarkable vocabulary. He is sad – with the sadness of the world's burdens. I will tell you about him some day.

And on 20 September he wrote in his diary:

A very long talk with the Prince of Wales. We talked for about an hour and a half alone. I let him have his say about the Navy; he is devoted to his old profession. How is it possible to have been so long a sailor, and not have got 'imbued with the spirit of it'? That was his question. His memory is excellent and his vocabulary unusual, and above all things he thinks his own thoughts. They are long thoughts too. He has opinions, and strong ones on naval matters, and he aired them all in grave fashion – views on types of ships, on a sailor's education, on strategy and naval policy.

He told me of his friendly relations with the officers and men with whom he had served, how he loved to talk with the men of their homes and their pleasures and their troubles. He was full of the 'responsibility' of midshipmen and young lieutenants, and eloquent on the merits of such a training. And presently we broke away from the past.

I asked him how if he were charged with the education of a Prince of Wales, he would plan it. This riddle he is going to think over. He said, 'I am not clever, not a bit above the average.' I asked him how he knew that. He replied by the test of examination. But he sees that this test is only half a test.

It is a charming mind – grave, thoughtful, restrained, gentle, kindly, perhaps a trifle obstinate and sombre for so young a lad.[8]

Sir Herbert Warren was the President of Magdalen when the Prince of Wales went up to Oxford. He was a fine scholar and a poet but he is remembered not for these qualities but because he was afflicted to an almost farcical degree with one of the most pathetic of human weaknesses. Another undergraduate, James Lees-Milne, has written of him:

I have met many obvious snobs in my life – in fact the majority of human beings, high and low, are snobs of one sort or another, which is what makes them so entertaining – but with the single exception of a restaurant proprietor in Moscow, I have never encountered a more blatant social snob than this eminent Professor ... Sir Herbert honestly believed that a title conferred a heavenly grace in which those poor handleless creatures were sadly and totally lacking. How anyone without a title, and there were quite a few, ever got into Magdalen during Warren's presidency, I am at a loss to explain. That the titled and untitled were regarded by him as sheep and goats I am quite certain.[9]

Dr Warren himself undertook tutorials for the Prince who, accompanied by six other undergraduates, visited his library once a week to study the humanities. Mr Charles Grant Robertson discoursed to the Prince on history and the Warden of All Souls, Sir William Anson, on constitutional law. He studied political economy with the Rev. Lancelot Ridley Phelps, French with M. Berthon and German with Professor Hermann Fiedler. None of these distinguished gentlemen had any greatly formative influence on him and, like other members of his family, he was inclined to take some pride in an aversion to books, boasting of a preference to learn from life.

As the Prince of Wales grew to manhood his relationship with his father suffered the strain inevitable between two strongly obstinate characters with widely differing tastes. It was when he went to Oxford that he first gave a demonstration of that stubbornness which had been a characteristic of every generation of his family since Queen Victoria, about whom Sir Charles Dilke once said: 'Her obstinacy constitutes power of a kind.'[10] Silently he rejected his father's right to choose his friends. Lord Derby's son, Lord Stanley, was sent as planned to Magdalen and the two young men spent two years there together, but at this time no friendship occurred between them. Randolph Churchill wrote:

Children often fail to embrace friendships which are planned for them by their parents and though the Prince of Wales and Lord Stanley spent two years at Magdalen together they did not in fact become intimate friends until they both joined the Grenadier Guards at the outbreak of the war in 1914. The Prince of Wales, during his Oxford days, had to endure the supervision of his former tutor Mr Henry Hansell and it may well be that he resented the benevolent conspiracy of his father and Lord Derby to subject him in addition to what he may have regarded as the chaperonage of Lord Stanley.[11]

This is politely understated and the truth is that the Prince was always unwilling to give his confidence to anyone who owed his introduction to him to the King. He believed that the disposition to please Majesty is limitless and he regarded everyone who was a friend or appointment of his father's as potentially a spy. At this time in his life he was merely a young man who intended to enjoy himself without encouraging the advent of a footman with a summons to the library. Later in life his distrust of his father's friends was to have more positive effects.

Another of the Prince's personal qualities which was to emerge at this time was his extraordinary interest in clothes. Later generations have learned that a fondness for personal adornment is a leading masculine characteristic, held in check for a short time at the beginning of the century by the unnatural fashions of the day; but the Prince had an interest in clothes far deeper and more extensive than a mere desire to dress himself up. This aspect of the matter made a great appeal to him, however, and it was in his own clothes that his fascination with the matter first declared itself. His personal tastes were for informal clothes and he liked bright colours and large patterns. Some people thought his taste very vulgar and first among those to whom it made little appeal was the King.

It was not so much that the King was indifferent to the question of men's clothes as that he too was deeply interested in it. For the Prince's addiction was an inherited characteristic. King Edward VII had an extreme and passionate interest in all the details of uniforms, orders and so on and could have his whole evening spoiled if one of his guests wore the wrong tie. At the same time he was something of an innovator in the matter of everyday dress, with a liking for bold checks and bright colours. The Prince Consort said of him as a young man that he took no interest in anything but clothes, and that even out shooting he was more concerned with his trousers than with the game. The Duke of Connaught was so much of an authority on the details of uniforms that he could tell at a glance if small details such as the spurs a man wore or the colour of his sword slings were incorrect. George v had a conservative taste in clothes but they were to him, too, an absorbing topic of conversation. Belonging, as has been said, to a generation who were apt to judge people's morals by the cut or the fit of their suits, he had, nevertheless, a certain weakness for colour, which showed itself in his country tweeds and his kilts.

'Wear the Balmoral kilt and jacket on weekends,' he once wrote to his eldest son, 'and green kilt and black jacket on Sundays. Do not wear the red kilt till I come.'[12]

But these were the King's only departures from the conventional, and the Prince has remarked that his childhood was 'buttoned-up' in every sense. He and his brothers invariably wore starched Eton collars and were never permitted to take off their coats. Even with shorts they wore long stockings right up to their thighs, the sight of the knees being acceptable only with kilts. When one of them as a small child went into the King's presence with his hands in his pockets, orders were immediately given to 'Lala' for the pockets to be sewn up. The King and all his generation always wore boiled shirts with a frock coat by day in London, and, when the Prince of Wales visited his father, he was expected to wear a morning coat, while, when he dined with him, he wore a tail coat with a white tie and the Star of the Garter.

It is not therefore surprising that at Oxford the Prince was enthusiastic about the fashion for more informal clothes, appearing in flannel trousers with sports coats and early versions of the garment called 'plus-fours', nor that he wore trousers with 'turn-ups' which were then the latest thing. He tells us that he disliked ceremonial dress and, unlike another member of his family, Kaiser Wilhelm, cared nothing for uniforms, but this is probably untrue. In any case, all his life he took great pleasure in his own clothes, and, so unscholarly in other ways, he made a serious study of the history and evolution of dress. It has sometimes been suggested that his choice of dress was influenced by a desire to provoke his father, and, if this were so, he was certainly successful, but, in fact, long afterwards when the clothes he wore were no longer of much interest to anyone but himself, Diana Hood reports him in the garden of his house in the South of France wearing crimson trousers one day with a light blue shirt and red and white shoes, and another day bright blue trousers with a canary yellow shirt and blue shoes.[13] And in his book *A Family Album*, which seems to have been intended as a book of idle memories, he returns compulsively to the subject of clothes again and again, until it becomes virtually a history of modern dress told through the persons of his own family.

When the Prince first arrived in Oxford he was diffident and lonely. He tells us that, surrounded by young men who had come up with friends they had made at Eton, Harrow, Winchester or some other public school, he felt nostalgic for the Navy. He was not of course alone in having very little learning, nor in the fact that he need not rely on an honours degree for his future career. And it does not seem to be true as Brian Inglis has said that 'the decision [to send him to Oxford] turned out to be even more ill-advised than putting the Prince through Osborne and Dartmouth.'[14] Most young men enjoy university life and once he had settled down the Prince was no exception. Steering clear at first of the public school boys, he earned a reputation for modesty in his choice of friends, but he soon disclosed where his real tastes lay. While the dons exerted all their brilliance and charm in an attempt to interest their Royal pupil, Major Cadogan had no difficulty in captivating his full attention. Major Cadogan had orders from the King to teach him to ride and he undertook this task with patience and skill. Soon the Prince, who had begun by complaining that riding was very dull and only necessary to please Papa, was hunting with the South Oxfordshire Hounds and appearing on the polo fields. He would never make a first-class horseman but he had unflinching physical courage and boundless enthusiasm.

In the Easter and summer vacations of 1913 he went to Germany to improve his knowledge of the language. His trips to this country were very different from his visit to France, because in Germany he stayed almost entirely with very close relations. The Prince was descended from a long line of kings, beginning with Egbert in 827, but genetically was almost pure German, while many of his enormous number of cousins and second cousins had married back into German families. In nearly all the small palaces of Germany there lived and reigned some close relation already well known to him. At Easter, travelling with Major Cadogan, Dr Hermann Fiedler and his valet, Finch, Prince Edward motored up the Rhine to Stuttgart, to visit King Wilhelm and Queen Charlotte of Württemberg (Onkel Willie and Tante Charlotte), and while staying with them he visited Count Zeppelin who showed him his latest model, the Z4. In the summer vacation he stayed at Neustrelitz with the Grand Duke of Mecklenburg-Strelitz and his mother (the Duchess of Mecklenburg-Strelitz was born Princess Augusta Caroline of Cambridge and was a sister of the Prince's grandmother, the Duchess of Teck). From there he visited Prince Henry of Prussia (Uncle Henry, the Kaiser's younger brother, in fact a first cousin once removed) and (another first cousin once removed) the Duke of Saxe-Coburg, by birth an Englishman and Duke of Albany.

From there, too, he paid a call on the Kaiser at Unter den Linden where, appearing in one uniform after another, each more dazzling than the last, this cousin received him first sitting on a wooden horse in his own sitting room, and later at dinner, after which he took him to the opera to hear *Aida*. It is not surprising that the Prince developed at this time a fondness for the Germans and an admiration for their good qualities which he retained all his life.

Back in England he returned to Oxford, although he had originally gone up only for one year. Even before he left the university his father had begun to find his energy and love of hard exercise excessive.

You certainly have been doing a great deal – the King wrote to him – hunting two days, out with the beagles twice, golf and shooting one day, besides all your work, which seems a good deal for one week. I only hope you are not overdoing it in the way of exercise.[15]

And indeed the Prince's sheerly physical prowess was quite exceptional. An American undergraduate who was at Oxford with him wrote an account of a day when he was out with beagles and, although in fact it refers to a day in November 1914, after he had left the university and when he was up only for a short time, it is a picture of him which is appropriate here. After referring to the fact that most undergraduates spoke of the Prince of Wales as 'the Pragger', he said:

When we had taken off some of our clothes, and I had changed to my running shoes, we started. I must say, however, the Pragger wore a muffler and a heavy cap all the time we were out. There was a long stretch of walking, with the farmer and his sons on horses to scout out the hares, and a number of village people in the rear. But when the hounds did strike the scent, the Pragger was at the front in a jiffy, and there he remained all the time. With my running shoes and all the force I could put into it, I could not possibly keep up with him, nor could anybody else.

After some time the hare threw the hounds off the trail and we were compelled to stand about waiting while the hounds frantically tried to pick up the scent again. Then, taking several breaths, I mustered up courage to say to the Pragger, 'You don't run as though you were out of training.' To this he answered that he had not run during the entire time he had been away from Magdalen.[16]

In his second year the Prince entered very fully into the life of his fellow undergraduates, wining and dining as well as entering, if sometimes only as a spectator, into the various sports. In June 1914 in an article in *The Times* a fellow undergraduate wrote of him as follows:

He plunged at once into a catholicity of interests and amusements. He was entertained and gave entertainments in return; and those present found that, though he was at first rather shy, he was a delightful addition to a dinner party, most attractive in the quiet and humble part he took in the conversation, but full of humour and with opinions at once decided and sane. His laugh and smile are, perhaps, particularly attractive. ...

He played football eagerly and perseveringly for the second eleven; he became a private in the OTC; he played golf and ran with the beagles. He was a zealous spectator of college competitions and in Eights week there was no more untiring follower of the boat from the tow path. ... There are no great animosities in Oxford, but the members of one set are not always too friendly to those of another. There must have been anxiety before he came up that the Prince would not be able to avoid being drawn too much into a particular group. Moreover, the removal of the privileges and distinctions of his rank necessarily involved his being placed in a position of equality in a society fastidious as well as appreciative, and critical as well as kindly. Again, if the Prince were to play so many games and take part in so many activities, he had to steer a middle course between an undignified obscurity and an embarrassing prominence. Finally, some must have wondered whether anyone could enjoy such a life of irresponsible equality and then pass on to the life of high position and formality and publicity. ...

He has gone with perfect simplicity to such public acts as the welcoming of the French President or a Garter ceremonial and then returned with equal lack of ostentation to Oxford.[17]

And in November 1914 after the Prince of Wales had left Oxford and joined the Army, Sir Herbert Warren wrote a report of his sojourn at Magdalen which he also sent to *The Times*. In this he said:

From the first he took his own line, with equal modesty and firmness, determined in his own mind that he would be really *par inter pares*, that he would seek and accept no tribute except on his merits, that he would take as habitual and as assiduous trouble to avoid deference and preference as others to cultivate it, desiring as the old Roman poet put it, 'that men should give what he wanted, but that they should be free to deny': *Quodque dari voluit, voluit sibi posse negari.* His natural dignity and charm, and it should be added, the good sense and feeling of his college companions, and of Oxford generally, that democratic aristocracy, enabled him to go far in this resolve without mishap or untoward result. Once having started on it he pursued this narrow, nice line with increased confidence until it seemed the most easy and natural and unconscious thing in the world. ... He did not want to spend any time at all, even a little, in being treated *en prince*.

And Warren concluded with the oft-quoted passage which begins 'Bookish he will never be'.

Bookish he will never be; not a 'Beauclerk', still less a 'British Solomon'. Kings, perhaps fortunately, seldom are this last. That is not to be desired, but the Prince of Wales will not want for power of ready and forcible presentation, either in speech or in writing. And all the time he was learning more every day of men, gauging character, watching its play, getting to know what Englishmen are like, both individually and still more in the mass.[18]

In the last passage of the undergraduate and the first passage of the

President the same thing is successfully attempted – to define for the contemporary reader the quality which enabled the Prince to conduct himself so easily in his unique and uniquely delicate position. The words of both writers might have been merely sycophantic – something of the sort would certainly have been written in any case – but, if they had been, they could hardly have been so convincing. And, in fact, we owe to these writers the first impressions of the very real talent this Prince had for natural feeling and natural behaviour in an impossibly artificial situation, of the 'narrow, nice line' that, pursued with increasing confidence, would soon carry him to amazing heights of popularity almost all round the world.

4

FIRST WORLD WAR

In his report on the Prince of Wales's sojourn at Oxford quoted in the last chapter, Sir Herbert Warren says that, but for the outbreak of war in August 1914, the Prince would have returned to Magdalen for the Christmas term. The Duke of Windsor has told us, however, that he had by now persuaded his parents that he had had enough of Oxford and won their agreement to a programme of travel for the rest of that year, after which he was to have joined the 2nd Battalion of Grenadier Guards in January 1915. Whatever the truth of this matter, the Prince's university career came to an end when he went in June, for the second time, to the summer camp of the Oxford Battalion of the Officers' Training Corps. In July he was attached to the 1st Life Guards for a short period because his father, still disapproving of his seat on a horse, wished him to learn from the riding master. Every morning from nine to eleven he paraded in the riding school with the recruits, a system which left him free to experience for the first time the pleasures of the London season.

From the very first he showed an uninhibited zest for night life, and in the world of dinner parties and balls very soon conquered his natural diffidence. On 7 July he attended his first ball, by 9 July he is recording in his diary that he has become fond of dancing and loves going out, and, by 10 July, that he has had no more than eight hours' sleep in the last seventy-two. In common with all his contemporaries he was soon to have his natural development distorted, his environment blasted, and his sight accustomed to scenes of tragedy and horror which in the whole history of the world had hardly been equalled.

His first reaction to the holocaust was to try and get into it, and it must be accepted that no emotion in his whole life was more sincere than his desire to serve and to suffer, if necessary to die, as every young man in the land might do except himself. On the outbreak of war the instructions he received from his father were to wait in London until suitable employment could be found for him, a situation he found quite intolerable. He wrote to his father telling him of his distress at not being allowed to serve his country and asking him for a commission in the Grenadier Guards. 'And dear Papa,' he wrote in his diary, 'never hesitated for a moment & immediately instructed Lord Stamfordham to notify this to the War Office.'[1]

On being gazetted to the Grenadier Guards he was posted to the 1st Battalion, at Warley Barracks, Brentwood, and detailed to the King's Company. Ten days later the 1st Battalion was moved to London and in mid-September forty-eight hours' leave was granted as a preliminary to its being sent overseas. To his intense chagrin the Prince was immediately transferred to the 3rd Battalion, stationed at the same barracks. He determined then to call on Lord Kitchener. Dressed in the uniform of a subaltern he ran up the marble steps of the War Office where he asked if he might see the Secretary of State for War. When Lord Kitchener received him, the Prince sat at the great table in the famous oak-panelled room that looks out on to Whitehall and pleaded to be allowed to go to France.

'What does it matter if I am killed?' he asked, 'I have four brothers.'[2]

But Lord Kitchener explained to him that the danger was not that he might be killed but that until there was a settled line he might be taken prisoner, a chance he was not prepared to take.

The Prince persisted in his attempts to be allowed to go to France until in November 1914 he was attached to the staff of Field-Marshal Sir John French, Commander-in-Chief of the British Expeditionary Force. Sir Dighton Probyn, writing to Sir George Arthur, said:

I saw the dear ... Prince of Wales yesterday. He came to wish me good-bye – and it was really delightful to see the change that had come over him since he had last been in this room. On the last occasion he really *cried* with sorrow at the idea of 'being disgraced', and he said he was not being allowed to go to the war. Yesterday his face beamed with joy. Do let Lord Kitchener know this.[3]

When the Prince arrived in France he was employed on paper work and tasks such as the carrying of despatches, designed, as he was quick to see, to conceal from him his non-combatant role. And soon he was complaining that his only real job was that of being Prince of Wales. This job he already performed with a natural distinction and in January 1915 Lord Esher noted in his journal:

The King sent for me in the afternoon: he had just heard from the Prince of Wales, who has been motoring all through the French lines in Alsace. He has seen all the French generals and was extraordinarily well received. This must have done a great deal of good.[4]

And on 3 February (speaking of a liaison officer in Paris) he wrote:

Doumayrou lunched with us; he is optimistic. He praised the Prince of Wales very highly. The Prince was asked by a General what he thought of the prospects of the war. The boy replied that he did not think there would be any *courbe* of the enemy's line, but that they would suddenly collapse. This was thought a felicitous phrase.[5]

But the Prince would never rest content with the life the authorities had chosen for him and he steadily opposed their plans by his determination to see more active service. In May 1915 his efforts were partially rewarded and he was attached to the General Staff of the 1 Army Corps near Bethune. Lord Claud Hamilton was appointed as his personal ADC, a position he fulfilled until the end of the war. From Bethune the Prince made a practice of slipping up to the front to visit the Guards and other regiments. His energy was as usual extraordinary and he thought nothing of walking six miles before breakfast. 'The Prince eats little and walks much: we eat much and walk little,'[6] Oliver Lyttelton, a brother officer, wrote. This same officer has given us one of the most convincing pictures of the Prince of Wales ever written.

By the beginning of August 1915, though still an ADC, I was back amongst my brother officers of the Guards division. I found that the Prince of Wales was an extra ADC. He was the most charming and delightful human being that I had ever known. He, too, chafed at being at HQ, and all the more because he recognized that he was unlikely ever to be allowed to serve in a battalion. He never stopped trying.

It was a hot and sunny month and our duties at HQ were light. One morning, HRH came into the divisional staff office and asked whether I was also dining with Desmond FitzGerald,* his great friend, then commanding the 1st Battalion Irish Guards. 'If so, we will go together.' I said, 'Yes, Sir, I am the other guest,' and was delighted because Desmond lived three or four miles away, and the road was nearly all up hill. The Prince's car would get us there in under ten minutes.

About 6.30 he arrived again in the staff office and said, 'By the way, you have got a bicycle, I suppose? If you haven't you had better get one, because we ought to start. Dinner is at 7.30 . . .'

It was still very hot when we set out. 'I never get off,' said HRH as we faced a mile or two of hilly road. 'It is one of the ways that I keep fit.' I was in good training, but after a mile I had sweated through my Sam Browne belt and had begun to entertain some republican inclinations. However, we had a gay and delightful evening: the Prince was happy, and in the highest spirits; we had replaced our lost tissue with some old brandy, and free-wheeled home to our cage like schoolboys.

It is rarely that I am given a chance to pay my respects to him in these days, but for me his spell has never been broken.†

He used to lend his large grey Daimler car to any brother officer who could find the courage to ask for it. After I had returned to duty, I later got some leave and asked to borrow the car to get to Boulogne, because by this means you could get

---

* Lieutenant-Colonel Lord Desmond FitzGerald.
† Written in 1962.

an extra day in England. He sent me a slip of paper agreeing at once, but asking me whether I would take a letter to 'my people' at home. This was how he described the King and Queen.

I had some trouble with the French territorial guards at the road barrier at the entrance to Boulogne, and it took a few minutes of my fluent French and some bluff to get through. As I reached the quay the leave boat had just cast off, but I was not the Prince's messenger for nothing, and waving his letter to the King, I persuaded the embarkation officer to order the ship to put back. I swept up the gangway in triumph, and delivered the letter at Buckingham Palace in a few hours.[7]

It was true that the Prince never ceased to try to get into the trenches. He kept up a steady pressure on everyone he thought might help him. In July he motored forty miles to see Lord Esher who was staying at GHQ.

We walked in the garden for a long time – Lord Esher recorded – and he told me what he had written to me, of his keen wish to be in the trenches with his Guards. There is an idea of giving him a post on the staff of the Guards Division, which is about to be formed . . . Nothing could look better than the boy; his very clear skin is tanned, and this throws into relief the unusually bright and clear blue eyes. When presently the Field-Marshal's motor drove up he had a funny look of shyness and hid behind an oleander bush until I dragged him out. The Field-Marshal treats him with a sort of paternal affection which makes their intercourse quite easy.[8]

In September 1915 the Prince of Wales got his desire and was appointed to the staff of Major-General Lord Cavan in command of the Guards Division. Almost immediately his new position was endangered, however, by a narrow shave in which his driver was killed. The Prince had accompanied Lord Cavan on a tour of the Divisional front-line sector before Loos in which he got his first real sight of war, and, emerging from the trenches 'a muddy pair', they had found both cars riddled with holes and the Prince's driver dead. When Sir John French heard of this incident he issued orders for the Prince to be transferred to XI Corps Staff, but several days later the Prince met the Commander-in-Chief riding in his Divisional area, and himself persuaded him to rescind the order. Soon afterwards Lord Esher wrote to the Prince as follows:

I have been some days with the Field-Marshal lately and he told me of his meeting with you in a muddy lane, and the talk you had. You were perfectly right, and he was much touched by all that you said and claimed. You can imagine that I had rather a cold shiver when I heard of your escape, and the disaster to your poor chauffeur. But in future, which may be full of unforeseen difficulties in the years far ahead, your gallantry and determination to live the life of a soldier and run the risks will never be forgotten. If it ever is, then our people will have lost all their noble traditions of regard for what is best in their princes and in the youth of our country. You know what I feel about you, and my feelings are widely shared by the army, which is no longer a select caste, but is composed of young men of all classes of those who will be your own people one of these days, and who will have grown up with you. Meanwhile take reasonable care of yourself!...

I hear that the King is coming out; and it is an excellent thing. He ought to be mightily proud of you. Bless you, always, and take some care![9]

About the same time Lord Esher visited the Queen and recorded:

I had two hours with the Queen. I told her everything that had been going on in France. She is proud of the Prince of Wales. I tried to make her see that after the war thrones might be at a discount, and that the Prince of Wales's popularity might be a great asset.[10]

King George v's children had been brought up out of the public eye, and the Prince of Wales first became known to the British people through the quality of his courage, energy and enthusiasm during the war. He soon became a byword. 'A bad shelling will always produce the Prince of Wales,' the officers of his regiment said, and the private soldiers wrote home of his courage and keenness. 'The Prince complained that his employment was artificial,' Kitchener's biographer summed up laconically, 'and it proved impossible to keep him out of the front line whenever he had the opportunity to go anywhere near it.'[11]

Writing of this time Brian Inglis has said that the Prince was continually compelled to test himself, 'not out of any craving for popularity or esteem – on the contrary, the notion that they could be bought so easily would have embarrassed him. It was not the world but himself that he wanted to reassure.'[12] Except in the sense that this remark has a general application and might be made about a great many people, there is really no evidence for it. One of the greatest contradictions of the Prince's strangely contradictory nature was that he was both diffident and self-assured. He was often shy and uncertain in his relationships with other people (although never when he wanted something badly), but he had unusual confidence in his own opinions and no apprehensions about his physical courage. King Edward VII was humiliated all his life because he was denied active service and his grandson belonged to a generation whose idealism caused them to rush to the sacrifice. The British ruling classes have often failed in the liberal virtues but seldom in the heroic, and the Prince's reaction was the simple one of a brave and ardent young man. He had felt the impact of the war in a personal way very early. His equerry, Major Cadogan, was killed, as were Prince Maurice of Battenberg and three of the King's Household, Lord Crichton, Lord John Hamilton and Lord Charles Fitzmaurice. The Prince could not bear to be the only man held on the sidelines.

The emotions which caused him to receive the following letter from the King were more complicated, however:

Ld Cavan has written to Bigge about your wearing the ribbon of the Legion of Honour. It is very silly of you not doing what I told you at Easter time, which was to wear the ribbons of the French and Russian Orders that were given you. I know the French order was given you in peace time, but I explained that if you had not had it, you would have been given it for war service, the same as Uncle Nicky sent you his order especially. The French naturally are hurt if you don't wear it. So get both ribbons sewn on your khaki at once.[13]

Yet it was characteristic of the Prince and one of his most attractive qualities that he found it deeply distasteful to wear war decorations which he was denied the opportunity of earning, while other men had to endure the battles and the terrible life in the trenches without recognition.

His father sympathized with his desire to visit the trenches and Lord Stamfordham wrote to Lord Cavan:

The King entirely agrees to the understanding that when the Prince goes up to the front under instruction neither you nor Gathorne Hardy will be held responsible for his personal safety. His Majesty realizes that Gathorne Hardy himself, acting in the spirit of the C-in-C's orders will run no unnecessary risks, but of course risks there must be. We can only hope and pray that all will be well and His Majesty feels that this change will be good for the Prince and also that his occasional presence forward will be appreciated by the men.[14]

In the spring of 1916 the Prince of Wales paid a six weeks' visit to the Middle East to inspect and report on the defences of the Suez canal. Here he met Australian and New Zealand troops recently evacuated from Gallipoli. Then he reported for duty to the XIV Army Corps Staff commanded by Major-General Lord Cavan. The XIV Army Corps was spared the battles of Arras and Messines but took part in the Battle of Passchendaele. And watching this great offensive, begun with so much enthusiasm, achieve nothing but death and exhaustion, the Prince of Wales shared the weariness and cynicism of the combatant troops and learned from his own experiences to fear and hate war.

In the autumn of 1917 the XIV Army Corps was ordered to Italy to bolster the Italian army in rout from Caporetto. Apart from six weeks' home leave in March to make a tour of the defence plants, the Prince stayed with it until May 1918 when he was attached to the staff of the Canadian Corps in France, where he remained until the end of the war.

A story went the rounds during the war of two soldiers detailed to accompany the Prince. 'It's all very well for him,' one of them said to the other, 'but if he gets killed, we shall get the blame.' This story, at first sight merely amusing, pinpoints in a dozen words the quality of ruthless single-mindedness which carried the Prince to the centre of the war. In this situation it operated almost entirely to the general good. There can be no pretence that his war was the same as that of other young officers in the British Army or that he ever ran the risks that they ran. But, owing to his exceptional keenness and determination, he understood what the survivors had endured, saw with his own eyes the horrors that afflicted them, and shared the overwhelming and indescribable experience which divided them from the civilians at home; and because of his naturalness and modesty he made an unforgettable impression on the suffering and dis-illusioned armies in France. He took to riding a green army bicycle and he pedalled hundreds of miles inspecting camps or ammunition dumps and home again to write his reports.

Even now – he wrote forty years later – after three decades, I still meet men who will suddenly turn to me and say, 'The last time I saw you, you were on your bicycle on the road to Poperinghe' – or Montauban, or any one of a hundred French villages.[15]

On the road to Poperinghe he was on his way to visit Talbot House, a hostel for the troops in the town run by the Reverend Philip – 'Tubby' – Clayton. Becoming known by its initials in the morse code – Toc H – this was the forerunner of a Christian movement, one based on the complete equality of its members. More than fifty years later there was emotion in Tubby Clayton's voice when he spoke of the Prince. 'The Prince of Wales *loved* danger,' he said. 'He used to come often. Sometimes on his bicycle, sometimes on his feet, occasionally in a car. He loved to be with the men.' And he added reminiscently: 'There was something so nice about his clothes. I don't know where he lived, but he was always so nice and clean, but not too smart.'*

Writing to Hector Bolitho some years after, Tubby Clayton said that it was at this time he began his development as a conversationalist:

Now I think he is the most accomplished conversationalist in the world. Think of the hundreds of people to whom he speaks, people with strong prejudices. They may be social, political, intellectual or racial prejudices. A phrase askew in the Prince's conversation would be a disaster; a friend of England lost and perhaps an enemy created. ...

It is not generally fluidity which makes his talk so versatile. It is because of his undimmed, never-wearying attempt to find out facts, which he sorts discerningly and puts in his astonishing memory. From this store the facts have an odd habit of popping out at the right moment, months or even years later. All sorts and conditions of men thus become attached to the Prince with a kind of loyalty and appreciation which is essentially personal and has nothing to do with his unique position.[16]

At the end of the war the Prince of Wales did not immediately leave the army but was attached to the Australian Corps in Belgium, from where he visited the occupation troops in Germany and made his first contact with the American Expeditionary Force. Then in February 1919 he returned home.

* The Prince lived in a château and Finch looked after him.

5

THE PRINCE IN LOVE

Anyone making a study of the life of the Duke of Windsor is bound to be struck by the contradictory accounts of his personality and behaviour given by different people at different times. It will later be argued that this was partly the result of distortions in the eyes of the beholders and partly of the unusually rigid, one might almost say departmentalized, nature of his responses to other people – that is between those people he liked and with whom he felt at ease and those with whom he had nothing in common. Above all it is impossible to understand either his history or his nature without knowledge of the extraordinary consistency he showed in one of the most ordinary but important of human situations.

The Prince was deeply in love three times in his life. The first time he was twenty-one. In the First World War the army was granted fairly regular leave from France, and the Prince had in addition duties which brought him home more often than his fellows. In spite of his war service he spent a certain amount of time in England, and in 1915 he began a romance which was to last for three years.

From the time when Edward VII first acquired Sandringham, each generation of the Royal Family had been on terms of intimate acquaint-anceship with the Lord Leicester of the day. At Holkham, the land made famous to agriculturalists by Coke of Norfolk was, for the initiated, equally famed for its shoot. The two families visited each other regularly and were in the special relationship of neighbours. Lord Leicester's daughter-in-law, Lady Coke, was twelve years older than the Prince of Wales when she became the object of his affections. He saw much of her when he was in England and when he was away poured out his love in letters to her. It is not known to what extent she returned his love but certainly she was pleased and flattered by it. In societies when chastity is imposed on young girls, love affairs between young men and older women

.are not exceptional, but in this case, small, lively, with an individual humour, above all married, Lady Coke was a portent.

Nevertheless, by the spring of 1918 she no longer received the Prince's undivided attention. In February and March he spent six weeks in England to make a tour of the defence plants and at this time it is sometimes said that he fell in love with Lady Rosemary Leveson-Gower, daughter of the Duke of Sutherland. On 2 March we find Lady Cynthia Asquith reporting in her diary:

Pamela Lytton ... told us of the wild excitement fluttering all the girls over the Prince of Wales who, 'unbeknownst' to the King, has taken to going to all the dances. So far, he dances most with Rosemary and also motors with her in the day time. No girl is allowed to leave London during the three weeks of his leave and every mother's heart beats high.[1]

It has been suggested that the Prince of Wales wished to marry Lady Rosemary but that there was opposition to the match on the grounds that the heir to the throne must marry a royal princess while at the same time Lady Rosemary was reluctant to accept a future which would have led to her being Queen. In any case she married Viscount Ednam, the heir to the Earl of Dudley and a lifelong friend of the Prince of Wales, in 1919. It is unlikely that the Prince had serious intentions towards her, and it was the only time in his life that he showed more than a passing interest in an unmarried girl. And even at the time Lady Cynthia wrote the entry in her diary, he had already turned aside to travel the path that led him on to his strange destiny.

On an evening in either February or early March 1918 a young married woman named Freda Dudley Ward walked through Belgrave Square with an escort known to her as Buster Dominguez. Mrs Dudley Ward was married to a member of the family of that Lord Dudley who married Lady Rosemary Leveson-Gower, and she had two children. Dudley Ward was a Liberal Whip and he spent so much of his time in the House of Commons that his wife was accustomed to going out in the evening without him. On this particular evening, as she and Dominguez strolled through Belgrave Square, they could hear from the noise and see from the lights of an open door that a party was going on in one of the houses, and, as they approached this house, the maroons that, like the sirens in the second war sent civilians running for cover, proclaimed the imminence of an air raid. No obvious shelter offered itself except the open door of the house where the party took place, and, when the maroon went off, Mrs Dudley Ward and her escort ran through this door and stood in the hall of the house. Almost immediately the people at the party came streaming down the stairs and their hostess, who later identified herself as Mrs Kerr-Smiley, realizing what had happened, called her two uninvited guests to accompany her down to the cellar. Thus they presently found themselves standing rather isolated in the cellar of a strange house among a large group of people they did not know. It was at this moment that in the semi-darkness a young man appeared at Mrs Dudley Ward's side and started an animated conversation with her. He asked her where she lived and she replied for the moment at her mother-in-law's house in London, and asked him in return where he lived, and he said in London, too, and sometimes at Windsor. When the air raid was over Mrs Dudley Ward and her escort tried to leave, but Mrs Kerr-Smiley came over to her and invited her and her escort to come upstairs and join the party.

'His Royal Highness is so anxious that you should do so,' she said.

So Mrs Dudley Ward went upstairs and danced with the Prince of Wales until the early hours of the morning, when he took her home, Buster Dominguez having at some time disappeared forever into the night. The next day the Prince of Wales called on Mrs Dudley Ward and, after a Cinderella-like sequence in which he established which Mrs Dudley Ward it was he wished to see, there began a relationship which was to last for sixteen years.

The coincidence of their having met in an air raid is matched by one equally improbable. The Mrs Kerr-Smiley in whose house this meeting occurred was the sister of that same Ernest Simpson who would figure so largely in the life of Edward VIII. No less a person than the Duchess of Windsor has written of this event as follows:

Indeed, and it is strange to have it to come back to mind after so many years, one of Maud Kerr-Smiley's favourite stories about the British Royal Family was that, at a ball she gave in her house in Belgrave Square, towards the end of the First World War, the young Prince of Wales, then a soldier Prince on leave, had met a beautiful young woman, who became his first true love.[2]

There was never any secret about his relationship, although it was conducted with complete discretion. It was known to hundreds of people, not merely to the friends of her friends and the friends of their friends, but to everyone who went about in London Society and saw this young couple dancing together at the Embassy Club, or at private parties, or on golf courses, at the races, or in country houses. Mrs Dudley Ward is as ineradicable a part of British royal history as Mrs Fitzherbert or Mrs Keppel. Lord Esher to whom she was connected by marriage immediately made this comparison. He was very fond of his nephew's wife and, worldly Edwardian that he was, he did not object to her friendship with the Prince of Wales. 'But be discreet,' he often said to her, 'be like Mrs Keppel. Be discreet.'

There have been few published references to Mrs Dudley Ward. One of the first was written by Lady Cynthia Asquith only ten days after the entry from her diary already quoted. On 12 March 1918 she wrote:

Saw the Prince of Wales dancing round with Mrs Dudley Ward, a pretty little fluff with whom he is said to be rather in love. He is a dapper little fellow – too small – but really a pretty face. He looked as pleased as Punch and chatted away the whole time. I have never seen a man talk so fluently while dancing. He obviously means to have fun.[3]

There are two imperceptive statements in this account. In the first place the Prince of Wales was not a little in love with Mrs Dudley Ward, he was madly, passionately, *abjectly* in love with her. If this is not understood, nothing about his whole life can be understood and it is thrown so much out of balance that people contemplating it have found it necessary to invent explanations – a certain immaturity, for instance, which prevented him falling in love or wishing to marry. From 1919, when he returned from the army, to 1934, the whole of his life has to be set against the background of the fact that when he was in London he went every day to see her, usually at five o'clock, often staying to dine or to take her out to dinner, but, if this was impossible because of his public engagements, returning to her house later in the evening. When she took a house at Sandwich for the summer, he took one too, when she went to other people's houses, he went with her, wherever she was he followed her, physically whenever possible, when not possible with his extreme devotion. Occasionally he had brief affairs with other women, notably the much publicized one with Lady Furness, but he was never more than superficially faithless, and Mrs Dudley Ward was during all this time the strongest influence in his life.

Lady Cynthia Asquith is imperceptive once more in describing Mrs Dudley Ward as a pretty little fluff. She was, in fact, one of the most attractive women of her generation, being gifted with charm as some people are gifted with a talent for music or acting. It is notoriously difficult to analyse charm but one of the concomitants often present is an almost innocent candour which prevents any trimming of the personality towards the conventional attitudes of the day. In the 1920s, when these attitudes were conspicuously arrogant, speech was clipped, and strangers complained that in English Society no one ever introduced anyone to anyone else, except occasionally and vaguely by a Christian name, Mrs Dudley Ward had an unpretentiously friendly manner and original opinions to which she habitually gave a droll expression. Very small, she matched the Prince in physical attributes and, although she was not beautiful, her looks were very pretty and delightful. In a pleasure-loving age, she was pleasure loving, but she was not superficial and later in life she was to exhibit serious depths. Her most individual characteristic was her voice, which was rather thin and high, but with unusual intonations which made it oddly attractive. All her life she was adored by servants, secretaries, telephonists, everyone who had anything to do for her. This was not due to any ordinary courtesy but was because she did not alter the tone of her conversation by a hairsbreadth no matter to whom she spoke; so that, when it was to a butler or secretary at the end of the telephone, she made in her strangely intonated voice the same jokes or observations she would have made to the master of the house. Her influence on the Prince was said to be entirely for his good in all ways except one. But that, after all, was a fairly important one. It was for Mrs Simpson that King Edward VIII renounced the Crown, but it was because of Mrs Dudley Ward that he was free to do so.

The Prince of Wales was in middle life to perform an act which, however one regards it, must be admitted to be without parallel in the history of the crown. Even the most amateur of psychologists may surely be allowed to see significance in the fact that he began at the earliest age the process which led to regal suicide by depriving himself of the opportunity to marry and have children. For this Prince, who declared that he would not marry except for love, would never again find attractions in anyone who was not already a married woman.

One of the strangest aspects of his history is the extent to which his personality apparently changed as he progressed through life. A member of his Household who was with him for years said: 'There were three different people: the Prince of Wales, the King and the Duke of Windsor.' In the pages of this book there will be much evidence of this shifting personality and it is impossible to conceive of the young Prince of Wales doing or saying some of the things which are attributed to the Duke of Windsor; nor can the change be accounted for entirely by the loss of kingship, although this proved far more bitter than he had expected, the accompanying losses far greater.

Some things remained constant throughout: confidence in his own opinion in dealing with the world in general; in personal matters an unshakable determination to have his own way combined with an unusual certainty about what he wanted; above all, a capacity beyond what is often found in a man to become engaged with and dependent on a woman. During almost all the years that he was Prince of Wales he was attached to Freda Dudley Ward.

Mrs Dudley Ward quite naturally and quite soon became *persona non grata* to King George V and Queen Mary. In the chapters that follow much strain in the relationship between the King and his eldest son will be recorded. Earlier in these pages the King has been defended against what might be regarded as a charge of deliberate brutality to his children. It is more difficult to defend his behaviour towards them, and particularly towards his eldest son, once they were men. There must be a strong element of spiritual pride in anyone who places exaggerated weight on the rights of parental authority, a feeling of revolt against any assumption of equality on the part of the so-recently-dependent child. One must assume that for the King of England all temptations of this kind are magnified a hundred times. The King loved everything old, the Prince loved everything new (possibly in reaction) and they were separated by a generational gap that had been unnaturally widened by the war. Yet the King seems never to have made any attempt to understand the younger man's point of view or to sympathize with his aspirations. He continued to hector his children long after, if this had ever been appropriate, it had ceased to be. His own biographer says:

His trust in the discretion of all his Household, high and humble, moreover, was so complete that he did not stop to mince his words even in the presence of the servants, and his loud and trenchant chaff or criticism would ring out, not sparing the object of his wrath, in a publicity which obviously increased the embarrassment of a youthful victim.[4]

Many people would sympathize with his son if he felt that he should not need to depend so much on the discretion of the King's Household.

Yet all observers are agreed that as his younger sons married the King's anxiety concerning them ceased, and he at last established a happy relationship with them. Nothing has ever been said of the disappointment and pain he must have felt because of his eldest son's unassuageable devotion to Mrs Dudley Ward.

6
CANADA AND THE UNITED STATES OF AMERICA

The Prince of Wales was nearly twenty-five when he returned from the war and it needed no great perspicacity to see that he was miraculously fitted for the job to which he had been born and bred. The fact that he had original views as to how to behave when carrying out his public duties and an ability quite unusual in royal personages to project a personality on to the world stage had not yet emerged; but, with the looks of a wistful choir boy and a small, slight figure on which his army greatcoat swung with the grace of *haute couture*, he would have been seized upon for the role of Prince Charming even in the idealized world of dramatic art. This, and the reputation which followed him home from the war, was enough to make him a national hero; while, for those who met him at close quarters, he had subtler charms. Probably the most winning of these was his ability suddenly to dispel the natural sadness of his face with a smile which lit it brilliantly from within. In his public appearances, speaking in a strong, clear voice and the unexpected accents of a stable boy, he seemed always enthusiastic and friendly and moved by an intense desire to please.*

The only problem to be decided was where to make the best use of him. At home there was much discontent and disillusion among ex-servicemen, too many of whom were on inadequate pensions and unable to find either a job or a home, and it was believed – not unnaturally in view of the fate of

---

* It has been argued that this is a meaningless statement, since a stable boy might speak with one of a number of accents according to where he came from. It seems satisfactory to several of the Prince's friends, however, and if one is pressed to evoke a more precise impression one can only murmur the word Newmarket. The Prince's friends, Lord Westmorland and Major 'Fruity' Metcalfe, spoke in the same way. At this date none of the Royal Family had strictly upper-class voices, the guttural accent of earlier generations having given way to an impure vowel sound. Writing in 1951, Harold Nicolson said: 'I go to the BBC to listen to recordings of King George's broadcasts. His voice is so like the present King's. Very virile, rather bronchial, very emphatic. I notice the closed "o" as in "those"; it is what the BBC would call "off-white", meaning slightly Cockney.'[1]

the Romanovs, the Hapsburgs, and the Hohenzollerns – that the British monarchy was less stable than it had been at the beginning of the war. As the King's representative, there was much that the Prince might do in his own country. However, Lloyd George had a plan for him to undertake immediately a series of tours in the Commonwealth countries to thank them for their contribution to victory and to strengthen their ties with Britain.

Before he could do anything it was necessary for him to appoint a staff. Lord Stamfordham – the King's secretary – had been concerning himself for some time about the necessity to find a good Private Secretary for the Prince and he wrote:

A really good man as P.S. is indispensable. Someone with brains, with some Colonial knowledge; a facile pen – a nice fellow.[2]

The Prince appointed Mr Godfrey Thomas, who left the Foreign Office to join him and who remained with him for seventeen years until his abdication. As equerries, he appointed Captain Lord Claud Hamilton, who had been with him during the war, and a brother officer in the Grenadier Guards, Captain Piers Legh. Later in the year, before the Prince set off for Canada, his father insisted on the appointment of an older man and, at the suggestion of Lord Stamfordham, the Prince appointed Rear-Admiral Sir Lionel Halsey, who had been Lord Jellicoe's Captain of the Fleet at the Battle of Jutland and whom he immediately liked. Sir Lionel Halsey, referred to by the Prince and his Household as 'the old Salt', was to remain with him for many years.

The Prince's own most immediate concern was to gain his parents' permission to leave the family home. His choice for himself fell on York House, St James's Palace, which had been the home of his family in his childhood. York House was old and rambling and the furniture was largely Victorian. Here and there were some very fine pieces, however, and with the aid of these and of Mrs Dudley Ward the Prince made it all that he wanted. A reasonably large room on the first floor became his sitting-room, off which he had a bedroom and bathroom. The walls in the sitting-room were decorated by survey maps of the world on which the British Empire was coloured red. These maps were always kept completely up to date. On the ground floor of York House there was a large dining-room, but, when he was alone or had intimates with him, the Prince had his meals on a table brought up in front of the fire in the sitting-room. He ate very little all his life and at the time when most people had luncheon he often ate only an apple. He moved into York House just before he left for Canada in August 1919 and his servant Finch, who had been with him since the nursery, became his major-domo. The Prince's cousin, Lord Louis Mountbatten, occupied some of the rooms at York House for a time, and when he got married the Prince's younger brother, Prince George, took these over.

In the early part of that year, while he was in England, the Prince of Wales began to perform the public duties which fell to him as the King's heir. One of the first things he had to do was to learn to speak well. On this matter he had some advice from Winston Churchill, who told him not to try to be clever when he had a point to make but to use a pile driver.

It has been a habit with biographers of earlier sovereigns to give a list of their activities in some given year to show the variety and scope. By 1919 times had changed – transport was much easier – and the Prince's activities even in a few short weeks of late winter and early spring would make a list of boring length. The following account of some of the things that it fell to him to do is therefore only a small part of the whole, intended to show the variety of his undertakings rather than the extent. He visited Belgium and France, reviewing troops in both countries, and in Paris visiting the Queen of Italy and dining with M. and Mme Poincaré. He became President of a great many hospitals, of the RSPCA and of the Royal National Life-boat Institution, he was elected a Fellow of the Royal Society, a member of the Jockey Club, and he was initiated as a Freemason. (In the whole history of Freemasonry since 1737 only two of the heirs apparent had failed to become a member of a Craft, one of whom was George V.) He received the Freedom of the Cities of London and Plymouth. He visited the New Zealand Force and part of the Australian Fleet and he took the salute at Australia House on Anzac Day. He visited ex-servicemen at Rhondda and lunched with Mr Lloyd George at the House of Commons. Among the speeches he made were one to the Canada Club on the part of the Canadian troops in the war and another to the Canadian Officers Club; he made a speech to the Grenadier Guards Old Comrades Association at Chelsea Barracks, to the Printers' Pension Corporation at the Connaught Rooms and to the Fishmongers' Company at Fishmongers' Hall. He entered the ring after the fight between Jimmy Wilde and the American, Joe Lynch, and after shaking hands with the victorious Englishman made a short speech. At the end of a speech on the effect of war on art at the Royal Academy dinner, he said that the art of camouflage owed a great deal to a Royal Academician and remarked that it was 'after all but the same idea which brought the Birnam Woods to Dunsinane'.[3] If those who are aware of the extent of the Prince's own knowledge of Shakespeare feel that credit for the felicity of the phrase should go to his speech-writer rather than himself, he had by now learned to speak with a natural ease and good humour which did the speech-writer justice.

The Prince made a six-day tour in Wales and another in the West of England during which he visited all kinds of civic undertakings and in both places the Royal Society's Agricultural Show. He visited the Handley-Page Aerodrome at Cricklewood and from there flew over London. The account of his visit to his own estate at Kennington (belonging to the Duchy of Cornwall) reveals some of the reasons for his great popularity.

He was accompanied by an architect and the officials of the estate and he received a deputation from the Lambeth Central Labour Party. He agreed with this deputation that in the schemes for housing on the estate there should in future be collaboration between the officials of LCLP and those of the Duchy of Cornwall and that the advice of the former should be asked and considered; that if possible the new houses should be larger than those already on the estate; that in all building contracts the clause as to the trade union wages and conditions should be observed; that consideration should be given to the setting up of a Duchy of Cornwall works department to carry out all repairs and building; and that he would privately visit the derelict sites and houses on the estate. Mr Lockyer, President of the LCLP, said that they knew that the Royal Family really knew nothing of the actual conditions under which the workers lived, but they were conscious that they desired to do their best for the people of England, especially those on the Duchy estate. He then pointed out that a number of empty houses in Kennington Road were made to appear as if they were tenanted when the Royal Family visited Kennington by having curtains put up. To this the Prince of Wales replied that he had realized the houses were empty. Mr Walter Peacock, Secretary to the Council of the Duchy, said the curtains were put up at the instigation of the Lambeth Borough Council, who complained of the dilapidated appearance of the road. Mr Lockyer then said that there were houses on the estate which had been in a disgraceful state for years and he urged that building operations should be begun at once. Remarking that he was receiving from the estate only about half what had been paid to King Edward and his father, King George, the Prince said that nevertheless he could not tell them how much he appreciated their kindness in laying the facts before him and assured them that these should have every consideration. He would be most happy, he said, to walk round the estate with them and to have their advice and collaboration. He had been away for three or four years but he thought things had improved and would improve in the future. 'We hope to alter the present state of affairs.'[4]

It must be added that the Prince of Wales was as good as his word. He poured money into the estate for building and improvements and the Labour Council presently declared him to be one of the best landlords in the country.

In 1919 he did not satisfy everyone, however. When he asked Sir Frederick Ponsonby how he thought he was getting on, the latter replied unhesitatingly that there was a risk in becoming too accessible. The monarchy, in his opinion, must always remain on a pedestal. The Prince replied that times had changed since the war and he felt that one of his tasks was to bring the institution nearer the people, but Ponsonby remained cold and unconvinced.

At about this time the King addressed himself to the same topic, and the young man who as a child had so often been warned not to think himself better than anyone else was now adjured to remember his position. The war, the King said, had made it possible for the Prince to mix freely, but he should not believe he could behave as other people.

We owe to the Countess of Airlie, for more than fifty years lady-in-waiting to Queen Mary, a picture of the Prince of Wales at this time which shows him nervous and frustrated and still in some ways rather immature. He 'dropped in' at her flat unexpectedly at about midday one day.

He sat for over an hour on a stool in front of the fire smoking one cigarette after another and talking his heart out. He was nervous and frustrated, pulled this way and that. The Queen had told me that she was urging the King to keep him in England – 'to learn how to govern' as she put it, and make up for the gap in his constitutional experience caused by the war. Mr Lloyd George on the other hand had evolved a plan for a series of Empire tours for the heir to the throne, to strengthen relations with the peoples of the Commonwealth. The King was inclining to this idea, and the Prince himself preferred it....

The Prince told Lady Airlie that he knew he would have to work to keep his job. 'I don't mind that,' he said, 'but the trouble is they won't let me have a free hand.' And he told her how delighted he was to have been able to persuade his father to let him have his own establishment at York House. 'I don't want to marry for a long time,' he said, 'but at twenty-five I can't live under the same roof as my parents. I must be free to lead my own life.'

At the time of this conversation the Prince was temporarily estranged from the Queen for the reason that he had asked her to talk to his father about a marriage for Princess Mary, but he believed she had done nothing. 'I'm so annoyed with her that I haven't been near her for over a week,' he said. Lady Airlie begged him to go to see the Queen, and her diary continues:

I knew how much she had his happiness at heart, and how often she put in a good word for him with the King, but she could never relax sufficiently to tell him so. She still remained tragically inhibited with her children. They were all growing up now; she loved them and was proud of them but with the exception of Princess Mary they were strangers to her emotionally – a nest of wild birds already spreading their wings and soaring beyond her horizon.*

The King too was proud of his sons but he was often harsh with them simply because he could not bridge the gulf between their generation and his. I remember him telling me once at Sandringham how angry he had been with the Prince of Wales for calling something he had done 'good propaganda'.

'I told him never to say anything like that again. I do things because they're my duty; not as propaganda.'

As the heir to the throne grew older the stream of paternal criticism increased, but the Prince's behaviour when his father hauled him over the coals for being

---

* A strange metaphor to apply to these nervous and essentially well-behaved young men.

the 'worst dressed man in London', and laid traps for him with orders and decorations, showed the utmost forbearance.[5]

In August 1919 the Prince left on HMS *Renown* for Canada, touching at Newfoundland on his way. He took with him in addition to his permanent staff, Captain Dudley North (later Admiral) and Lieutenant-Colonel Edward Grigg (later Lord Altrincham).

At the time that the Prince of Wales left on the first of his Empire tours, it had already become plain that the most important function of modern royalty is to be seen. With the advent of the young Queen Victoria, the unpopularity of the Georges had lifted a little, but in the years of her long retirement it settled heavily down again and the republican movement gained strength. In the climate of that time it was possible for ambitious politicians such as Sir Charles Dilke and Mr Joseph Chamberlain seriously to advance republican views and sentiments. (Almost ever since it would have been regarded as a sign of such unstable judgment as to preclude any possibility of political advancement.) The republicans appealed to the self-interest of the country when they said that the Royal Family was altogether too expensive, not worth the money that it cost. Yet as Geoffrey Dennis has so aptly pointed out: 'The discontent with the Queen was not because England wanted less monarchy, but because England wanted more.'

She was paid to perform a great function and she did not fulfil that function. She was salaried as a mighty Queen and she lived, dingy and concealed, like a stingy private matron in a republic. The nation kept its side of the bargain. She did not keep hers. The nation said: We are getting too little monarchy for our money.[6]

During all the years of her retirement the Queen worked assiduously at her papers and carried out her constitutional rights and her duty 'to advise, to encourage, and to warn' to their extreme limits and beyond. The country quite rightly cared nothing for any of this and would not have paid a hundredth part of the money that went to the upkeep of the monarchy to any other permanent official for the performance of these services. As soon as she began to show herself in public, however, the republican movements disbanded, no more was heard of the expense of the Royal Family and the people began to express their hitherto unrevealed hunger for the mystery and magic of monarchy.

Harold Nicolson has pointed out that the influence which any British king or queen is able to exercise is derived not only from the personal qualities of an individual sovereign but also from the respect and affection with which the monarchy as an institution is today regarded. Such is the strength of feeling towards the latter, however, that whatever the personal qualities of the individual sovereign these will grow in the esteem and affection of the public, who require with any certainty only two things – that the king or queen shall be a respectable, God-fearing character, and that he or she shall be seen. Thus at any particular moment the sentiment of the public for the monarchy as an institution and for the personal qualities of the sovereign or for his heir will be inextricably mixed. The warmth and affection which is felt for the Royal Family always has a strongly personal element in it which must be felt in a personal way by those who are the object of it, and, since these are human, presumably welcomed and in some sense returned. 'Everyone said that the difference shown when *I* appeared and when Bertie and Alix drive, was *not* to be described,' Victoria wrote. 'Naturally for *them* no one stops, or *runs*, as they always did, and *do* doubly now, for me' – a statement which was quite untrue since Princess Alexandra, although in the third position, was idolized by the British public for her beauty, charm and unaffected manners.

When King George v visited the Commonwealth as Duke of Cornwall it was a turning point in his life. He worked so hard and put so much of himself into each and every occasion and almost for the first time tasted the pleasures of a personal success. 'As the tour proceeded and the strain increased, he gained in experience and rose to every occasion.... He and the duchess always appeared to be *interested*, never revealed traces of impatience, of fatigue, of hurry; showed constant courtesy, zeal and pleasure. The impression they left behind them was everywhere happy and satisfying.'

Far more important, nevertheless, were the impressions he received.

Among the impressions of lasting importance made on the Duke were, first and foremost, the loyalty to the Crown shown by all classes and creeds and races in every Colony he visited. It surprised him to hear from the lips of those who had never seen England even in childhood, constant and loving references to Home. ... It was forced in upon him that nothing had contributed so much to produce those unmistakable manifestations of loyalty and of love of England as the life and example of Queen Victoria. Everywhere she was a legend; among the more primitive races she had become invested with almost divine qualities. ... Her grandson now formed from what he heard and saw a lasting impression of the importance which must henceforth attach to the private lives and examples of those called on to fill her place and assume the power and symbolism of her great office.[7]

And of his tour in India, his biographer says:

He was thenceforth in no doubt about the importance of the Monarchy and the heavy responsibilities of a democratic sovereign, and the purpose and policy of his life were founded from these days on that knowledge. The key to the achievements of his reign was cut in India. ... He saw then the extent to which the whole Empire might stand or fall by the personal example set from the Throne, and to assure the integrity of that example he was to sacrifice much that men hold dear, much that makes life sweet.[8]

George V was the first member of the Royal Family to pay an extended visit to the Commonwealth and Empire. It was not surprising then that he regarded himself as an authority upon them. Now he sent his eldest son forth to represent him.

It was thus a foregone conclusion that throughout his tour the Prince would be met by cheering, enthusiastic crowds, that he would drive through lanes of loyal subjects, bowing, smiling and waving his hand, and that he would come back to England impressed by the strength of the feeling for the Crown. Was there, in addition, anything particular about this particular visit? Did he by his own qualities arouse some particular enthusiasm or particularly genuine emotion? The answer to these questions, which must in each case be 'yes', can be given with some confidence. There are many witnesses to its truth.

One of the most convincing of these is a few reels of film that have been incorporated into the film made from the Duke of Windsor's book *A King's Story*. When he arrived in Canada the Prince immediately inaugurated a new function which he put into practice as far as possible on all his tours and which became famous. Everywhere he went, in the large cities or at stations where there was little more than a platform and an elevator, although always a crowd waiting for him, he held an open, public reception at which all and sundry could come and shake him by the hand. In the film of *A King's Story* he can be seen at one of these functions, standing at the end of a kind of wooden platform. People file by him in a never-ending stream and, as each passes him, he extends his hand to shake theirs (at one point on his tour his right hand became so bruised and sore that he had to use his left) and for each separate individual he has a separate smile. Suddenly, as man after man passes by him, one of them halts and speaks a few words. Instantly the Prince's face, which has never lost attention or recognition of the uniqueness of each meeting, lights up with a more particular response and he answers the man immediately with some words that cannot be heard. The man who spoke to him nailed for all time his awareness of those others passing him and the intensity of his desire to please.

There are two other incidents in this film which, although they have no direct bearing on these tours, bear on the character of the Prince. One shows him performing one of his first public duties. He is seen, still a child, tapping a commemorative foundation stone four times with a mallet or hammer, once at each corner. What is touching about this otherwise ordinary action is the seriousness and anxiety of the Prince, which are out of all proportion to the difficulty of his task. Tap, he hits the stone, and tap again, as though his life and some part of the nation's welfare depended on this tapping.

The second thing, which no one who sees the film can fail to notice, occurs when the Duke of Windsor speaks a commentary on the film. He is seated in a chair in his own house and he is now a man of seventy. The camera returns to him again and again and he talks about what is happening. He speaks in a strong controlled voice with some American accent and he has an air of easy confidence; but all the time at the level of his waist his hands on his knee can be seen clasping and unclasping while the fingers and thumbs continually move against each other. In his writings and in this spoken commentary the Duke of Windsor often manages to give a rather complacent impression. This may be because autobiography is a difficult task for someone who is not an artist with the pen; or it may be that in his long exile complacency grew upon him to protect him against his thoughts. All one can say is that there is nothing complacent about the little boy tapping the stone or the continually moving hands.

Compton Mackenzie once wrote: 'If one may so put it, King George had all the talents but none of the genius of royalty. If his son may have lacked some of the talents he had the genius of it beyond any except a dozen princes in the history of man.'[9] At the time Mackenzie was in a mood for chivalrous hyperbole. If one paraphrased him to say that King George had the character for royalty and the Prince all the talents 'beyond any except a dozen princes in the history of man', a great many people would feel that it was not an exaggerated statement.

On the first of his tours the Prince touched down in Newfoundland and then landed in Canada at the port of St John and, travelling through Halifax, Charlottetown and Quebec, boarded a train just outside Quebec put at his disposal by the Canadian Pacific Railway which carried him through Canada, stopping not merely at the major cities but also at dozens of small stations, at every one of which people were gathered, often having come a long way to meet him. The train was a kind of hotel de luxe on wheels in which the Prince had a dining-room, drawing-room, bedroom and bath as well as room for all his staff. He went to Toronto and from there to Ottawa, paid a short visit to Montreal, then travelled on through North Bay, Sudbury, Saulte St Marie and through the wild and splendid scenery of the Algoma country to Nipigon. From Nipigon he went on in the train through Port Arthur and Fort William to Winnipeg, then through the prairies to Edmonton and Saskatoon, to Alberta and Calgary, and on to the Rocky Mountains. From Vancouver he went back to Montreal, for a more extended visit.

At all the big cities he attended functions, luncheon and dinner parties, made speeches, shook hands, smiled and bowed, untiringly willing, physically strong. At Nipigon he spent a few days roughing it in a camp with some Indian guides eating Indian food and fishing for trout. At Saskatoon he watched a demonstration of bronco-busting and achieved everlasting fame by mounting one of the broncos and staying on it until the end of the course. At Calgary he wrote 'Some ranch!' in the visitor's book of the owner of the biggest ranch in Canada, and at Alberta he bought a ranch for himself. Most striking of all, he received as great a welcome from the French-speaking population as from the English. Everywhere he met companies of men who had fought in the war and one of his chief functions was to review men who regarded him as an old comrade.

Hundreds of thousands of words were written about him. Newspapers all over the world were in those days prepared to devote columns to a description of such ceremonies. The accounts of journalists covering a tour of this kind seldom survive the event they are written about and nothing is so stale as the cheers of yesterday. Here and there, however, some writer was so struck by what he witnessed that he recorded the event in words sufficiently fresh to convey the spirit of it. Here are two excerpts from the account of the special correspondent of *The Times*:

Some of his speeches he reads; sometimes he speaks from notes which he hardly looks at; sometimes he just talks as a friend to friends. When he is on his feet he loses all self-consciousness. You hear without effort every word he says. He has a happy knack of saying the right thing in the right way, and his clear boyish voice has a quality of sympathy and sincerity which makes the speaker one with his audience.

The speech after luncheon yesterday was a severe test. He had to speak after Sir Robert Borden and before Mr MacKenzie King, both practised orators between whom he was sitting. The audience consisted of the Governor-General and the foremost statesmen, lawyers, soldiers and Consular representatives in the province. Never at a loss for a word, with hardly a glance at the notes on the table, he talked with an ease and happiness of thought and expression that any of them might have envied.[10]

And on 4 September 1919 at Winnipeg in an account of a ceremony at which the Prince bestowed decorations on returned soldiers or on their nearest relation, this correspondent wrote:

For each old mother or father, all of whom seemed to look into his face as if he himself was their son, for each pathetic widow, for each wounded soldier he had an especial word of sympathy and praise and understanding ready, and not a short one either, so that before he gave them his left hand to shake after pinning on the medal won in the great struggle, he never stopped talking for a moment. ... For him and for the Empire this gift of human sympathy and kindliness is a very great and valuable possession.[11]

And here is what Mr Everard Cotes, who travelled with him through Australasia, had later to say:

To be of the imperial present with its dignity and untarnished splendour, to come to the royal past with its long discipline of duty and decoration of anointed names, and to let it all sink as the Prince lets it sink into the simplest background of his personality is an achievement ... which makes at once the happiest appeal to human nature, the world over.[12]

Yet, however much the Prince pleased his hosts, he seems not to have entirely pleased his parents. His mother wrote to him on 7 September from Balmoral Castle.

One's head almost reels at the amount you are doing. I feel angry at the amount of handshaking and autograph writing you seem compelled to face. In one place I see you had to give yr. left hand as the right was swollen! This does not sound dignified, tho' no doubt the people mean it well. . . .

And in reply the Prince wrote almost apologetically that it was not his fault if the crowds went mad, but that he could be trusted not to let down the King's position or his own.

The King wrote to him from Buckingham Palace on 12 October:

You might take things easier during the last month of your visit & give yourself more spare time and more rest from the everlasting functions & speeches which get on one's nerves. I warned you what it would be like, these people think one is made of stone & that one can go on for ever; you ought to have put your foot down at the beginning & refused to do so much. [But he added] All I wish to say now is that I offer you my warmest congratulations on the splendid success of your tour, which is due in a great measure to your own personality & the wonderful way in which you have played up.[13]

At the end of his Canadian tour at the invitation of President Wilson the Prince crossed the border into the USA and travelled to Washington arriving there on 11 November, Armistice Day. The President was ill and was unable to receive him formally, but he was met by Vice-President Marshall, the British Ambassador Lord Grey, and General Pershing, whose hand he grasped with a broad smile, and he attended an Armistice dinner that night.

During the few days he was in Washington he visited the President who received him sitting up in Lincoln's bed, which had also been slept in by Edward VII, he visited the Red Cross Headquarters and a hospital where he talked to war veterans, and he went to Mount Vernon to lay a wreath on George Washington's tomb. (At Mount Vernon, where he was shown a photograph of his grandfather, he took a particular interest in the fact that he wore a 'plug hat'.)

Then he went for a few days' rest to Sulphur Springs, where he played golf and astonished the local population by his ability to turn a somersault off a diving board.

On 18 November he travelled to New York. Because the official welcome was to take place in the harbour his train was sent to Jersey City where he boarded an Admiral's barge and sailed across the harbour, through scores of vessels blowing their whistles in welcome, to Pier A, the Battery. As he came off the barge, his hand at the salute, the colours of the guard of honour slowly dipped to a roll of drums, while all the time guns boomed and the crowd cheered. From the Battery he drove to the City Hall where he was welcomed by the Secretary of State and the Mayor of

New York and where he was given the Freedom of the City. On his route he drove in an open motor-car, and as he passed beneath the offices of the stockbroking community he was greeted by streams of ticker tape floating down from the windows. In response he rose from his sitting position in the car and stood up bowing and smiling. That night he went to a gala at the Metropolitan Opera House where Caruso sang and also Rosa Ponselle. The next day the *New York Tribune* devoted twelve columns to describing his welcome. Here is an excerpt from it.

A week ago the Reception Committee planned every step and stage of the ceremonies to be used at the City Hall, where he was made a Freeman of New York, up to the minute last night when the Royal Barge took the tired young man to the battle cruiser allotted him. That programme was followed through yesterday but the men and women of New York rose up and overwhelmed it. They drowned the sound of brass bands with the din of their voices shouting their welcome. They obscured the decorations hung along Lower Broadway with blizzards of torn paper, they fought the heavy police guards to get close to his car, and in the Aldermanic Chamber at the City Hall they broke through to cheer him frenziedly.[14]

And the *New York World* said:

It was not crowd psychology that swept him into instant popularity but the subtle something that is called personality. Three months ago the *World* correspondent wired from St John, N.B., 'New York will fall in love with this lad'. New York did.[15]

During the next four days the Prince visited West Point, to review the troops and cadets, decorated American soldiers, dined with the Pilgrims of the USA, attended a ball at Mrs Whitelaw Reid's and went to a luncheon party at the Piping Rock Club. On the Friday afternoon, 21 November, he gave a tea party on the *Renown* for a thousand New York school boys and girls and on the Saturday morning he held an investiture. He stood in naval uniform between two members of his suite in the full dress of the Guards with bearskins. Behind him the officers of the *Renown* were drawn up in a semicircle. He distributed over one hundred decorations. Then he moved aft and began a farewell celebration to hundreds of people. Later he went over the side and stepped into a barge to review five thousand Boy Scouts drawn up on the river bank and afterwards returned on board for a farewell luncheon party. That afternoon the *Renown* sailed for home.

In the USA, as much as in the British Dominions and Colonies, the Prince of Wales, by his personality and behaviour, lifted his hosts off the horns of their dilemma. They longed, like humanity everywhere in the world, to be allowed to idolize royalty; yet to do so was against their whole culture and philosophy, against the idea they wished to preserve of themselves as citizens of the New World. In the aftermath of the war the revulsion against the forms and ceremonial of European society, a society which had so conspicuously broken down, was particularly strong. Democracy was thought of not so much as a political method, but as a romantic ideal. If a kingly figure had come among the peoples of the West dressed in ceremonial costume, holding himself aloof and silent, bowing and waving, they would no doubt have been moved to much the same emotion, but there would have been a sense of unease and shame in showing it so openly. When they saw this smiling, friendly, handshaking boy with his obvious desire to please and his intense awareness of each and everyone, they were able to adore in him qualities they believed in and which they felt it respectable to praise. In all the countries that he visited the same words and phrases could be heard. 'A real democrat', 'a good sport', a 'Prince with no pretence', 'Sailor Prince', 'Democratic Prince', 'Our Prince', and more formally: 'The frank democracy of the Prince had a strong appeal in Washington', 'The Prince showed a boyish enthusiasm and interest', 'Behind the formal expression there is the genuine sentiment', and so on.

All courtiers and most royal personages have believed that if the 'mystery and the magic' are to be preserved, royalty must remain on a pedestal. There has never been much evidence for this view. A story is told (and much approved) about Queen Alexandra who, when visiting a hospital, noticed one man who looked particularly downcast. She inquired about him and was told that he had been wounded in the leg and had just been told that his knee would be permanently stiff and useless. Immediately the Queen went to his bedside. 'My dear, dear man,' she said, 'I hear you have a stiff leg; so have I. Now just watch what I can do with it' – and lifting up her skirt she swept her lame leg over the top of his bed-side table.[16] There was nothing very aloof about this, yet this Queen inspired a spontaneous love in the English as possibly no one except her grandson has ever done. It is clear, however, that it is safer to remain on a pedestal. To come off it, to behave in a natural and human way, to let the mystery and magic take care of themselves requires an unusually unaffected nature, a lack of a narrow kind of vanity, a real interest in other people. The odds against these qualities being part of the equipment of a member of the Royal Family must be very high indeed.

The Prince of Wales had them. He also had another quality which reinforced these and which was to prove less fortunate in the long run. Like his father before him he was exceptionally opinionated. He believed that he understood his own generation, the generation that had been through the war, as none of his family or their advisers could. Now, as he sailed home on the *Renown*, he was able to reflect that it was exactly by ignoring the views of his father and his courtiers and going his own way that he had made a success of his tour beyond anything that had ever been seen before.

7
NEW ZEALAND AND AUSTRALIA

The Prince of Wales spent the first two and a half months of 1920 in England, starting on a strenuous round of public duties immediately after Christmas. Although so little of his adult life had been spent in this country, the success of his tour had preceded him home and his reputation had grown proportionately.

In a single year – Lord Curzon of Kedleston said, moving the address of thanks in the House of Lords following the King's Speech – the Heir to the Throne, after modestly concealing his services and ability in the strenuous occupation of war, has sprung into fame as one of those forces which are likely to be of the greatest good in the future both to his country and the Empire as a whole.

The British population of that day – proud of their Prince and anxious to welcome him home – were personally captivated as much by his choice of leisure occupations as by his strenuous attention to duty. Today no member of the Royal Family can be seen with a pack of hounds without arousing controversy because large sections of the public have an intense antipathy to blood sports, but hunting was regarded then with uncritical affection as a national sport, and the Prince's courage as he hurled himself across country did as much to please the population here as riding the bronco had done to please the crowds in Canada. 'I started off to pilot the Prince,' Captain Drummond of the Pytchley Hunt confessed to the Press, 'but before we had gone very far he was piloting me.' And it pleased the public to read – sandwiched between accounts of his appearance at public luncheons and dinners, his visits to various parts of the country and his continuous speech-making – an account of the Prince's appearance in the final of the Squash Rackets Handicap at the Bath Club. Playing off a handicap of seven (half a game or the equivalent of 30-love at lawn tennis) he met Captain Eric Loder (a well-known sportsman of the day and Master of the Pytchley Hunt, who once walked to Brighton in a match against Captain Buckmaster – Buck of Buck's Club – and won it).

The Prince keeps his elbow up – *The Times* reporter recorded – and his shoulder too. Granted he plays the strokes very accurately, though the strain must be enormous. Captain Loder hammered away at his opponent's backhand and that in the end beat him. The strain was too great and in the end he made a mistake in hitting the ball too low. ... Whoever takes on the Prince has got to be a good player as well as a hot one before the match is finished.*[1]

However recently we have been given evidence that there was a good deal of strain behind the scenes at this time. On 22 January 1920 Frances Stevenson (afterwards Lady Lloyd George) wrote in her diary:

D. [David Lloyd George] says there has been a quarrel between Grigg & Halsey who went to Canada with the Prince, & the Prince has taken Halsey's part. D. says this is a great pity, as Halsey lets the Prince do as he likes, while Grigg is far the abler man. They are all three coming here tomorrow morning.

And on 23 January:

D. had a tough time with the Prince today. The latter was determined to have his way about giving Halsey political authority during the tour. The P.M. was as equally determined that Grigg should have this authority, & eventually had to insist as Prime Minister that the Prince should agree to it. Eventually he did, but objected that the question of where he should go to was not a political matter & that therefore it could be left to Halsey. The P.M. had to point out that it was essentially a political matter.[2]

From Lady Lloyd George we also learn that there was trouble of a more serious kind. The intention in the early part of 1920 seems to have been that the Prince should go to Australia and New Zealand in the spring and on his return set off almost immediately to India in order to arrive there in the autumn in time to open the new constitution. On 12 February 1920 Lady Lloyd George wrote:

The Prince of Wales ... was there. ... He is very sick at having to go off on another tour, & when I said it was hard luck, said: 'Well, you tell the P.M. that!' He evidently thinks D. is largely responsible for it. I said it was most important that he should be in India to inaugurate the reforms, & of course they could not be delayed. He said: 'Well; I hope it will do some good.'[3]

On 16 March of the same year she continued:

D. went to see the Prince of Wales off this morning.† The King & Queen are very sniffy with D. because the latter has been listening to the Prince's objection to going to India after his Australian tour, & to the suggestion that Prince Albert should go instead.

---

* In fact *The Times* reported with a bias in favour of royalty. The Prince's handicap speaks for itself and he had little natural skill at squash or any other game, in spite of enormous enthusiasm.
† To New Zealand and Australia.

Anyhow the Prince when he came last Friday to see D. again touched on the question of India, & begged D. to get him out of it, & to send his brother. It is certainly hard lines on the boy to be away from England practically till next July twelve-months. D. said he would think about it. Apparently the Prince went to the King & Queen & told them about it, & they were furious that D. had discussed the subject with the Prince before discussing it with them. On the station this morning they were extremely frigid with D., indeed D. says that the Queen would scarcely shake hands with him, and seemed openly to resent D. making a fuss of the boy. However, it only amuses D., who is really very fond of the Prince, who appears to be just as fond of him.[4]

It is a matter of history that the Duke of Connaught travelled to India that autumn to open the new constitution in place of the Prince, the reason being given that the Prince needed a rest for the sake of his health and would delay his visit to the following year. In spite of this there is another entry in Lady Lloyd George's diary on 18 June 1921; a year later.

Went to Cuckoo Belville's party on Thursday night – lots of celebrities, including the King of Spain and the Prince of Wales, who had come up from Windsor after his father's dinner party and intended returning there before morning. He must have had one of his gloomy fits, for he came up to me and remarked: 'There's more trouble about India – have you heard?' For the moment I thought he meant a rebellion, but then it occurred to me that he must mean his visit there, & I said: 'But I thought it was all settled. Don't you want to go?' 'Of course I don't want to go,' he replied petulantly – 'I know,' I replied, 'but I thought you had become more or less reconciled to the idea.' 'Oh! I suppose I can become reconciled to anything,' he replied. 'Does the P.M. think I ought to go?' I could not understand why he brought the subject up again, as I knew it had all been settled ages ago, but I suppose he must have been feeling particularly depressed about it. Apparently he had been having an argument with his father about it, for I heard that the Prince said he would ask the P.M. whether he really wanted him to go. Whereupon the King said: 'I don't care whether the P.M. wants you to go or not. I wish you to go & you are going.'[5]

This evidence opens up a whole field for speculation. Were the King and Queen without feeling for their gifted if wilful son, who had worked so hard and known so little of the pleasures of youth? And, if they were ready to sacrifice him personally to the monarchy, were they unheedful of the need to nurture the heir to it? Probably not entirely. We know that in the end the Prince's visit to India was put off for a year. Nevertheless, there is plenty of evidence that the schedules for his tours were exhausting and that the King agreed to programmes that were nearly impossible to undertake.

And what of the Prince himself? It is early days to be told of his 'gloomy fits'. Later in life his moodiness was a factor to reckon with, and he often disappointed people he could so easily have delighted. It is usually assumed that this was because he became spoilt and easily bored but there is also evidence of a genuine melancholia. Were his remarks as reported by Lady

Lloyd George simply the result of a 'gloomy fit', or is it possible that he was cast in so private a mould that he had no public ambition, that he did not enjoy the excitement of his tours, the exercise of his natural talent, his popularity, and the feelings he aroused in other people in the way one would naturally assume he did. Given hindsight one may believe that his enjoyment was less, his demands on life more complex than his public appearances, standing smiling in uniform to receive the cheers of the crowds, would suggest. For the rest he was young and loved above everything the pleasures of youth – dancing and night life, hunting and polo. It does not require much explanation if he sometimes longed to have time to himself. Above all, he was in love. At this time in his life he was forced sometimes for years at a time to put his public work before his strongest desires. His cousin, Lord Louis Mountbatten, had been attached to him as a personal aide for the tour of New Zealand and Australia (officially Flag-Lieutenant to Admiral Halsey). On 16 March 1920 he called for the Prince at Mrs Dudley Ward's house to drive him to Victoria station on the start of this long journey. The Prince was in tears when he came out to join him.

'Have you ever seen a Post Captain cry?' he asked his cousin, and Lord Louis confessed that he had not.

'Well, you'd better get used to it,' he said, 'you may see it again.'

People stood cheering in the streets as they drove to the station, and at Victoria a crowd of two or three thousand people broke through the barriers erected on the platform and raced cheering towards the Royal party. They were held back by a quickly formed chain of police and Australian soldiers but they crossed the line and stood on the opposite platform, waving farewell to the Prince, who stood to attention and saluted them. In Portsmouth crowds again waited to see him board the *Renown*.

The *Renown* entered Auckland Harbour on 24 April. On her way she went through the Panama Canal and called in at San Diego and the Hawaiian Islands as well as at the Barbados and Fiji. At Barbados the sugar pickers called to each other: 'Come! It's a too sweet boy,' and the Prince replied to a rumour that the islands were to be sold to America by saying: 'I need hardly say that the King's subjects are not for sale to other governments.' At Fiji he accepted the homage of the chiefs, looking 'very young, fair-haired and courteous'.

He landed at Auckland on the eve of Anzac Day and it was said that he was flushed and seemed embarrassed by the depth of the welcome he received. His first act was to attend the service at St Mary's Cathedral in commemoration of the men who had died five years before, and throughout his tour of New Zealand as in Canada and later in Australia he was continually met by small groups of ex-soldiers and sailors, with some of whom he had served at the front. He travelled on a train through much of New Zealand, standing as before on the back platform, smiling and waving to the people who stood beside the railway line to see him, and visiting twenty-one towns and cities before he reached Wellington. On 26 May the *Renown* sailed into Melbourne Harbour where the fog was so great that the Prince had to transship to the *Anzac*, sent out for him, before he could land.

It is not proposed to follow him on his tour of these two great countries, where he spent the whole summer, visiting over two hundred different places and travelling by sea and land a total of nearly forty-six thousand miles. From Auckland he went to Christchurch and presently to Melbourne, Sydney, Canberra, Perth, Adelaide; then to Hobart in Tasmania, back to Sydney, to Brisbane and back to Sydney for his departure. On the way home he visited Fiji, Samoa, Mexico, Panama, Trinidad, British Guiana, St Lucia, Grenada, Dominica and Montserrat. Everywhere he went his popularity increased and everyone found him irresistible. He had by now become exceedingly professional and he had the great gift of a naturally clear voice. At Melbourne where he was to speak at a State Banquet in the Hall of Parliament House he was warned by the Prime Minister, Mr Hughes, that he would find both the acoustics and the audience difficult, and the Prime Minister himself, speaking before him, failed entirely to surmount the first of these difficulties. The Prince then rose and, speaking in a quiet and natural tone, made every word audible, thus creating conditions in which his modest, smiling and unaffected manner scored overwhelmingly. But wherever he went it was above all his talent for the easy exchange, the touch of personal interest that raised the natural enthusiasm of the crowds to a pitch of adoration. The Australians had believed the accounts from Canada exaggerated but they were soon behaving as though it was they who had discovered him.

'They told me,' one man said to the Press, 'I would have to wear a top hat and I swore I would not wear anything but ordinary clothes. They are good enough for me and good enough for anyone. I went and I watched this boy carefully and I soon made up my mind that he was all right and that it was the people who had talked about having to wear a top hat who had put their foot in it. They were out of touch with the Prince but I was not.'[6]

And above all they were moved by his capacity to be moved himself. One man told *The Times* reporter that he had been near the Prince and seen his eyes fill with tears again and again as working women and small children filed past him in an interminable stream. 'He could not have spoken then however much a Prince he was.'

The Nation – *The Times* correspondent wrote from Australia – regards the Prince as simple and generous-minded, without 'side'. It is disposed to think that his staff is inclined to check these impulses, an idea which the staff will do well to be careful to dissipate, for it is the chief threat to the success of the tour.[7]

And so on this occasion the staff were forced to adopt the Prince's method and let the mystery and the magic look after themselves.

Two things must be emphasized. The first, that while as it turned out no opportunity could have been more propitious, probably no one in our history has ever had so marked a power as this young Prince to rivet the ties of emotion and sympathy between the Mother Country and the millions of men, women and children in the outlying commonwealth of nations. The emotions felt for England could never be explained merely by political or economic advantage, and there is no doubt that the monarchy was the greatest single influence in welding these disparate nations together and in creating the feeling of integration and patriotism which was so remarkable and so spontaneous in each of the great wars. After the first war, when the monarchical principle proved in Europe too weak or too unpopular to hold the allegiance of the people, it would have been easy to predict that the young countries of the western world would soon outgrow its influence. The effect of the Prince of Wales's tours can never be exactly measured, but he aroused emotions then which attached the people to the Crown, survived the restlessness of the post-war years, the abdication crisis, and the transfer of loyalty to the new King and Queen, and brought the Dominions in to stand unquestioningly by Britain's side on the declaration of the second war. The populations of the countries he travelled through would no doubt have found much to love in any royal personage who visited them, but the manners and the personality of this young prince were in tune with a philosophy they cherished deeply and were marvellously reassuring to the sense of uncertainty and insecurity inevitably felt by the citizens of these aggressively young countries.

His physical energy was extraordinary, and in addition to his public functions he was always ready to join enthusiastically in any sport provided for his entertainment. While at Christchurch he went hare hunting, and, although he twice fell off the dark brown show-jumper on which he had been mounted, he finished the day as strongly as anyone in the field. In New South Wales he hunted kangaroo and on one occasion he gave a demonstration of his exceptional physical powers by riding all day and then deciding that he would finish the last eight miles home on foot, a feat he proceeded to perform at a swinging pace. That evening he attended a small dinner and dance at Government House.

Violent physical exercise seemed necessary to him all his life, but this fact should not be allowed to minimize the physical and mental strain of these tours, the real slogging hard work he undertook. He was never for long at one place, while he had to speak, lunch, dine, receive addresses, shake hands, smile, wave, for day after day, week after week at a time. In Melbourne, for instance, he replied to twenty-six addresses. Although his speeches were largely written for him, he always introduced interpolations and his own figures of speech. The enthusiasm of the people and particularly of the Australians was sometimes expressed in ways that must have become difficult to bear. Writing many years later, he said that in Australia even a car was often no protection against his welcoming hosts, who would snatch him out of it and pass him from hand to hand in the streets. Worst of all was the touching mania which caused crowds to close round him and, pushing and shoving and treading on his feet, to aim the end of a folded newspaper at him if they could not reach him with their hands. On all public occasions he drove himself to do all that was required of him and showed an almost obsessive desire to give to each individual and every occasion.

Nevertheless, on this tour and in his twenty-seventh year he began to exhibit a duality in personality and behaviour. Genuine hardship seems to have been caused him, here as elsewhere, by the determination of private people to entertain him, and it is impossible not to sympathize with the young man, who at the end of a long day was expected to appear, fresh and convivial, at private parties. But he responded to the pressures put upon him by a personal selectiveness which, as the years went on, involved the disappointment of very many people and which, in the circumstances, was really not acceptable. The letter which follows has been chosen because it is well authenticated and because it describes an event which occurred thus early in his career, but it is typical of many letters which are part of a post bag following newspaper serialization of the history of his early life, and described similar events all over the world.

My in-laws in Queensland – the writer says – organized a large dance when he was out there in 1920 and invited him to stay for it, & in fact had built on to the house! but he never came having said that he would – making out that the rains had made the roads impassable when in fact he had found the Bell girls in Boonah more to his liking and didn't want to leave them. Various people motored over the road to prove that it was passable – but he never came, and hurt a great many feelings in consequence.*

Two further observations must be made of this time. First, his cousin Lord Louis Mountbatten, who at this time was as close to him as anyone living, bears witness to a genuine streak of melancholia. Writing many years later, he said: 'On this journey I got to know my cousin very well indeed. I soon realized that under that delightful smile which charmed people everywhere, and despite all the fun that we managed to have, he was a lonely and sad person, always liable to deep depressions.'

When these depressions were on him the Prince would sometimes pass whole days by himself in his cabin on the *Renown*, seeing no one except his cousin and hardly eating. Lord Louis Mountbatten wrote to his mother: 'I am having a great time, but it is very difficult to keep David cheerful. At times he gets so depressed, and says he'd give anything to change places with me.'[8]

And writing of the Indian tour which took place over a year later, he speaks of the Prince as still tired after the previous tour.[9]

* Letter to the author from Mr Ian Scott.

The Prince himself by the time he left Australia was physically and mentally exhausted. On the way home he had time for reflection and for the first time he saw clearly the nature of his official life.

> Lonely drives through tumultuous crowds, the almost daily inspection of serried ranks of veterans, the inexhaustible supply of cornerstones to be laid, the commemorative trees to be planted ... sad visits to hospital wards, every step bringing me face to face with some inconsolable tragedy ... always more hands to shake than a dozen Princes could have coped with. ...[10]

And he reflects that he was 'a wayfarer rather than a sojourner', while as soon as he began to know places or people he was forced to move on.

These words were written many years after the event, but if they really represent – and there is some reason to believe they do – the thoughts of the young Prince of Wales as he sailed home to England, it suggests that, whereas the cheering populace can easily dispense with, or compensate for, the 'mystery and the magic' of monarchy, some elemental faith in it is necessary to the man himself. When one contrasts the Prince's perfectly reasonable and understandable words, his all-too-realistic visions of cornerstones and commemorative trees, with the awe experienced by his father in similar circumstances, the almost sacrificial sense of dedication, one cannot feel moved to the award of praise or blame; but one must pity the young Prince, born in so many ways so suited to his inexorable fate, but with a clarity, a *practicality* of vision which, in some spheres most valuable, was here such a desolating gift.

8

INDIA

From the autumn of 1920 until the autumn of 1921 the Prince spent a year at home. His own recollections of that year are chiefly concerned with the splendours of the London season and, characteristically, with the fact that full-dress uniform was restored to the Household Troops, who mounted guard in red tunics and bearskins. This was the year of the coal strike and the first post-war slump, but it was also the year in which a full return to peace-time conditions was attempted. The wealth and splendour of the 1920s would never approach that of the years before 1914, particularly in relation to the numbers of servants kept and the plurality of houses in full commission, but servants in livery once more served food on gold and silver plate in the great houses of London and a whole society gave itself up to entertaining. The Prince of Wales belonged to a generation of *jeunesse dorée* who danced with a feverish determination to shut out the memories of the terrible past.

In the winter of 1920–1 he started hunting fairly regularly, sometimes with the Household Drag Hounds, sometimes with the Pytchley, and at least once with the Quorn. He never acquired a strong seat on a horse and, without this, but with an absolute determination to surmount every obstacle that came in his way, he earned a reputation for the ease with which he parted company with his horse as well as for the courage with which he continued to invite this fate. But he rode very good horses and was very light and, when in the spring he started to ride in point-to-point races, he did so with some success. His first race was the Grenadier Guards Race at the Guards Point-to-Point at Warden Hill. Riding a horse called Pet Dog, he came third in a field of sixteen, and he achieved this feat in spite of falling off at the second fence. Then he won the lightweight race at the Pytchley Hunt Point-to-Point on Rifle Grenade from a field of fourteen runners, leading by five lengths over the last fence and winning by a length. On Rifle Grenade he was also second at the Quorn. But his greatest triumph – and a real one – came on 1 April, when, on Pet Dog, he won the Welsh Guards Challenge Cup at Hawthorne Hill, riding over a steeplechase course and under National Hunt Rules. The King and Queen, the Duke of York and Prince Henry were present to witness his success, as was also Lord Stamfordham. Lord Stamfordham said that he was the first Heir Apparent to ride in a race, much less ride a winner, but he added that he hoped HRH would never run such a risk again. In the spring the Prince took up polo with the same enthusiasm, playing at Hurlingham, Roehampton or Ranelagh whenever he got the opportunity.

In spite of all this, what is most notable in the record for the year is still the rigour with which he performed his public duties. Once more he drove himself beyond what even the strongest physique could endure, and, in addition to the endless round of speeches, dinners, luncheons, horse shows, ex-service men's associations and so on, he undertook a series of special visits to the provinces. He spent three days in Glasgow, ten days in Devon and Cornwall, visiting the Scilly Isles, Bristol and Bath, and four days in South Wales. In July he went to Knowsley for a five-day visit to south and west Lancashire. Randolph Churchill tells us that Lord Derby was also extremely energetic but says that even the capacity of these two remarkable men must have been under a strain on that occasion. In the five days they visited Ormskirk, Southport, Formby, Great Crosby, Waterloo, Litherland, Bootle, Liverpool, Ashton-under-Lyne, St Helen's, Manchester, Salford, Eccles, Irlam, Prescot, Fleetwood, Clevelys, Blackpool, St Anne's, Lytham, Kirkham, Mowbreck, Hale, Preston, Leyland, Chorley and Wigan. Enormous and wildly enthusiastic crowds attended them throughout the tour.

Writing to the Viceroy of India, Lord Reading, about the plans for the Prince's coming tour, Lord Stamfordham said:

For the moment the Prince's health is suffering from the bodily and mental strain of the life which he almost insists upon following, and I am certain that when he comes to India he will have to take things much easier than he has done hitherto, either at home or in the Dominions. . . . I would strongly urge that his programme allows ample time for rest and recreation.

But in a later letter he said:

Lord Derby's speech was unfortunate. The Prince had had no doubt a trying tour in Lancashire: but, as someone remarked, he was able each evening to play several sets of lawn tennis before dinner! HRH is now perfectly well and I think looking forward to his tour.[1]

The speech which had earned Lord Stamfordham's disapproval was delivered by Lord Derby to the Lancashire Division of the National Unionist Association on 9 July. He said:

I realize that my demands on HRH's health and strength were more than I should have made. .... He was absolutely exhausted each evening but his only thought was whether he had left undone anything that he ought to have done. After I left him last night I felt that if I had my way I should say to him: 'Look here, young man, your spirit is willing. You are giving up the whole of your leisure to fit yourself for the task which will some day be yours. You have no right to give up your health which is as much value to the nation as to you. You have got a strenuous month in front of you, and after then, take a holiday until April. Do nothing. Knock out even the voyage to India.'

And he added:

Speaking seriously, I think something should be done to prevent the Prince doing what he is only too ready to do in giving up the whole of his time and health to the people and the country.[2]

This speech did, in fact, have an unfortunate effect in India. The Prince had originally been expected the year before to open the new constitution, and it was now widely believed that there would be a further postponement. However, all through the summer the plans progressed for the Prince's visit in spite of some uncertainty caused by the political disturbances in India.

The anxieties of the authorities as well as the importance attached to the Prince of Wales's tour were because it took place in the aftermath of the massacre at Amritsar. This is not the appropriate place to go into the details of that horrifying episode, one of the most tragic and shameful in British Indian history, and it is enough to say that it is chastening to read about it today. Only less terrible than the massacre itself were some of the cruelties and humiliations to which Indians were subjected during the period of martial law which followed it. These things were condemned by the Hunter Committee and by the House of Commons, where Edwin Montagu, the Secretary of State, described the events at Amritsar as 'terrorism' and Winston Churchill as 'frightfulness', the latter adding: 'by "frightfulness" I mean inflicting great slaughter or massacre on a particular crowd of people with the intention of terrorizing not merely the rest of the crowd, but the whole district. .... Frightfulness is not a remedy known to the British.'[3] But this came too late and it is impossible to over-estimate the effect of Amritsar in India.*

In 1920 Gandhi and the Congress organization struck a temporary alliance with the Moslem community and launched a movement of non-co-operation with the Government. At one time a complete boycott of the Prince of Wales's visit was threatened, though later Gandhi issued a state-

---

* Nor was there unanimous support for Churchill's opinion. The House of Lords rejected the view of the Commons and defeated the Government on a Motion deploring the conduct of the case by General Dyer (the General in command of British forces).

ment that it should not be marked by *hartals** or other active signs of disapproval, only by abstention from official celebration. There was naturally some anxiety about the tour and many different opinions. On 21 April 1921 the Secretary of State telegraphed the Viceroy:

I do not think if you will forgive me, that I shall approach the Palace at the moment about date on which we must know about his visit. I will leave them to agitate... My reason is that they are being lobbied. Alwar writes to Winston protesting that on no account should the visit be postponed. Lloyd writes home protesting against HRH's visit. Patiala says that on no account should the visit take place either this year or next without boons.[4]†

King George himself cut through the general agitation by instructing Lord Reading, the new Viceroy, on his departure for India to assess the situation and come to a decision by June at the latest as to whether the Prince's visit should take place. In fact, in the circumstances of the time, there was less choice than this uncertainty suggests and the Viceroy finally put the matter in these words to the Secretary of State:

No sufficient reason could be given for a further postponement except that the country is too disturbed. If this reason for postponement were given, non-cooperatives would regard it as a tremendous triumph. ... I cannot believe that it would be wise to postpone the visit on this ground. It would be a confession of the impotence of the King-Emperor's Government in face of the Gandhi opposition.[5]

Next there was some indecision as to where the Prince should land. Bombay was the obvious choice both because it was the Gateway to India and the first great city to have grown into prosperity under British rule, and because it was here that both King George and his father, King Edward, had landed. However, for several months it had been the scene of acute labour troubles and disturbances accompanied by some loss of life. In Bombay the Indian community over-shadowed the English in wealth and prestige and there was a natural tendency for them to employ their resources to support political agitation. However, it was not seriously believed that there was much danger of a hostile demonstration to the Prince, although it was feared that he might be received merely with a polite show of respect. Once more official opinion stood firm.

Finally there was a little difficulty about the date on which he should arrive, and Lord Cromer, Chief of the Prince's Staff for the Indian tour, wrote to the Viceroy's Secretary as follows:

* Hartal: Literally a 'closing' (of the shops) but popularly a period of mourning imposing the duty of remaining at home. Preached in the name of religion, it was also enforced by threats and a *hartal* was often the occasion for mob violence. During the Prince's visit it was only once or twice imposed with success and even then, as at Peshawar, the markets were sometimes closed yet the people appeared on the streets.

† A boon: An edict announcing some benefit: traditionally, the release of prisoners, some constitutional concessions or temporary suspension of taxes.

H.M. said that November 9 was the date on which both he and King Edward had landed in India ... and he did not understand why the same traditional date was not adhered to ... I explained that November 9 was in point of fact the date originally selected ... but that owing to representations made from India and not from this end, the date had been deferred. ... The King's chief concern is, in my private opinion, that in the ordinary course of things H.M. will be at Sandringham during the latter half of October, and the Prince's departure on October 26 will necessitate the King coming up to London to see H.R.H. off at the station.[6]

In view of the King's overriding devotion to tradition, this may seem to have been a rather unfair opinion, but it is true that on this occasion his natural preferences reinforced each other.

During the summer months he talked to his son at some length about his forthcoming journey, dwelling on his own experiences in India and of the necessity for a more elaborate display of pageantry and more ceremonial behaviour in the orient. He observed that, although he himself could not approve of the Prince's informal approach, he had to admit that it had succeeded very well in Canada, New Zealand and Australia. Nevertheless he said that in India his son was to do exactly what the British authorities advised him, because what went down in the western world would not do so there.

Since his last tour some changes had been made to the Prince's Staff, and, apart from Lord Cromer's appointment as Chief of Staff, Lord Claud Hamilton, who went to join the King's Household, had been replaced by the Hon. Bruce Ogilvy; Colonel Grigg had left to return to politics, and Captain Alan Lascelles had been appointed Assistant Private Secretary. The Prince now asked for his cousin Lord Louis Mountbatten, who since the last tour had returned to his naval career, to join him once more.

The *Renown* dropped anchor in Bombay very early in the morning on 17 November to the salute of guns of the ships of the East India Squadron. For two or three weeks before advertisements had been appearing in the Bombay newspapers urging the public to refrain from welcoming the Prince, to abstain from attending public functions and to maintain themselves in their houses as a sign of national mourning. The streets were placarded with notices calling for a boycott. Yet for two or three days streams of vehicles of every kind, from luxurious motor-cars to humble phaetons, had been blocking the land approaches to the Gateway to India, and at dawn on the day of the Prince's arrival dense crowds were to be seen making their way to every part of the route the procession would take, until, in spite of the long wait that must follow under the dangerous Indian sun, every inch of standing room was occupied. When the Prince landed at the Apollo Bunder, dressed in the uniform of a naval captain, he was met by the Viceroy, Lord Reading, the Governor of Bombay, Sir George Lloyd, and the Heirs Apparent of ten of the Indian princes who were to attend him during his tour. Crowds of Indians stretched as far as the eye could see.

After inspecting the Guard of Honour he was conducted down a broad processional route, between white columns topped by golden lions, to a small amphitheatre. From here he delivered a message from his father, the King-Emperor – and added some words of his own. Then he entered the royal barouche and, accompanied by his staff and preceded by his escort, he drove through the busiest and most populated thoroughfares. When he left the amphitheatre thousands of Indians rushed to prostrate themselves before the chair in which he had sat and to kiss the dust over which his car had passed. And, if there was any uneasiness as he passed through the cheering multitudes, it was noticeable that he did not share it. He stood up in his car and called to the guards not to press the people back.

In the meantime in the back streets of Bombay there was some street fighting. This was attributed not so much to the non-co-operators themselves as to the unintended result of their agitation on hooligan elements in the city, as well as to the opportunity that presented itself because of the withdrawal from these areas of large numbers of police and military to the processional route. Indeed Gandhi himself, although too late, did his best to stop the violence by personal appeals and a series of proclamations calling on all communities to exercise forbearance. But, although these disturbances were regarded rather as a sign of the general unrest in India than of any lack of warmth in the welcome to the Prince, they did serve to underline the element of risk that would attend the whole of the Prince's tour in British India. However, if the success of his visit was ever in doubt, this was dispelled during his visit to Poona. The principal event of this visit was the laying of two foundation stones, the first of the Maratha War Memorial and the second of a memorial to Shivaji, the hero of the Marathas. When he had performed the second of these acts the Prince said in his clear voice:

A few minutes ago I laid the foundation stone of a Memorial to the Maratha soldiers who laid down their lives in the Great War, men who proved that the spirit which animated the armies of Shivaji still burns bright and clear. From this spot the statue of the founder of Maratha greatness will look with pride across the river which commemorates the latest exploits of the abiding valour of his people. And what could be more fitting than that the glory of the past and of today should be inaugurated in the presence not only of the representative of the house of Shivaji but also of those princes and chiefs who are descended from the soldiers and statesmen of the Empire which he founded.

When this speech was translated so that everyone present could understand it, it provoked shouts of victory, Maratha battle cries, blessings on the Prince's head, invocations of victory to his sword in such a volume of sound as to be absolutely deafening. And as he left the enclosure those who were not near enough to touch him threw gold and silver coins in his path so that the royal feet might tread on them.

That afternoon he attended the races and, after watching for about two hours, he left the Royal Box and walked through all the enclosures, followed by a crowd shouting in an ecstasy of delight and enthusiasm. On his way back through Poona his route should have been guarded only by the police, but of their own accord men of the units of the Indian Army stationed in Poona and in Kirkee turned out and lined the road, giving him a wildly enthusiastic reception. Later on the same evening, the soldiers again turned out, this time with torches, to speed him on his way to Kirkee Station.

News of this personal triumph at Poona, following so quickly on that at Bombay, made a great impression throughout India and did much to ensure the success of the rest of the tour. Back in Bombay it soon became noticeable that wherever HRH was due to pass crowds began to collect at street corners to welcome him. Most significant of all was the fact, often referred to by the official historian of the Indian tour, that these crowds, usually not much inclined to be vocal, began now to cheer him as he passed with the heartiness of an English crowd. Here is a description of the Prince's drive round the stadium in Bombay at the naval and military display.

The whole great mass of spectators rose in their seats, waved hands and hats in an ecstasy of enthusiasm, and cheered him to the echo. When he stood up in his car and waved in response to the cheering, popular delight knew no bounds. No one who witnessed this spectacle can possibly entertain the theory that Indian crowds are not vocal. At the exit hundreds of young men and boys surged round his car cheering him madly. Nothing like this scene has ever been witnessed in Bombay before; and no doubt remained in the heart of anyone who saw it that the Prince's conquest of the great city was complete.[7]

While the Prince was in Bombay an incident occurred that was to add unexpectedly to the success of the tour, and in addition to introduce to him someone who was to become a lifelong friend. He was disturbed one afternoon during a siesta by a young Indian Cavalry officer who entered without ceremony and stood by his bed. This was Captain Edward Dudley Metcalfe, popularly known as 'Fruity'. He made his mark without difficulty on this hot afternoon by telling the Prince that a number of maharajas were anxious to lend him some polo ponies and asking him whether he would like to play.* As a result of this conversation twenty-five polo ponies and a third train to transport them were added to the Prince's retinue, and for the rest of the tour the ponies were unshipped wherever possible and the Prince and his staff played polo. These games became a very important part of the tour. The Indians are good judges of horses and

* This is the Duke of Windsor's own account. In fact Captain Metcalfe had been temporarily attached to the Prince's staff for the purpose of organizing this side of his life.

riding and it is in accordance with their traditions for ruling princes to exhibit their prowess before the eyes of their subjects. The games attracted large crowds, and even at Allahabad, where the orders for non-co-operation were successfully imposed, the Indians, having satisfied their sense of duty by staying off the streets in the morning, rushed wreathed in smiles to cheer the Prince on the polo ground in the afternoon.

As long as he lived Captain Metcalfe was to be one of the Prince's favourite companions and one of the major influences upon him. His charm lay partly in his skill with horses but chiefly in his gaiety and good humour. When the Prince returned to England Metcalfe accompanied him and was put in charge of the Prince's stables, hunters and steeplechasers as well as polo ponies. Like everyone else he was completely correct in his manner to HRH in public, but in private his natural good fellowship overlapped the limits of formality and he fulfilled, as probably no one else ever did, the Prince's need for a masculine relationship on equal terms. In a letter written to Metcalfe from Balmoral in the following year (1922) when the Prince was twenty-eight, he endeavoured to tell him how much he missed his company and to express his affection and appreciation of a marvellous friendship. The writer constantly checks himself from becoming 'sloppy', but, written in a round boyish handwriting and in round boyish words, the letter is more than a pact of friendship, it is an expression of gratitude and love.

There are indications in it that the Prince fears he may have difficulty with his father in securing a permanent appointment for Metcalfe, but his insistence that his friend should not return to his regiment or to India but should stay to look after his stables and to carry on being 'his greatest man friend' might be construed as a personal guarantee.

In London the presence of Metcalfe soon came to be recognized, like that of Mrs Dudley Ward, as a sign that the Prince of Wales was probably near. He accompanied him on his night life as well as out hunting and at polo, and he shared his interest in clothes. In 1925 he married Lady Alexandra Curzon, a daughter of Lord Curzon of Kedleston.

King George had paid a vigorous attention to the matter of clothes throughout all the Prince of Wales's tours. He had written to New Zealand complaining because the Prince wore a turned-down collar in white uniform, with a collar and black tie. 'I wonder whose idea that was, as anything more unsmart I never saw.'[8]

And to New Zealand he wrote too: 'I think you ought to censor Brookes' photos that he sent to the papers, as you and Dick* in a swimming bath together is hardly dignified, though comfortable in a hot climate, you might as well be photographed naked, no doubt it would please the public.'[9] Now he wrote to India:

* Lord Louis Mountbatten.

I have just seen in the papers different pictures of you in India and ... I am surprised to see that you and your staff are wearing blue overalls with your white tunics. A most extraordinarily ugly uniform. I wonder when the order was given, as white overalls have always been worn with white tunics by the Army in India. The regulations ought never to have been altered without my approval. I will find out from the C-in-C when these orders were given, as I consider that the white uniform has been entirely ruined, besides being very uncomfortable in that weather.[10]*

Another of the Prince's aides had ideas for his instruction and entertainment. Lord Louis Mountbatten proposed to the Prince, who was, he says, quite keen on the idea, that they should attempt to contrive a meeting with Gandhi themselves. Here they came up against the Government of India, however, who were adamant that nothing of the sort should take place. Years later, as Viceroy, Mountbatten told Gandhi of this abortive attempt.

On the evening of 22 November the Prince left Bombay for Baroda. He spent the next three weeks in Rajputana (today called Rajasthan) as a guest of the princes of India. Then he went to Lucknow, from there to Allahabad and from there to Benares. From here he went to Nepal, an independent kingdom on the southern ranges of the Himalayas and the home of the Gurkhas, back to British India at Patna, and from there to Calcutta. Next he went to Burma and from Rangoon he went by ship to Madras. Then travelling by train and motor-car, he visited Bangalore and other parts of Mysore, travelled on to Hyderabad and then by way of Nagpur, Indore, Bhopal, Gwalior and Agra to Delhi. After a short stay at Delhi he went to Patiala and Lahore in the Punjab, and into the great state of Jaman, stopping at Satwari Cantonment because of an outbreak of the plague at the winter capital of Jammu. Then he crossed into the Frontier Province at Attock, and from Peshawar drove through the Khyber Pass as far as the Afghan Frontier. Re-crossing the River Indus, he returned to Rawalpindi and, passing through the small state of Kapurthala, to Delhi. From here he went through miles of the Sind desert back to the sea at Karachi. He left India exactly four months after he had landed at Bombay.

Immediately following the triumph of his arrival at Bombay, he spent three weeks in Rajputana staying in turn with the Indian princes. Here he was the guest of some of the richest men in the world. He fulfilled his usual heavy programme, replying to addresses of welcome, driving through gaily decorated streets and under triumphal arches, reviewing troops, visiting colleges, attending banquets, garden parties and so on, amid scenes of unbelievable splendour and in country of surpassing beauty. This visit, contrary to the belief expressed by some people, was one of the

---

* It was a Naval custom to wear a blue coat with white trousers, and the blue overalls were of a softer and more comfortable material. The Prince and his staff now abandoned the practice, although according to the Duke of Windsor certain units of the Army in India continued to follow it.

most successful and at the same time enjoyable of all his tours. His hosts showed unusual tact and understanding and they kept formal functions to a minimum and even cancelled some when they realized he was over-tired. He managed to invest everything he did with the element of simple friend-liness which is characteristic of Indians themselves, and they rejoiced in his informality and obvious interest in everyone he met. His love of sport stood him in good stead and, as he played polo, shot duck and got his first pig, he gave great pleasure to his hosts and their subjects.

During his absence from British India, as a result of the activities of bands of Congress volunteers, who directly defied a Government order, certain leaders of the non-co-operation movement had been arrested and imprisoned, and these included Pandit Motilal Nehru.* At Lucknow, the first town through which the Prince passed after he left Rajputana, attempts to damp the popular enthusiasm entirely failed; but Allahabad was Nehru's home and his arrest had produced a change in the atmosphere which had previously been enthusiastic to welcome the Prince. Now, for the first and almost the last time, the non-co-operators successfully prevented any display of public rejoicing on the streets.

But, although the *hartal* was successful only at Allahabad, the Prince was far from satisfied with the arrangements for his tour. From Nepal on 16 December he wrote to his father saying that he was very depressed and felt he was doing no good. The main reason for this was the activities of the non-co-operators but an important factor was the extent of the pre-cautions taken by the police. The Prince wrote complaining of the police to the Viceroy as well as to his father saying that they had 'the wind-up unnecessarily', and objecting to the fact that he was seldom allowed to drive through the bazaars or native quarters. The Indians, he said, were crowded together and guarded by police who faced 'outboard' to protect him.[11] In a very long letter, written on 9 January 1922, Lord Reading re-plied. He began by pointing out that in undertaking the tour of India the Prince was performing a far greater service than by his visits to Australia and Canada, and he went on to say that he himself bore the main responsi-bility for the advice that the visit should be made. He continued:

I trust you will forgive me, Sir, if I say that although the political conditions have deteriorated since the decision was announced ... yet I remain strongly of opinion that Your Royal Highness's visit is doing real good – infinitely more than you think – and I trust that events will convince you of this before you leave India.

Lord Reading then went on to explain that it was impossible to leave any discretion as to relaxation of precautions to subordinate officers and indeed it would be ineffective to do so, since naturally they would take no risks.

* Father of President Jawaharlal Nehru and a close associate of Gandhi's.

And then he came to the crux of the Prince's complaint. 'You suggest that the police themselves feel that the protection is overdone, but that they dare not relax the precautions because of the very strict orders from Delhi.' Yet these orders, he explained, were based on the rules observed for the protection of the Viceroy and it would not be possible to give a general order to the effect that less stringent precautions were to be taken for the Prince than were actually taken for the Viceroy. He proposed, nevertheless, to write to the Governor of each of the Provinces still to be visited and suggest that whenever it was reasonably safe, 'i.e., where there is no special reason to anticipate trouble', that 'a freer opportunity should be afforded to the Indians of welcoming Your Royal Highness'. And he added: 'There is more danger when there is a public announcement of the route you will take; there is, I think, the minimum of danger when without announcement or previous knowledge by the crowd you take your opportunity of going amongst them. May I say without flattery that no one could make better use of such opportunities, if they were afforded, than Your Royal Highness.'[12]

The Viceroy was as good as his word and he issued instructions of the kind suggested to the Governors of the Provinces the Prince was to visit. In February, after the Prince's visit to Delhi, the Viceroy wrote to the King: 'I found H.R.H. in a much better frame of mind as regards his visit than when he wrote his letter from Calcutta to me; indeed he told me he felt quite differently about it now.'[13]

But to the Secretary of State, speaking of the Durbar held in Delhi, he made the following remarks which add a detail to the picture we are given of the Prince.

The Prince made a very good speech which he delivered well and scarcely a trace of nervousness. Altogether, I noticed during his visit that he was certainly far less nervous in manner than I had been led to believe and as I gathered from reports during the earlier parts of his trip.[14]

However, the Prince remained acutely sensitive to any interference between himself and his own interpretation of his duty. In Peshawar the non-co-operators succeeded in getting all the shops shut although spectators thronged the streets. The Prince and his companions became aware of some change in the official programme when they suddenly noticed to their surprise a complete absence not merely of spectators but even of police. Sir John Maffey, Chief Commander of the North-West Province, wrote later to the Viceroy's Secretary the following explanation of what had happened:

After consulting the GOC and the Deputy Commissioner and the Police before leaving Government House, I had told the Prince's staff that I would not send HRH back along the *hartal* route, but ... straight out of the city by the opposite gate from that which he entered. The whole programme was successfully put through on these lines. HRH, however, is most acutely hurt at having been sent out by what he calls the back door. Nobody but himself has this feeling.[15]

And indeed the Prince had been both hurt and angry, regarding Sir John Maffey's action as an insult to his courage and honour.

Students here, as elsewhere and at other times, were easily attracted to political agitation and on more than one occasion his visits to universities disappointed him. A visit to Aligarh University was cancelled as the Prince was disinclined to go there with the memories of other visits to universities present in his mind. The Viceroy realized that he felt the absence of students very keenly and decided not to subject him to a further risk of this kind.

But on the whole the Prince's tour was a triumphal progress throughout the land. 'In my most sanguine moments,' the Viceroy wrote to the King of the visit to Bombay, 'I never expected such a complete success as has happened and this is due to the Prince himself.'[16] And of the visit to Delhi he wrote to the Secretary of State: 'He himself is delighted with his visit and in these matters he is rather hard to please for he sees through all attempts at camouflage and is over-keen to detect them.'[17]

The Prince's love of sport was of particular value in India where both the native population and the British Army shared it. At Lucknow he rode in four gymkhana races and won two, one of them in a close finish, while coming second in the other two. And at the famous Kadir Cup Meeting (which attracted all the hardest and best horsemen in India) he capped everything by winning the lightweight hog-hunter's race. The course was nearly four and a half miles over very rough country. *The Times* correspondent describing the race said: 'The two Hog Hunters Cups usually mean a lot of grief, for the pace is what is called a "cracker". .... One year, out of 22 runners 10 fell, one man fractured his skull, and four or five others were also carried in.'[18]

The Prince rode against the wishes of some of his staff and the news of his win spread like wildfire across the country. In England his horsemanship was regarded with (an often affectionate) contempt, but his record in competitive events would have won esteem even for a private citizen. In the circumstances of his tour and combined with his obvious pleasure at the approbation of the crowds, it raised his popularity to heights which had really never been seen before.

Characteristically, he remained suspicious to the last. On 10 May Sir Almeric Fitzroy recorded in his diary an account of a conversation given in a letter from his daughter in India (who was private secretary to Lady Reading). One of the police officers attached to the royal party during the tour told her that just before he sailed the Prince drew him aside and asked him 'as an honest man' to say what he had thought of his tour. In reply the police officer told him, and possibly more important, later Sir Almeric's daughter, that he had believed it to be the greatest possible mistake to bring him out at all, but 'the tour itself had convinced him he was wholly wrong in his view, that it had gone infinitely better than he had thought possible, and that the good it had done was incalculable'.[19]

With stops at Ceylon, the Malay Peninsula and Hong Kong, the Prince now travelled on the *Renown* to Japan where he stayed for four weeks as the guest of Prince Hirohito. Then after calling at the Philippines, British North Borneo, Penang and the naval base of Trincomalee in Ceylon, the *Renown* sailed across the Indian Ocean to the Red Sea. The Prince left her as she went through the Suez Canal and travelled by train to Cairo to pay his respects to King Fuad. On 20 June, after being away for eight months, he reached England.

No personal qualifications – *The Times* leader remarked – even though joined with happy circumstances of fortune and station, would by themselves account for the depth of esteem which the nation feels towards the Prince, were it not for his pre-eminence in the princely virtue of courage. *Habemus principens:* we have in him a Prince who lives up to the name, as a true leader of men, endowed with the prime requisites of leadership.[20]

So much for the public side of the tour. There is no doubt that in British India it was as brilliantly successful as the foregoing account suggests. Now, for the first time, however, criticisms of the kind that had already been heard in Australia began to reach a small circle in England. It is also necessary to deal with the suggestion made by Helen Hardinge (Viscountess Hardinge of Penshurst) that the Prince's naturally informal manner was far less immediately sympathetic to the Indians than it had been to the democratic civilizations of the West. She writes:

Behaviour which had been so enthusiastically acclaimed in the new civilisation of North America went down badly in the ancient, complex Orient. Before he went, the Prince had not seemed to take much trouble to study the strange and sophisticated society into which he was going, and he relied for his effect mostly on his then famous personal charm and his 'glad hand' approach ... But, as his father had discovered when he had gone to New Delhi ten years previously to be crowned in the Coronation Durbar, the Indians liked their King-Emperor – and consequently his heir – to behave like one. The regulations that governed their own society were very strict, and their public conduct formal in the extreme.

Some of the Indians among whom the Prince moved were teetotallers. This is an article of faith, both with Hindus and Moslems. Of course, they do not all keep these rules, but representatives from the West are expected to exert great discretion where alcohol is concerned. The Prince of Wales, accustomed to the freedom of the cocktail shaker – as most of us were by that time – did not exercise this discretion. And when he tried to repeat the success he had achieved in other parts of the world by cutting through the elaborate protocol and making his own direct and informal approach to people, there was consternation. For that protocol had been devised not, as he appeared to imagine, by a group of haughty Englishmen in Viceroy's House, but by the Indians themselves, through their own traditions.[21]

It has not proved possible to find much corroboration for this account and, as far as British India is concerned, it is impossible to believe that the Prince's informal manner, his total lack of fear of crowds, and his willingness to go among them were unwelcome to the vast mass of ordinary people, or to those educated Indians who still smarted under the humiliation inflicted on their nation in the aftermath of Amritsar. But India has the reputation of being a country of ceremonial and to the ordinary Englishman there seems an inherent probability in what Lady Hardinge says, at least if it is applied to purely formal contacts with Indians of high birth. Fortunately we have the account of an eye-witness to this tour. Professor Rushbrook Williams is an authority on the Indian States, and at the time of the Indian tour he was Director of Public Information and a Deputy Secretary to the Government of India. At the instigation of a committee supervising the preparations for HRH's visit and containing a number of prominent Indians, Lord Reading appointed him Official Historian of the tour. These are his personal comments written fifty years later:*

I do not entirely agree with the impression which the sources that you mention leave on my mind. About HRH's attitude to the tour, for one thing. Godfrey Thomas told me that he was really tired of all the Empire touring, but he faced the Indian tour with his usual sense of duty. The King (with all due respect), remembering his own visits, was very stiff in his instructions, some of which did not fit in well with the conditions which HRH actually encountered. Above all, he sanctioned a programme which was much too heavy; we all of us, let alone HRH, were almost dead of exhaustion by the end of it.

It is important, I think, to distinguish between the impression which HRH made on Indians, and on the British community – particularly the official community. I never knew an Indian who had met HRH who was not charmed by him – he was human, informal and genuinely interested in them. Again and again I heard the remark: 'If only all you Europeans were like him!' The fact that he did not go down well with the officials, particularly their ladies, is explained by the fact that in many of the places which we visited, the local high officials 'tagged on' to us for several days. HRH was often obliged to take into dinner the same elderly British 'burra mem' for four or five nights in succession! Above all, he *wanted* to meet and to get to know Indians; he was far more interested to find out all about them than about his own countrymen. It is true that he began to drink a bit before the tour was over; but after a heavy day, with not a minute of respite, he had to nerve himself to face an enormous official gathering in the evening! He did like girls, particularly pretty and gay ones, but he was allowed to meet so few that when he saw one – and this applied to Indian girls as

* In a letter to the author.

well – he was rather apt to break protocol and dance with them, leaving his very senior British partner fuming. It was all very human and rather pathetic to watch. The princes loved him – they found that they could talk to him as man to man; and as they were for once in a position to do what they liked in their own territory, they ruthlessly cut down the tiring list of official functions, and gave him riding, polo and shooting instead. In weighing up the tour as a whole, please do not forget that it took place in face of an official boycott launched by Gandhi and the Congress Party. In spite of this, the number of Indians who wanted to meet him was enormous, and the effect of the tour on *them* – which was what really mattered – was all good . . .

Lord Reading was enormously sympathetic with the Prince's feelings – they got on very well. So also was Lady Reading. Neither would listen to a word against him in public. Lady Hardinge does perhaps not realize that, except on state occasions, the Indian aristocracy are *completely* informal. The British kept up protocol the whole time! This surprised many Indian princes a good deal – they could not understand how British officials, from the Viceroy downwards, could actually *live* in an atmosphere of protocol which they themselves, the living exponents of the ancient Indian way of life, adopted only on quite infrequent and traditionally-prescribed, formal occasions. I shall always remember the remark which HH the late Maharaja Ganga Stugh of Bikaner – our host at the time – made to me while HRH was teaching some of the younger princes, who were our fellow-guests, to play Billiard Table 'Slosh' (they broke three windows between them!): 'Look at that now! He is a real *Shahzada* (son of the Emperor) – but they wouldn't let him do that in your British India! What a pity you British are so formal!'

Professor Rushbrook Williams's letter is of great value both for the picture he gives of the India of the time and as evidence for the defence. He puts the extenuating circumstances in a most sympathetic light. Nor should the realities of the Prince's dilemma in being so often driven beyond what it was possible for him to achieve be minimized, because the frustration caused him was one of the elements of his ultimate development. Nevertheless, the kind of criticism that began in Australia (when he met the Bell girls at Boonah) cannot be disregarded, because, gathering strength in India, it could presently be heard all round the world. It would not be easy – and indeed would be presumptuous – to suggest how the Prince might best have dealt with the pressures created by a combination of his own personality and conduct with the heavy schedules agreed to by the all-powerful, insatiable and unimaginative King, but it is clear how he did deal with them. He developed a callous irresponsibility to those parts of the programme he found unrewarding and a stony disregard for the feelings of people whose hospitality or welcome proved inconvenient. He began to be ruthlessly unpunctual and his staff were often in real difficulty to explain his absence or delayed appearance at public functions. He had become very spoilt – how should he not? – and he had been as Robert Sencourt so aptly puts it 'subjected to a tension too unique, too subtle, too varied and too continuous for his character to ripen and strengthen'.[22] Melancholy by nature and easily bored, when he was forced to appear at public functions which did not interest him, by his unresponsiveness and air of discontent, he gave colour to the kind of rumour that he was 'still suffering from a hangover from the night before' or 'was drunk at the time', while his passing flirtations were given more importance by offended civil servants and their wives than possibly, at least while he was young, they deserved. (At this time in his life he was very much in love and it was a surprise to one of his travelling companions to have it suggested that he was less than absolutely faithful.) Nevertheless, it is beyond doubt that from the time of his Indian tour he troubled less and less if he gave offence on dull or very formal occasions although he never lost his ability to magnetize crowds. In a postbag following newspaper serialization of the history of his youth some of the writers speak of their disappointment when he either failed to turn up or arrived several hours late and conducted himself with an air of boredom and discontent, while others wish to record an unforgettable memory of his miraculous goodness and charm.

9

THE PRINCE AT HOME

In a television interview with Kenneth Harris in 1970 the Duke of Windsor betrayed an interest in the word 'establishment'. Asked what he thought it meant, he replied: 'Well, the establishment was a new word to me until about fifteen years ago when I heard it and I asked people to explain it to me. It's not easy to explain, it's rather an obscure word, but it must always have existed. I think it means authority, authority of the law, of the Church, of the, well, I suppose, the monarch to a certain extent. And universities and maybe the top brass of the army and navy.'[1]

The Duke's definition misses a little of the subtlety in the use of the word today. In its modern sense it means an inter-related power, not only the direct power wielded by the people the Duke mentioned, nor even their combined power, but an extra power generated by the connection between these groups and others in key positions – in politics, in the City of London, in the higher ranks of the Civil Service, everywhere that power resides. Even today in embassies all over the world, in public and government offices, at cocktail parties, concerts, race meetings, men can be heard saying to each other: 'What are you doing here?' or 'You don't remember me?' remarks which open doors, set underlings to work, avoid hours of time-consuming routine, produce seats on aeroplanes and so on. What is in doubt is whether the 'old boy net' any longer wields any real power, the power that governs the country, and whether the establishment in its old form any longer exists. In the early years of this century there was no doubt about this, no doubt that it existed and was extremely powerful, or that the climate of opinion was formed within its unmarked boundaries.

King Edward VII was at the very centre of the establishment, both as Prince of Wales and as King. For years without any real political power, he was influential in exactly the way the word has been stretched to express. George V was also a part of it, but probably only when he became King.

He was a family man by nature who did not seek power of any kind, and, as Duke of York, even as Prince of Wales, he appeared little on the social or political scenes. When the Duke of Windsor first came across the word 'establishment' there is no doubt that he welcomed it, with its slightly but unmistakably disrespectful air, as a delightful generic term for a great many things he disliked.

This is typical of an immaturity of outlook which he never outgrew. All his life he tended to view his fellows as might a schoolboy, setting a demarcation line between himself and kindred spirits on the one hand, and authority and the friends of authority on the other. His failure to develop in depth may be partly attributable to heredity. According to John Gore, his father's immaturity in his youth caused concern, while according to many authorities, his three younger brothers developed fully only with marriage. What is beyond doubt, however, is that the most important influences of his childhood and youth – his relationship with his parents, his restricted education, the arid discipline of the Naval Colleges, the lack of close contact with civilized minds, as well as the freak of birth which placed him in a unique position of isolation and pre-eminence in which, if we are to believe modern psychologists, his primary function was to assuage the infantile longing of the rest of mankind for a father figure – all contributed to it. As a young man such stability as he might have achieved in this unparalleled position came under a continual barrage from the hectoring and complaints, the bombardment of instructions to which his father subjected him, as well as the insurmountable fact that he could never please the King.

While the Prince was a child there were many signs of the fondness that existed between his father and himself but they were incompatible in taste and in a different sphere they would have gone their separate ways. As it was, the King's authority was absolute and he wished to live the life of a family man with his wife and children around him. His dictatorial attitude spoiled to some extent his relations with all his sons and the happy family existed only in his imagination. 'The King is in a very good form,' Lord Hardinge wrote once to his wife, 'which I hope will survive the arrival of his sons.'[2] It is constantly said that his attitude to his children changed completely with their marriage, but there seems also to have been a well-defined difference in his feelings for his first and second sons beforehand.

'You have always been so sensible & easy to work with,' he wrote to the Duke of York at the time of his marriage in 1923 '& you have always been ready to listen to any advice & to agree with my opinions about people & things, that I feel we have always got on well together (very different to dear David)'.[3]

In return there was some ambivalence in the Prince's feeling for his father. We are told that he talked almost excessively about him, telling stories which reflected admiration and respect. Nevertheless he can often be seen attempting the forlorn task of cutting the King, indeed all the Royal Family, down to size. Thus arriving at Trent and being shown Lytton Strachey's recently published *Queen Victoria*, the Prince said: 'That must be the book the King was talking about this morning. He was very angry and got quite vehement over it.' 'P of W had not seen the book,' Lady Lloyd George continues, 'so we showed it to him & presently he was discovered in roars of laughter over the description of the Queen and John Brown.'⁴

Much damage was done to the relationship between the King and his heir by the fact that the former managed to keep himself so well informed of the latter's movements and behaviour. The Prince came to regard with dislike and distrust people who might have his father's ear, particularly, it is said, those who were members of his own staff. In December 1935 when the old King was clearly dying, Lord Esher went to Tom Jones* with the object of asking him to impress on the Prime Minister the importance of the choice of a successor to Lord Stamfordham when the new King came to the throne. 'The Prince can be obstinate,' Lord Esher said. 'He takes violent likes and dislikes. He has got rid of several of his staff because he suspected them of carrying tales to his father.'⁵

There is an inherent probability in this statement yet curiously enough there is not much evidence for it. There were remarkably few changes on the Prince's staff and the only ones of any note were in 1924 when Lieutenant W.D.C. Greenacre succeeded Captain Metcalfe: in 1929 when Hugh Lloyd Thomas replaced Captain Lascelles: and in 1930 when Bruce Ogilvy was replaced after nine years' service by Major J.R. Aird. Of these, Captain Metcalfe had had only a temporary appointment and one can be quite certain that this was not willingly terminated by the Prince but due to pressure from his father; Captain Lascelles left of his own accord and Bruce Ogilvy was a close friend. Any lingering suspicion one might have of the last on the grounds of his access to the King through his mother Lady Airlie, Queen Mary's lady-in-waiting, must be dismissed when we find that he and his wife were among the Prince's party when he went skiing in 1935 with Mrs Simpson. And if it is not easy to see whom the Prince could have sacked, neither is it obvious which of his staff had the King's ear. Admiral Halsey we have seen earlier was appointed by the King and, although he called him the 'old Salt' the Prince had no great affection for him. However, this was probably more because he regarded him as 'a bore' than because he thought of him as a spy.

Of the others, Godfrey Thomas was one of the Prince's earliest and most trusted friends. He entered the Diplomatic Service in 1911 or 1912 and was

* Thomas Jones, universally known as Tom Jones, served in the Cabinet Offices from their formation in 1916 to 1930, first as Assistant Secretary and later as Deputy Secretary under Sir Maurice Hankey. His importance to the history of the Abdication is a result of his unique relationship to Baldwin, whom he served as devil's advocate as well as friend and adviser. See Keith Middlemas's introduction to *The Whitehall Diaries*.

in Berlin as a junior attaché when the Prince went there in 1913. As the youngest member of the staff he was detailed to look after HRH and a friendship grew up between them. In the war Thomas was unable to join the army because of poor eyesight and whenever the Prince was on leave he received permission from the Foreign Office to join him. At the end of the war, when HRH set up his own household at St James's Palace, Thomas gave up his diplomatic career and became his Private Secretary. He remained in this position until, on Edward's accession, having refused to become Private Secretary to the King, he became Assistant Private Secretary to Major Alexander Hardinge. He was a quiet man and, unlike most of the Prince's close friends, his interests were of an intellectual kind. He was a golfer, however, and often accompanied his young master in this capacity. The Prince returned his affection, on occasion attempting, as with Metcalfe, to express this in letters to him.

Captain Lascelles was another matter. Aristocratic by birth and temperament, a man of integrity and serious disposition, proud and rather unbending, he is an exactly typical figure of the old 'establishment'. Of a far higher level of intelligence than the man he served, his interests are literature and music. He left the Prince's household in 1929, and it is widely known that he did so because he could stand no more of him, but a few years later he found his way back into royal service as Assistant Secretary to George v himself. As a result he returned to Edward's service in time for the Abdication and later served George vi, first as Assistant-Secretary and later, on Sir Alex Hardinge's retirement, as Private Secretary.

It is easy to believe that he and the Prince of Wales were incompatible in character and temperament and it is well known that hostility grew up between them, and that in later years Lascelles's distrust and dislike of the man who was now Duke of Windsor grew into considerable bitterness in consequence of difficulties between him and his brother the King. Nor is there any doubt that his feeling was fully returned. In the later years of his life when the Duke of Windsor spoke of Sir Alan Lascelles, he made the name sound like a whip. Yet there is no evidence of dislike or disagreement between them when they were young, and Captain Lascelles performed one enormously important function. For eight years he wrote all the Prince of Wales's speeches and in 1936 he wrote the King's. Because the Prince made interpolations when he was speaking and was quick in response to the needs of the moment, it had been put about – and naturally not contradicted – that he worked on his speeches himself. There is no truth in this and the Prince, who had neither the capacity nor the will for such tasks, depended entirely on Captain Lascelles.

Lastly there was Brigadier-General G.F. Trotter, known to his friends as 'G'. Although considerably older than the Prince of Wales, he was to be found in his company only less often than Metcalfe. It has been suggested that his age recommended him to George v as a companion for his son, but it is difficult to believe he was appointed by anyone other than the Prince himself. His post was that of Assistant Comptroller, but his association with the Prince was also of a more personal kind and he soon became a constant companion. This is what the Duke of Windsor said about him: 'I learned from "G" Trotter that life should be lived to the full.'[6]*

People have differing ideas of how to live life to the full. It is impossible to understand the Prince of Wales's tastes and pursuits without reference to the time in which he lived. From the beginning of the war there had been a tendency to react to the unbearable strain by escaping into triviality in everyday life. Such records as Lady Cynthia Asquith's diaries give an astonishing picture of the superficiality of the civilian upper classes. Then in the aftermath of the war there occurred a transitional period between the old rich civilization and the poorer and more democratic world of the future. Bereaved and uprooted and emotionally exhausted but with an entirely new freedom from convention, large sections of society spent their time in the pursuit of pleasure with a single-mindedness which marks this generation off from almost every other in history. In spite of his position and his essentially unreal relationship with his fellows, the Prince was a genuine product of his period. Indeed it is impossible to refrain from speculation as to whether he could have progressed so inexorably to his fate if he had been born at any other time – one of the very few fields for speculation in a progress which was soon to take on the predestined air of a Greek tragedy.

The pursuit of pleasure was conducted against a background of booms and slumps, of the homeless and the jobless, the first Labour Government in 1924, the General Strike, the betrayal of agriculture and later under the shadow of the great army of unemployed. This increased the air of cynicism and superficiality, but did not entirely account for it.

It can now be seen that the 1920s were not lacking in talent – years that recall Joyce, Yeats, Eliot: Bloomsbury and the Diaghileff ballet with all that these terms imply: Lawrence, Forster, Huxley and Waugh. It was nevertheless a philistine age. For reasons that have never been analysed but partly because of the war and partly because personal wealth was changing hands, the youth of this generation were singularly uneducated. Boys of eighteen had left school to fight, while the schools themselves were kept going by the old and the invalid. Foreign travel and the education given girls at 'finishing schools' in Europe ceased for the duration of the war. After the war educational facilities were stretched to accommodate the rising class of *nouveaux riches*, and girls, who might previously have been well taught by governesses at home, were sent to schools where the quality of the teaching was often so poor that they grew up virtually uneducated.

---

* 'He is indeed a trotter,' was the comment of a Boston dowager to Sir John Balfour.[7]

But the most extraordinary thing about the post-war years was the dancing. All over London, hotels were forced to hire bands and, clearing part of the restaurant floor, provide room for dancing, and at the same time dozens of new establishments opened their doors. These were called night clubs often inaccurately, because many of them were also open for dancing at tea time. The most famous and the one which the Prince attended night after night was the Embassy Club in Bond Street. He has described it as 'that Buckingham Palace of night clubs', an inapt description for what' was simply a long underground basement, however luxuriously furnished. The Prince attended the balls at the great London houses, but later in the evening, or on nights when he had no other engagements, he could almost always be seen at the Embassy Club, often accompanied by his brother, Prince George. The Embassy Club was run by a famous *maître d'hôtel* called Luigi, and more than anywhere else it reflected the mood of the day.

The swing doors of the restaurant opened on the long side of a well-proportioned room. All round the walls above the sofas and the tables looking-glasses reflected the scene. The whole of the centre of the room was a dance-floor, but late at night, when the restaurant was full, and almost always at luncheon, tables placed uncomfortably close together would fill the middle of the room, until there was almost no space left in the centre. At one end of the room, on a balcony above the floor, was the bandstand.

To this room night after night for years came dukes and earls and princes and their wives and the women they loved, writers, actors, Press-lords, politicians, all the self-made men from the war who were trying to break into Society, all the riff-raff and the hangers-on. At home in many of the houses in which these people lived there were cooks and kitchen-maids waiting to cook a dinner, butlers and footmen waiting to serve it. But their masters and mistresses at the Embassy Club sat at their tables only until the waiters served the soup, and then, as though mechanically activated, they all got up and began to dance. In this restaurant one could eat as well as anywhere in the world, but the food was always crammed down between dances, drowned with gin-and-tonic, blown over by cigarette-smoke.

At dinner time, and most people dined late at about nine o'clock, the room would be reasonably filled. It was later, after the theatre, that the tables were jammed together over almost every available inch of floor. Early in the evening, when the whole room could be seen with a relatively unimpeded vision, it would have been possible for an acute observer to watch the rules of an older society gradually being broken down. For the first time in history the British upper classes were opening their ranks and allowing wholesale ingress to rich men, famous men or women, notorieties, anyone who could add a scrap to their entertainment. And very largely it was this that was causing the crush and the excitement, that made Luigi's tyrannical rule a possibility. At the Embassy the clientele he favoured all knew each other, and met there as in their own drawing-rooms. The nod-ding and waving and calling out and transferring to one another's table that went on gave opportunities for social climbing from outside this group which were unequalled.

Most of London's great hostesses could be seen here and all the beauties – Lady Cunard, sitting most nights with Sir Robert and Lady Abdy; Mrs Richard Norton and Lady Louis Mountbatten, Miss Paula Gellibrand, later to become the Marchesa da Casa Maury, whom many people thought the most beautiful of them all, Lady Loughborough and Miss Poppy Baring, Miss Tallulah Bankhead on her very best behaviour, and many other male and female stars from the theatre.

Historically the women of this generation are always represented as wearing a kind of bandeau on their heads and smoking cigarettes through long jade holders. Mademoiselle Lenglen, the tennis champion, wore a bandeau, and on the stage women representing sirens smoked through long holders. At the Embassy Club the women had short, unadorned, shingled hair (sometimes longer hair was curled up at the back to achieve the same effect), and they smoked Turkish cigarettes without holders. Here is a deliberately stylized description of some of them from *The Green Hat* by Michael Arlen.

Nearby was a corner-table of eight young people. ... They were four married couples, and they had all been boys and girls together, and they had a son and daughter apiece, and they all went to the same dentist. The women had white oval faces, small breasts, blue eyes, thin arms, no expression, no blood; literally of course, not genealogically. One of them stared right into people's faces and blinked vaguely. She was lovely. ... Presently, a prince of the blood joined them, there was a little stir for a minute or two, a little laughter, and then he rose to dance with the girl of the blind blue eyes. As she danced she stared thoughtfully at the glass dome of the ceiling. She looked bored with boredom.[8]

It is noticeable that Arlen regarded the Prince of Wales as part of the scene. The blind blue eyes belonged to Mrs Richard Norton whose physical appearance and many of whose characteristics served this author again in his portrait of Lily Christine, another of his heroines who also dined at the Embassy Club.

They dined late, at about the hour when Harvey and his wife had usually finished dinner and were beginning to yawn. The place was crammed with people, many of them smiling across at Lily Christine and her friends. ...

Where did all the money come from? he wondered. For years now one had been hearing how poor these people were, how they were overtaxed, how they could not live as they used, how they were being deprived almost of the necessities of life. ... But here all these people were, and one gathered pretty regularly here, dining without an anxious thought at two to four pounds a head. Of course, these well-set-up young men were all working at one job or another, but only very few of them could be earning enough to live on this scale as the fancy took them. Then where did all the money come from?

It disturbed one a little to think that the fathers of these young people quite easily 'faced the necessity for the fact that in the present state of industrial depression the wage earners must learn not to ask too much'.[9]

The question of money had great relevance to the scene. The young people whom Michael Arlen is describing had been brought up in the Edwardian age to an aristocratic role. They had an absolute if discreet belief in their own superiority and their natural right to certain material things; yet their role, their lands and their incomes were all diminished. They adjusted themselves as best they could. They lived in small houses in Westminster, they sold the gold plate and they managed without a footman, sometimes without a kitchen maid (servants were becoming very difficult to get even if one could afford to pay them). They dined out, they said, because they could not afford to dine in – by which they meant they could not entertain on the scale of their parents. They seemed to themselves to be making endless economies, constant adjustments, and they could not go further or faster in one generation. This, as much as their desire for entertainment, caused them to open their doors so easily to many people they still regarded as their inferiors – the ability to pay being less rare and even more necessary than wit.

Michael Arlen was himself a phenomenon of the 1920s. At the height of his popularity he was one of the most sensationally successful novelists ever known and he was widely read outside the ordinary public for a best-selling novel. He romanticized the world that Evelyn Waugh was to satirize, but he did something else as well. 'He happened,' his son wrote, 'to strike one of those chords which a very few writers strike each generation or semi-generation.'[10]

The chord Michael Arlen struck was the death knell of the Edwardian codes of behaviour. He had a natural talent but he wrote a lush and fantastic prose and in a few years, when what he had to say had been heard often enough no longer to evoke a response, his popularity unexpectedly dropped away from him. Lily Christine was the type of his heroine and, in the scene when she goes to see Mrs Abbey, Arlen distils the romantic ideals of a generation. Mrs Abbey, who is the anti-hero, is an actress, very beautiful, immensely respected, outwardly rather bluff and jolly, but very secret and much concerned with her reputation. She represents the old ideas of sexual morality and she is suddenly shown as poisonous in her shocked and prurient attitude to Lily Christine. Lily Christine is gallant, reckless, chivalrous, unconcerned with any of the things Mrs Abbey holds dear. Honesty and generosity are glorified at the expense, not of chastity, which is not at issue, but of discretion.

In as much as Arlen had really got hold of something which was important to the new generation, the young married couples at the Embassy

Club, who were his physical models, were not otherwise representative of it. The Prince of Wales's generation grew up before the war and, although they saw themselves as very up to date, they were conditioned in Edwardian schoolrooms. Most of the women took lovers – women who dine out every night inevitably do – but, although they were moved by the courage and honesty of Michael Arlen's heroines, they did not make any serious attempt to emulate them. It is a fact, and one that may have some significance here for its effect on the Prince's mind, that sexual promiscuity is often far more widespread when some discretion is observed than in even the most permissive societies.

For the rest, this society like all others was composed of individuals. Individually some were very rich, some hard-working. Some would become conventionally and uncompromisingly staid when they inherited from their parents, while a few had a great future to fulfil. Collectively they presented a slightly raffish air.

It was almost certainly then as much from taste as because of their access to his father that the Prince avoided the big guns of the establishment. Probably he was not much interested in politics (this will be argued in more detail at an appropriate place), although he showed such a lively response where he was personally touched and had, like most people born at the centre of things, an unwarranted confidence in his own opinions and judgment. In any case, except in the course of his public work, he was seldom to be seen in the company of members of those great political families who for generations had played their part in the government of the country, or of the lesser nobility who undertook the serious work of the counties. These, in return, began quite early to adopt a somewhat scornful attitude towards him. It would be too crude to say that he regarded them as 'stuffy' while they regarded him as 'rather vulgar', but these words do represent the spirit of the thing.

In this matter the Prince played unwittingly if unconcernedly into the hands of his critics. One of the oddest things about him – until one remembers the isolation of his youth – is that he was singularly uninformed about all those shibboleths which go to make up what has been so conveniently and compactly labelled for later generations by the single letter 'U'. The Prince was in some ways surprisingly 'non-U'.* This was most noticeable in the clothes he wore. It was not merely that the upper classes agreed with his father in disliking the loudness of his tweeds and the cut of his clothes: the Prince wore his top hat on the side of his head out hunting, a thing even schoolboys at Eton or Harrow knew was done only by cads. And he gives another rather delightful example of his ignorance of the customs of

---

* For a full explanation of this see *Noblesse Oblige* edited by Nancy Mitford. Hamish Hamilton, 1956.

the tribe himself in *A Family Album*. He tells us that when he was in America in 1924 he found that people glanced at his feet with embarrassment, and finally someone told him that the suede shoes he wore were regarded in America as effeminate. He explained that in England they carried no such stigma, but he forebore to wear them again. Yet in England at the time these shoes, as also the brown and white brogues he often wore, were regarded as a totally reliable sign of a cad. These things were all taken with the utmost seriousness then, not for themselves but for what they told people about one another in a class society which was deeply divisive and made possible only by the complete acceptance of the superiority of one class over another. People whose behaviour was quiet but 'non-U' were regarded by the 'U' classes as 'very middle class', but, with the exception of the Prince of Wales, people whose behaviour was spirited – the cads – were treated in a fairly punitive way.

Yet we can be sure all these things were forgiven him whenever he chose to exert himself, partly because no one in England of any class can resist overtures from a member of the Royal Family, but also for qualities of his own. Before we can decide what these were we must follow him into the society of the people he trusted and loved.

In contrast to his attitude of rebelliousness and mistrust to any kind of masculine authority, in his relationship with first one and then the other of the two women for whom he cared deeply the Prince seemed, on the contrary, to be actively seeking a dominating, quasi-maternal partner. There was a slavish quality in his devotion that prevented it being fully returned by any woman who sought a lover rather than a son. Mrs Dudley Ward was extremely fond of him and she exercised an enormous influence over him, but he must always have been aware that the intensity of his love was not returned. Yet, although after 1924 he had several short affairs and at least one more permanent association – with Lady Furness – his basic attachment to Mrs Dudley Ward remained the same.

Throughout the years he telephoned to her regularly every morning (for some reason no longer on record her household spoke of this as 'the baker's call'. 'Has the baker called yet?' and so on), and he usually visited her house some time during the day. If she had loved him more than she did, or if she had been insensately ambitious, history might have been, not completely different, but altered, because it seems possible that from the earliest time the Prince regarded his predestined role as not inescapable, and viewed the Duke of York much as one brother might another in the case of a family firm. In later life he was to reject any suggestion that he had not wished to be King, and he pointed to how hard he had worked as Prince of Wales. Nevertheless, at the time he often suggested to Mrs Dudley Ward that they might go away together. She was asked in her old age whether she thought he had been serious in these proposals and she replied rather sharply: 'I don't know. We didn't go into it.' Nevertheless, one cannot ignore the probability that, even at this time, he regarded the options as open to him and accepted his future only on his own terms.

People speaking of these years almost invariably remark of Mrs Dudley Ward that 'she was very good for him', and, asked for a more specific account, explain that, although in public her attitude towards him was extremely correct, in private she 'teased' him (counteracted a tendency to become rather spoilt), and took a strict view of his obligations.

She had two little daughters (she was legally separated from her husband at this time although she divorced him in 1931), and it became her boast that 'ours was the first house without a green baize door'. Mrs Dudley Ward's children lived with their mother in the front of the house, and her guests accepted their presence on many occasions when their own children would have been in the nursery. The Prince of Wales adored these children, particularly Angie. They called him 'Little Prince', a prettier name than the Keppel children's 'Kingy', and, as Angie grew up, she often accompanied him. She attended a day school but she had several special classes in languages, dancing and so on. Discovering that it was impossible for the mistresses of the school to be quite sure when these extra classes took place, she would sometimes play truant. When this happened she would wait on a seat on the road outside the school until a car drew up and the chauffeur, Ladbroke, got out and told her that 'His Royal Highness' would like her to go to tea at St James's Palace, or to play golf, as the case might be. If golf, they would drive off to Coombe Hill, where for an hour or so they shared the attention of the professional, Archie Compston.

Mrs Dudley Ward's maid, McCann, has said that the servants both in their household and in the Prince's were devoted to him and that his popularity with them was at least as great as with the public, and she told a rather charming story about him. He owned a cairn terrier called Cora which McCann used to look after when he was away from home. Presently Cora had a son called Johnnie which was given to Mrs Dudley Ward, and again looked after by McCann. On one occasion, when McCann and her mistress were going to be away, the Prince offered in his turn to look after Johnnie. McCann was rather worried because she knew that Johnnie was very spoilt, and she said to her mistress that she hoped she would ask the Prince not to be angry if he behaved badly and begged at meals. It was not really his fault. That evening, when the Prince arrived at the house, Mrs Dudley Ward said in her curiously intonated voice: 'Now tell His Royal Highness what you said this morning.' And McCann repeated her worries about Johnnie. The Prince listened gravely and, when she had finished, he replied: 'Well, all I can say is that I am the President of the RSPCA.'

Most illuminating of all is the phrase by which Mrs Dudley Ward's daughter remembers him: 'Anything to please,' he would say when her mother made some proposal to him, 'anything to please.'

People whom he trusted or loved almost invariably speak of his essential simplicity, and they use a word about him that is also used about his father. 'We liked him,' Mrs Colin Buist said, 'because he was so straightforward.' And she added: 'You know, I have known him all his life and I have never seen him angry. If he hears something he doesn't like or doesn't understand, he never speaks strongly. He just says: "Oh! well I suppose he thinks...."' His preferences were always for a private life. He liked to dine two or four – alone with the woman he loved or with one other couple. One reason for his addiction to night clubs was that there people dined in small parties.

Instances are given of his generosity. Lord Mountbatten, as a young naval officer, was sitting with him in his room at St James's Palace when he opened an envelope containing a cheque for £300, a back payment for his services as an officer in the war. 'This is not much use to me,' he said to his cousin, 'but I dare say you could do with it.' And he threw the cheque over to him. Lady Hardinge speaks of his generosity both to charities and individuals, and she says: 'He used, long ago, to be lavish with tips. A shockingly bad, but brave rider, he was reputed to give a five-pound note to anybody who opened a gate for him out hunting. A story circulating at the time said that his route across country was marked by attentive members of a famous banking family, each one holding open a gate.'[11]

But the qualities for which above all he was famous were his exceptional ability to handle a crowd and a quite irresistible personal charm. About the first there is no doubt at all and there are hundreds of witnesses to it from all over the world. He had the gift of command combined with a special quickness and adroitness in extemporization and a flair for saying something tactful to each and every person. The second is equally well attested, not merely by immense numbers of simple people, but again and again in the memoirs of courtiers and others with a wide experience of meeting people.

'He had an absolutely magnetic charm,' Lord Mountbatten has said, while a typical comment is this one taken from the autobiography of the Duchess of Atholl. 'We also saw a little of the Prince of Wales lately returned from his trip to India. I think it was the first time I had met His Royal Highness and I began to realize something of his great charm.'[12]

And dozens of stories are told to illustrate how instinctively he performed his duties, saying and doing exactly the right things without prompting and invariably winning over members of the Labour Party and other people whose politics made them regard him with distrust. A very remarkable instance of this is given by David Kirkwood in *My Life of Revolt*. The Prince showed much anxiety to meet him at a time when there was trouble on Clydebank, and finally talked to him alone, in a sitting-room put at their disposal while a party took place at Lady Astor's house. According to Kirkwood's account the Prince did little more than question him and listen sympathetically to his answers, but at the end of the interview Kirkwood says: 'I felt, as I feel when I see an expert engineer at work, that I had been in the presence of a man who has a big job to do, and is earnest and determined to do his job well.'[13] And Kingsley Martin speaks of Kirkwood as 'a bold and sincere man, who thought himself an uncompromising revolutionary, [but] ended up in the House of Lords, and became an enthusiastic monarchist after meeting the Prince of Wales.'[14]

Thus, although the Prince already gave cause for some anxiety to those nearest to him, if one reads only the accounts written and published when he was young one gets a consistent picture of an exceptionally attractive young man, eager to succeed at his job, spoiled and moody and of small intellectual capacity, but quick, imaginative and responsive. There are, however, other accounts which, although written from hindsight, cannot be ignored. Here is an account by Lord Davidson of a meeting with him:

When I was still working in the Colonial Office as Private Secretary to Lulu Harcourt, I remember at his instance going to lunch in some rooms in St. James's Palace to meet the Prince of Wales. This must have been I suppose in 1912, and the purpose of the operation was that I should be looked over with a view to my becoming the Prince's Private Secretary. Lulu Harcourt pressed me very much to accept the post, but I realized from the atmosphere of the luncheon party and the conversation, or rather what emerged during the conversation, that it was no job for me. I was not a yes-man or a lick-spittle and I would have made a very poor courtier; nor did I quite like the personality of the Prince of Wales, charming in some ways as he was – and certainly to me. ... From then onwards, studying the Prince of Wales and meeting him from time to time, I formed the conclusion that he was an obstinate, but really a weak man, in whose pastimes I could have taken no share, and whose friends, male and female, I would not wish to have known intimately. ... I never felt that he could make a king in the same class as King George V, who was a man of highest character and sobriety and a devoted husband. ... From the earliest days I had grave doubts whether the Prince of Wales would ever succeed to the throne or become an adequate King of England.[15]

This passage has been chosen because it is typical of a kind of easy contempt with which some people have allowed themselves to speak of the Prince from the time he became Duke of Windsor. It may not be thought absolutely damning to him and his friends that Lord Davidson did not like them, but it seems highly unlikely that this description of them would have been written if he had remained on the throne. Certainly more care would have been taken about details. In 1912 the Prince was eighteen and going up to Oxford. Some anxiety was felt at that time to choose the right man as his equerry, but it was not until seven years later when he returned from the war that the question of a Private Secretary arose. And it was not until 1919 that he moved into the rooms in St James's Palace to which Lord Davidson presumably refers. These are unimportant mistakes but they occur in a passage which includes the words: 'From the earliest days I had grave doubts whether the Prince of Wales would ever succeed to the throne.' Nothing but abdication could have prevented the Prince succeeding (he did, of course, succeed) and Lord Davidson is here claiming precognition of an event which took even those closest to the Prince by surprise.

Another and more important witness, who is also writing from hindsight, is Lady Hardinge. Here is her description of him.

Everywhere he went – she says – he brought his almost overwhelming charm into play. Not a natural charm, but a force at his command, it was a quality all the more remarkable because he could switch it on and off at will – this was sometimes rather unnerving for those under its influence. Through it, in a room full of people, he could maintain himself as the centre of attraction long after the initial curiosity which usually surrounded the Prince of Wales had worn off. If he wished, he could completely change the whole atmosphere. It is impossible to exaggerate the strength of the spell he could cast; mostly it was a question of moods, although later on calculation came into it, and a curious boyish mischievousness.

The charm was reinforced by an astonishing memory for detail. As a child, he had been unusually quick and precocious in this respect, and long afterwards his memory of his early years was remarkable. His quickness at recognizing faces and recalling names gave satisfaction to large numbers of people at home and abroad.[16]

This is a rather curious account and one that conflicts with much that has been written by other observers. Yet it is clearly the result of a serious attempt at analysis.

One should probably not be misled by the assumption that after a while people in a room with the Prince of Wales lose 'their initial curiosity', because this is tantamount to a suggestion that after a while his charm can be isolated from his royalty and considered separately. It is surely one of the special disadvantages suffered by the Royal Family that people in a room with them seldom lose a special alertness to their presence, although they may react differently. 'Either they slap you on the back, or they get under the table,' Prince George said, speaking of naval officers, but with a wider reference; and Mrs Dudley Ward said: 'It was difficult for them [the Prince of Wales and Prince George] to meet any of the nice people. I often noticed that at parties. All the nice people stood round the walls while the pushing people pushed up to them.' It is impossible to dissociate the person from something which is as much a part of personality as a pretty face and as much a barrier to easy conversation as imperfect knowledge of a language.

The primeval emotions aroused by royalty have been explained by psychologists as the result of a father-fixation on the person of the monarch. 'The ordinary citizens,' Harold Nicolson says, 'learnt to regard King George both as the father of his people and as the reflection and magnification of their own collective virtues.'[17] And this theory has been enlarged to include an entire idealized and idolized family. Even so it seems inadequate. It is entirely prosaic and takes no account of the glamour and the glory, the jewels and the uniforms, the limelight on the slim groomed figure gravely receiving homage; or of man's upward strivings, his sense of beauty, his ordinary human failings. Suffice it to say that the emotions aroused by the monarchy are not subject to such influence as class or education and can be seen at their purest equally among members of the higher aristocracy as in the humblest folk. Men of intelligence and wide opportunity are never wanting to spend their lives in the service of the Royal Family, while left-wing intellectuals, like Harold Laski and Kingsley Martin, who regarded themselves as absolutely cold to the magic of monarchy and write of it from the sidelines, nevertheless seem to become captivated by the subject and return to it again and again. When people who have previously believed themselves to be immune to the attractions of royalty find themselves in its presence, they are often taken by surprise by the ecstasy of pleasure and appreciation they feel. The easiest way to rationalize this pleasure is to invest the royal personage with qualities that account for it – thus intelligent people can often be found repeating with a radiant expression the most ordinary expressions of humanity, the most moderate examples of the royal wit. Yet even when these can be shown to be the commonplaces of every day, it does not alter anything – for how can it be that this person, subject to such extraordinary influences, can yet speak and behave in an ordinary way?

However, if the charms of any member of the Royal Family cannot be separated from their royalty, there may, nevertheless, be charms that are particularly suited to set this off. From most accounts of Edward VIII as Prince of Wales, it seems he had qualities which, attractive in anyone, become irresistible in a member of the Royal Family. In attempting to analyse these one cannot disregard his looks. His fair face under his thatch of yellow hair was both exceptionally beautiful and ineffably sad in repose. 'He is sad,' Lord Esher had said, 'with the sadness of the world's burdens.' And we know from Lord Mountbatten that this air of having been blighted by some vision too immense for him to bear did represent a genuinely melancholy temperament. This suggested vulnerability, which is attractive in almost anyone, but in a royal personage was enough by itself to account for the sympathy he aroused. Then on occasion the sad, royal face would light up with an intensity of desire to please which transformed the expression to one of youthful, almost conspiratorial gaiety. And, although there were other qualities – the natural manner, the mild sense of humour, the infallible memory – it was this desire to please that was found irresistible by the populations of whole continents and also by individuals quite accustomed to displays of exceptional charm.

However, one cannot spend the whole of one's life in an effort to please, and, as the Prince grew older and more confident of his powers, he began to lose the desire to please everyone he met. It was not that the youthful spring died within him but that it became more and more concentrated on the few people he loved. 'Anything to please,' he said to Mrs Dudley Ward, 'anything to please.' Yet, spoiled and moody, he was uneasy with his parents and their friends and in the palaces of the King.

If one takes a further passage from Lady Hardinge it becomes easier to understand the contradiction in her account. Here is her description of their first meeting when she was nineteen and he already twenty-six.

> He seemed to be quite as frightened of me as I was of him, although he was seven years older than me, and fidgeted his way through dinner. I do not think he ever felt really at home at Windsor or at Buckingham Palace.[18]

The Prince, like so many other people, was a different person with those he liked and trusted from when he was ill at ease. Other people besides Lady Hardinge have spoken of his switching on his charm, but one must reject the charge that there is anything very unusual or sinister about this. When the Prince was uneasy or bored, he either sat melancholy and aloof (as time went on he more and more often chose this alternative), or he 'switched on' an imitation of feeling and behaviour which experience had taught him was effective. If almost the whole of one's duty is publicly to please people, it cannot be considered a crime to counterfeit emotions which never could be at command. What was sad, and unusual in his family, was that as he grew older these emotions became less and less spontaneous; almost as though he had worn out the whole stock in the exceptional ardour of his youth. But at the time of which Lady Hardinge speaks, she might have formed another view of his charm if she had followed him into the ballroom where half an hour later in a different mood he was to be found embarrassing the young ladies he met by returning the curtsies they dropped him.

For there is really no doubt that he had a genuine simplicity and naturalness of manner. Inasmuch as Lady Hardinge's account seems to contradict this, one is forced to reject it. There are too many anecdotes on record in which the element of simplicity is *apparent* – as he rides on his bicycle, runs with the beagles, answers a passer-by or enters Toc H.

> I saw the young Prince of Wales yesterday – Lord Esher wrote in 1928 – His journey to the north moved him quite a lot. Nellie and I lunched with him the other day. Just a round table wheeled up to the fire in the sitting-room. Who would credit such a proceeding by the light of the Prince Consort?
> This boy is a Stuart, not a Brunswick.[19]

And at St James's Palace the servants were dressed in black and changed into the royal livery – sometimes rather hurriedly – only when it was known that the King or Queen was coming there.

From the time when he was a child playing football with the village children at Sandringham, the Prince seems always to have suffered from a genuine uneasiness about his enforced elevation, and from a desire, no less honourable for coming sometimes into conflict with other desires, to enter on equal terms the world from which he felt shut out. It was this sense of being shut out that accounted for much of the duality of his nature. His books are full of sentences expressing his dislike of ceremony, his consciousness of the loneliness of his lot, and of a wistful envy of the ordinary man. Certain aspects of his character give these sentences the ring of half-truth, but this should not obscure the fact that they were half true.

The difficulty arose not so much because his natural simplicity, so admirable in itself, was in some ways inconvenient in the heir to the throne, as that because of his immaturity of mind he was unable to reconcile it with the exceptional demands life made upon him, or even with other aspects of his own character. Thus we have the much-quoted story which first saw the light of day in Compton Mackenzie's *Windsor Tapestry*. This book was written soon after the Abdication with the expressed intention of defending the ex-King against what the author regarded as 'the abominable treatment which HRH the Duke of Windsor had received and was still receiving'....[20] Among the least satisfactory of this author's works, it was written at a white heat of loyalty and indignation, and it is therefore ironic that almost the only thing in it to survive is the following:

Allusion has been made to his suddenly turning 'royal', and this was often held against him when he was Prince of Wales. He was accused of being too familiar one moment and then turning suddenly on people he fancied were presuming on his familiarity. A little imagination would help in judging those apparent inconsistencies of behaviour.

To take an example known to the writer. On several occasions the Prince of Wales went up to Oxford for a day or two in after years. Once on entering the Junior Common Room at Magdalen he bade everybody be seated, telling them he was a Magdalen man and did not wish to be treated ceremoniously but as a member of the College. The next time he went into the J.C.R. nobody stirred, and he asked sharply if that was the way to treat the heir to the Throne. It sounds inconsistent. But surely the instinct of those undergraduates should have led them to pay him the courtesy of rising and allow him to put them at their ease a second time.[21]

Although this story has been so often quoted, Compton Mackenzie appears to be telling it at second hand – 'To take an example known to the writer' – and there is an improbable neatness about it. Yet even if it is difficult to believe as it stands, it illustrates a charge which has been frequently made. Those who knew him best defend him against it. 'About the royal snub,' Lady Laycock volunteered. 'I never saw any of that in all the time I knew him.' And when questioned, her mother, Mrs Dudley Ward, replied: 'No. I don't remember that,' but added reflectively, 'Of course, he was very spoilt.' However other people as well if not so closely placed to observe have retorted: 'There was never any doubt about it. I have seen it dozens of times myself.' In this case it might be wise to reverse the usual rule and give greatest weight to the views of those who knew him least, because clearly the temptation to indulge the 'royal snub' would be at its weakest with those who knew him best.

Probably every member of the Royal Family who attempts to break the rules of isolation from the rest of the world will be compelled from time to time to administer the 'royal snub', and this would be true irrespective of any natural tendency to arrogance. If the rules are kept on one side they will be kept on the other, but, if they are waived, too much is left to the judgment of any and every man. The Prince may not have been arrogant by nature but he was extraordinarily spoilt and self-indulgent. He was clearly very haughty when his ideas for fulfilling his public duties were interfered with.

Many rumours and anecdotes of doubtful truth have grown up around the person of this Prince. A story of his visit to a hospital after the war – some say in the war – has had a tremendous circulation. It seems to have reached print for the first time in 1926 in the Memoirs of Sir Almeric Fitzroy, who had written it in his diary on 1 May 1923. Since then it has appeared again and again. Here is what Sir Almeric says:

A very remarkable story is told me of an act of mercy performed at his own inspiration by the Prince of Wales while in Belgium this week. One of his tasks was to visit a hospital for the special treatment of English soldiers suffering from facial disfiguration, the greatest difficulty of which is the extreme sensitiveness of the victims to any suspicion of curiosity or recoil on the part of a visitor. The Prince had seen all the cases produced and, noticing that there were only twenty-seven present out of the twenty-eight known to be in the institution, asked for the twenty-eighth. The officer in charge proceeded to explain that his was a case of such a frightful, not to say repulsive character, that it was not thought well to include him with the rest; whereupon the Prince said he had undertaken the job and refused to have anyone deprived of his sympathy who had, it seemed, the highest claim to it. He was at once taken to the patient's room, went straight up to the man and kissed him. Surely an act of compassion entitled to live in history with Philip Sidney's cup of water on the field of Zutphen. He who can so bear himself in the dread presence of extreme misery must have a genius for pity.[22]

All other printed versions of this story were written, as far as has been ascertained, after Sir Almeric's and all have in common with his the lack of any very sound attribution – no name of the hospital or place where the incident occurred, no eye-witness and so on. There is also something improbable about the way it is told – why, for instance, with twenty-seven men present should the Prince have counted them? It has to be true or untrue – it is too extreme to be one of those stories which even if apocryphal are useful in illustration of a truth – and for years it has had so great a hold on so many people's imagination that one feels almost apologetic in exposing it as a mere invention. However, unfortunately it is not true and in the Prince's youth it was well known to his Household that nothing so irritated him as to be told it.

Another story about him took the form of a poem and mouldered in the British Museum until it was included in a collection of poems and verses published in 1964.* Now that it has been released it must be dealt with because it has so many of the hallmarks of a candidate for perpetual circulation. On one of his visits to the west country estates of the Duchy of Cornwall, it was suggested to the Prince of Wales that he should visit Thomas Hardy. Hearing of this incident Max Beerbohm wrote the following:

> ### A Luncheon
> Lift latch, step in, be welcome, Sir
> Albeit to see you I'm unglad
> And your face is fraught with a deathly shyness
> Bleaching what pink it may have had.
> Come in, Come in, Your Royal Highness.
>
> Beautiful weather? – Sir, that's true,
> Though the farmers are casting rueful looks
> At tilth's and pasture's dearth of spryness –
> Yes, Sir, I've written several books. –
> A little more chicken, Your Royal Highness?
>
> Lift latch, step out, your car is there,
> To bear you hence from this ancient vale.
> We are both of us aged by our strange brief nighness
> But each of us lives to tell the tale.
> Farewell, farewell, Your Royal Highness.[23]

Max Beerbohm seriously under-rated the attractions which royalty has even for poets. There was no question of the Prince of Wales lifting the latch. Thomas Hardy sat in the covered stand to watch the Mayor and Corporation of Dorchester welcome him, and later, wearing 'a very alert and cheerful expression', drove with him to his house at Max Gate.

One cannot leave the subject of rumour without referring to the fact that it is widely believed, by many people who should know better, that the Prince customarily drank too much. This is completely untrue. The Prince had an obsession with physical fitness, and he ate very little, often nothing at luncheon, and drank nothing until after seven o'clock in the evening except tea, a beverage for which he had an enduring passion the whole of his life. A story is told of how on one occasion both his pilots,

* Twenty-five copies of this poem were printed in 1946 of which Number 17 went to the British Museum.

Flight Lieutenant Edward – 'Mouse' – Fielden* and Flight Lieutenant Hugh Mellor were with him in his aeroplane when they had to make a forced-landing. Sick with apprehension themselves, they found their anxiety relieved by the obvious enjoyment of their passenger in the back, and, later by the fact that, to keep him happy while arrangements were made for their rescue, it was necessary only to introduce him to the cottage of a woman who made him a cup of tea.

Nor can one close this account of the impression made by the Prince in his youth without one more quotation from Lady Hardinge, a truthful witness but one by no means biased in his favour.

'Never think,' she said, 'never think there wasn't quality there.' And she waved her hand in the air. 'He only had to arrive at Windsor. . . .'†

It is often argued that although the King showed none of the jealousy of his successor-designate characteristic of Queen Victoria, he arrested the development of both his elder sons by his unwillingness to allow them adequate opportunities to acquaint themselves with the affairs of the realm. Sir John Wheeler-Bennett says that, on the Duke of York's return from his world tour in 1928, both his own advisers and the King's believed it desirable that he should be given information about certain of the inner workings of international and Commonwealth affairs as disclosed in the reports of British representatives, and he goes on to say:

Here, however, the opposition of King George was encountered. His Majesty was averse to such a procedure, holding that it was no part of the duties of his eldest sons to have access to such confidential information, yet ignoring the fact [here he paraphrases the Duke of Windsor himself] that they were expected, in some indefinable manner, to appear conversant with world affairs and to give the impression of being informed and knowledgeable. Not even in the case of his heir, the Prince of Wales, did the King permit his presence at audiences granted to Ministers nor to peruse the contents of those ever-present dispatch boxes containing the submissions of the Prime Minister and the heads of Government departments, and he discouraged his association with political leaders. The only privilege which he would concede to the Prince and the Duke of York was permission to see a very limited selection of Foreign Office and Dominion Office telegrams – and this only with the greatest misgivings and after considerable resistance.[24]

And King George VI is reported as saying to his cousin Lord Louis Mountbatten on the first night of his reign, 'Dickie, this is absolutely terrible. I never wanted this to happen; I'm quite unprepared for it. David has been trained for this all his life. I've never even seen a State Paper.'[25]

When considering the development and history of the Prince of Wales after his return from his tours in 1922, historians have been inclined to sug-

* Later Air Vice-Marshal Sir Edward Fielden.
† In conversation with the author.

gest that, by his unwillingness to allow him access to the affairs of state, the King obstinately deprived his son of any worthwhile work to do at this important stage of his life, when for the first time he had the opportunity to settle down. The tendency is to compare the Prince of Wales with King Edward VII and this period of his life with the long 'locust years' of the former. The comparison is not valid, however, partly because Edward VIII ascended the throne at the age of forty-two while Edward VII was almost sixty when his mother died, but chiefly because of the change in the world situation and in the situation of the Crown in the intervening years.

At the time when the rulers of almost every country in Europe were closely related to the English Royal Family, it was obviously necessary that the Prince of Wales should be well informed of the policies of his own country, and indeed it became the practice of Foreign Ministers to take him (Edward VII, when Prince of Wales) into their confidence in spite of the Queen's wishes. Even then it was doubtful whether an emissary at large with no particular powers and too much opportunity to say the wrong thing, was necessarily of great advantage to the state; just as it has never been proved that Edward VII's good relations with the French outweighed the hostility between him and his cousin Wilhelm or that either of these things affected the march of events one way or the other. However that may be, by the nineteen-twenties the world had changed, the sheer volume of work undertaken by the central government was immeasurably greater, and both foreign and internal politics were too complex and too highly charged to be treated as the training ground for Kings. Under a constitutional monarchy the King himself can commit no public act except on the advice of his ministers and since he can do nothing without their advice they are responsible if mistakes are made; while the duties and rights of the King by George V's day had become well defined as 'to advise, to encourage and to warn'. Because of the continuity of his service – he remains while governments change – it is clear that a wise king might at any moment exert a valuable influence over his ministers, but this is a one-man job, not one that can be shared or delegated to his heir. Yet the perusal of state papers, which must be in the main a very dull activity although intensely and dramatically rewarding at times, would not be undertaken purely as an academic exercise except by a very determined student of politics.

In all the circumstances, then, it is surely possible to hold the view that King George was perfectly correct in being unwilling for his sons to see anything except a 'very limited selection of Foreign Office and Dominions Office telegrams', and right, too, to discourage their association with political leaders. In any case, although the experiment of allowing the heir to the throne access to ministers and ministerial policy has not in recent history been tried, it does not require much imagination to envisage the difficulties which in modern times it might create.

Nor, although one can understand the feelings of the Duke of York on his elevation to the throne, need one sympathize too greatly with him for his ignorance of state papers, partly because as King he would have a first class secretariat to instruct and advise him, but even more because the duty 'to advise, to encourage and to warn' is surely one that can be learned only in its performance, not by watching from the sidelines in a state of total discretion.

In discussing his life as Prince of Wales, the Duke of Windsor himself seems to accept that these are the facts of the situation, rather than to suggest that what he describes as 'the rather curious nature of my position', was due to any obstinacy or ungenerousness on the part of his father. The Prince of Wales is the King's deputy, he says, but otherwise has no prescribed state duties. And then he goes on to the sentence paraphrased by Sir John Wheeler-Bennett.

In retrospect the Duke of Windsor seems to have worked up a small degree of self-pity for his years as Prince of Wales, but it is very doubtful if he really felt this strongly at the time. It is only in the last thirty years, since the outbreak of the Second World War, that work as distinct to the opportunity to make a living has been elevated to its present importance to the dignity of mankind. In the nineteen-twenties, although by then sons of gentlemen were in no way prohibited from working in trade or at one of the professions, they felt neither guilt nor a sense of ill-treatment if interesting work was not part of their birthright. Of the Prince of Wales's upper-class contemporaries, a great many went into one of the Guards Regiments for a short period when they first grew up and then settled down to the life of a country gentleman, appearing at White's Club or Buck's Club in the middle of the week, but otherwise occupying themselves as Masters of Hounds, owners of racehorses, or, in the case of the elder sons or the more serious-minded, as magistrates, High Sheriffs, Lords Lieutenant and so on; while they spent a great deal of time on exactly those jobs which fell in such profusion to the Prince of Wales – speaking at public banquets, opening agricultural shows, laying foundation stones and opening bazaars. At the same time, it must be remembered, none of the daughters of the well-to-do went to work, so that they were always free to lunch or dine out, play golf or ride to hounds. In the country such activities as tennis parties were by no means confined to weekends. The idea of pitying royalty because their work, although of infinite benefit in the encouragement of all those voluntary associations which civilize society as well as of charitable institutions, is not of major political importance is a modern conception. In the nineteen-twenties, although the Prince of Wales would have had ideas appropriate to his station rather than to his capabilities, that is to say having been born at the apex of society, he would have tended when considering the question of work to have concerned himself with only the most important and interesting spheres, it is nevertheless doubtful whether, unless under the influence of a direct comparison with Edward VII or temporarily thwarted of something he seriously wished to do, he really expected or even desired to anticipate the responsibilities of the King.

Brought face to face with the appalling poverty of the late nineteen-twenties and early thirties, to his infinite credit his distress was genuine and spontaneous. Under the influence of this he was inclined to make a-political statements and to believe that something could and should be done to alleviate the desperation he found. As a result, it has sometimes been thought that he had a genuine interest in politics, even that this was of a progressive, almost radical kind. Nothing could be further from the truth. He was concerned, as almost everyone is, with certain political questions and by the nature of his work his attention was drawn to these again and again, but, if allowance is made for this, it can be seen that his serious interest in the government of the country was hardly greater than that of any other easy-going, under-educated, unintellectual young man. The King was responsible for discouraging his association with professional politicians but he could hardly have prevented, and indeed would not have wanted to prevent, his gravitating towards those noble families, such as the Stanleys and the Cecils, to whom politics was the stuff of life. This, as has been said in a different context, the Prince notably failed to do.

Again, it is perfectly clear that, as far as he was a political animal, he was as unthinkingly conservative in outlook as ninety out of every hundred young men born outside the working class. His books are restrainedly but quite definitely full of nostalgia for 'the good old days', while his accounts of political occasions are couched in the language of a faded reactionism which, although it expresses sentiments still held by many people of his class and age, falls oddly on the modern ear. Here is what he had to say about the General Strike of 1926:

What was unique about the strike of 1926 was the reaction of the upper and middle classes. They regarded it as a blow aimed at the constitutional foundations of English life. In response to the Government's appeal thousands left their business desks and their suburban homes or emerged from their landed estates, their clubs, and their leisure, determined to restore the essential services of the nation. The people I knew felt they were putting down something that was terribly wrong, something contrary to British traditions. And they put on a first-class show.[26]

He goes on to say that his father, who clearly had difficulty in deciding whether the strike fell within the ordinary meaning of party politics or was of a more revolutionary nature, was anxious that his sons should keep out of it. This he found impossible to do, and he adds that he hopes he will not at this late date be accused of party politics when he says that he lent his car and chauffeur, George Ladbroke, to transport the *British Gazette*, the Government newspaper edited by Winston Churchill, to Wales.

What he does not say but which is greatly to his credit is that he also contributed to the miners' relief fund. The Prince took an absolutely genuine, deep and imaginative interest in the welfare of the working man and in particular of ex-servicemen towards whom he felt a very real comradeship. Whenever he was in England he supported Toc H and the British Legion, never failing to attend their functions, to take part in their ceremonial occasions and to give them a warmth of interest and patronage which clearly exceeded a mere attention to duty. Toc H, founded in the house at Poperinghe, spread rapidly after the war and branches were formed all over England and in the British colonies. It is a religious movement and each year has an annual Birthday Festival and a ceremony of the lighting of a lamp. Its founder 'Tubby' Clayton wrote to Hector Bolitho as follows:

The Prince has led the building of Toc H, and he guided it in many overseas developments. He has visited houses of Toc H in every part of London, in Birmingham, Manchester, Sheffield, Newcastle, Halifax, Hull, Southampton and as far off as Buenos Aires. On his way back from Melton he has twice turned aside for a friendly glimpse of the house at Leicester. He has lit every lamp from his own, and never missed a chance of showing kindness to great or tiny meetings.[27]

Mr Clayton is also responsible for the following rather charming story of the Prince. Arriving late at one of the meetings of a branch of Toc H he came quietly up some back stairs on to a platform on which a group of men were singing, and joined in their song. His presence became generally known only when one by one the men backed shyly away from him, leaving him standing by himself.*

The British Legion was the result of the decision of five different associations, which had sprung up to represent the interests of the ex-servicemen, to unite under the Chairmanship of Earl Haig. It was formed in 1921 and it stood for the maintenance of world peace and the international co-operation of ex-servicemen. Its annual festival ceremonies at the Albert Hall and the marches to the Cenotaph commemorated those who died in the Great War and reminded those who remained of the horrors of war. The King and Queen and indeed the whole Royal Family gave their support to this institution, and the Prince of Wales, who became patron, took a very personal interest in it. Through the years he visited the branches and was present at the great ceremonial occasions whenever his duties allowed.

During all its early years it was forced by the conditions of the time to concern itself chiefly with the day-to-day interests of the ex-servicemen, representing them on every front and continually pressing the Government on issues concerning them. Right from the start unemployment was the biggest problem with which it had to deal, but it also took up such matters as the pensions paid to ex-servicemen, their rights in cases of ill-health, housing, and so on. Grants were made to enable ex-servicemen to

* Conversation with the author.

open or re-open businesses in which they would employ other ex-servicemen, and wherever the British Legion failed to secure government action it made every attempt to give practical aid itself.

In this world of ex-servicemen's associations and working men's clubs, the Prince of Wales found a sphere of genuine interest. 'I feel more at home with the Legion than anywhere else,' he said once, and, whether or not this was completely true, he succeeded in making the people of Britain feel it was. In those days the Prince could not captivate the whole nation by one or two television appearances, but, by his continual visits to the branches and headquarters of the working men's associations, he earned the love of large sections of the population.

If his father can be said to have contributed to his subsequent develop-ment, it is surely not because he prevented him playing politics, but be-cause, even in this sphere where his son was so obviously successful, his attitude was invariably churlish and discouraging. The members of Toc H had a uniform blazer which was worn on festival occasions and at the light-ing of the lamps. The Prince earned the equivalent of a summons to the library as a result of a press photograph showing him dressed in this blazer. And, while the King often gave the Prince formal praise for some obviously successful public appearance, he could never put much warmth into his speech because he felt nothing but irritation and disapproval of his methods. Lord Stamfordham once wrote to Sir Godfrey Thomas on the subject of humour: 'The King argues,' he said, 'that he never made jokes in any of his public speeches.'[28]

10

ABROAD

Towards the end of the Duke of Windsor's life someone who had served him for many years remarked in tones of humorous affection: 'Of course, New York was his undoing.'

In 1924 the Prince of Wales broke his journey to his ranch in Canada to stay with Mr and Mrs James Burden of Syosset, Long Island, in order to see the international polo matches between Great Britain and America. After his long and strenuous years he was in holiday mood and his affinity with what had almost overnight become the richest and the most undemanding society in the world was immediately apparent. In the early days of their supremacy the American nation required of a visitor only that he should be 'a good fellow', and that he fully deserved this appellation the Prince had demonstrated all over the world. He now set about his holiday-making with an assiduousness and a carefree lack of particularity which startled his staff and his father even though it delighted his hosts. His own account of the King's reaction to this visit is among the most disingenuous passages in his book. He quotes a headline 'Prince Gets in with the Milk-man' and then blames the American Press for the fact that his father refused after this to let any of his sons visit America again. The King did not openly ban a return to America but, whenever this was suggested either by the Prince of Wales or his brothers, he managed by some means to prevent it.

The Prince was nothing if not an original personality; no faceless royalty he, and, if it is not always possible to catch the exact mixture of talent, charm, obstinacy, flair for public relations and callow lack of judgment which combined to make him unique, it is not because of any attempt at disguise on his part. The contemporary newspapers give a very animated account of the impact he made on this visit to America.

In Long Island his American hosts had no difficulty in arranging a welcome for him and his staff and he remarks that, compared to the creature comforts Americans took for granted, the luxury to which he was accustomed seemed almost primitive. And so great was the interest in his visit that from 30 August, when he arrived on the *Berengaria,* dressed in a grey double-breasted suit with wide lapels and the famous tan suede shoes, the USA Press, including such serious organs as the *New York Times, New York Herald-Tribune* and *Chicago Tribune,* devoted every day a front page column to his movements as well as a further column on the inside pages, sometimes two or three.

Thus the *New York Times* on 1 September, after calling him 'the indefatigable vacationist', told its readers that the morning before in very hot weather the Prince had practised polo for more than two hours, running three ponies into a lather and exhausting two companions (Major Metcalfe and Captain Frank Miller, official referee of the Meadow Brook Club), and went on to say that for hours in the afternoon no one had known where he was, 'no one that is except the Prince and a few boon companions who knew that he was streaking it up Long Island in one of the fastest motor boats extant'.

There were other hours last night when the Prince was lost – this account continued. When he got back to the Williams' place he telephoned to the Burden House that he would not be in for dinner. Naturally no one asked him where he would dine. He got into an automobile with members of his party and was whirled away. He stayed out until after 11 o'clock. At least at that hour his movements had not been officially reported and it was said at the Burden Place that he had not come home. And everyone seemed to think it rather a lark, nor did anyone doubt that the Prince was highly delighted at having got clean away.[1]

On the following day the Prince went to a luncheon party given by Mr and Mrs Harold Irving Pratt where two hundred guests were assembled to meet him and where dancing had been arranged. From there against the advice of his staff and his hosts who warned him of the heat and the holiday crowd, he went to the races at Belmont Park.

There had been no advance warning of his intention but a thousand persons observed his progress to the box of August Belmont. The band struck up God Save the King and the Prince stood up, doffing his hat and so exposing to the bright sunlight his famous head of straw-coloured hair.

Inside the paddock the crowd became a mob and the scene that followed might have made David W. Griffiths envious. The photographers who had been trailing the Prince for days without any breaks climbed aboard the opportunity with cries of glee.[2]

On 3 September he is reported as having gone to a dance and stayed out until six o'clock in the morning, and on 4 September as having disappointed many people by failing to turn up for a drag hunt arranged for five o'clock in the morning, for the good reason that he had only just gone to bed. The

New York Times commented that the most startling fact of the day that followed was that he went from rising to bed time without taking any exercise. That afternoon he went to the W.G.Grace estate to watch the American polo team putting a last edge to their game. From his first arrival in the USA he had been much concerned to avoid the public and the Press and had constantly implored them to leave him alone. On this occasion he arrived at the far end of the field on the side opposite to that frequented by spectators, squirmed through a hole in the fence and perched on the low boards edging the field.

'There he sat swishing his stick, contentedly chewing a blade of grass, eyes on the players who were doing things very neatly and oblivious of those who were gradually searching him out. When at last he arose he was ringed by a half-hundred sub-debs and their escorts all gazing at him in naive admiration.'[3]

The most elaborate of the dances arranged for the English Prince was that given by Mr Clarence Mackay at Harbor Hill. The house was built at the top of a hill and was a reproduction of a French chateau, suggesting according to one newspaperman the famous Maison Lafitte, with formal gardens and terraces resembling those at Versailles. The Prince of Wales spent the day visiting this house and being shown the art treasures. Describing it later he wrote that whereas the 'paintings, tapestries, old china and armour would have been commonplace enough in an English country house … what was surprising was to find a squash-rackets court, a gymnasium, an indoor swimming-pool, and a Turkish bath'. The word 'commonplace' must be regarded as an ornament even in the general context. The Duke went on to say that for this party the music was provided by two bands directed by the famous Paul Whiteman 'who at a later stage was inspired to lead his musicians in a march around the hall, weaving in and out of the shadowy figures in armour'.[4]

In spite of these attractions the Prince left Harbor Hill at 2.30 in the morning and went once more to some destination unknown until about 5 a.m. when he returned to bed. The following day a reporter in the *New York Times* remarked:

The Prince already had made it three straight by going to the Cosden Place from Piping Rock on Wednesday night and dancing until 5 o'clock in the morning. Those who knew his vacation tastes thought that he probably was making it four straight by dancing all night somewhere else last night.[5]

On 5 September the Prince disappeared once more and late that night was still absent from the Burden house.

On 6 September he played polo and surprised the American crowd by his unique method of resting between the chukkas. He would bend over and touch his toes with his knuckles and remain in that position for the full minute and a half between periods. Then he would rise and leap into his saddle apparently completely refreshed. In the afternoon he went once more to the races. On this occasion he stood by one of the fences, where a newspaper report gives the following account of his actions.

When the steeplechasers approached the barrier where the Prince stood, he touched his fingers to the ground and half kneeled. As Damask, the leader, jumped, the Prince lifted himself and swung around, going through the motions of a rider, and evidently in his imagination helping the horse over the barrier. A second later he helped Duettiste in the same way, and then did the same service for Carabiniere.[6]

That night Will Rogers (a famous comedian) came as a guest at a great party given by the Piping Rock Club. He had been personally asked for by the Prince. Interviewed afterwards, Rogers said: 'Why yes he's a great boy, no kidding. And at that dinner! Why say I couldn't have hired a straight man to do straight for me what he did. You know at a dinner like that where there's a great man present the people always watch him. And whether your stuff goes over or not depends a good deal on how he takes it ...'[7] 'He was sitting on my right and he'd think up gags for me to spill. And laugh – Gosh. He'd just double up. And every time the Prince would laugh, everyone in the house would laugh.' And he added: 'The Prince is a good kid. Too bad I can't afford to carry a guy like that around with me. I'd have a swell act if I could.'[8]

Rain caused a certain amount of trouble to the Prince's staff because twice the International polo games had to be postponed. After the first postponement Captain Lascelles announced that the Prince of Wales might delay his trip to Canada a day or so to see the three games. On 10 September the game was again postponed and Captain Lascelles was asked whether the Prince would cancel his trip to Canada entirely. To this suggestion he replied: 'Absurd,' and also 'Poppycock.' The Prince's schedule had been planned long ago, he said, and would be rigidly adhered to.[9] However, on the next day a new announcement was made by someone else that the Prince had no plans which could not be altered and was prepared to wait ten days if necessary to see the game. At about this time Captain Lascelles made two further announcements. He had seen, he said, mistaken accounts as to the Prince's late rising. The truth was that he was out of bed by ten o'clock every morning, and began his day with a swim in the Burden Pool. Again, it was a mistake to think that the Prince was a pleasure-lover and a sportsman only, an idea based on his diversions while on an American holiday, and to counter this suggestion he made known something of the Prince's literary tastes. In spite of his many social and sporting engagements the Prince had been reading during his stay in America *The Life and Letters* of Walter Hines Page. And he added that HRH had not authorized publication of a series of articles written about him in one of the weekly magazines but had given his consent to an old army acquaintance only on the condition that they were submitted for approval.

Other attempts were made to counter the air of frivolity which between them the Press and the Prince had contrived to give. On 18 September he visited in New York the Julia Richman High School, the Museum of Natural History and the offices of the *New York Times* and *Herald-Tribune*, the following day paying a visit to Wall Street. And on 19 September it was announced that he was anxious to return to the USA at a later date to visit great industrial centres and farms and become acquainted with American working conditions and American men and women.

On 22 September the Prince finally left for his Canadian tour. Before he left the *Chicago Tribune* had asked its female readers what sort of a husband they thought the Prince would make. Among the replies were the following:

1. A nice fellow but thinks too much of himself to appreciate anyone else.
2. Too conceited and too spoiled from too much publicity.
3. He would be impossible as a husband. I imagine he's an 'I'm crazy about myself' sort of person. The world likes people who can forget their own selves.
4. He's too frivolous; thinks too much about polo and that sort of thing. He doesn't show any inclination to get down to solid business. We like to see fortunately situated people apply themselves to something of value to the world.[10]

In the spring of 1925 the Prince travelled in the *Repulse* down the west coast of Africa, stopping at Gambia, Sierra Leone, the Gold Coast, Nigeria, arriving at Cape Town on 30 April. Here he was welcomed by General Hertzog and General Smuts. Dressed in naval uniform and cocked hat, he was received by a crowd estimated at 190,000 of the 200,000 population of Cape Town as well as another 30,000 people from other parts of South Africa. He then set out on a 10,000-mile tour of South Africa, the most complete State tour ever undertaken. His own acquaintance with the country was to a large extent limited to what he could see from the railway train, but whether stopping in large towns or at small railway stations dressed in the red uniform of the Welsh Guards or more informally in a grey suit and soft hat, he still enchanted the waiting throngs, the Afrikaners as well as the English, by his charm, his friendliness and his fearlessly straightforward behaviour – as when at Colesberg, finding that a Commando of Dutch Farmers had turned out to do him honour, he immediately mounted a horse and rode into town at their head. In Durban he insisted as usual in moving about among the crowd at the racecourse, and in Johannesburg one of the travelling journalists wrote of his welcome:

One might have thought it had snowed people, for besides carpeting the ground to the maximum capacity of human congestion, they lay in great precarious drifts along roofs and balconies; they fringed every cornice, ledge and coping-stone, and in the form of clumps of small boys, they dangerously overweighted the branches of spindly trees.[11]

He visited diamond mines and battlefields, witnessed tribal ceremonies, and whenever he was given freedom to do so played his usual arduous rounds of golf (at Port Alfred he played forty-five holes on the first day of the weekend as well as having a lesson from the club professional). Then on the afternoon of 29 July the *Repulse* left the British base at Simonstown and sailed across the South Atlantic to South America. The Prince was returning the State visit of the President of the Argentine Republic and, according to his own account, had also the underlying purpose of stimulating interest in the products of British industry. On 16 October 1925 he arrived back in England at the end of his last official overseas tour, having visited forty-five countries and travelled a distance of 150,000 miles.

On 17 October *The Spectator* devoted an article to the Prince of Wales's return in which, after saying that everywhere he went he left behind most pleasant memories of his charm, modesty and friendliness – 'We do not exaggerate for the sake of serving a desirable convention' – the writer referred to certain criticisms that had been made of him in the Argentine newspapers. This article is remarkable in two ways – for the astonishing servility of its language, and because it marked one of the few occasions on which criticisms quite often heard abroad were openly referred to in the British Press.

The writer speaks of a day when the Prince was due to visit a school at eleven in the morning. The building had been specially decorated and the children taught to sing in English 'God Bless the Prince of Wales' and also another English song, while one child was prepared to make a speech in English. Two ministers were at the school to receive the guests. The assembled company waited for some time and then one of the two ministers, Dr Sagarna, went to the Prince's house where he was merely told without explanation that the engagement had been cancelled. The writer goes on to say that, in his opinion and the opinion of the correspondent he quotes, it was inconceivable that the Prince himself was responsible for this blunder, but that, in spite of this, it was impossible to prevent people from talking and drawing comparisons between his apparent willingness to attend supper parties into the small hours of the morning and his failure to keep an engagement a few hours later. Then, in slavishly apologetic tones, he suggests that, whatever the difficulties, the Prince should avoid giving people the excuse to say he was either unduly restless or exhausted by giving to amusements too many of the hours which might have been spent in preparation for work that was necessarily exacting and tiring. And he went on to say that the Prince would do well to attach himself seriously to some public cause entirely beyond and above faction.

Following this article A.G.Gardiner drew attention to it and, having first catalogued with perfect sincerity the Prince's many good qualities, continued as follows:

All that has been said about the Prince's charm of manner, friendliness of spirit, and good nature is gladly and universally recognized, but behind this ground for satisfaction is a widespread and growing doubt as to whether other qualities no less necessary to the great place he holds and the still greater place which he will in all probability one day hold, are being cultivated with equal zeal.

There is a feeling that there is a lack of seriousness which, excusable and even natural to healthy youth, is disquieting in the mature man. This implies no disapproval of the Prince's love of sport, of fun and of innocent amusement. Nor does it imply a demand that the heir to the throne should have intellectual tastes that nature has not endowed him with. Least of all does it imply that the qualities of a snob would be a desirable exchange for the Prince's high spirits and companionable temper. But it does mean that the public would be relieved to read a little less in the encomiums of the Press about the jazz drum and the banjo side of the Prince's life. . . .

The Prince's future is not a personal affair only, but an affair of the nation and of the world. His apprenticeship to life is over. His career is henceforth in his own hands. He commands an affection and goodwill on the part of the nation that cannot be overstated and that a man of his genuine kindliness of heart must wish to repay. He can repay it by emulating the admirable example which is offered by his parents of how a modern democratic throne should be filled. It is the general wish, now that his travels are over, that he should take up some task which will reflect his interest in the weightier matters of the national life and that will prepare him for the heavy responsibilities which will one day fall upon him. And finally, it is proper to say that the nation would be gratified and relieved to find that the heir to the throne, like Dame Marjorie in the song, was 'settled in life'.[12]

The British Press were presently to show themselves capable of imposing upon themselves a quite extraordinary degree of reticence in relation to the affairs of this royal young man. The fact that these articles were published reflects the growing understanding of the defects in his character which, alongside his popularity, continually increased.

I I

NO DOUBT OF THE YOUNG MAN'S CAPACITY FOR GOODNESS

The trouble was that as the Prince neared middle age the polarity between his response to people and occasions that awoke his interest and imagination and those which failed to do so became increasingly obvious. More and more often he gave demonstrations of an immature callousness and indifference to other people's feelings, and he troubled less and less to control the weariness and sadness with which he went about so much of his work. Yet, in that part which he undertook from choice, he still had a marvellous capacity to please and he made a genuine contribution to the evolution of the role of modern royalty. Because of this the late twenties and early thirties were the years in which his reputation shone most brightly but also those in which a solid body of rumour and criticism grew.

As Prince of Wales he had a duty to attend certain ceremonies and functions – the State opening of Parliament, the winter and spring levees held by the King, the Courts at which the year's debutantes were presented and so on. In addition he inherited from his father and grandfather many honorary positions. In fulfilment of these duties he constantly found himself at public banquets, charity balls, the unveiling of memorials and the like. But it was in the spheres of his own choice that he particularly shone.

Because, during the period he was King, he proved unable to undertake the volume of work required of him or to measure up to the magic of monarchy, either by following the old safe paths laid down by his predecessors and his courtiers, or by carrying off a new conception of his role, it is often taken for granted that Edward VIII would have been in all circumstances temperamentally unfitted for the throne. And this may be so, but as

131

Prince of Wales he showed a tremendous appetite for work, and in his departures from practice he was almost entirely successful.

As the great depression of the late twenties and thirties hit first one industry and then another and the vast armies of unemployed men and of under-nourished children stood on the streets, a living condemnation of modern civilization and government, the Prince no more than any other man could offer a political solution to the problems that beset his country. But it would be wrong for this reason to underestimate the very real contribution he made to the relief of human unhappiness. Whether calling in at branch meetings of the Legion, or leading thousands of ex-servicemen from the Albert Hall to the Cenotaph in a torchlight parade, he succeeded in giving sincerity and genuine enthusiasm to the performance of what might have been a purely dutiful role. He spoke to the men on his travels in tones of equality as well as concern, and in return they openly adored him. It was not uncommon for scenes of spontaneous enthusiasm to be evoked by the mere mention of his name.

In 1928 he became patron of the National Council of Social Service, an event which according to its official historian was to lead to some diversion from its original broad aims and purposes through concentration on one specific type of activity. From now on the work the NCSS undertook on behalf of the unemployed was to take precedence over everything else. It is not a polite exaggeration to say that the Prince inspired a great deal of this work, that other people were fired by his enthusiasm or that he constantly suggested new spheres where he might be of use to the institutions working in this field.

Nor did he ever spare himself physically. He travelled continually all over the worst areas of Wales, the Tyneside, Lancashire, the Midlands and Scotland, and to quote the historian of the NCSS:

The Prince knew more than some of his Ministers about the problems of the derelict valleys and the silent mills. Nor were the endless ceremonies, openings and presentations accomplished without personal cost in nervous strain and sheer fatigue. On one occasion, worn out with day-long travelling in Wales and the pain of helpless sympathy, the Prince slept exhausted on the shoulder of Sir Percy Watkins, chief NCSS officer for Wales, waking dutifully each time Sir Percy warned him that the car was approaching groups of children waiting to see their Prince.[1]

The sphere which the Prince made his own was that of voluntary service. He helped to raise funds where necessary but his heart was in the effort to raise volunteers. It says much for the achievements of the Welfare State that to a later generation his appeals seem rather naïve against the background of the depression and the appalling numbers of unemployed. At that time, however, even the hospitals were dependent to a very large extent on voluntary effort and, if any help was to be given to individuals other than that of a purely economic kind, it had to be done by voluntary workers. These were unable to touch the basic problems but they made an enormous contribution to the welfare of thousands of people. Because of his immense personal prestige the Prince was able to co-ordinate the work of the various institutions with far more ease than is usually possible. Thus we find him writing to the President of the British Legion, Sir Frederick Maurice, to emphasize the importance of co-operating with the National Council of Social Service. Sir Frederick is reported in *British Legion* as saying: 'His Majesty's Government have selected the National Council of Social Service as a general clearing house for voluntary effort for providing opportunities for recreation and useful occupation for unemployed men and women, and His Royal Highness particularly wishes that we should co-operate with that body as far as possible.'[2]

On 27 January 1932, prompted once more by the Prince, the National Council of Social Service organized a meeting at the Albert Hall at which he addressed an audience of the representatives of every type of school from the elementary stage to the universities, and all those organizations concerned with juvenile, educational, health and rural work which made up the social services of the country. His speech was broadcast to meetings in over two hundred and sixty towns and villages all over the country. In it he said:

You cannot hope to influence directly the trend of international affairs, but close at hand is a domestic problem, vast and baffling if looked at in the mass, though easier to help when broken up into individual pieces. . . I am thinking now of each member of the unemployed population as a single, separate personality, beset by depression, labouring under a sense of frustration and futility.

It was in this spirit that the Prince appealed for volunteers and that the NCSS went about the work of aiding the unemployed men and their families.

The response to the appeal was immediate and indeed temporarily overwhelming. By the autumn the NCSS was in touch with seven hundred schemes. By the following year, 2,300 centres had been opened catering at the peak for a quarter of a million men and women. All owed their existence to local initiative, much of it from the unemployed themselves, and all aimed at relieving the unhappiness and depression of the vast numbers of rejected and unwanted men and women, who were encouraged to take over the organization of their own activities.

It is not possible here to refer to or even to list the activities of the NCSS but mention must be made of their concern with physical fitness, for the wives of the unemployed, and specifically of the Welsh Land Settlements where unemployed families lived and worked farms varying from quite small market gardens to several hundred acres of agricultural land on a co-operative basis. The organizers of this work have never forgotten the nature of the Prince's personal contribution to it. In 1971 Sir George Haynes, who succeeded Captain Lionel Ellis as General Secretary, wrote:

I can still see him very clearly as he was then – so alert, keen to see and understand, and most direct in his contacts with all sorts and conditions of men. I am enclosing an old photograph I have kept of his visit to the University Settlement, Liverpool in late 1931 when I was the Warden. It shows better than any other I have seen the Duke's way of approach, his transparent interest and concern, and the immense regard people had for him. He had a charisma in those days which was unique ...

My main impressions are of the deep affection in which he was held, the genuine pleasure of the large crowds which lined the routes, the directness and sincerity of his approach. He knew what he was trying to do was only touching the surface, but, perhaps more than he knew, he brought a sense of personal concern for unemployed people and their social conditions which was widely appreciated by ordinary people.*

The Prince's interest and concern for the unemployed overlapped into his private life. Returning from a tour of the depressed areas in the early thirties he told Mrs Dudley Ward that more ought to be done for the families of the unemployed. There were many clubs and centres, he said, but too often they were run by the wrong kind of people. 'People like you ought to run clubs,' he told her. As a result of this remark, the First Feathers Club, using as insignia the Prince of Wales's Feathers, opened at Ladbroke Grove in 1934. The Club was originally conceived to aid the unemployed but it was soon felt that it should not be confined to these. Other Feathers Clubs followed – at one time there were eight – and also the Feathers Club Association. Mrs Dudley Ward remained Chairman of this Association for thirty years, attending every day at its offices and always present at the management committee of each of the Clubs, while she was largely responsible for raising the money needed to run them. Three Feathers Clubs remain in London to this day, although they are now concerned with rather different problems.

It would have seemed bewildering then to those who worked with the Prince in the fields where his enthusiasm combined with his natural flair for casual communication to make him one of the best-loved figures in modern history, if they had known that elsewhere so much anxiety was felt. In 1927, when he was thirty-three, a member of his own household expressed this anxiety in a letter to Baldwin in which he asked the Prime Minister to use his influence with the Prince. For 'There is no doubt,' this writer said, 'of the young man's capacity for goodness.'†[3] The Prime Minister's re-

* Letter to the author.
† This writer remains anonymous but the magisterial tone suggests Captain Lascelles.

sponse to this letter, according to some accounts, took an unexpected and rather exaggerated form. In 1927 the Prince, accompanied by his brother, Prince George, visited Canada for the Diamond Jubilee of the Confederation and Baldwin travelled with them. His biographers state that 'even then Baldwin was preoccupied with the problems which the Prince's behaviour and attitudes suggested would become acute when he became King',[4] and they quote Lord Eustace Percy on the subject. Speaking of what he describes as Baldwin's 'apparently eccentric judgment of which things really mattered and which had better, for the moment, be allowed to take their course', he says:

The most eccentric act of his whole public life was surely his determination, in the late summer of 1927, to leave a deeply divided Cabinet to clear up the wreckage of the Geneva Conference while he accompanied the Prince to Canada. Undoubtedly he overrated both his influence with the Prince and the opportunities of influence which this voyage would offer him; but, undoubtedly, too, the Prince, with his usual charm, had given him some cause to miscalculate thus. We are here in a region of personal relationships, where the truth could be known only to two people and will now probably never be known to anyone else, owing to the loyal reticence of one of the actors and the bad memory of the other; but no one who was at all in Baldwin's confidence at the time could mistake either his deep anxiety about the problem or his sense of personal responsibility for averting the danger that he foresaw. He failed to avert it, but, when it came in 1936, he was at least prepared for it and his manner of dealing with it would have been less sure if he had not brooded on it so far in advance of its coming.[5]

There is no very good evidence that Baldwin really took such an exaggerated view of the problems created by the Prince or of his own personal responsibility in the matter. His son, Earl Baldwin of Bewdley, believes that he travelled to Canada at this time for the simpler reason that he had been invited to the Diamond Jubilee celebrations and had accepted at a much earlier date. Whatever the truth of the matter, Baldwin was quite quickly given an example of the kind of behaviour that had upset so many people. The Prime Minister, his wife and someone who travelled with him, were invited to dine at Government House where the Prince of Wales and Prince George were staying. Arriving punctually for dinner, they passed on their way into the house the two brothers dressed in shorts and shirts going out to play a game of squash. The whole party was then kept waiting until, the game being over, the princes had had time to dress for dinner.

Since the irresponsible, almost hostile attitude to obligations which bored the Prince and the immaturity exhibited by his choice of leisure pursuits were so well-guarded from the British public and are so important to an understanding of his character, and also of the critical, sometimes contemptuous tone of much of the informed comment about him, one more example from the postbag following the newspaper serialization will be given, although chronologically it is out of context. This describes a visit to Bermuda in 1931.

I well recall – the writer states – a visit by the Prince of Wales in a warship . . . when he was due to come ashore and trot round the island in a carriage through the admiring throngs.

The anticipatory admiration, however, soon waned when his arrival was delayed and delayed. Crowds along the route grew restless and rumour swept the island that the Prince, after a heavy night, was immured in his cabin with a hangover, was sulking in his tent and refused point-blank to disembark. At long length, after much persuasion of how much offence he was gratuitously giving, he agreed to go through with the performance, came ashore, and was duly driven through the streets in his carriage (no cars were allowed in Bermuda then), with a face like thunder, refusing to look right or left. His route lay right past our home in Cedar Avenue, so we all got a good look at that grey, sullen visage. . . .

What fascinated me on reading your narration of this tour was that this contre-temps may have resulted not from a hangover – as all Bermuda furiously believed – but from one of the black depressions you describe. At all events, it helps illustrate perhaps that the world abroad, and the Empire in particular, was *not* entirely at his feet!*

Other people speak of the Prince playing the ukelele in his rooms all night with a total disregard for people who wished to sleep, or say that his black moods were not confined to his Empire tours, but that the 'grey, sullen visage' might increasingly be seen in England, at agricultural shows and so on.

However, to end on this note would give an unbalanced and inaccurate picture of the impact which by and large the Prince made at this time. In fact his popularity with the public was equalled by the strength of his hold on the imagination of individuals – many of them people of experience and knowledge of the world. Nothing illustrates this better than Baldwin's own account of an incident which occurred on the Prince's return from a tour of East Africa in the year of 1928.

On this tour the Prince had travelled in a semi-private capacity. His first purpose was an extended shooting expedition, but Sir Edward Grigg, his equerry on his earlier tours who was by now Governor of Kenya, was anxious the Prince should visit him. Accompanied by a small staff, consisting of Captain Lascelles, the Hon. Piers Legh and Brigadier-General Trotter, and travelling out with his brother the Duke of Gloucester, the Prince visited Kenya and Uganda and then started on safari to Tanganyika. At Mombasa, the Gateway to Kenya, he said:

For me it marks the completion of what I know to be the most significant chapter of my whole life hitherto. Ever since the conclusion of the Great War, ten years ago, I have taken every possible opportunity of seeing for myself some

---

* Letter to the author from Mr David Shelley Nicholl.

unit of the Empire, until there remained only this wonderful land of promise in Eastern Africa. Today I have reached the land and the circle is complete.[6]

The Prince's trip was in the main a holiday one, however, and he proceeded to enjoy it in characteristic fashion. He played golf on nearly every course in East Africa and hunted game in Uganda, in Kenya and in Tanganyika. He was joined in Nairobi by Lady Furness, who accompanied him on the Governor's safari and was alone in a car with him when he fell ill with malaria. Her presence did not apparently inhibit the Prince from showing his normal interest in other women, except during the time she was with him, and it is said on good authority that the safari was sometimes brought to a halt for several days while the Prince indulged a lighthearted fancy. In any case it was after this trip that Captain Lascelles resigned his appointment on the Prince's staff for the reason, it was believed in a small circle, that he could stand no more of it.

The Prince's safari to Tanganyika was interrupted by news that the King was seriously ill and by cables from the Prime Minister, Admiral Halsey and Godfrey Thomas, all urging his immediate return. The light cruiser *Enterprise* was ordered to proceed from Aden to Dar-es-Salaam to pick the Prince up and she completed the journey to Brindisi in eight days. Mussolini sent his own train there to meet him and gave orders for the tracks to be cleared to the Swiss frontier.

When he arrived at Folkestone he was met by Baldwin who travelled to London by train with him. There then occurred a conversation that has become famous.* Monica Baldwin's account of how her uncle told it to her is given here, because while in the main particulars this account differs from no other, the Prime Minister added something to it.

When we had to call him from Africa at the time of the old King's (George v) first serious illness, I had gone down to Southampton† to meet him with the delicate task of explaining to him exactly how the land lay. We had dined together as we travelled up by train to London and during the meal we had talked more or less indifferently of this and that. At last he said to me:

'You know, Prime Minister, I should like you to remember that you can always speak of anything to me.'

I seized on this and I answered: 'Sir, I shall remind you of that!'

And as I said it a most curious impression came over me, a feeling of certainty that one day I almost certainly *should* have to 'say something to him' – and that it would be about a woman. And then, as suddenly as it had come, it was gone.

. . .

When he arrived at Sandringham (? or was it Buckingham Palace)‡ he was told that he might not on any account go *near* his father, who was, we all thought,

---

* Baldwin invariably repeated himself when telling a story, saying the same thing at the same point to different people.

† Baldwin's memory was at fault. He arrived at Folkestone.

‡ Buckingham Palace.

near death, for at least 48 hours. He simply took no notice, damned everybody and marched in. The old King, who had for nearly a week been practically un-conscious, just opened half an eye, looked up at him and said:

'Damn you, what the devil are you doing here?' And from that moment he turned the corner and began rapidly to get better. It was exactly like the scene in 'Henry IV' when Prince Henry tries on the crown. . . .[7]

It will not be found possible to reconcile Baldwin's version of the Prince's arrival at Buckingham Palace with that given by the Duke of Windsor himself. Yet even if Mr Baldwin is in error, as people speaking from memory so often are, the passage shows how romantic was the feeling he still had for the Prince a year after the Abdication.

It has been argued that King George cannot be criticized for refusing to allow his sons access to confidential information concerning affairs of state or for discouraging them from an active interest in political affairs. A hypothetical case can be made, however, that the King had an adverse in-fluence on his eldest son's future through his continual interference with his leisure pursuits, an influence which can be seen at its strongest after his illness in 1928.

The Prince most enjoyed two things: the life in the night clubs in London and hunting. And he found nothing as exhilarating as riding a good horse and taking a line of his own across country. A legend has grown that he was an extremely bad horseman, indeed Lady Hardinge has said a shocking one. This is absurd. In the seasons of 1927–28 and 1928–29 he rode six winners, was second five times and third once, all in good point-to-points. This is a record which no bad horseman could possibly achieve. The belief that he was so completely unskilled seems to have grown up because he was often reported as falling off. His seat on a horse may not have been strong but it is perhaps not generally realized that someone who rides unflinchingly at a fence with the single intention of getting to the other side is apt to be unseated if he experiences some check.* The Prince seems to have ridden keen, hard-pulling horses and his method when racing was to jump into the lead and hold it as long as he could. His success in this field was immensely important to him because it was his only oppor-tunity to compete with the rest of the world in circumstances that could by no conceivable means be weighted in his favour.

One of his more charming characteristics was his genuine love of the country and his passion for violent exercise. When he first came home from his travels he took Easton Grey, a house in the Duke of Beaufort's Hunt, and later he had rooms and stables at Craven Lodge, Melton Mowbray. It seems possible that had he continued to hunt he might have bought an agricultural estate in the deep country when he felt the urge to have a

---

* Small falls by other horsemen were not so often reported.

house of his own, and devoted his leisure to those country pursuits which both his father and grandfather had enjoyed above everything.

However, this was not to be. From the time in the autumn of 1924 that he had a rather bad fall in the Army point-to-point at Arborfield Cross, he was under constant pressure from his family, from the Press and even from politicians (Ramsay MacDonald wrote him a personal letter of appeal) to give up the hazards of steeplechasing. Then, at the time of his father's illness in 1928, his mother made it a personal point that with his father so ill he should give up race riding and be content with hunting. And he told her that he would of course do as she asked.

Relating this, the Duke of Windsor says that the question of his continuing to hunt was academic because his string of horses was built round steeplechasing, a remark which at first sight seems unconvincing. It would be natural to feel that these great point-to-point horses were rather wasted merely on hunting but in such circumstances most people would keep the old favourites and gradually exchange the others for horses better suited to the hunting field. In the case of the Prince of Wales, he was not free to hunt two or three days a week but had to fit in occasional days between his public duties. He may well have felt that without the climax of the spring point-to-points, the few days' hunting he would get were not worth the trouble and expense.

In any case in the winter he sold all his horses and gave up his rooms at Craven Lodge. The anxiety of his parents and the continual pressure brought upon him is perhaps understandable. Nevertheless, one of its effects was to narrow his vision to the golf courses round London, and Fort Belvedere.

Fort Belvedere is a 'Grace and Favour' house situated on land bordering Windsor Great Park near Sunningdale. A strange castellated house begun in the eighteenth century and twice enlarged, it had been neglected for many years when the Prince first saw it. He says that it was a 'pseudo-Gothic hodge-podge' and that the garden was untended and the surrounding woods wild and untidy. Here is Lady Diana Cooper's impression of it:

He had turned a royal folly near Virginia Water into a liveable house, where he could rest from his labours at the week's end. It was called Fort Belvedere and was a child's idea of a fort. Built in the eighteenth century and enlarged by Wyatville for George IV, it had battlements and cannon and cannon-balls and little furnishings of war. It stood high on a hill, and the sentries, one thought, must be of tin.[8]

Mrs Dudley Ward was with the Prince when he first found Fort Belvedere in 1930 and it was she who helped him with the alterations and decoration. It is associated, however, a little with Lady Furness, with whom he had a short, not very serious, love affair, but famous because it was here that he brought Mrs Simpson and here he conducted so many of the conversations that led in the end to abdication.

The garden at Fort Belvedere satisfied the Prince's inordinate desire for violent exercise. Like many another keen gardener, he loved best the hard work, and he personally cleared laurel and undergrowth, cut paths through the woods and planted the borders. As time went on the creative pleasures of gardening came to replace his love of hunting and even to some extent of golf. He entertained at the Fort a great deal at weekends and friends such as the Metcalfes and members of his staff such as the Thomases stayed regularly there. But, as naturally domestic as the rest of his family, he was happy in this house even when alone or nearly alone. On the adjoining estate belonging to Lord Derby the wail of the bagpipes could often be heard late into the night, and Lady Furness tells us that once when he found her working at *petit point*, he became fascinated with the technique and asked if he could do it too. His first project was a paper weight for his mother, embroidered with the royal crown and the initials M.R. in gold, his second a backgammon board for Lady Furness, the background beige, the points in the Guards' colours red and blue.*

For anyone seriously interested, Lady Furness, who like Mrs Simpson was an American, has written the story of this romance in *Double Exposure* with much candour and detail. Here it must be said that she did not arouse the self-protective instincts of a whole society in the manner of her successor. Lady Furness is widely remembered, even in Court circles, as a good sort. Quiet and some say rather dull, she must go down to history as uncalculating and not very much on the make. Her claim to attention is simply that she was responsible for bringing Mrs Simpson into the Prince's life.

There are many accounts of their first meeting, both the Duke and Duchess of Windsor themselves having given their recollections of it. Here Lady Furness's version will be given because it covers the more important facts, while the comments she makes seem shrewd in a situation where, in any case, nothing was said that would have seemed worth repeating had not one of the people involved been of royal blood. Putting the meeting in the later part of 1930 or early 1931 she says:

I went over to Wallis, took her to the Prince, and introduced her. This meeting has been the subject of an enormous amount of fiction. It has been written, for example, that the Prince, on being introduced to Wallis, asked her if, in England, she did not miss the comforts of central heating, and that she had answered, 'I'm sorry, sir, but you have disappointed me. Every American woman who comes to

---

* The Duchess of Windsor says that when as Mrs Simpson she first saw the Prince of Wales tatting and showed surprise he told her that he had been taught by his mother. 'At Sandringham my brothers and sister and I used to sit around her at tea-time. While she talked to us, she was either crocheting or doing some kind of embroidery; and because we were all interested she taught us *gros point*.'⁹

your country is always asked the same question. I had hoped for something more original from the Prince of Wales.'

Had this been true, it would have been not only bad taste but bad manners. At that moment Wallis Simpson was as nervous and as impressed as any woman would have been on first meeting the Prince of Wales. Another apocryphal story is that when the Prince first met Wallis an electric tension was set up between them, and he then and there decided he could not live without her. This is utter nonsense. Wallis and I became great friends; actually I came to regard her as one of my best friends in England, and the Prince and I often would include Wallis and her husband in our parties. The Prince, consequently, saw her at least once a week for the next three and a half years. It was only after this that he discovered she was more important to him than the throne.[10]

In conversation, diaries or letters people have left many an impression of the Prince of Wales in the late nineteen-twenties and early thirties. Thus he is seen trying with Ivor Novello to recapture an escaped flock of parakeets in a garden, dancing with Lady Cunard who wears 'a fatuous air of luxurious abandon'[11], recognized from his backview by Sacheverell Sitwell, although he was unaware he was in the room, by his likeness to Gilray's cartoons of the Prince Regent,* dining with Lady Astor and playing against her in the parliamentary golf handicap at Walton Heath.

Her handicap was twenty, his twelve. . . . The match took place at Walton Heath on 5 July 1933. . . . He gave out that he particularly disliked a crowd of spectators, but a huge crowd assembled, as was inevitable because it was not every day that one could watch the Prince of Wales playing a match against Lady Astor in the semi-finals of a famous competition. The Prince was very nervous. He drove well, but his putting got worse and worse until on one green he took four. Just before the turn he was two down and seemed to be going to pieces. Lady Astor, who did not want to beat the heir to the throne under such embarrassing circumstances, sought to calm and cheer him. She was always very good at cheering people and in this case was so successful that he pulled himself together. He drew level and when she lost the seventeenth hole, he won the match, two up and one to play. The Prince, always partial to gay clothes, wore a blue check shirt, grey plus-fours, check stockings and black-and-white shoes.[12]

Twice we have a picture of him in full dress uniform during a presentation ceremony at Buckingham Palace. In 1931 he was heard by Mrs Simpson, as yet merely an acquaintance, to say to his great-uncle, the Duke of Connaught: 'Uncle Arthur, something ought to be done about the lights. They make all the women look ghastly.'

Later that evening, at Lady Furness's house, over a glass of champagne which 'he barely touched', he complimented Mrs Simpson on her dress. 'But, sir,' she responded, 'I understood that you thought we all looked ghastly.'

* Letter to the author.

141

'He was startled. Then he smiled. "I had no idea my voice carried so far." '[13]

The second occasion was two years later when his favourite, Angie Dudley Ward, was presented as a debutante. In those days it was the habit of journalists to select each year one of the girls making her debut and, concentrating publicity on her, to make her the debutante of the year. In 1933 the name of the debutante who received this treatment was Primrose Salt. During the whole of the early summer this had been the subject of a joke between Angie and the Prince of Wales. 'You had better get your hair done,' he would say to her, '(or sit up straight, or go and change, or lower your voice) or you will never be able to beat Miss Primrose Salt.'

But on the evening in 1933 when she was to be presented at Court, sitting in her mother's house, he said: 'Now tonight we will huff Miss Salt. Because, when it is all over, and I come down among you, it will be you I talk to, not Miss Salt.'*

* Conversation with Lady Laycock.

12

WALLIS WARFIELD

' "You'd think," said Aunt Bessie with some heat, "that we'd all come right out of *Tobacco Road*." '

Mrs Merryman was speaking at the time of the Abdication of King Edward VIII, and she referred to what the Duchess of Windsor has called 'the wild canards being circulated that my family had come from the wrong side of the tracks in Baltimore, that my mother had run a boarding-house'.[1] And it is true that large sections of the British people were, and have remained convinced that, in addition to the obvious disadvantage as a prospective wife for the King of England of having been twice married, Mrs Simpson had also that of being of lowly, even disreputable birth. This conviction seems to have been arrived at without much knowledge of the facts but through a kind of complacency which caused the English of that day to be easily persuaded that a twice-married American woman might also be of low birth. Yet this was particularly irritating to Mrs Simpson as well as to Mrs Merryman, because, although in childhood and youth she had known poverty and insecurity, no one had ever before questioned her breeding.

Her birth was the result of the union of two American families both of which could trace their descent to the earliest Colonial times, and an accident of geography made it doubly sure that she would grow up conscious of being well-born. Her father, Teackle Wallis Warfield, was a Warfield of Maryland, her mother Alice Montague, a Montague of Virginia. The state of Maryland did not secede from the Union during the Civil War but the sympathy of most of its principal families was with the Confederate cause. On the outbreak of the war, her grandfather, Henry Mactier Warfield, a member of the Maryland legislature, was arrested by the Federal Department Commander in Baltimore along with several others to prevent the Legislature from considering a resolution on secession. He was held prisoner for fourteen months, during the whole of which time he refused to take the oath of allegiance in return for his freedom. When his son married a Virginian, it became natural that his granddaughter should regard herself as a Southerner – something, she has explained, that in her childhood she regarded as a matter of life and death importance. Yet a fact less easily understood by the average Englishman but actually of even greater significance is that she belonged to one of the first families of Baltimore.

The populations of the eastern seaboard towns of America are largely descended from the first English settlers. As a result they have often maintained a tightly cohesive society, with a well-defined class-system, which considers itself to have a superior culture and higher moral principles than the rest of the nation. To the outside world Boston is the best-known example of what is meant, but the people of Philadelphia, Baltimore, Charleston and New Orleans feel a pride in their descent and birthplace at least equal to that of the Bostonians. This attitude owes something to the intellectually absurd and provincial mentality which makes people of different districts in England refer to men who have lived among them for twenty years as 'strangers to these parts', and even the more sophisticated of those who come from Baltimore are apt to emphasize the insularity of the 'Baltimoreans' with a deprecatory humour that ill conceals pride. Yet there is also a solid basis to it, in that families who can trace their descent for more than two hundred years in one place customarily place greater weight on birth and breeding than, as in the rest of the United States, on money. This has made for a development which is essentially different from that of the populations of the cities of the north and west and the cultivation of the virtues, if also the vices, of a genuinely aristocratic society. Wallis Warfield's father died a few months after she was born leaving her mother with almost no money. This was one of the two major facts of her childhood, and it was both partially offset and heavily underlined by the other – her unquestioned status in the society in which she lived.

The marriage of her parents was opposed by both their families because her father's health was such that he could neither work for his living nor support his wife. We do not know what were the charms that caused a beautiful and spirited girl to marry him, but when her child was born a year later the young couple were at a summer resort named Blue Ridge Summit in Pennsylvania, where they had gone on account of his health to escape the summer heat of Baltimore, and five months later he died. The future Duchess of Windsor was born on 19 June 1896, almost exactly two years after in England the Duchess of York gave birth to her eldest son.* She

* From time to time attempts have been made to dispute this date of birth, notably on one hilarious occasion when the American Press tried to find facts to substantiate a slip of the tongue by Aunt Bessie Merryman which suggested that the Duchess of Windsor was seven years older than she professed to be. But it is confirmed by Baltimore contemporaries who knew her in their prams or at school.

arrived a few weeks before she was expected and her first clothes had to be borrowed. She was named Bessiewallis, in accordance with the Baltimore habit of giving children two names and running them together – Wallis after her father and Bessie after her mother's sister. She disliked the name Bessie, however, which she associated with cows, and as she grew up, this was dropped in favour of the more simple Wallis. When her father died she and her mother were left dependent on their relations.

Something more must be said about these relations. The Baltimore Warfields were successful businessmen, bankers and public servants, and they were puritanical and proud. The Montagues on the other hand were good-looking and naturally attractive but more easy going and worldly. At this particular time the Montagues suffered, as did other Southern families, from having inherited a style of living which their means would no longer support. So strong was the family-feeling in both these families that Wallis was taught to relate all her own developing characteristics to one or other of them.

If the Montagues were innately French in character – she writes – and the Warfields British, then I was a new continent for which they contended. All my life, it seems, that battle has raged back and forth within my psyche. Even as a child, when I misbehaved, my mother taught me to believe it was the Montague deviltry asserting itself; when I was good, she gratefully attributed the improvement to the sober Warfield influence.[2]

When someone reaches a position in life which for any reason sets him or her apart from the majority of his contemporaries, it becomes a matter of interest to isolate those influences which have contributed to the development of the adult personality. This can never be an entirely objective exercise because we seek an explanation of aspects of the personality we already know.

In the case of Wallis Warfield much has disappeared into the mists of time. Destiny, which cut the lightest word of the little boy in England on to the memories of those who came in contact with him, did not mark out the little girl in Baltimore. One thing seems clear, however. From the youngest age she received an almost daily illustration of the power of money.

No elite, however much it prides itself on higher things, can survive without money, while an elite that has survived a century or two is likely to be inter-related and clannish. Bessiewallis Warfield was surrounded by solidly wealthy relations. Uncle Solomon, Uncle Henry and Uncle Emory Warfield all had farms in the country where the little girl was sent for the long summer holidays, and the two latter sons or daughters who grew up in houses with spacious verandahs and rambling rooms, waited upon by Negroes, with horses in the stables behind and cattle that grazed the land.

On the other side of the family her mother's first cousin had a country house in Virginia which became a gathering place for the Montagues. Of the Warfield uncles, Uncle Sol is by far the most important to this story. He was the only one unmarried and he took it upon himself to see that his niece was educated as befitted a Warfield child, sending her, if not to the best, to the second best school in Baltimore. Thus, among her own relations and also among the girls she met at school, she alone knew the pinch of poverty and deprivation.

For the first four or five years after the death of her father she and her mother lived with the dead man's mother and elder brother. Uncle Sol was a banker and an entrepreneur. He was the dominant male influence in Wallis's life and she was frightened of him. 'For a long and impressionable time,' she writes, 'he was the nearest thing to a father in my uncertain world, but an odd kind of father – reserved, unbending, silent. Uncle Sol was destined to return again and again to my life – or, more accurately, it was my fate to be obliged to turn again and again to him, usually at some new point of crisis for me and one seldom to his liking. I was always a little afraid of Uncle Sol.'[2]

Wallis loved her grandmother, however, and even after she had left her house never ceased to visit her almost daily. In this household there was also an Irish nurse named Joe who had brought up earlier generations of Warfields and a coloured footman-valet, both of whom were devoted to the little girl. For the first years of her life she lived in the style of most of the other children of upper-class Baltimore families. Even here there were certain differences, however, and one of her memories of her grandmother's brownstone house was that the third floor was divided between Uncle Sol and her mother and herself, but, whereas he had a bedroom and private bathroom, they shared her grandmother's bathroom on the floor below.

When she was four or five years old this arrangement came to an end. Hostility grew up between her mother and her grandmother because, after a suitable period of mourning, the younger woman began to go out with men – 'suitors' is the word used by the Duchess of Windsor, an oddly chosen word with overtones it is difficult to be sure of. The Duchess also suggests in a tentative fashion that this hostility may have been much increased because 'perhaps against his will, perhaps without ever realizing it' Uncle Sol might have wished to count himself among these suitors. In any case from now on life became far more obviously hazardous.

They continued to rely on Uncle Sol's support and every month he placed a sum of money in Mrs Warfield's bank account. Every month the amount was different, however, sometimes barely covering the rent, at other times increased to include a few other things. The Duchess writes that she never knew whether this was his way of reminding 'a gay and (by Warfield standards) frivolous widow' of her dependence on him, but that it inevitably complicated life for her mother and herself. She was disturbed also by the awareness that her mother was unhappy.

For the first time I came to know loneliness – she writes – as loneliness can only be known in the excruciatingly sensitive perceptions of childhood. There is no way, in my opinion, of explaining how a child is able to sense the unhappiness and despair of grown-ups; but the phenomenon occurs – I experienced it. A shivery feeling comes, as when on a crisp fall day the sun is momentarily obscured; and the tenuous apprehensions that now assailed me took the form of a dread of being left alone, even for a few hours, as if my mother, too, might vanish.[4]

After a while mother and child were rescued from the frightening dreariness of life in a cheap hotel by Aunt Bessie Merryman, that same Aunt Bessie who was to accompany and chaperone her niece through the extraordinary crisis of her life, and who now invited them to make a home with her. Aunt Bessie it should be said was a Montague not a Warfield – an important difference. However, when Bessiewallis was six or seven years old her mother decided that she must have an apartment of her own and moved again, this time to the Preston Apartment House on Preston Street.

There is a slight discrepancy in the accounts of Mrs Warfield's exact status in the Preston Apartment House. Thus in recalling Wallis Warfield as a child in this house, one of the other tenants spoke of 'my landlady's'[5] little daughter who used to help her mother serve the meals, and it is almost certainly from this period that there arose the stories, 'the wild canards' that Mrs Warfield ran a boarding house. According to the Duchess of Windsor's own account the situation was somewhat different. Her mother was a beautiful seamstress and a marvellously good cook. For some time she had been using the former gift as a source of pin-money, but becoming tired of it and finding that most of her fellow tenants ate out, she invited them to become her paying guests for dinner. Unfortunately her talent for cooking far outran her financial sense and before long 'the simple dinners grew into banquets – terrapin, squab, prime sirloin steaks, and soft-shell crabs, fresh strawberries, elaborate pastries'.[6] Once more Aunt Bessie was forced to rescue them, this time by settling with the tradesmen and disbanding the dining club. There is no reason to disbelieve this version of the story. One cannot imagine that Mrs Warfield had the resources to become 'the landlady' of the Preston Apartment House.

A few years later she had acquired some, however. Their next move was to a house of their own, 212 Biddle Street.* Her mother wished, the Duchess of Windsor says without further explanation, to try her hand at real estate. But her new-found wealth was not unconnected with the fact that soon after this Mrs Warfield broke the news to her daughter that she had decided to marry again. John Freeman Rasin was a member of a rich

* This is the house with which the Duchess of Windsor is chiefly associated and for a short time after her marriage it was opened to the public.

and politically prominent Baltimore family, the son of the Democratic Party leader. He was well known to Wallis because he had often visited her mother, but she was much upset by the suggestion that she must in future share her mother's affections with him. Their fortunes considerably improved after her mother's marriage, however, and in time she grew fond of her step-father, although she continued to address him as Mr Rasin. She never quite understood him. He appeared to have no occupation but to spend most of his day smoking and reading.

Uncle Sol felt it his duty to see that his niece was educated in a manner befitting her class, and he paid for her schooling. As a result, after attending a small day-school for boys and girls, she went to a girls' school called Arundell. Every writer on the subject, including the Duchess, has felt it necessary to record that Arundell was neither as fashionable nor as expensive as Bryn Mawr (not to be confused with the college of that name) but second to it. From her own account of her schooldays we know that she worked hard and with the aid of what she has described as a 'twenty-four hour memory' (an asset of value to her for the rest of her life), she did well in examinations. What is more interesting, since in reality she had almost no fondness for games of an athletic kind, is that her desire to belong to a team, no longer to stand apart was so great that by drive and ambition she gained a place in the baseball team. She tells us that so fierce were her longings that when this objective was achieved she experienced an elation seldom equalled in all her life – a strong statement if one stops to consider her life. Strange words too for a child who, although small and by no means a beauty, already had the gaiety and vitality, as well as the gregariousness and love of a party, which are such assets to people who wish to belong to a team. Above all, from the time she was about fourteen Wallis attracted boys so easily and so deliberately that, always surrounded by them, she was bound also to have a following of girls. Why then did this child, so well endowed to become the centre of any adolescent society, feel so strongly the sense of 'standing apart'?

One of her contemporaries has answered the question in the following way. When as a child she put Wallis's name down on the list of girls she wished to ask to her party, she found it scratched off. On protesting to her parents that Wallis was a friend and an asset at a party she had it explained to her, that, although Wallis herself might be welcome at the house, if as a result of the invitation she was asked to return the visit, she could not be allowed to go. In her sad and poverty-ridden widowhood Wallis's mother had committed a sin unforgivable in the eyes of Baltimore society and taken a lover Mr Rasin, who finally married Mrs Warfield, had been visiting her for some time before this happy event took place. Nor was this all. Mr Rasin, who, his step-daughter believed, sat at home reading and smoking, also according to contemporary accounts 'drank more than was good for him'.

It is not difficult to imagine that the general disapproval and hostility towards the wife of this man was as nothing to that felt by old Mrs Mactier Warfield and Uncle Sol. In this predicament the latter did his duty to his brother's child and proposed to remove her from her mother and bring her up in his own household. This was a turning point in Wallis's life. She might at one step have removed all the reasons for her isolation and, it is interesting to speculate, possibly altered the whole of her future career. She chose to remain with her mother.

Among the few memories her school fellows have of her is that she was always very well and neatly dressed. Her mother made her clothes or gave the patterns to a dressmaker, but both mother and daughter had such a natural sense of clothes, both how to fit and how to wear them, that she did not suffer on this account. She is remembered as 'very strong'. Mrs Hartman Harrison, who taught the dancing class which she attended, always looked forward to the evening when she came, because she was so co-operative and, dancing with the best boy, led the other children with seriousness as well as grace. There was, however, a reserve in her dealings with other people, although, if this concealed ambition and a certain ruthlessness, it held no malice. Wallis was a 'good fellow' and out for a good time. One of her schoolfellows, David Bruce, later among the USA's most distinguished Ambassadors, thought of her with affection all his life because, older than him, she was kind to him then. In general, however, her school-fellows respected her but regarded her with something of her own reserve. It is a curious fact, which could not escape the attention of anyone meeting her childhood friends, that it is difficult to find any among them who has read the Duchess of Windsor's autobiography or has the most elementary knowledge of her career. Admittedly this is a line which Baltimoreans like to take up, professing to have no interest in all these goings on with a man who may have been King of England but was a 'stranger to these parts'. Yet it shows a very surprising lack of curiosity which surely could not be sustained without owing something to envy or hostility.

The truth is that Wallis had too much success with the boys to be very much loved and, while one of the reasons for this was that she was naturally very attractive to the other sex, she was also, according to most accounts, 'rather fast'. Here again is a word difficult to translate into the idiom of the present day, since the qualities it describes are no longer regarded with much disfavour and certainly attract no penalties from the rest of society. It was used to suggest an unbecoming interest in the other sex and a greater freedom of behaviour than was permitted to well-bred young ladies of the time.

However, Wallis was not without close friends. At the age of sixteen she was sent to a boarding school named Oldfields, which seems to have been the equivalent of what in England was known as a 'finishing school'. Here she met two girls, Mary Kirk and Ellen Yuille, with whom she made great friends. The first should be remembered because her future and Wallis's were to be curiously inter-twined,* the second, as Mrs William Sturgis and then as Mrs Wolcott Blair, remained among her greatest friends to the end of her life.

Speaking of her time at Oldfields the Duchess of Windsor has told us that the thought of going to college never occurred to her. 'It just didn't exist for girls of my age.' And in reply to her own question: 'What, then, was life supposed to hold for us?' She answers 'marriage'.

Not only was marriage the only thing we had to look forward to, but the condition of marriage had been made to seem to us the only state desirable for a woman – and the sooner the better. The fact that few, if any, of us were in love or were even the recipients of concentrated masculine attention had nothing to do with the case. It was marriage itself, conceived in the most poetic and romantic terms, that we aspired to.[7]

From which it can be seen that the education of the young ladies of Baltimore differed in no important respect from that of their counterparts in England.

While she was at Oldfields her step-father died, leaving her mother and herself once more alone in the world. A combination of Uncle Sol's continuing generosity and her own social talents ensured that the next stage in her career, her debut in Baltimore society, was carried through with unqualified success. There is an annual function in Baltimore the social importance of which it is impossible to exaggerate. The Bachelor's Cotillon is a men's club formed in the nineteenth century for the purpose of giving cotillions. Every year the first two of these dances are the coming-out balls and of these two it is a life-and-death matter to be asked to the first. When Wallis received her invitation for this she felt her future was assured, and at her first ball she found herself in an element where she would be happy and successful for the rest of her life.

In 1916 Wallis married Earl Winfield Spencer Jr., an officer in the air arm of the United States Navy, a not very ambitious choice. Pondering the question: 'Is our fate in our stars or does it lie within ourselves?' the Duchess of Windsor tells us that Aunt Bessie Merryman 'insists that I have always had a plan germinating in the back of my mind for everything I have done'.[8] There seems to have been no very far-reaching strategy in her mind when she made her first marriage and to do it she broke her own candidly declared intention to marry money. Earl Winfield Spencer – Win to his wife – had neither very much money nor any great career in front of him. Wallis found him physically attractive and she had been brought up to get married. One of her contemporaries, when asked why Wallis had married Spencer, replied with an air of surprise at being asked the question: 'Why she wanted to get out of it, of course.' It certainly is not im-

* Mary Kirk became Mary Raffray and at the end of her life the third wife of Ernest Simpson.

probable that Wallis, like thousands of other girls from the beginning of time, took the first reasonable opportunity to get away from home.

Two glimpses of Wallis as the young wife must be recorded here. The first is of her listening to the sound of the crash gong, which announced that somewhere an aeroplane had crashed, and living through the hours that followed before the name of the pilot was announced. This had a lasting effect on an already nervous girl. The second is of her first dinner parties when, armed with a cookery book called *Fannie Farmer's Cookbook*, she prepared the food herself. 'She became my bible,' the Duchess writes. 'I followed her to the letter. If she told me to tie the asparagus with two pieces of string, I tied it with two, not one or three. Whatever reputation I may have since acquired as a hostess began with her.'[9]

For the next twenty years of her life we have to rely almost entirely on the Duchess of Windsor's own account. Several biographies have been undertaken but none of them impress one as accurate or well informed. However, Lord Brownlow is quoted by Robert Sencourt as saying that the Duchess's account is written with 'an almost blinding veracity',[10] and, although there is plenty of evidence that she tells us only what she wishes us to know and is capable of fairly obvious subterfuge when she chooses, she does on the whole tell the story of the next twenty years with such astonishing candour that there is no reason to doubt the details.

Her first husband soon turned out to be a neurotic alcoholic and obsessively jealous. 'I am naturally gay and flirtatious,' the Duchess writes, 'and I was brought up to believe that one should be as entertaining as one can at a party.... My gaiety, and even more the response of others to it, made Win jealous.'[11] Win had a propensity for practical jokes and this now took a sadistic turn. He used to lock his wife up in a room for hours on end. Spencer was unhappy about his career since, when the USA entered the war, he was kept on administrative duties and denied the chance of combat flying. In a few years he took openly to drink. Once more Wallis had the humiliation of having the circumstances of her private life a matter of public knowledge.

Then one afternoon Spencer locked his wife into the bathroom for hours at a time and left her there into the night. Next morning Wallis went to see her mother, who was living near her, and told her that she felt the only honest course left to her was divorce. It is a matter for astonishment to the English reader at this point to be told by someone who two divorces later aspired to marry the King of England that on both sides of her family the consternation was extreme. The English when discussing the Abdication invariably put down the King's and Mrs Simpson's fatal preference for marriage over the time-honoured arrangement usual in such cases very largely to the fact that she was an American. Americans, they argue, have to get married and do not mind about divorce; we, on the other hand, are not always marrying but we do mind about divorce. In this they show a total ignorance of the difference between Hollywood and Baltimore – a difference it is not necessary to understand however in order to appreciate the coolness with which the Duchess of Windsor relates what followed. Wallis's mother and her Aunt Bessie both believed that marriage was indissoluble – or if not indissoluble, indissoluble by a Montague. Aunt Bessie said that she must go away for a while, or, as a last resort agree to a temporary separation, but on no account get a divorce. 'The Montague women,' was her unanswerable dictum, 'do not get divorced.' Uncle Sol's reaction was predictably stronger. 'I won't let you bring this disgrace upon us!' he said. 'The Warfields in all their known connections since 1662 have never had a divorce. What will the people of Baltimore think?'

And he told her that any divorce action she might take would have to be done with her own resources. No help of any kind could be expected from him.

Her husband's reaction to her decision was rather different. ' "Wallis," he said slowly, "I've had it coming to me. If you ever change your mind, I'll still be around." '[12]

At the time of her decision to leave Spencer, he had a staff appointment at Washington and, when he was ordered to the Far East, she merely remained behind – a lone young woman in an apartment in Washington. She tells us that the 1920s were a particularly hazardous era for a lonely woman 'especially on sofas and in rumble seats'. 'I had … a code,' she says 'which was never to allow myself to drift into light affairs of the moment. But one must pay the price – many evenings alone.' Having delivered herself of these excellent sentiments she goes on to give a description of her experiences of Washington society which seems to leave very little time for evenings alone. The diplomatic circle was in those days, she tells us, comparatively small and was carried on by men of a cultured background. Even the Third Secretary of a legation 'was a personality in his own right, a young man of charm, an accomplished dancer, worldly-wise without being world-weary, sophisticated without being cynical'. And she adds that the surplus of attractive unattached men made the diplomatic service a paradise for women on their own. In this circle brilliant conversation was carried on at luncheon and dinner parties, and also Sunday night suppers, impromptu excursions to little country restaurants, picnics in the Virginia countryside.[13]

At this time in her life Wallis Spencer fell deeply but rather unsatisfactorily in love. Here is what she says herself:

This is not to say that my heart was never stirred. It became involved in Washington. There was a young diplomat attached to the embassy of a Latin-American country. Only a little older than I, he was already marked as a man of great promise. . . . For a time he was only a gay escort, somebody to take me to th s party or that. Then he came to mean much more. Perhaps without realizing it he acted both as teacher and model in the art of living. He took me out of the world of small talk and into the wider world of affairs and diplomacy. This may well have been what was worrying my mother. I was not yet divorced – indeed, I had made only tentative gestures in that direction. I was conscious of drifting dangerously, and yet I was reluctant to free myself from so beguiling a current. I knew that I could not continue to have it both ways. I must go through with my divorce or return to Win.[14]

In the event she did neither. Her young diplomat married someone else and she cajoled five hundred dollars out of Uncle Sol and sailed for Paris with a Montague cousin and friend, now a naval widow, called Corinne Mostin. In Paris the diplomatic service once more provided escorts for the two young women. The Assistant Naval Attaché was a friend of Mrs Mostin's and he invited them to dinner at once and brought with him the First Secretary of the Embassy, Elbridge Gerry Green. 'The dinner proved the happiest kind of beginning. We became a foursome. Our escorts were extremely knowledgeable about cathedrals and chateaux as well as cafés and restaurants, and soon our evenings were taken up with exploring the city while our weekends were solidly booked for trips through the French countryside.'[15]

Something nevertheless seemed to be missing. All this time Win Spencer was writing to his wife pleading with her to forget the past and return to him. He told her she could board a naval transport at Norfolk and travel to his station in China at government expense. When an American woman friend invited her to accompany her home on the *France*, Wallis agreed to this suggestion with an eagerness that surprised herself, and July 1924 found her one of a number of naval wives travelling to China to join their husbands.

When, as was inevitable, she left her husband for the second time, she went to Shanghai to try to get her divorce from the US Court for China. Soon after her arrival she posted a letter of introduction to an Englishman at the embassy there which someone had given her in Washington on her way through. A day or so later a basket of mangoes arrived for her followed shortly afterwards by a young man called 'Robbie'.

We had a drink together, very pleasant. Then he suggested dinner, and it proved to be even more pleasant. This was the simple beginning of a delightful friendship. Robbie knew everyone in Shanghai. . . .[16]

From knowing nobody she was once more drawn into the world of garden parties, race meetings, dancing by moonlight to 'Tea for Two' and so on. . . .

Next Mrs Spencer went to Pekin with the intention of 'shopping around for silks and porcelain'. Here however she had an important encounter. Accompanied by Colonel Louis Little and his wife, whom she had known in Washington and by that Gerry Green, who had been her escort in Paris and who was now stationed here, she went to a dance at the Grand

Hotel de Pékin. Across the room she saw Herman and Katherine Rogers, who not much more than ten years later would be waiting to welcome her at the end of a flight across France.* At this time they had a house in Pekin and, equally hospitable, they insisted on her leaving the hotel and going to stay with them. She tells us that there was a simplicity, a still-deep peacefulness about life in Pekin that imparted an air of timelessness to one's thoughts and actions; also that her impression was that bachelors outnumbered unattached women by a ratio of at least ten to one and that her poker was good enough for her to be able to supplement her too modest income. She says: 'I came to love Pekin as I have loved only one other city – Paris.'[17] Nevertheless: 'An inner voice, which I suppose was the voice of conscience, began to speak to me. It spoke rather severely. It said that I was deluding myself; that I was beginning to confuse a lotus-eater's illusion for reality; that I had better give thought to returning to my own people and winding up the unfinished business of my marriage to Win. I did not want to listen, but I did. ... So early in the summer somewhat in the mood of a female Ulysses, I left Japan to take ship to the West Coast.'[18]

When Wallis arrived in Washington a family friend who was a lawyer told her that at a cost of about three hundred dollars and after one year's residence she could obtain a divorce in Virginia on the grounds of desertion after three years' separation from her husband. He recommended to her a small but comfortable hotel in a little town called Warrenton in the Fauquier County. The Warren Green Hotel boasted only one room with a bath and Wallis achieved this only when she had outstayed all other claimants. Until then she lived in a single room on the second floor back.

She tells us that the year she spent here was the most tranquil of her life. She read a great deal – poetry which she loved and the novels of Sinclair Lewis, Somerset Maugham and John Galsworthy. 'However,' she writes, 'I do not want to give the impression that Warrenton was for me a distaff Walden where my days were dedicated solely to books, solitary meals and afternoon walks with the philosophical Mr Mason [a sixty-year-old fellow guest]. After a time I ran into an old acquaintance, Hugh Spilman, who worked in the local bank, and whom I had known in Baltimore. He took me in tow and launched me in the social whirl of the local horsey set. He was also possessed of an old three-pedal, rattling flivver. The two of us must have made quite an impression as we rolled up to the porticoed mansions for formal dinners.'[19]

At this time there also occurred a more important introduction. Wallis used to go to New York occasionally to shop for clothes at the small side-street speciality shops and on these occasions she stayed with Mary Kirk

* She had met Katherine Rogers earlier in Coronado as a young widow named Katherine Bigelow.

now married to Jacques Raffray. With the Raffrays she met Mr and Mrs Ernest Simpson.

Ernest Simpson was the son of an English father and an American mother and he was born in New York and graduated at Harvard. As a child his summer holidays had been divided between England, where he had an older married sister, and Europe, where he travelled with his father. While still an undergraduate, Ernest crossed to England and joined the Grenadier Guards as a second lieutenant. Later he became a British subject. At the time of his meeting with Wallis Spencer his first marriage was already in difficulties. This is the impression he made on his future wife.

Reserved in manner, yet with a gift of quiet wit, always well dressed, a good dancer, fond of the theatre, and obviously well read, he impressed me as an unusually well-balanced man. I had acquired a taste for cosmopolitan minds, and Ernest obviously had one. I was attracted to him and he to me.[20]

In the summer of 1927 Aunt Bessie Merryman took her niece on a trip to Europe, a trip which was enlivened by the presence on board ship of a sedate young Philadelphia lawyer who decided that on holiday 'life was meant to be lived' but ended unexpectedly by a cable announcing the death of Uncle Sol. When Uncle Sol's will was read, it was found that in the first place his fortune had been grossly over-estimated and in the second it had been left to found and support a home for impoverished ladies of gentle birth. His niece was left with a small trust fund that was to cease in the event of her remarriage. Nothing in her own account can be said to suggest that she was taken unpleasantly by surprise by her uncle's will, but the reader is nevertheless left wondering about it. Were the terms a result of the repeated failure of her uncle and herself to agree on the lines of conduct open to her? This suggestion is denied by those who have studied the terms of his will. Solomon Warfield wished to commemorate the memory of his mother, to whom he had given a lifetime of devotion, and he defined very explicitly, even movingly, his reasons for endowing this charity, which exists to this day and is run by a trust administered by some of Baltimore's leading citizens.

In December 1927 Wallis Spencer's petition for divorce from Winfield Spencer was granted and in July 1928, having spent some intervening time with the Herman Rogers in a villa near Cannes in order to consider her future, she married Ernest Simpson.

Ernest Simpson had by now transferred to the London office of his father's firm. He and his wife were comfortably off and they took a flat for a short period and then the short lease of a house, No 12 Upper Berkeley Street, while looking for a more permanent home. Presently they found what they wanted in a flat, No 5 Bryanston Court.

They seem to have been happy together. His wife describes Ernest Simpson as a man with quiet rather scholarly tastes who loved reading, the theatre, opera and ballet. He also enjoyed sight-seeing, and at weekends he and Wallis, who as yet knew few English people, spent their weekends together in small hotels sight-seeing all over England. They also shared an interest in antique furniture and, when they moved to Bryanston Court, Mrs Simpson was able for the first time to indulge the taste for fine things which was to be a source of happiness to her for the rest of her life. At this time she could not afford to go to the more famous and expensive antique dealers, but she haunted the little shops in Kensington and Chelsea where in those days genuine bargains could be found. She employed the services of an interior decorator to help her with Bryanston Court into which she fitted an eighteenth-century Dutch secretary, an Italian table painted yellow and black, a William and Mary walnut chest and several Queen Anne pieces which she had bought in the first flush of her new enthusiasm. She already exercised much trouble and ingenuity in getting what she wanted. We are given an example of this in her account of the furnishing of her dining-room. It was, she says, rather small – seating only ten people – and the question of ventilation was a problem because she was determined to dine by candlelight, candles in sconces on the walls, and in candlesticks on the table. She solved this problem by sitting herself at the head of the table with her back to an open window and putting her husband at the foot. The same attention to detail was given to food.

In planning a dinner, I wanted each item whether it was trout, partridge, or grouse, to be of the same size. I had noticed that this small detail, besides making for symmetry, has the merit of reducing a hostess's area of possible embarrassment. With everything the same size there is no chance of the platter arriving at the far end of the table bearing only a token; and, conversely, there is no necessity for the hostess to make conversation while the guest-of-honour probes an irregular assortment for a modest helping. I cannot say that my fishmonger was immediately sympathetic to this desire of mine: nor was he visibly elated by my habit of pressing the breast-bone of a fowl to see whether it was tender, nor was the greengrocer other than disapproving at my punching and squeezing the fruits and vegetables to determine their quality. I knew all the cuts of beef; and, when the butcher failed to cut me the T-bone steak I wanted, I produced for him my *Fannie Farmer Cookbook*, with a diagram showing how to cut a steak the way I liked.[21]

When Mrs Simpson first arrived in London she knew almost nobody to ask to her dinner parties, but Ernest Simpson's sister (that Mrs Kerr-Smiley at whose house in Belgrave Square the Prince of Wales first met Mrs Dudley Ward) took her under her wing. One gets the impression, nowhere stated, that Mrs Simpson found neither her sister-in-law nor her sister-in-law's friends entirely sympathetic and soon she began to make friends of her own, among them American expatriates and Americans from the embassy. These included Benjamin Thaw and his wife, the former Consuelo Morgan, the sister of Thelma, at this time Lady Furness, and of

Gloria Vanderbilt. Some time in the autumn of 1930 Lady Furness introduced her to the Prince of Wales.

There are several accounts of this meeting and the memories of the protagonists vary a little. The Duchess of Windsor tells us that she was very nervous. One thing she was able to rely on even here, however, was the confidence of a woman who knows from experience that she is extremely attractive to men. After her first meeting it was six months before she saw the Prince again and then six months more,* and it is sometimes said that when he first met her he did not like her very much, although there seems not to be much evidence for this. He was invariably pleasant to her, and out of the blue in January 1932 he sent her an invitation to Fort Belvedere. Here is her first impression of it.

It was dark when we approached the Fort. Our headlights picked out a gravel driveway winding in graceful turns through a wood; suddenly there materialized a fascinating shadowy mass, irregular in outline and of different levels, the whole surmounted by a soaring Tower bathed in soft light thrown up by concealed flood-lamps. Even before the car ground to a stop, the door opened and a servant appeared. An instant later the Prince himself was at the door to welcome his guests and supervise the unloading of our luggage, an attention which I was to discover was a habit with him. The Prince led us through a narrow hallway into an octagonal hall with white plaster walls in each of the eight corners of which stood a chair upholstered in bright yellow leather. The floor was of black and white marble. We then moved into the drawing-room. . . . I was instantly struck by the warmth of the room which, like the hallway [sic] was octagonal. Curtains of yellow velvet were drawn across the tall windows; the walls which were panelled in natural pine, were hung with handsome paintings which I later identified as Canalettos; the furniture by my now quite experienced eye recognized as mostly Chippendale, except for a baby grand piano and a gramophone; and opposite the fireplace on one wall were shelves of books in beautiful bindings.[22]

The Prince himself escorted his guests to their bedroom, appraising it personally with the glance of a careful host.

The next day the Prince took all his male guests, including Ernest Simpson who was not normally addicted to violent physical exercise, to spend the morning clearing the undergrowth in his neglected woods to make way for shrubs and rhododendrons. While waiting for her husband to fetch a sweater, he escorted Mrs Simpson into the garden himself and showed her the view to Virginia Water and the semi-circular stone battlement in which thirty odd eighteenth-century Belgian cannon were placed. Below the battlement on one side was a tennis court and on the other a swimming pool.

This was the first of many visits to the Fort. At first Lady Furness was always present and acting as hostess, and Prince George was often a fellow

* This is according to her own account. According to Lady Furness they met at least once a week for three and a half years before he discovered she was more important to him than the throne.

guest. In June 1933 the Prince gave a party at Quaglino's for Mrs Simpson's birthday and in July he dined for the first time with the Simpsons at their Bryanston Square flat. Then in January of the following year Lady Furness left on a visit to America. The day before she sailed she asked her friend Wallis for a cocktail. This is Mrs Simpson's version (slightly different from Lady Furness's account) of what was said then:

We rattled along in our fashion; as we said good-bye she said, laughingly, 'I'm afraid the Prince is going to be lonely. Wallis, won't you look after him.'[23]

The Duchess says that in spite of this conversation she was not even sure that she would see the Prince while Lady Furness was away and this may well be true. Soon after she first came to London, discovering that in England people did not drop in without arrangement as they had in the United States, she had started a habit of being at home to her friends every evening after six o'clock for drinks. She was now considerably elated when the Prince asked her if he might visit her sometimes at this time, and even more so one evening when, outstaying the rest of the guests, he remained so long she was forced to offer him potluck. After that he came often informally for dinner, choosing, apparently by chance, the very evenings on which Ernest Simpson had brought papers home to work on. When this had happened several times, Simpson adopted the habit of leaving his wife alone to entertain their royal visitor. Finally the Prince asked the Simpsons whether they would like to bring some of their friends to the Fort.

Lady Furness was in America from January to March 1934. While she was away she behaved sufficiently indiscreetly for the attentions paid her by Prince Aly Khan to reach the Prince's ears. We have her account of what happened on her return and also the Duchess of Windsor's. Neither strike the reader as completely candid. Lady Furness tells us that the Prince dined with her once and also asked her to the Fort but that his manner to her, although formally cordial, was personally distant. Unable to understand what had come between them, she visited her friend Wallis Simpson to ask her advice. There is some discrepancy about what happened then, because Lady Furness puts the visit at a time when she was still on terms with the Prince even if these were rather frigid, whereas from the Duchess's account it is clear she believes it occurred after the Prince had ceased to see Lady Furness altogether. The Duchess's account is given here because by now the curtain was falling on Lady Furness's appearance in history.

It was an unhappy call. She told me that the Prince was obviously avoiding her – she couldn't understand why. He would not speak to her himself on the telephone. No more invitations to the Fort were forthcoming. Finally she asked me point-blank if the Prince was interested in me – 'keen' was the word she used.

This was a question I had expected, and I was glad to be able to give her a straight answer. 'Thelma,' I said, 'I think he likes me. He may be fond of me. But, if you mean by keen that he is in love with me, the answer is definitely no.'[24]

13

MRS SIMPSON

In May 1934 Mrs Dudley Ward's elder daughter had an operation for appendicitis, followed unexpectedly by complications. For several weeks she was seriously ill. During these weeks her mother thought of little else and spent most of her time at the nursing home. Only when her daughter was out of danger and on the way to recovery did she begin to consider the fact that, for the first time in nearly seventeen years, although the Prince of Wales was in England, a period of weeks had gone by without his visiting her house or telephoning her. She put a call through to St James's Palace. The voice on the switchboard at the other end was that of a friend. For years these two had spoken to each other nearly every day, Mrs Dudley Ward always addressing the other in terms of an easy-going equality which exceeded ordinary courtesy. Now when the telephonist heard her voice, she immediately replied in tones of the greatest distress. 'I have something so terrible to tell you,' she said, 'that I don't know how to say it.' And when pressed to continue she said sorrowfully: 'I have orders not to put you through.'

In the spring of the same year Angie Dudley Ward was driving a car down to Windsor in the early hours of the morning, one hand on the wheel, the other round the neck of the man she would presently marry, Lieutenant Robert Laycock, when a policeman on a motor bicycle swung in front of them and waved her to a halt. Instantly Angie understood the seriousness of her offence, not in relation to such matters as her own driving licence, but in relation to her future husband's career. At the very least, she believed, he would look intensely foolish if the facts were to be published through a court case. She began to plead with the policeman to overlook it, using all her youth and charm as well as her very real anxiety to persuade him. He could not be deflected from his obvious duty, however, and he proceeded to take her name and address.

When she got back to her home, Angie was intensely worried, and, used to having her own way, she thought of the man who, for as long as she could remember, had been her special friend. She, too, put a call through to the Prince of Wales. She spoke to the butler, Osborn, who told her that His Royal Highness was out, and she left a message that she urgently wanted to speak to him. Getting no reply, she wrote the Prince a letter telling him what had happened and begging for his help. When this, too, went unanswered, she tried once more to speak to him on the telephone and once more she was told he was out. Then she went to her mother.

Mrs Dudley Ward was not particularly sympathetic to her daughter's problem and said she thought she would have to suffer for being so silly. Then she added: 'Anyway, I don't think you'll get much help there. Haven't you noticed anything? Haven't you noticed that he hasn't been here for weeks?'

Mrs Dudley Ward would never see the Prince again, Angie not for many years.

Within a matter of weeks the gist of these matters was widely known. When a new favourite arises it causes great excitement because people not previously in the inner circle recognize an opportunity. Speculation and gossip about Mrs Simpson had begun long before this, soon after Lady Furness left for America. Thus Chips Channon on 17 January in a couple of paragraphs throws light on the period.

Emerald Cunard swept into tea and stayed two hours. I had never seen her so brilliant. She now gives off an ambience that completely lights up her pretty wrinkled Watteau face. She had had a dinner party last night (to which we were bidden and refused) for Diana Cooper.

At 11.30 the front door bell had rung and there was the Prince of Wales accompanied by Mr and Mrs Simpson. It was an imprévu visit: the Prince was as charming as only he can be sometimes, and now is so rarely. Later he took them all to the Embassy Club for supper. Diana and the Prince talked politics for 2 hours. Emerald said, 'The little Prince talked like a Prophet and drank Vichy water', and she said to him: 'You are not David, Sir, but Daniel'. She is in an excellent mood.[1]

We have several descriptions of Mrs Simpson at or about this time. One of these was written by her defeated rival, Lady Furness.

She did not have the chic she has since cultivated. She was not beautiful; in fact she was not even pretty. But she had a distinct charm and a sharp sense of humour. Her dark hair was parted in the middle. Her eyes, alert and eloquent, were her best feature. She was not as thin as in her later years – not that she could be called fat even then; she was merely less angular. Her hands were large; they did not move gracefully, and I thought she used them too much when she attempted to emphasise a point.[2]

Chips Channon describes her as 'a jolly, plain, intelligent, quiet, unpretentious and unprepossessing little woman', but he adds: 'She has already the air of a personage who walks into a room as though she almost expected to be curtsied to. At least she wouldn't be too surprised. She has complete power over the Prince of Wales, who is trying to launch her socially.'[3] And in another passage he refers to her as 'a nice, quiet, well-bred mouse of a woman, with large startled eyes and a huge mole'.[4] However, it is not long before he is telling us that she is 'a woman of charm, sense, balance and great wit, with dignity and taste ... never embarrassed, ill at ease, and could in her engaging drawl, charm anyone'.[5]

It does not seem to have been very quickly perceived that Mrs Simpson had a strong and also a magnetic personality, although this is positively asserted by people who know the Duchess of Windsor. Possibly she was not aware of her own potentiality at this time, but the ability to adjust personality to changing circumstances is a not uncommon female characteristic. It seems unlikely that the attractions she so quickly acquired were entirely in the eye of the beholder.

In her book she has disclaimed any notion of being an 'intellectual' but implicit in everything she writes there is confidence that she is a wit, an assumption which we have seen Chips Channon thought justified. Different people have different ideas of wit, so it is fortunate that a good many examples of the Duchess of Windsor's have been preserved for us. Thus Chips Channon writes that she said: 'she had not worn black stockings since she gave up the Can-Can'[6] and tells us that this was typical of her humour: she herself illustrates what she calls her mother's 'trigger-wit' first by telling us that, having fallen down in a five and ten cent store, she replied to the girl who asked if she might help her: 'Yes. Just take me at once to the five and ten cents coffin counter',[7] and secondly by the fact that soon after her third marriage she signed a visitor's book on the Fourth of July: 'Here on the Fourth with my third.'[8] She says that a friend of hers will 'long be remembered' for her remark when her husband was knighted: 'Well, it took King George to make a lady of me!'[9]; the Duke of Windsor tells us that she referred to his habit of buying the coats of his suits in London and the trousers in New York as 'pants across the sea'[10]: Sir John Balfour that when asked the name of the man who sat next to her at dinner, she replied: 'I have often been accused of avoirdupoix but this is the first time I have sat next to a Levi Mirepoix', while on the same evening she thanked him for picking up her bag with the remark 'I like to see the British grovelling to me'.[11]

It is impossible to over-estimate the gain to even the lightest statements from being accompanied by the attributes of an attractive personality, and, although in hindsight Mrs Simpson may not be regarded as a very great wit or a very distinguished intelligence, she was naturally attractive to men, she had much vitality and gaiety, frankness of speech and an uncalculating manner, she was kind and thoughtful to those she found about her. There is no doubt that all her life people of intellectual ability sitting next to her at dinner found her clever and amusing. Thus Colin Coote: 'Speaking for myself on the few occasions when I met her, her charm and intelligence seemed very evident.'[12] And Lord Templewood: 'She may well have thought me very dull – if so, she did not show it, and could not have been more agreeable. I well remember not only her sparkling talk, but also her sparkling jewels in very-up-to-date Cartier settings. In the notes that I made at the time I described her as very attractive and intelligent, very American with little or no knowledge of English life.'[13] The most interesting account of a meeting with her was given by Lord Beaverbrook. He said:

She appeared to me to be a simple woman. She was plainly dressed and I was not attracted to her style of hairdressing.

Her smile was kindly and pleasing, and her conversation was interspersed with protestations of ignorance of politics and with declarations of simplicity of character and outlook, with a claim to inexperience in worldly affairs. Throughout the evening she only once engaged in political conversation, and then she showed a liberal outlook, well maintained in discussion, and based on a conception which was sound.

I was greatly interested by the way the other women greeted her. There were about six women who were present at the dinner or who came in afterwards. All but one of them greeted Mrs Simpson with a kiss. She received it with appropriate dignity, but in no case did she return it.[14]

Chiefly she was a perfectionist. As Duchess of Windsor she would earn a just reputation for the beauty of her houses and the splendours of her food as well as for the elegance of her dress. Earlier in this narrative we have seen her weighing and measuring, tying the asparagus with two strings, 'not one or three', because Fannie Farmer told her to. These are the hallmarks of the perfectionist. The artist sloshes food into a bowl, stirring confidently and tasting occasionally: the perfectionist makes absolutely sure. Chips Channon writes of Mrs Simpson's first essay in interior decoration which had been so much trouble and pleasure to her: 'She invited us for a cocktail at Bryanston Court where she was living in a dreadful, banal flat.'[15] Yet she had a strong latent taste and was immensely educable. In her later years everything in every room of hers was superb and quite soon she would make no mistakes in judging whom to employ and where to buy, judgment which the mere possession of money cannot give, although vast expenditure may be needed to satisfy it.

It is often said that, before she got caught up in a whirlpool of events she could not control, she exerted a very good influence on the Prince of Wales. One of the reasons for this, both he and she have told us, is that among her attractions for him was that she was the first woman ever to take an interest in his work. If this had been true it would have been merely a commentary on his personal taste, because in England there is no shortage of women who are interested in public work. In fact it was not true and might have seemed ironical to Mrs Dudley Ward, who at that moment was immersed in the arrangements for the opening of the First Feathers' Club and the raising of money for several more. The second reason is that the extent to which he drank before he met her has been very much exaggerated. Many of his friends deny it altogether, and stories that he was constantly and seriously the worse for drink seem quite without foundation. Finally, the idea that Mrs Simpson improved him has been much put about, notably by the two diarists – whose talents give their opinions a quite unjustified weight. Thus Chips Channon:

Mrs Simpson has enormously improved the Prince.[16]

We went to the opera. ... and were joined in Emerald's box by the Prince of Wales and the Ménage Simpson. I was interested to see what an extraordinary hold Mrs Simpson has over the Prince. In the interval she told him to hurry away as he would be late in joining the Queen at the LCC ball – and she made him take a cigar from out of his breast pocket. 'It doesn't look very pretty,' she said. ...[17]

She encourages the King to meet people of importance and to be polite; above all she makes him happy. The Empire ought to be grateful.[18]

She confessed to Honor that she always kicks him under the table hard when to stop and gently when to go on. Sometimes she is too far away and then it is difficult.

a statement which is made even more absurd by the words that follow it:

I like the King very much. He is so manly, so honest and far shrewder than people pretend.[19]

Harold Nicolson also accompanied Mrs Simpson to the theatre. He describes her as 'bejewelled, eye-brow plucked, virtuous and wise', and goes on: 'I was impressed by the fact that she forbade the Prince to smoke during the *entr' acte* in the theatre itself. She is clearly out to help him.'[20]

Yet to those not bewitched by the immediate presence of royalty it is exactly these proprietary attentions that seem so inappropriate. One has only to visualize Mrs Keppel pulling at the King's cigar, and ordering him about with the confidence which only intimacy can give, to realize how little Mrs Simpson was equipped to be Queen of England or even for the role of King's mistress.

Within a matter of weeks more gossip and scandal had been created than in the whole of his previous forty years. Until now, although he had followed his inclinations in his private life and at times had stretched the resources of his household in covering lapses due to his idiosyncrasies and unpunctuality, while he had obstinately refused to follow the conventions suggested to him by his father and his father's court, there is no doubt that he had added more to the brilliance of the crown, to the magic of the monarchy, than he had taken away. From now on he was to behave with a senseless recklessness in minor matters, an imperviousness to other people's opinions and feelings, which, carelessly and publicly proclaimed, could not for long have been covered by his household and must in the end have undermined even his extraordinary popularity.

Almost immediately they had London society by the ears. Initially this was because, if we are to believe Chips Channon, there was a rift between the Prince's old friends who had been given such short shrift, and all those struggling to get on the bandwaggon* but chiefly owing to the childish ostentation with which the Prince and Mrs Simpson conducted themselves. Mrs Simpson's appearances in society were designed to invite gossip about the unprecedented splendour of her jewels. Diana Cooper described her as 'glittering', and said she 'dripped in new jewels and clothes',[21] and Chips Channon variously as 'simply dressed but with a new parure of rubies',[22] and 'in a simple black dress with a green bodice and dripping with emeralds – her collection of jewels is the talk of London',[23] 'literally smothered in rubies',[24] and 'wearing new jewels – the King must give her new ones every day',[25] while probably the most amusing account of her appearance – at a weekend dinner party in the country – is given by Marie Belloc Lowndes.

She wore a very great deal of jewellery, which I thought must be what is called 'dressmaker's' jewels, so large were the emeralds in her bracelets and so striking and peculiar a necklace. . . . Several of my fellow-guests asked me what I thought of her. I said what had struck me most were her perfect clothes and that I had been surprised, considering that she dressed so simply, to see that she wore such a mass of dressmakers' jewels. At that they all screamed with laughter, explaining that all the jewels were real, that the then Prince of Wales had given her fifty thousand pounds' worth at Christmas, following it up with sixty thousand pounds' worth of jewels a week later at the New Year. They explained that his latest gift was a marvellous necklace which he had bought from a Paris jeweller.[26]

Marie Belloc Lowndes nevertheless put firmly on record the fact that she liked Mrs Simpson, and an interpolation is justified here to give her impressions at her first meeting. Before this she had discussed the subject of so much gossip with her friend, Lady Colefax.

Of course I know, Marie – the latter had said – that people are speaking in a very horrid way of the poor Prince and Mrs Simpson. It's awfully unfair, and pure jealousy on the part of the women he has liked in the past, and who all of them made him dreadfully unhappy. Not one of them was even ordinarily faithful to him. Almost all of them had lovers and of course that made him feel wretched. Mrs Simpson is quite a different sort of woman. She doesn't pose as being young and in fact must be nearly forty. She is clever and intelligent and is interested in everything that interests the Prince, including gardening.[27]

---

* See pages 45, 46 and 53 of *Chips. The Diaries of Sir Henry Channon*.

Following this conversation Mrs Belloc Lowndes met the Prince with both Mr and Mrs Simpson at Trent. Her main impression – apart from her wonder at the costume jewellery – was of Mrs Simpson's anxious concern for her husband: 'Twice she said to her host: "I think Ernest would like to meet ——." The first time this happened it was quite obvious that —— did not wish to meet Ernest, and I could not help feeling sorry for her.'[28]

She also records her conviction that Simpson was not *un mari complaisant* although later she says: 'Little by little the two began to "shed" Mr Simpson. He was less and less with them, and people of a certain type began giving dinner parties and evening parties "to have the honour of meeting His Majesty the King and of course Mrs Simpson". This was specially the case with some women who were American by birth, but married to Englishmen. The most prominent of these ladies was Lady Cunard. She constantly entertained Mrs Simpson, both with the King and without him.'[29]

Lady Cunard demands some attention, as does Lady Colefax, since theirs are two of the names most frequently mentioned as members of a 'circle' into which Mrs Simpson is sometimes thought to have introduced the Prince of Wales, a circle so trivial and corrupt that they were actively responsible either for persuading him that he might marry a woman with two living husbands, or, if not this, for having lulled his conscience and his senses to sleep so that he was deluded about what public reaction to his marriage would be. Thus Brian Inglis, having mentioned Lady Cunard specifically by name, says:

She [Mrs Simpson] liked moving in society. Edward did not like it, nor did it provide him with the kind of social intercourse he really needed... People who secured introductions to him were usually would-be social lions or lionesses, and at their parties, individuals whose company he would have relished were often too inhibited – or even sorry for him, that he should be visibly so bored. They assumed that the Prince had been caught up in 'that raffish group' – a contemporary critic's view, which Compton Mackenzie quoted – 'which now lords it over London society, that mongrel pack of mainly immigrant aliens, naturalized or otherwise, the Invaders, the most heartless and dissolute of the pleasure-loving ultra-rich, the hardest and most hated people in England.'[30]

This is a fantasy. In the first place it is an entirely naive view that London society was at any time divided into tight little groups or circles such as are suggested here. It might conceivably be regarded as made up of members of overlapping circles but a hostess on the grand scale such as Lady Cunard entertained no 'mongrel pack of mainly immigrant aliens' but most of the leading writers, musicians and painters in England, many of the leading politicians, more than half the aristocracy. However, other people believed that Mrs Simpson did harm to the Prince of Wales by taking him so much into society. Harold Nicolson, in the description of his meeting with them already quoted from, goes on to say:

The Prince is extremely talkative and charming. I have a sense that he prefers our sort of society either to the aristocrats or to the professed highbrows or politicians. Sybil* imagines that she is getting him into touch with Young England. I have an uneasy feeling that Mrs Simpson, in spite of her good intentions, is getting him out of touch with the type of person with whom he ought to associate.

Go home pondering on all these things and a trifle sad. Why am I sad? Because I think Sybil is a clever old bean who ought to concentrate upon intellectual and not social guests. Because I think Mrs Simpson is a nice woman who has flaunted suddenly into this absurd position. Because I think the P. of W. is in a mess.

And because I do not feel at ease in such company.[31]

Harold Nicolson's uneasy thoughts reflect, as do the fantastic accounts of the other writers, the fact that a loss of virtue occurs through too much indulgence in social life, a thing harmless in itself and indeed necessary to most people (although it was untrue to think that the Prince could be got out of touch with persons with whom he ought to have associated, because, as has already been shown, he had never been in touch with them). But his uneasiness is as much that Sybil, who is 'a clever old bean', should waste her time on the Prince of Wales as that the Prince should waste his time on her. And if Lady Colefax was a clever old bean, Lady Cunard was an even cleverer. 'Bookish he will never be,' Sir Herbert Warren had said about the Prince of Wales. Lady Cunard was very bookish indeed; an immensely cultivated woman, quite unusually well-read, witty and talented. Apart from her husband, Sir Bache Cunard, whom according to her biographer she married as 'a necessary springboard to broader horizons', she had an intimate relationship with only two men in her life – one was George Moore, the other Sir Thomas Beecham. Here is what Osbert Sitwell has to say about her:

In the world of opera and ballet, Lady Cunard reigned alone. Her boundless and enthusiastic love of music places all those who enjoy opera in her debt; for it was largely her support, and the way she marshalled her forces, that enabled the wonderful seasons of opera and ballet in these years to materialise. There appeared to be no limit to the number of boxes she could fill. Her will-power was sufficient, her passion for music fervent enough, to make opera almost compulsory for those who wished to be fashionable. .... And much as I loved the opera and ballet I was often sorry when the hour came for us to leave her house, because her airy and rather impersonal alertness, and her wit, which consists in a particular and individual use of syllogism, so that it was impossible beforehand ever to tell to what conclusion any given premise might bring you, made her drawing-room unlike any other, gay, full of life. But she would never be late for the opera, if she could help it, albeit she would find it difficult, I think, in other matters to be punctual. Again, whereas the majority of London hostesses love dullness for its own sake, and without hope of reward, and whereas, moreover, one is continually surprised to find how little literary hostesses have read, Lady

* Lady Colefax.

Cunard loves to be amused, and her passion for books is obvious. She takes the pleasure in a volume that is new to her that a child finds in a toy, and when the talk turns on abstruse subjects, you will find that she has read the most unlikely works on them. ... But she tires so quickly of dullness, even of dullness new to her, that she has developed her own method of combating it. She can goad the conversation, as if it were a bull, and she a matador, and compel it to show a fiery temper. ... In addition to the fashionable near-art world, the eminent of many kinds, politicians, and occasionally a statesman, as well as writers, painters and musicians, frequented then, and still frequent, her drawing-room.[32]

From this it can be seen that the suggestion that she was in any social sense the inferior of the Prince of Wales or Mrs Simpson cannot possibly be sustained. In style, personality and wit, she was infinitely more distinguished, and, if it had not been that despite all her talents she shared with Lady Colefax the overpowering weakness that at the very thought of royalty her brain and her heart turned to jelly, they would have had nothing to offer her. By bringing the Prince and London's hostesses together Mrs Simpson may have acted as a catalyst of corruption, but she showed once more an absolutely unerring instinct for the best, if by the best is meant the most intelligent and entertaining.

By the summer of 1934 Mr and Mrs Simpson had become an almost permanent part of the Prince of Wales's private life. They were constantly at the Fort, where by now, rather to the chagrin of the servants, Mrs Simpson had begun to take an interest in the arrangement of the furniture, the running of the household and the menus for the meals. When they were in London the Prince's chauffeur, Ladbroke, waited often for hours outside her flat. In August the Prince took a house in Biarritz and invited the Simpsons to accompany him. Ernest Simpson had already arranged to go to the USA on business, and now for the first time Aunt Bessie Merryman took his place and acted as chaperone. The other guests included the Prince's Assistant Private Secretary, Hugh Lloyd Thomas, and his equerries John Aird and 'G' Trotter and Lieut-Commander and Mrs Colin Buist. Soon the Prince and Mrs Simpson formed the habit of leaving the others once a week and dining alone in one of the little bistros in Biarritz; and, when presently the whole party took a short trip on Lord Moyne's yacht *Rosaura*, the Duchess tells us that, sitting alone together on deck in the evenings, she and the Prince crossed the boundary between friendship and love. When they reached Cannes, although the party had been meant to disband there, the Prince, unable to bring his happiness to an end, decided to continue on the *Rosaura* to Genoa and from there to travel by train to Lake Como. In the ecstasy he felt, he showed a reckless disregard of the conventions which should have bound his behaviour and an insensate determination to break the barriers which stood between him and isolation in a world with this woman who had succeeded in appeasing his everlasting need for fulfilment, not as a Prince, but as a human being. On the *Rosaura*, as later on the

Nahlin, he showed that he lacked the maturity to accept easily the role of a lover and combine it with that of a man of affairs – his childish exhibitionism taking the form, as often as not, of stripping off his clothes; the clothes which, ever since his pockets had been sewn up to prevent him putting his hands in them, had been a bone of contention between himself and his father. Thus he appeared in shorts and sandals, not merely on the yacht and on the beaches, but when visiting the Borromeo Palace, where, instantly recognized though posing as a tourist, he was welcomed by the Prince Borromeo in a morning coat and striped trousers.

The Duchess's reflections on this trip, although they show her at her most honest and attractive, nevertheless underline the fact that in spite of his genuine simplicity and real dislike of ostentation, he took absolutely for granted that, while indulging his every like and dislike, he might nevertheless continue to wield all the appurtenances of power – a belief that in the long run would cause him an infinity of pain. She could not, she tells us, find any reason why this most glamorous of men should have been so much attracted to her. She was not a beauty and she was no longer young. 'In my own country I would have been considered securely on the shelf.'[33] On the other hand, and it is this paragraph that is so revealing, she found no difficulty in explaining why the Prince should be so overwhelmingly appealing to her.

Over and beyond the charm of his personality and the warmth of his manner, he was the open sesame to a new and glittering world that excited me as nothing in my life had ever done before. For all his natural simplicity, his genuine abhorrence of ostentation, there was nevertheless about him – even in his most Robinson Crusoe clothes – an unmistakable aura of power and authority. His slightest wish seemed always to be translated instantly into the most impressive kind of reality. Trains were held; yachts materialized; the best suites in the finest hotels were flung open; aeroplanes stood waiting. What impressed me most of all was how all this could be brought to pass without apparent effort: the calm assumption that this was the natural order of things, that nothing could ever possibly go awry. . . . It seemed unbelievable that I, Wallis Warfield of Baltimore, Maryland, could be part of this enchanted world. It seemed so incredible that it produced in me a happy and unheeding acceptance.[34]

Those who cannot understand and sympathize with this passage should not judge the Duchess. Yet judged she must be because the extent of her hold upon the Prince of Wales and the completeness of his subjection to her were soon to be remarked by every perceptive observer.

No one – Walter Monckton wrote after the Abdication – will ever really understand the story of the King's life during the crisis who does not appreciate two factors: The first, which is superficially acknowledged by many of those who were closely concerned in the events of these days, was the intensity and depth of the King's devotion to Mrs Simpson. To him she was the perfect woman. She insisted that he should be at his best and do his best at all times, and he regarded her as his inspiration.[35]*

Because of Edward's obsessed absorption in his love for Mrs Simpson and more especially because of the Abdication, it has become widely believed that the bond between them was a purely physical one and that she was the only woman to satisfy this side of his nature. It is clearly not very easy to find evidence for or against this theory, but people who hold it must reconcile it with the fact that it comes as a surprise to those who travelled with him on his tours as Prince of Wales and had so often to deal with situations created by a healthy interest in the other sex. Indeed it might be true to say that during the whole of his youth the Prince was criticized for over-indulgence in the sexual act while ever since he has been believed incapable of it until he met his wife.

For some people the purely sexual explanation of a relationship which inspired an act unique in history and also the slavish devotion of a lifetime is in any case too simple. It is interesting, therefore, that, following the passage just quoted, Walter Monckton recorded the view that it was a great mistake to assume that the Prince was merely in love in the ordinary physical sense. 'There was an intellectual companionship, and there is no doubt that his lonely nature found in her a spiritual comradeship.'[36]

Some time during the abdication crisis one of Mr Baldwin's entourage amused himself by sending a specimen of Mrs Simpson's handwriting to a graphologist and it is not necessary to have any considerable belief in graphology to be struck by this particular example of it.

A woman with a strong male inclination in the sense of activity, vitality, initiative. She *must* dominate, she *must* have authority, and without sufficient scope for her powers can become disagreeable. She needs a large field of organization, of influence ... primarily all she does comes from her wish to be important.

In the pursuit of her aim, she can be inconsiderate and can hurt – but on the whole she is not without some instinct of nobility and generosity. She is ruled by contradictory impulses; there is a certain restlessness in the writing, a sign that the satisfaction she gets is not strong enough to harmonize her life. She is ambitious and demands above all that her undertakings should be noted and valued.[37]

All his life the Prince of Wales had sought 'a woman with a strong male inclination' and one of the most enduring links between these two was that, in the context of this relationship although apparently in no other, he was made for domination, while she was made to dominate. He and Wallis Simpson were quite unusually suited to each other, two parts of a whole

---

* Monckton must be referring to the same kind of thing which had so much impressed Nicolson and Channon. One cannot accept that she insisted he should do his best at all times.

and it was her misfortune as well as his that, when two complementary natures join, it is not merely the best in each that finds completion. The time might come in the crisis that was to follow – although even here the evidence is not strong – when she would temporarily lose her power to influence his behaviour, like someone who, having whipped up a sensitive horse, momentarily loses control of it, but she must bear a large responsibility for everything that follows, because his greatest happiness in life was by now to obey her slightest wish.

Yet there seems little doubt that he misled her. For different reasons, her euphoria was as great as his, and nothing in her character, background or experience enabled her to see beyond hotel suites and yachts to the realities of power, or recognize that the choice was not between being Queen of England or the King's mistress, but between mistress of the King and exile. It may be argued that too much can be made of this. Some Americans have a predilection to divorce and remarriage as compared with the less binding relationships, but Mrs Simpson came from two families with English traditions and had already learned the penalties these exacted, while the issue was not one of such great complexity. Yet, even if it is an intellectual absurdity to attribute to the whole American nation an inability to understand that divorce constitutes a total prohibition on becoming Queen of England, all the evidence suggests that Mrs Simpson did not understand it. She did not understand it in her bones, as every English woman would have done, and this, more than anything else, may have accounted for his obsession. So many people were deceived as to his true nature because in all his life he had seriously loved only married women. Yet he was exceptionally domestic and was presently to show that for true satisfaction he needed not merely the durability and dependability of marriage but the delight of shared household goods and household chores which only the long habit of married life affords. When he asked Mrs Simpson to marry him he almost certainly made her believe that what he offered was in his power to give. Whether he believed it himself no one will ever know. For almost as long as he could remember he had defied tradition and the views of the King's household, and, in the phrase which he is said to have favoured himself, 'had got away with it', and he certainly saw himself as standing for the principles of the young against the old and well established. At this period of his life, it is possible that in a dangerously superficial way – which was to leave him at a loss when he came up against reality – he believed that he could get away with even this.

All this implies that they discussed it – a point hardly worth making if it had not been so much put about that the King merely got the bit between his teeth and galloped away, and if it were not for the fact that behind the red boxes and the rest of the paraphernalia the sight of two ordinary human beings was lost. So it has become necessary to ask whether it seems likely that two people who have been in love for two years, during which time one of them has been determined on marriage while the other has arranged the divorce without which this would not be possible, should, nevertheless, have never discussed the matter. Yet if Mrs Simpson believed she might be Queen because the King encouraged her to think so, then she had some right to feel aggrieved when the storm broke and to wish to avoid incrimination in all that followed. In that case, too, she did not deliberately risk abdication and exile but simply failed to understand the odds against her. It is irresistible, if this is so, to speculate on what she might have done if she had understood the true nature of the choice before her, but not relevant. All that can be said is that throughout history the favourite of the King has been regarded as an honourable position and one that few women would have dared to look beyond.

It is not intended to suggest that there and then on the yacht *Rosaura* thoughts of becoming Queen occurred to Mrs Simpson, but that the narrative which follows will be more readily understood if one believes that ideas of the sort began gradually to have a stronger and stronger hold on her, while at the same time she continued to abandon her will to what she called a 'happy and unheeding acceptance' of the strange fate that was hers.

In the autumn of that year, at a reception given at Buckingham Palace a day or two before the wedding of the Duke of Kent, she was presented to the King and Queen for the first and last time. This wedding marked the end of the particularly close relationship between the Prince of Wales and his younger brother which, outside those with women, must be regarded as the only important relationship of the elder man's life. The Duchess of Windsor tells us that as the wedding drew nigh a visible sadness grew upon him. She also tells us that after this only one member of the Prince's family remained a fairly constant visitor at the Fort – Lord Louis Mountbatten.

In February of the following year – 1935 – the Prince asked Mr and Mrs Simpson to accompany him to Kitzbühl for the winter sports and again Mr Simpson refused on the grounds of business in New York. Once more, at the end of the prearranged fortnight's skiing, the Prince could not bear to return home, and he and his party were now transported to Vienna and, after a brief interlude there, continued on to Budapest. It is not surprising that when Mrs Simpson returned to her flat in Bryanston Square she found that her relationship with her husband had undergone a change. Here again we owe to her own revelations our knowledge of what passed in her mind.

I was troubled, but my concern was no more than a tiny cloud in the growing radiance that the Prince's favour cast over my life. I became aware of a rising curiosity concerning me, of new doors opening, and a heightened interest even in my casual remarks. I was stimulated; I was excited; I felt as if I were borne upon a rising wave that seemed to be carrying me ever more rapidly and even higher. Now I began to savour the true brilliance and sophistication of the life of London.[38]

We have already admired the Duchess's honesty and sympathized with her situation. It seems reasonable, however, to expect that she would tell us something of what passed in her mind about the work and the unique public position of the man who opened the doors of all these hotel suites and society houses. Curiously enough there is not one word on these matters. From what she tells us, and we must accept that it may be all she chooses to tell us, her life with the Prince of Wales was merely one long, glorious, extended holiday.

In July 1935 Lady Diana Cooper wrote to Conrad Russell from Fort Belvedere:

This stationery is disappointingly humble – not so the conditions. I am in a pink bedroom, pink-sheeted, pink Venetian-blinded, pink-soaped, white-telephoned and pink-and-white maided.

The food at dinner staggers and gluts. *Par contre* there is little or nothing for lunch, and that foraged for by oneself American-style (therefore favoured, bless him).

We arrived after midnight (perhaps as chaperones). Jabber and beer and bed was the order. I did not leave the 'cabin's seclusion' until 1 o'clock, having been told that no one else did. HRH was dressed in plus-twenties with vivid azure socks. Wallis admirably correct and chic. Me bang wrong! Golf in the afternoon, only the Prince and Duff playing, Wallis and me tooling round. It poured and we took shelter in a hut and laughed merrily enough with other common shelterers.

The social life at the Fort centres round the swimming pool, which has an elaborate equipment (better than Bognor's)* of long chairs, swabs, mattresses and dumb-waiters bearing smoking and drinking accessories in abundance. It is some little way from the house, so showers cause a dreadful lot of carrying-in and bringing out again for the next fitful sun-ray.

Everything is a few hours later than other places (perhaps it's American Time. 'The huntsmen are up in America, and they are already past their first sleep in Persia'). A splendid tea arrived at 6.30 with Anthony Eden and Esmond Harmsworth. Dinner was at ten. Emerald arrived at 8.30 for cocktails, which she doesn't drink although the Prince prepares the potions with his own poor hands and does all the glass filling. She was dressed in a red-white-and-blue walking-dress, with tiny blue glass slippers and toes showing through.

The Prince changed into a Donald tartan dress-kilt with an immense white leather purse in front, and played the pipes round the table after dinner, having first fetched his bonnet. We 'reeled' to bed at 2 a.m. The host drinks least.

The house is an enchanting folly and only needs fifty red soldiers stood between the battlements to make it into a Walt Disney coloured symphony toy. The comfort could not be greater, nor the desire on his part for his guests to be happy, free and unembarrassed. Surely a new atmosphere for Courts?

Spirits excellent. Can it be due to proximity to royalty? Surely not. I think it's being entertained and resting from the strain of entertaining. The Prince reminds

* The Duff-Coopers' own house was at Bognor.

me of myself at Bognor – over-restless, fetching unnecessary little things jumping up for the potatoes or soda-water.[39]

That summer the Prince of Wales and Mrs Simpson repeated their holiday of the previous year – with slightly different companions, Lord and Lady Brownlow, Lord Sefton, Mrs Evelyn Fitzgerald, the Buists and John Aird, and at Cannes instead of Biarritz. They cruised this time on the Duke of Westminster's yacht, *Cutty Sark*, to Corsica; and later on Mrs Reginald Fellowes' yacht, *Sister Anne*, along the coast. Later still the Prince of Wales decided that they ought to revisit Vienna and Budapest and it was October before he and Mrs Simpson were back in London.

In his autobiography the Duke of Windsor tells us that he was by now conscious of the overwhelming love and surpassing need he had for Mrs Simpson, and he tells us that his dream of being able to bring her permanently into his life was, although quite vague, extremely vivid. He discusses the attitude that in Court circles is likely to be taken on the question of the divorce and tells us that he wished to discuss the whole thing with his father. Then he says quite openly that he did not discount the possibility that he might have to give up the Crown and took comfort in the fact that his brother, Bertie, was temperamentally so much more like his father. He says that he did not talk to his father because a concatenation of events prevented him doing so, and he lists such objections as the Silver Jubilee celebrations, the holiday season, his brother's – the Duke of Gloucester's – wedding, a general election and the death of his father's sister Princess Victoria. At Christmas at Sandringham the King seemed too old and too ill to be worried. Only the last two of these objections seem entirely valid. All the rest are in the category of the kind of event which might be expected to occur at any time. It is very hard to believe that the Prince could ever have found the courage to face the father whom he had been so conditioned to fear with the news that he intended to marry a married woman, already once-divorced, and that in order to do this he would if necessary renounce the throne.

What is more curious is that King George did not speak to him. News of the Prince's latest love had quickly reached the Palace and the anxiety that it caused the King spoiled the last year of his life – some believe hastened his death. We know that he discussed this matter with the Archbishop of Canterbury, Cosmo Lang, to whom he said that he was much concerned about the Prince of Wales's 'latest friendship'. The Archbishop said that the Prince had had previous friendships, like most young men, and especially those who had grown up during the war. But the King replied that he believed this affair was more serious than any of the others. We know too that he appealed to the Duke of Connaught to intervene and that he asked the advice of the Prime Minister, Stanley Baldwin, to whom he made the dramatic statement: 'After I am dead the boy will ruin himself in twelve months.'[40] And finally we have been told that only a few weeks before his death he exclaimed passionately: 'I pray to God that my eldest son will never marry and have children, and that nothing will come between Bertie and Lilibet and the throne.'[41] In the aftermath of the Abdication criticisms were levelled at certain people – Stanley Baldwin and Lord Hardinge of Penshurst in particular – because they had not spoken sooner to the King (Edward VIII) on the matter of Mrs Simpson. Very little attention has been paid to the fact that neither his father nor his mother ever spoke to him at all. George V had never ceased to hector his son about such things as his clothes and his deportment, and at this very time he spoke critically to him about his duty in relation to foreign affairs (see pp. 194–5), but on this matter, which he was well aware sapped at the life of the monarchy itself, he could not bring himself to intervene. This is surely a commentary not merely on the relationship within this family but on any tendency to criticize others in contact with Edward who intervened, if at all, very late. The truth is that the Prince of Wales, whose obstinacy in any case 'constituted power of a kind' was in this matter so early armed by certainty of purpose as to check advice or warning on the lips of those who tried to utter them. When he chose he was a formidable personality.

On Thursday 16 January 1936 the Prince of Wales was shooting in Windsor Great Park when a letter was brought to him from his mother asking him to propose himself for the week-end at Sandringham because, although there seemed to be no immediate danger, Lord Dawson was not too pleased with his father's health. The Prince flew to Sandringham in his own aeroplane the next morning, and on the Sunday he motored to London to inform the Prime Minister that the King was not expected to live more than a few days. On the Monday night the famous bulletin was issued – 'The King's life is moving peacefully to its close', and George V died in the presence of his wife and children. Hardly was the King dead than Queen Mary taking the hand of her eldest son, kissed it. 'The King is dead, long live the King.'

PART 2
THE KING

14

KING EDWARD

According to many accounts of Edward VIII's reign it began with an act almost as difficult to explain as the one with which it closed, and which to a small circle and on a small scale was as unpredictable and shocking. At Sandringham, where George V died, the clocks had always been kept half an hour fast ever since the days when Edward VII assembled his guests in the morning for shooting. It was done to ensure their punctuality but it must also have acted as a forerunner of daylight saving. On the night the old King died, Edward VIII is said to have left his bedside and gone immediately downstairs to give orders that the clocks should be altered to normal time. More attention has been given to the lack of feeling in this extraordinary gesture than to the lack of reason. Yet there is a senselessness about this early exertion of an unquestioned power that surely needs explanation.

A small error of fact is important. According to Mr Daniel Burlingham, the clockmaker in charge of the clocks at Sandringham, the order was given, not immediately after George V's death, but some time before it.

On the night when George V lay dying – he writes* – and it was announced by the BBC that 'the King's life was drawing peacefully to its close', the Prince of Wales thereupon ordered that the clocks should be put back to Greenwich Time immediately. I received instructions by telephone and, by the time I arrived at Sandringham (getting on for midnight) by taxi and accompanied by the clockman, the King had died.

I returned home during the small hours and the clockman stayed until first light to attend to the Turret Clocks at the House, Stables etc.

We owe to a member of the Prince of Wales's staff the most probable explanation. During the long hours while the King's death was awaited

* Letter to the author. Robert Sencourt was responsible for the research which revealed the true version of this event but for some reason he omitted in his book to explain the details.

177

some small mistake occurred because of the discrepancy between Sandringham time and real time. 'I'll fix those bloody clocks,' the Prince cried angrily, and without further consideration gave the order. This explanation loses nothing in credibility because it suggests a near-hysteria and is much more likely than that any sane man would leave a room, where his father had that moment died and his mother kissed his hand, to go down to give an order about clocks. Yet the effect was horribly offensive and can be explained only by the idea that the Prince was so closely imprisoned in his own personal crisis that he had no thoughts for anyone else. And it was a presage of all that was to follow that this man, who for so many years had seemed to have an unerring flair for doing and saying the right thing, should in the first minutes of his reign have disturbed and distressed everyone about him and alienated the sympathies of servants who had been with his family for years.

This strange and callous act was accompanied in private by excessive emotion. Lady Hardinge has described his grief as 'frantic and unreasonable' and says 'it far exceeded that of his mother and three brothers'.[1] And here again the intensity of his suffering suggests a subjective involvement different from grief or even from the guilt which might be normal to a son whose relationship with his father had steadily deteriorated. The King had made up his mind to marry Mrs Simpson but he had allowed himself to drift into a situation in which, since he resolutely refused to face facts, the pressures must have been intolerable. During the whole course of his reign this inner tension remained and his public as well as his private behaviour must be related to it.

His public appearances were cushioned by his enormous popularity which it is impossible to overstate. The strength of the monarchy had steadily grown from the reign of Queen Victoria and had reached a climax with the jubilee of King George v. As Prince of Wales, the new King had become known all over the world, largely through his own efforts, the beauty of his appearance, and his ability to please; but also with the help of modern transport and communications not previously available. His personal popularity was something that had never been seen before, and, in the numbers of those who loved and looked up to him, has not been seen since. Nor was it as yet understood how suddenly and completely popularity, which had taken years to build up, could be dissipated.

Even among those people who are not deeply moved by the concept of monarchy or concerned in its doings, there was interest in the new King, whose character and history suggested change. Would he, as he was expected to do, succeed in democratizing the monarchy and bringing it nearer to what were conceived (the subsequent history of the monarchy suggests wrongly) to be the requirements of the modern age? All in all no man ever came to the throne in more propitious circumstances. *The Times* leader said:

His winning smile, 'the smile that conquered Canada', his laughter-loving boyishness, sometimes nervous, but always self-possessed, his attractive habit of identifying himself with the different nationalities of the United Kingdom and the Empire, his thoughtful tact, his kindness and sympathy, his affection for children, his delightful sense of humour, his bodily activity and love of sport, his ready memory for faces, his freedom, for all his dignity, from personal or official side, his powers of conversation, and his remarkable talents of voice, memory and quick resourcefulness as a public speaker in other languages besides English ... have endeared him to all whom he met on our tours.

But it is not only in the nations of the Empire overseas that he has won the hearts of unnumbered men, women and children. Here, at home, in countless ways, he has no less securely established his hold on the affections of his people. Day in and day out he has never spared himself. He has traversed and studied the country from end to end, has made friends with all sorts and conditions of its workers, has gained an inside knowledge of its industries and has taken his place under the King, his father, at the head of every national movement for the relief of sickness and suffering and want. As a man he has a real British love for sport and every form of healthy exercise, and to all outward appearance does not seem to know the meaning of physical fear. As a King the people will be able to look up to him as one who has a statesmanlike knowledge and sympathetic understanding of the people of all creeds and races over whom he has been called to reign. ...

As an epitaph to the Prince of Wales, no one, even his most severe critic, could say that this was untrue or exaggerated.

The King began his public duties with his accustomed flair and with words that gave hope, even to his critics, that he might be capable of rising to the new demands to be made of him.

The first public act of a new King is to present himself before an Accession Privy Council. More than a hundred Councillors assembled in the Banqueting Hall of St James's, and, after referring to the irreparable loss of his father, Edward addressed them as follows:

When my father stood here twenty-six years ago he declared that one of the objects of his life would be to uphold constitutional government. In this I am determined to follow in my father's footsteps and to work as he did throughout his life for the happiness and welfare of my subjects.

I place my reliance upon the loyalty and affection of my peoples throughout the Empire, and upon the wisdom of their Parliaments, to support me in this heavy task, and I pray God will guide me to perform it.

Afterwards the King told Baldwin he had not been overwhelmed by his first Council as his father had confessed to being but had looked upon it as 'just business to be got through'. But Baldwin told Tom Jones that he held the paper he read first in one shaking hand, then in both, and then he put it to rest on the table.[2] And Attlee recorded that he looked 'very nervous and ill at ease'.[3]

That night he dined with Mrs Simpson.

The following day the Accession was proclaimed at four different points in London – first by Garter King of Arms at St James's Palace, then by Heralds at Charing Cross, Temple Bar and the Royal Exchange. And immediately the new King made a characteristic departure from precedent. He had arranged that certain friends of his, including Mrs Simpson and Mrs Evelyn Fitzgerald, accompanied by his Private Secretary, Godfrey Thomas, should watch the Accession ceremony from a room in St James's Palace. The thought came to him he was later to say, that he would like to see himself proclaimed King, a thought almost certainly made urgent by the fact that he would inevitably be parted from Wallis Simpson for the next few days and one that he immediately obeyed. As he stood talking to her by the window, a photographer caught them, so that the next day she appeared in the newspapers, a strange and nameless woman for the first time by his side. And, as he escorted her down at the end of the ceremony and she thanked him for arranging for her to see it and said she realized how different his life would now be, he told her that nothing could ever change his feeling for her.

After this he returned to Sandringham where his father's body rested in the little church, watched over by gamekeepers and other servants, who paid their last tribute to him. Next morning the coffin was placed on a gun-carriage drawn by a Royal Horse Artillery team and taken to Wolferton Station where a special train waited to take it to London. The King and his brothers followed the gun-carriage on foot; Queen Mary and Princess Mary in a carriage. When the royal train arrived at King's Cross that afternoon the same family procession walked behind through the streets across Trafalgar Square to Westminster. Here is a description by Tom Jones who watched it pass.

From the window of my second-hand bookseller, Gaston, I saw the mournful little procession pass on its way from King's Cross to Westminster Hall – perhaps 40 men in all counting mounted and on foot. The King plodded heavily along weighed down by a thick long overcoat, looking utterly done. The only patch of colour was the Royal Standard on the coffin. The absence of the military and of music, the walking of the King and the Dukes, the fewness of those taking part, the intense quiet of a thronged street, made the sight a most moving one. I suppose it could happen in this simple way nowhere but in London.[4]

The Royal Crown had been taken from its glass case in the Tower and secured to the lid of the coffin over the folds of the Royal Standard. The jolting of the heavy gun-carriage must have caused the Maltese cross on the top of the crown – set with a square sapphire, eight medium-sized diamonds and one hundred and ninety-two smaller diamonds – to work loose. At the very moment the small procession turned into the gates of Palace Yard the cross rolled off and fell on the road. Two members of Parliament – Walter Elliot and Robert Boothby – stood on the pavement watching the procession. As a company sergeant-major, bringing up the rear of the two files of Grenadier Guardsmen flanking the carriage, bent down and in a swift movement picked up the cross and dropped it into his pocket, they heard the King's voice say: 'Christ! What will happen next?' 'A fitting motto,' Walter Elliot remarked to his companion, 'for the coming reign.'

There was no lack of people willing to see this incident as an omen (just as there were plenty to whom the parallel with Henry IV occurred. 'One wonders whether it is going to be a case of the Prince in Shakespeare's Henry IV and the King in Henry V.')[5] Baldwin had expressed his anxiety to Attlee at the Accession Council and his doubts as to whether the new King would 'stay the course'. Later he enlarged on this in conversation with Tom Jones, which the latter recorded in a letter to Lady Grigg:

You know what a scrimshanker I am – the Prime Minister said – I had rather hoped to escape the responsibility of having to take charge of the Prince as King. But perhaps Providence has kept me here for that purpose. I am less confident about him than Lucy is. It is a tragedy that he is not married. He is very fond of children. . . . He had been to see Mrs S. before he came to see me. She has a flat now. The subject is never mentioned between us. Nor is there any man who can handle him. I have seen Halsey and Godfrey Thomas.

Jones adds that he put the other point of view to the PM, mentioning the King's quick intelligence, his freedom from humbug, his social sympathies and sense of duty when on a job. 'I pressed my view that he'll rise to the new responsibilities though he may discharge them in his own way.'[6] Violet Markham writing to Jones said: 'You and I have seen three accessions and remember the fears that greeted two of them. May one's present sinking of the heart be as fully falsified as earlier forebodings. I am glad he is on good terms with S.B.'[7]

But probably J.H.Thomas lamenting to Harold Nicolson about the death of the old King put with the greatest precision the sense of uneasiness felt by so many people. 'And now,' he said, ' 'ere we 'ave this obstinate little man with 'is Mrs Simpson. Hit won't do, 'arold. I tell you that straight.'[8]

However the King began by giving proof of his talent for public gestures. As long as his father's coffin lay in Westminster Hall, officers of the Household Troops, together with the Gentlemen-at-Arms and the Yeomen of the Guard, maintained a continuous vigil, while members of the public in enormous numbers filed by to pay their last respects. At midnight on the evening before the King's body was taken on its last journey to Windsor, people still moved past the coffin in spite of the lateness of the hour. A few minutes later four figures in full-dress uniform descended the staircase and took their place around the catafalque between the officers already on vigil and, bent over their swords, stood there motionless for twenty minutes – the new King and his brothers, Prince Albert, Prince

Henry and Prince George.* It was a fine romantic action which caught the imagination of the public and gave great pleasure to Queen Mary.

There is a notion, fostered to some extent by himself, which has never lost its hold on the public mind, that Edward came to the throne with serious intention of reforming and democratizing the monarchy and that he was prevented from doing this alternatively by the emotional crisis that cut short his opportunities, or because of obstruction from the court circles and the 'establishment'. In a passage in his book in which he deals with the latter suggestion he says that he quickly became aware that his popularity was not quite so complete as public expression made it sound. There was, he says, no actual hostility or animosity, merely something in the air – the first nip of an autumn frost. And he goes on in a passage of stunning super-ficiality to analyse the differences between himself and the old King which he felt were the cause of an air of disapproval which could be felt in Whitehall as well as at Court. Everyone was accustomed, he says, to a King who went regularly to church, seldom missed the Two Thousand Guineas or Cowes Regatta, shot grouse in August and, when he dined out, did so only with noblemen. The new young monarch, although he worked hard at his duties, took his pleasures differently, preferring golf to yachting and taking his holidays at Biarritz or at Eden Roc. He shot partridges in Hungary with Regent Horthy rather than in England, and spent his free evenings with small parties of friends at the Embassy Club. And so, be-cause he had departed from what had come to be accepted as the King's regular mode of life, many people had begun to shake their heads.

This passage is one of several which lend colour to the view that, far from having any concrete ideas for reforms of any significance, 'he had never thought in advance of a situation ... which could not be long deferred ... He appeared to be entirely ignorant of the powers of a constitutional sovereign and of the lines on which a King's business should be carried on.'[9]

Something must be said about the Household. At the death of a King his Household continues to serve his successor for six months during which time the new King will appoint his own. Lord Wigram was George V's Private Secretary but he was of retiring age† and he asked to be replaced after the funeral ceremonies were over.

There were two Assistant Private Secretaries, Major Alexander Hardinge and Captain Alan Lascelles. Captain Lascelles had served the Prince of Wales for nine years before asking permission to leave his service, and in this way returned to it, but Major Hardinge was the senior of the two. When considering what new appointments he would make Edward offered

* The Dukes of York, Gloucester and Kent respectively.
† We have seen earlier Lord Esher's anxiety that he should be replaced by the right person when the new King came to the throne.

the post of Keeper of the Privy Purse to Major Ulick Alexander (who accepted it) and that of Private Secretary to Godfrey Thomas who had been his own Private Secretary for almost the whole of his public career. Thomas refused the post on the modest grounds that he was not qualified to fill it and remained on as Assistant Private Secretary. It was then offered to Alexander Hardinge, who accepted it.

Once Thomas had refused the post, Hardinge was the obvious choice. He had been Assistant Private Secretary to George v since 1920 and was well versed in the Palace ways. He had a natural talent for constitutional affairs and, because of his family and background, a particular interest in foreign affairs. But he was nevertheless a 'George v man' and his appointment was a reversal of almost everything Edward had been expected to do and a sign of his deep pre-occupation with other things.* 'It is high time,' Chips Channon had written of Hardinge two years before, 'that such dreary narrow-minded fogies were sacked, as, indeed, they will be, in the next reign.'[10]†

Of the post itself much has been written. It is obviously of the greatest importance, since, in addition to the administrative work, it is the Private Secretary's job to keep the King fully informed on political, economic and international affairs and to keep him in touch not merely with the views of the party in power but also of the Opposition and the back-benchers in the House of Commons, the senior civil servants, the leaders of public opinion and those in touch with foreign affairs. It is his responsibility to explain to the King the implications and possible consequences of any action he may be contemplating, and after the Statute of Westminster, the Dominion Prime Ministers being no longer answerable to Downing Street but to the Governor-General, reports went straight from the Governors-General through his Private Secretary to the King. 'The secretary to the Monarch, occupies to the Crown,' Harold Laski wrote, 'much the same position that the Crown itself occupies to the Government: he must advise, encourage and warn.'[12]

Laski also wrote: 'Half of him must be in a real sense a statesman and the other half must be prepared, if the occasion arise, to be something it is not very easy to distinguish from a lacquey.'[13] We have also seen Lord Davidson

---

* It is fairly clear that Edward reappointed most of the old household because he had no idea what else to do. It is not so easy to understand why, since the evidence suggests that they disapproved of his conduct and complained of his treatment of them, so many of them accepted the appointments. The most charitable explanation, also the most likely, is that by the time the appointments were made the King had been on the throne for nearly six months and it had become clear that without them his business could not have been carried on.

† Sir Henry Channon's expressions on these matters need not be taken too seriously. There were many people in London society who were not attracted to him, and, highly sensitive to disapproval, he had a tendency to describe all these in terms such as he applied to Major Hardinge. Thus Oliver Stanley, who is remembered by many people as one of the wittiest and most distinguished politicians of his day, is described 'as that gloomy Oliver Stanley – Snow White as we all call him.'[11]

congratulating himself on not being a lickspittle. This is probably a misconception of the psychology of those who take a place in an exalted hierarchy, and bears comparison with the suggestion that every army officer below the CIGS has on occasion to behave like a lacquey. According to Lady Longford, Sir Henry Ponsonby 'peremptorily refused' Queen Victoria's orders when he did not approve of them, and the history of Private Secretaries suggests that they have generally performed the ritual side of their duties with a good deal of relish just because it has not occurred to any of them that anyone could mistake him for a lacquey. But ritual depends on the rules being kept, and, if they are challenged or ignored, the self-respect of every man in the hierarchy comes into question, and the unrest goes deep. During the whole of his reign the stresses produced by the ambivalence of Edward's feeling for the crown were felt by those who served him and from the outset his Household was in considerable disarray.

In the early part of his reign the King did not wish to disturb Queen Mary, who, before moving to Marlborough House, had to pack or dispose of the accumulation of a lifetime. The offices of his secretariat therefore remained at Buckingham Palace but he continued to occupy York House and to spend much of his time at Fort Belvedere.

In retrospect it is apparent that only the small enclosed world of Fort Belvedere really mattered to him and his self-engrossment was such that he felt the presence of those who were outside it not more than an actor feels the presence of his audience, who, although living, sentient creatures, are bystanders to the theme which stirs the emotions and stops the breath. His situation was unique in that nothing checked his growing exaltation or his increasing divorce from reality, because whichever way he turned he was confirmed in the validity of his fantasies. He continued at times to respond to crowd scenes which sustained him in the central role and when this happened he had lost none of his power to bewitch. But to a dangerous extent he reacted to the outside world only with anger and impatience because it kept him from the woman on to whom he had transferred his emotional needs.

'It was scarcely realized at this early stage,' Hardinge was later to write, 'how overwhelming and inexorable was the influence exerted on the King by the lady of the moment. As time went on it became clearer that every decision, big or small, was subordinated to her will. . . . It was she who filled his thought at all times, she alone who mattered, before her the affairs of state sank into insignificance.'[14]

It would be some time too before it was understood that 'the lady of the moment' was not an adequate description of Mrs Simpson. The estrangement of the Prince of Wales not merely from his father but from all those who surrounded him meant that almost none of those who had to deal with him really knew him. They believed Mrs Simpson to be merely the last of a succession of passing affairs, and since they had not witnessed the extent of his dependence on Mrs Dudley Ward, or understood the importance of his relationship with her, they were completely unaware both of his need to submerge himself in a domestic situation and of his fidelity.

Proofs of Mrs Simpson's power were soon forthcoming. In the first place the King surrounded himself only with people who were friends of hers and cut out of his life even those who had been closest to him unless they were part of this company. Even Fruity Metcalfe, his closest man friend from whom for years he had been inseparable and who for long had been promised a place in the King's Household, was hurt and disappointed to be overlooked. 'G' Trotter who had also been close to him for years was sacked, gossip said for no better reason than that he had refused to give up his friendship with Lady Furness, and Admiral Halsey was completely out of favour because he had the fortitude to attempt a discussion of the King's relationship with Mrs Simpson.

Members of the Household were not expected to go to the Fort unless sent for and those who had been accustomed to go there as guests were no longer invited. At the time of the abdication crisis this greatly increased the isolation of the King and the lack of communication between him and those who might have been expected to advise and warn him, while at the beginning of the reign it added considerably to the difficulties under which they worked.

His staff complained of his unpunctuality, inconsequence and conceit, most of all of his lack of consideration. He worked at odd hours and thought nothing of calling his secretaries from their dinner, their baths or their beds. Lord Wigram asked permission to resign after the period of mourning because of the irregularity of his temper and hours and he gave Baldwin his reasons. Worst of all was a lack of method with state papers. All his life Edward had been accustomed to watch his father 'doing his boxes' which he later described as 'the relentless grind of the King's daily life', and when he first came to the throne he made a great show of carrying out this part of his duty, working assiduously through the papers and initialling everything he read. His first enthusiasm was soon his undoing, however, and a shortage of initials betrayed him. This acquired a serious aspect because the red boxes were invariably taken to Fort Belvedere, where there was no responsible person in charge of them, and it was often days, as time went on sometimes weeks, before they were returned. Given the negligence of the King there could be no absolute certainty that no one besides himself had access to them, a circumstance which for reasons discussed in the next chapter caused considerable alarm.

He was full of ideas and he liked change for change's sake but there were only a few things in which his interest was sustained. He showed a continuing and almost pathological preoccupation with finance. At the end of any regime which has lasted a long time many abuses will usually be found to have crept in on the one side and a certain indulgence on the other.

There was plenty of room for reforms in the palaces and at Sandringham and Balmoral, and the Duke of Windsor makes a convincing case in his book for the need to cut down, particularly at the two latter. But in his desire for retrenchment he betrayed a small, compulsive stinginess and a lack of regard for men who had rendered long and faithful service, which contrasted oddly with the splendour of his almost daily gifts to Mrs Simpson, and lost him a great deal of sympathy. Thus there was understanding for the servants at Buckingham Palace, who resented having their beer money cut down at a time when they were often employed loading cases of champagne, or furniture and plate destined for Mrs Simpson's flat. At the beginning of the reign a sanction was obtained, although with difficulty, that no man should be dismissed without alternative employment, but after the formation of the new Household even this rule was dropped. Reforms at Sandringham were suggested in a report drawn up by the Duke of York at the King's request (most of these were gradually carried through in the next reign), but on a visit to Balmoral later in his reign the King undertook the work himself.

Changes of personnel and establishment were also effected by King Edward at Balmoral, during a brief visit to Deeside – Sir John Wheeler-Bennett writes – In this case, however, the decisions were taken by His Majesty in consultation with the Crown authorities alone, and without reference to his brother, although the latter was in residence at Birkhall.

The Duke of York was pained at being thus ignored. He was also disturbed at the nature of the King's decisions regarding his Scottish home and its retainers.

And Sir John quotes the following letter from the Duke of York to his mother:

David only told me what he had done after it was over, which I might say made me rather sad. He arranged it all with the official people up there. I never saw him alone for an instant.[15]

However, the strangest demonstration of an obsessive concern with even quite small sums of money took place not at one of the royal palaces but at Fort Belvedere. One day King Edward sent for his head-housemaid and asked her what happened to the guests' soap after they had left the house. She replied that it was taken to the servants' quarters and finished there. The King instructed her in future to bring it to his rooms for his own use.

There is an odd little pendant to this story. One evening, more than twenty years later, the Duke of Windsor confided in amused tones to a guest at dinner in his house in Paris that his wife had a strange little foible. All soap from the guests' rooms was gathered up, he said, and taken to her room where she used it up herself.

In *A King's Story* the Duke of Windsor tells us he began his reign with a good heart and high aspirations and believed that 'the same energy and the same quality of mind' which had brought him success as Prince of Wales might find useful employment in discharging his duties as King. He denies any ambition to be a great reformer and says he would have been content to be an innovator 'to throw open the windows a little and to let into the venerable institution some of the fresh air that I had become accustomed to breathe as Prince of Wales'.[16]

Yet in spite of the Duke's eminently judicial tones the first thing that must strike any informed reader of his book is that in his long exile he had learned almost all the criticisms that have been made of his conduct and in a search for self-justification had made small adjustments to the past which render his version of it unreliable.* These pages are notable for the razor-edged skill with which, using the methods both of *suppresso veri* and *suggestio falsi*, he carries the war into the enemies' camp. A perfect example of this technique concerns the Sandringham clocks. He begins by saying that in reality the King remains immune from criticism only as long as he gives no cause for it, and then he goes on:

Even so innocent and logical an action as my turning back the clocks at Sandringham to Greenwich time produced a shaking of old heads and a muttering in the beards over my presumption in tampering with an old family idiosyncrasy.[17]

The point here is that the shaking of heads and the muttering in beards was produced not by an action which most people would agree was essentially innocent and logical, but because the order for it was given while his father lay dying and carried out while his body was still warm.

In reality the near-hysterical impatience which is apparent in the alteration of the clocks was noticeable in many of his actions. If one takes only those criticisms against which he is concerned to defend himself in his book, we find the following instances of behaviour which gave needless offence at the time and which must sooner or later have undermined even his popularity:

Very early in his reign he offended many people by the manner in which he decided to receive what are known as The Privileged Bodies (leading corporate elements of the community, including such bodies as Oxford and Cambridge Universities, the Corporation of the City of London, the Governor and Company of the Bank of England, the Archbishop and Clergy of the Province of Canterbury, the Royal Academy of Arts and so on). Having been told that there were twenty such bodies, each of which he would be required to receive separately and to the address of each of which he would be expected to reply, he decided to telescope the whole proceedings by receiving all twenty together and addressing one reply to them all.

* Not merely as King. He deals with criticisms of his conduct as Prince of Wales with very slight and incredibly neat alterations of fact.

Then, because of the period of court mourning, the four annual courts, at which women of position and debutantes were presented to the King, had been postponed, creating a backlog of some six hundred ladies waiting for presentation. It was therefore decided that presentations should take place at two garden parties at Buckingham Palace in July. For some reason which is not now clear, no adequate arrangement seems to have been made in case of rain. At the first of these functions, while the debutantes passed the King one after another, a storm broke out. He immediately gave orders that the presentations were to be taken as made and disappeared into Buckingham Palace. The shower soon passed over but the King did not reappear. This incident affected very few people directly, but it made history because, as the curtseying girls passed the King, a photographer caught the look of thunderous boredom on his face and the Press next morning revealed to the world the picture of a monarch clearly failing in one of the most elementary of his duties. The childishness which is apparent in this photograph was sometimes more endearingly revealed, however, and even the most censorious of his staff were amused when the King, wishing to avoid a meeting with Lord Wigram, climbed out of one of the windows of Buckingham Palace and went off to see Mrs Simpson.

Probably his most serious omission, however, was that, in spite of the exhortations of his staff, he went to church only two or three times throughout the whole summer.

Yet when he was good he was still very very good. If he felt in the mood he still performed what he called his 'field work' with the energy and enthusiasm and the happy knack for which he had become famous. In July he accompanied a band of Canadian Pilgrims at a ceremony at Vimy and following this gave a reception for them at Buckingham Palace. He had expected to be away on holiday by this time but owing to a change of his plans he was still in London. The Duke and Duchess of Gloucester therefore acted as hosts, but he made a surprise appearance and by his natural and friendly behaviour bewitched his guests as he had their countrymen in his youth. An incident which increased his enormous popularity occurred when he was returning from presenting the colours to three Guards regiments, the Grenadier, the Coldstream and the Scots. He noticed at the top of Constitution Hill a slight commotion in the crowd, and a moment later a man pushed through the police line and what later turned out to be a loaded revolver struck the pavement beside him and skidded under his horse's hooves. The police had actually been watching the man and when he raised his arm one of them had fallen upon him and caused the gun to jump out of his hand. The King believed that an attempt had been made on his life, but with courage that was a part of his nature and one of the most striking attributes of his family he rode on without flinching.

And in his private life, at Fort Belvedere, where fantasy merged with reality, and in London where he was always accompanied by Mrs Simpson, most people found him delightful. Because of his royalty his extraordinary immaturity passed as naturalness, an endearing lack of 'side'. Thus Chips Channon:

> Afterwards we played a game, introduced by the King. He gave us each ten matches and we sat huddled in a circle on the floor, and an empty bottle was sent for and the idea was to pile matches on the top, in turn, without letting the pile collapse. It seems silly and it was, but it was most innocent and enjoyable.[18]

And Lady Diana Cooper from Fort Belvedere:

> The King unchanged in manners and love. Wallis tore her nail and said 'Oh!' and forgot about it, but he needs must disappear and arrive back in two minutes, panting, with two little emery-boards for her to file the offending nail.
>
> His Majesty's evening kilt was better than ever. I think it was a mourning one, although he denied it – anyway pale dove-grey with black lines, and his exquisitely fitting jacket rather Tyrolled-up in shape and improved buttons, and instead of that commonish white lace jabot that is generally worn he had most finely pleated Geneva bands like John Wesley. On Sunday by request he donned his wee bonnet and marched round the table, his stalwart piper behind him, playing 'Over the sea to Skye' and also a composition of his own.

The King's composition, which had been written some years before, is described in *The Heart Has Its Reasons*. It pleased Mrs Simpson but it brought the wrath of George v down on his son's head.

> The servants are a bit hobbledehoy – Lady Diana goes on – because HM wants to be free of comptrollers and secretaries and equerries, so no one trains them. Last night one brought in the evening paper which carried something about the Ascot Enclosure coming to an end, and said 'Lord Gran*ard* (mispronounced) has just telephoned to ask Your Majesty if you know anythink at all about it?' 'Well, I must say,' said the King, 'I call that the top!! I really can't have messages of that kind. Can you see King George having that asked him?'[19]

Lady Diana was to say later that 'What would King George think of that?' was a favourite question of the King's and also that his desire to be free of fuss was sometimes embarrassing. 'Diana, will you have a glass of champagne?' 'Well, Sir, I'd much rather have white wine if there is any.' 'Yes, of course,' and off he would go and fumble about for too long looking for it himself.* One of the odd things about Fort Belvedere was that it seems to have been accepted ever since the days of Lady Furness that one of the women of the party should act as hostess. This was a convention not often observed in bachelor households in England except in a slightly embarrassed and half-hearted way by whoever knew the host best, and even then only in relation to such matters as the whereabouts of the lavatory, and her observance of it led Mrs Simpson to give a certain amount of offence. When she apologized to members of the King's Household, or

---

* Conversation with the author.

other people who had been his friends for years, for not being present to welcome them, and then warmly pressed them to a drink, what was intended as a courtesy was often resented as an insolent show of power. The division between Mrs Simpson and her friends – nowadays the King's friends – and everyone else grew more and more complete.

15

THE KING
AND NAZI GERMANY

One of the strangest aspects of Edward's reign is that he spent much of it under the surveillance of security officers. Mrs Simpson was the primary object of these attentions, but, since they were so often together, it was impossible to take this kind of interest in one of them without extending it to the other.

The idea that Mrs Simpson had German relationships which might make her a bad risk appears to have arisen in the first place because of certain of her social acquaintances, but, in a small area at a very high level, it was taken seriously.* In the period intervening it has never been disposed of. Middlemas & Barnes, having said that the government's main fears about the King were of indiscretion, continue: 'About Mrs Simpson greater fears existed'; and there is no reason to suppose they distort the relative weight of the anxiety felt.[1]

It would be difficult today to say exactly who the social contacts were that gave rise to such apprehension. Middlemas & Barnes say that she was believed to have close contacts with 'German monarchist circles' but looking back it is not easy to see to whom this particular term could be attached. There is a belief that she was on terms with the ex-Crown Prince, but again absolutely no real evidence for it. It was thought that Ribbentrop had made approaches to her, but she has stated categorically that she met him only twice and both times in the public atmosphere of a luncheon or dinner party. This leaves the fact that the German Embassy attempted to flatter

---

* Writing on the day of the Abdication, Blanche Dugdale recorded: 'Lunched at Ritz with Jack Wheeler-Bennett. ... [He] talked about Germany. He is convinced that Ribbentrop *used* Mrs Simpson but proofs are hard to come by. But I think Government and *Times* have them.'[2] It is most unlikely that *The Times* had them, although some members of its staff hinted darkly at the time. If the Government had them, all one can say is, the German Government had not.

the Prince of Wales by asking her to a great dinner party on 10 July 1935 as the only certain evidence that interest was taken in her.

It is not suggested that the precautions taken were superfluous, merely that there is no evidence that Mrs Simpson had contacts which would by themselves have justified them. That they were not superfluous needs no underlining when one turns to look at her unrivalled opportunities for securing information and the enormous publicity which by now surrounded her. No foreign embassy in London could have been quite without interest in her.

The vague uneasiness which was felt as long as her companion was Prince of Wales hardened to a shocked alertness once he was King. From now on the red boxes, the King's lack of method, the fact that none of his staff accompanied him to Fort Belvedere added up to an enormous security risk. To combat this, for the first and last time in history papers were screened in the Foreign Office before the red boxes went off to the King.

There is no doubt that in the state of the world at the time and on such evidence as was known of the King's state of mind and his life at Fort Belvedere, such precautions were necessary and reasonable. Whether the suspicions of Mrs Simpson were justified is a totally different matter. One can only repeat that no evidence has ever been made available to suggest that they were.

Among the captured German documents there are a good many which will later be shown to report the King in private conversations with members of the German Diplomatic Service and agents of the Third Reich. Secondly, there are the accounts given in the memoirs of German agents in London in 1936. Thirdly, there is an important memorandum from Ribbentrop to Hitler after the King abdicated. None of these so much as mentions the name of Mrs Simpson, while in later documents she is mentioned only as Duchess of Windsor because she accompanied the Duke.* There may be other documents which have not been found, or if found not published. Yet the point to be made here is that, if she was in contact with German agents or acting as an intermediary between Germany and the King, one would expect to find her name mentioned in at least some of the documents which have been found and published.

Nor, when one looks back at the period, can one think of a single reason why she should have added to her ambitions that of furthering the cause of the Third Reich. For most of the period with which we are concerned we know that she was engaged in binding Edward to her side and all the evidence suggests she believed she might become Queen of England, or at the very least the King's wife. How could she have hoped to further those extraordinary projects by giving aid to Nazi Germany?

It seems almost certain that the only danger to be feared from her was through her influence over the King. In this regard, there is a difference of

* See Chapters 27 and 30.

opinion as to whether she was in any way concerned with politics, many people arguing that her interests were of a purely social kind, while others, who knew her when Edward was on the throne, insist that she did show an interest in current affairs. (We have Lord Beaverbrook's evidence on this matter.) What seems likely is that she was ambitious for the King and that her role was the feminine one of wishing to find a sphere of interest for her man. It is not impossible that she urged him to strike out for himself, to ignore the stupidities of the politicians, to play an active part in saving the world from war: and not improbable that she admired the regimes that made the trains work. For more than this there is no evidence of any sort.

But, if the suspicions against Mrs Simpson seem to have been based on very little, there is no lack of evidence of the King's indiscretions. First there is the direct evidence of the captured German Foreign Office documents and the memoirs of the German agents in London. These often show a naive misunderstanding of where power resides in England and it is easy to dismiss each individually as the unimportant vapourings of a German agent who wished to ingratiate himself with the Nazi regime. Together they add up to a considerable body of evidence that the King differed from his Ministers in many aspects of their Foreign Policy and allowed himself a freedom of expression which was completely unconstitutional, creating in Germany an impression of warm sympathy and an exaggerated idea of his power and influence. In addition, as will be shown, it is possible to find corroboration by more trustworthy witnesses for almost everything that was reported to Germany.

The Ambassador to London at that time was Leopold von Hoesch, a member of the old regime who never became a Nazi, but who was, nevertheless, loyal to the government he served. Hoesch had spent most of his official life in Paris or London and he had been for many years on terms of friendship with many people in London society, including the Prince of Wales. He died in April 1936 ostensibly of a heart attack, but it was widely rumoured that he had been liquidated by his Nazi bosses. Thus Lady Diana Cooper writes (of a luncheon with Hoesch in 1934):

> It was in his instructive arms that I had waltzed all 1912 and 1913 and I was fond of him through war and peace. Two years later he was liquidated – through foul play, I have personally no doubt. Duff would never agree with this, but there is good evidence. Besides, Leopold Hoesch was no Nazi.[3]

It is scarcely necessary to underline the fact that, if the Nazis were responsible for his death, they killed a man whose long contacts and special position with the British aristocracy gave him unrivalled opportunities to learn and judge British feeling.

As early as April 1935 Hoesch reported to the Reich Chancellery that the Prince of Wales had inquired in great detail about the progress of the Anglo-German conversations then taking place in Berlin and was critical of the 'too one-sided attitude of the Foreign Office', while he had once again shown his 'complete understanding of Germany's position and aspirations'. During this conversation the Prince is also reported as saying that he had long foreseen that, if there were no general disarmament, Germany would one day take it upon herself to decide the scale of her armaments; but, in speaking of the German demand for the return of colonies, he had advised that 'in the interests of retaining Britain's sympathies', Germany should not put forward a formal demand with regard to the British mandated territories. However, Hoesch says this:

The Prince added that his first-hand experience of events during and after the war had firmly convinced him that in our era wars were, quite apart from their destructiveness, no longer a means for solving political problems. The subjugation of a vanquished people by victorious States was no longer conceivable. Therefore, war simply meant the destruction of one another by nations who were in fact created to work together. When it was over, war left behind a heap of ruins, and even when it proved possible to clear them away, no generally satisfactory solutions could in the nature of things be found between victors and vanquished, with the result that new causes for future conflicts were created. The fact that he had come to realize the futility and hence the reprehensible character of clashes of arms, however, by no means meant that he was a pacifist. Far from it. He desired his homeland to remain strong and to command respect, and he therefore understood very well that the Reich Government and the German people were inspired by a similar desire. He fully understood that Germany wished to face the other nations squarely, her head high, relying on her strength and conscious that Germany's word counted as much in the world as that of other nations.

I told the Prince in reply that what he had just said corresponded, as it were, word for word with the opinion of our Führer and Chancellor, such as I had heard it myself from his own lips.[4]

In June 1935 two months after this interview the Prince made a public statement which drew a reproof from his father. Speaking at the Annual Conference of the British Legion on 11 June he said:

There is one point which your President, when I was speaking with him the other day, brought up, and which also commended itself to me, and that was that a deputation or a visit might be paid by representative members of the Legion to Germany at some future time. I feel that there could be no more suitable body or organization of men to stretch forth the hand of friendship to the Germans than we ex-service men, who fought them and have now forgotten all about it and the Great War.

On the afternoon of the day on which he made this statement the Prince was sent for by the King who, reminding him how often he had told him not to mix in politics, especially foreign affairs, went on to say that the views the Prince had expressed were contrary to Foreign Office policy, and that he must never speak on controversial matters without consulting the government.

That the King's remarks were not merely correct in principle, but timely, was borne out by the reception given to the Prince's statement by the world Press. In England it was reported but received very little comment, such as it got being almost entirely favourable. In France there was a good deal of comment of a reserved and unenthusiastic kind; in America it was welcomed as an augury of a new era in Anglo-German relations bound to result in mutual benefit; but in Germany it was given a welcome out of all proportion to its importance. It received headlines in most newspapers, *Der Angriff* (founded by Dr Goebbels) giving it two lines of large type on the front page – The British Friendly Hand. An Appreciative Gesture by the English Heir Apparent – and it was widely treated as being a well-considered statement of some importance. The Berlin correspondent of the *Morning Post* summed up the German reception of the speech in these words:

As it is universally accepted here that the key to peace is in London ... the declaration by the Prince of Wales is regarded by Germany as being the seal to the friendship agreement between the two countries.... The fact that the Prince of Wales is accustomed to exercise extreme reserve in his public utterances, it is pointed out, gives stronger effect to his pronouncement yesterday.[5]

However, in his history of the British Legion, Graham Wootton is at great pains to clear the Prince of Wales of any personal initiative in this matter. The British Legion 'foreign policy' had for long rested on the belief that the ex-servicemen of all countries, including ex-enemy, had a part to play in the preservation and promotion of international friendship but their desire to see German ex-servicemen admitted to FIDAC (Fédérations Interalliées des Anciens Combattants) had been thwarted first of all by continental delegates, chiefly Belgian, and later by Hitler's rise to power. By 1935 Hitler was seriously interested in the possibilities of Anglo-German friendship and he sent Ribbentrop to London to try to promote it by any means. But, given that both the British Legion and the Prince of Wales had for long believed sincerely in the value of a rapprochement between the British and enemy ex-servicemen, it is unlikely that they would have the prescience immediately to change their policy merely because Hitler now endorsed it.

In addition, Colonel Crosfield, the Legion's 'Foreign Secretary', consulted Anthony Eden, then Lord Privy Seal, but always in touch with foreign affairs, as to the advisability of a visit to Germany by representatives of the Legion. The interview took place on 1 March 1935 and Eden informed Colonel Crosfield that there was no objection on the part of the Foreign Office to contact between the British Legion and the 'Front Kampferbund', but he warned him that he and those who went with him to Germany must expect to be the subject of a considerable amount of propaganda. It was only after this that the Chairman of the British Legion approached its Patron, the Prince of Wales, and asked him to commend the policy of establishing friendly contacts with ex-enemy ex-servicemen.

Evidence that the Prince was himself taken by surprise by the reception accorded to his speech comes once more from the German Foreign Office files. On 14 June Hoesch sent a telegram to the Foreign Office in which he said that the Prince's speech had been favourably commented on in the Press, and also in all the conversations he had had, although he had heard that Winston Churchill disapproved of it. And he said that at a Court Ball held the day before the Prince had talked to him at some length about his pronouncement, saying that he had not realized that it would have such a sensational effect, as it had seemed to him a perfectly natural statement and the expression of a widely held view. He added that he had encountered criticism in some quarters, especially in France, but that he was 'not retracting and was convinced that he had said the right thing'.[6]

The last words are illuminating. The Prince of Wales had made a mistake, one which, as has been shown, was understandable, yet nevertheless one which had had unexpectedly wide repercussions, which his father had recognized instantly,* and which would be remembered by many people for a long time; but he was 'not retracting and was convinced that he had said the right thing'.

In 1935 many people in England were under the influence of a strong feeling of guilt towards the Germans because of the Versailles Treaty, while at the same time, although there was already plenty of evidence of the inhumanities of Hitler's rule, it was still just possible in England to be ignorant of it (in 1936 many people who were later to be ardently anti-Nazi were still able to have ambivalent views about the German occupation of the Rhine).† It is understandable that the Prince of Wales in common with so many young men of his generation should have been looking for a cause, a philosophy which held out some hope for the future. (It is irresistible continually to refer to him as a young man – he was at this time forty-one.) In hindsight it is extremely unsympathetic that he should have found what he sought in Nazi Germany. Yet in justice it must be remembered that many another idealist found it in Soviet Russia, and that identification with either involved blindness, or at the very least confused thinking, in the face of murder, oppression and callousness on an unprecedented scale.

* Not only his father. Chips Channon wrote immediately afterwards: 'Much gossip about the Prince of Wales' alleged Nazi leanings; he is alleged to have been influenced by Emerald (who is rather éprise with Herr Ribbentrop) through Mrs Simpson. The Coopers are furious, being fanatically pro-French and anti-German. He has just made an extraordinary speech to the British Legion advocating friendship with Germany; it is only a gesture, but a gesture that may be taken seriously in Germany and elsewhere.'[7]

† When, in the war, details of the Nazis' treatment of Jews and political enemies were much publicized in England in order to arouse enthusiasm for the war, there were many people who expressed horrified surprise, although the evidence had been available for years.

It cannot be forgotten that most of the Prince's relations were German and that he had been happy there in his youth, and, even more important, that he had seen far more than most people of the effects of a weak democratic government on the poorest of his countrymen. But it has been remarked before that he was much subject to the temptation, common to people born at the centre of power, to measure his abilities by his proximity to able men rather than by any impartial estimate of his own qualities. Talking of America and lamenting that we did not send our best men there, he said to Harold Nicolson: 'What can I do? They will only say: "Here's that bloody Prince of Wales butting in." '[8]

And immediately following the British Legion speech, in direct defiance of his father's instruction not to speak on controversial matters, the Prince went out of his way at Berkhamsted School to give his views on a ban by the LCC on the use of guns, even wooden guns, by boys in the Cadet Corps of schools within their jurisdiction, describing the members of the LCC as cranks and their views as misguided. This speech also made a fairly wide impact and was not forgotten.

Least of all were these things forgotten by the Germans, who took an exaggerated view of the importance of Edward's accession. The first evidence of their interest is in a despatch by von Hoesch from London, dated 21 January 1936, in which, speaking of the new King, he says, as he has done before, that he is not a pacifist and desires a strong Great Britain but believes that war no longer affords a means for settling international disputes; he is convinced, moreover, that a fresh European war must result in the ruin of Europe, its submergence in Bolshevism and the destruction of all civilization. Then he goes on:

> You are aware from my reports that King Edward, quite generally, feels warm sympathy for Germany. I have become convinced during frequent, often lengthy, talks with him that these sympathies are deep-rooted and strong enough to withstand the contrary influences to which they are not seldom exposed.

And in a later passage he continues:

> King Edward will naturally have to impose restrictions on himself at first, especially in questions of foreign policy, which are so very delicate. But I am convinced that his friendly attitude towards Germany might in time come to exercise a certain amount of influence on the shaping of British foreign policy. At any rate, we should be able to rely upon having on the British throne a ruler who is not lacking in understanding for Germany and in the desire to see good relations established between Germany and Britain.[9]

At about the same time a report was apparently sent to Hitler himself by the Duke of Saxe-Coburg-Gotha.* Charles Edward, Duke of Coburg, had

---

*A carbon copy of this document was found together with a covering letter from the Duke of Coburg's Chief of Staff, Herr Nord, to Göring's Private secretary, Herr Gritzbach, of which the

a curious, rather sad life. A grandson of Queen Victoria, the son of Prince Leopold, he began life as an Englishman and inherited from his father the title of Duke of Albany. When he was fifteen and a schoolboy at Eton, the heir to the House of Saxe-Coburg-Gotha died and the Duke of Connaught, the next in succession, declined the honour for himself and his heirs. Queen Victoria herself intervened and decided that Charles Edward, to whom the succession descended, would have to be trained for the dukedom. This involved his being taken from Eton and brought up in Germany. As Duke of Saxe-Coburg-Gotha he rose to be a general in the Prussian Guard and in the First World War the duality of his inheritance shattered his life. He was denounced in Germany for being English and in England for being German. In England his name was struck off the roll of the Peerage and his Garter removed. Then in the Revolution of 1918 he was forced to abdicate the dukedom of Saxe-Coburg. From now on he was to be found in almost every reactionary or militarist organization which sprang up and in 1932 he took part in the creation of the 'Harzburg Front' in which the Deutschnationale (Conservative) Party associated itself with Hitler and his hitherto socially inadmissible Nazi Party. He joined the Brownshirt organization of which he was a Group Leader and became a Hitler man. It is improbable that he was ever admitted to the Inner Council of the Nazi Party but he paid a terrible price for his allegiance to it, being imprisoned at the end of the second war by the Americans and spending the last years of his life in poverty and indignity. He was the last duke of the historically distinguished House of Coburg.

In 1936 he was staying with his sister Princess Alice, Countess of Athlone, at Kensington Palace. According to her account, he had come to England to watch a football match between Germany and England; according to his own he was there as President of the Anglo-German Fellowship and was hoping to engage in consultations with a view to strengthening the Fellowship arrangements and extending them to other countries. In reality, he seems to have had some kind of roving commission to report to Hitler on the possibilities of Anglo-German agreement. He was excellently placed to meet people of importance many of whom were asked to meet him at dinner at Kensington Palace, but his membership of the Nazi Party was, nevertheless, well known.* The tone of his memorandum is unctuous and conspiratorial and suggests a desire to impress the Führer with his personal advantages. Several people are referred to as 'Eton schoolfellows

---

relevant passage reads: 'The Duke gathered from the conversation he had the day before yesterday that there was a certain interest on the part of the Colonel-General [Göring] for his mission in England. On the Duke's instruction I enclose herewith the January report to the Führer, which is perhaps somewhat revealing concerning a number of persons.'

* Visitors asked to Kensington Palace included Anthony Eden, Duff Cooper, Neville Chamberlain and 'Mr Astor' (described as Editor of *The Times* but presumably the Hon. J. J. Astor the proprietor of *The Times*, later Lord Astor of Hever).

of mine', a term which denotes an old Etonian whether a contemporary or not. In the case of Duff Cooper he begins his report:

Invited to dine at Kensington Palace. Was very unforthcoming at first, then became increasingly talkative when it emerged that we had been contemporaries at school at Eton.

He had several conversations with the King, (his first cousin once-removed) and he begins his report on these as follows:

First conversation on the day after the death of King George V on the occasion of carrying out the Führer's commission; a little more than half an hour (with pipe at fireside). Following this I accompanied him on his journey to Buckingham Palace.
Second conversation during my visit to Her Majesty the Queen at tea.
Third conversation between State dinner and reception at Buckingham Palace.

The opinions he attributes to the King include:

(1) An alliance Germany–Britain is *for him* an urgent necessity and a guiding principle for British foreign policy. Not, of course, against France, but, of necessity, including her. In this way safeguarding European peace. ...
(2) The League of Nations was a farce. Only a few nations decided things in the world – Germany, England, France, Japan, the United States. All other conferences, whether at Geneva or elsewhere, gave a false picture.
(3) Complained during second conversation about Russia and Litvinov, with whom he had, 'unfortunately', just had to shake hands.
(4) To my question whether a discussion between Baldwin and Hitler would be desirable, he replied in the following words: 'Who is King here? Baldwin or I? I myself wish to talk to Hitler, and will do so here or in Germany. Tell him that please.'
(5) Praised Ribbentrop's activity and conduct of negotiations on the naval agreement.

And the Duke of Coburg ends this remarkable document with the following sentences:

The King is resolved to concentrate the business of government on himself. For England, not too easy. The general political situation especially the situation of England herself, will perhaps give him a chance. His sincere resolve to bring Germany and England together would be made more difficult if it were made public too early. For this reason I regard it as most important to respect the King's wish that the non-official policy of Germany towards England should be firmly concentrated in one hand and at the same time brought into relations of confidence with the official policy. The, in this respect, peculiar mentality of the Englishman must be taken into account if we want to achieve success – which undoubtedly is attainable.
The King asked me to visit him frequently in order that confidential matters might be more speedily clarified in this way. I promised – subject to the Führer's approval – to fly to London at any time he wished.[10]

One aspect of the peculiar mentality of the Englishman is that he finds it extremely difficult to take seriously statements couched in language like this. Any credence he might be inclined to place on the word of the Duke of Coburg is dissipated by sentences like: 'Who is King here? Baldwin or I?' Nevertheless, there is ample evidence from more reliable sources that the King sometimes expressed opinions which could form a basis for this account.

For confirmation of his scorn for the Government's policy in backing the League of Nations, one need go no further than the Duke of Windsor's own memoirs. He tells us that when, after the Italian conquest of Ethiopia, Haile Selassie arrived in London, Anthony Eden suggested to him that it might be a popular gesture for the King to receive him. 'Popular with whom?' the King asked. 'Certainly not with the Italians.' He then refused to do as his Foreign Secretary asked, although, in order that he should not go away completely empty-handed, he designated his brother, the Duke of Gloucester, for the task. Following the description of this incident he says that there was an unspoken difference of opinion about Italy between himself and his Ministers.

> They had embarked on a futile policy of coercing Mussolini, which had utterly failed of its purpose and was only forcing him into ever closer relations with Hitler. ... I could see no point in indulging in half measures that could not succeed. It was more important in my eyes at this stage to gain an ally than to score debating victories in the tottering League of Nations.[11]

For the fact that the King was warmly pro-German one need look no further than the memoirs of people very close to him at the time. In the summer of 1936 Duff Cooper made a speech at the annual dinner in Paris of the Great Britain-France Society. In this speech, which was approved after certain changes by the Foreign Office, he said that Great Britain and France were bound to stand together, that their interests were identical and they were threatened by the same danger. The speech caused a sensation in the British Press and it was said that the Secretary of State for War had proposed a military alliance with France and openly threatened Germany. After recounting this Duff Cooper writes:

> The day after my return from Paris I met the King at dinner. As he approached me I saw that his face was heavy with displeasure. I expected a rebuke and I think he was preparing one, but suddenly the frown fled, giving way to his delightful smile as he laughed and said: 'Well, Duff, you certainly have done it this time.'[12]

Evidence that the Duff Coopers took the possibility of the King's anger seriously and with some apprehension is the fact that Lady Diana Cooper also writes an account of this meeting and in almost identical terms.

For the views the Prince is said to have expressed about Litvinov there is no independent evidence but no one who read his book with any attention would find them in the least unlikely.

Finally corroboration for the idea that the King had resolved to concentrate the business of government on himself can be found in *Chips*. Sir Henry Channon, as has been shown, was not an entirely reliable witness, but he had the opportunity to observe the King at the time and, unlike the Duff Coopers, he was not the least anti-German, hardly could he be said to be anti-Nazi. He cannot therefore be regarded as having any bias which might inspire criticism of the King on this particular matter. Yet in November 1936 we find him writing (admittedly immediately following an absurd suggestion that Winston Churchill might create a new party and rule the country):

> The King is insane about Wallis, insane. He, too, is going the dictator way, and is pro-German, against Russia and against too much slipshod democracy. I shouldn't be surprised if he aimed at making himself a mild dictator, a difficult task enough for an English King.[13]

In March 1936 German troops re-occupied the left bank of the Rhine, breaking the Versailles Treaty, signed under duress, but also the Locarno Pact which guaranteed the French, Belgian and German frontiers, with Britain and Italy as additional guarantors, signed voluntarily in 1925, which Hitler had promised to stand by. The question immediately arose should Britain and France reverse the situation by force of arms – the French army had an overwhelming superiority at the time – or should they accept a situation for which, because of feelings of guilt about Versailles, there was considerable support in the country.

In London at the time was a representative of the German News Agency (DNB), who was also a press attaché, named Fritz Hesse. In *Hitler and the English*, he describes in much detail conversations alleged to have been held between von Hoesch and Edward VIII immediately following the occupation of the Rhineland. Von Hoesch, he says, decided to use his long and intimate friendship with the King to appeal to him in the hope that he would preserve peace and he went to see the King (according to Hesse, secretly one night) with a memorandum he had prepared, of which the chief points were that the Franco-Russian pact contradicted the essential terms of the Treaty of Locarno, that the re-occupation of the left bank of the Rhine affected German territory only, and that Hitler was ready to replace the old Locarno Treaty by a new one and return to the League of Nations if the Rhineland question were happily solved. Hesse says that von Hoesch told Prince Bismarck and himself what passed at the interview. He had persuaded the King, he said, to send for Mr Baldwin. Then Hesse goes on:

I was with von Hoesch when the telephone rang. Von Hoesch whispered to me: 'The King!' and handed the second receiver to me, so that I could listen to the conversation.

'Hallo,' a voice called, 'is that Leo? David speaking. Do you know who's speaking?'

'Of course I do,' replied von Hoesch.

'I sent for the Prime Minister and gave him a piece of my mind. I told the old so-and-so that I would abdicate if he made war. There was a frightful scene. But you needn't worry. There won't be a war.'

Von Hoesch put down the receiver. He jumped up and danced round the room. 'I've done it, I've outwitted them all, there won't be a war! Herr Hesse, we've done it! It's magnificent, I must inform Berlin immediately.'[14]

It is not easy to take seriously the piece of jolly Germanic English attributed to the King. Nor indeed need one do so. It is necessary to deal with Hesse's evidence here because it has been so much quoted, but he is not a reliable witness, being given to exaggeration and distortion. Moreover, the use of the name 'David' makes the whole account highly suspect. His Majesty may have been called 'David' by the women he loved, but apart from this the name was never used except by members of his family. Even old and close friends such as the Metcalfes invariably addressed him as 'Sir'. Nevertheless, it seems likely that, even if the whole telephone conversation was his invention, Hesse did hear something in the course of his duties which inspired it. In any case on 11 March von Hoesch sent the following telegram to the Foreign Ministry:

Today I got into indirect touch with the Court. The view prevailing in the authoritative quarter is that our proposals could well constitute a basis on which to construct a lasting peace system; in other respects, too, there is understanding for the German point of view.

The directive given to the Government from there is to the effect that, no matter how the details of the affair are dealt with, complications of a serious nature are in no circumstances to be allowed to develop.[15]

There is also in the German Foreign Office Documents a Minute of a telephone conversation between a Dr von Stutterheim, Foreign Correspondent of the *Berliner Tageblatt* and Paul Scheffer, its editor, which had a marginal note. To be submitted to the St[ate] Secretary and Foreign M[inister] Aschmann, and which reads as follows:

The King is taking an extraordinarily active part in the whole affair; he has caused a number of important people in the Government to come and see him and has said to them: 'This is a nice way to start my reign.' [Quoted in English in the original.] The King won't hear of there being a war. He is absolutely convinced that what must now be done is to get over the 'breach of law' as quickly as possible and get on to the practical discussion of the Fuhrer and Chancellor's proposals. In view of the tremendous influence possessed by the King and his immense energy, due importance must be attached to this where Germany is concerned.[16]

On 8 May, the German Ambassador to Italy sent the Foreign Ministry a copy of a memorandum by 'a reliable confidant' about a conversation which took place 'about a week ago between the King of England and the Italian Ambassador'. The enclosure was as follows:

About a week ago an exhaustive conversation took place between the King of England and the Italian Ambassador, Grandi, at the house of a mutual friend. During this conversation the Italian Ambassador is said to have tried to give the King of England a very exhaustive account of the Italian Government's policy, emphasizing in particular that Italian policy did not in any way run counter to British interests, but was, on the other hand, determined to force the Abyssinian conflict to a conclusion even at the risk of a European war. He, Grandi, could only confirm quite unequivocally that Mussolini's determination and his decision must be regarded as his last word. But Grandi also attached extreme importance to convincing the King of England that the Italian Government wished to uphold and respect absolutely British rights and interests, as they resulted from the various protocols.

In reply the King allegedly expressed profound regret that such serious tension should have developed in Anglo–Italian relations.

In his view, however, the prestige of the British Empire was not at stake in the present conflict. The British Empire, where its status and prestige were concerned could not be identified with the policy of any one Government or with the Parliamentary policy of a particular period. For peace in Europe it was absolutely essential that two great nations, Germany and Italy, should be afforded full satisfaction by granting them, with full realization of their needs, the necessary colonial markets.

There is a footnote to the document at this point referring to an important marginal note. This is in von Neurath's* handwriting and reads: 'The King had expressed this view with regard to Germany to me, too.' The document then continues:

This should be done in such good faith as to make possible a policy of complete cooperation and complete understanding between Britain, France, Germany and Italy. The King could not say how much he had already done in this sense as Prince of Wales or what he intended to do in this sense in the future. Although under the parliamentary system the government was not in the King's hands, he would continue to try to do what appeared to him to be possible and necessary. The King considered an armed conflict between Britain and Italy over Abysinnia to be absolutely out of the question. He hoped, rather, that an understanding would speedily be reached on this problem. The League of Nations, as at present organized, must, in his judgment, be considered dead.[17]

Grandi's report on his conversation with the King of England, which was sent by special courier to Rome, is said to have greatly impressed both Mussolini and Suvich, though both refrained from expressing any opinion.

Edward also figures in what historically is regarded as one of the most important documents of the pre-war era. This is a memorandum from

* German Foreign Minister from 1932–8.

Ribbentrop to Hitler dated 2 January 1938, headed *The Possibilities of Agreement with Great Britain. Memorandum for the Fuhrer.*

Ribbentrop came to London as Ambassador in 1936 in order to make a last attempt to reach an understanding with England which would leave Germany free to make war in the East. 'The aim of German Foreign Policy,' he says in his memoirs, 'was to convince Britain that if a choice had to be made between a general alliance against Britain and an Anglo-German alliance, Germany would prefer the latter.'[18] By the end of his stay he no longer believed in the possibility of any agreement and in the memorandum of 2 January 1938 he sets out his reasons for the opinions he had reached. The importance of this document is that it marks the change in Hitler's policy towards Great Britain. In future he would look for his friends elsewhere. On the narrower subject of Edward VIII, it shows the extent of German misunderstanding of his power and influence. In his conclusion Ribbentrop writes:

I have worked for friendship with England for years, and nothing would make me happier than the possibility of its achievement. When I asked the Fuhrer to send me to London I was sceptical about the likelihood of success, but, because of Edward VIII, it seemed that a final attempt should be made. To-day I no longer have faith in any understanding. England does not desire in close proximity a paramount Germany, which would be a constant menace to the British Isles. On this she will fight. National Socialism, however, is thought capable of anything. Baldwin already apprehended this and Edward VIII had to abdicate, since it was not certain whether, because of his views, he would co-operate in an anti-German policy.[19]

There is therefore so much evidence that the government had reason to apprehend 'indiscretion' by the King that, however one evaluates any particular document, one cannot ignore either the quantity and variety of the witnesses or the similarity of their evidence. But none of it was available at the time or for that matter for many years after. How then were the King's sympathies so well known in England – if only in what is called informed circles? Every writer about his reign has had to deal with the rumours, while it is common in memoirs or other published papers to come across remarks expressing relief at his abdication because of fear of his pro-German sympathies.

The answer is that in a general way and as far as social gossip is concerned it was learned from the King himself. Edward was straightforward in all things and he was obtusely, obdurately opinionated. His gifts for handling a crowd or charming an individual, more especially his unique position, had given him a quite unreal idea of his own capacities and mental equipment, and to the end of his life he never saw any reason to refrain from the expression of views which were quite out of tune with the policies of his country. He had only the haziest notions of the behaviour proper to a constitutional monarch and Chips Channon is completely correct in describing him as 'against too much slipshod democracy'. He also had a quite irrational attitude towards Soviet Russia. On the eve of the 1945 General Election Marietta FitzGerald, a young American journalist assigned to write about it, sat next to the Duke of Windsor at dinner in New York, and asked him for his views.* 'One thing you can be certain of,' he told her, 'if Labour wins you can tear up your piece because Russia will take over the country in a few days.' To the end of his life he felt no diffidence in expressing the view that in the Second World War 'England had not known who her friends were', and in his book published in 1951 he sees nothing inappropriate in witticisms at Anthony Eden's expense because the latter had not wished him to travel in Italy in 1936. Less widely known and more unattractive is the fact that this man, who is sometimes believed to have earned the enmity of the British Government by being too radical in outlook, was 'against too much slipshod democracy'. Towards the end of his life he used to astonish Englishmen by dissertations on the advantages that might accrue to the United States of America through the election of Senator Goldwater.

In 1936 it was not, of course, a question of patriotism, which does not enter into it. The duties of a patriot may be differently understood by different people. Edward VIII has often been compared to Lindbergh, and, while it is unlikely that his influence was anything like as great, there is some validity in the comparison. Both were youthful heroes. Both had exceptional opportunities to form erroneous judgments. Both believed in the power and might of Germany. Neither understood that this had to be fought, if necessary to the death.

But, if Edward made no bones about his sympathies either as King or as Duke of Windsor, it would be wrong to believe that his views on Germany had any influence on the attitudes or actions of the government at the time of the Abdication. Anthony Eden could not help being aware of them, because there seems no doubt that the King pressed them upon him himself.† However, the degree of departmentalization in government is much greater than most people realize and, although Baldwin at least must also have known of the King's tendencies, it is improbable that the rest of the Cabinet knew much more about these matters than anyone else in the direct path of gossip. According to Hugh Dalton the Opposition took account of the 'widespread rumours that he [the King] was unduly sympathetic to the German Nazis, and a general feeling that, for a constitutional monarch, he was inclined to hold, and to express, some dangerously

---

* Later Mrs Ronald Tree.

† Both Brian Inglis and Middlemas & Barnes refer to a despatch from Jan Masaryk to Benes reporting a conversation with Eden in which the Foreign Secretary disclosed how worried the Foreign Office was with the King's increasing and disturbing intervention in foreign affairs. Eden is said to have remarked that if the King went on like that, there were ways and means of compelling him to abdicate. Much persistence and nearly three years of research have failed to turn up this document.

personal views'.[20] But one can be certain that the matter was never discussed in Cabinet. The minutes of the Cabinet of 27 November 1936, which sat to consider the crisis, and those of seven subsequent Cabinet meetings are officially closed until the year 2037. But Mr Montgomery Hyde has already pointed out that, as several Ministers, notably Neville Chamberlain and Samual Hoare, kept a private record of the meetings, and as the Index of the Cabinet conclusions as well as two long letters from Lord Zetland (in the India Office) to Lord Linlithgow (Viceroy of India) somehow escaped the net, it has been possible for fairly complete reconstructions of these meetings to be published.* Lord Beaverbrook always had early and accurate information of what had taken place (his informant is said to have been Samuel Hoare), while Baldwin gave Tom Jones his reasons for telling only five men – Chamberlain, Halifax, MacDonald, Simon and Runciman – of his second meeting with the King, as follows: 'You can't,' he said, 'tell a thing like that to the whole Cabinet. Out it would come.'[21] The government were extremely anxious to confine the issue to the simple one of marriage and there is no doubt that they succeeded.

* *Baldwin: The Unexpected Prime Minister*, pp. 476, 486, 489, 494 and 501.

16

THE *NAHLIN*

In the early days of the King's reign it did not occur to anyone that he intended to marry Mrs Simpson. In the first place, she was married to Mr Simpson, and this by itself made the idea so unlikely that it only gradually began to take hold of men's minds. Even Walter Monckton who, long before the abdication crisis when he represented the King, was on terms of close friendship with him, recorded that he always under-estimated the strength of the King's devotion and 'of their united will'.* And he says in words which are the nearest to criticism he ever comes:

I thought, throughout, long before as well as after there was talk of marriage, that if and when the stark choice faced them between their love and his obligations as King-Emperor, they would in the end each make the sacrifice, devastating though it would be.[1]

Yet there were signs which, if they had been believed, would have made the King's intentions perfectly plain. One, so odd that it was barely understood by those concerned, was that in the long discussions about the new Civil List, the King laid much emphasis on the provisions to be made for a Queen, concentrating on this aspect more than any other. A second, which was also disregarded, was a strange story told by Sir Maurice Jenks, a former Lord Mayor of London, to Baldwin.

He said that, some time before, Ernest Simpson had applied for admission to a Masonic Lodge over which he, Jenks, presided, his candidature being supported by the Prince of Wales. Simpson was refused entry and

---

* Walter Monckton, who was to play a considerable part in the abdication crisis and whose notes kept at the time are invaluable source material, was in later life to have a distinguished political career – during the war at the Ministry of Information and afterwards at the Ministry of Labour where he initiated the policy of conciliation which ruled industrial relations until 1970. At the time of the abdication he had a great reputation as a barrister, and he owed his position as adviser to the King to the fact that they had made friends when at Oxford together.

the Prince of Wales, who naturally demanded an explanation, was told that it was against the Masonic law for the husband of his mistress to be admitted. The Prince gave his word that this was not the situation and Simpson's candidature was accepted. Now Simpson had come to see Jenks – 'the mari complaisant is now the sorrowing and devoted spouse' – and told him that the King wished to marry his wife. Simpson had said that he would like to leave England but that would make divorce easier and Jenks suggested that Baldwin should see him. Baldwin refused flatly, saying that he was the King's adviser not the Simpsons', but he saw Wigram with Davidson present, and told him all he had heard. Walter Monckton was also told, first by Sir Maurice Gwyer and later by Sir Lionel Halsey. Monckton writes:

> I did not know Mr Simpson, nor indeed have I ever spoken to him, but I confess that I was afraid (and so, I think, were my informants) of the possibility of blackmail upon an extravagant basis; and I did not believe that the King had said what was attributed to him at third hand: nor was I at liberty to pass the rumour on to him.[2]

However, years later, after the war had begun, Walter Monckton met a man named Bernard Rickatson-Hatt, editor-in-chief of Reuters and an old friend of the Simpsons. Rickatson-Hatt then told him that he had been at York House with the King and Ernest Simpson. When he had got up to go, Simpson had asked him to remain, and turning to the King had made a dramatic statement. Wallis, he said, would have to choose between them; and he asked the King what he intended to do about it? Did he intend to marry her? The King then rose from his seat and said: 'Do you really think that I would be crowned without Wallis by my side?'[3]

Walter Monckton in reporting this goes on to observe that Rickatson-Hatt's account fitted the dates of Sir Maurice Jenks's story to Baldwin. So curious was the whole atmosphere of the Abdication that this version of what happened is generally accepted and no one has ever questioned the preposterous words attributed to the King in speaking to another man about his wife.

Rickatson-Hatt also gave Monckton the following analysis of Mrs Simpson's character which the latter wrote down because 'he clearly has a considerable knowledge of the parties – apart perhaps from the Duke [of Windsor] – and a completely objective outlook together with a good memory, and some considerable insight into the character of Mr and Mrs Simpson'.

> I asked him about her attitude towards Simpson. He said that Simpson was extremely fond of her but that she was incapable of being in love with any man. She was extremely attractive to men, amusing and kind on most occasions but capable of hardness. She had often used the same technique which I think has used with the Duke, namely making him supremely unhappy and then over-

whelming him with kindness and affection in making up the difference. He remained and I think still remains extremely fond of her. Rickatson-Hatt says she is not the sort of woman who could be relied upon to stand by a man in poverty or misfortune. She likes the good things of the earth and is fundamentally selfish. He thinks her intention was to have her cake and eat it. She was flattered by the advances of the Prince of Wales and the King and enjoyed his generous gifts to her to the full. She thought that she could have them and at the same time keep her home with Simpson.

Long before February 1936 Simpson had tackled her on the matter though he had never up to then, apparently, made a direct approach to the King. She had always told him that he could trust her to look after herself; she enjoyed the attention she received and there was no harm in it. Rickatson-Hatt himself thinks that but for the King's obstinacy and jealousy the affair would have run its course without breaking up the Simpson marriage.[4]

Whether or not the King spoke the words to Simpson attributed to him by Rickatson-Hatt, he began now with the utmost coolness to thwart conventional ideas of discretion in his relationship with Mrs Simpson, and to make it plain that she was to occupy a position never before accorded to the King's favourite. On 27 May he gave a dinner at St James's Palace to which were invited Lord and Lady Louis Mountbatten, Lord and Lady Wigram, Mr Duff and Lady Diana Cooper, Lord and Lady Chatfield, Mr and Mrs Baldwin, Mr and Mrs Lindbergh, Lady Cunard and Mr and Mrs Simpson, and he placed Lady Cunard and Mrs Simpson one at each end of the table. This admixture of the two worlds he was usually so anxious to keep separate seemed designed to cause comment. The following morning the King made quite sure of it by publishing the list of his guests in the Court Circular, an official and wholly unusual method of announcing his friendship with the Simpsons.

Before the first of these dinner parties, at the end of May, the King had said to Mrs Simpson: 'Sooner or later my Prime Minister must meet my future wife.'[5] This, according to her account, was the first time he mentioned marriage to her, although later in the year he told Walter Monckton that he had intended to marry her ever since 1934. At about the same time Mrs Simpson discovered that her marriage to Ernest Simpson was dead, that he had found a new emotional centre, in short another woman. She therefore decided on divorce, a decision which she imparted to the King.

It would be wrong, the Duchess of Windsor tells us, dropping into the sententious, woman's paper style which, so open about much of her early life, she invariably uses when speaking of the King or the Abdication, it would be wrong he told her for him to try to influence her in any way. 'You can only do what you think is right for you.'[6] But he arranged for her to have legal advice. According to her own account she went to see Sir George Allen but this is almost certainly a mistake. Walter Monckton says that the King and Mrs Simpson visited him several times at his Chambers during the summer to discuss the divorce and the King said that he was not going to allow her friendship with him to prevent her from obtaining release from her husband. He asked Monckton to advise her whom to consult.

I had a talk with them both at tea at York House and it was as a result that she came to my Chambers and I introduced Toby Matthews, a partner in Charles Russell & Co., to her. She told me in answer to a direct question, and I think she told Toby too, that she wanted to be free of her present marriage; that she was getting older, but might well meet someone with whom she might happily marry. She said to me in the little lane behind the exits of Harcourt Buildings that it was ridiculous to imagine that she had any idea of marrying the King. At that time I thought so too, but I knew that the divorce proceedings would be likely to cause increased risks of publicity damaging to the King, and I was not altogether surprised when Toby told me that after discussion with his partner Gerald Russell he had decided that his firm could not act. It was as a result of this decision that I introduced Mrs Simpson to Theodore Goddard who acted for her throughout the proceedings.

Monckton says that by the end of June he became seriously disturbed 'not by the prospect of the King marrying Mrs Simpson if and when she got her freedom, but about the damage which would be done to the King if he continued to make his friendship with her even more conspicuous'. Eventually he decided to ask Winston Churchill for advice, and found him extraordinarily sympathetic and ready to help.

He told me how he refused to sit at dinner with people who criticised the King. But he was plainly anxious about what I told him. He was all against divorce proceedings in which he saw no advantage; the existence of Mr Simpson was a safeguard. Moreover he was anxious that I should make plain to the King how important it was that his friendship should not be flaunted in the eyes of the public. He particularly said that Mrs Simpson ought not to go as a guest to Balmoral, although no doubt if the King wanted to see her while he was there she could stay with someone else nearby.

At the dinner given by the King on 10 July at York House Churchill let him know that he had seen Monckton who had confided to him his anxieties and the King then sent for Monckton who told him Churchill's views.

He [the King] made the old answer about divorce, that he didn't see why Mrs Simpson should stay tied to an unhappy marriage simply because she was his friend. And as to the suggestion of keeping the friendship quiet, he said he thought I should have known him better; he was not ashamed of his friendship, and he was not going to hide it or try to deceive people.[7]

None of these things was known at Buckingham Palace until several months later, but the King's Household had other things to worry about. Edward showed a total disregard, even a lack of comprehension, of the lines he was expected to draw between his public and official position and his private life. An innovation for which he was responsible and which survived the test of time was the foundation of what is today known as the Queen's Flight. For the sake of economy he arranged that the Air Ministry should take over the upkeep of his aeroplane and the salaries of his pilot and mechanics. Yet he continued to use it for the benefit of his friends and even for the importation of goods on which duty should have been paid. This almost innocent assumption of his inalienable right to do as he pleased was paralleled by the use he made of the two detectives provided for his protection by Scotland Yard, one of whom as often as not was detailed to look after Mrs Simpson. His staff were nervous that a question might be asked on these matters in the House of Commons which they were afraid would produce an awkward situation, but they, nevertheless, still believed that they were dealing with different manifestations of the new King's irresponsibility and lack of understanding of his constitutional position, and did not understand that these were deliberately flown signals of his intention to raise Mrs Simpson to a position where the attentions he bestowed on her would become appropriate. No one could control the King, indeed no one seems to have been able to speak to him, and the only hope therefore lay in the idea, which seems to have occurred to almost everyone concerned with the events of this time, that sooner or later he would tire of 'the lady of the moment' as he had of others, and that, once freed from his obsession, all the capacity for good, the genuine devotion to duty, the straightforward nature, the extraordinary charm and flair for public life, would reassert themselves and balance the immaturity and lack of discipline, the instinctive and genuine dislike of so much of his job and the life he had to lead, and enable him with the aid of a well-trained staff to make a good King. Since no one could solve the problem, the temptation was strong to hope that, if one refrained from looking at it for a while, it might go away.

However, this reckoned without the King, who now went on holiday. He had originally wished to go to the South of France and had intended to rent a villa. However, there was a good deal of social unrest in France in the summer of 1936, and a combination of sit-down strikes and the proximity of the Spanish Civil War persuaded the Ambassador to Paris that it would be unwise for him to stay in that country. Edward therefore chartered a large yacht, the *Nahlin*, owned by Lady Yule, and invited a party to accompany him on a cruise along the Dalmatian coast. The numbers of this party fluctuated a little but at one time or another Mrs Fitzgerald was there, Mr and Mrs Humphrey Butler, Lady Diana and Duff Cooper, and among the King's staff, Captain Lascelles, Godfrey Thomas and John Aird.

The King had originally intended merely to take a holiday and he ventured forth, under the romantic rules of an earlier century, as the Duke of Lancaster. This fiction had soon to be dropped because he was given a vociferous welcome wherever he went, and because, in addition, his journey acquired a semi-official aspect owing to the necessity for him to fall in with the wishes of the Foreign Office. He had proposed to join the *Nahlin* at Venice but the Foreign Office objected to his passing through Italy at that time.* They made no objection to his visiting the Greek islands and were actually in favour of a visit to Istanbul. In Athens he was met by the Prime Minister, General Metaxas, with whom he had an interview lasting two hours, and afterwards the diplomatic representatives in each of the capitals he visited naturally wished to bring him into contact with the political leaders. In Istanbul he had two meetings with Kemal Ataturk and other cabinet ministers and diplomats, and, travelling home by train, he was joined by King Boris in Bulgaria, who accompanied him to Sofia, where he was welcomed by members of the Bulgarian Government. On his journey through Yugoslavia he was accompanied by the Prince Regent, Prince Paul, and met by Dr Stoyadinovitch, the Prime Minister, and in Vienna he paid a call on President Miklas and received the chancellor, Dr Schuschnigg, in a half-hour audience at the British Legation. In retrospect it was apparent that a journey with so many political and diplomatic aspects should not have been undertaken without the Foreign Secretary in attendance, but this was no fault of the King's, who, apart from a slight over-enthusiasm for Ataturk with whom he conversed in German, and whom he was said to have asked to London, carried out his part with great success, creating goodwill wherever he went; while once more it was no fault of his if, in the atmosphere of the time, this was of purely temporary effect.

However, it is not for its diplomatic results that the King's holiday will be remembered but for the holiday voyage of the *Nahlin* along the Dalmatian coast and through the Greek waters to Turkey. For this journey was the beginning of what would so shortly be the end, the point at which every historian writing of the Abdication must inevitably start.

The King and his party made a night journey by train to Yugoslavia, crossing the border at Jessenice where they were met by Prince Paul and the British Chargé d'Affaires, Mr Balfour,† and where their coach was coupled up to the Yugoslav royal train. They then travelled on through Zagreb and reached the port of Sibenik the following morning, 10 August. Here there awaited them not merely the yacht *Nahlin* and the two destroyers the *Grafton* and *Glow Worm*, which were to accompany the yacht, but in addition a mob of about twenty thousand peasants dressed in native costume assembled to welcome them. And it was immediately remarked that this laughing, shouting mob were as much interested in Mrs Simpson as they were in the King, a curious circumstance considering that no English crowd would have recognized her and a tribute to the efforts of American pressmen, who now proceeded to follow the yacht wherever she went.

*An objection which the Duke of Windsor still saw as a fit subject for pleasantries at Anthony Eden's expense when he wrote his memoirs.

† Later Sir John Balfour, he had a series of meetings with the King, now and later, which he has recorded in a paper called *Encounters with the Windsors*, much quoted here.

This exuberant welcome was to be repeated at every port of call, on one occasion the whole of the King's party being nearly pushed into the sea by the crowd as they returned to the yacht: while in Dubrovnik they were greeted with a cry of 'Zivila Ljubav', the Yugo-Slav equivalent of 'Vive l'amour'.

The couple who were the occasion of this enthusiasm were elated by a sense that all the world loves a lover and, whereas they might have been expected to feel some anxiety, even some guilt, at this extraordinarily public recognition of their relationship, they felt only happiness. 'It delighted both of us that strangers of uncomplicated hearts should wish us well.'[8]

Lady Diana Cooper now joined the party to christen the two destroyers which guarded the yacht the 'Nanny-boats', and to give us the following authentically charming glimpse of her host:

There's no traffic in Ragusa and there are baroque and gothic churches and palaces and monasteries. The people were mostly in national dress and on this occasion they were all out in orderly rows, both sides of the streets that the Consul had mapped out for our tour of the sights. They were cheering their lungs out with looks of ecstasy on their faces.

The King walks a little ahead talking to the Consul or Mayor, and we follow, adoring it. He waves his hand half-saluting. He is utterly himself and unself-conscious. That I think is the reason why he does some things (that he likes) superlatively well. He does not *act*. In the middle of the procession he stopped for a good two minutes to tie up his shoe. There was a knot and it took time. We were all left staring at his behind. You or I would have risen above the lace, wouldn't we, until the procession was over? But it did not occur to him to wait, and so the people said: 'Isn't he human! Isn't he natural! He stopped to do up his shoe like any of us!'[9]

In retrospect there may appear something almost purposeful about the conduct of the King on the *Nahlin*. Everywhere they went he and Mrs Simpson were photographed together, passing through Salzburg, driving in Athens, bathing in the sea, and on one occasion in a small boat, her hand on his arm and he looking down at her. Every line of his face and body told, and still tell, of his unutterable devotion.*

Once more the King defied the conventions of the day and worried his staff by removing most of his clothes. Passing through the Corinth Canal he stood on the bridge wearing nothing but shorts and a pair of binoculars while the yacht passed so close to the cheering crowds on the banks that it seemed they could have touched him. And at Athens he insisted, against strong protests from his staff, on dining with Lord Dudley in a little café in the port.

After Athens the boat continued leisurely in stages to Istanbul. But now, so different is life from how we imagine it, no one any longer enjoyed the

* See page 228.

holiday. The King had relapsed into a mood which subdued and disheartened his guests. Anxiously they searched their memories. What could have happened? What had been said? Desperately they tried at meals to amuse or interest him, even to keep up some show of the amity which had gone from their association. No lip service to courtesy disturbed his melancholy, no concern for his guests diminished an unrelenting fit of the sulks.

'What are the plans for the day, Sir?'

'Wallis, what are the plans for the day?'

It will never be known what passed in his mind. Two possibilities suggest themselves. The first, that he simply considered his position. Perhaps at this moment, in spite of the deliberate exhibitionism, the determined indiscretions, he reflected on his future: on the sacrifice that must be made in one direction or the other, of the dereliction of duty which had become inevitable, either to the woman whose name he had so completely and publicly associated with his own, or to the crown.

There is another possibility however. While the yacht rested in Greek waters the conversation turned one night to the relationship between King George of Greece and a woman who was his constant companion.

'Why doesn't he marry her?' the American, Mrs Simpson, asked.

Upon which one of the guests replied in astonished tones with a simple statement of fact: it was impossible for the King to marry a woman who was both a commoner and already married. No one ever related this innocent answer to the King's mood (although the impact of both question and answer were strong enough to be communicated thirty years later) because no one had any idea what passed in his mind, no smallest inkling of his intentions. Yet he had already given several demonstrations that those who were not with him were against him, as well as of an absolute disregard for old ties or outworn affections. Did he in his disturbed state feel the irrational anger which can be provoked in an undisciplined mind by a messenger with bad news?

It might have been so, or it might have been a mixture of the two, one being a starting point for the other. As long ago as when he toured India with his cousin Mountbatten, the King had had fits of melancholy.

In any case the party broke up without regrets and the King travelled through Bulgaria and Yugoslavia to Vienna and from there to Zurich, where Wing-Commander Fielden flew him home in an aeroplane of the King's Flight.

Arrived in England, he went straight to Fort Belvedere but after an hour or two he left and went to Buckingham Palace to dine with Queen Mary. He told her at dinner that he meant to spend the last two weeks of September at Balmoral, which he says was a source of pleasure to her, signifying as she thought a return to traditional ways. If this was so, her pleasure was short-lived. It was customary for the list of guests at Balmoral to record the names of Cabinet ministers, bishops, admirals, generals and so on. In 1936 the King, who felt he gave sufficient of his time to such dignitaries when in London, asked whom he pleased. Among his guests there were many people who bore names that had been among those of the guests at Balmoral through the years – the Duke and Duchess of Marlborough, the Duke and Duchess of Buccleuch, the Duke and Duchess of Sutherland, the Mountbattens and the Roseberys. The Duke and Duchess of York were at Birkhall, and the Duke and Duchess of Gloucester at Abergeldie, near by. The King had nevertheless decided in the words of his future wife 'that this grouping would be improved by a leaven of less exalted but nonetheless stimulating people'[10] and her name as well as that of Mr and Mrs Herman Rogers were recorded in the Court Circular. So also was that of Mr Esmond Harmsworth.

Nor was this all. If one had to choose one example to illustrate the extent of the King's alienation and oblivion to everything except the emotion which dominated his life, one could hardly choose better than the action with which he began his holiday. Months before he had been asked to open some new hospital buildings in Aberdeen on a day in September, and with ineffable negligence had refused on the grounds that he would still be in mourning for his father (there had been no mourning at Ascot in June and it was part of his whole philosophy to reduce the traditional mourning), deputing his brother the Duke of York to take his place (although one would suppose that what applied to one brother applied also to the other). On the day that the Duke undertook this task the King himself was seen openly arriving at Ballater station to meet Mrs Simpson, whom he put into the front of his car beside him, while the Herman Rogers got into the back. This became extremely widely known, indeed exaggerated, and not merely in Scotland. Chips Channon recorded a month or so later:

The Mediterranean cruise was a Press disaster, the visit to Balmoral was a calamity, after the King chucked opening the Aberdeen Infirmary, and then openly appeared at Ballater station on the same day, to welcome Wallis to the Highlands. Aberdeen will never forgive him.[11]*

The rest is mainly surmise. According to one authority, 'the Duchess of York openly showed her resentment at being received by Mrs Simpson',[12] and certainly, if the latter carried as far as Balmoral her belief that one of the women in a bachelor household should act as hostess, one can understand that it might be regarded as very insolent indeed.

However, by now it did not need personal or private antipathy for the King's family to regard Mrs Simpson with anxiety and horror, because the American papers were in full cry. Almost daily articles and photographs appeared showing the two together, while rumour became more and more scurrilous. On 23 September the *New York Woman* pointed out that if

* The King did not 'chuck' the visit to which he had never agreed.

Ernest Simpson should wish to divorce his wife the King could not be sued for adultery in England.

Meanwhile at Balmoral the King took the opportunity to devise economies, and Mrs Simpson to introduce the three-decker toasted sandwich to the kitchens.

By 1 October the King was back in London and this time he went straight to Buckingham Palace. He hated Buckingham Palace and he makes the surprising statement that it had a dank and musty smell which assailed him every time he set foot inside the King's Door. He never lost the feeling of not belonging there and he says that he made few changes because of a presentiment that he would not live there for long.

And Walter Monckton wrote:

He could not bear to feel that he would be cooped up in Buckingham Palace all the time within the iron bars. They must take him as he was – a man different from his father and determined to be himself. He would be available for public business and public occasions when he was wanted, but his private life was to be his own and was, as far as possible, to be lived in the same way as when he was Prince of Wales. The Fort was to remain a retreat for weekends and for rest.

But he added:

He never spoke to me of any doubt or hesitation about accepting his position as King. It was only later on in the year, when the controversy was upon him, that he would sometimes say that they must have him for what he was or not at all and that, if they were wanting someone exactly reproducing his father, there was the Duke of York.[13]

17

THE DIVORCE

When the King returned from his holiday it seemed to his staff that his nervous condition was greatly improved and he began to talk of visiting the provinces during the coming winter. Plans were discussed for visits to the Black Country and to South Wales. Nevertheless anxiety about him continually grew because, although the national newspapers still refrained from any gossip, American newspapers now began to find their way into England as well as into the Dominions, and, even more, because letters of a most critical kind began to reach Buckingham Palace, Queen Mary, the Prime Minister and other Cabinet ministers, the Archbishop of Canterbury and many other leading men. During the whole course of the abdication crisis a selection of those reaching Buckingham Palace were sent to the King at Fort Belvedere, so that it is not true, as is so often stated, that he was later taken completely unaware by the attitude of the government and his subjects.

All through the summer Major Hardinge had found it impossible to get Baldwin to address himself to the serious situation which he believed to be developing. 'The Prime Minister's natural reluctance to interfere in the private life of the Sovereign,' Hardinge wrote later, 'in spite of the pressure that was already considerable, was reinforced by the fact that no constitutional issue could arise as long as Mrs Simpson remained married to Mr Simpson.'[1] Yet on 14 October, while waiting to see the King in connection with his forthcoming visit to the Fleet, the Prime Minister volunteered to Hardinge that he was increasingly anxious over the King.

Baldwin too had been on holiday and on his return he had had a great shock. At the beginning of the Parliamentary recess he had been in a dangerous state of nervous exhaustion. 'It is the responsibility that kills. ...' he told Tom Jones. 'It broke Bonar Law in 1921.'[2] And in a year which included the Hoare-Laval Pact, the occupation of the Rhineland and the outbreak of the Spanish war, as well as such small but pregnant signs of the times as the public exhibition of a gas mask, * Tom Jones listed among the causes of the Prime Minister's condition both the death of the old King and anxiety about the new. All through the summer letters of protest about the King and Mrs Simpson had been sent by British citizens abroad and members of nations of the Commonwealth to the Prime Minister but these had been largely kept from him by his staff because of his nervous exhaustion. On his return there awaited him on his desk the accumulation of several months of letters as well as all the American press cuttings and the photographs of the King and Mrs Simpson among cheering crowds, walking, or driving, or alone on the beaches, and he had learned during two or three hours' concentrated reading of the world-wide scandal surrounding the British crown.

Anthony Eden, calling on the Prime Minister at this time to bring him up to date with the national scene and to tell him of his own initiative in applying an embargo on the supply of arms and aircraft from Britain to Spain, found Baldwin's attention wandering. Presently the Prime Minister interrupted his Foreign Secretary to ask him whether he had received any letters about the King.

'I expect you have some,' he said. 'I fear we may have difficulties there.' And then he made the astonishing statement: 'I hope that you will try not to trouble me too much with foreign affairs just now.'⁴

Eden, suspecting, he has said, that this was merely 'another example of Baldwin's reluctance to face the unpleasant realities which were our daily fare at the Foreign Office', returned to his office where he found the conversation explained by the number of letters he had received in a similarly critical strain.

Baldwin proceeded slowly and when in his conversation with Hardinge at Buckingham Palace, the Private Secretary warned him that the day would come when he would be forced to intervene, he replied that he agreed but was hoping to stave it off until after the Coronation, an astounding remark considering the Coronation was still six months off. However his conversation with Eden had been in the opposite sense and it seems likely that he was merely warding off pressure to act before he was ready to. His hand would soon be forced.

Once Mrs Simpson had decided to divorce her husband, she had taken a house in Cumberland Terrace (one of the Nash terraces in Regent's Park) and another at the small seaside town of Felixstowe. The reason for the latter was because her divorce suit had been put down for hearing at Ipswich and it was necessary for her to comply with a residential qualification. It has always been assumed that the divorce suit was heard at Ipswich

* "Today I saw for the first time a gas mask. It was in one of the Whitehall windows of the United Services Museum fixed on the face of a wax figure of a young man and labelled, "official gas mask".⁹

because of a desire to avoid publicity, although it has never been sufficiently explained how this result could have been achieved in that way. The truth seems to be that the London courts were full for more than a year. The evidence of Ernest Simpson's adultery had been provided at a hotel at Bray, so that the witnesses to prove the case were at Maidenhead. Theodore Goddard therefore attempted to get the case tried at Reading Assizes and, only because divorce cases were not being taken there, set it down for hearing at Ipswich. He retained the services of Sir Norman Birkett, KC (then Mr Birkett, KC) with the object, he said, of preventing any suggestion that Mrs Simpson was trying to avoid publicity. (Mr Birkett lunched at Fort Belvedere with the King to discuss with him the conduct of the case. 'Norman,' wrote Walter Monckton, 'was deeply impressed with the King's straightness and kindness and devotion to Mrs Simpson, and was captivated by his charm.')[5] Goddard, nevertheless, saw a great deal of difference between normal publicity to the actual proceedings and press comment beforehand and, when he received a telephone call from Lord Beaverbrook, who as it happened was an old friend of his, and who told him that he proposed to publish a statement in the *Evening Standard*, he went to see him to dissuade him.

Lord Beaverbrook had learned of the impending divorce 'in the ordinary way of news gathering', that is to say before knowledge of it reached the public, or, in this case, the Prime Minister, and, since by now Mrs Simpson's name was beginning to be known to a great many people, her divorce was undoubtedly news. He was not much impressed with Goddard's representations and the solicitor left him without having received any assurance that publication would be withheld. In consequence he went on the following morning, in company with Walter Monckton and Mr Allen, the King's solicitor, to see the King at Buckingham Palace where he told him exactly what had happened. He suggested that the King should telephone to Lord Beaverbrook himself and 'make it clear that there was no desire whatever to stop any report of the proceedings but merely to stop press announcements beforehand'.[6] With this suggestion he ensured Lord Beaverbrook a place in the history of the Abdication.

On Tuesday, 13 October, the day before Baldwin's visit to Buckingham Palace, the King telephoned to Lord Beaverbrook and asked him to go to see him and to name his own time. Lord Beaverbrook seems to have been in no hurry to reply to his request, and, suffering rather mysteriously from toothache, he became 'so heavily engaged with his dentist' for the next two days that the interview did not take place until Friday, 16 October. (According to an editorial footnote to Lord Beaverbrook's account, there is no record in his diary of an appointment with his dentist on either of the intervening dates, although at five-thirty on 15 October there occurs the name Mr Ernest Simpson.)

The King knew Lord Beaverbrook only slightly, although they had met on at least two occasions, once at dinner at St James's Palace and once at Stornoway House, Lord Beaverbrook's London home, which was almost next door. He now went much further in his request than Goddard had suggested, asking for help not merely in suppressing all comment in advance of the Simpson case but also 'in limiting publicity after the event'. He stated his case calmly, Lord Beaverbrook says, and with considerable cogency and force.

The reasons he gave for this wish were that Mrs Simpson was ill, unhappy and distressed by the thought of notoriety. Notoriety would attach to her only because she had been his guest on the *Nahlin* and at Balmoral. As the publicity would be due to her association with himself, he felt it his duty to protect her.[7]

Lord Beaverbrook found these reasons satisfactory and he undertook to do what the King wanted. In company with Walter Monckton he called on Mr Esmond Harmsworth (son of Lord Rothermere, the owner of the *Daily Mail*, who was Chairman of the Newspaper Proprietors' Association) who it will be remembered had stayed with the King at Balmoral. They then approached the other British newspapers who consented without much difficulty to a policy of discretion.

While I was engaged in these activities directed to regulating newspaper publicity – Lord Beaverbrook writes – I had no knowledge that marriage was in the mind of the King. He himself had given me no hint of the matter, and, at the same time, I had been told by Mrs Simpson's solicitor, Mr Theodore Goddard, that His Majesty had no such intention. I repeated that assurance to other newspaper proprietors. And I believed it.

Even if I had known that he did propose marriage, I would still have done what I did. But the fact remains that I did not know, although I was having conversations with the King almost every day.[8]

On Friday, 16 October, the day that Lord Beaverbrook called on the King, Baldwin went in company with his wife to Cumberland Lodge, a house in Windsor Park, to stay the weekend with Lord FitzAlan, a former Conservative Chief Whip and Viceroy of Ireland. He found staying there the Duke of Norfolk, Lord Salisbury and Lord Kemsley, another Press lord. The main topic of conversation was naturally the Simpson divorce (although the facts do not support the suggestion sometimes made that this house-party had been gathered together to discuss the worries about the King). There had by now been sufficient evidence that the King might be intending to marry Mrs Simpson for it to be immediately obvious that the latest event brought the prospect of a constitutional crisis uncomfortably near. It was calculated that, if Mrs Simpson received a decree nisi on 27 October, this would be made absolute on 27 April, just in time for the King to marry her before the Coronation in May.

On the following morning Major Hardinge arrived to see Baldwin to beg him to see the King and urge him to prevent the divorce going

Top At Sandringham in 1902. *From left to right* Prince Albert, Princess
Mary, Prince Edward, Prince Henry and the future George V
Below The boys' room, Marlborough House, 1905

As 'Chief Morning Star' during his tour of Canada, 1919

Mrs Dudley Ward

Top By the swimming pool at Fort Belvedere. *From left to right* The Hon
Mrs Jock Gilmour, Lord Louis Mountbatten, the Duke of York, Prince
Gustav Adolf of Sweden, Princess Ingrid of Norway, Princess Sybilla of
Sweden, The Duchess of York, Lady Furness
Below The Prince of Wales with Fruity Metcalfe, the Metcalfe children and
Lady Furness

Top The King with Mrs Simpson in a motor-boat off the *Nahlin* during their Dalmatian holiday, 1936
Below Farewell from Windsor

The Duke of Windsor at Schloss Enzesveld

Top After the Wedding at Château de Candé. *From left to right* Mrs Bedaux, Mrs Rogers, Lady Alexandra Metcalfe, Mr Dudley Forwood, the Duke of Windsor, Fruity Metcalfe, Herman Rogers
Below Walter Monckton, Fruity Metcalfe and the Windsors after the wedding

The Duchess of Windsor at a party in New York

through and to avoid flaunting his friendship with Mrs Simpson in public. He believed that Baldwin was the only person who could do this, and he thought it of vital importance that the King should be given a warning.

If the King desired to marry a woman who was twice divorced there would be two people primarily concerned, Stanley Baldwin, as Prime Minister, and Cosmo Gordon Lang, the Archbishop of Canterbury and head of the Church. The King is not as is sometimes thought 'Head' of the Church but he is bound by an Act of Settlement of 1701 to be a member of the Church of England and he is officially designated 'Defender of the Faith'. The Church regards marriage as indissoluble and does not accept divorce and remarriage. After the Abdication an idea gained ground that these two men, the Prime Minister and the Head of the Church (the names of Geoffrey Dawson, the Editor of *The Times*, and Alec Hardinge, the Private Secretary, are sometimes joined to theirs), plotted together to rid themselves of the King for unworthy political motives not connected with his wish to marry a twice-divorced woman. There is no real evidence for this theory, in fact the reverse, but, vaguely held by a great many people, it has led to the equally false idea that the King was too 'radical' for the leader of the Conservative Party and the Leader of the Church. The King was accustomed to make unconstitutional interventions on domestic as well as on foreign affairs and internally the most important question of the day was the vast army of unemployed, for whom his genuine sympathy cannot be called in question. He was accustomed to speak of his ministers loudly and critically at semi-public functions such as dinner parties. None of this made him a 'radical' however, and it is unbelievable that any politician who had any real acquaintance with him ever mistook him for one.

It would be pleasant to cast Lord Beaverbrook as inventor of the plot and villain of the piece, and indeed he made a bid for the role in his account of the Abdication. But in fact it grew up years before this account was published and, except through his influence as a proprietor of newspapers, and, of much greater importance, his influence on the Duke of Windsor in exile, he cannot be held responsible for it. What makes it worthy of discussion is that it seems to have had a natural attraction for all those who, being unable to believe that the King gave up his crown merely for the sake of a woman, needed some more complicated explanation of it.

The history of the Abdication, which has been written about so often and by so many people that almost every detail has been filled in, entirely absolves the Prime Minister. The very qualities which made him a dangerous leader for England in the peril that menaced her became the rarest of virtues in his dealings with the King. He was an experienced and cunning politician – thought shrewd or crafty according to the eye of the beholder – but he was a kindly man and he was fond of the King. By temperament slow, some said lazy, he was never precipitate and he relied very much on his instincts, which were for the most part good. He remained completely and marvellously free from the indignation so many people felt and the consequent wish to chasten the King. Again and again he can be seen warding off the attempts of others to speed events or administer rebukes.

In his account of the Abdication the Duke of Windsor gives the impression that from the first he saw Baldwin as an enemy. These are the broodings of exile, however, and none of the accounts written at the time suggest that the dealings between him and the Prime Minister were anything but frank and friendly. On the other hand, it is probably an exaggeration to say that he had real affection for Baldwin (as a result of his charm and his desire when in a good mood to please, people who met him on formal or public occasions almost invariably overrated his liking for them). Beaverbrook says that he found Baldwin 'something of a bore'[9] – an expression the Prince used far more often than other people's accounts of their relationship with him would lead us to believe – and, in any situation other than that of Prime Minister and King or Prince of Wales, this is what one would expect.

If Baldwin was not plotting, there could be no plot. Nevertheless, since other names are sometimes mentioned in this connection it must also be said that they are almost invariably those of men who were exceptionally devoted to the monarchy, taking for granted its power for good and the damage to the Commonwealth that would follow any damage to the crown. In hindsight it can be seen that the loyalty of the British public was so much to the institution that one King could be removed and another take his place without a tremor of hesitation in the transfer of feeling. But that could not be known beforehand, and no one has ever attempted to explain how it was intended to remove the monarch without risk to the monarchy.

Cosmo Gordon Lang, the Archbishop of Canterbury, who with Baldwin had most cause for concern, was perhaps not so strong in Christian charity and patience as the Prime Minister. He had for many years been a friend of George v and Queen Mary and Edward had known him – even felt affection for him – as a child. He was too close both to the old King and to his Private Secretaries to retain the young man's friendship when he grew up, and he had shown himself singularly inept when Edward came to the throne. Calling at Buckingham Palace on the day after the funeral to pay his respects to Queen Mary, he had asked to see the King and then in a clumsy attempt to come to terms with him had said that he supposed the other must be aware that he had often been the subject of discussion between his father and himself. He asked the King not to misjudge him, however, because he said he had invariably done his best to reassure his father when criticisms of his conduct arose. The King quite reasonably resented the implication of these remarks, and his dislike of the Archbishop was strong at the time and not, as in the case of Baldwin, a later growth.

He can't endure any kind of cleric – Baldwin told his niece. One day, at the Fort, when the Duke of Kent and the Archbishop of Canterbury and I had all been at him during the entire morning, the Duke of Kent came into the room where I was waiting alone until the Archbishop's interview with the King was ended.

'He is,' said the Duke, 'damning the whole root and stock of the Episcopacy. He has just shoo'd the Archbishop of Canterbury out of the house.'

And even as he spoke, the King came in looking ruffled, and the Archbishop's car went snorting down the drive.* [10]

All through the summer the Archbishop, like other public figures, received press cuttings and photographs and letters from overseas expressing dislike and dread of the King's behaviour and he felt that 'the monarchy was being vulgarized and degraded, that mud was being thrown on sacred things'. The Archbishop had the appalling personal difficulty that he would have had to crown the King if he had succeeded in his purpose of marrying Mrs Simpson and retaining the crown. 'As the months passed ... the thought of my having to consecrate *him* as King weighed on me as a heavy burden. Indeed, I considered whether I could bring myself to do so.' [11] He would undoubtedly have liked to intervene. In fact he could do nothing.

I made repeated suggestions about seeing him [the King] but he was very emphatic that on the subject of his relations with Mrs Simpson he would listen to nobody but Mr Baldwin, who had a right to speak to him and advise him. [12]

Baldwin kept the Archbishop informed but otherwise, in the words of his biographer, 'he could only watch and wait'.

To return to the day in October when Baldwin stayed at Cumberland Lodge, he had previously received a letter from Major Hardinge telling him of the impending divorce and begging him 'to see the King and ask if these proceedings could not be stopped, for the danger in which they place him [HM] was becoming every day greater'. [13] Baldwin had therefore arranged with his host Lord FitzAlan, to invite Hardinge and his wife to luncheon, and afterwards he retired with Hardinge to discuss the matter. The Private Secretary confined his requests to two things: that the Prime Minister should ask the King (1) that the divorce proceedings be dropped and (2) that he should cease to flaunt his association with Mrs Simpson publicly. The Prime Minister did not immediately agree but he suggested to his host that the Hardinges should return again to dinner, and after dinner he told him that he had in the end decided to ask for an audience.

This proved easier said than done. Baldwin telephoned Hardinge the following morning to say that the King had left Fort Belvedere for

---

* Something in Baldwin's memory of this event is almost certainly incorrect. The Archbishop by all accounts was never at the Fort during the abdication crisis and this must therefore refer to some earlier occasion. Yet it is difficult to see why on an earlier occasion they should all have been 'at him during the entire morning'.

Sandringham and was not available. He asked Hardinge to arrange an appointment for the following morning (Tuesday). At Sandringham it was said that the King had sent word that he would be late arriving, upon which it was assumed – correctly – that he had gone to see Mrs Simpson at the house at Felixstowe. Hardinge left a message at Sandringham late that night saying that he had tried to get him on urgent business since 9 a.m. and would telephone again the next morning. The King finally reached Sandringham at 4 a.m. the following day but he telephoned to Hardinge punctually at 9 a.m. On being told the subject the Prime Minister wished to talk to him about, he seemed taken aback and said that Mrs Simpson's divorce was not a matter on which he or the Prime Minister could intervene. However he agreed to see Baldwin and, after he had been told that, although the Prime Minister was quite willing to go to Sandringham, he was anxious that no one should know of his visit and that their talk should be in complete privacy, he agreed to go back to Fort Belvedere. He received the Prime Minister there at 10 a.m. the next day.

Thousands of words have been written about the Abdication and every event, every detail of what happened is known.* The only thing about which there will always be room for surmise is what was in the King's mind. Fifteen years later he purported to tell us, but by then fifteen years of exile and the persuasions of other people had intervened and he no longer remembered himself. Only one thing can be said with absolute certainty. The King was in every way more sympathetic, more considerate of the feelings of others, more honourable and more likeable than the picture he painted of himself. Throughout the crisis he behaved with a sincerity and straightforwardness which forced the respect and earned the affection of those who worked for him. In the notes other people made of their dealings with him there is never any trace of the self-satisfied sarcasm which so mars his later account.

His account of what happened when Baldwin first arrived has been generally accepted. The King was in the garden and the Prime Minister complimented him on the beauty of the grounds and the arrangement of the garden. Soon they repaired to the octagonal room and Baldwin, who was clearly nervous, became very restless and finally asked for a drink. When the butler brought the tray the Prime Minister rose and picking up the decanter and a glass asked the King to say 'when'.

'As gravely as I could,' the Duke of Windsor writes, 'I hoped even severely, I answered, "No thank you, Mr Baldwin; I never take a drink before seven o'clock in the evening." '[14]

However, there is a note in Harold Nicolson's diary which, although clearly wrong in several details (although not more wrong than gossip tends to be), and probably telescoping the events of more than one occa-

*In *Baldwin: the Unexpected Prime Minister*, H. Montgomery Hyde has disposed of the idea that when the cabinet papers are released in 2037 they will reveal much we do not already know.

sion, has this in common with the Duke's account, that the two men met in the garden (all recorded accounts of their other meetings place them in the evening and this was December) and that Baldwin asked for a drink.

7th December.
Oliver Baldwin came to see me this morning. He told me that his father and the King walked round and round the garden at Fort Belvedere discussing the business, and then returned to the library having agreed that HM must abdicate. Stanley Baldwin was feeling exhausted. He asked for a whisky-and-soda. The bell was rung: the footman came: the drink was produced. S.B. raised his glass and said (rather foolishly to my mind), 'Well, Sir, whatever happens, my Mrs and I wish you happiness from the depths of our souls.' At which the King burst into floods of tears. Then S.B. himself began to cry. What a strange conversation-piece, those two blubbering together on a sofa.[15]

The rest of the conversation has been re-constructed again and again.* Baldwin began by reminding the King that when they met at Downing Street on the eve of the King's death he had said that he was glad Baldwin was Prime Minister and he recalled an earlier occasion when they travelled up from Folkestone together and the King (as Prince of Wales) had said that he was to remember he could always speak freely to him about everything. Did that – he asked – hold good when there was a woman in the case?

The King made some gesture of assent and Baldwin went on to speak of his regard for him as a man and his belief that he had the qualities which might make him an admirable monarch during the transition period the country was going through, and he said: 'You have all the advantages a man can have. You are young. You have before you the example of your father. You are fond of your house and you like children. You have only one disadvantage. You are not married and you ought to be.' Then he told the King he had two great anxieties. The first was the effect of a continuance of the kind of criticism that appeared every day in the American Press and the effect this would have in the Dominions, particularly in Canada where it was widespread, and the effect it would be bound to have in this country. Recollecting the substance of this interview for the benefit of the House of Commons, Baldwin said:

And then I reminded him of what I had told him and his brother in years past. The British monarchy is a unique institution. The crown in this country through the centuries has been deprived of many of its prerogatives, but today, while

* Baldwin's biographers have had access to his own notes of what was said and to Lucy Baldwin's diaries. Mrs Baldwin regularly made notes of her husband's conversation and, where accuracy is at stake, her version is usually accepted. Tom Jones also kept notes of Baldwin's conversations which have been published and Lord Citrine quotes a conversation in which Baldwin gave him the most complete of all the accounts of this interview. The author has had the benefit of Miss Monica Baldwin's account. Most of these versions are similar in many particulars, as Baldwin had a trick of repeating the same words again and again. In addition, there is his own account to the House of Commons and the Duke of Windsor's version.

that is true, it stands for far more than it ever has done in its history. The importance of its integrity is, beyond all question, far greater than it has ever been, being as it is not only the last link of Empire that is left, but the guarantee in this country so long as it exists in that integrity, against many evils that have affected and afflicted other countries. There is no man in this country to whatever party he may belong, who would not subscribe to that. But while this feeling largely depends on the respect that has grown up in the last three generations for the monarchy, it might not take so long, in face of the kind of criticisms to which it was being exposed, to lose that power far more rapidly than it was built up, and once lost I doubt if anything could restore it.[16]

And he went on to say: 'You may think me Victorian, Sir. You may think my views out of date, but I believe I know how to interpret the minds of my own people; and I say that although it is true that standards are lower since the war it only leads people to expect a higher standard from their King. People expect more from their King than they did a hundred years ago.'

In his account of this interview the Duke of Windsor says that it slowly dawned on him that the Prime Minister's real object was to persuade him to use his influence with Mrs Simpson to stop the divorce. This may be regarded as literary licence because the reason for the interview had been explained to him by his Private Secretary before it took place.

Baldwin told the King of the large correspondence he had received on the subject of his friendship with Mrs Simpson. And he produced, and later left with His Majesty, a folder containing many samples of this correspondence. And he said: 'The American newspapers are full of it and even the Chinese vernacular newspapers are carrying stories about your behaviour. The effect of such comment in the American Press would be to sap the position of the throne unless it were stopped.'

Then he said: 'I don't believe you can get away with it', a phrase he was very proud to have thought of, and repeated to everyone he afterwards told of this conversation, because it was one the King often used himself. And when the King asked him what he meant he said: 'I think you know our people. They'll tolerate a lot in private life but they will not stand for this kind of thing in the life of a public personage and when they read in the Court Circular of Mrs Simpson's visit to Balmoral they resented it.'

To this the King replied: 'The lady is my friend and I do not wish to let her in by the back door, but quite openly. . . .'

And then, as it was now Baldwin's turn to be silent, he said, 'I hope you will agree that I have carried out my duties with dignity.'

To which Baldwin, understandably, if rather weakly, replied: 'I do agree and all the more as I know that the duties of royalty are not much to your liking.'

The King then said, 'I know there is nothing kingly about me but I have tried to mix with the people and make them think I was one of them.'

Baldwin came to the point. 'Cannot you have this coming divorce put off?'

'Mr Baldwin,' the King replied, 'that is the lady's private business. I have no right to interfere with the affairs of an individual. It would be wrong were I to attempt to influence Mrs Simpson just because she happens to be a friend of the King.'

Baldwin was later to say that this was the only lie the King ever told him, and Beaverbrook that, although it was a perfectly proper reply provided the King had no feelings except those of friendship, 'if he had deeper feelings, and an intention to marry, it was no reply at all'.[17]* The King seems always to have been quite satisfied with it however and as Duke of Windsor he repeated it in his account of the interview with an effect of pride.

Before he left Baldwin pointed out the danger of the divorce proceedings. If a verdict was given that left the matter in suspense (by which he seems to have meant a *decree nisi*, after which it would be six months before the decree was made absolute), everyone would then be talking, and when the Press began, as it must begin some time, a most difficult situation would arise. 'There might be sides taken and factions grow up in this country in a matter where no factions ought to exist.' And he urged that Mrs Simpson should be asked to leave the country for six months, hoping, as he later told Tom Jones, that in the meantime the King's passion might cool and that other influences might be brought to play on him. (Almost everyone who spoke to the King during these weeks invariably urged delay in one form or another for the same reason.)

These were the main points of the interview but when Baldwin left the King he was aware of his exaltation and he told his wife that the King had said that Mrs Simpson was 'the only woman in the world and I cannot live without her'. It is curious that, presented with this opportunity, he did not ask him exactly what he meant, but perhaps at this stage he did not want to be told. He was satisfied to have got through the interview and 'broken the ice'. He had made sure that the King knew the extent of the Press comment and the tone of the letters he was receiving and he had done this without personally antagonizing him. When he left the King had said to him (as he was to say many times in the days that followed): 'You and I must settle this matter together. I will not have anyone interfering.'

Major Hardinge was less satisfied. He felt that Baldwin had failed in not mentioning the subject of marriage and emphasizing the dangers of any idea of the sort. In the following week he discussed this with some of the

* Beaverbrook also accuses Baldwin of 'deceit and dishonesty' at the same interview because he says he knew at the time of the intention of the King to marry Mrs Simpson and concealed that knowledge, and he gives as evidence for this remark the fact that Lord Templewood in his account says that Baldwin had been told by two of the new King's advisers after the funeral of the old King that he 'had made up his mind to marry Mrs Simpson'. A further perusal of Lord Templewood's account makes it fairly plain that, although Baldwin like almost everyone else had begun to fear this might be true, he still hoped to avert it.

heads of the Civil Service and it was decided that Mrs Simpson should herself be warned. Theodore Goddard (who it will be remembered had given his word that marriage was not contemplated) was persuaded to undertake the task and he travelled to Ipswich for the purpose. On his return he reported that Mrs Simpson had derided any question of marriage to the King and that the divorce would go on.

On 26 October *The New York Journal* – a newspaper belonging to William Randolph Hearst – printed an article under the headline KING WILL WED WALLY. This stated unequivocally that eight months after her divorce Edward would marry Mrs Simpson and that after the Coronation she would become his consort. Having pointed to the marriage of the Duke of York to 'a commoner, so-called' it went on to say that Edward believed that 'the most important thing for the peace and welfare of the world is an intimate understanding and relationship between England and America, and that his marriage with this very gifted lady may help to bring about that beneficial co-operation between English-speaking nations'. Two things added to the impact of the article. The first that until now the Hearst papers had been singularly quiet on this topic, and the second that Hearst had recently been in England, where he was believed to have visited Fort Belvedere. It was immediately assumed that this was something in the nature of an inspired leak. (In fact, as Brian Inglis has pointed out, there was little in the story that could not have been formulated by putting two and two together.) In any case the idea that Edward might intend marriage had now appeared for the first time in print and the sensation this made was by no means confined to America. (American newspapers were entering England, if only to subscribers who received mail copies, and the story spread quickly by word of mouth.) One effect of it was greatly to increase the difficulties and doubts of the editors of English newspapers, who were confined to Beaverbrook's 'gentleman's agreement', but only as to comment on Mrs Simpson's divorce. Brian Inglis has analysed the motives which were to keep them silent on all aspects of the greatest newspaper story in history for many days to come. Since not all the newspapers and magazines came under the control or influence of Beaverbrook or Rothermere, he asks, why was the story not broken by some editor craving a scoop to put his paper on the map?

The temptation must have been considerable, particularly for papers that needed a circulation boost. But for once their managerial sides were not keen on the idea. They were afflicted by fear of the unknown. What would the reaction be, should a paper take a chance and spring the story? Obviously its sales for that issue, and probably for the next few issues, would be prodigious, but what thereafter? Suppose the public, though avid for the story when it appeared, thought badly of the paper for having printed it. ... And what of advertisers? The weight of official and unofficial disapproval at such an act of lèse-majesté might well lead to the withdrawal of promised advertisements. What, too, of the legal position? A single false step, a misstatement, an unguarded innuendo, and swingeing damages could be expected against the transgressor. No, on the whole it was safer to wait.

The position of the 'quality' papers, London and provincial, he goes on to argue, was rather different. And he quotes Tom Jones as saying that their silence 'is not enforced by government, but by a sense of shame'.

No quality newspaper cared to be the first to break the story. And their reluctance to take the risk can only be attributed to the prevailing belief that on this issue, the lead should be given by the government – or by *The Times*, as it could be assumed that *The Times* would not pronounce without government sanction.[18]

The position of the editor of *The Times* was therefore a particular one and Geoffrey Dawson had told Tom Jones on 21 October that *The Times* would have 'to do something about the King and Mrs Simpson but that the PM must tell him what he wanted done'.[19] The reply to this was that Baldwin would like him to continue to do nothing.

Geoffrey Dawson was later to be accused of having been in collusion with the government against the King. The great difficulty in examining the charge is that no one has ever seemed to be quite clear what is meant by it. Thus Inglis, having said that *The Times* would not pronounce without government sanction as a statement of fact of which he does not seem to disapprove, goes on almost immediately to remark that if anything should have warned the King that the continued Press silence on Mrs Simpson was a fatal mistake, it was the fact that Baldwin was imposing it.

Geoffrey Dawson was later to be at pains to dissociate *The Times* from collusion with the government, but his own diaries make it clear that he allowed himself to be restricted from broaching the issue by Baldwin.[20]

The truth is that the issue is constantly muddled by the difficulty of distinguishing between Edward himself and his position. Baldwin was quite clearly not plotting to remove the King from the throne. He was on the other hand perfectly certain that he could not both remain on the throne and marry Mrs Simpson, an attitude which although it cannot be regarded as plotting did not commend itself to Edward. However, although Geoffrey Dawson probably never went outside his duty, he does in retrospect seem a little assiduous in the performance of it, in exactly the way that Baldwin was so splendidly not. On 26 October – the day on which the Hearst newspaper article appeared – he received a letter from an Englishman living in the USA signed Britannicus in Partibus Infidelium which described so perfectly the damage being done to the crown and the indignation of Britons abroad that Lord Beaverbrook was afterwards to say that it was written in the offices of *The Times*. (Brian Inglis who went into the matter says that this is not so, that the writer's name and a New Jersey address was on it.) The letter which is very long and not a little prosy began by saying that the writer could not expect to see it published, 'touching as it does on what is in England a forbidden theme' yet 'I cannot help unburdening myself by bringing certain facts, for whatever the effort may be worth, to the attention of the organ that is traditionally regarded as the chief moulder of British public opinion. ...'

He was, the writer went on to say, 'a Briton who had been resident in the United States for several years' and who had a 'deep and continuous interest in everything bearing upon Anglo-American relations'. He had always sought to contribute to this by depicting British public life in the most favourable way.

It has therefore been with great regret, and even with dismay, that I have watched in the course of the last few months the development of a situation that gravely lowers British prestige in American eyes. I refer to the poisonous publicity attending the King's friendship with Mrs Simpson.

I am one of those who had a deep admiration for the present monarch when he was Prince of Wales; and looked forward to the day when he would bring a new vision and a new inspiration to the task of kingship. In common, I fear, with a great many others, I have been bitterly disappointed. The doings of the King, as reported in the American Press, have in the course of a few months transformed Great Britain, as envisaged by the average American, from a sober and dignified realm into a dizzy Balkan musical comedy attuned to the rhythm of Jazz.

The writer then goes on to say that the American man in the street sees other countries through the medium of some outstanding personality played up by the Press. 'To him Italy is Mussolini, Germany is Hitler, Russia is Stalin; for many years Great Britain was George V.' A democratic monarchy can have many advantages over a democratic republic he observes and he points out that while France has failed to make much impression on American public opinion because of her lack of an outstanding personality, every American knows the name of the King of Great Britain.

But, by the same token, a monarchy filled by an individual who has made himself the subject of cheap and sensational gossip can be of incalculable harm by adding to the difficulties of international understanding....

I am not in a position to know whether British opinion at home considers Edward VIII is satisfactorily carrying on his father's tradition. But the prevailing American opinion is that the foundations of the British throne are undermined, its moral authority, its honour, and its dignity cast into the dustbin. To put the matter bluntly George V was an invaluable asset to British prestige abroad; Edward has proved himself an incalculable liability.

For several months now the American public has been intermittently titillated with unsavoury gobbets of news about the King and Mrs Simpson; but in the course of the last three or four weeks there has come a perfect avalanche of muck and slime.... First we had the news despatches, suitably and abundantly illustrated by photographs: Mrs Simpson accompanies the King on a yachting cruise, Mrs Simpson accompanies the King when he goes to consult a Vienna ear specialist, Mrs Simpson accompanies the King to Balmoral, Mrs Simpson accompanies the King on the train back to London, the ubiquitous Mrs Simpson is in the King's company on every conceivable occasion. ...

One journal ... gives the alleged details of a conversation in which the Prime Minister reproves the King for his carrying on, and the latter curtly tells him to mind his own business. Another asserts that Queen Mary is being ousted from Buckingham Palace in order to clear the way for Mrs Simpson's installation as the King's official hostess. ... Advertisements in railway trains and other places scream out exhortations to buy this or that publication to get the inside story about the King and Mrs Simpson. Distinguished Britons landing on American shores are beset by pressmen who ask them what the British people think about it all; and the next day appear accounts describing with malicious glee how the distinguished Britons struggled amid confusion and embarrassment to evade the question. ...

The writer goes on at very great length to describe the effect of all that has happened at a time 'when Britain's prestige has suffered severe reverses, especially through the setbacks endured by her diplomacy in the Italo–Abyssinian conflict' and finally concludes with the following:

It may be presumptuous, and even impertinent, for a person far removed from the centre of events to suggest a remedy; but I cannot refrain from saying that nothing would please me more than to hear that Edward VIII had abdicated his rights in favour of the Heir Presumptive, who I am confident would be prepared to carry on in the sterling tradition established by his father. In my view it would be well to have such a change take place while it is still a matter of individuals, and before the disquiet has progressed to the point of calling in question the institution of monarchy itself.[21]

The writer was right in thinking that *The Times* could not publish his letter but Geoffrey Dawson decided to make use of it nevertheless. He therefore went on the day he received it to see Major Hardinge at Buckingham Palace (the Archbishop of Canterbury also called on that day to discuss the situation with the Private Secretary), and he took with him the Britannicus letter and asked Hardinge to read it and then to show it to the King. The Private Secretary had a duty to keep the King informed of the trends of opinion everywhere and it is hardly possible to argue that this letter, which arrived on the same day as Hearst published the statement that the King would marry Mrs Simpson, could have been withheld from him. In any case Hardinge agreed to show it to him.

On the following day, 27 October, Mrs Simpson's divorce suit was heard at Ipswich and evidence was brought of Ernest Simpson's having stayed at the Café de Paris at Bray with a lady named Buttercup Kennedy. A decree *nisi* was awarded with costs against Simpson. Too much can be made of the fact that the divorce suit smacked of collusion because the actual mechanics of many divorces were contrived at that date (the real co-respondent being guarded from unpleasant publicity by an artificial arrangement with another woman), but there were, nevertheless, circumstances which were unusual. Two press photographers had their cameras smashed by the police, who also forcibly prevented reporters from following Mrs Simpson; while Ladbroke, the King's chauffeur, had to execute a skilful manœuvre to get her away from the court.

The following morning the British Press kept the gentleman's agreement and reported the divorce only in the most formal way. Not so in America, however, where the Press had a field-day even by their own standards, the palm being awarded to the oft-quoted headline KING'S MOLL RENO'D IN WOLSEY'S HOME TOWN.*

The first phase on the road to abdication was over.

---

* The connection of Wolsey with Ipswich had also been noticed by Baldwin who told Tom Jones he could quite understand why people were put in the Tower in the old days, and he would gladly put Mrs Simpson there if he could.[22]

18

THE LETTER

On 3 November the King opened Parliament, giving short shrift to the first part of this ceremony and a display of his natural talent in the second.

Traditionally the King drives from Buckingham Palace to Westminster in a gilt state coach drawn by eight grey horses and escorted by the Household Cavalry, through streets lined by loyal subjects come to assuage their desire for ceremony, for mystery and magic. And, although this drive is strictly a sideline, a by-product of the main occasion, it is, nevertheless, of the essence of modern majesty.

On the day when Edward VIII opened his only Parliament it poured with rain and by now it might in any case have begun to be noticed that the 'Queen's' weather, so marked a seal of Heaven's approval of previous sovereigns from Queen Victoria onwards, had deserted this one. Edward underscored the fact by cancelling the state procession and driving to Westminster in a closed Daimler. Pageantry, he would write later, requires sunshine, and there are few sadder sights than a dripping cortège splashing down a half-empty street – a remark which shows him careless of the fact that those who half-filled the streets stood in the soaking rain merely for a glimpse of him.

Arrived at the Houses of Parliament, however, he was anxious to do well. He had witnessed the ceremony so often that he did not fear the part he had to play but he was aware that here he found himself with a sophisticated and critical audience and above all one which knew of the reports in American newspapers and even of Mr Baldwin's interview with him. He was determined to do his best.

The opening of Parliament is the only occasion – apart from the Coronation – on which the King wears his crown. Edward having not yet been crowned decided to wear the cocked hat of an Admiral of the Fleet, and he appeared among their Lordships (the ceremony takes place not in the House of Commons, but in the House of Lords) looking, according to one witness, 'exactly as he did in 1911 at the investiture at Caernarvon. Not a day older, a young, happy Prince Charming, or so he seemed'.[1]

As this was his first Parliament he had to make what is called the Declaration ensuring the maintenance of the Protestant Faith by the Crown.

I, Edward VIII, do solemnly and sincerely in the presence of God profess, testify and declare that I am a faithful Protestant, and that I will, according to the true intent of the enactments which secure the Protestant Succession to the Throne of my realm, uphold and maintain the said enactments to the best of my powers according to law.

This duty was repugnant to him and he found it wholly inappropriate to an institution supposed to shelter all creeds, but, since it was mandatory, he had decided not to make an issue of it. As he mounted the steps to the throne he tells us that his strongest impression – and one cannot help wondering whether any other sovereign has ever felt the same – was of the smell of moth-balls from the peers' robes.

The Lord Chancellor approached bearing the Gracious Speech, and Edward, placing his cocked hat on his head, took it from him. Confidence grew as he began to read and there welled up inside him a feeling almost of defiance.

'The King,' Harold Nicolson writes, 'looked like a boy of eighteen and did it well. He referred to the "Ammurican Government" and ended "And moy the blessing of Almoighty God rest upon your deliberoitions". '[2]

A young King has made his first speech from the Throne (*The Times* leader said next day). Not alone the fact that his was a Throne by itself, but his whole Royal demeanour bade one feel that in himself was all his state.[3]

Nine days later the King turned the rain which still splashed down on him to better account. On his visit to the Fleet at Southampton he won the hearts of the Navy because, unlike Sir Samuel Hoare, the First Lord of the Admiralty, he would not wear a waterproof while inspecting men in the rain – 'A small thing, but sailors take note of small things, and in this they saw the real difference between the Politician and the Monarch'.[4]

And in Sir Samuel Hoare's account of the same occasion we find Edward, almost for the last time in his life, exhibiting those qualities which, in spite of everything, will ensure him a small place in history and make him of everlasting interest to the psychologist and the biographer.

I had a unique opportunity of seeing the most attractive side of his personality – Sir Samuel Hoare wrote – If, on the one hand, he was, as many thought, wayward and irresponsible, on the other hand, no one could deny his surpassing talent for inspiring enthusiasm and managing great crowds. He seemed to know personally every officer and seaman in the fleet. On one of the evenings there was a smoking concert in the aircraft carrier *Courageous*. No officers except Chatfield, the First Sea Lord, Roger Backhouse, the Commander-in-Chief of the Home

Fleet, and Louis Mountbatten were present. The vast underdeck was packed with thousands of seamen. In my long experience of mass meetings I never saw one so completely dominated by a single personality. At one point he turned to me and said: 'I am going to see what is happening at the other end.' Elbowing his way through the crowd, he walked to the end of the hall and started community singing to the accompaniment of a seaman's mouth-organ. When he came back to the platform, he made an impromptu speech that brought the house down. Then, a seaman in the crowd proposed three cheers for him, and there followed an unforgettable scene of the wildest and most spontaneous enthusiasm. Here, indeed, was the Prince Charming, who could win the hearts of all sorts and conditions of men and women and send a thrill through great crowds.[5]

Lord Templewood adds that the whole visit had been one long series of personal triumphs for the King and says that he was amazed by his liveliness as they travelled back after two days of continuous inspections in the worst possible weather.

The King had every cause to be pleased with himself as weary and cold he entered the doors of Fort Belvedere. He was met by his butler who told him that there was a letter from Major Hardinge who was anxious that he should read it without delay. And there on top of the usual red boxes was the document marked 'Urgent and Confidential'. Putting aside for the moment the thoughts of the bath he had looked forward to, the King opened it slowly and read it. This is what he read:

> Buckingham Palace,
> 13th November, 1936.

Sir,

With my humble duty.

As Your Majesty's Private Secretary, I feel it my duty to bring to your notice the following facts which have come to my knowledge, and which I *know* to be accurate:

(1) The silence of the British Press on the subject of Your Majesty's friendship with Mrs Simpson is *not* going to be maintained. It is probably only a matter of days before the outburst begins. Judging by the letters from British subjects living in foreign countries where the Press has been outspoken, the effect will be calamitous.

(2) The Prime Minister and senior members of the Government are meeting to-day to discuss what action should be taken to deal with the serious situation which is developing. As Your Majesty no doubt knows, the resignation of the Government – an eventuality which can by no means be excluded – would result in Your Majesty having to find someone else capable of forming a government which would receive the support of the present House of Commons. I have reason to know that, in view of the feeling prevalent among members of the House of Commons of all parties, this is hardly within the bounds of possibility. The only alternative remaining is a dissolution and a General Election, in which Your Majesty's personal affairs would be the chief issue – and I cannot help feeling that even those who would sympathize with Your Majesty as an individual

would deeply resent the damage which would inevitably be done to the Crown, the corner-stone on which the whole Empire rests.

If Your Majesty will permit me to say so, there is only one step which holds out any prospect of avoiding this dangerous situation, and that is for Mrs Simpson to go abroad *without further delay*, and I would *beg* Your Majesty to give this proposal your earnest consideration before the position has become irretrievable. Owing to the changing attitude of the Press, the matter has become one of great urgency.

I have the honour, etc., etc.,

ALEXANDER HARDINGE.

P.S. I am by way of going after dinner to-night to High Wycombe to shoot there to-morrow, but the Post Office will have my telephone number, and I am of course entirely at Your Majesty's disposal if there is anything at all that you want.[6]

Writing about his reactions to this letter fourteen or fifteen years later the Duke of Windsor says that he began by being shocked and angry, shocked by its suddenness, and angry because it suggested that he should send 'from my land, my realm', 'the woman I intended to marry'. And he says that the longer he read the letter the more puzzled he became by the motives that had prompted his Private Secretary to write it. He did not question his right to address such a communication to his sovereign, indeed if a Cabinet crisis impended over any issue, it was his duty to warn his master. But having said that what hurt was the cold formality of the letter he goes on in language absurdly inappropriate to the nature of the issues involved to ask himself what this could mean. Was it a warning or an ultimatum? Who but the Prime Minister could have suggested all this to his Private Secretary, and, if the Prime Minister, what was his purpose? He speaks of himself as a man in love and says if their intention was to make him give up Mrs Simpson they had misjudged him. 'They had struck at the very roots of my pride. Only the most faint-hearted would have remained unaroused by such a challenge.'[7] And he says he has decided to come to grips with Mr Baldwin and the 'nebulous figures' involved. In order to do this he decided that, although the normal channel of communication between the Palace and No. 10 Downing Street is the King's Secretary, because of Hardinge's attitude he must establish a new connection.

One must have some sympathy with the King's desire to appoint a personal representative in the coming negotiations, but for the rest it is surely a matter of amazement that, in the words which are said to be his own favourite, the Duke of Windsor to a very large extent 'got away with' this. Books and articles have been written for the sole purpose of refuting the inexplicit but unmistakable charges he seems to be making (which are continually reinforced by other passages in his account of the Abdication), of collusion and bad faith and of disloyalty or at least hostility on the part of the Private Secretary; while no biographer of Baldwin has been happy to ignore the implication of his words entirely.

Yet the King, unless his mind was completely unhinged, could not possibly have been surprised or shocked. From the time of his return from the *Nahlin* Major Hardinge had done everything possible in fulfilment of his duty to keep him informed of the trends of public opinion. Day after day cuttings from the American Press and letters from his subjects resident abroad had been selected and sent to him. The Prime Minister had been persuaded to see him; and, although at this interview he had failed to bring up the question of marriage, he had made absolutely plain the damage which in his opinion was being done to the crown and the dangers which threatened it unless the King prevented the divorce and ceased to flaunt the friendship; while before leaving he had given him a folder of cuttings and letters the general effect of which had been to frighten Baldwin himself into believing that in the year 1936 it was his duty to leave foreign affairs to his Foreign Secretary, while he dealt with this more pressing matter.*

Hardinge had then arranged that Goddard should go to Ipswich to warn Mrs Simpson that any idea of marriage could never succeed, and only a few days before he had sent to the King the Britannicus letter with its graphic description of the effect of his recent behaviour on American opinion and its suggestion of abdication. Whatever the feelings of the King he cannot surely have been unprepared for his Private Secretary's letter.

It is necessary for the moment to digress from the King to examine the events which had led Hardinge to write the letter at this particular moment. Baldwin had spent the time since his interview with Edward 'in the steadily diminishing hope that the King would listen to his warnings'.[8] He had employed himself in testing opinion in private conversations. Among the most important of the people he saw at this time were Clement Attlee, the Leader of the Opposition, and Sir Walter Citrine, the general secretary of the Trades Union Congress. If one reads only Attlee's account of his first interview with Baldwin one gets the impression that he called on the Prime Minister merely to ask for information, but Citrine's account makes it fairly plain that the Leader of the Opposition also gave his own views, and indeed it is highly improbable that he did not. Attlee's opinions are known from a later interview to coincide with those of the Prime Minister, and Citrine, who had recently returned from America, was even stronger. He had been humiliated by the fact that 'newspapers in other countries were carrying discreditable stories about the King',[9] and he agreed with Attlee that the Labour people in the country would not countenance the idea of Mrs Simpson becoming Queen. There is no record of an interview with Sir Archibald Sinclair, Leader of the Liberal Party, but it must be presumed that Liberal opinion was tested in one form or another. Lord Beaverbrook was soon to learn Sir Archibald Sinclair's views, which again largely coincided with those of the Premier.

* The King's own thoughts at the opening of Parliament show him to have been well aware of all this.

By the beginning of November many people began to be frightened of Baldwin's policy of inaction, since it was clear that in view of the foreign Press the English newspapers were bound soon to break their self-imposed silence. In what Middlemas has called 'a most striking exercise of back-stage power', certain civil servants, including Warren Fisher and Horace Wilson, 'attempted to jump Baldwin into an ultimatum', by composing a draft for him to submit to the King. This draft read as follows:

Unless steps are taken promptly to allay the widespread and growing mis-givings among the people, the feelings of respect, esteem and affection which Your Majesty has evoked among them will disappear in a revulsion of so grave and perilous a character as possibly to threaten the stability of the nation and the Empire. The dangers to the people of this country of such a shock, the disunity and loss of confidence which would ensue at a time when so much of the world is looking to the United Kingdom for guidance and leadership through a sea of troubles, cannot but be obvious to Your Majesty. In Mr Baldwin's opinion there is but one course which he can advise you to take, namely to put an end to Your Majesty's association with Mrs Simpson.[10]

This draft was shown to Hardinge who regarded it as very drastic and made some suggestions for amending it. It was then passed to Neville Chamberlain (Chancellor of the Exchequer and known to believe Baldwin should take a hard line with the King) who amended it as follows:

I have before me an official communication in which the advice of Your Majesty's Government is formally tendered, to the effect that in view of the grave dangers to which, in their opinion, this country is being exposed, your association with Mrs Simpson should be terminated forthwith. It is hardly neces-sary for me to point out that should this advice be tendered and refused by Your Majesty, only one result could follow in accordance with the requirements of constitutional monarchy, that is, the resignation of myself and the National Government. If Mrs Simpson left the country forthwith, this distasteful matter could be settled in a less formal manner.[11]

These drafts make it clear that but for his Private Secretary in the first place, and the Prime Minister (who when he saw them suppressed them) in the second, the King might well have had real cause for complaint.

On 11 November the Prime Minister received a warning from the Editor of *The Morning Post* that the Press could no longer stay silent unless the government had the matter in hand, and Geoffrey Dawson, the Editor of *The Times*, went to Downing Street to discuss the possibilities and dangers of publication. In the meantime Hardinge had learned that two affidavits had been filed requiring the intervention of the King's Proctor in the Simpson divorce case on the grounds of collusion.*

---

* As the law stood at the time the fact that two people both wished to divorce each other was an absolute bar to their being able to do so. Thus if it could be proved that the divorce was arranged 'collusively' between the two parties, the application would fail. It was for this reason that evidence had to be provided of the physical unfaithfulness of one party or the other, and

Possibly more important than any of these things, Hardinge, who on 15 October had written confidentially to the Governor-General of Canada, Lord Tweedsmuir, asking if there were any marked reaction in Canada to articles in the American Press (which found its way freely over the border) and whether there was any evidence of damage to the prestige of the monarch, received a reply. In this Lord Tweedsmuir pointed out that, although he had done his best to collect opinions through his staff, this was not a matter which he, as the King's representative, could broach directly with anyone in Canada. His impression was, however, that the Canadians, whose reaction had at first been one of incredulity and indignation 'especially at the impertinence of a paper like *Time*', had come to an unwilling belief in these stories. Canadian opinion intensely disliked the American element in the stories and the Canadian, although very friendly to the American, was quick to resent interference or patronage and felt his dignity hurt in having his King so closely associated with gossip of an American flavour.

'The monarchy under the late King,' Tweedsmuir wrote, 'was exalted into a kind of palladium of the domestic virtues.' It provided a standard of conduct for the ordinary man which, although he might not personally follow it, he profoundly admired. 'He feels that the British monarchy is the one stable centre in the anarchic world and he is in dread of anything which might weaken that stability.'

Then, having said that the country had originally been settled, so far as the British population was concerned, largely by Scots and United Empire Loyalists, that is by Presbyterians and Methodists, and had retained far more of the Victorian tradition in thought and conduct than any other part of the Empire, he went on to make a special point in relation to the King's personality.

He is really idolized here. Canada feels that he is, in a special sense, her own possession. It is wonderful how strong the personal affection is in all classes, from guides and trappers and prospectors and small farmers up to commercial and political leaders. Any smirching of their idol is felt as almost a personal loss. I am told on all sides that this feeling is especially strong in the younger people. Canadian youth is by no means strait-laced, but the King has become to them an ideal figure which has captured their imagination and their affection. They have the feeling of their elders about the sanctity of the throne, but they have also this sense of personal intimacy. Like all devotees, they are unwilling to believe that any clay can enter into the composition of their god. And if they are compelled to admit this there will be a most unfortunate reaction.[12]

For all these reasons, the Governor-General summed up, 'the condition

---

why this was so often provided by the respondent being found in bed at a hotel with someone hired for the purpose.

Legal opinion which was later sought was that there were no grounds for treating the divorce as collusive but Hardinge did not know that at the time.

of Canadian opinion seems to me to be most anxious and disquieting'. He also wrote in the same strain to Baldwin although it is doubtful whether the Prime Minister had yet received this letter on 13 November when Hardinge wrote to the King.

In any case, both men came to the conclusion that the time had come to act. Baldwin called a meeting of some of his senior colleagues, MacDonald, Chamberlain, Halifax, Simon and Runciman and began discussions with them: Hardinge decided that it was his duty to warn the King.

On the morning of 13 November he had composed a draft of the letter he was eventually to send when Dawson arrived to see him, to show him the draft of a strongly-worded leader he had written for *The Times* and to warn him that the Press could not be held for more than a few days longer and that *The Times* should be in the forefront. Hardinge, who was later to write 'The King's Private Secretary is a solitary figure, and ploughs a lonely furrow', and 'At this moment of anxiety and distress I desperately needed an outside opinion as to the general wisdom and propriety of my letter, as well as its accuracy', showed his letter to Dawson who found no fault with it.*

Hardinge then called at Downing Street to ask the Prime Minister's authority to tell the King of his meeting with senior ministers and to ask whether Baldwin could postpone the meeting until they learned the King's reaction. Baldwin replied that he could postpone no longer as the pressure was overwhelming.

One further event must have influenced Hardinge. On that day he lunched with Stanley Bruce, the High Commissioner for Australia. As a result of this luncheon Bruce sent a communication to the Prime Minister in which he indicated the views of Australia which were that 'if there was any question of marriage with Mrs Simpson the King would have to go, as far as Australia was concerned'.[13] This communication had a great effect on the Prime Minister and two days later (15 November) he had luncheon with Bruce. At this interview Bruce found Baldwin's mind confused and he later wrote him a letter in which he summarized the position as he saw it, advising him as to where in his opinion his duty lay. Speaking of Baldwin's meeting with the King on 20 October he said:

You did not deal specifically with the question of the King contemplating the madness of marrying the woman, and make it clear that the consequences of such an action would be such as to leave no alternative but for him to abdicate. Nor did you warn him that if he contemplated such a thing you would be forced to tender your resignation. If I rightly comprehend the position, you at this first

---

* In an article in *The Times* of November 1955 Lord Hardinge says that Geoffrey Dawson 'called and showed me the leading article which he had written for his paper', a slightly equivocal sentence. In *The History of The Times* it is stated that Hardinge asked the Editor to call. It does not seem of very much importance, unless one believes in a plot against the King. Hardinge may be criticized for asking advice; but his reasons for doing so carry conviction and he could certainly have been criticized if he had sent off so important a document without any man's advice.

interview gave to the King a broad picture of the undesirable reactions of this country and the Empire and the damage to British prestige abroad which his conduct abroad was causing, and made the strongest appeal to him to mend his ways. Your hope was that this appeal would be successful and the position would right itself gradually and that no more drastic action would be necessary. I gather that, for a week after your interview, you inclined to the view that it was having the effect you hoped for, but that now you are convinced it is not and that further action on your part is necessary. Your preoccupation is the time and character of such action. The answer as to the time is clearly – at once. With the certainty that the Press will restrain themselves little longer, and the evidence of the possibility of the King committing himself to some irrecoverable action afforded by the divorce proceedings, any delay is dangerous.

In considering what action should be taken, Bruce went on to say that the overwhelming importance of the distinction between a marriage and a liaison must be kept in mind, but that there was sufficient evidence to suggest that the King might be contemplating marriage. If he said that he had such an intention, then Bruce thought Baldwin would have to advise him what the consequences would be, and these he outlined as follows:

That the people of this country and of the Dominions would not accept this woman as the Queen and would demonstrate both against her and the King himself – that the House of Commons would probably take drastic action with regard to the Civil List – that because of the perils both to the Throne and the Empire the King's conduct had created, there would be a demand for his abdication that he would find it impossible to resist. ... You would have to tell him that unless he was prepared to abandon any idea of marriage ... you would be compelled to advise him to abdicate, and unless he accepted such advice you would be unable to continue as his adviser and would tender the resignation of the Government.[14]

Hardinge had not seen this letter at the time of his own to the King but, since he had luncheon with Bruce on the day he sent his to Fort Belvedere, he must have been completely informed of the High Commissioner's views. Considering this and the attitude of leaders of the Opposition and Sir Walter Citrine, the restiveness of the Press, the draft memoranda of backbenchers and civil servants, and of the meeting of senior members of the government, how better could he have performed his duty than by the letter he sent to the King?

The King thought less coldly, or so he would later write, with more sympathy for the fact that he was in love. Yet he had cut himself off completely from Hardinge and the rest of his household who could not approach him except in the line of duty, and he had made it plain that no man might address him on the subject of Mrs Simpson. (See Godfrey Thomas and Halsey to Baldwin p. 181, and see his treatment of General Trotter p. 185.) The idea that he was hurt because Hardinge did not approach him in person or in a less formal way simply will not do.

The truth is he found Hardinge personally unsympathetic and would probably never have appointed him had his mind been less distracted. There was no approach the Private Secretary could have made which he would not have found distasteful. But he did like Godfrey Thomas who had served him for years. Nevertheless, when shortly after this Thomas felt that he must make an attempt to save his master from the future he so clearly intended for himself, he, too, could only write. It is often said that none of the King's servants ever attempted to dissuade him or to tell him the truth about where he was heading, but this is completely untrue. And, although Thomas wrote informally and with sympathy and love, speaking not merely of the King's duty to his country but in graphic and moving terms of the inevitable consequences to himself of abdication, his letter had no greater effect than Hardinge's. Neither man ever received an answer.

19

'SOMETHING MUST BE DONE'

The King was correct in believing that many people now knew that Baldwin had been to see him and also that increasing numbers had seen, or seen reports of, the gossip in the American Press. By Friday, 13 November, when he returned from his visit to the Fleet, Tom Jones was writing, 'There is only one topic in London – Mrs Simpson',[1] and Chips Channon, 'We are faced with an impasse. The country, or much of it, would not accept Queen Wallis, with two live husbands scattered about,'[2] while on the following day he recorded that the House of Commons was openly talking of abdication.

Mrs Simpson was awaiting the King at Fort Belvedere accompanied by Aunt Bessie Merryman, but he did not immediately tell them of the letter he had received. During the night he decided that, although the Private Secretary was the normal channel between the Palace and No. 10 Downing Street, he could no longer work through Alex Hardinge. He therefore asked Walter Monckton to meet him on Sunday afternoon at Windsor Castle and motored there to meet him.

Lady Colefax had motored down to Fort Belvedere for the day and finding herself alone with Mrs Simpson she had a long talk with her, later reporting her to be 'really miserable'.

All sorts of people had come to her reminding her of her duty and begging her to leave the country. 'They do not understand,' she said, 'that if I did so, the King would come after me regardless of anything. They would then get their scandal in the far worse form than they are getting it now.'

And at some time during this conversation Lady Colefax asked her whether the King had ever suggested marriage. Mrs Simpson 'seemed surprised' and said: 'Of course not.'[3]

The King had already taken Monckton into his confidence and, one evening about a week before he met him at Windsor Castle, he told him that he meant to marry Mrs Simpson. On that occasion Monckton, like everyone else when first confronted with this intention, counselled delay in making any decision, particularly as there was no possibility of marriage before 27 April, still six months off. The King then explained to him that he could not go forward to the Coronation meaning in his heart to make the marriage whatever happened, and deceiving both the government and the people.

At the meeting at Windsor Castle he showed Monckton the letter he had received from his Private Secretary. (The room in which the interview took place was the same in which the King would make his last broadcast less than a month later.) Walter Monckton's biographer remarks that it is difficult, reading this letter today, to understand the King's resentment because, although it was frigid it was not peremptory, and put forward disagreeable but nevertheless unquestionable truths. The evidence tends to suggest that Monckton himself shared some of the King's feeling. He afterwards wrote:

That letter informed him that the Press could not be kept quiet much longer and (inaccurately) that the Cabinet were already discussing the association and urged him to send Mrs Simpson abroad at once. [In this passage it is Monckton himself who is inaccurate. Hardinge had not said that the Cabinet were already discussing the matter but that the Prime Minister was meeting senior members of the government to discuss the matter, and in this he was correct.]

The King had never given Major Hardinge the opportunity of discussing Mrs Simpson with him, but he had reason to think that Major Hardinge, his first private secretary, was criticizing his conduct widely and in the strongest terms, and this he bitterly resented.[4]

The King, Monckton goes on to say, regarded the letter as forcing the issue (which it undoubtedly was) and thought that it compelled him to take some action, either to dismiss Major Hardinge or in some other way to bring the matter to a head. Monckton advised him not to dismiss Hardinge – as this would indicate a breach over Mrs Simpson – and 'to wait and be patient'.

In another passage, Monckton, after claiming a long friendship with Hardinge which he says made the difficulties of their positions easier, goes on to say:

I used to think Hardinge took too pessimistic and critical a view of the relationship and of the King's conduct: I am sure that he expressed his opinion too emphatically and widely to have any hope of retaining the King's confidence when the crisis came.

The result was that the King was confirmed in his policy of not confiding his feelings and his ideas on this subject to any of his staff. He felt he could not go behind Hardinge even to Godfrey Thomas: and he was in any case reluctant to mix what he hoped might still be his private affairs with his public duty and thought he might embarrass his Household by discussions.[5]

On any objective study of the facts Hardinge cannot be criticized on the score of his official duty, but this is apparently a charge of a more personal sort. It is too late successfully to investigate it (and Hardinge now passes into the background of the story) except to say that it was to a large extent his job to talk – in the sense of informing himself of opinion – and also that the King had a tendency at this time to regard any disagreement about what he wanted to do as a hostile act. It would not be surprising however if Hardinge was more censorious than Monckton himself. Monckton was a very remarkable man with a talent for negotiation which allowed him to conduct the delicate affairs of the Abdication without losing a friend or making an enemy and at the end of it to receive as much favour from the new King – George VI – as from the old. But he was romantic and emotional by nature, and in certain circumstances might also have found the world well lost for love (which is not the same as saying that he would have failed in his duty or sacrificed other people to himself, merely that he had an understanding and sympathy for the King's obsession denied to most people). This made him unrivalled in this situation as a negotiator but a trifle biased as a witness.* It is most unlikely that, but for Hardinge, the King would have gone to Godfrey Thomas, and completely ignores the facts to say that he still hoped not to mix his private with his public affairs. Monckton himself goes on to a far more acute analysis.

Moreover he was intensely and naturally suspicious on the whole matter, and made such confidences as he did in water-tight compartments. I am sure this was largely due to anxiety to avoid making anyone's position uncomfortable by too much knowledge. But in part it was no doubt because he realized that if anyone in his service sufficiently clearly appreciated what he wanted to do, his plans would probably be frustrated.[6]

On that afternoon at Windsor Castle Monckton agreed to act as the King's adviser and liaison with Baldwin in this crisis 'thus temporarily taking over Hardinge's principal duty as the constitutional link with the Prime Minister and the Cabinet'.[8] And Edward then told him that he proposed to send for Baldwin and tell him that if the Government were against his marriage with Mrs Simpson he was prepared to go.

'He will not like to hear that,' Monckton said gravely.

'I shall not find it easy to say,' the King replied.[9]

When he got back to the Fort the King showed Hardinge's letter to Mrs

---

* His own biographer says of him: We may infer that his friendship with the King led him always to place the most favourable interpretation possible upon his character. Where others detected an abnormal obstinacy he preferred to find strength and resolution.[7]

Simpson who, according to her own account, 'was stunned' and said she thought the only thing for her was to follow the Private Secretary's advice and leave the country. The King was adamant that she should not do that and he said that Hardinge's letter was 'an impertinence'. And he told her that he had discussed it with Monckton and was going to send for Baldwin on the next day. 'I'm going to tell him that if the country won't approve our marrying, I'm ready to go.'[10]* And on the next morning the King asked his secretaries to inform Mr Baldwin that he wished to see him at six-thirty that evening.†

In the meantime he telephoned to Stornaway House to find Lord Beaverbrook, and, on being told that the latter was on the high seas on his way to the USA, he appealed to him by telegram and telephone to return immediately. Lord Beaverbrook was appalled by the freedom with which the King talked to him on the telephone on the ship and even on one occasion in a newspaper office – 'The conversation was of course monitored. I asked that secrecy should be observed. Fortunately Mr Patterson was a man who would not make public use of a private conversation, but the King was not to know that.'[12] Nevertheless, he turned round in New York and took ship back to England.

At some time, and the indications are that it was probably before this second interview, Baldwin sent for the Attorney-General, Sir Donald Somervell, and asked for his advice on three matters – Marriage, Abdication and the possibility of an intervention by the King's Proctor. On the question of marriage the Attorney-General gave the opinion that the King's marriage was outside the Royal Marriages Act but that it would be unconstitutional for him to marry contrary to the advice of his ministers and he quoted Queen Victoria's sentence to her uncle, Leopold of the Belgians, to the effect *'Lord Melbourne, who I have of course consulted throughout and who approves'*. If he did marry contrary to, or without advice, he would be acting unconstitutionally, as if he did any other public act without or contrary to advice.

This does not seem to have been the view that was adopted. The precedent of Queen Victoria was invoked in an article in the *Daily Telegraph* of 5 December 1936 by W. Ivor Jennings, a Reader in English Law at the University of London, in the opposite sense. The engagement of Queen Victoria was not discussed in Cabinet, Mr Jennings said, and, although Lord Melbourne was cognisant of the proposal, no Prime Minister has ever

---

* The accounts of the King, Mrs Simpson and Walter Monckton differ. Walter Monckton says: 'I wanted him once more to wait and be patient, but he discussed the matter with Mrs Simpson after leaving me and decided to send for Mr Baldwin and tell him of his intention to marry.'[11]

† The King actually told Hardinge to arrange for Baldwin, Chamberlain and Halifax to come to see him and added that he would be glad if the Prime Minister would let Hoare and Duff Cooper come as well. Baldwin replied that he would come alone, saying that as the matter had not yet been before the Cabinet, he could not single out two of his ministers to accompany him.

been in that confidential, almost paternal relationship in which he stood to the Queen. The Queen subsequently announced her engagement to the Privy Council, but she took the decision on her own account.

It is a difficult question but the history of the Abdication seems to prove that the sovereign is free to choose his own consort providing his choice is approved by the Prime Minister and government of the day. If on the other hand he chooses someone generally regarded as unsuitable to be Queen, it in fact becomes a constitutional matter.

On the question of the Abdication, Sir Donald Somervell said this could be done with the King's Assent by an Act of Parliament; and on the question of the King's Proctor he took the view that it would be contrary to the constitutional position of the King for the King's officer in the King's courts to investigate allegations against the King, but he added that this view was debatable.*

Baldwin arrived at the Palace at six-thirty to be warned by Hardinge that he might expect something dramatic, and the King came straight to the point. 'I understand that you and several members of the Cabinet have some fear of a constitutional crisis developing over my friendship with Mrs Simpson.'[13] Baldwin replied that this was true. In his account of this second interview with Baldwin, the Duke of Windsor says that it was the Prime Minister who then introduced the question of marriage and this is what Baldwin himself said in a speech to the House of Commons made some weeks after the interview and without notes. It is not what Lucy Baldwin recorded in her diary on the evening of the same day. According to her account it was the King who introduced the subject – which is not only more likely but (along with certain other small points) has led historians to the neat deduction that when he wrote his account, although his memories were in some ways vivid, the Duke of Windsor, having no written record of what occurred, relied on Baldwin's speech to the House of Commons.†

In any case during the course of the interview Baldwin told him that he did not think this 'particular marriage was one that would receive the approbation of the country'.

I pointed out to him that the position of the King's wife was different from the position of any other citizen in the country; it was part of the price which the King has to pay. His wife becomes Queen; the Queen becomes the Queen of the country; and, therefore, in the choice of a Queen, the voice of the people must be heard. . . .[14]

When Baldwin had said this the King said to him: 'I want you to be the first to know that I have made up my mind and nothing will alter it – I have looked at it from all sides – and I mean to abdicate to marry Mrs Simpson.'

* Sir Donald Somervell's views on these and related matters are given in full in H. Montgomery Hyde's *Baldwin: The Unexpected Prime Minister*.

† Middlemas & Barnes.

To this Baldwin replied 'Sir, this is a very grave decision and I am deeply grieved.'[15]

According to Lucy Baldwin's account, Baldwin then went on to tell the King that in the view of some legal opinion the divorce ought not to have been granted, that there were certain aspects of it that in any ordinary case would not have gone through. And Mrs Baldwin says: 'His Majesty, I gather did not exactly like that.'[16] This is a little obscure because it is not clear what Baldwin was referring to (unless to the two affidavits alleging collusion which Hardinge had been told of) but His Majesty was probably quite right not to like it. (See p. 247 above for Somervell's opinion on an intervention by the King's Proctor against the King and p. 283 below for the issue of collusion.) Baldwin therefore turned to a nobler theme, telling the King that Mackenzie King of Canada and Bruce of Australia both agreed that the throne was the one thing that held the Empire together and that this might break it up. The King repeated that he intended to marry Mrs Simpson as soon as she was free. If he could marry her as King well and good; he would be happy and in consequence perhaps a better King. But if on the other hand the government opposed the marriage, as the Prime Minister had given him reason to believe it would, then he would go. Baldwin replied that this was most grievous news on which he could not comment that day.*

Then the King said that he meant to go and tell his mother of his decision that evening and he gave Baldwin permission to tell two or three Privy Councillors whom he trusted.

All the time the King was most charming – Lucy Baldwin wrote that evening – but S. said the King simply could not understand and he couldn't make him. On leaving, the King held Stanley's hand for a long time and there were almost tears in his eyes when he said good-bye.[16]

And at this interview Baldwin was more than ever conscious of the other man's exaltation. 'The King's face wore at times such a look of beauty', he told his family, 'as might have lighted the face of a young knight who had caught a glimpse of the Holy Grail.'[17]

Out of courtesy – the Duke of Windsor wrote fifteen years later – I escorted Mr Baldwin to the Garden Entrance. Standing under the glass canopy, I watched him wriggle into the same undersized little black box in which he had made his first descent on the Fort.† As the box with its portly occupant shot away into the dark, it began to take on the guise of a sinister and purposeful little black beetle. Where was it off to now?[18]‡

* This is the Duke of Windsor's version. Baldwin's does not differ in any material way.
† A reference to an earlier description of Baldwin's car, which was in fact a police car.
‡ This was, it is true, a busy day for Baldwin. Before seeing the King, he had received a deputation consisting of Lord Salisbury, Lord Derby, Lord FitzAlan and Sir Austen Chamberlain who urged him to decide on a policy and acquaint the King with it. To this he replied that he would think it over, and he seems to have been more impressed when he heard that Winston

That night the King went to dine with his mother, having asked that his sister Mary should be present. His new sister-in-law, the Duchess of Gloucester, was also there when he arrived, this having been arranged before it was known that he would come, but she left him alone with his mother and sister as soon as dinner was over.

Edward – David to his family – then told them of his love for Wallis Simpson and his determination to marry her and of the opposition of the Prime Minister and other members of the government. Presently he made it clear that he intended to abdicate.

This was not completely unexpected to Queen Mary who had lived in an agony of shame and apprehension for months. Even before her husband died she had realized that there was a dangerous recklessness in her son's feeling for Mrs Simpson, and in the last months she had learned of his total disregard for the dignity of the crown like everyone else from American newspapers. Because of the long silence of the British Press it is hardly realized in England how much suffering the King inflicted on his family, not merely by leaving the throne but by the manner in which he went.

The Queen, who had so long and so painfully failed in communication with her children, now implored her son to reconsider his decision. In July 1938 she wrote him the following letter:

You ask me in your letter of the 23rd June to write to you frankly about my true feelings with regard to you and the present position and this I will do now. You will remember how miserable I was when you informed me of your intended marriage and abdication and how I implored you not to do so for your sake and for the sake of the country. You did not seem able to take in any point of view but your own. ... I do not think you have ever realized the shock, which the attitude you took up caused your family and the whole Nation. It seemed inconceivable to those who had made such sacrifices during the war that you, as their King, refused a lesser sacrifice. ... My feelings for you as your Mother remain the same, and our being parted and the cause of it, grieve me beyond words. After all, all my life I have put my Country before everything else, and I simply cannot change now.[19]

Queen Mary refused her son's plea that he might bring Wallis Simpson to see her. She was both shocked and angry. In the following account, which Baldwin gave his niece, some of the shock is apparent:

Queen Mary is one of the shyest women I have ever met in my life. This shyness puts a kind of barrier between her and you which it is well nigh impossible to get across.

I had suffered rather from this, though she was always very nice to me. But I was always expected to keep the conversation going; and it sometimes flagged.

Churchill had been asked and refused to join the deputation than by the views of those who did join it. In the evening after leaving the King, he met Neville Chamberlain, Lord Halifax, Simon, MacDonald and Runciman and informed them of what had happened at his audience with the King.

She had a way, too, of standing at the end of the room when one was shown in at Buckingham Palace; and she would remain there like a statue while you made your bow and walked over a sometimes very slippery floor to kiss her hand. But all that was one day changed quite suddenly and I will tell you how. . . .

The first time I was sent for to see her at the beginning of this Simpson story, I had a tremendous shock. For, instead of standing immobile in the middle distance, silent and majestic, she came trotting across the room *exactly like a puppy dog*: and before I had time to bow, she took hold of my hand in both of hers and held it tight. 'Well, Prime Minister,' she said, 'here's a pretty kettle of fish!'

After that, I can assure you, my dear, the barriers were down. [20]

We know from her biographer that if Queen Mary was shocked she was also humiliated and very angry.

It can be simply stated that Queen Mary greeted her son's decision to give up the throne with consternation, with anger and with pain. . . . No single event in the whole of her life – which, we may recall, had not been an invariably happy one – had caused her so much real distress or left her with so deep a feeling of 'humiliation'. [21]

And again:

The plain fact was that, as well as feeling miserable, Queen Mary was likewise feeling angry. 'H.M. is still angry with the Duke & I really think that helps her to bear what she called "the humiliation" of it all,' wrote an old friend several months later. [22]

Nevertheless, at the time the Queen wrote her son this letter:

As your mother, I must send you a line of true sympathy in the difficult position in which you are placed – I have been thinking of you all day, hoping you are making a wise decision for your future – I fear your visit to Wales will be trying in more ways than one, with this momentous action hanging over your head. [23]

On the following day the King told each of his brothers of his decision. The Duke of York, he says, was so taken aback that he could not bring himself to say anything, while the Duke of Gloucester seemed to be considering how this news would affect himself. The Duke of Kent, 'because he had had better opportunity than the others to observe the nature of my love for Wallis', [24] was more reconciled to his decision. His assessment of his eldest brother's reaction is probably correct, as it may be of his second brother's. The evidence does not suggest that the Duke of Kent was 'reconciled'. 'Besotted. That was what the Duke of Kent called it over and over again,' Baldwin told his niece, and: 'Another time the Duke of Kent came in looking furiously angry. "He is besotted on the woman," he said, "one can't get a word of sense out of him." ' [25]

At his meeting with Baldwin the King had also asked whether he might, without a breach of constitutional practice, seek the independent counsel and advice of other members of the Cabinet. He still had some hope that, even though the senior members of the Cabinet were behind Baldwin, there might be among the younger ones, particularly those who were his personal friends, someone who could be persuaded to speak for him. When Baldwin agreed, he asked to see Sir Samuel Hoare and Mr Duff Cooper, and he saw them both on the following morning, 17 November.

Sir Samuel Hoare had been not an intimate, but an acquaintance of his for some time. As Prince of Wales he had been in sympathy with Hoare when the latter had been forced by public opinion to resign over the Hoare-Laval pact, and as King he had asked him to Sandringham to shoot,* and had spent several days in his company on his recent visit to the Fleet. Predictably the King failed to win him as an ally. Hoare, who says that on his way to the interview he was as nervous as when he first met Gandhi, told him that Baldwin was in command of the situation and the senior ministers solidly behind him. If the King were to press his marriage on the Cabinet he would meet a stone wall of opposition.

The Duke of Windsor said that Duff Cooper (with whom he was on far more intimate terms) was as encouraging as Hoare was discouraging, but this seems to be a misinterpretation of Duff Cooper's attitude. He began by asking whether it was any use trying to dissuade the King from his intention or whether his mind was made up.

He said that it would be quite useless, and I believed him. I then suggested postponement. ... I thought that if they would agree not to meet for a year, during which he would be crowned and perhaps attend a Durbar, of which there seemed some possibility at the time, he would at the end of that period have grown more accustomed to his position and more loth to leave it. I also secretly thought that he might in the interval meet somebody whom he would love more. He never has.[26]

In answer the King made an explanation which is important because in the first place it exposes exactly what Duff Cooper's suggestion would have meant, and in the second it outlines an attitude from which he could never be persuaded to depart.

The Coronation, he said, is essentially a religious service. The King is anointed with oil; he takes the Sacrament; and as Defender of the Faith he swears an oath to uphold the doctrines of the Church of England which does not approve of divorce.

For me to have gone through the Coronation ceremony harbouring in my heart the secret intention to marry contrary to the Church's tenets would have meant being crowned with a lie on my lips. ... Whatever the cost to me personally I was determined, before I would think of being crowned, to settle once and for all the question of my right to marry.[27]

On the same day, 17 November, Miss Ellen Wilkinson asked a question in the House of Commons of the President of the Board of Trade.

* Sir Samuel Hoare had been at Sandringham on 16 October when the King left to see Baldwin at the Fort.

Can the Right Hon. Gentleman say why in the case of two American magazines of the highest repute imported into this country in the last few weeks, two
and sometimes three pages have been torn out; and what is this thing the British
public are not allowed to know?[28]

To this Mr Runciman answered: 'My department has nothing to do
with that.'

Since Miss Wilkinson knew, as by now did every member of the House
of Commons, why these American magazines had been censored, the question must have seemed to the watching Press a warning that, if they remained silent much longer, the news of the King's love for Mrs Simpson
might break for the first time elsewhere. Nevertheless, the Prime Minister
had sent for Geoffrey Dawson after his interview with the King the night
before and 'made it clear for the first time that any Press comment at this
moment might weaken his influence such as it was'.[29]

And the Press were in a further difficulty. ... 'If newspaper criticism
were to begin before these engagements,' Geoffrey Dawson wrote, speaking of the intended visit to Wales and also of the visit to the Fleet, 'it
might be taken as an attempt to undermine H.M.'s popularity in advance; if
immediately after them as an attempt to minimize his influence. It was a very
difficult problem on which S.B. professed himself quite unable to give
advice.'[30]

The King began on 18 November the journey through South Wales
which, more than anything else he ever undertook, has lingered in the
minds of his fellow countrymen. He was attended on this tour by his
Private Secretary, Major Alexander Hardinge. The King showed no sign
of any animosity towards Hardinge, indeed he was completely friendly.
Major Hardinge wrote later that he believed the animosity the Duke of
Windsor showed him after the Abdication was entirely artificial and the
shock and surprise caused by his letter manufactured subsequently.[31]

In one of the blackest periods of British industrial history South Wales
was the blackest part of the country. In the Rhondda and Monmouth
valleys, against a background of slag heaps and shuttered and empty shops,
hosts of men stood on the road or at abandoned works to meet the King,
and these men and their families were short of food and clothing and many
of them had been out of work for years. As he moved among them, the
King spoke to dozens of men directly, showing the utmost concern for
their plight. A hundred times an hour his obvious sympathy encouraged
sad-faced, ill-clothed men to speak to him of their troubles. And he showed
even in these unpropitious circumstances the old flair for public relations,
the same instinct for maximum effect. He entered Merthyr Labour Exchange at a time when it was full of men waiting hopelessly for work and
moving up to the grill spoke to them individually, showing openly his
sorrow for their plight; and he ended his already long day almost an hour
late because he made a detour, not in the original schedule, to visit the

Bessemer Steel Works at Dowlais. Here nine thousand men had been employed a few years before, while now it was a vast derelict area. Hundreds of men awaited him, sitting on piles of twisted and rusting metal where demolition had taken place, and when he arrived they arose and sang an old Welsh hymn. The King stood bareheaded, his face grave and set, plainly intensely moved. Turning to an official, he said: 'These works brought all these people here. Something must be done to find them work.'*

That night he dined with Malcolm Stewart, former Chief Commissioner for the Special Areas and Sir George Gillett, his successor. Ernest Brown, Minister for Mines, and Sir Kingsley Wood, Minister of Health, who accompanied him throughout the tour, were also there. At this dinner he was told something of the plans for re-starting derelict pits and steelworks in South Wales and Monmouthshire.

On the following day, 19 November, the King carried out an almost equally arduous tour. At a housing estate at Pontypool he said: 'You may be sure that all I can do for you I will; we certainly want better times brought to your valley.' And at Blaenavon he told the Chairman of the Unemployed Men's Committee 'Something will be done about unemployment.'†

When the King left South Wales he left hope behind him, and by his outspoken comments he probably did, as *The Times* put it the next day, 'greatly help to concentrate attention on the state of the distressed areas and the failure of the industrial revival to penetrate the economic backwaters that are particularly affected.'[32] He had given a demonstration of his capacity for sympathy, of his genuine distress at the misery which surrounded him and he had brought something very like happiness (however fleeting) to men who for so long had known only despair. He had spoken words that have ensured him a place in history and which have led many people to jump to the conclusion that he had some real affinity with the Left Wing political parties. More than for anything else, he is remembered for the simple reaction: 'Something must be done.'

Yet how many people remember that these words and those which followed them – 'You may be sure that all I can do for you I will' – were spoken a bare three weeks before he left England for good? And how many people have ever known that when he spoke them he had already told the Prime Minister, his mother and his three brothers of his intention to abdicate the throne?

The King arrived at Paddington at seven o'clock in the evening of the second day of his tour. That night he dined with Sir Henry Channon. The

---

* This has been variously reported as 'Something ought to be done', and 'Something must be done'. 'Something must be done' are the words which have been remembered.

† There was some real justification for this remark because the government, at last recognizing that these appalling conditions could not go on, had already got plans for injecting money into these areas and re-starting some of the derelict works.

day before he had found time to telephone from Wales to say he would like decorations to be worn and he arrived in good spirits. Chips wrote:

At once I saw that he was in a gay mood – no doubt a reaction from his depressing Welsh tour, two dreadfully sad days in the distressed areas. ... The King was jolly, gay and full of cracks. He returned only tonight from the distressed areas, and must have felt as elated as I do after two or three days in my constituency.[33]

THE MORGANATIC
MARRIAGE PROPOSAL

Baldwin, who had been in Scotland while the King had been in Wales, returned on the same day, and on going down to Chequers the following day he found a letter from Walter Monckton.

> You will find his decision unchanged on the main question – Monckton wrote – And he is facing the rest and considering all that is involved, with a real appreciation of the interests which you would wish him to have in mind. I think he will want to see you about Tuesday or Wednesday. I shall no doubt see him before then and I will let you know anything worth reporting. At present his ideas are a little fluid, but I shall remember what you said to me and do my best. He will not do anything precipitate or selfish, saving *il gran refiuto*.[1]

And on the same day Hardinge recorded that he had seen Monckton after he had had an interview with the King and that Monckton looked on HM's decision to marry and abdicate as irrevocable, although he added that Duff Cooper's influence had not helped. Monckton said that he was urging the King to get it over quickly and go out of the country.

The King was nevertheless undecided. He gave the impression that, although he had made up his mind on the main issue and was at peace with himself, he had neither come to a decision as to procedure, nor even entirely given up hope of finding backing for his belief that he might marry Mrs Simpson and also remain on the throne. A lack of decision on the first of these things seemed natural at this early stage, but his reasons for not abandoning hope soon became apparent.

The *Daily Mail* had given great publicity to the King's visit to Wales and on Monday, 23 November it appeared with a leader under the headline *The King Edward Touch*. This leader, having said that the magic of personal leadership had never been better shown than by the King's visit to South Wales, continued:

The King was openly disturbed and afflicted by his survey. The lot of the humblest people has always been his nearest anxiety and continual pre-occupation – and the people of South Wales realised that here was a man who cares supremely for their wellbeing. He has started a fresh chapter of endeavour for the distressed areas. The King does not consider his mission fulfilled by the pilgrimage to derelict mines, extinct forges and forlorn villages. Already he has talked to his Ministers and prompted them into real activity. ... The King has called for action. He will want to review the Government's plans and to be kept posted of their progress.

The royal technique repays study. In the first place he approached the difficulties of South Wales resolute to find a remedy however novel the methods of treatment might be. He went to see for himself, personal investigation being the basis for every job of work the King touches. Then, once he had settled in his own mind the extent and urgency of the dilemma, he called for all the evidence available. ...

The contrast to the way in which national questions are customarily approached can escape nobody. There is consultation, committees are appointed and conference takes place in the solemn apartments of Whitehall, but how often does a Minister as a preface to this consecrated and lengthy procedure, go boldly forth to see for himself and measure the problem by independent judgment, following this with action.

If only Ministers would say in the House of Commons: 'I am going to see for myself and act forthwith' instead of 'The matter is receiving attention', at what a refreshing pace the nation's affairs would move! Even such deadweight lethargy as surrounds Britain's most vital need – rearmament – would yield to the King Edward touch.

Surely those who have recently confessed that they dared not tell the people the truth three years ago and have accomplished so little towards defence will realize the gulf between their conduct and the King's methods in Wales.*

This leader made it plain that an attempt to form a King's party would be made and its effect cannot be properly appreciated unless it is remembered that it did incidentally express a general attitdue towards government held by increasing numbers of people. These were the days of the Popular Front, of the Spanish Civil War, of a growing awareness of what was happening in Germany and Italy: this was the generation of the thirties who above everything were tired of the complacency and lethargy exemplarized by the National Government. King Edward VIII could hardly have retained the reputation for championing the cause of the unemployed against the government if it had not been for the growing belief

* On 12 November in the debate on the Address Baldwin had made the 'appalling frankness' speech, in which he said: 'Supposing I had gone to the country and said that Germany was rearming and we must rearm, does anybody think that this pacific democracy would have rallied to the cry at that moment? I cannot think of anything that would have made the loss of the election from my point of view more certain.'

of his subjects that a champion was needed to counter the apathy shown in the face of the appalling conditions in the distressed areas.

The *Daily Mail* leader was immediately countered by a leader in *The Times*.

It is right that the King's contribution to this awakening should be applauded. But it is a wholly mischievous suggestion, and one altogether alien to the spirit of the Constitution, which would set his well-known sympathy with the distressed areas against the measures taken by the Government, and which by implication would drive a wedge between the Monarch and his Ministers. The King's Ministers are His Majesty's advisers, and to contrast his personal and representative concern for the well-being of a section of the people with the administrative steps of his advisers is a constitutionally dangerous proceeding and would threaten, if continued, to entangle the throne in politics.

And after quoting at length from the *Daily Mail* leader, it went on:

To write in that way is to strike at the very root of the Monarchy: for if the Monarch is to be dissociated for the purpose of political argument, from some actions of his Ministers, then by inference he must bear a more direct responsibility for all the rest. The King's constitutional position is above and apart from party politics, and those who cherish the institution of the Monarchy will always strive to keep it so.

And on the following morning, 25 November, *The Times* leader counter attacked both more subtly and, to those who understood it, more openly.* A new Governor-General, Patrick Duncan, had just been appointed for South Africa and *The Times* criticized the appointment, not on the grounds of Duncan's personal qualities but on the grounds that he had been too much involved in South African politics and that this would make it difficult for him to remain above the political battle there. Then it went on:

It is the position – the position of the King's deputy no less than of the King himself – that must be kept high above public reproach or ridicule, and that is incomparably more important than the individual who fills it. ... the King's deputy, like the King himself, should be invested with a certain detachment and dignity, which need not at all preclude his contact with all sorts and conditions of people, but which are not so easily put on as a change of clothes.

The *Daily Mail* leader was clearly inspired by its owner, Lord Rothermere, whose son Esmond Harmsworth we have seen visiting the King at Balmoral and who had joined Lord Beaverbrook in arranging the discretion of the Press over Mrs Simpson's divorce suit. In the absence of Lord Beaverbrook on the high seas, these two formed the spearhead of the King's party, and they now made themselves felt in an unexpected way.

Mr Esmond Harmsworth invited Mrs Simpson to lunch with him at

---

* Lord Beaverbrook was later to say that this leader 'intimidated the King in code'.[2]

Claridge's.* His purpose in doing this was to ask whether she had ever considered the possibility of marrying the King morganatically. He explained that a morganatic marriage was one between a member of the Royal House and a woman not of equal birth, in which the wife does not take the husband's rank, and her children are without rights of succession, while their claim on their father's estate is restricted to his personal property. Harmsworth asked Mrs Simpson whether she would be willing to marry the King under these conditions.[3]

'Wallis,' the Duke of Windsor tells us, 'replied that the matter was hardly one upon which she could with propriety comment.'

However, in spite of this and one or two other improbable remarks, Mrs Simpson almost certainly favoured this idea as a compromise way out of a situation into which she and the King had so light-heartedly drifted. She immediately explained it to the King, who, although he was not at once attracted to it, nevertheless sent for Mr Harmsworth. He also asked Walter Monckton to look into the legal precedents. Monckton advised him that even in the unlikely event of the Cabinet approving a morganatic marriage, special legislation would be required and there was little prospect of such a Bill passing Parliament. It is symptomatic of the King's state of mind that in spite of this advice he sent Mr Esmond Harmsworth off to expound the idea to the Prime Minister. Here is the account of this interview which Baldwin later gave his niece.

Harmsworth, the editor of the *Daily Mail*† (which, my dear, with the *Daily Express* I always call 'the Devil's' press), managed to get an interview with him at Fort Belvedere shortly before the end. It was he who suggested the morganatic marriage to the King. The King at once sent for me and told me what Harmsworth had said. I assured him that the British people would never agree to it, and left him to digest that. . . .

Harmsworth then called upon me.. . . I told him that he and his filthy paper did not really *know* the mind of the English people: whereas I *did*. And I explained to him that a morganatic marriage would mean a special Bill being passed in Parliament; and that Parliament would *never* pass it.

Harmsworth said:

'Oh, I'm sure they would! the whole standard of morals is so much more broadminded since the War.'

I replied:

'Yes: you are right: the ideal of morality and duty and self-sacrifice and decency certainly *has* gone down since the War: but the ideal of Kingship has gone *up* – in fact, never in history has it stood so high as now. And I tell you that the English people will never accept the thing that you suggest.

* There is some doubt about when this luncheon took place. The Duchess of Windsor dates it as while the King was in Wales, the Duke of Windsor appears to think it was after he came back. Lord Beaverbrook says it was on 21 November, and although this was a Saturday, Lord Beaverbrook may have kept a note at the time, whereas the other two clearly did not.

† Esmond Harmsworth, now the 2nd Lord Rothermere, proprietor of the *Daily Mail*, was not in fact the editor.

Harmsworth was frightfully funny, though he did not realize it.[4]

Reporting to the King on this interview Harmsworth said that Baldwin had seemed 'surprised, interested and non-committal'. However, he had promised to refer the plan to the Cabinet.

Two days later, having heard nothing from the Prime Minister, the King asked him to come and see him.

He asked at once what Baldwin thought of this new proposition and Baldwin replied that he 'had not considered it'. He explained that by this he did not mean that he had given it no thought but that he had not considered it officially. If, however, the King wanted 'a horseback opinion', he thought that Parliament would never pass the necessary legislation. He then explained that if the morganatic marriage proposal was to be 'considered' it would have to be submitted not merely to the British Cabinet but to the Dominion Cabinets as well. He asked the King if he wished him to do that and the King replied that he did.*

Under the Statute of Westminster, by which the crown was the legal connecting link between England and the Dominion countries, the question should have been put to each self-governing Dominion through the Governor-General, but it was agreed that the matter was too delicate and too personal to be handled by the King himself and Baldwin undertook to determine their views.

On the following day Lord Beaverbrook landed at Southampton and motored straight to the Fort, where special dishes had been prepared for his luncheon to accord with his latest diet.

Lord Beaverbrook was horrified to hear of the morganatic proposal. 'Mrs Simpson,' the King said, 'preferred the morganatic marriage to any other solution of the problem.' He also told Beaverbrook that Harmsworth had already laid the morganatic proposal before the Prime Minister. 'In speaking of Mr Harmsworth, the King confessed to some embarrassment. Harmsworth had asked him if I was returning home, and the King had not told him that he himself had recalled me. He asked me to protect him on this point.'[6]

Lord Beaverbrook's dislike of the morganatic marriage proposal was a result of his belief that the politicians had no status at all in the main issue of marriage. The King was free to marry whom he chose and the government had no power in law or in precedent to forbid the banns. But he was not free to make a morganatic marriage because this would require legislation. If the Prime Minister refused time for the necessary Bill (or presumably if Parliament refused to pass such a Bill) the King must accept open humiliation or dismiss his ministers and seek new advisers in the House of

---

* 'Mr Baldwin had hoped, and thought to frighten the King' – Chips recorded from information he describes as 'true, though not six people in the Kingdom are so informed' – but 'found him obstinate, in love and rather more than a little mad'.[5]

Commons. Lord Beaverbrook then gave the King his recommendations, which were: (1) to withdraw the proposal for a morganatic marriage. (2) To find some friend in the Cabinet who would represent his case. (3) Not to let the Cabinet reach any decision on any issue until he had measured the strength on either side. He then went off saying that he would discuss these suggestions with Monckton and also that he would see Sir Samuel Hoare hoping to persuade him to be the advocate for the King. He found that Monckton agreed with his views and that Hoare could not be persuaded to represent the King, even in the limited role of an advocate who did not necessarily approve of his intentions.

That night, when Lord Beaverbrook at last got to bed after his labours, he was woken at two o'clock in the morning by a telephone call from the King, who was anxious to hear the outcome of his talk with Hoare. 'A conversation took place that greatly embarrassed me. The King spoke, as on a previous occasion, with such freedom that I was positively alarmed, and he, in turn, was impatient of the guarded nature of my replies.'

The King then told Beaverbrook once more that, although he approved of his plans and endorsed his recommendations, 'Mrs Simpson preferred the morganatic marriage to any other solution'.

'When he made this statement I knew that the agreement between us was null and void. Whatever he might assent to in his mind, it would not have the agreement of his heart. ... A morganatic marriage was what Mrs Simpson wanted, and what Mrs Simpson wanted was what the King wanted.'[7]*

Baldwin seems on this occasion to have agreed with Beaverbrook.

The King agreed to go out quietly – he told Tom Jones – and he afterwards told this to his Mother and his brothers. But he has clearly now gone back on that. Mrs S. was down at Fort Belvedere over the weekend and has talked him out of it, because on Friday he was where I left him. Walter Monckton wrote telling me that, with the King's knowledge. At our interview the King said he could do nothing without the woman.

And he added:

There is a 'set' which is backing the marriage. I don't know but I suspect the Beaverbrook–Rothermere Press will take that line.[8]

In fact there was never any chance that the Cabinet would endorse the proposal. According to Middlemas, because of his own dislike of the idea, Baldwin was genuinely anxious to see that it was fairly considered, and he had discussed it informally with senior ministers after Harmsworth had put the proposal to him.

---

* In his introduction to Lord Beaverbrook's account, Mr A. J. P. Taylor suggests that a belated tribute should be paid to the generosity and unselfishness of Mrs Simpson in giving up the idea of being Queen and insisting on the proposal for a morganatic marriage.

It was agreed – Neville Chamberlain recorded – that we must act cautiously, and find out attitude of Opposition and of Dominions before committing ourselves. S.B. should point out various difficulties but not turn anything down. I have no doubt that if it were possible to arrange the morganatic marriage this would only be the prelude to the further step of making Mrs S. Queen with full rights.[9]*

Sir Donald Somervell put the main objection to the idea succinctly if rather cruelly as follows:

I confirmed what of course he knew that the wife of the King is Queen, that it would require an Act of Parliament to prevent this result. I remember adding that it would have been an odd Act. If it had been an honest recital it would start Whereas the wife of the King is Queen & whereas the present King desires to marry a woman unfit to be Queen – be it hereby enacted etc.[10]

And later on when all this became public *The Times* put it in rather the same way: 'The constitution is to be amended in order that she may carry in solitary prominence the brand of unfitness for the Queen's Throne.'[11]

Even before he saw the King on 25 November Baldwin had taken the precaution of calling Attlee and Sinclair (the two leaders of the opposition parties) and Winston Churchill together, and putting to them the question: 'Would they be for or against the government if it came to resignation?' Attlee and Sinclair replied without equivocation that they would refuse to form an alternative government if asked and Churchill that 'although his attitude was a little different he would certainly support the government'.[12] And in fact Baldwin would have been prepared to resign on this issue. 'Is this the sort of thing I've stood for in public life?' he exclaimed to Tom Jones. 'If I have to go out, as go I must, then I'd be quite ready to go out on this.'[13]

On 27 November Baldwin told his colleagues what had taken place between himself and the King, and explained that, although the King might himself have consulted the Dominion governments through the Governor-Generals on the spot, he 'was loath to employ this channel, since he felt that the matter was much too personal, too delicate to be handled by the King himself.'[14] Baldwin said that he was not asking for a decision but that his colleagues should think it over before the next regular Cabinet meeting on 2 December. Meanwhile telegrams would be sent to the Dominions asking them for their views. The Dominions were asked to choose between three possible courses.

(1) That the King should marry Mrs Simpson and she should be recognized as Queen.

---

*And indeed in *A King's Story* the Duke of Windsor tells us that he immediately reflected that it is not the form but the content of things which matters and that a lesser status would not prevent Wallis from fulfilling the many duties of a King's consort.

(2) That he should marry her and she should not become Queen (the morganatic proposal).

(3) That the King should abdicate in favour of the Duke of York.

Baldwin was later to be accused, by Beaverbrook and others, and in effect by the Duke of Windsor, of slanting the telegrams against the King. In fact, although he signed them, they were drafted in the Dominions Office, as were all subsequent cables between Whitehall and the Dominions, by Malcolm MacDonald, the Secretary of State, and Sir Henry Batterbee, the Permanent Secretary, with some help from Neville Chamberlain and Sir John Simon. Eden is quoted as saying that they were 'worded with a scrupulous impartiality, which would have defied the reader to guess the judgment of the government at home'.[15]

However, Baldwin's biographers have felt it necessary to defend him against a charge of having plotted to secure an answer from the Dominions which, left to themselves, they would not, or might not, have given, and they have probably made too much of his impartiality. Baldwin was perfectly entitled to make it known that the feeling of the British Parliament would in all probability be against the morganatic proposal and he was also in the position of having to get answers from the Dominions which were not merely unequivocal but could be seen to be so. If by 'impartial' it is meant that he did nothing to influence the Dominion Prime Ministers on a matter which he believed to be fundamental to the future of the monarchy and which was extremely urgent, then he was not impartial and it surely would be unproductive to expect any politician in his position to be so. In any case Brian Inglis quotes Stanley Lyons in a statement to the Australian Parliament as saying that the British government's proposals had come in the form of a secret and personal cable from Baldwin [presumably the cable drafted by Macdonald]

informing me that he had had conversations with his Majesty the King about Mrs Simpson, and that his Majesty had stated his intention of marrying Mrs Simpson, but that at the same time his Majesty had said that he appreciated that the idea of her becoming Queen and her children succeeding to the Throne was out of the question, and that consequently he contemplated abdication and leaving the Duke of York to succeed on the throne. His Majesty has subsequently asked Mr Baldwin's view on a new proposal, namely, that a special legislative provision should be made for a marriage to Mrs Simpson, which would not make her Queen and would not entitle her issue to succeed to the Throne. Mr Baldwin informed me that he had advised His Majesty that he did not think there was any chance of such an arrangement receiving the approval of Parliament in Great Britain, also that the assent of the Dominions would be essential to the carrying out of such an arrangement. He invited my personal view.[16]

If the replies which were returned were not in fact unequivocal, it seems to have been more because of an element of the 'backwoods' in their composition, than because of any great difference of view. Thus we are told that Savage, of New Zealand, who replied that 'his country would not quarrel with anything the King did, nor with anything his Government did to restrain him', had never before heard of Mrs Simpson and had had to go to the Governor-General for enlightenment. In India, which enjoyed a more limited measure of self-government than the other Dominions, opinion was divided on religious grounds, the Muslims being in favour of the King-Emperor's marriage and the Hindus against it; and from Ireland, de Valera, who had his own axe to grind, replied that the United Kingdom and the older Dominions must settle the matter as they thought best, but whatever happened Edward VIII could not remain King of Eire.

However Canada, Australia and South Africa were perfectly definite, although Mackenzie King merely backed Baldwin in whatever decision he chose to make. The strongest reply came from Lyons, the Prime Minister of Australia, who said that 'in his view His Majesty could not now re-establish his prestige or command confidence as King', while the proposal that Mrs Simpson should become Queen would 'provoke widespread condemnation, and the alternative proposal, or something in the nature of a specially sanctioned morganatic marriage, would run counter to the best popular conception of the Royal Family'. Hertzog of South Africa was almost equally strong, replying that, while abdication would be 'a great shock', a morganatic marriage would be 'a permanent wound'.[17]

Baldwin once more sounded out Attlee, who replied that, while Labour people had no objection at all to an American becoming Queen, he was certain that they would not approve of Mrs Simpson for that position and would object to a morganatic marriage.

I told him that it was important not to think that London was typical of the country as a whole, and that opinion in the Commonwealth was likely to coincide with that of the provinces rather than of the metropolis. I found that I had correctly gauged the Party attitude. Despite the sympathy felt for the King and the affection which his visits to the depressed areas had created, the Party – with the exception of a few of the intelligentsia who could be trusted to take the wrong view on any subject – were in agreement with the views I expressed.[18]

Baldwin also sent Sir Samuel Hoare to explain to Lord Beaverbrook the Government's attitude (Sunday, 29 November). No breach existed, he said, all the ministers stood with Mr Baldwin. And he added that the Prime Minister hoped that when the publicity broke, as it soon must, the Press would also present an undivided front. To which the Press Lord replied in his usual picturesque way that he had taken the 'King's shilling' and was a King's man.

The Cabinet met on 2 December and a general discussion took place. Duff Cooper, alone and in vain, pleaded for delay, suggesting, as he had to the King, that the whole thing might be dropped until after the Coronation and raised again in a year's time. The rest of the Cabinet were unanimous that the morganatic plan was both impracticable and undesirable.

When Baldwin went to see the King on the evening of Thursday, 4 December, it was therefore to report to him in this sense. By then, however, the whole situation had changed because the British Press had at last broken silence on the King's marriage. It is true, nevertheless, as Brian Inglis has remarked, that 'the abdication of King Edward VIII was virtually settled before millions of people in Britain were aware that it was even contemplated, or that there was a crisis of any kind'.[19]

21

THE PRESS
BREAKS SILENCE

By the end of November, although the silence of the Press was still un-broken, Mrs Simpson's presence in the King's life and physically at Cumberland Terrace began to be very widely known. She could not go about the streets without people turning to stare, strangers loitered about peering at her house, and she even began to receive letters, some of them anonymous.

In other countries, particularly in America and France, the King's abdication and marriage to Mrs Simpson have often been presented as a Great Romance – the Love Story of the Century. In England very few people have at any time taken that view. Those who were in favour of allowing the King to marry her and remain on the throne were more in-clined to take up a modern and democratic attitude to the monarchy – 'Let him marry whom he pleases' – than any idealized or exalted view of the relationship. Most people saw the Abdication as an incomprehensible and shabby dereliction of duty. 'There are circumstances in the present pro-posal which freeze the very pulse of Romance,' a writer in the *Daily Telegraph* remarked.[1]

For Mrs Simpson therefore the cheers which had so much warmed her heart in Yugoslavia had given way, like the Mediterranean sun, to Eng-land's chillier climate. She felt a mounting menace in the air and many of the letters she received were openly threatening. She was an exceptionally nervous woman and the King was exceptionally nervous for her. When he heard a rumour of a plot to blow up her house, although he believed it to be ridiculous, he arranged for her and her aunt, Mrs Merryman, to join him at the Fort, where they would automatically be guarded. Thus the King and Mrs Simpson were together when the Press broke the long silence.

This came about in a manner which had all the by-now-recognizable hallmarks of the abdication crisis – that is to say, it was not the result of a co-ordinated plan, but happened because in a long period of drift so much steam had been built up that almost any movement of air would be bound to blow the lid off it.

On the morning of 1 December the Bishop of Bradford, Dr A.W.F. Blunt, delivered an address to his Diocesan Conference. According to his and other later statements, all he intended was a rebuke of Bishop Barnes of Birmingham (a churchman who constantly upset his colleagues by his unorthodoxy and who had suggested that the Coronation should be secularized) and a lament that King Edward was not a more regular churchgoer.* What he managed to do, after a dissertation on the religious nature of the Coronation ceremony – 'it is a solemn Sacramental rite, linked up as an integral part in a service of Holy Communion' – was to make some highly equivocal remarks about the chief participant in it. 'The benefit of the King's coronation,' he said, 'depends under God upon two elements – firstly on the faith, prayer and self-dedication of the King himself. On that it would be improper for me to say anything except to commend him and ask others to commend him to God's grace, which he will so abundantly need – for the King is a man like any other – if he is to do his duty properly.

'We hope,' Dr Blunt went on, 'that he is aware of this need. Some of us wish that he gave more positive signs of such awareness.'

The following morning 2 December these remarks of a provincial Bishop passed unnoticed in the London newspapers but the *Yorkshire Post* had a leader commenting on it, which had been given circulation to other newspapers, several other provincial papers likewise commented, while the *Manchester Guardian* published a selection of these comments.

> Dr Blunt must have had good reason for so pointed a remark [the *Yorkshire Post* said]. Most people by this time are aware that a good deal of rumour regarding the King has been published of late in the more sensational American newspapers. It is proper to treat with contempt mere gossip such as is frequently associated with the names of European royal persons. The Bishop of Bradford would certainly not have condescended to recognize it. But certain statements which have appeared in reputable United States journals, and even we believe in some Dominion newspapers, cannot be treated with quite so much indifference. They are too circumstantial and plainly have a foundation in fact.

For this reason an increasing number of responsible people is led to fear lest the King may not yet have perceived how complete in our day must be that self-dedication of which Dr Blunt spoke if the Coronation is to bring a blessing to all the peoples and is not, on the contrary, to prove a stumbling block. . . .

* Two days later Dr Blunt was quoted by the Press as follows: 'What I had referred to was the fact that, to all outward appearance, the King seems to live entirely indifferent to the public practice of religion. He may have a private religion of his own, but he does not show the world he has one and I think it is a pity.' As to the rumours, the Bishop said, his address had been written six weeks earlier. 'I did not know of them. I did not know of their existence. . . . I studiously took care to say nothing whatever of the King's private life, because I know nothing about it.'

One other great event had taken place on 1 December – in London the Crystal Palace had burned down and once more people were not slow to see this as an omen. Thus the *Nottingham Journal* commenting on the Bishop of Bradford's words, said: 'They seem all the more emphasized by being uttered on the day when a great monument of Victorian tradition lies shattered in a smoking ruin.'

On the morning of 2 December the Cabinet had taken the formal, and with the exception of Duff Cooper, unanimous decision to reject the morganatic proposal on the grounds that it was both impracticable and undesirable. Lord Beaverbrook, lunching immediately afterwards with a member of the Cabinet, learned without difficulty of this decision, and hurried to the Palace in a state of agitation which surprised the King.*

He told him that he had placed his head on the execution block leaving Baldwin with nothing to do but swing the axe.†

Lord Beaverbrook asked the King if he had seen the cables to the Dominions, and hearing that he had not, he told him that they had been sent to all the Dominions and that they had been framed in the same rigid way as Baldwin had presented the case to the Cabinet, in effect, 'Do you recommend the King's marrying morganatically? Or, if the King insists on marrying, do you recommend abdication?' He then begged the King to stop them, saying that as a Canadian he knew the Dominions, and their answer would certainly and swiftly be no. (Apparently neither Lord Beaverbrook nor the Duke of Windsor appreciated the significance of this opinion.)

The King also learned of the Cabinet decision from Walter Monckton who had been informed by Baldwin.

During the day he saw the provincial papers and in the afternoon Lord Beaverbrook telephoned to warn him to expect sensational disclosures in the metropolitan morning papers and an attack in *The Times* from Geoffrey Dawson's fluent and pitiless pen. And he begged to be allowed to lift the restrictions imposed on the newspapers friendly to the King, saying that there were many besides himself who held that there was nothing wrong in the King marrying a woman who had divorced her husband and that a strong case could be made. But the King could not see it that way and in his own account he makes it plain that he did not desire the responsibility of dividing the nation and was determined to protect Mrs Simpson from the kind of publicity a newspaper campaign of this kind would be sure to provoke.‡

* The Duke of Windsor dates this as 27 November, the date of the first Cabinet meeting when Baldwin informed his colleagues of the proposal but when no decision was taken. He has clearly mixed it with the Cabinet of 2 December.

† Mrs Simpson, showing an unsuspected knowledge of the constitution, made almost the same remark. According to her account, the King replied: 'I've got to do something. At the very least I'll get my head in a more comfortable position on the block.'²

‡ Beaverbrook says his appeal was made and rejected on the evening of 1 December after the

When Baldwin called on the King at six o'clock that evening he found him very anxious to hear the replies from the Dominion governments, and he told him that, although these were not yet complete, they had gone far enough to show that neither in the Dominions nor at home would there be any prospect of such legislation being accepted. And he showed him Lyon's telegram.

'What about Parliament?' Edward asked.

'The answer would, I am sure, be the same.'

When the King persisted that Parliament had not been consulted, Baldwin replied that he had caused inquiries to be set on foot in the usual manner and the response had been such as to convince 'my colleagues and myself' that the people would not approve of a marriage to Mrs Simpson. He then summed up for the King the three choices before him

(1) He could give up the idea of marriage.
(2) He could marry against the advice of his ministers.
(3) He could marry and abdicate.

The Prime Minister prayed that he would take the first course. The second course he described as 'manifestly impossible', and he explained that, if the King married in face of the advice of his Ministers, he could not remain on the throne. If he would not abandon his project, there was really no choice before him but to go.

The King then said that it seemed in reality he was left with only one choice, and to this Baldwin replied with obvious sincerity that both he and his colleagues hoped he would remain as King. Edward then said explicitly that he would marry Mrs Simpson even if he had to abdicate to do so.

At this interview Baldwin made the first of several appeals to the King to consider his duty, and that evening he told his wife: 'To all arguments based on responsibility towards his people, the King did not react, not feeling any responsibility which should dictate or influence his conduct.' And he said that the King had said again and again: 'Wallis is the most wonderful woman in the world' and that he could not live without her.[3]

He seemed considerably unnerved by the provincial press, however. Picking up a copy of the *Birmingham Post*, he said: 'They don't want me.'[4]*

There is no doubt that both the King and Mrs Simpson were shattered by the comments of the British Press. The tone of even the most scurrilous

---

report of the Bishop of Bradford's address had been circulated to the Press but before it had been published: the Duke of Windsor says it was on the afternoon of 2 December.

* The leader in the *Birmingham Post* said, 'The Bishop of Bradford's words are words of reproof – such reproof as no one, whether cleric or layman, has thought proper to address to the King for many a long day.' And it concluded a discussion on whether the Bishop had acted in the public interest or not with the following: 'He must be allowed to speak but the truth when he gives warning – as in effect he does – that in the eyes of the people of this country, as in the eyes of the subjects of the Crown overseas, the private and public life of the King–Emperor are inseparable'.

articles appearing in America and elsewhere had always been friendly, even at times admiring. They had counted absolutely on his popularity, and they had never imagined a situation in which neither his power and position, nor the deference and love of his people would be strong enough to shield them from criticism.

The King had that almost pathological dislike of the Press which, not unknown in other members of the Royal Family, is the result of being of perpetual interest to it.* He had been particularly upset by Beaverbrook's suggestion that there would be a critical leader in *The Times* the following morning and he had convinced himself that Dawson would attack Mrs Simpson. At this interview with Baldwin he had been insistent that the Prime Minister must prevent this.

In the late evening, as I was struggling with the paper – Dawson recorded – he [Baldwin] rang me up twice himself – the only time, I think, that I ever heard his own voice on the telephone – to say that His Majesty was worrying him to find out, and if necessary stop, what was going to appear in *The Times*. He understood that there was to be an attack on Mrs Simpson and 'instructed' the Prime Minister to forbid it. In vain S.B. had explained that the Press in England was free, and that he had no control over *The Times* or over any other newspaper. When he spoke to me, full of apologies, the second time, it was to say that the King would now be satisfied, and leave the Prime Minister alone, if the latter would read the leading article for him. Could I possibly let him see it for the sake of peace?[6]

The paper was just going to Press but Dawson sent a proof of the leader round to Downing Street, where, by the time it arrived, the Prime Minister was in bed and asleep. But the King need not have worried because, although *The Times* devoted a column and a half to a leader on the crisis, it said very little and did not mention Mrs Simpson by name. 'The storm breaks,' Harold Nicolson wrote in his diary. 'A fine leading article in the *Telegraph* and a confused muddled jumble in *The Times*. I suspect that when Geoffrey Dawson sees a vital crisis he writes the leader himself, and the result is an amalgam of tortuous and pompous nothings. The other papers write in sorrow rather than in anger.'[7]

Dawson's prominence in the history of the Abdication is due to the accusation that he plotted with Baldwin against the King. In fact by now he had no access to the Prime Minister who 'began to withdraw behind the formal front of the government,'[8] and it was the *Daily Telegraph* not *The Times* which emerged with most credit from the crisis.† On 3 December it

---

* Chips said: The King is at his worst with Fleet Street – off-hand, angry and ungracious; he never treats them in the right way, or realizes that his popularity largely depends on them.[5]

† The Deputy Editor of *The Times*, R. Barrington Ward, had 'an informed source' in touch with the King's affairs who kept him posted, and who is referred to in *The History of The Times* as 'A' and by Lord Beaverbrook as Walter Monckton. J.C.C.Davidson wrote: 'One of the most interesting features of the crisis was the fact that it was the making of the *Daily Telegraph*. For the first few days of the crisis Robin Barrington Ward was in charge of *The Times* and was magnificent;

was the *News Chronicle* which attracted attention because it was the only paper to mention the morganatic proposal.*

The Press comments had had an even greater effect on Mrs Simpson than on the King, and had convinced her, as Hardinge's letter had failed to do, that she must leave the country. The King, who had been worried by threats of danger to her, was also anxious for her to leave.

After some discussion it was agreed that she should go to the Villa Lou Vieie at Cannes, the house of her old friends the Herman Rogers, and the King arranged for his chauffeur, Ladbroke, to drive her there and his friend and Lord-in-Waiting, Lord Brownlow, and his personal detective, Inspector Evans of Scotland Yard, to accompany her.

They left England on the evening of 3 December, followed by the 'hounds of the Press'.[10] These gentlemen did their level best to live up to the Duchess's description of them and she has told in detail of the extraordinary chase across France which had all the ingredients of a film sequence but must in reality have been an unpleasant experience. Lord Brownlow fitted admirably into the scenario since he turned out to be present in the role of 'double agent'.

At a meeting at Lord Beaverbrook's house the evening before, at which Walter Monckton and Mr Allen, the King's solicitor, were present, it had been agreed that the best, if not the only, method of keeping the King on the throne was to persuade Mrs Simpson to make an act of renunciation.† Lord Brownlow was the chosen agent and his task was to urge her to leave the country. Consequently, he was considerably taken aback to be asked by the King the following morning to escort her to France.

Then, as a result of a conversation he had with the King before leaving, Lord Brownlow realized for the first time how far things had already gone, and he changed his tactics. On the journey to Newhaven instead of persuading Mrs Simpson to leave the country, he urged her to stay and go with him to Belton, his country house, on the grounds that if she left England the King would follow her. But Mrs Simpson replied that she could not see how going to Lincolnshire instead of to Cannes could affect the situation.

My separation from David would be nearly absolute, whether the actual distance between us was one hundred miles or seven hundred. Knowing David

---

but when Dawson came hastening back from Canada the newspaper lost its character and even its information became forty-eight hours out of date. I thought it essential that one respected newspaper should be properly informed so that it could give the nation a lead; I accordingly saw to it that the *Daily Telegraph* was kept completely informed ... it was very striking how accurate was the information carried by the *Telegraph* and how out-of-date was that carried by *The Times*.'[9]

* Middlemas & Barnes suggests that this may have been because it was the only paper which did not realize that the morganatic scheme was already dead.

† Lord Beaverbrook has denied that he, at any rate, meant this to be more than a temporary measure to ease tension and gain time.

as I did I was more than doubtful that anyone, including me, could change his mind. If I stayed and my pleas failed, I should always be accused of secretly urging him to give up the throne. I told Perry, therefore, that I did not see how his plan could work. If I were to go to Bolton ... and if, in the end, the King should decide to abdicate, the blame attaching to me would be even more bitter than was already the case. It would be said that I was afraid of losing the King; that, having left him at the Fort, I had lost heart and run back in order to hold him.

'You must remember,' I said, 'that until this morning I was an utter stranger to all but a handful of people in Great Britain. There is no one to speak up for me. I am sure there is only one solution: that is for me to remove myself from the King's life. That is what I am doing now.'[11]

22

A KING'S PARTY?

When the Duchess of Windsor wrote that the solution to the problem was for her to remove herself from the King's life – 'That is what I am doing now' – she used the words as a kind of literary flourish, a statement which did justice to her feelings as she travelled with Lord Brownlow towards Newhaven on that memorable night. She did not, of course, intend to be believed.

All through France at every stopping place she telephoned to the King and, as soon as she reached the Rogers's home at Cannes, there began the daily telephone conversations which were to continue for nearly six long months. Only a few days later she explained to Lord Brownlow why it would be wrong for her even to attempt to leave the King, and in the meantime she had left him behind at work on a scheme for an appeal against the verdict of his Prime Minister – the only one for which he ever appeared to have much personal relish. A few days before he had said to her that, if there were only some way of making his position known to his people, their decent and loyal sentiments would be felt and the situation reversed, and she had suggested he should deliver a broadcast in the manner of President Roosevelt's 'fireside chats'. The King adopted her idea with enthusiasm and began to work on a speech. He seems to have been fired by a project that gave him both scope for his special talents and something to do.

The Duke of Windsor says that he sought no special privileges, merely something that the fundamental laws of his realm allowed to his subjects but the Prime Minister proposed to deny to him. He would tell his people that he was determined to marry Mrs Simpson but he did not insist that his wife should be Queen. All that he asked was that 'our married happiness should carry with it a proper title and dignity for her, befitting my wife'.[1] He then made the naive and unconsidered suggestion that he should leave

England for a while so that the country could reflect 'calmly and quietly, but without undue delay' on this matter, and he wrote later that he had tentatively fixed on Belgium as a convenient place to await his people's verdict. This proposal had the two insuperable disadvantages that to ask his subjects to make this decision over the heads of his ministers would have been unconstitutional and that it required them to arrive at a majority decision by some unspecified means. Astonishment at the extraordinary lack of judgment the King revealed was tempered by the knowledge of his psychological and emotional state. Fifteen years later the Duke of Windsor was still showing the same confidence in the propriety and practical possibility of this scheme.

As soon as he had finished the draft the King left Fort Belvedere and drove straight to Buckingham Palace to receive Baldwin who had been summoned to hear his new proposal. He was dead tired and without wasting words he thrust the draft of his speech into the astonished Prime Minister's hands. Baldwin read it and said that he would consult his colleagues, but added that he had no doubt what their opinion would be. And he told the King that an appeal to the people over the head of the government would be unconstitutional. The King's answer was rather confused.

'You want me to go, don't you?' he said. 'And before I go, I think it is right for her sake and mine, that I should speak.'

To this Baldwin replied:

What I want, Sir, is what you told me you wanted: to go with dignity, not dividing the country, and making things as smooth as possible for your successor. To broadcast would be to go over the heads of your Ministers and speak to the people. You will be telling millions throughout the world – among them a vast number of women – that you are determined to marry one who has a husband living. They will want to know all about her, and the Press will ring with gossip, the very thing you want to avoid. You may, by speaking, divide opinion; but you will certainly harden it. The Churches are straining at the leash; only three papers would be on your side, the *News Chronicle*, the *Daily Mail* and the *Daily Express*.[2]

And Baldwin then tried to explain to the King the danger of the King's Proctor intervening before the Simpson divorce was made absolute.

He left, having promised to call a special Cabinet meeting to consider the broadcast and, because he did not wish to provoke the King, having agreed that he might consult Winston Churchill. (The following morning he told his colleagues that he thought this was his first mistake.)

When he had gone the King sent for Walter Monckton and Mr Allen who were in the Palace and asked them to take a copy of his broadcast to Lord Beaverbrook and ask for his comments and advice, with a message that he would also like Mr Churchill to see it. (Both these men returned the opinion that his idea would almost certainly be resisted as 'an appeal by the King to the people over the heads of the Executive'.)[3]

And then tired as he was he drove to Marlborough House to see his mother. She told him she had found the newspapers somewhat upsetting particularly as she had not seen him for ten days. To this he replied that his aloofness had been due to a desire to spare his family from being involved in a matter which he must handle alone, a bland explanation which could not disguise the enveloping egotism and total lack of concern for his family which was characteristic of the King at the time. Although the decision he would finally make would affect the life of his brother as much as his own, and, although his mother still mourned his father, all his family were excluded from his councils and even denied access to him except when he chose on rare occasions to see them. The Duke of York seems never to have been consulted about his willingness to take up the duties his brother threw down. The following record in his diary speaks for itself.

The Prime Minister went to see him at 9.0 p.m. that evening and later (in Mary's and my presence) David said to Queen Mary that he could not live alone as King & must marry Mrs —— When David left after making this dreadful announcement to his mother he told me to come & see him at the Fort the next morning [Friday December 4th]. I rang him up but he would not see me and put me off till Saturday. I told him I would be at Royal Lodge on Saturday by 12.30 p.m. 'Come & see me on Sunday' was his answer. 'I will see you & tell you my decision when I have made up my mind.' Sunday evening I rang up. 'The King has a conference & will speak to you later' was the answer. But he did not ring up. Monday morning, December 7, came. I rang up at 1.0 p.m. and my brother told me he might be able to see me that evening. I told him 'I must go to London but would come to the Fort when he wanted me.' I did not go to London but waited. I sent a telephone message to the Fort to say that if I was wanted I would be at Royal Lodge. My brother rang me up at 10 minutes to 7.0 p.m. to say 'Come & see me after dinner.' I said 'No, I will come & see you at once.' I was with him at 7.0 p.m. The awful & ghastly suspense of waiting was over. I found him pacing up & down the room & he told me his decision that he would go.[4]

The truth is that at this time the King's family also found him 'rather more than a little mad'. After the Abdication was over Queen Mary told more than one person that to all her appeals he had answered: 'All that matters is our happiness,' and repeated this over and over again.

On the evening of 3 December when the King had returned to Buckingham Palace he announced to Walter Monckton his intention of going to the Fort, and Monckton, horrified that he should be alone, so tired and so late, went with him. The King left Buckingham Palace that night never to enter it again as King, and he remained at the Fort until the crisis ended. He was by now completely out of touch with the household, owing to his estrangement with his Private Secretary, and Monckton used the Windham Club as an unofficial London headquarters for the King's business, a room being set aside for him. Monckton and Sir Ulick Alexander slept at the Fort, as did Mr Allen sometimes, and they were often joined by Sir Edward

Peacock, the Receiver General of the Duchy of Cornwall, who had a house nearby. Two of them, Walter Monckton and Sir Edward Peacock, made notes of the events of those days and have left us a picture of the all-male society at Fort Belvedere in the last days of the King's reign.* All four men worked for the King, none of them approved of his decision, all believed that he failed in his duty, but they made no appeals to him, nor did they question his right to do as he pleased. They served him faithfully and willingly and felt affection and concern for him. In the seclusion of his chosen group he was as charming as ever; on every issue except the main one he behaved impeccably and he clearly suffered an appalling strain.†

He almost certainly gave up any serious intention of retaining the throne on the morning of 4 December after Baldwin had warned him that the Cabinet would not consent to his broadcast. On that day Monckton informed Lord Beaverbrook that he could see him no more. 'He was engaging on negotiations with the government on the terms of abdication and must dissociate himself with those who were in the other camp. He did not wish to endanger the financial conditions of the Abdication by maintaining contacts of which Baldwin disapproved.'[6] And, although poor Lord Beaverbrook then appealed to the King for an interview, his appeal was firmly rejected.‡

On the same day the King sent for Sir Edward Peacock to discuss the question of pensions in the Duchy of Cornwall and the appointment of Sir Lionel Halsey as liaison officer between the King and the Duchy, and to him he said: 'I am by no means sure that I am going but wish to clear these points just in case.' And Peacock noted: 'Winston C had seen His Majesty that day and urged him to fight for the morganatic marriage, and assured him that he would get strong support. This had, I think, momentarily unsettled His Majesty ... but, as soon appeared, this hesitation was short-lived.'[9]

Churchill himself had been unsettled by the events of the night before. He had been the chief speaker at a rally at the Albert Hall the purpose of which was to attack the government for its failure to re-arm, and he announced beforehand that he would incorporate in his speech an appeal on behalf of the King. Beaverbrook warned him not to do this and Citrine said he would leave the platform if he did, and, although he gave the text of his speech in *The Gathering Storm*, he did not actually make it. Nevertheless, he was much inspired by the fervour with which the crowd sang *God*

---

* Sir Edward Peacock's notes have been preserved with Walter Monckton's.

† Monckton & Allen splendid – Sir Edward Peacock noted – the King liked them very much & they spoke to him with great frankness & courage when necessary.[5]

‡ 'Poor' only in this context. When Randolph Churchill asked Beaverbrook why he intervened in the abdication crisis he replied: 'To bugger Baldwin.' But A. J. P. Taylor has dismissed this as 'late night gossip by Randolph Churchill, not the most reliable of sources'[7] and believes that Beaverbrook gave up his holiday and returned to England in answer to the King's appeals. Lord Beaverbrook himself is forced to admit that to dislodge the Prime Minister from Downing Street would have been no more than 'a welcome by-product'.[8]

Save the King at the end of the meeting and the next day he issued the text of his speech to the Press.

The rally at the Albert Hall has been taken by several historians to be the starting point of what they have seen as a movement of support for the King and a moment of real danger of a constitutional crisis. It is extremely difficult to assess what actually occurred. Monckton for instance says: 'Between Thursday and Sunday 6th there was a great wave of sympathy for the King and a desire in many quarters to retain him at all costs.'[10] And both Middlemas & Barnes and Montgomery Hyde report the danger of a King's party at the end of this week. Yet on the night that Churchill was so moved by the singing of *God Save the King* at the Albert Hall, Harold Nicolson, speaking of an address on biography which he gave in a chapel at Islington, wrote:

At the end Paxton asked them to sing the 'National Anthem' 'as a hymn'. They all stand up and there are no protests, but only about ten people out of 400 join in the singing. Poor Paxton is much upset. 'I never dreamt,' he said after-wards, 'that I should live to see the day when my congregation refused to sing *God Save the King.*'

And Nicolson added:

I do not find people angry with Mrs Simpson. But I do find a deep and enraged fury against the King himself. In eight months he has destroyed the great structure of popularity which he had raised.[11]*

Of the other diarists, Chips Channon seems divided on the point, writing on 3 December that 'the sentiment of the House of Commons is pro-Government and pro-Baldwin; it feels that the King has no right to plunge us in this crisis and that the Dominions would not stand Wallis as Queen, even if England did,'[12] and on 4 December 'London is now properly divided and the King's faction grows';[13] while Tom Jones reported as late as 8 December that 'the country is split in two',[14] a statement which according to most commentators bore no relation to the facts.

Crowds formed outside Buckingham Palace, Downing Street and St James's Palace and people carried boards announcing that they wished the King to stay or Baldwin to go. However the Duke of Windsor himself says: 'the crowds were not large or particularly demonstrative',[15] although he adds that their sympathies were unmistakeably with the King. Finally Oswald Mosley declared for the King – a circumstance which Middlemas believes had some influence on Edward's decision – 'Especially he would not put himself at the disposal of Mosley's Blackshirts'[16] – and one which would certainly not have worried the government.

* There was obviously a great discrepancy in the numbers at the two meetings. On the other hand, since the Albert Hall audience were there to press for armaments, it must have been largely made up of people who were anti-Government. This was almost the lowest point of the National Government's reputation. It could also be argued that an audience of middle-class intellectuals come to hear Nicolson on biography was not representative.

Whatever the real division of opinion, it was certainly at this time that the King's supporters made some kind of a bid. On 4 December Churchill issued the text of the speech written for the Albert Hall meeting to the Press. It was in essence an appeal for patience but it accused the government of having solicited assurances from the Leader of the Opposition that he would not form an alternative administration in the event of their resignation (Attlee promptly denied this) and thus confronted the King with an ultimatum. And all this week the Beaverbrook–Rothermere press and the *Daily Mirror* spoke for the King directly and published articles presenting Mrs Simpson in an attractive light. (The American Press, delighted at being proved right, devoted more space than ever to the story.) The *News Chronicle*, strongly non-conformist in character, surprised everyone by supporting the King, particularly, as we have seen, the morganatic proposal, but the *Daily Herald* supported Baldwin and the constitutional argument.*

On the morning of 4 December Baldwin called a Cabinet to discuss the King's request to broadcast at which it was unanimously decided that it would be impossible, while he was King, to allow him either to broadcast or make any other public utterance which had not been approved by his ministers, since constitutionally they must be responsible for his words. And Simon drafted a paper to this effect. Then once more the Cabinet attempted to induce Baldwin to deliver an ultimatum warning the King that the matter could not drag on and saying that they must have an answer by midnight. And once more Baldwin rejected their advice. But, speaking of the Cabinet, Middlemas says: 'Not one of them, when the moment came, wished to force the King to abdicate; even Chamberlain accepted the need to give him time.'[17]

During this meeting of the Cabinet a message was brought from Attlee. The day before, 3 December, he had asked the Prime Minister at Question Time whether any constitutional difficulties had arisen and whether he had any statement to make and the Prime Minister had replied: 'While there does not at the moment exist any constitutional difficulty, the situation is of such a nature as to make it inexpedient that I should be questioned about

---

* *The Times, Telegraph, Morning Post* and *Manchester Guardian*, the *Sunday Times* and *Observer*, and, with the exception of the *Western Morning News*, virtually all the provincial papers supported Baldwin. Among the papers which supported the King for sectional reasons were the *Catholic Times* and the *Tablet*. The former, arguing from the premise that no such person as Mrs Simpson could exist and referring to her as Mrs Spencer, arrived at some conclusion not easily understood by Protestants and demanded the re-establishment of the monarchy as an active force in the country. In *Reynolds News*, on 6 December H.N. Brailsford argued that, if the King had lent himself to the manœuvres of the Youth Guard, 'under that somewhat portly youth, Mr Churchill,' with the Die-hards and Oswald Mosley to back him, it might have 'brought Fascism upon us in a peculiar English guise, with a Royal Fuhrer'. And he said: 'Meanwhile against the background of this sour comedy, looms up the tragedy of Madrid.'

Of the weeklies, the *Spectator* supported the government, the *New Statesman* the King, Kingsley Martin offering his services at one time for a special article, and being at first encouraged, then restrained; and arguing in favour of the morganatic marriage.

it at this stage.'[18] Mr Churchill had then asked for an assurance that no irrevocable step would be taken before a formal statement had been made to Parliament. Attlee now warned that he could not avoid putting a further question and it was agreed that Baldwin should be in his place to answer it. At eleven o'clock when the House met he replied to Attlee that he had nothing to add to his statement of the previous day and once more Mr Churchill asked for an assurance in the terms he had used the day before. However at four o'clock on the same day, immediately before the House adjourned for the weekend, in response to 'widely circulated suggestions as to certain possibilities in the event of the King's marriage', the Prime Minister made a statement on the morganatic proposal. Having explained that there was no such thing as a morganatic marriage in English law and that the Royal Marriages Act of 1772 had no application to the King himself, he said:

> The Act, therefore, has nothing to do with the present case. The King himself requires no consent from any other authority to make his marriage legal, but, as I have said, the lady whom he marries, by the fact of her marriage to the King, necessarily becomes Queen.

This he explained would mean that she would enjoy all the status, rights and privileges which attach to that position and that her children would be in the direct line of succession to the throne.

> The only possible way in which this result could be avoided would be by legislation dealing with a particular case. His Majesty's Government are not prepared to introduce such legislation.[19]

When he said these words cheering broke out all over the House and, according to the political correspondent of the *Daily Telegraph*, 'rose to a striking demonstration so prolonged that, for a little while, Mr Baldwin could not continue'.*

At four o'clock when the House adjourned for the weekend, Baldwin, accompanied by Major Dugdale, his Parliamentary Private Secretary, drove to Fort Belvedere to inform the King of the Cabinet decision and to show him Simon's draft opinion on the question of his broadcast. After the King had read it, he dropped the matter and never mentioned it again, but it was the turning point after which he decided to abdicate. He wished now to bring the audience to an end, but Baldwin went on to warn him that the

---

* Several authorities have said that Winston Churchill rose to ask a supplementary question and that there were then counter cheers which suggested support for a King's Party: and Middlemas & Barnes that Baldwin himself sensed that his own reception was a degree less warm. But Churchill asked the supplementary question in the morning when the Prime Minister had refused to give a statement, and there is no record in Hansard of a further intervention in the afternoon. Even the *Daily Express* correspondent, who cannot be thought to have had a bias, reported on 5 December that Baldwin 'was cheered, so far as anyone could judge from the Press Gallery, on every side of the House. It seemed that Mr Baldwin was putting forward the case on behalf of the Cabinet which the House of Commons as a whole was prepared to support.'

sooner he came to a definite decision the better because of a danger of a constitutional crisis, but he added that it was the prayer of himself and his colleagues that the King would change his mind. After he had gone the King reflected that for him to change his mind would mean publicly renouncing the woman he had asked to marry him, a surrender that would cause the crown, 'that noble ornament', to 'rest upon a head forever bowed in shame'.[20]

At the time he merely said that he would let the Prime Minister know as soon as possible. Baldwin did not press him further because, as he afterwards told the Cabinet, 'However great the inconveniences and even risk, the decision when taken must be the spontaneous decision of the King.'[21]

Two things temporarily weakened the King's resolution to end the crisis. The first, as we have seen, was the influence of Winston Churchill, who dined at the Fort on the Friday and Saturday, 4 and 5 December. His advice was that the King should ask for time. Monckton wrote:

He said that he could not say that the King would win through if he stood and fought, but that he ought to take time in order to see what measure of support he received. His presence was a great encouragement to the King who liked him, and mimicked his mannerisms superbly without the smallest malice: 'We must have time for the big battalions to mass. We may win; we may not. Who can say?'[22]

But both Monckton and Peacock are agreed that his influence was only temporary, and Peacock says that two days later, at dinner on Sunday, 6 December, the King said that Winston had been very amusing but was quite wrong in what he suggested, and that such a course would be inexcusable. And Peacock added: 'He spoke with gratitude of Stanley Baldwin's kindness and help.'[23]

The second and more important influence was that of Mrs Simpson on the telephone from Cannes. Walter Monckton says that the King spoke to her every day, sometimes twice a day.

These telephone calls, with a bad line at a long distance, will never be forgotten by any of us. The house is so shaped that if a voice is raised in any room on the ground floor it can be heard more or less distinctly in the whole house.[24]

And Sir Edward Peacock, more explicitly:

There was evidently a certain wavering in the King's mind for a short time after Winston's call, based upon the hope inspired by Winston that something could be done, and also, as I know, upon the insistence over the telephone of the lady that he should fight for his rights. She kept up that line until near the end, maintaining that he was King and his popularity would carry everything, etc. With him this lasted only a very short time; then he realized the falsity of the position, and put it definitely aside, saying that under no circumstances would he be a party to a constitution crisis, or any other move that would weaken the constitution or cause trouble between the Crown and its Ministers.[25]

Mrs Simpson, misled for so long by the King himself, could not fail to be influenced by the views of Lord Beaverbrook and Winston Churchill, and undoubtedly believed that, if the King would only fight, he would win. Churchill, unaware of the change in the King's attitude, wrote to the Prime Minister:

My dear P.M.

The King having told me that he had your permission to see me as an old friend, I dined with him last night and had a long talk with him. I strongly urged his staff to call in the doctor. HM appeared to me to be under a very great strain and very near breaking point. He had two marked and prolonged blackouts, in which he completely lost the thread of his conversation ... although he was very gallant and debonair at the outset, this soon wore off and his mental exhaustion was painful to see. Even to hardened politicians, the combination of public and private stress is the hardest of all to endure. I told the King that if he appealed to you to allow him to recover himself and to consider, now that they have reached their climax, the grave issues, constitutional and personal, with which you have found it your duty to confront him, you would, I am sure, not fail in kindness and chivalry. It would be a most cruel and wrong thing to extort a decision from him in his present state. ...[26]

The belief that Edward, both as Prince of Wales and as King, was either occasionally or habitually the worse for alcohol has become so widespread that it is necessary to digress in order that nothing in his physical or mental state at this time should be attributed to that cause. When people have believed something for a very long time it often seems that nothing that can be said will alter their opinion. For future generations it is therefore necessary to say that it is impossible to meet anyone who knew HRH well who believes that he was any more addicted to alcohol than any ordinary man who drinks for pleasure or when tired or under stress. Thus Walter Monckton:

I have heard it suggested since that the King was, during the days that followed, in no state, because he was drinking so much, to reach any decision. Nothing could be more ridiculous. Life was for all of us disorganised, a series of interruptions with snatches of sleep. I certainly drank more than the King, but among all the great men who saw us both constantly throughout those days I never heard of one who thought either of us had been drinking! More half-consumed whiskeys poured out than I have ever seen.[27]

Churchill had also endeavoured to put some heart back into Lord Beaverbrook. He drove straight from dinner with the King to Stornoway House. The King telephoned himself to Beaverbrook to tell him of Churchill's coming and Beaverbrook concluded 'that he had changed his mind and was ready to fight for his Throne after all'.[28] But he was both better informed and less optimistic than Churchill and on the morning of the 5th he received news that the King had sent Walter Monckton to London to tell the Prime Minister of his formal intention to abdicate.

The responsibility – he wrote later – was the King's. Throughout all the days of public controversy he shackled the Press that was favourable to himself. He would allow us no liberty in expressing our views or in arguing for his cause. His chief desire was to secure a minimum of publicity for Mrs Simpson. He was also anxious to avoid any suggestion of conflict with Baldwin. As a result, the pro-Baldwin Press had the field all to itself.[29]*

At the time he said to Churchill: 'Our cock won't fight.' And, unable to convince the other, he added: 'No dice.'[30]

* The main interest of these words is for the light they throw on the King. Lord Beaverbrook is assuming that if he had been given a freer hand he might have altered the course of events, an assumption that is not justified. Many people read the *Daily Express*, but, as on other occasions, they did not necessarily accept its opinions. J.C.C. Davidson wrote: 'Whenever Max was involved in a battle like this he never pulled his punches, and the truth was not in him. With a great newspaper he had a very strong weapon, but it was not strong enough to make a real breach. ... The *Daily Express* and the *Daily Mail* are not siege weapons for they have no real weight, and it was very striking how the British people refused absolutely to be stirred up to a pro-King hysteria at the behest of the old Rothermere–Beaverbrook Alliance.'[31]

23

THE LAST DAYS

Lord Beaverbrook's information was correct and on Saturday afternoon, 5 December, Monckton formally told Baldwin of the King's decision to abdicate. Thus the crisis was over. On Monday, 7 December, it could be seen to be over, the King and his subjects having separately reached a decision which too closely coincided for any further disruption or interruption of their intentions to be possible. When Members of Parliament returned from their constituencies after the weekend, they returned in a mood of solid agreement. Whether or not there had been any real danger of a constitutional crisis the week before, it quickly became clear that Attlee had been right, and, once the situation was fully understood, the country as a whole felt quite strongly that the King could not marry and remain on the throne.

The House of Commons showed their solidarity by turning on Churchill at Question Time. His Press statement had made him unpopular and, when he once more attempted to ask the Prime Minister for an assurance that no irrevocable step would be taken, he was actually howled down. It is an appalling thing to have several hundred men unexpectedly turn and yell at one, and Churchill was horrified and suitably chastened. His ill-judged championship of the King did great, if only temporary, harm to his political career. 'I think he is done for. In three minutes his hopes of return to power and influence are shattered. But God is once more behind his servant, Stanley Baldwin.'[1]

A new diarist had now appeared on the scene who gives us an account of the King's mood on the same day which cannot be surpassed.*

December 7th.
Lunched at Club with Walter [Elliot] who explains the King's *one* idea is Mrs Simpson. Nothing that stands between him and her will meet his approval. The

---

* Baffy Dugdale.

Crown is only valuable if it would interest *her*. He must have marriage because then she can be with him always. Therefore he has no wish to form a 'Party' who would keep him on the Throne and let her be his mistress. Therefore he has no animosity against Ministers who are not opposing his abdication. ... What really got him was Baldwin's parting remark yesterday. 'Well, Sir, I hope whatever happens, that you will be happy.' He is very upset by the newspapers, never having seen anything but fulsome adulation in all his forty years! Baldwin will be very careful not to press him. So the situation will remain as it is for some days, though this is bad, for unrest must grow. Nevertheless, I do not think, in light of this knowledge, that there is much danger of a King's Party. It is impossible to be 'plus royaliste que le roi'.³

Nevertheless, the last week of the King's reign was not uneventful. Both his own advisers and the government had for some time been increasingly worried by his vulnerability if he abdicated to an intervention by the King's Proctor in Mrs Simpson's divorce suit. Monckton says: 'I was desperately afraid that the King might give up his throne and yet be deprived of his chance to marry Mrs Simpson.'³*

On Saturday, 5 December, at luncheon at the Windham Club he suggested a solution to Sir Horace Wilson, Mr Thomas Dugdale and Mr George Allen, and in the afternoon of the same day he repeated it to Baldwin when the Prime Minister visited the King at the Fort. His proposal was that there should be two Bills – one giving effect to the King's wish to renounce the Throne and the other making Mrs Simpson's *decree nisi* absolute immediately. And he wrote: 'This would finally have cleared up a grave constitutional position affecting the whole world and have left no ragged ends or possibilities for further scandal.'⁵

Describing the scene at Fort Belvedere when Monckton made his suggestion to Baldwin, the Duke of Windsor wrote that Baldwin himself thought it a just accommodation but said that some opposition must be expected from his colleagues. He promised his own support and then said that in the event of the Cabinet refusing the second Bill he would resign.

---

* The King's legal advisers continued to take very seriously the threat of an intervention on the grounds of collusion in the Simpson divorce or of Mrs Simpson's adultery with the King. However, since the publication of Mr Montgomery Hyde's *Baldwin: The Unexpected Prime Minister* it has become clear that, because the King's Proctor (Mr Thomas Barnes) was bombarded with abusive letters after the Abdication, he, together with Sir Donald Somervell, the Attorney-General, decided to make all the usual enquiries applicable in such a case. Mr Montgomery Hyde quotes Sir Donald Somervell as follows: 'He (Mr Thomas Barnes) had already with my approval seen some of the apparently more responsible of his correspondents who admitted they had no evidence but were repeating the gossip of the Clubs & the Temple.' And, having said that Barnes interviewed countless people, members of the crew of the yacht, servants, hall porters, etc, he concludes: 'By this time Barnes was convinced we should get nothing. Whether or not they had ever committed adultery is a question on which I believe those who know him will differ. It became, however, obvious that if they had done so they had not done so openly and had also not publicly indulged in the familiarities which normally indicate cohabitation. Our inquiries also confirmed the view that the divorce – even if it had some collusive fact – e.g., the willingness of Mrs S. that her husband should be unfaithful – was not a collusive divorce in the ordinary or any provable sense.'⁴

Biographers of Baldwin naturally assumed that the Duke's memory was mistaken – 'He made no such promise,' Middlemas says, 'nor is it conceivable that a man of his political experience should have even considered one.'[6] However, when Birkenhead's *Walter Monckton* appeared it became clear from Monckton's account that Baldwin had made the promise.

On Sunday morning there was a meeting of senior ministers at which Baldwin did what he could to urge his colleagues to accept Monckton's suggestion. However, the others feared an outcry of one law for the rich and one for the poor and thought that to rush the decree through would publicly confirm the worst about Mrs Simpson and give the appearance of a bargain. Neville Chamberlain put the reasons against it as follows: (1) It could not be denied that the King regarded the Bill as a condition of abdication, and it would therefore be denounced as an unholy bargain; (2) it would irretrievably damage the moral authority of the government at home and in the Empire; (3) it would be looked on as an injury to the marriage law in general; (4) it would injure the respect for the monarchy.

By this time, too, the Cabinet, and particularly Chamberlain, were anxious to get the whole matter wound up. It was hurting the Christmas trade (incredibly this seems to have been true), 'holding up business' and 'paralysing our foreign policy'. And Chamberlain at least was also tired of the continued opportunity given to 'the Simpson Press' to misrepresent what was happening. He complained that

the public is being told that we are engaged in a fight with the King, because we have advised him to abdicate and he has refused. That is quite untrue, and we must say so. He asked us to examine the morganatic marriage proposal, we told him we could have nothing to do with it, and he has accepted that view. The public is also being told that we are trying to rush the King into a decision that he has no time to think over. That is equally untrue. He has been thinking it over for weeks, though he has been unwilling to face up to realities.[7]

When Monckton was called in to be told that the Cabinet could not agree to the second Bill he said that the decision would greatly disappoint the King who, in the light of it, would undoubtedly ask for additional time for thought. And, on being asked how many days he thought the King would need, he replied not days but weeks – rousing Baldwin to say that it would have to be settled before Christmas. But Monckton's response had come from the depths of his deep disappointment because at Fort Belvedere preparations for the Abdication went on. (When asked directly by the 3rd Earl Baldwin whether his father had promised to resign if he could not persuade the Cabinet, but had not kept his word, Monckton made it plain that the Prime Minister had offered his resignation but he had assured him that 'he was perfectly certain that the King would permit no such action, and persuaded S.B. not to consider it further.' And he said he confirmed this with the King immediately after.)

The events of Monday, 7 December, are obscure and likely to remain so because everyone gives a different account.

In Cannes, under the influence of Lord Brownlow, Mrs Simpson prepared a statement for the Press. This read:

Mrs Simpson, throughout the last few weeks, has invariably wished to avoid any action or proposal which would hurt or damage His Majesty or the Throne. Today her attitude is unchanged, and she is willing, if such action would solve the problem, to withdraw from a situation that has been rendered both unhappy and untenable. [8]

Lord Brownlow doubted that this statement was sufficiently strong and wished for a forthright declaration that Mrs Simpson had no intention of marrying the King. But she shrank from dealing him so cruel a blow. She also telephoned to the King to tell him of her decision and to read him the statement.

After I finished there was a long silence. I thought that David in his anger had hung up. Then he said slowly, 'Go ahead, if you wish; it won't make any difference.'[9]

The Duke of Windsor's account is not very different, although he leaves out the anger.

It did not occur to me that she was asking to be released. Yet that was what she meant. And others read into her statement the same thing.[10]

However, according to both Monckton and Sir Edward Peacock the King was a party to this statement and it was given to the Press with his approval.

Meantime – Monckton says – he was most anxious that Mrs Simpson's position should be improved in the eyes of the public, and it was with his full approval that she made her statement on Tuesday, December 8, from Cannes that she was willing to give up a position that had become both unhappy and untenable. This, when published, was looked upon as being perhaps the end of the crisis, but we at the Fort knew of the statement before its publication, and that his intention was quite unchanged.[11] *

And Sir Edward Peacock:

She apparently began to think of her own unpopularity, and a statement was suggested, which she issued from Cannes. The King approved, well realizing that this would to some extent divert criticism from her to him, the very thing he wanted.[12]

On the same day that this statement was circulated to the Press, Theodore Goddard learned that another affidavit was about to be served on the King's Proctor by a private individual, to the effect that the intervener was

* The *Daily Express* published it under the headline: End of Crisis.

in a position to show why the decree should not be made absolute 'by reason of material facts not having been brought before the court and/or by reason of the divorce having been obtained by collusion'.* Goddard felt that he ought to see his client (some say because of the intervention, others because she had begun to issue statements to the Press) and he told Monckton that he proposed to go to Cannes. However, when Monckton told the King, he sent for Goddard and forbade him to go. On hearing this from Sir Horace Wilson, Baldwin then also sent for Goddard. Of what followed one thing is clear – Baldwin wanted Goddard to go to Cannes to see Mrs Simpson. His reasons for wanting this are obscure and have been given different interpretations, but there is evidence that he encouraged Goddard to go in Monica Baldwin's account.

And then began a series of comic episodes. For in all great tragedies, Monica, there are *always* comic episodes. . . .

Mrs Simpson began communicating with the Press. And this very much worried her lawyer, because she did *not* consult *him*. He, you see, was getting the divorce affairs wound up.

He was a fellow called Godard [sic] – a man whom every crook in London employs by reason of his cleverness; everybody who gets into a mess applies immediately to Godard, who gets them out at once.

He is, I may say, a man of blameless reputation but extraordinary ingenuity.

Well, Godard didn't like this, and he said he *must* see her as it compromised him when she made statements to the Press unknown to him. So he wanted to follow her to France. But the King forbade him. So Godard came to see me.

Well, he was shown up – a big, burly chap, with a large face, 'plain and pale like a ham'. . . . He told me his trouble. And I was very wily indeed. I said:

'Mr Godard, the relation between a lawyer and his client is the most sacred in English law. Even the *King* cannot come between them. Do you consider it your duty to your client to follow Mrs Simpson to Cannes?'

He said: 'I do.'

I said: 'Then don't ask *my* advice, Mr Godard, but do your duty to your client and take no notice of the King.'

So this man who had never set foot in an aeroplane in his life got in at Croydon and flew across the sea.

Some of the European papers got hold of the story – or rather the fringe of it – and reported that an obstetrician of world repute had left England for the Rogers villa at Cannes.[13]†

But why did Baldwin want Goddard to go? His biographers believe that he 'made a last and almost certainly genuine attempt to get Mrs Simpson to give up the King' by withdrawing her divorce action. Other

---

* The intervener was an elderly solicitor's clerk named Francis Stephenson, who later decided not to proceed with his application. No one has ever inquired into his action for which the motives are unknown.

† Goddard suffered from a heart ailment and he took with him not merely his clerk but also his doctor. The Press reported that he was accompanied by a gynaecologist, giving rise to the rumour that Mrs Simpson was pregnant.

motives have been attributed to him, although only Lord Beaverbrook managed to think of one that was discreditable. (Lord Beaverbrook believed that he did it because, if Mrs Simpson could have been persuaded to withdraw, he would have been absolved without shame from his promise to resign – a likely motive for someone who had been plotting for weeks to bring about the abdication of the King.)

Another solution which has had quite a wide circulation is that Goddard's reason for going was not directly connected with either the Abdication or the intervention of the solicitor's clerk. According to this story, when Mrs Simpson left England she took with her the emeralds which Queen Alexandra brought from Denmark at the time of her marriage, and Goddard was sent over simply to get them back. For obvious reasons it is not possible to get corroboration for this. All one can say is Lord Davidson believed it, and told it to more than one person.

And certainly without some explanation of this kind Baldwin's action seems incomprehensible. Why should he, when after weeks of negotiation he had reached an agreement which, even if it was not entirely satisfactory, brought a much needed end to the crisis,* and done this without putting pressure on the King or dividing the country, why should he try to re-open the whole thing by sending Goddard on this errand to Mrs Simpson. Two things give weight to the idea that this was, nevertheless, what he did. The first is that the Duchess of Windsor's account confirms it. The other is the rest of his conduct at the time.

In many ways a humorous man, Baldwin had great areas of unsophistication, one might even say insensitivity, and he invariably overrated his influence with the King. On the day that Goddard left for Cannes he decided that Edward must consult his conscience and that he was the man to make him do it. 'He must wrestle with himself in a way he has never done before,' he is reported to have said, 'and, if he will let me, I will help him. We may even have to see the night through together.'[15] And packing his bag and accompanied by Dugdale, he set off for Fort Belvedere.

The King was surprised when Monckton told him of the Prime Minister's proposed visit, remarking that he thought everything had already been said, but he agreed to receive him.

On arrival at Fort Belvedere, Walter Monckton who travelled down with the Prime Minister, saw at once that the King was in a state of utter exhaustion and 'seemed worn out'. He also showed obvious signs of distress at the sight of Baldwin's suitcase. Monckton then went to Sir Edward Peacock, who was in the house, and arranged for him to ask the Prime Minister to stay with him at his own house, Bodens Ride. However, as

---

* 'For two precious months, while the Duce's son-in-law Ciano was at Berchtesgaden, while Germany signed the anti-Comintern pact with Japan, and while Fascist soldiers entered Spain, our ministers could attend to only one thing, the determination of King Edward VIII to marry an American citizen, who was bringing divorce proceedings against her second husband.'[16]

soon as this suggestion was made to Baldwin, he said it would be better for him to return to London.

In recounting this episode in *A King's Story*, the Duke of Windsor is at his most hostile to Baldwin, charging him with paying this visit merely because it would make his own part in the crisis sound better if he could claim to have made a 'humble and sincere' effort to get the King to change his mind. And he goes on:

> But I had already had quite enough of Mr Baldwin; his part in my life was over, and I did not propose to have him on my hands that night, snapping his fingers, storing up little homely touches for his report to Parliament.[16]

And he goes on to say that he went to Sir Edward Peacock and asked him to take Baldwin away. This account gives a good deal of interest to the notes Sir Edward made at the time.

> He [the King] said to me that at the moment he felt unable to have people about & seemed completely done. I suggested that I take the Prime Minister & Dugdale away & give them dinner at Bodens Ride, but he said immediately: 'I could not do that. The Prime Minister has been so kind as to come here to help me, I could not let him leave without giving him dinner. He must stay.' I finally secured his assent to arrange with the Prime Minister that he & Dugdale should go home after dinner, but he was urgent that I should not do so unless I was sure that it would not hurt the PM's feelings.[17]

Here is Monckton's account of the interview that took place between Baldwin and the King.

> Once again when the audience took place I was present with the Prime Minister and the King. The Prime Minister was a little deaf when he was tired, and on this occasion it had a curious result, as when the Prime Minister had urged once again all that he could to dissuade the King, for the sake of the country and all that the King stood for, from his decision to marry, the King wearily said that his mind was made up and he asked to be spared any more advice on the subject. To my astonishment, Mr Baldwin returned to the charge with renewed vigour and, I thought, put the position even better than before. He asked me immediately afterwards if I thought he had said all that he could, and when I explained that I thought he had done even more, it was plain that he had not heard the King's request to him to desist.
>
> The audience took place in the drawing-room with its large windows facing the garden and looking away to the woods – though of course the blinds were drawn and the lights on. I can see them sitting there now, the King in his chair in front of the fire, Mr Baldwin at right angles to him on the sofa, and myself on a chair between them. It was the room in which the Abdication was to be signed in three days time.[18]

That night there were nine to dinner, the Dukes of York and Kent, Monckton, Peacock, Allen, Ulick Alexander, Baldwin, Dugdale and the King. Monckton had suggested to the exhausted King that he should dine in his bedroom before himself going up to change. The rest of the party seem actually to have sat down to dinner without him, when the King appeared – jolly as a lark.

This dinner party – Monckton wrote – was, I think, his *tour de force*. In that quiet panelled room he sat at the head of the table with his boyish face and smile, with a good fresh colour while the rest of us were pale as sheets, rippling over with bright conversation, and with a careful eye to see that his guests were being looked after. He wore his white kilt. On Mr Baldwin's right was the Duke of York, and I was next to him, and as the dinner went on the Duke turned to me and said: 'Look at him. We simply cannot let him go.' But we both knew there was nothing we could say or do to stop him.[19]*

Next morning Baldwin told the Cabinet that the King seemed 'happy and gay, as if he were looking forward to his honeymoon'.[21] And he told them it was useless to try to do any more.

In the meantime in Cannes it seems likely that Mrs Simpson understood for the first time the inevitable end of this affair and did indeed agree to do anything that might prevent the King from abdicating. She was ready to surrender everything, even to withdraw her divorce petition. Goddard telephoned to Baldwin the following message.

I have today discussed the whole position with Mrs Simpson – her own, the position of the King, the country, the Empire. Mrs Simpson tells me she was, and still is, perfectly willing to instruct me to withdraw her petition for divorce and willing to do anything to prevent the King from abdicating. I am satisfied that this is Mrs Simpson's genuine and honest desire. I read this note over to Mrs Simpson who in every way confirmed it.

Signed Theodore Goddard
counter-signed Brownlow.[22]

But this whole absurd adventure had been begun days, even weeks, too late, and, if it had been successful, could only have resulted in the King losing both the throne and his future wife. By now the King was absolutely determined and surely he was right to believe that, if he had given up Mrs Simpson for the crown at this juncture, it would have rested on a head 'forever bowed in shame'. No one could alter his decision.†

However, now it was the turn of the Cabinet, previously so anxious for an ultimatum, to have second thoughts, although this may have been the result of a wish to safeguard themselves. A formal message was sent to the King:

* 'My brother was the life & soul of the party – is the Duke of York's version – telling the P.M. things I am sure he had never heard before about unemployed centres, etc (referring to his visit to S. Wales). I whispered to W.M. "& this is the man we are going to lose". One couldn't, nobody could, believe it.'[20]

† In *A King's Story* the Duke of Windsor gives an account of a further attempt on Mrs Simpson's part to make him give her up. But there is a suggestion in the papers of the time that this was not wholly sincere or creditable, whereas the message through Goddard was almost certainly genuine.

Ministers are reluctant to believe that Your Majesty's resolve is irrevocable and still venture to hope that before Your Majesty pronounces any formal decision, Your Majesty may be pleased to reconsider an intention which must so deeply distress and so vitally affect all Your Majesty's subjects.

The King replied:

His Majesty has given the matter his further consideration but regrets he is unable to alter his decision.

Nothing remained but the formalities and the arrangements for the King's future rank and finance.

On 9 December Monckton and Peacock went to see the Duke of York at 145 Piccadilly where they reported to him 'and secured his assent to His Majesty retaining Royal Rank & that if and when he is allowed to come to England he should have the Fort to live in. The Duke of York authorized Monckton to tell this to the King.'[23]

Later on the same day Monckton and Simon drafted the King's Message to Parliament – although Monckton remarks 'I say "we drafted" but in fact the draft was substantially his – though I was responsible for it.'[24] And later still Monckton went back to Downing Street where arrangements were made for the instrument of Abdication and the Messages to be distributed throughout the Empire at the right time and place. He also had an interview with Queen Mary who said to him: 'To give up all this for that!'*

Monckton arrived at Fort Belvedere with the draft Message and the draft Instrument of Abdication at 1 a.m. the next morning. Sir Edward Peacock was already there and had told the King of a Cabinet decision that he should stay out of England for a period of not less than two years.

Lord Birkenhead goes on:

He had seemed to agree. It had been the longest and most exhausting day for Walter since the crisis began. At twenty minutes to three in the morning Peacock told the King that they ought to go to bed: 'He insisted on taking me up to my room, and there talked for a while longer. I begged him to go to bed. As he went away I heard him say to poor Walter Monckton, who was dead beat: "I want just a word with you." I learned next day that the "word" went on until well after three o'clock.[26]†

On Thursday morning, 10 December, the Instrument of Abdication was signed and witnessed by the King's three brothers as also the King's Message to the House of Commons. Six copies of the Abdication were

* 'Bertie arrived very late from Fort Belvedere,' Queen Mary wrote, 'and Mr Walter Monckton brought him and me the paper drawn up for David's abdication of the throne of this Empire because he wants to marry Mrs Simpson!!!!!'[25]

† Years later the Duke of Windsor told a visitor to his house in Paris that he always slept well and he said that this was true even during the Abdication. 'The others used to go off to London in the morning and I used to go to bed and go to sleep. There was nothing else for me to do.'

signed and seven of the Address as in the case of the latter one copy went to the House of Commons and one to the House of Lords.*

That afternoon the Speaker to the House of Commons read the King's Message to a packed House and, speaking from notes, Baldwin then made one of the most famous speeches of his whole career.† Here is Harold Nicolson's account of it.

The Prime Minister then rises. He tells the whole story. He has a blue handker-chief in the breast-pocket of his tail-coat ... His papers are in a confused state ... and he hesitates somewhat. He confuses dates and turns to Simon, 'It was Monday, was it not, the 27th?' The artifice of such asides is so effective that one imagines it to be deliberate. There is no moment when he overstates emotion or indulges in oratory. There is intense silence broken only by the reporters in the gallery scuttling away to telephone the speech paragraph by paragraph. I suppose that in after-centuries men will read the words of that speech and exclaim, 'What an opportunity wasted!' They will never know the tragic force of its simplicity. 'I said to the King. ...' 'The King told me. ...' It was Sophoclean and almost unbearable.[27]

When *A King's Story* appeared it became clear nevertheless that the speech left the King with a grievance. That morning Baldwin had asked Walter Monckton whether there were any special points the King would like him to mention and the King had sent him two notes; one asking him to say that he and the Duke of York had always been on the best of terms as brothers and 'the King is confident the Duke deserves and will receive the support of the whole Empire'; the other asking him to say that 'the other person most intimately concerned had consistently tried to the last to dis-suade the King from the decision which he had taken'.[28] Baldwin read out the first note but he did not mention the second. In the same way the first note was found among his papers, the second was not. To anyone who has studied what Baldwin felt, it seems obvious that whereas the King would undoubtedly have sent such a request, Baldwin would have found it im-possible to comply with it. How easy, if that were so, to crumple it up in one's pocket.

Baldwin's speech was received with solemnity and Attlee asked that the sitting should be suspended until six o'clock.

The financial arrangements for the future Duke of Windsor were initially discussed by the Cabinet, and Hardinge pressed the Prime Minister through Walter Monckton to combine in the Instrument of Abdication the pro-vision for an income of £25,000 a year with an undertaking on the ex-King's part not to return to the country without the consent of the King and the government of the day. And Monckton makes it plain that he

---

* The Message and the Instrument of Abdication will be found in the Appendix.
† This speech has been extensively quoted from in the account given here of the meetings between Prime Minister and King.

believed that if the King had made up his mind earlier he would have negotiated from greater strength. Writing on 6 December, he says:

> I felt that there was at any rate a strong element in the Cabinet who as early as this felt that his immediate abdication upon generous terms was desirable. I think there is little doubt that due provision would have been made for an income and title if he had expressed his willingness to go at once.[29]

However, in the end the financial arrangements were made not with the government but with the Duke of York. Probably the chief reason for this was that any settlement had to take into account the peculiar position of Balmoral and Sandringham, of which, under the wills of Queen Victoria and King George V, Edward VIII was a life tenant. Any satisfactory financial settlement had to be based on the transfer of those to his brother. Naturally no one but their financial and legal advisers was a party to the settlement, but informed guesses put the figure for Sandringham and Balmoral at one million pounds and the yearly income paid by George VI to his brother at £60,000. Over and beyond this the Duke of Windsor is believed to have taken substantial sums out of the country from other sources.

On 10 December Monckton and Peacock secured what Monckton later described as a general settlement of the money affairs at a meeting at which were present the Duke of York, Wigram, Sir Bernard Bircham, Mr Allen and Ulick Alexander. Right from the start there were difficulties and this family was no more immune than any other to misunderstandings over money. But the technicalities were immensely complicated and everyone seems to have been agreed that there was no lack of generosity on the Duke of York's part, merely at times a difficulty in understanding the arrangements, and at others in deciding between the views of his different advisers.

> The discussion threatened to become heated as sentiment and legal fact were getting rather mixed – Peacock wrote – so I intervened to shift this, then had a short talk with the Duke of York and Bernard Bircham alone. I removed the technicalities which were perplexing the Duke & stated directly & simply what I believed would be his desire should certain eventualities occur. I said that if I was right I was sure the question re B and S could be settled to his & everybody's satisfaction. ... He agreed.[30]

And the Duke of York's version of the same interview.

> Wigram was present at a terrible lawyer interview which terminated quietly & harmoniously. E.R.P. was a very great help.[31]

At Fort Belvedere only one thing seriously upset the King. This was a message from Sir John Simon saying that in the changed circumstances he would feel bound to withdraw the detectives who had been guarding Mrs Simpson at Cannes. The King was so greatly distressed that Monckton protested to Simon who, possibly as a result of this, decided to bear the brunt of any criticism himself and reversed the order.

The day ended with what Lord Birkenhead has described as 'an emotional and somewhat embarrassing evening'. Mr and Mrs Hunter, who were friends of the King's, had been invited to dinner and Monckton, who was not present, received the following account of what happened from Peacock:

In a short time the butler came in to say that Mrs Hunter was of the party at the Fort and wanted very much to see me. So I drove over and saw Kitty Hunter, who burst into tears and explained to me how Mrs S. had fooled her to the last, declaring that she would never marry the King. Her account of the dinner suggests that the poor King must have had a pretty difficult time, because apparently Kitty and George wept into their soup and everything else during the meal, in spite of the King's heroic efforts to carry off the dinner cheerfully.[32]

Once he had decided to abdicate immediately, the King determined to fulfil his desire to broadcast to the nation. He tasted at once the joys of being a subject of the King because the government no longer could restrain him. However, he instructed Walter Monckton to inform Baldwin that as a matter of courtesy he would allow the Cabinet to see in advance what he intended to say. On the evening of the 10th he worked late into the night and he was up early on the 11th to finish his speech. Then he invited Winston Churchill to luncheon to wish him good-bye and to show him the draft. (During this luncheon he ceased to be King.) The Duke of Windsor has said that it is not true that Churchill wrote his broadcast speech – he wrote it himself – but he was responsible for one or two phrases which the student of Churchilliana should be able to spot.

As Churchill stood on the doorstep saying good-bye to the ex-monarch there were tears in his eyes and he gave a fresh association to Marvell's famous lines on the beheading of Charles I.

> He nothing common did or mean
> Upon that memorable scene.*

The ex-King's decision to broadcast to the nation made urgent the question of his future rank and titles. 'The pundits were confounded,'[33] Sir John Wheeler-Bennett writes, and they sought the counsel of the new King. In a memorandum annexed to his record of the Abdication crisis, George VI gives an account of an interview with Lord Wigram and Sir Claud Schuster (as representative of the Lord Chancellor), who came to ask his view on the matter. The question, the King was told, was urgent because Sir John Reith, the Director-General of the BBC, was proposing to introduce the ex-King on the air as Mr Edward Windsor. The King said

---

* Horatian Ode upon Cromwell's Return from Ireland. 1.57.

that this would be quite wrong but that before going any further it was necessary to know what his brother had given up by the Abdication. Upon Schuster replying that he was not quite sure, King George, who is normally represented as being completely bowled out at this time by his sense of his own inadequacy, gave a convincing exhibition of regal testiness as well as the solution of the problem.

I said, It would be quite a good thing to find out before coming to me. Now as to his name. I suggest HRH D of W[indsor]. He cannot be Mr E.W. as he was born the son of a Duke. That makes him Ld E.W. anyhow. If he ever comes back to this country, he can stand & be elected to the H. of C. Would you like that? S replied No. As D of W he can sit & vote in the H of L. Would you like that? S replied No. Well if he becomes a Royal Duke he cannot speak or vote in the H of L & he is not being deprived of his rank in the Navy, Army or R. Air Force. This gave Schuster a new lease of life & he went off quite happy.[34]

King George also gave instructions as to how his brother should be described on the radio that night and it was on his specific command that the ex-King was introduced as His Royal Highness Prince Edward. That evening he visited his brother to tell him that he had decided to create him a Duke as the first act of his reign. 'How about the family name of Windsor?' And the following morning at his accession council he announced his intention to create him the Duke of Windsor, although it was not until after the Coronation that style and title were given legal form. See p. 322.

During the day the ex-King received what he has described as 'a hint' from the Prime Minister that he would be gratified if he would stress that he had at all times received every possible consideration from him; a hint about which the Duke of Windsor writes bitterly, after brooding for years on the fact that Baldwin had refused his own request to do justice to Mrs Simpson. And during the day it was arranged, through Mrs Simpson on the telephone, that he should go to Baron Eugene de Rothschild's house, Schloss Enzesfeld, near Vienna – the last stages of the Abdication having been conducted at such speed that not until now had any consideration been given to the ex-King's future.

That evening he dined with his assembled family at Royal Lodge and after dinner Walter Monckton fetched him and drove him to Windsor Castle from where he was to broadcast. At the Castle he was met by Lord Wigram as Deputy Constable and Lieutenant-Governor of the Castle. Mounting the Gothic staircase to a room in the Augusta Tower, he met Sir John Reith. So that his voice might be tested he read a newspaper report of a reference by Sir Samuel Hoare to the fact that the new King was an ardent tennis player. Then Sir John Reith announced: 'This is Windsor Castle, His Royal Highness Prince Edward,' and he spoke to the listening world in a voice which, gradually gaining confidence, ended on a high note of courage.

At long last I am able to say a few words of my own.

I have never wanted to withhold anything, but until now it has been not constitutionally possible for me to speak.

A few hours ago I discharged my last duty as King and Emperor, and now that I have been succeeded by my brother, the Duke of York, my first words must be to declare my allegiance to him. This I do with all my heart.

You all know the reasons which have impelled me to renounce the throne. But I want you to understand that in making up my mind I did not forget the country or the Empire which as Prince of Wales, and lately as King, I have for twenty-five years tried to serve. But you must believe me when I tell you that I have found it impossible to carry the heavy burden of responsibility and to discharge my duties as King as I would wish to do without the help and support of the woman I love.

And I want you to know that the decision I have made has been mine and mine alone. This was a thing I had to judge entirely for myself. The other person most concerned has tried up to the last to persuade me to take a different course. I have made this, the most serious decision of my life, upon a single thought of what would in the end be the best for all.

This decision has been made less difficult to me by the sure knowledge that my brother, with his long training in the public affairs of this country and with his fine qualities, will be able to take my place forthwith, without interruption or injury to the life and progress of the Empire. And he has one matchless blessing, enjoyed by so many of you and not bestowed on me – a happy home with his wife and children.

During these hard days I have been comforted by my Mother and by my Family. The Ministers of the Crown, and in particular Mr Baldwin, the Prime Minister, have always treated me with full consideration. There has never been any constitutional difference between me and them and between me and Parliament. Bred in the constitutional tradition by my Father, I should never have allowed any such issue to arise.

Ever since I was Prince of Wales, and later on when I occupied the Throne, I have been treated with the greatest kindness by all classes, wherever I have lived or journeyed throughout the Empire. For that I am very grateful.

I now quit altogether public affairs, and I lay down my burden. It may be some time before I return to my native land, but I shall always follow the fortunes of the British race and Empire with profound interest, and if at any time in the future I can be found of service to His Majesty in a private station I shall not fail. And now we all have a new King. I wish him, and you, his people, happiness and prosperity with all my heart. God bless you all. God Save the King.

After the broadcast he returned to Royal Lodge to say good-bye to his family. It was late and his mother and his sister Mary left quite soon, but the four brothers and Walter Monckton sat on until midnight when the Duke of Windsor and Monckton left to drive to Portsmouth. As he took leave of his brothers he bowed to the new King, a gesture which led the Duke of Kent to cry out: 'It isn't possible. It isn't happening.'

All the way down to the coast he talked quietly and composedly to

Walter Monckton about their early friendship at Oxford and about the First World War.

At Portsmouth the ex-King had been expected hours before he arrived, and a Naval Guard with rifles and fixed bayonets had been paraded, while the *Fury* waited alongside and ready for sea. A young naval officer present at the time kept a record of that evening.

As time wore on the feeling of drama began to wear off. The Commander-in-Chief of Portsmouth, Admiral Sir W.W.Fisher was there, Captain Victor Danckwerts, the Guard of Honour and myself, just waiting and waiting. The Captain of the *Fury* with his Officers likewise were waiting on deck with everyone on board at their stations for slipping and proceeding to sea.

After about an hour and a half and much telephoning it was eventually learned that the King had left Windsor late.*

When the King's car at last reached Portsmouth shortly after one-thirty in the morning it entered through the Main Gate instead of, as it should have, through the Unicorn Gate nd Admiral Fisher, the Commander in Chief Portsmouth, himself drove after it to intercept it and to direct the chauffeur to where *Fury* was docked and where Piers Legh, Ulick Alexander and Godfrey Thomas stood waiting. There were tears in Sir William Fisher's eyes as he said good-bye for the Navy but the King seemed in the same good spirits he had shown all the week, and, if he felt any emotion appropriate to the enormity of the occasion, he gave no sign of it. His friends and members of his household escorted him down to his cabin to say good-bye. 'Godfrey had served him for 17 years,' Monckton wrote, 'and felt that in some way he had failed in his duty, and that what was virtually his life's work had been shipwrecked.'

Fury sailed immediately and anchored in St Helen's Roads for the night, in company with *Wolfhound*, proceeding in time to cross the Channel and arrive in France in the morning.

* Letter to the author from Rear-Admiral C.D.Howard Johnstone, CB DSO DSC.

24

AFTER THE ABDICATION

The immediate aftermath of the Abdication is chiefly remembered for three things: the indelicate speed with which the erstwhile friends of the ex-King and Mrs Simpson scuttled: the broadcast of the Archbishop of Canterbury: the placidity with which the British people accepted the event.

Of the first, which is relevant to this biography, there is unhappily no doubt. No defence can disguise the fact, vouched for by dozens of witnesses, that in the weeks following the Abdication almost no one could be found who had ever been on terms of intimate friendship with the ex-King or Mrs Simpson. All eyes were turned longingly to the occupant of the throne. Osbert Sitwell commemorated this sad state of affairs in a poem which has never been published and of which the title *Rat Week* is perhaps the best part. The only thing that can be said in extenuation of this exhibition of human weakness is that not many of the King's friends had understood that he meant to marry Mrs Simpson and would abdicate if necessary to do so: and, of the few who had ever asked the direct question, none had received a truthful reply.

The Archbishop's intervention is not easier to defend. Lang had suffered from his inability to give any guidance during the course of the Abdication and he now felt that he could not merely say 'kind, and of course true things about the late King's charms and manifold services' and that he was bound to refer to the surrender of a great trust. On Sunday, 13 December, he broadcast to the nation in words which gave offence to very many people.

What pathos, nay what tragedy, surrounds the central figure of these swiftly moving scenes! On the 11th day of December, 248 years ago, King James II fled from Whitehall. By a strange coincidence, on the 11th day of December last week King Edward VIII, after speaking his last words to his people, left Windsor

Castle, the scene of all the splendid traditions of his ancestors and his Throne, and went out an exile. In the darkness he left these shores. . . .

From God he had received a high and sacred trust. Yet by his own will he has abdicated – he has surrendered the trust. With characteristic frankness he has told us the motive. It was a craving for private happiness. Strange and sad it must be that for such a motive, however strongly it pressed upon his heart, he should have disappointed hopes so high and abandoned a trust so great.

Many people found 'in the darkness he left these shores' a self-indulgent and uncharitable flight of fancy, and the rest of the opening passages, although they expressed in well-chosen words what others felt, were spoken at a time when the general tone (in the Press, for instance) was funereal rather than critical. What followed was even worse.

Even more strange and sad it is that he should have sought his happiness in a manner inconsistent with the Christian principles of marriage, and within a social circle whose standard and way of life are alien to all the best instincts and traditions of his people. Let those who belong to this circle know that today they stand rebuked by the judgment of the nation which had loved King Edward.

(Lord Brownlow expressed his personal indignation to the Archbishop himself and Walter Monckton wrote: 'To be frank, I have not myself enjoyed much the comments which have reached me attributing the Archbishop's rebuke to myself. It merely shows that if one speaks deliberately to millions of people and recklessly includes unguarded words intended to attack an ill-defined group, one ought to know that one will wound many whom one would wish to leave untouched.')[1]

The Archbishop concluded:

Yet for one who has known him since childhood, who has felt his charm and admired his gifts, these words cannot be the last. How can we forget the high hopes and promise of his youth; his most genuine care for the poor, the suffering, the unemployed; his years of eager service, both at home and across the seas? It is the remembrance of these things that wrings from our hearts the cry: 'The pity of it, O the pity of it.' To the infinite mercy and the protecting care of God we commit him now, wherever he may be.[2]

A torrent of abuse fell upon the Archbishop from all sides and the broadcast seems to have had only one beneficial effect. It added to the literature of the Abdication, not very strong in wit, the following neat little squib:

> My Lord Archbishop, what a scold you are!
> And when your man is down how bold you are!
> Of charity how oddly scant you are!
> How Lang, O Lord, how full of Cantuar!*

* This was composed by Gerald Bullett, had a wide circulation by word of mouth, and was published in his *Collected Poems* in 1959.

Most memorable of all, however, was the speed at which the British forgot the ex-King and turned to the new (and, although this is the complaint against the ex-King's friends, in the unambitious public it seemed a virtue). There were several reasons for it, of which the most important, essentially in normal times forgotten, is that it is the institution itself which enslaves the mind. It would not be correct to say that one King is as good as another, because there are very large limits to this, and because, although it may be true that no human being could in his own person sustain the weight of idolization, it is also true that, for all the rich paraphernalia, the solemn and bolstering pageantry, the ramifications of the King's business, the monarchy remains only as strong as its hold on men's imaginations. It is a question of faith. HRH Prince Edward had disturbed this faith a little, and the public, longing for reassurance, turned eagerly to his successor.

The English are usually represented as being passionately involved in the crisis and some indeed were. Speaking for one section of these, an officer in the Royal Fusiliers, of which the Prince of Wales had been Colonel-in-Chief, said:

'We loved him. We would have drawn our swords for him. And then, by God, *didn't he let us down*!!'*

Others simply felt sad. Speaking of a dinner on 28 January 1937, at which Lionel Ellis was present, Tom Jones wrote:

We were bidden to discuss future relations of the [Unemployment Assistance] Board and the National Council of Social Service, but throughout dinner and for an hour after we talked of nothing but the recent Palace crisis. This is unusual – the subject has dropped out, but Ellis was still full of grief for the fall of his Prince, with whom he had worked closely from the inception of the Albert Hall meeting on unemployment onwards. ... He developed at great length a theory to explain the ex-King's conduct. He was an artist. He did not wish to be King, but finding himself one he wanted to fill the part in a modern way, revealing himself as unconventional, spontaneous, and the friend of the common man. But when on his father's death he moved into Buckingham Palace he found himself in the grip of the most powerful and rigorous ceremonial machine, from which he constantly escaped to Fort Belvedere and Mrs Simpson. When he realized that he could not be the sort of King he wished to be he abdicated, as the only honest course open to him, and left the job to a brother who would find its duties and restrictions far less irksome.[8]

But the majority of British people, far less personally involved, would have been pressed to explain exactly what they felt. Their emotions may have been summed up in a cartoon which appeared soon after in a British newspaper. In this a workman throws down his tools and turns to his mate with the question: 'How can I do my work without the help and support of the woman I love?'

* In a letter to the author from Sir Martin Lindsay of Dowhill.

In any case, the people of England forgot King Edward VIII until in the summer of 1972 his body was brought home for burial.

There will always be room for speculation about the Abdication. The Duchess of Windsor has told us that when she and the Duke were first married only one thing marred their happiness. 'After the first burst of joy in rediscovering each other and being together we found our minds turning back in interminable post-mortems concerning the events leading up to the Abdication. . . . This endless re-hashing of the lost past became almost an obsession with us until one evening David said despairingly, "Darling, if we keep this up we are never going to agree, so let's drop it for good." Then and there we vowed we never would discuss the Abdication again, and to this day we never have.'[4]

If the two principals could not agree, it is unlikely that any writer will ever be allowed the last word on the subject. Nevertheless, there are one or two aspects of the Abdication which have received little attention.

It is always taken for granted that Edward VIII was incapable of the sustained work which is required of the monarch, and was in character and temperament ill-equipped for the role. *Capax imperii nisi imperasset* runs the tag from Tacitus used about the Abdication. 'Had he never been emperor, no one would have doubted his ability to reign.' And it is almost inevitable that this will be the final verdict on him, for on what is he to be judged if not on his actual performance?

Yet during the whole of his reign he was under maximum strain and at times near the edge of a breakdown. He was not in a mental state to be judged and, while it may be true that under his particular stars his character made him unsuitable to the throne of England, it might nevertheless be argued that under a happier configuration he could have made a good King.

One of the main complaints against him was that he was incapable of the sustained work which is required of a monarch, a complaint which must seem extraordinary to anyone who has knowledge of the immense programmes he undertook as a young man, of the eagerness to serve which he exhibited in all his contacts with the unemployed and the working men of Britain, of the trouble he took over his speeches, both as Prince of Wales and later, after the Abdication, as Governor of the Bahamas.

It may be true that he had no taste for paper work and could never have spent the necessary hours on the eternal red boxes. But surely some means could have been found to alter the procedure so that he was presented with précis of only the most important documents. His grandfather, King Edward VII, disliked formal audiences with his ministers and by 1905 had almost ceased to give them to anyone 'with the exception of the Prime Minister, the Foreign Secretary and Arnold Forster occasionally – when he forced himself upon him'. A committee of seven, which it will be remembered included Mrs Keppel, was formed to perform for the King 'the kind

of service which the Prince Consort had performed for Queen Victoria'.[5]*
Surely in different circumstances it would not have been beyond the wits of
Edward VIII's secretaries to supplement his good qualities and overcome
his bad.

But to make a good King it is necessary to have the will for it. From the
earliest age the Prince showed a lethal inability to find attraction in anyone
but a married woman, and, when he finally met the woman to whom he
was to devote the rest of his life, she had two husbands living and, because
she was an American, no natural understanding of the limits of the King's
power, or of the discretion and devotion to duty required of the woman
whose fate is linked with his, either as Queen or in any other relationship.

From the moment he fell in love with Mrs Simpson he proceeded wil-
fully and entirely unnecessarily to compromise both her and his own position. If one can imagine a man secretly but determinedly intent on the unlikely task of making a divorced commoner (the fact that she was an
American was here irrelevant) Queen, or if not Queen a morganatic consort, how would one expect him to behave? Surely with the greatest possible discretion and a considered attempt to gather a band of serious and
experienced advisers around him. Yet it was not so much that the Prince
drifted on to his fate, as that he went out of his way to feed the world
Press with gossip and scandal, covering his loved one with jewellery,
flaunting her everywhere he went and in the Court Circular, showing a
reckless disregard for the conventions and a complete indifference to the
feelings of his family, above all to any chance of gaining sympathy for his
project. On the *Rosaura* in 1935 and again on the *Nahlin* a year later he
seemed to be insisting on attention.

Then, how is it possible to explain that, when the crisis broke, until his
anger with Hardinge induced him to employ the services of Walter
Monckton, without either advisers or a plan of campaign, almost the only
thing he could think of to do was to send for Lord Beaverbrook?

Again, we have been told so much of his desire to democratize and
modernize the monarchy, and, if not to confront the establishment, at least
to reform it. Yet during the course of his reign there is almost no evidence
that he had given any real thought to these exceedingly interesting and in
many ways necessary projects. He succeeded, through impatience and more
or less by accident, in suggesting one or two reforms which have since
been thought desirable, and he effected some economies which had become
necessary, although in doing this he showed what to some observers seemed
a lack of consideration for old and loyal servants and an unacceptable
meanness. These were the sum total of his achievements.

The truth seems to be that his mind was never given to the task that by
inheritance and years of training was his. There is no indication that the

---

* Mrs Keppel said about the Abdication: 'The King has shown neither decency, nor wisdom,
nor regard for tradition.'[6]

mental strain from which he suffered during the crisis was due to a prolonged struggle between his conscience and his inclinations. Indeed rather the reverse, he seemed to fear only that something might hurt Mrs Simpson or separate her from his side. Here is what Stanley Baldwin said about him to his niece.

He is an abnormal being, half-child, half-genius. It is almost as though two or three cells in his brain had remained entirely undeveloped while the rest of him is a mature man. He is not a *thinker*. He takes his ideas from the daily press instead of thinking things out for himself. He never reads – except, of course, the papers. No serious reading: none at all.

He is *reasonable*: that is to say, when he really *sees* a thing, he does it. You might say he is amenable to reason – except, of course, on that one subject. . . .

I did a thing which I don't expect your Reverend Mother would have approved of. I said to him, was it absolutely necessary that he should *marry* her? In their peculiar circumstances, certain things are sometimes permitted to royalty which are not allowed to the ordinary man.

To this he replied immediately:

'Oh, there's no question of that. I am going to marry her. . . .'

After that began an unforgettable period. . . .

The King was in a curious state of mind. He kept on repeating over and over again:

'I can't do my job without her. I am going to marry her, and I will. . . .'

What rather shocked me, if I may say such a thing, was that there seemed to have been no *moral* struggle at all.

The last days before the Abdication were thrilling and terrible. He would *never* listen to reason about Mrs Simpson. From the very first he insisted that he would marry her. He had *no* spiritual conflict *at all*. There was no battle in his will. I tell you this and it is true. He is extraordinary in the way he has no spiritual sense; no idea of sacrifice for duty. *That* point of view never came before his mind.

I set it all before him. I appealed to one thing after another. Nothing made the least impression. It was almost uncanny: like talking to a child of ten years old. He did not seem to grasp the issues at stake. He seemed *bewitched*. . . .

He has no religious sense. I have never in my life met anyone so completely lacking in any sense of the – the – well, what is *beyond*. And he kept on repeating over and over again: 'I can't do my job without her – I am going to marry her, and I will *go*.' There was simply no moral struggle. It appalled me.

For once in his life Baldwin was in agreement with Lord Beaverbrook. 'Our cock won't fight.'

Yet the King had been reared to an understanding of the constitutional position. Subconsciously he must have known, as everyone else did, that there was no question of his marrying Mrs Simpson and remaining on the throne. ('The real puzzle,' Sir Colin Coote was to write, 'was how anybody could ever have thought it possible for her to become Queen of England, and of seven British Dominions as well.')[7] Although for a week or two he appeared to be negotiating with the Prime Minister, he accepted a negative answer to every proposal with such docility that the only way in which one can explain his attitude and actions is if one believes that, whether he completely understood this himself or not, he was instinctively aware when he first decided to marry Mrs Simpson that this would involve giving up the crown: and that his unprecedented, completely unexpected and otherwise inexplicable decision to marry her was partly inspired by a deep longing to escape the terrible responsibilities of the role he had inherited; a role to which he was in some ways temperamentally unsuited, and for which he had from his earliest youth shown some distaste as well as the conviction that it was not inescapable.

Walter Monckton has asserted that the King had a religious side to his nature but he adds: 'One sometimes felt that the God in whom he believed was a God who dealt him trumps all the time and put no inhibitions on his main desires.' And he also says: 'Once his mind was made up one felt he was like the deaf adder "that stoppeth her ears; Which refuseth to hear the voice of the charmer." '[8]

Both at the time of the Abdication and for the rest of his life the King would always show the most extraordinary obtuseness in relation to the facts. He believed that his abdication of his duty would be seen as the honourable course in the situation in which he found himself; and he held to this view forever after. Yet to people reared to the moral concept which inspired the poet Lovelace: 'I could not love thee (Dear) so much, Lov'd I not honour more', and who were between two wars in which when necessary they would die for it, his conduct could never seem anything but contemptible. It was this profound difference in understanding which would bedevil his relations with his country and his family for the rest of his life.

The belief that the pressures of the King's life had built up an instinctive desire to escape the throne – and it must be remembered that he managed immensely to increase the burden he had to carry because of his temperamental inability to be guided by his courtiers down safe, traditional paths – will naturally run into objections. One of these is that, according to Lord Beaverbrook, on the night he left England he said to one of his companions: 'I always thought I could get away with the morganatic marriage.' Yet there is no way in which the morganatic marriage proposal can be shown to have an important bearing on the King's conduct, more particularly on his subconscious motives. It was suggested to him for the first time by Esmond Harmsworth less than three weeks before the end, and he understood almost immediately that it was unlikely to be accepted. As we have seen he persisted in it merely because 'I've got to do something. At the very least I'll get my head in a more comfortable position on the block'; a statement which, if we can believe it, might reasonably be given in evidence for the view expressed here.

But if the King simply bowed out, what of the plot? And what of Baldwin's great skill? If the first was nonexistent, perhaps the second has been overrated. In 1965 Sir Ulick Alexander, who it will be remembered was one of the small staff who resided at Fort Belvedere during the crisis, wrote a letter to *The Times* in which he said:

I was of course not present at the private discussions between the Prime Minister and the King during this period, but what was said was always discussed afterwards by the King with the three of us* and I found it, and I know at least one of my colleagues found it, extremely difficult to decide on what line Mr Baldwin was proceeding.[9]

And in truth Baldwin never seems to have been quite certain what he should do. He was forced into action in the first place by Hardinge and Davidson and the party at Cumberland Lodge: he had to have both his situation and his duty analysed for him by Bruce: on almost every occasion it was the King who sent for him and initiated the next stage of the negotiations (although he always dealt admirably with the suggestions made to him): and at the very last he was apparently willing to endanger the agreement which had been reached, by sending Goddard to Cannes and going himself to reason with the King at Fort Belvedere. Harold Nicolson saw artistry in the fact that he dropped his notes and asked for confirmation of dates during his speech to the House of Commons, but he was in a very nervous and exhausted state and earlier he had left his notes behind and had had to send Dugdale back to fetch them. It is so easy in hindsight to think of the Abdication in the context of the smoothness with which it passed and with which the new King commanded the loyalty of his subjects and to see Baldwin as manœuvring skilfully in the background. But at the time those most intimately concerned with it greatly exaggerated the danger to the monarchy and had no feeling of manipulative power. It seems far more likely that Baldwin behaved as most politicians do in a crisis and followed his nose; and that his success was due to a happy combination of his best and his worst qualities. He emerges as a man of large character, kind, devoted to the monarchy and fond of the King. He also had a constitutional inertia in face of a crisis. This forced the King to lead again and again, and, since he had made up his mind to marry Mrs Simpson, and was a man of determined bad judgment, virtually all Baldwin needed to do was to show the patience and lack of aggression which came naturally to him. Against this view there can be put one or two remarks he made at the time, but history is at its most misleading when pinning down the small change of everyday life, particularly when this is between men who share some common experience but are otherwise strangers to each other.

When the Duke of Windsor left England he sent Baldwin a friendly personal message and it was only after many months of the influences of exile that he began to believe in the existence of a plot against himself.

* Presumably the other two were Walter Monckton and Allen.

Nevertheless, since the charge has been made, it is as well to point out that it could only have had substance if Baldwin had represented a minority view. In fact, his view was shared by the Cabinet, by the leaders and almost all members of all political parties, by everyone except a handful of MPs, by the vast majority of his countrymen and of the populations of the Dominions.

In his long exile the Duke went very near falling into the trap his father had warned him about so long ago, and confusing his person with his position. It was to the last that the loyalties of the Prime Minister and the government belonged. Once they despaired of saving the monarch, it was their duty to save the monarchy.

PART 3
THE DUKE OF WINDSOR

25

SCHLOSS ENZESFELD

On the night in December 1936 when the ex-King left England to travel across the Channel, he left the historians behind him. In abdicating the crown he forfeited their attention, and in future, drawing one chapter to a close, they would turn in the next to his brother. But the interest of the biographer was not in any way diminished; rather the reverse, for from now on he would have the field to himself. What does an ex-King think? How does he feel? Has he regrets? What does the future hold? A human curiosity about these things may be unexpectedly well repaid.

Two days before the Abdication Baron Eugene de Rothschild received a message in a light code asking whether 'David' might go to Schloss Enzesfeld, his house near Vienna. After consulting the head of his family he replied that he would be glad. The Duke of Windsor knew only an hour or two before he left where he would go, but he travelled straight to Schloss Enzesfeld and stayed there until the end of the winter. His host left the house to him but his hostess, Baroness Kitty de Rothschild, stayed on until the beginning of February.

The Duke had not intended to stay at Schloss Enzesfeld so long. He had hoped to go to France to be nearer Mrs Simpson but his lawyers insisted that in view of the intervention of the solicitor's clerk, Mr Stephenson, it was more than ever necessary that they should keep a frontier between them until her divorce was made absolute. All the intensity of feeling that had brought the Duke to this place could therefore be assuaged only during long daily telephone calls to Cannes. All day he waited for the evening; every day he waited for the end.

In the early part of January the Duke's oldest and greatest friend, Fruity Metcalfe, was skiing with his family at Kitzbühel. There had been a short break in this friendship during the last year or so and Fruity, who had reasonably expected a job in the King's household as soon as Edward came to the throne, had been overlooked. His genuine affection and loyalty for the man who was now Duke of Windsor had survived the disappointment, however, and, at exactly the time when in England Osbert Sitwell was inspired by events to write *Rat Week*, he telephoned to the Duke at Enzesfeld and asked him whether he would like him to go for a short stay. 'Ah!' the Duke replied, 'Would I like you to? ...' Metcalfe was a gifted letter-writer, acute and observant, always telling us exactly what we want to know. In a series of letters he wrote to his wife from Schloss Enzesfeld, later from Cannes and in the war from Paris, we get closer to the subject of this biography than at any other time. At Schloss Enzesfeld, then, he takes up the story.

Schloss Enzesfeld. 21 Jan. 1937

I arrived after a rather uncomfortable journey, as the train was overcrowded all the way, to be met by an army of press photographers. I felt like a cinema star!! Kitty, Boysie,* Chas. Lambe & HRH only here. HRH in wonderful form, happy, jolly, amusing & very easy. Sat up very late that night talking. Never have I found him easier or more charming, he is at his very best, & quite like his old form. He couldn't be more thoughtful and kind in every way. We went off the next morning to the Semmering – just Lambe, HRH and myself plus a horde of police & detectives in a car behind. Picked up a world champion ski teacher (very spoilt & stupid young man) on the way, & kept on at this skiing till dark! Never have I seen such energy – he never stops for one second – he is quite good, not nearly your form, still a long way ahead of me. Lambe is very good. Played poker that night. HRH is in his old Sunningdale–Epsom form.† I've never seen him better. *Happy cheerful* has no regrets *about anything*. He talked to W for hours after we'd finished playing poker. The conversation did *not* seem to go so well. Talks of marriage early in May. No date fixed. Has no idea of returning to England for a year or two at least. Wants to get a place out here. Do not think he misses England or *anything* connected with it *one little bit*. He seems glad to be free of it all.

I think Kitty has got on his nerves – she won't leave – he gets quite short with her at times. Says he wants men only & doesn't want any women about. Three times Kitty said she was leaving but never does. (He takes over the place, servants & all when she does.) Yesterday spent day in Vienna – turkish bath all morning – he & I – then shopping, then big cocktail party at the Embassy – I never leave him. Lambe left today for England but Greenacre has just arrived. He was sent out from England before they knew I was coming. I'm glad as he does the letters etc. We went off very early to Semmering. Kept at it all day till dark. Got back at 8.30 p.m. *Worn out*. Tomorrow go up again.

Tonight he was told at dinner that HM wanted to talk on phone to him. He said he couldn't take the call but asked it to be put through at 10 p.m. The answer to this was the HM said *he would talk at 6.45 p.m. tomorrow* as he was *too busy to talk*

---

* Count Rex.

† At different times the Metcalfes had taken houses at Sunningdale and at Epsom and HRH had spent many weekends with them as Prince of Wales.

any other time. It was pathetic to see HRH's face. He couldn't believe it! He's been so used to having everything done as he wishes. I'm afraid he's going to have many more shocks like this. He is just living through each day till he can be with W. (the 27th April is the date), he ticks off each day on a calendar beside his bed. He's terribly in love. He has become very foreign – talks German all the time – he seems to have absolutely no worries and is as I said before in his very best form. Lots of people are marked down – never having heard from them, etc. Hugh & Helen & Emerald he's mentioned.* He tells me he didn't know until about an hour before he left England where he was going to. He had thought of going to some hotel in Switzerland! . . .

PPS – He seems to only see one thing & has the whole thing out of proportion.

Schloss Enzesfeld.   Sunday 24th inst. (Jan)

Today HRH decided to take an easy, so we didn't go to Semmering. I must say I was glad as it really isn't so much fun. You see it's a long drive both ways and when you do get there I think the skiing isn't up to much – There is one slope and you have to walk it every time – there is very little snow & a great deal of ice. He of course says its much better than Kitzbühel – how he can possibly think this I don't know. After skiing we drive to an hotel and have a bath and tea, which is the best part of the day. We lead a very quiet life here. Kitty has been very good and never asks anyone out here although I know she has a very difficult time putting people off. . . . I personally think she couldn't be sweeter or more charming but between ourselves she gets on HRH's nerves & he is longing for her to leave. He says that she is always *saying* she is going but will not do so, he is frightfully keen to have the place to himself. You know how he loves to run his own show. . . . Well I am very happy & HRH just couldn't be a more delightful companion. He's not had one bad day since I arrived. I must say he's been awfully sweet to me. We sit up very late every night talking about all sorts of things we've done together. His memory is astonishing. Of course he's on the line for hours & hours every day to Cannes. I somehow don't think these talks go so well sometimes. It's only after one of them he ever seems a bit worried and nervous. She seems to be always picking on him and complaining about something that she thinks he hasn't done or ought to do. (This sounds as if I heard all the conversations. Of course this is not so but as my room is next to his & he talks terribly loudly its awfully difficult not to hear a certain amount that he says.) He is like a prisoner doing a time sentence. All he is living for now is to be with her on the 27th April. As we come back every night after skiing he says, 'One more day nearly over.' It's very pathetic. Never have I seen a man more madly in love. (I had to stop as he came into my room & sat for 3/4 hour – this is always happening just as I am writing about him! It's very tricky!!). . . . I think he wants me to stay on with him for another few weeks but I'll see how things go. . . .

I am feeling very jaded as we never seem to get to bed & then out all day somewhere. If it's not the Semmering its Vienna. There is a lot of work to be got through as the telephone never stops & his mail is enormous – sometimes 300 letters, etc., mostly from mad people! Gosh but some of them are abusive. We never show him any of those of course. They come from all over the world.

* Lord Sefton, Mrs Evelyn Fitzgerald, Lady Cunard.

When Greenacre leaves Jack Aird comes out and then Joey* .... I *do* wish you were here but there is no chance – He won't have any women at all.

Schloss Enzesfeld. 27th Jan. 1937 2 a.m.

I hope I can get this letter off to you but I doubt it as I'm sure to have a visitor at any moment. He will *not* go to bed that is true. He is in & out of his room till 4 AM nightly. How the devil he's as well as he is beats me – because he *is* well – as I've said before I've never seen him better. You can contradict any rumours to the contrary. We've been over the Semmering all day – skiing hard – No lunch! He never seems to tire. We leave about 10 a.m. & don't get back till 8.15 p.m. then dinner at 8.45 p.m. (marvellous food as you know). He is [unintelligible word] at this infernal skiing & really has got it. I am not much better than when I left Kitzbühel. I do try to do Christies but I'm on my behind most of the time. I don't think anything of the instructor he's got. To start with he can't talk English – so what a hope I've got. There is very little snow on the Semmering but the hell of a lot of ice. I always seem to find the ice. Tomorrow we go to Vienna for the day, he has a meeting with Selby in the afternoon, the rest of the time will be spent shopping (buying presees for Wallis) haircut, feet, etc. There is a lot of work here & no time to do it as we are always out somewhere. The daily mail brings *hundreds* of letters which have to be opened and dealt with some way. (Gosh some of these letters are abusive the things they write about W are unbelievable) Greenacre does 3/4 of these while I am in attendance but I get enough believe me. I don't know how long HRH wants me to stay. I've offered to go when Princess Mary and Harewood arrive but he said he'd like me to stay on. Jack Aird comes out next. I'm enjoying it all greatly but I can't get any sleep. I don't get to bed till all hours & always wake terribly early as usual – result is I am *awfully* tired....

You thought Kitty had left for Paris. *Not* on your life – she's here & intends to stay at least another week. HRH is longing to get the place to himself. He is frightfully close about money, he won't pay for anything – it's become a mania with him. It really is not too good.... Now I must stop as I hear HRH coming along from his room.

Later.

Once more let me say that HRH is 100% & the most delightful companion as he is now to be with. If he'd remain as he is I'd give up everything to serve him for the rest of his life. I really am devoted to him. You've no idea how sweet he is about our children. He loved reading David's letter & the letters the twinnies wrote – isn't he odd?

Schloss Enzesfeld. 29.1.37.

We've had an 'easy' today, no Semmering as HRH thought he'd take a day off. I couldn't have been more delighted as my old ankles are dreadfully swollen; indeed I'm sore all over as I've taken a few good 'uns in the last few days. I'm afraid I'm never going to be much good at the game. HRH has improved a great deal even since I've been here. Tonight we've got the Selbys, old Mensdorff & several other diplomats dining. It's the first party we've had of any kind. On the

* Sir John Aird and Mr Piers Legh.

3rd Feb there is a big show at the Embassy. HRH is making a great fuss over decorations. He has sent for all his orders etc to put on. He says he must keep up his dignity. It's so funny this coming from him who never cared if he had them on or not. I've mentioned several times you might be coming over to Mittersill but he has never suggested your coming here even for a few days. I do wish he would but I fear it's no good. .... HRH has asked me to stay on but I can't make out how long he would like me to stay. I think I should make a move before the 15th Feb don't you think? Princess Mary & Harewood arrive the end of next week!! Lovely! I suggested going (and would very much like to!!) before they arrived but he said he wanted me to help him out. I believe he has an idea (& I know he is working on it hard) that he should get permission to go to some place between here & Cannes about the middle of March to arrange things, etc. with W. He says he only asks for a few days! I bet he will fix it. This is all being done through his lawyers. They are also trying to get the time limit (27th April) cut down.

3 A.M. HRH came in & stopped till now. I will not have time to write more as we are to leave for skiing at 8 am to do our first run.

Hotel Bristol. Wien.   3rd Feb.

We're in here today as there is a big show at the Legation tonight.

Kitty left yesterday!! *Terrible show!* as HRH was late getting dressed owing to his infernal telephone call!! *& missed her! Never saw her to say good-bye or thank her!* She was *frightfully hurt* & I don't blame her. He *is* awfully difficult at times & this is the worst thing he's done yet. I went down to the station with a letter which I got him to write & that made things a bit better – He also never saw the servants to tip them and thank them etc!! (all due to more d—n talking to Cannes. It never stops). ...

He was very hurt at not being made personal ADC to the King in the Honours List. He said just now: 'Well I suppose I have no standing of any kind now – I used to be a Field Marshal & an Admiral of the Fleet – but now I'm nothing' – It's very pathetic – These sort of things are beginning to upset him a bit I fancy. He talks of my going with him to the Munster's place to see it later on, as he thinks he might take it for a year or two if it's suitable.* I can't get any definite date how long he wants me to stay but I shd think about another 2 weeks, maybe longer. I of course *love being with him* as he is so wonderful to me. He said that later on you & I must come out & stay with him & W! I hope he means after the wedding!! ...

Schloss Enzesfeld.   4.2.37.

Last night's party at the legation was a 'corker' it was a musical show!! You can imagine what he felt about it! However he was wonderful as he always is when he really tries. Never has he played up more or been in better form. Selby was delighted at the success of the evening. All the foreign Ministers were present. HRH spoke to everyone of importance and got away with murder! von Papen had a long talk with him & it seemed to go very well. Re my returning here in March or April I think it very unlikely. I'll stay on about another 10 days or perhaps 2 weeks but it's all very uncertain as he may get tired of me being here so

* Wasserleonburg which the Duke took for the following summer.

long & want a change. He said *he'd tell me* when he'd like me to go. I'm rather dreading his sister & Harewood arriving. It will be terribly stiff & formal & they are not easy to get on with. ...

Schloss Enzesfeld.   7.2.37.

We've had no skiing the last few days as weather conditions at the Semmering have been very bad. ... When there is no skiing the days are very long as you know how restless he is. The evenings lately have been *dreadful* he won't think of bed before 3 AM & now has started playing the accordion and the bagpipes!! You can imagine how I love it. He has been going through all his old letters etc. some of them awfully interesting. I was very touched when he showed me the letter we wrote from Jamaica on his father's death. He said he'd *always* keep it as it was one of the nicest he had received. The Princess Royal, Harewood arrive today. *Great* preparations. He is determined to make this visit a great success & you've no idea the trouble he is taking over little detail. He's been round their rooms here 20 times altering furniture etc. etc. We all go to the station to meet them, picking up the British Minister & Lady Selby on the way – Press photographers are arranged for!! He *wants* to have *plenty of* publicity made about their visit. They will be here a week – we'll do a lot of sight seeing (& skating, she is *very* keen I believe – isn't this terrible? You know my form on the ice!)

I believe the Duke of Kent is coming out at the end of the month. He goes first to stay with Paul of Servia & then comes on here – Perry Brownlow is coming on the 27th. HRH had a long talk with him last night. It seems Mrs S likes Perry better than any of the staff, & he is to go down to Cannes after being here a bit.

Last night there was a bit of trouble – in fact almost a row on the phone. He got in a *terrible* state. Their conversation lasted nearly 2 hours! He came in to my room very late & poured out all his troubles! ... I'm going to be in difficulties about money I'm afraid as I'll have to buy my return ticket & pay for this servant (who is utterly useless) which I had to get as the servants here are so hard worked. HRH pays for as *little* as he can when we go anywhere.

Metcalfe continued to write regularly until he left for home towards the end of March. On 14 February he reported the success of the Harewood visit. All the week they went sight-seeing – 'there's no doubt sight-seeing with Royalty is all right with me!' At night they played poker and Fruity began to find Princess Mary 'sweet & simple but terribly shy', while 'I got on well with him, he was calling me Fruity by the end'. Then he adds 'Kitty is *out* completely – all due to W who apparently was very jealous of her. Isn't it staggering?'

On 17 February he reports a thaw. 'I hope to goodness we get some more snow or our life will be extremely difficult – if he's not doing something he gets *very moody* & *irritable* & things are by *no means easy*. There appears to be *lots of difficulties* cropping up as regards money & his family etc. & he has sent urgently for his two solicitors to come out. ...' Fruity says again that he has asked HRH when he would like him to go & once more received the reply: '*I'll tell you* when I want you to go.'

In his next letter he reports that HRH would like him to stay until he leaves Enzesfeld for good. At this time the Duke of Windsor believed that he would go to the Duke of Westminster's place, Chateau St Saens, and a large part of Metcalfe's time was taken up on the arrangements for this. In the end the Duke's solicitors vetoed the whole idea. Metcalfe had by now become anxious to see his wife, if not to go home, and much of his letters are devoted to this theme. On 1 March he says: 'I *long* to see you & suggested your coming out for a few days. It seems that he *wouldn't like this idea at all* as I mentioned it to him today & he said I'd rather you didn't have Baba out to Vienna as it would get in the papers. He won't have any women connected *in any way* with him & his staff at present. I am really very unhappy at the prospect of another month at least of this life. It is a *dreadful* strain & I am definitely feeling it. However he needs me & wants me so I must do it for him ...'

On 1 March he reports that Lord Brownlow has arrived and that Sir Godfrey Thomas will follow him. And he goes on:

P.G. [Prince George the Duke of Kent] left last night after 5 hectic days – we were on the go the whole time sight-seeing & skiing. On Monday last HRH & I went up to Paul's [Count Munster's] place*. We had a lot of fun going up together in the train – & he was in grand form & the visit a success, he liked the house & has taken it for June July August. ... Since Jack left I've been alone on duty here till Perry arrived & there has been a great deal to do. He still gets about 500 letters which have to be dealt with etc. I get *dead beat* as one has to go on very late at night, because we're out all day doing something or other.

Then on 2 March:

HRH is being wonderfully sweet & kind & seems to love having me with him. I wish to God HRH hadn't minded you coming out here. It was awfully sweet of you to offer to do it.

On 6 March he writes:

I've had a very long spell here & it is not a very restful life to say the least of it. I'm beginning to feel it a bit I'm afraid. However it's been decided that I make the move with him & I'll have to stick it. ... Latest plans are we leave here on the morning of the 22nd & take train to Amiens & from there motor. We don't go near Paris & unless I went on from Amiens (which means leaving him with Godfrey to move in etc) I don't see that I'll be able to meet you. I'm afraid I'd better give up the idea. ... Perry is here now ... He leaves on the 10th & Godfrey arrives on the 12th. It's going to be a hell of a business getting out of this place & as no one talks a word of English you can imagine how I'm going to get on! Getting into Bendor's place & engaging servants etc is going to keep someone very busy! I don't know how good Godfrey is at this sort of job but I admit I don't fancy myself much at it!! You see the trouble is that HRH has got no permanent staff at all & thinks he can do everything himself. It's absolutely absurd. We've not been able to go skiing for days now as the snow is gone for

* Wasserleonburg.

the time being. So we are stuck here all day unless we go to Vienna. I'm so bored with the hundreds of letters we still get every mail, of course half of them are rubbish but they still have to be gone through.

Metcalfe continued to write until he left for home at the end of March, often reverting to the by now well-established themes of his desire to get home, of the exhausting nature of his life and the difficulties of finding a staff. 'When I get back,' he wrote once, 'I'll have to write HRH a *marvellous* letter. You must give me your ideas & help in this.' And he adds with pardonable pride: 'I've carried on here & made a great success of it I know, & HRH is deeply grateful to me....' In an undated letter in the middle of March he reports that 'Dickie' is here for two or three days and on the 17 March that 'HRH has now been fixed up with a permanent equerry; a young fellow from the Legation.'*

Lord Louis Mountbatten had several long conversations with his cousin during his visit and brought away memories (as so many other people have) of his extraordinary obtuseness about the realities of his life. He spoke airily of returning home and of the kind of work he would like to do there, and Lord Louis, by nature very straightforward, could not persuade him of the change in feeling for him among the ordinary people of England. During this visit Lord Louis twice offered to be best man at the Duke's wedding. The Duke thanked him but declined the offer. 'This will be a royal wedding,' he explained. 'My two younger brothers will come over as supporters.'1†

One other person visited Schloss Enzesfeld at least once during these months, although curiously enough Fruity Metcalfe does not report it. (This may merely mean that all his letters have not survived.) Walter Monckton was sent over on what must have been one of the most delicate missions of his whole life, and the long sad history of the Duke's relationship with his family began with this visit.

The first reason for Monckton's mission was to try to smooth over difficulties that had arisen between the King and his brother as a result of negotiations for a settlement of the Duke's financial affairs. It will be remembered that the Duke's solicitors in company with Sir Edward Peacock had to some extent secured the arrangements for a general settlement at a meeting with the then Duke of York, accompanied by Lord Wigram and Sir Bernard Bircham, at the time of the Abdication. Monckton says he was always convinced that the Duke could rely on his brother for a generous settlement but 'the advice the King was getting prevented him

---

* Mr Dudley Forwood, later Sir Dudley Forwood Bt.

† Conversation with Lord Mountbatten. A royal bridegroom has two supporters, not a best man. Many years later when the Duke of Windsor and Lord Mountbatten met and had a long conversation the Duke said: 'I have always had a bone to pick with you. You didn't come to my wedding.' And Lord Mountbatten reminded him of this conversation. As a result of it Major Metcalfe acted as best man to the Duke. Thus HRH was best man to Lord Mountbatten, Lord Mountbatten to Metcalfe, and Metcalfe to HRH.

making the immediate and unqualified promise he would have liked'.[1] Anyone who has been in a situation of this kind must sympathize with the Duke of Windsor, particularly as everything in his earlier life contributed to an utter defencelessness against the feelings of impotence and isolation which he now experienced. Monckton's task was to reassure him, and, in fact, a settlement satisfactory to the Duke was eventually reached, although only after he had suffered months of frustration and anxiety.

However, if one sympathizes with the Duke, one must sympathize even more with Walter Monckton. He had a second and most formidable task.

In 1966 the Duke of Windsor contributed six articles to the *New York Daily News*. In these he wrote of his time at Schloss Enzesfeld. At first, he says, he used regularly to speak to his brother on the telephone.* Then one day the King told him that these telephone calls must cease. The Duke asked him if he was serious and the King replied that he was, adding that the reason for this must be clear to his brother. The Duke says it never was. He refers to the legal difficulties over his property rights which he says were irksome to his brother but a matter of life-and-death to him, but he makes it clear that he believes there was another and graver reason for the King's decision. All his life the Duke would blame any lack of enthusiasm for himself that he met with in England as due to what he describes here as 'that staid, tightly linked aristocratic bureaucracy which had hedged in the Monarchy since Queen Victoria's time'. He says now that this section of the Court wished to be rid of him, and in an even more significant phrase, that 'those closest' to his brother were not displeased that this should be so.[3]

However the Duke's memory is probably at fault. According to Walter Monckton, it was he who at Schloss Enzesfeld had the appallingly delicate task of persuading HRH to abandon the habit of telephoning regularly to his brother. Ever since the Abdication the Duke had taken it upon himself to advise the King on the questions of the day. 'This advice,' Monckton writes, 'often ran counter to the advice which the King was getting from his responsible ministers in the government. This caused him trouble which no one would understand who did not know the extent to which before the Abdication the Duke of Windsor's brothers admired and looked up to him.' The Duke, Monckton adds, was particularly quick in understanding and the King both slower and troubled by the impediment in his speech. Conversation on the telephone was exceedingly hard for him, particularly when questions arose affecting Mrs Simpson.[4]

The Duke accepted Monckton's advice but the bitterness he felt emerges sharply from the pages of the article he wrote thirty years later.

At the end of March he left Schloss Enzesfeld, in spite of being unable to

---

* According to Fritz Wiedemann these conversations were monitored by the Germans who found them mainly about social matters and uninteresting.[2]

move over to France. He was determined at all costs to avoid the trouble he thought there would be if his hostess, Baroness Kitty de Rothschild, returned to her own home. He therefore went to a small hotel near Ischl. Then at the beginning of May the long vigil at last ended. On the day he heard that Mrs Simpson's divorce had been made absolute, he left for the Chateau de Candé.

26

THE WEDDING

King George VI was finally responsible for the choice of the Chateau de Candé for his brother's wedding. Various suggestions were made but the choice was narrowed down to La Croë, a villa in the South of France, and the Chateau de Candé before the matter was put to him. He chose the Chateau near Tours rather than La Croë because of the reputation of the Riviera as a playground for the rich.

It is improbable that either he or his advisers understood the circumstances in which the Chateau de Candé was placed on the list. It belonged to a French-born naturalized American named Charles Bedaux who had made an enormous fortune through a system of industrial efficiency. At the time of the Abdication he had offered his chateau to Mrs Simpson as a holiday house and a refuge from the Press. The offer was made through Herman Rogers, whom he had met once or twice, but Bedaux was surprised to be told some weeks later that his chateau had been selected for the wedding ceremony. He went there nevertheless to welcome his guests, arriving there after Mrs Simpson but before the Duke. Asked at a later date about his friendship with the Windsors he replied in what Janet Flanner called 'his occasionally troubled English', 'I never met them until I got to Candé as to her; as to him, until he arrived at Candé.'[1]

Neither the ex-King of England nor his future wife, nor any of their advisers apparently saw any reason why the loan of this house for their wedding should not be accepted from a man they had never met and about whom only the most cursory inquiries had been made. Everyone was to pay for this, Bedaux in the direct line of consequences with his life.

Candé was a rebuilt, turreted, Renaissance castle in Touraine on which Bedaux lavished a fortune. According to Janet Flanner, he had bought a house in Monts merely because he had been told that the wrought-iron balconies would make good consoles at Candé. On the estate he had con-structed a network of brooks to encourage duck, a swimming pool, an enclosed badminton court, archery butts and a golf course. The castle remained a rather ugly and, according to Lady Alexandra Metcalfe who stayed there, not very comfortable example of its type.

Mrs Simpson went to Candé early in March accompanied by Herman and Katherine Rogers. They were received by Bedaux's wife, Fern, a tall, refined, quiet and rather beautiful woman. There is a discrepancy in the accounts about what happened next. The Duchess of Windsor says that Mrs Bedaux showed her to her own room and said that since she would not be there she hoped her guest would use it as her own. There is nothing in the Duchess's account to suggest that the Bedauxs were ever again at Candé during her stay. But we know that not only Mrs Bedaux but also her husband was there, and that it was at Candé that the Duke of Windsor began the long conversations with Bedaux which led to the events of the next chapter.

Mrs Simpson was alone with the Rogers at Candé for much of April, however, except when other of her friends came to visit her. One of these, Bernard Rickatson-Hatt, was with her when Slipper, the little dog the Duke of Windsor had sent her, was bitten by a viper and died. Then on 3 May news of her decree absolute reached her and on the next day her fiancé arrived.

On 17 May the Duke of Windsor wrote to Fruity Metcalfe and asked him if he would be best man at his wedding.

'David longed to have his sister and his brothers, and most of all his mother, near him at his marriage. ...' the Duchess of Windsor writes. 'But ... the unspoken order had gone out: Buckingham Palace would ignore our wedding. There would be no reconciliation, no gesture of recognition. That also meant that many of the friends with whom David had made his life would find it awkward to come to Candé.'[2]

It would have been hard for any member of the Royal Family to attend the wedding because the religion of their country did not recognize divorce and its clergy usually refused to officiate at the re-marriage of divorced persons. It was not part of their duty to flout this religion, still less in so public a manner as by attending the Duke's wedding. The word 'usually' has been used in connection with Church of England practice in relation to the re-marriage of divorced persons because there was a famous clergyman at the Savoy Chapel in London who regularly re-married the innocent party to a divorce. It was in the light of his practice that the offer to marry the Windsors which came from an unknown clergyman, the Reverend R.A. Jardine of Darlington, was seen and gladly accepted, and not merely the Windsors but many of their friends were innocently pleased that they should have the benefit of something other than the French civil ceremony. Someone might have felt suspicious of Jardine, however, the one man who could be found to break the laws of his church.* In any case he turned out to have what Walter Monckton would later call 'a marked weakness for self-advertisement' and he toured the United States on the strength of having married the Windsors.†

On 1 June Major and Lady Alexandra Metcalfe arrived and on 2 June the Reverend Jardine and Walter Monckton. Mrs Constance Spry came for the day to arrange the flowers and Cecil Beaton to take photographs. He was at Candé twice and has left a fascinating account of his visits in *The Wandering Years*. Lady Alexandra Metcalfe kept a diary of her visit there. In this she records that her fellow guests on the first night were Mrs Merryman, Mr and Mrs Rogers, Mr and Mrs Bedaux, Mr Allen, the solicitor to the Duke, and Mr Dudley Forwood, HRH's equerry. Lady Alexandra had not seen Mrs Simpson for some time and she was struck, as so many other people were at other times, by how little her physical characteristics matched her extraordinary role. Cecil Beaton, who was an admirer of Mrs Simpson (although he is responsible for the following description of her: 'She twisted and twirled her rugged hands. She laughed a square laugh, protruded her lower lip. Her eyes were excessively bright, slightly froglike, also wistful'),[3] tells us that she was not at her best on the day before her wedding. 'Wallis hovered about in yellow, slightly more businesslike than usual; with her face showing the strain: she looked far from her best.'[4]

Of Herman Rogers, Lady Alexandra says that 'he was nice, quiet & efficient' but obviously knew nothing of England and world opinion. Of the Bedaux she says: 'Infinitely better than expected. She is like a borzoi & is not at all common & he is brilliant & very astute, but unattractive. They are very retiring & might be guests.' Then she goes on:

We sat around & chatted in the library until HRH came in in his shirt sleeves from the office where he was competing with letters, telegrams & presents. He could not look better or be in better spirits. Outwardly he appears just the same as a year ago as King at the Fort. The evening at dinner (I sat between Allen the Solicitor & HRH) went off very easily, but one has no feeling of being at a unique occasion or witnessing a page of history. . . .

HRH is in marvellous form, obviously happy, much easier to talk to, has made no allusion to England, family, staff or friends. Wallis & he disappeared after

---

* Two Bishops disowned Jardine. Dr Hensley Henson, Bishop of Durham, said that if the marriage had been taking place in his own diocese he would have considered himself bound to inhibit any clergyman from officiating but he could not control Mr Jardine on the Continent. Presumably, he added, Mr Jardine had permission from the responsible Anglican Bishop. The Bishop of Fulham, whose jurisdiction covered the Anglican Church throughout Northern and Central Europe, issued a statement saying that if it were true that an Anglican clergyman had undertaken to perform a religious ceremony in connection with the marriage of the Duke of Windsor, he wished it to be known that this action had been taken without his knowledge or consent.

† According to Iles Brody, a very unreliable witness, Jardine and his wife were arrested six years later in Los Angeles, where they maintained a Lilliputian Church called the 'Windsor Cathedral', and charged with having overstayed their permit. They turned to the Duke of Windsor for help and he replied that he could do nothing for them.

dinner with Allen & we carried on a desultory conversation till we went to bed. The telephone rings a lot & Herman makes dates to meet the Press.

The list of presents is rather pathetic. So far Kent & Gloucester are the only members of the family who have sent presents or letters.

(One of the letters was from Stanley Baldwin. After expressing the hope that the Duke would find happiness and triumph over the difficulties of his new life and assuring him of the understanding and sympathy of himself and his wife, Baldwin said:

Through all that time in the early winter, you ran dead straight with me and you accomplished what you said you would do: you maintained your own dignity throughout: you did nothing to embarrass your successor, nor anything, as might so easily have happened, to shake the monarchy more than was inevitable in the circumstances.)[5]

Lady Alexandra Metcalfe continues:

He sees through Wallis's eyes, hears through her ears & speaks through her mouth.

This morning the parson arrived, a gallant little fellow called Jardine from Darlington. He wrote & offered to come as he felt the way the marriage was being treated by the bishops, etc, was appalling. HRH is so pleased to be having a religious ceremony. We found a chest suitable for an altar, put a lame and lorn table cloth of Wallis's round it & with the aid of Mrs Spry's flowers it looks quite pretty.

Cecil Beaton arrived to take photos – Herman Rogers was going to give a list of present givers to the Press but Fruity got him to give up the idea. Bedaux, Aunt Bessie, Mrs Rogers, Fruity & I went to lunch at Sembeaucy, a gargantuan meal. I like the Bedaux more & more, they have done fascinating trips & are very interesting. . . . Walter Monckton arrived at tea time.

Monckton was the bearer of evil news. He carried with him a letter from King George VI in which he informed his brother that he had been pleased by Letters Patent 'to declare that the Duke of Windsor shall, notwithstanding his act of Abdication ... be entitled to hold and enjoy for himself only the title, style or attribute of Royal Highness, so however that his wife and descendants, if any, shall not hold the said title or attribute.' The Duke of Windsor was to be HRH: his wife was not. The King hoped that this painful action he had been forced to take would not be regarded as 'an insult'.

'When I arrived,' Monckton wrote, 'he received the news almost in the same words his brother had used when he sent me off. "This is a nice wedding present." ' And Monckton said he sympathized with the Duke over this. 'When he had been King he was told that he could not marry Mrs Simpson because she would have to take his status and be Queen, so he gave up his Kingdom and Empire to make her his wife. He could not give up his royal birth, or his right to be called "His Royal Highness" which flowed from it. It was a little hard to be told, when he did marry her, that she would not have the same status as himself.'[6]

Monckton wrote to Sir John Simon, the Home Secretary, warning him not to under-estimate the bitterness this act would create. He believed that if the King had been left to himself he would never have assented to this course because he knew how it would affect his brother and he believed, too, that if it had been left to the Cabinet they might have taken his advice. Walter Monckton says he was later told 'though at second hand', that the Dominions, in particular Canada and Australia, were not satisfied that the Duchess should have a royal title.

This idea has never been contradicted and is often put forward. No doubt it has this much truth in it that there was a general consensus of opinion. But the Dominions were not a single entity capable of conceiving of this departure from ordinary procedure and they once more gave their opinion in answer to a question from London. Baldwin's latest biographer, Mr Montgomery Hyde, has stated that Baldwin did not want to sign the telegram to the Dominion governments but got Simon to persuade his successor-designate Neville Chamberlain to do so. Mr Montgomery Hyde also says: 'It should be noted that there was no design to deprive Mrs Simpson of the rank of Duchess on her marriage by restricting her to some such style as "Mrs Windsor", since this would understandably have conflicted with the Peerage law. But, as King George VI reminded Baldwin at the time, once a person has become a Royal Highness there is no means of depriving her of the title.'[7]

This last sentence is the crux of the matter and the explanation for what, unexplained, seems so incredibly mean. Neither the King and Queen nor anyone close to them understood this couple well enough to be sure the marriage would last. They knew little of Mrs Simpson except that this was her third marriage and that she had been instrumental in the King leaving the throne. And they knew little of him. They had always exaggerated his passing affairs and underestimated his essential faithfulness. Now he had shown himself completely unpredictable. Baldwin's last words to his niece were: 'His family are all wondering what will become of him when at last he opens his eyes and sees the sort she really is.' And what would become of her? Where would 'Her Royal Highness' go? What do? Once the idea enters one's head the possibilities are limitless. Would there be marriage and re-marriage? More than one Royal Highness? The new King and those nearest him were still under shock from the Abdication. Was there no limit to the possible damage to the throne?

The Duke of Windsor received the news as he would have a wound in battle. It struck at his deepest emotions and it altered him as gunshot might have altered him. From now on he would live with this fact and never forget it, any more than a man who lives in pain can forget it, although for short periods he may sometimes feel it less. He had so secured himself from within that he was more than ordinarily vulnerable to blows from without. When he said in his farewell broadcast: 'You must believe me when I tell you that I have found it impossible to carry the heavy burden of responsibility and to discharge my duty as King as I would wish to do without the help of the woman I love,' he believed he had made all plain, said all there was to say and that his abdication would be seen as the only honourable course in the situation in which he found himself. So obdurately was he armed against any other point of view, any understanding of the magnitude of his dereliction of duty, that the actions of his family and the government of his country were to him incomprehensible and completely unexpected. In the months at Enzesfeld before he wrote to Fruity Metcalfe to ask him to be best man, he learned something of his position, at least that his family would never bless his union. 'The drawbridges are going up behind me,' he said to his future wife on arrival at Candé, 'I have taken you into a void.'[8] As time went on he would suffer blow after blow until, game as he was, he was punch drunk, but nothing ever hit him like this calculated meanness, this hideous discourtesy to his wife. It would be some years before, accepting his situation although still not understanding it, he would give up hope of a public life. During that time, as he travelled about Europe and then from France into Spain and on to the Bahamas, no word he spoke, no act of his can be understood or judged except in the light of the news he received at Candé on the day before his wedding.

Yet neither at the time, nor in the company of his wife forever afterwards, could it spoil his happiness. Lady Alexandra Metcalfe takes up the tale.

Wallis lost no time in explaining to me that she lived in the other end of the chateau from the Duke & he called it W1 & W2. The night before his wedding when she went to bed she shook hands and curtsied and said 'Goodnight, Sir' in exactly the same way as she said good-night to all of us. I gather he understood his staff not coming but took Perry's back out the worst. Her not being made HRH was the worst blow. When he knew this he said he wanted to give up his own title. He has written a letter to the King saying he will not *admit* the fact of Wallis not being HRH. . . .

I've never seen him happier or less nervous, but try with all one's might & main when looking at her one can't register that she can be the cause of the whole unbelievable story. One almost begins to think there is nothing incredible, unique or tragic about it as they are so blind to it all. Except for the Press, which one does not see as they are only allowed as far as the gate, one might be attending the wedding of any ordinary couple.

June 3rd.

The bitterness is there all right.

He had an outburst to Fruity while dressing for dinner. The family he is through with. The friends, staff & Perry have also been awful. He intends to fight the

HRH business as legally the King has no right to stop the courtesy title being assumed by his wife. Monckton & Allen agree but let's hope he does nothing.

Wallis had lots to say about the staff, Perry & HRH to me. She said it didn't matter to her but she minds a great deal really & says Monckton has made her sign just Wallis on the documents today. She said that she realized there was no insult they hadn't tried to heap on her. She thanked me effusively twice for having come & said she thought it was sweet of me.

Two never to be forgotten scenes. On Wednesday & Thursday morning a figure in a dressing-gown with tousselled hair sitting on the floor going through the mail helped by Mr Carter, his old clerk. The second, even more memorable perhaps than the ceremony today, was the rehearsal before dinner last night. A small pale green room with an alcove in one corner. The organist, Dupres, from Paris trying out the music in the room next door. Fruity . . . with HRH stands on the right of the alcove, Wallis on Herman's arm comes in – under the tutelage of Jardine, a large-nosed red-faced little man, they go over the service – HRH's jaw working the whole time exactly the same as I saw the King's all through the Coronation. Walter Monckton, Allen & I watch with such a mixture of feelings. The tune played for 'O Perfect Love' is not the lovely one, so I sing it to the organist who writes it down as easily as I am writing this. Mr Bedaux keeps calling Jardine 'The Reverend'.

Dinner. Kitty & Eugene & Randolph Churchill came to dine. I sat on HRH's right with Monckton on the other side. I couldn't like him more. He is devoted to him. Seven English people (Fruity, Monckton, Allen, Randolph Churchill & Hugh Thomas, Lady Selby & myself) present at the wedding of the man who six months ago was King of England.

3.30

It's over & it's true. I felt all through the ceremony that I must be in a dream. It was hard not to cry & in fact I did. In the room besides the guests already mentioned there were a number of French officials & wives. The civil ceremony took place first, at which only Fruity & Herman R. were present.

During that time we sat & waited talking ordinarily as nothing unusual was happening, the organ playing from the room next door. Jardine came in first followed shortly by the Duke & Fruity who stood two yards from my chair. Throughout the ceremony Fruity held for him the prayer book Queen Mary gave him when he was 10 with 'To darling David from his loving Mother' written in it. Wallis on Herman's arm came in the other door. She was in a long blue dress short tight-fitting coat blue straw hat with feathers & tulle, the loveliest diamond & sapphire bracelet which was his wedding present.

Jardine read the service simply & well. . . . His responses were clear & very well said. . . . Her voice . . . lower but clear. It could be nothing but pitiable & tragic to see a King of England of only 6 months ago, an idolized King, married under those circumstances, & yet pathetic as it was, his manner was so simple and dignified & he was so sure of himself in his happiness that it gave something to the sad little service which it is hard to describe. He had tears running down his face when he came into the salon after the ceremony. She also could not have done it better. We shook hands with them in the salon. I realized I should have kissed her but I just couldn't, in fact I was bad the whole of yesterday. . . . If she occasionally showed a glimmer of softness, took his arm, looked at him as though she loved him one would warm towards her, but her attitude is so correct. The effect is of a woman unmoved by the infatuated love of a younger man. Let's hope that she lets up in private with him otherwise it must be grim.

June 4th

A very nice telegram came from the King & Queen and one from Queen Mary. The Press and photos are good.

No one will ever know to what extent Wallis was at the bottom of everything. Baldwin is supposed to say that as a schemer & intriguer she is unsurpassed. My opinion is that she must have hoped to be either Queen or morganatic wife as if she had realized she would get neither she would & could have stopped him putting forward the whole idea. Nevertheless, although I loathe her for what she has done, I am unable to dislike her when I see her.

On the evening after the wedding the Duke of Windsor and his wife left for Count Munster's house, Wasserleonburg, where they spent most of the summer.

27

THE DUKE OF WINDSOR
VISITS GERMANY

In his farewell broadcast Edward had said: 'I now quit altogether public affairs,' but almost in the next sentence: 'If at any time in the future I can be found of service to His Majesty in a private station, I shall not fail.' There is no doubt that, although at the time he gave no great thought to his future career, he never questioned that after a short period abroad he would return and be given some post which made use of his talents and training. It might be too much to say that he saw himself as merely changing places with the Duke of York, but he certainly envisaged a situation far nearer to that than to what was actually in store for him. All Walter Monckton's qualities were once more fully employed when he visited the Windsors at Wasserleonburg.

The Duke's anxiety and resentment about financial matters had diminished, but, added to the permanent bitterness about the title, there were new difficulties because he was already worrying about when he would return to England and what work would be found for him there. Monckton records that he became uneasily aware of the Duke's boredom and eagerness to return and also of his wife's discontent at the ambiguity of his position. 'She, I think,' he wrote, 'was in some sense beating against the bars. She wanted him to eat his cake & have it. She could not easily reconcile herself to the fact that by marrying her he had become a less important person.'[1]

While the Windsors were at Wasserleonburg there occurred an incident which further opened the Duke's eyes to the feelings of his family. The Duke and Duchess of Kent were in Austria on a short holiday. Realizing that he would be somewhere close to the Windsors the Duke of Kent had wanted advice as to what he ought to do, and Monckton had told him that it would cause trouble if he visited the Windsors without taking his wife with him. When the time came the Duke of Kent, nevertheless, proposed to visit his brother on a day when his wife would be away. 'By all means,' the Duke of Windsor replied to his suggestion, 'and bring Marina with you.' The Duke of Kent said that she would be visiting her family that day, and to this Windsor replied: 'Well, put off your visit for a day or two and bring her with you.' The Duchess of Kent absolutely refused to go and so the Duke referred his difficulties to the King, who, on Monckton's advice, directed both him and his wife to call on the Windsors. However, the Duchess still refused to go, and as a result a coolness grew up between the Duke of Windsor and the brother who had been so close to him.[2]

About the same time the Windsors paid a short visit to their new friends the Bedauxs, not at Candé but at a castle in Hungary called Borsodivanka. We know a good deal about Charles Bedaux because in three *New Yorker* Profiles Janet Flanner left a record of him for posterity rather as Rebecca West immortalized other unheroic figures.* He was one of those strange manic types who appear from time to time on the financial or industrial scene, make a large fortune and a brilliant reputation very quickly, and end, as often as not, in trouble. Bedaux, who was, according to the American trade union, the CIO, the 'father of one of the most completely exhausting, inhuman "efficiency" systems ever invented', had at one time a network of 'efficiency offices' all over the world. Janet Flanner says: 'How much he profited from his system was always less interesting to him, however, than how much his clients believed in it. Feeling that he was an industrial saviour, he wanted his ideas and methods to dominate the workings of an organization long after his engineers had gone on to another task.' She describes him as having 'a boldly battered face, dominated by his fine dark eyes', and says that 'Men, women, children and animals all found Bedaux attractive. He had eloquence and French charm. He dramatized everything he said, and believed everything, true or false, he heard himself say.'[3]

HRH seems to have taken a fancy to Bedaux and there is no doubt that they spent hours talking together at Candé, while we have already seen that the Bedauxs were present at the wedding. (It was said that he and Jardine instantly recognized each other as kindred spirits – both there for what they could get out of it.) Bedaux and the Duke had one real interest in common – labour conditions and the working man. Bedaux was afterwards to say that the Duke was 'insatiable' and that 'only the life of labour is interesting to the Duke'.[4] As a result of a conversation which took place at Borsodivanka the Duke and Bedaux formed a plan. The Duke's plan was simple – he merely wanted for his own edification to make a tour first of Germany, then of his wife's country, the United States, to study labour

* The facts of Bedaux's history as given here should not necessarily be attributed to Janet Flanner as other sources have also been used.

conditions. Bedaux had a more complex plan and here one cannot improve on Janet Flanner.

What Bedaux doubtless did not tell the Duke was that in 1933, when Hitler came to power, the Nazis had promptly suppressed Bedaux's German company on the grounds that it was an interference with their Strength-through-Joy movement; that in 1935 Bedaux had used Count Joseph von Ledebur as a high-powered private agent to try to have the suspension annulled; that for two years Bedaux himself had been vainly finangling with Hitler's higher-ups to get his company back into business; and that in July of that year, 1937, just after the publicity he had enjoyed as host to the Windsor wedding, he had finally been granted an interview with the Nazi banking genius, Dr. Hjalmar Schacht. As a result of this interview, it was arranged that for twenty thousand dollars in what the Nazis called, in Party double-talk, 'reinvestment money' and thirty thousand dollars in what they called 'penetration money' – or bluntly, for fifty thousand dollars in American cash, of which thirty thousand would go into the slush fund of the Nazi Party – Bedaux could open up again. But he could do that only by putting himself under the wing of, and by giving a permanent cut of his possible business profits to, the notorious Dr Robert Ley. Thus, in that summer of 1937, the Duke's interest in Nazi labor must have seemed providential to Bedaux.[5]

Bedaux had several uses for the unsuspecting Duke. He had become convinced – nor was he alone at the time – that the Duke had long-term political possibilities if he could stage a comeback. More immediately he thought of the joy the Duke could give the Nazis through the discomfiture of the British if he toured Germany under the auspices of the infamous Dr Ley, and of the benefits this might bring to himself.

Soon after the Windsors' visit to Germany, Bedaux was indeed on intimate terms with many of the Nazi leaders. His widely dispersed efficiency officer gave him the entrée to industrial plants all over the world, and he was in an ideal position to undertake industrial espionage. From the autumn of 1937 Bedaux would never be seen again in the United States until, in 1943, he was flown from El Biar in Northern Africa to Miami, under arrest and in military custody, and there turned over to the Department of Justice. At the time of his arrest he had been engaged on a scheme to lay a pipeline through the African desert with the object of bringing peanut oil to the Nazis. On his person he carried many incriminating documents, including an Ausweis – or exit visa – from Vichy France on which he was described as 'attached to the German Military Occupation High Command'. In answering questions he impressed officials by the exuberance with which he made statements damaging to himself concerning both his actions and the philosophy which lay behind them.

First his citizenship had to be decided, because he had been out of the USA and in the land of his birth for long enough for this to be in doubt. Rather than be deported to French Africa, where he would have been shot without trial, Bedaux spent a month convincing the American authorities that he was still a citizen of the United States. Six weeks later he was committed for trial on a charge of treason and of communicating with the enemy.

During the whole period of Bedaux's imprisonment – in which he had succeeded in charming most of his guards – he had asked to be issued with two sleeping pills every night. On the night he was told of the Grand Jury indictment he swallowed the lot and he died in hospital early the next morning.

But this was all in the future. In the summer of 1937 he busied himself arranging for the Duke of Windsor to see labour conditions in Nazi Germany.

Before leaving Candé on his wedding day the Duke of Windsor had addressed himself to the world Press. He realized, he said, that it was better to be open with the Press and, if they would respect his private life, he would inform them of any plans of his which might be of public interest.

On 3 September through the mouth of Mr T. H. Carter (the Duke's old Clerk, now Chief Clerk Accountant of the Privy Purse and on a visit to the Windsors) there issued the following ineffable communiqué:

In accordance with the Duke of Windsor's message to the world Press last June that he would release any information of interest regarding his plans or movements, His Royal Highness makes it known that he and the Duchess of Windsor are visiting Germany and the United States in the near future for the purpose of studying housing and working conditions in these two countries.

According to Geoffrey Bocca the Windsors were not without advice as to what the effect of their visit might be. He states that their friends in London were appalled at the idea and, according to Brigadier Michael Wardell, that Lord Beaverbrook flew to Paris to dissuade them from going.[6] Some colour is lent to this statement by the fact that in the aftermath of the visit the *Daily Express* joined the rest of the world Press in admonishing the Royal couple. In her autobiography the Duchess merely says that Bedaux assured the Duke that the visit would be under the auspices of private citizens and there would be no question of their being involved in Nazi propaganda schemes. If they believed this, the Windsors were to be quickly disillusioned.

When they arrived at the Friedrichstrasse Station in Berlin on 11 October, they found waiting for them the Third Secretary of the British Embassy who handed them a letter from the Chargé d'Affaires, Sir George Ogilvie Forbes, which informed them that the British Ambassador, Sir Nevile Henderson, had unexpectedly left Berlin and that he himself had been directed to take no official cognizance of their visit. Also on the platform was a delegation of German officials headed by Dr Robert Ley.

From this time on, the visit was something of a nightmare for the poor

Windsors. Dr Ley, their guide to labour conditions in Germany, was a fairly advanced alcoholic and the Duchess a notoriously uncourageous traveller. For the next few days she was driven in a black Mercedes Benz at breakneck speed through the city and on the open road, with Dr Ley sitting between her husband and herself.

Then the Windsors were taken by a Luftwaffe officer to have tea with Field-Marshal Göring and his wife at their house about forty miles from Berlin. The Görings had had some conversation about their expected guests before they arrived, Emmy Göring saying to her husband that an abdication seemed to her something like a capitulation. 'I don't understand this woman not giving up her marriage in view of everything that was involved.' Göring, however, was firmly convinced that the marriage was simply a pretext to get rid of the King, 'a man who understood the signs of the times and knew how to interpret them'. 'He [Göring] did not conceal the fact that the German government had earnestly hoped to see the Duke as King of England. The natural opposition between British and German policy, which the German government was doing everything to remove, could, said Herman, easily be set aside with the aid of such a man as the Duke.'

Nevertheless, although the Duke and Duchess seemed enthusiastic about all they had seen, the Duke wished only to discuss the primary cause of his visit to Germany. He showed himself very well informed and talked exhaustively about plans he had had to improve the social position of the British working man – plans which had caused offence in England because, according to opinion there, such matters were not the concern of the throne.

Emmy Göring thought the Duchess amazingly well dressed. 'I could not help thinking that this woman would certainly have cut a good figure on the throne of England.' She was also astonished that they both refused a drink. 'I thought once again how one simply cannot believe everything one reads in the newspapers.'[7]

The Duchess for her part was surprised by the elaborate weight-reducing apparatus in the Field-Marshal's gymnasium and the Duke by a map on the wall which showed Austria as already a part of Germany.*

Under the aegis of Dr Ley the Windsors then visited workers' houses, hospitals and youth camps in Dresden, Nuremburg, Stuttgart and Munich. They met Himmler, Hess and Goebbels and they were given a gala dinner by the Duke of Coburg in a house at Nuremburg belonging to Streicher. Streicher was away but spokesmen denied that the Duke had refused to meet him. Everywhere they went the welcome given them by the German crowds was tremendously and unexpectedly enthusiastic. The Duke responded with what the reporter to the *New York Times* described as a modified Nazi salute – something between the real thing and a wave. On two

* Surprised, but not apparently sufficiently shocked.

occasions, however, he was reported as giving the full Hitler salute – the first time at a training school in Pomerania when a guard of honour from the Death's Head Division of the Hitler Elite Guards was drawn up for his inspection, the second time for Hitler himself. On the last day of their visit the Windsors were told that the Führer would like to meet them and they travelled obediently to Berchtesgaden. At the station they were met by Hitler's car and, among others, Dr Paul Schmidt, Hitler's interpreter.

There was a difficulty because the Windsors' train was an hour earlier than expected and the Führer was known to be taking his afternoon nap. But, although the Windsors were kept waiting, they were courteously treated and taken for a drive, until Hitler was ready to receive them in the large room with the view towards the Untersberg where he later received Chamberlain. Paul Schmidt says:

The Duke expressed his admiration for the industrial welfare arrangements he had seen, especially at the Krupp works in Essen. Social progress in Germany was the principal subject of conversation between Hitler and the Windsors during the afternoon. Hitler was evidently making an effort to be as amiable as possible towards the Duke, whom he regarded as Germany's friend, having especially in mind a speech the Duke had made several years before, extending the hand of friendship to German ex-servicemen's associations. In these conversations there was, so far as I could see, nothing whatever to indicate whether the Duke of Windsor really sympathized with the ideology and practices of the Third Reich, as Hitler seemed to assume he did. Apart from some appreciative words for the measures taken in Germany in the field of social welfare the Duke did not discuss political questions. He was frank and friendly with Hitler, and displayed the social charm for which he is known throughout the world. The Duchess joined only occasionally in the conversation, and then with great reserve, when any question of special interest to women arose. She was simply and appropriately dressed and made a lasting impression on Hitler. 'She would have made a good Queen,' he said when they had gone.[8]

The English dailies treated this visit with a good deal of reserve but the American newspapers covered it thoroughly. On 23 October 1937 the *New York Times* reporter said:

The Duke's decision to see for himself the Third Reich's industries and social institutions and his gestures and remarks during the last two weeks have demonstrated adequately that the Abdication did rob Germany of a firm friend, if not indeed a devoted admirer, on the British throne. He has lent himself, perhaps unconsciously but easily, to National Socialist propaganda. There can be no doubt that his tour has strengthened the regime's hold on the working classes. ... The Duke is reported to have become very critical of English politics as he sees them and is reported as declaring that the British ministers of today and their possible successors are no match for the German or Italian dictators.

However, it was an Englishman, Herbert Morrison, who in the Labour magazine *Forward* best expressed the impatience most people felt. It was impossible to refrain from public comment on the Duke, he said, because 'he would not retire in peace'. He had always failed to realize that in a constitutional monarchy neither the heir to the throne nor the King can publicly manifest opinions on controversial matters.

We Labour people can the more easily say these things because some of his activities were 'up our street'.

His visits to the distressed areas and his indications of impatience with the situation – even the Government – were bound to be pleasing to our people. But they were constitutionally dangerous and not inconsistent with those Fascist tendencies with which (quite possibly unjustly) he is credited.

Referring to the Duchess of Windsor as Mrs Simpson, Morrison said that nothing had been known about her political opinions and tendencies, 'although there were rumours'.

Who are the Duke's advisers? – he went on – I do not know. But either they are very bad ones or he will not take good advice. If the Duke wants to study social problems he had far better quietly read books and get advice in private rather than put his foot in it in this way. .... Although what he is going to do with this knowledge I do not know, for he cannot be permitted to re-enter public life – in this country at any rate. ....

The choice before ex-Kings is either to fade out of the public eye or to be a nuisance. It is a hard choice, perhaps, for one of his temperament, but the Duke will be wise to fade.[9]

The circulation of the Labour magazine was not very great but this article was extensively quoted in the *New York Times*.

More was to follow. Bedaux, once having arranged it, had stayed out of the German tour, but now he began to make preparations for a similar tour of the United States. It quickly became apparent that, not merely were a large part of the American Press and public against the tour on account of the publicity given to the German visit, but that the labour unions, led by those of the Duchess's home town, Baltimore, were going to use the opportunity for an attack on Bedaux.*

'Finally,' Janet Flanner wrote, 'the great American public, acting like a stentorian-voiced, million-mouthed court chamberlain admonishing a still favourite royal pair about the bad company they were keeping, began roaring to the Windsors to get rid of their new palace favourite or else.'[10]

The general hostility and the shock of finding both himself and his companies in so much trouble prostrated Bedaux physically and mentally. During the next few weeks he was persuaded by the acting head of his American companies to sign an agreement not to interfere with their operation, and later he relinquished his voting rights. On 10 November he

---

* The Baltimore Federation of Labour described Bedaux as the arch-enemy of labour and, speaking of the Windsors, announced their refusal to 'co-operate with such people, whether emissaries of a dictatorship or uninformed sentimentalists'.

fled to Canada and from there to Europe, never to set foot again in the United States until he was flown there in 1943.

As for the insatiable Duke, he had at last had enough. He cancelled the trip to the United States and he and his wife stayed at the *Meurice*.

28

MARRIED LIFE

When one reads what they have both written about this period of their lives, one gets the impression that the Windsors were unable to understand the comparatively simple facts of the abdication crisis, and that she, at any rate, felt that if they could return and juggle the events a little everything would fall out differently. This feeling, that it was in some way their own fault for playing their cards badly, would gradually give way to bitterness and an equally irrational sense of having been manipulated by other people – the growth of these emotions being accelerated as the actualities of their new situation became apparent to them.

From the beginning the matter of the title caused trouble. Who would bow to the Duchess and who would not? Walter Monckton began it by giving the Duchess a deferential and unmistakable bow immediately after her wedding ceremony. He found, he said, that his head 'bowed easily'. This would, nevertheless, be a difficult decision for the English, not least for those who took the monarchy most reverentially. Yet on the whole people seem to have decided it less on logic than on the kind of temperamental grounds that influenced Walter Monckton. Lady Diana Cooper (as Lady Norwich) curtsied in greeting the Duchess when her husband was Ambassador to Paris, so did Lady Dixon, so did many rich Republican Americans. Nevertheless, some of the Windsors' friends felt genuinely unable to extend this courtesy to her.

In their own household it was made known that the Duke wished his wife to be addressed as Ma'am and referred to as Her Royal Highness and their own secretaries were instructed when writing to her to begin the letter 'Madam', and end it 'I am, Madam, Your Royal Highness's devoted and obedient servant'.

Then I came down to the villa – Harold Nicolson wrote to his wife in August

1938 – had a bath, shaved, put on my best clothes. Because the late King of England was coming to dinner. Willy Maugham had prepared us carefully. He said that the Duke gets cross if the Duchess is not treated with respect. . . .

She, I must say, looks very well for her age. She has done her hair in a different way. It is smoothed off her brow and falls down the back of her neck in ringlets. It gives her a placid and less strained look. Her voice has also changed. It now mingles the accents of Virginia with that of a Duchess in one of Pinero's plays. He entered with his swinging naval gait, plucking at his bow tie. He had on a *tussore* dinner-jacket. He was in very high spirits. Cocktails were brought and we stood round the fireplace. There was a pause. 'I am sorry we were a little late,' said the Duke, 'but Her Royal Highness couldn't drag herself away.' He had said it. The three words fell into the circle like three stones into a pool. Her (gasp) Royal (shudder) Highness (and not one eye dared to meet another).

Then we went into dinner. There were two cypresses and the moon. I sat next to the Duchess. He sat opposite. They called each other 'darling' a great deal. I called him 'Your Royal Highness' a great deal and 'Sir' the whole time. I called her 'Duchess'. One cannot get away from his glamour and his charm and his sadness, though, I must say, he seemed gay enough. They have a villa here and a yacht, and go round and round. He digs in the garden. But it is pathetic the way he is sensitive about her. It was quite clear to me from what she said that she hopes to get back to England. When I asked her why she didn't get a house of her own somewhere, she said, 'O.ie never knows what may happen. I don't want to spend all my life in exile.'[1]

The Windsors had difficulty in deciding where to live, not only because they still retained some hope of eventually returning to England, but also because he preferred the country, she the town. They spent the winter of 1937–8 partly at the *Meurice*, partly at a furnished villa at Versailles, the Chateau de la Maye. Then in the spring of 1938 they took a lease of the villa La Croë at Antibes. Later in the same year they took a long lease of 24 Boulevard Suchet near the Bois de Boulogne and they moved into this in January 1939.

For nearly two years the Duchess was occupied with the decoration and furnishing of these two houses. La Croë was already partly furnished, and crates of furniture, china, glass, plate and linen were sent there from Frogmore, where the contents of York House and Fort Belvedere had been stored, but the decoration of both houses and the furnishing and decoration of Boulevard Suchet took up much of her time and talents for many months. It is a matter of common knowledge that throughout her life the beauty and splendour of her houses was equalled only by the quality of her food. The house on the Boulevard Suchet was made for entertaining. It had four rooms leading one from the other on the first floor and the Duke's and Duchess's apartment above. All Paris contributed to the furnishing of these. The interior decoration was put in the hands of a famous firm, Maison Jansen, but the Duchess planned and directed, and supervised every detail. For months she visited antique shops, searching for furniture, chandeliers, candelabra, pictures, china and glass. She was not easily satisfied and rooms that did not please her were repainted, while the antique dealers came and went so that she might try the effect of their goods in her house. No trouble was too much for her, no expense too great.

She spent hours, too, in the salons of the great Parisian dressmakers, and the clothes she wore were as much a result of art as the furnishing of her rooms. She went nearly every day to the hairdresser or to have her face done, and, when she went to La Croë, a hairdresser from Paris accompanied her. Every evening he re-set her hair and he was available for her guests.

If one asks why the King of England gave up his throne for her, one must look for the answer in himself. But if one wants to know how she succeeded in making him happy, it was very largely through her domesticity. Towards the end of her life one of her few close friends said of her: 'The only thing that could be said against Wallis is that in all her life she never did anything except keep house.' The juxtaposition of the homely phrase and the Boulevard Suchet is astonishing. This was 'keeping house' on an unimaginable scale. Yet, if it had been the fate of Wallis Warfield to live in some modest sphere, she might have scrubbed and swept and polished, sewed and baked, haunted junk shops, attended sales, weighed and measured as she had in the old days of Fannie Farmer. As it was she interviewed the chef, discussing not merely the menu but the individual dishes, moved the furniture here and there until it pleased her, attended all the smallest details of the welfare of her guests, scrutinized with efficient and calculating care all the household accounts.

All these interests her husband shared. Sometimes he went shopping with her, sometimes not, but they discussed endlessly the colour schemes and the arrangements of the rooms. Both were meticulous, perhaps too meticulous to be much loved – the curtains must fall just so, the chairs, the lamps, the pepper pot stand, not here or here, but here. He shared, too, her love of clothes, and he never tired of adding to her jewels. Most of all he loved her authority.

One of the secretaries they employed at the time, Diana Wells Hood, has since written a book about her experiences. This is a little spoiled by being padded with anecdotes she learned at second hand, but when she is writing from her own observation she gives a fascinating account. Her picture of the Duke's happiness with his wife is absolutely convincing.

His wife was constantly in his thoughts. If he went out alone he looked for her the moment he returned home. If she went out without him and remained away for any length of time, he became nervous and pre-occupied.

He never made any attempt to conceal his feelings. He was frankly demonstrative. More than once I saw him take her impulsively in his arms and kiss her tenderly. At the house in Boulevard Suchet when she went out without him he used to accompany her to the front door. A small lift connected the private suite with the ground floor. As the lift disappeared on its downward journey he could be seen putting his arms around her.

He bought her exquisite jewellery and other beautiful gifts. Nothing was too good for her. He sought in every way to make her happy. He himself was happy and light hearted in her presence.[2]

Miss Hood says that HRH addressed the Duchess as 'Darling', or 'Sweetheart'. If she called him from some other part of the house he would leave what he was doing and go to her immediately. Once he got up and ran to his wife in the middle of a haircut.

The Duke behaved on occasion with an almost childlike impulsiveness. I have seen him lean out of his bedroom window on the first floor of his Paris residence and call down to a friend who had just left the house. One afternoon he called out in this way to his valet on the pavement outside. The Duchess, happening to come into the room, simply said, as to a wayward child, 'David!' He turned quickly from the window to explain. 'It's the dogs, darling. They might have been run over.'[3]

The dogs too were much loved – cairn terriers, Pookie and Dette and Prisie (from the French *surprise*), they accompanied the Windsors everywhere.

When the two houses were finished the Windsors began to entertain their closer friends at La Croë and all Paris, as the saying is, at Boulevard Suchet. In Paris they stood at the top of the staircase, very close together to receive the obeisance of the passing guests. From the royal livery of the servants to the banner of the Garter which decorated the hall at La Croë, everything proclaimed the appreciated value of exactly those aspects of the ex-King's inheritance which had received so little respect in the days at York House when the servants wore black.

Miss Diana Hood had been engaged as secretary at a salary she did not regard as 'princely' and she owed her job to the fact that she had been called in to help the Duke with a speech when he visited Rio de Janeiro as Prince of Wales and that he remembered her. She remembered him. She had been so nervous on the first occasion when she went into the room. But he had come forward smiling and, installing her in a chair, had made some reassuring remarks before they began to work. On her first morning at the *Meurice* she thought it natural to ask permission to sit when she began to take dictation, and she received it. Presently Mrs Bedford, the Duchess's secretary, came into the room and later she expressed her astonishment. No secretary ever sat in the royal presence. After that, while the erstwhile democratic Prince sat in a low armchair with his papers on the floor all round him, or later in his own house even with his feet up on his desk, Miss Hood stood erect to take dictation, sometimes for an hour at a time, putting her papers on the nearby furniture or, like him, on the floor.

Apart from the household servants the Windsors employed two secretaries (later a third, Miss Arnold, joined them), two chauffeurs, and were guarded by two detectives – one English, Storrier, and one French – who followed them everywhere. When the Duke entertained in his own home he was attended by an equerry, sometimes Mr Colin Davidson, more often Mr Dudley Forwood.

The secretarial staff seem to have been employed almost entirely on household or social work (although the letters from fans still took up a lot of time), paying the wages, haggling with the dealers, making appointments, sending out invitations. One gets the impression nevertheless that they were poised for better things.

In the months following his marriage the Duke of Windsor consulted Sir William Jowitt as to the legality of the King's action in restricting the title of Royal Highness to himself. There is and, since it has not been tested in court, always will be great doubt as to the legality of the act. The case for believing that it was not legal was outlined by Mr Patrick Montague-Smith in an introduction to Debrett's Peerage of 1973. Mr Montague-Smith argues that when the Duke of Windsor made his farewell broadcast, on the instructions of the new King he was introduced as 'His Royal Highness Prince Edward'. 'We may therefore accept that either he reverted to this style when he abdicated, or that, as his style was uncertain, it was clarified by King George vi, being then "the fount of all honours".' He then asks the following questions.

(1) Can one receive a title or style which one already has by birth and membership of the House of Windsor *without restriction*, and yet subsequently, in May 1937, be restricted by Letters Patent to such a title or style for himself only? (2) If one accepts that the title or style of HRH emanates from the Sovereign following the Abdication, *again without restriction*, can this legally be restricted at a subsequent date to himself only? (3) Is it legal to prevent a wife holding the same titles and styles permitted to her husband?

Mr Montague-Smith goes on to say that there are certain circumstances in which the sovereign, even though the fountain of honours, is powerless to act. One is to alter the destination of a peerage already created, its precedence, its alienation or its surrender. And he points out that the Peerage Law sanctions that the wife of a peer becomes noble, provided she remains his wife or widow and does not re-marry.

'I know of no other case,' Mr Montague-Smith writes, 'where such a restriction was applied.' And he then goes on to make a point which must have weighed heavily on the Duke of Windsor. When King George vi, as Duke of York, married it was announced in the *London Gazette* that his wife would take the title, style or attribute of Royal Highness 'in accordance with the settled general rule that a wife takes the status of her husband'.

At an earlier date Mr Philip Thomas had argued, in Burke's Peerage of 1967, that the depriving Act, the Letters Patent of 1937, started by quite falsely representing the Letters Patent of 1917 as applying only to princes in the lineal succession to the crown – which by abdicating the Duke of Windsor was not – and then purported to grant the Duke the qualification of Royal Highness, something which was already his under the Grant of 1917. 'At most, all it did was to make him a fresh grant of that qualification. It did not deprive him of what he already had, and the provision that it should not be enjoyed by his wife applied only to the qualification then granted, not to that which he already had. As a consequence the Duchess is entitled to say: 'I claim to be Royal Highness as consort of the Duke by virtue of the Grant of 1917 under which he enjoys that qualification and which has never been revoked.'

Mr Montgomery Hyde replied to the case made by Mr Montague-Smith in the letter to *The Times* quoted in an earlier chapter. He did not argue the case in any detail but relied on the fact that the leaders of the government, Sir John Simon, Lord Hailsham and Sir Donald Somervell, were quite satisfied with the decision which he states with complete certainty 'accorded with the wishes of King George VI and Queen Mary'. He also says that even Sir Walter Monckton did not object on legal grounds. However, while it is true that Monckton made no public objection – and one may be sure he would have advised the Duke against doing so – it does not follow that he was convinced of the legality of the procedure. His biographer says that he 'deplored this step, that his affection for the Duke caused him to see it as a mean and petty gesture', which suggests that he saw it as a depriving act.[4] In addition, Lady Alexandra Metcalfe recorded in her diary written at the time that he did not agree with what may be termed the 'lineal' view, that under the Letters Patent of 1917 the title was granted only to heirs to the throne.

In 1937 when the Duke applied to Sir William Jowitt for an opinion he was advised that there was considerable doubt as to the legality of the King's action. No action was ever taken on this advice it is said because the war prevented it. It was stated in the *Sunday Telegraph* column 'Albany at Large' of 4 June 1972 that, when after the war Jowitt became Lord Chancellor, the Duke reminded him of his opinion and 'hoped that in his position he would now be able to see justice done'. Jowitt did nothing.

One must have considerable sympathy for the Duke of Windsor. Doubt as to the legality of the Act must have immensely increased his feelings of impotence and rage.

At the same time he suffered from a sense of rejection. The Duke and Duchess of Gloucester visited the Windsors at the *Meurice* but ministers of the crown and other important people visiting Paris were inclined to avoid him because of fear of being misunderstood by the Royal Family at home. From time to time he was involved in ludicrous incidents, as when Joseph Kennedy, the American Ambassador to London, playing golf behind him at Antibes was clearly anxious to avoid him. In this situation the Windsors behaved with the minimum of circumspection and made matters much worse by giving way too publicly to their feelings. Soon accounts reaching England through reliable sources reported their abuse of the Royal Family and of Lord Baldwin, and their praise of the Fascist regimes. Walter Monckton, emollient as ever, visited them himself and persuaded the Prime Minister (Chamberlain), Lord Halifax, Winston Churchill and Duff Cooper to call on them. He writes 'Their visits were welcomed and improved the atmosphere.'[5]

But the Duke wished to return to England. It had never been his intention to become an expatriate or to abandon entirely public work. He was maddened by being unable to find out to whom and in what way to present his case and by non-committal answers to his letters. Monckton visited him several times and tried unavailingly to help. Staying with the King and Queen at Balmoral he talked to Neville Chamberlain about these problems. He wrote:

> The Prime Minister thought that the right course was for the Duke of Windsor to be treated as soon as possible as a younger brother of the King who could take some of the royal functions off his brother's hands. The King himself, though he was not anxious for the Duke to return as early as November 1938 (which was what the Duke wanted) was not fundamentally against the Prime Minister's view. But I think the Queen felt quite plainly that it was undesirable to give the Duke any effective sphere of work. I felt then, as always, that she naturally thought that she must be on her guard because the Duke of Windsor, to whom the other brothers had always looked up, was an attractive, vital creature who might be the rallying point for any who might be critical of the new King who was less superficially endowed with the arts and graces that please.[6]*

In these circumstances the Duke succumbed to his sense of injury.

It is impossible not to feel some sympathy with him but he became the victim of his intense feeling of grievance. All his capacity to feel, his charm, his eagerness and his desire to please were enchained to his wife: his thoughts were given up to the consideration of his own injuries. In 1938 and 1939 Great Britain stood on the edge of war, her people poised for the greatest disaster in her history. The Duke wrote letters to the harassed Prime Minister, his mother and his brother pressing his own claims.

Worse than this were his periodic public appearances. He continued to show the lack of sense which had taken him to Germany in 1937. His first forty years had totally unfitted him for the life of a private citizen, but this would not have been disastrous but for his desire for self-justification and

---

* Monckton's view is not necessarily correct. In March 1937 Lady Lloyd George recorded in her diary the following conversation between Lloyd George and King George VI. 'H.M. is most anxious that the Duke should not return to this country, but D. told him that he did not take that view and thought H.M. would be wiser not to oppose it. "She would never dare to come back here," said H.M. "There you are wrong," replied D. "She would have no friends," said H.M. D. did not agree. "But not you or me?" said the King anxiously.'[7]

his determination to see justice done to his wife and to find a sphere of interest for himself.

Soon after his marriage he became involved in newspaper publicity concerning two distinguished authors. Compton Mackenzie had sent him a telegram wishing him long life and happiness on his wedding day and to his surprise he received an answer. He then wrote to the Duke 'to offer his pen to write a book which would put his case fairly to the world.'[8] Incredibly HRH accepted his offer and promised to meet him in Paris in the autumn to discuss the synopsis. In the ordinary course of publishing practice the serial rights of the book were then offered to *The Sunday Pictorial* before it was even written. Mackenzie was immediately worried by the amount of money this newspaper was prepared to pay if the Duke gave the book his approval. He felt strongly that the Duke had been wronged and his intentions were entirely chivalrous, not in the least commercial. *Windsor Tapestry* is full of indignation and sarcasm and illogical scores against those he took to be the Duke's enemies and is almost unreadable. But, although he was acting entirely in good faith, he could no more than anyone else stop the publicity that inevitably followed. Walter Monckton and Mr Allen, the Duke's solicitor, saw Mackenzie in October of that year and in two interviews made it plain that the Duke could not approve or authorize the book (although he said that the Duke's advisers had had difficulty in persuading him of this) but since by now the whole of Fleet Street knew of the project, they were too late to stop a great deal of publicity. In November *The Sunday Dispatch* had a front-page article *The Truth About the Duke of Windsor Book*, which was largely quoted in other newspapers and which was followed by statements from Compton Mackenzie's publishers and by the Duke's solicitors. This gave further opportunities of the kind *The Duke Repudiates Compton Mackenzie*. According to his later recollection Compton Mackenzie issued five writs for libel.

It was unfortunate that almost at the same time the Duke of Windsor was engaged in a libel action against Geoffrey Dennis, who in a book called *Coronation Commentary* defended the Duke with almost as much passion as Mackenzie himself but inadvertently broke the laws of libel by repeating calumny in order to refute it.

Most foolish of all were the Duke's appeals for peace. The first of these was made in a broadcast to America on 8 May 1939 from the battlefields of Verdun. It seems probable that the Duke was what the Americans call a 'sucker' for Mr Fred Bate of the National Broadcasting Company. Mr Bate had been striving to get him on the air ever since the Abdication and finally devised a scheme the Duke found irresistible. Great secrecy surrounded the project and the Duke's secretary, Miss Hood, believes he composed his speech and even typed the final version himself. It was literate, one might almost say literary, but in the context in which it was delivered, completely banal. War and peace are majestic themes that do not lend themselves to the tongues of private citizens. Above all, with his unerringly unfortunate sense of timing, it was made as the King and Queen journeyed across the Atlantic on a goodwill visit to Canada and to the United States. It was banned by the BBC and once more Lord Beaverbrook issued a reproof.

The decision of the Duke of Windsor to broadcast – the *Daily Express* leader said – is to be regretted. The King is on his way to America. Any word spoken to the United States at present should have come from him. It would have been better, therefore, for the Duke to wait. It is reported that the Duke will make an appeal for peace in his broadcast. Such an appeal would have been uttered more appropriately after the King's peace mission to the Dominion had been brought to a conclusion.[9]

These rebukes did not discourage the Duke from making one last effort for peace in a telegram to Adolf Hitler in August 1939.

As a matter of fact none of these things was very important or made much impact. The vast majority of the people of England had lost interest in the Duke of Windsor and were never to regain it until after his death when his body came home for burial. Probably not one in every twenty people alive at the time remembers any of these events. But the Duke's antics were watched by the King's household and they did not inspire confidence.

There was a lighter and happier side to life. During that last summer at La Croë the Windsors were visited by many of their old friends, and Miss Hood, installed with the other secretaries at the lodge, gives us a picture of the beauty and luxury of their house, and describes the splendour of the food and entertainments. Among the guests were Major Metcalfe, his wife, Lady Alexandra Metcalfe, and his son David, Mrs Evelyn Fitzgerald, Lord Sefton and Mrs Gwynne, later to become Lady Sefton, Mr Colin and Lady Rachel Davidson, Commander and Mrs Colin Buist. The Duke, who seldom ate lunch, went off to play golf at midday, or dressed in the bright coloured trousers and shirt earlier described, dug and hoed in the garden.

In the middle of August Lady Alexandra Metcalfe and her son went home, but Fruity, who had been ill, stayed on. In a letter of 15 August he tells his wife how much she and David are missed. Then he goes on:

La Croë, Cap d'Antibes. A.M.
15 August 1939.

Things here go on much as usual but yesterday afternoon was something out of the ordinary!! HRH's surprise! I heard terrible wailings coming from the woods about 5 pm & first of all thought that one of the little dogs had got a slight go of rabies; but after listening intently I thought I must be – anywhere but where I was – the sun beating down etc. I heard the bagpipes!! Well I knew the worst then. At 6 pm some very strange people arrived evidently some 'old time' friends of Wallis. American – Baltimore or roughly about there. A man & 2 women – one old & the other not so old & married to the man, who turned out to be the Assistant French representative of Pan-American Airways. The Rogers family also arrived. Then HRH appeared escorting Wallis (I acted up to this as A.D.C. in waiting – introducing etc.). His appearance was magnificent – if indeed a little strange considering the almost tropical heat. He was completely turned out as the Scotch Laird about to go stalking. Beautiful kilt, swords & all the aids. It staggered me a bit. I'm getting used to blows & surprises now. Then from the woods rushed what might easily have been the whole Campbell family – of course very complete with pipes & haggis etc. Women as well as men. I inquired where they sprung from & was told they were folklore dancers (paid by a society in England & of course Scotland *not* including Southern Ireland). The object of these visiting dancers is I believe to promote better International feeling. Personally, *I* think if they get into Germany then I really wouldn't blame Hitler if he attacked any country & started off the European conflict. I felt like helping to do so myself last evening. They piped & danced & made merry till 7.15 pm. We all had to admire & applaud by order of the All Highest. HRH himself took photos of the merry throng. It was awe-inspiring. By now close on 7 pm the heat was dying down & indeed so was I & I fell into one of those long chairs & grasped my iced tomato juice firmly – but not for long. The clarion call to duty. I was told to please get up & help with the guests, and so to dressing time to dine with the Earl of Dudley. . . .

The Windsors had a man servant who was no good and who rejoiced in the name of Simpson. Fruity complains that his room is full of the clothes he had 'taken off since yesterday'. And then goes on:

Eric Dudley's dinner was a fiasco from Eric's point of view. HRH was as if he was lying on a wet slab in a fishmonger shop – the same old greasy eye & limpness. He was Not trying. Wallis was, on the other hand, but it was no good, he won the day.

Eric had done wonders with the Coin d'or (spelt wrong) the pool was practically overflowing – cocktails, champagne etc were to the 'right & left of 'em', flowers from the South Seas were littered in abundance everywhere. Food – masterpieces of everything, soufflés that rose almost to the stars on touch. A three-man band in the shrubbery – at least they started off as three – then one unlucky one who played the accordian fell into a small pond not illuminated by error. This reduced the orchestra to the two but they made up for it by working extra time. I may here mention that even this comic interlude failed dismally to bring even a little smile to the face of our late (retd) Sovereign Monarch. I did think he could have done this. The party broke up early as you can imagine. I went to the Casino to watch other strange things happen. So now you know all.

Miss Hood, whose recollection of the visit of the Highland troop is infinitely more respectful but otherwise identical, tells us that they were led by Pipe-Major Macdonald Murray and that he, unexpectedly delayed in Nice, came over one afternoon in the following week to tune the Duke's bagpipes. The Duke, she says, was delighted to have an opportunity for practice and the wailing of the bagpipes could thereafter be heard in the lodge.

Pipe-Major Macdonald Murray returned to England but the Duke continued assiduously to practice his bagpipes. Almost every night Elizabeth [Miss Arnold] and I could hear him either on the roof of the chateau or walking about the gardens blowing robustly with unaffected enjoyment. Once or twice when there were urgent telephone calls to be put through to London he came piping over to the lodge where we made the connections from our switchboard. We were sometimes in bed when this happened, but the heralding pipes gave us time to slip into our clothes to receive HRH.[10]

29

THE WAR

The war began almost as peace had ended with a letter from Major Metcalfe to his wife.

La Croë, Cap d'Antibes. A.M. France.   September 3rd 1939.
Well I wonder when you will ever get this. We seem to be entirely cut off from the rest of the world, & we know 'd—n all' of what is happening. It's all *very* odd. Anyhow we've declared war on Germany. H.M's speech was *not* heard here by anyone. I've just talked to Herman R. on the phone & he gave me the gist of it.

Certain people here are *quite extraordinary*. No one could understand how their minds work. On Friday it had all been settled for a plane to be sent out early Sat morning to bring us home, etc. At about 1 am or 2 am Walter spoke again. The conversation had to be in French which didn't help any, as Walter is about as bad as the Master here! It went on in the library. I went on reading my book in the drawing-room as I could not think that anything *could* go wrong. It all seemed plain sailing to me. (I have become adviser in chief and the only person who is getting anything done here now & indeed they realize it. I, it was, who got all the servants off, 8 of them & 1 secretary. It took some doing I can tell you as Cannes stn was Hell on earth. . . . Well anyhow they came in to me after about ½ hour & said 'We are *not* going – the plane is coming for *you* & Miss Arnold tomorrow. I looked at them as if they really *were* mad—— Then they started off – 'I refuse to go *unless* we are invited to stay at Windsor Castle & the invitation & plane are sent personally by my brother etc' – I just sat still, held my head & listened for about 20 minutes & then I started. I said *I'm* going to talk now. First of all I'll say that whatever I say is speaking as *your best* friend, I speak only for your good & for W's, *understand that*. After what I've said you can ask me to leave if you like but you're going to listen now. You *only* think of yourselves. You don't realise that there is at this moment a war going on that women & children are being bombed & killed while you talk of your *PRIDE*. What you've now said to Walter has just bitched up everything. You talk of one of H.M's Govent planes being sent out for Miss Arnold & for me.!! You are just nuts. Do you really think for one instant they would send a plane out for me &

Miss Arnold? It's too absurd even to discuss. I said a lot more in the same strain. They never uttered. After this I said now if this plane *is* sent out to fetch you, which I doubt very much then get into it & be b——y grateful. I went to bed then. It was 3.15 a.m. Well at 7.30 I was wakened by *her maid* telling me to get up! to arrange for a car to go to the flying field, etc. I went down in pyjamas & got hold of the French car cleaner. . . . to go to go to pick up Mouse *if* he was there. I knew d——n well he wouldn't be there. Then at 8 a.m. HRH came in *fully* dressed to my room & said we've decided to go in the plane. I said O.K. *if* it comes & now I'll have a bath!!

Of course there never was a plane as I knew they'd never send it & of course Walter would have repeated all the rot talked on the phone. If Walter had any sense he shd *never* have repeated one word of this, as it was all temper & didn't make any sense & Walter shd have realized this & to whom he was talking but I guess he's done it. I know he has in fact. . . . They are in a *panic* about flying. Every ½ hour it is 'I won't go by plane we will motor to Paris,' or to Boulogne, etc. I point out the impossibility of doing that – roads blocked with troops, no hotels, etc., etc.

Today we talk of a destroyer to be sent out. Oh God, it's a mad house. Today's talk with Walter hasn't helped any. He said something about not being able to send a plane for 4 or 5 days as it would be safer then. I can't follow this at all. Now Winston is head of the Admiralty he will, I think, send a destroyer if the little man here asks for it. It seems *she* wd rather go in a boat – *anything but* a plane. She is terrified & so is *he*! We've got no servants at all except Marcel & Robert & a pantry boy & 2 French maids. You shd see him packing, it really is funny. Simpson was *very bad* stuff. He is a *rotten* type. His face all this last 2 weeks has been like a sour lemon. He has the jitters.*

I am to be with & go with 'the boss here' *wherever* he will go in this war – *So please do this for me*. Get in touch with Scotland Yard & let Major Wattle or Whittle (the awful thing is that his correct name has clean gone out of my head but it is something like 'Wittle') know that I am going to do this for the war & therefore I *cannot do* special constabulary. . . . Also get from R—— tailors Burlington St *all* my khaki uniform sent to Wilton Place (I don't want them to alter or make anything – They are bad).

We know the other end of the story from Walter Monckton. 'The decision about the Duke's immediate future was therefore added to the Prime Minister's other anxieties,' his biographer writes. 'He directed that Edward could return only if he was prepared to take one of two posts that would be offered to him, either Deputy Regional Commissioner to Sir Wyndham Portal in Wales, or Liaison Officer with the British Military Mission No. 1 to General Gamelin under General Howard Vyse.'[1] We are also told something that may be a clue to the matter of the aeroplane which Major Metcalfe could not follow. It was decided to fly Walter Monckton out to Antibes to convey to the Duke the decision about his future but to send him in an aeroplane in which the Windsors would be reluctant to make the return journey, leaving Monckton to languish in France. When

---

* A servant who had apparently been recommended by Lady Alexandra Metcalfe.

the Duke saw the small Leopard Moth which was used, he remarked that it looked as if both tyres were flat and the aeroplane tied up with string.

Finally the Duke and Duchess, accompanied by Major Metcalfe, motored to Cherbourg in circumstances which the Duchess has quite aptly described as 'cloak and dagger', stopping on the way to telephone the British Embassy for directions as to where to go. They took with them the usual quantity of luggage, this time supplemented by innumerable cardboard boxes in which the Duchess had decided to wrap 'certain valuable possessions' to save weight and space. They were also accompanied by the three cairns, Pookie, Prisie and Dette.

At Cherbourg they were met by Lord Louis Mountbatten who, on Winston Churchill's instructions, had brought the destroyer HMS *Kelly* to take them home. He was accompanied by another old friend, Randolph Churchill, in the uniform of a lieutenant of the 4th Hussars (his spurs strapped on upside down).

The *Kelly* left Cherbourg at dusk, and when she arrived at Portsmouth it was in the pitch darkness of the blackout. 'At 8.30,' Lady Alexander Metcalfe wrote in her diary, 'a message came to say the destroyer would be in about 9.30. We went down to the dock, everything in inky blackness except for a ghastly Very light. A guard of honour by a hundred men with tin hats & gas masks were drawn up & lots of red carpets & gangways. We stood about waiting in nervous tension. This part of the show was done bang up & all due to Winston who had given orders for him to be received with all due ceremony.'

From on board the *Kelly* the result was dramatic. As Lord Louis, with difficulty and skill, brought the ship alongside the Duke went to the bow of the ship, the guard of honour was revealed and the band of the Royal Marines played *God Save the King*. The quay on to which the Duke stepped to inspect them was by a chance the same from which he had left England in 1936.

When this formal reception was over the Duke and Duchess were welcomed to England by Walter Monckton and Lady Alexandra Metcalfe. No member of the Royal Family awaited them, no messenger, no message. As far as the ex-King's family were concerned their return to England might not have happened. How much the Duke's response to the plan to send an aeroplane to fetch him had contributed to this display of frigidity is not known. In any case, it was complete. Lady Alexandra had arranged to send her own car and chauffeur to collect the Windsors' luggage but Walter Monckton had telephoned to the Palace to ask for a car to be sent to fetch the Duke and Duchess. This was unequivocally refused, and Lady Alexandra therefore drove Monckton to Portsmouth herself in a second car and, on the next day, drove the Windsors back to her house at Hartfield.

When they first arrived in Portsmouth Monckton and Lady Alexandra had gone to the Grand Hotel 'which the ABC recommended as the most spacious and luxurious of the dreary hotels' and booked 'a large red plush bedroom' for the Windsors. However, Admiral James, C-in-C of Portsmouth under orders from Winston Churchill, invited the Windsors for the night and the large red plush bedroom was occupied by the Metcalfes themselves. The next day the whole party drove to South Hartfield House.

The Duke never *once* gave the impression of feeling the sadness of his return – Lady Alexandra wrote in her account of these days – as with everything else the blind has been drawn down & the past is forgotten.

They arrived on the 12th & today is the 25th. The visit has gone easily & well. There have been moments when the ice has seemed dangerously thin & ominous cracks have been heard but the night has brought a thickening & we have skated on again. He saw the King – a stag party & nothing personal crossed the lips of either. P.M., Winston, Belisha & Edward Halifax have all been visited with uneventful success. His job has materialized & Fruity is on his personal staff. This was done as usual not with tremendous grace.

Most days we have come up to this house [the Metcalfes' London house, 16 Wilton Place]. There is only the sitting-room open & Anna in a permanent daze. All business is transacted from this ridiculous house. Clerks, secretaries, war office officials, hairdressers, bootmakers, tailors, with a sprinkling of friends stream in & out. They have sandwiches & tea from a Thermos for refreshment. The first few days 200 to 300 letters arrived every day, the percentage of bad ones was only six. ... Walter has to be up with his son so we have every evening a quatre. It's been difficult on more than one occasion not to shout 'Stop, stop, stop, you've got everything all wrong', but considering all they have been very grateful & sweet & completely simple.

I see endless trouble ahead with the job in France as I don't think he will think it big enough & I doubt his getting on with the 'Wombat'.* Wallis going to make La Croë into a convalescent home. At first it was to be for vetted officers who were a little tired & needed rest. . . . If the Duke goes to say goodbye to his mother it will be at my door for good or bad, as during one of our lengthy talks I put it over strong to Wallis & the day after she told me she had got HRH to agree to do so. Her arguments were all wrong but the object was achieved. ... I do think the family might have done something, he might not even exist but for one short visit to the King. Wallis said they realized there was no place ever for him in this country & she saw no reason ever to return. I didn't deny it or do any pressing. They are incapable of truly trusting anybody therefore one feels one's loyalty is misplaced. Their selfishness & self-concentration is terrifying. What I am finding it difficult to put into words is the reason for his only having so few friends. One is so perpetually disappointed.

The Duke of Windsor had been offered the choice of two jobs – Deputy Regional Commissioner in Wales and Liaison Officer with the British Military Mission to General Gamelin. He chose the former. Without any more discussion of the matter than had become the practice between the King and his brother, the offer was dropped and the Duke was summoned

* Nickname given to General Howard Vyse.

to the War Office to be informed by the CIGS, General (later Field-Marshal) Sir Edmund Ironside, that he was to be assigned to the British Military Mission at Vincennes and was to report for duty as soon as possible.

At the same time the Minister for War, Leslie Hore-Belisha, received a letter from the Palace which said that the King thought that the Duke would be most suitably employed as a member of the Military Mission to France and that the Duke who was a Field-Marshal in the British Army was prepared to revert to the rank of Major-General for the duration of the war. The Duke called twice at the War Office to see Hore-Belisha. On his first visit he began by saying that he did not want to give us his baton, to which Hore-Belisha replied that it was unique for a Field-Marshal to take the rank of a Major-General. The Duke then said that before he went to France he would like to be attached to the different Commands in England so that he could be in contact with the soldiers again and added that he wanted to take the Duchess with him. Hore-Belisha writes: 'I began to see difficulties, so I said I would see what could be done. He then referred to the Duchess's desire to give her villa in the South of France as a convalescent home for British officers. I said I thought she wanted to run a hospital on the south coast of England but he replied "No," he wanted her to be with him in Paris.'

On 16 September Hore-Belisha recorded in his diary:

The King sent for me at 11 am. He was in a distressed state. He thought that if the Duchess went to the Commands, she might have a hostile reception, particularly in Scotland. He did not want the Duke to go to the Commands in England. He seemed very disturbed and walked up and down the room. He said the Duke had never had any discipline in his life.

At an interview with Hore-Belisha later on the same day, the King also remarked that all his ancestors had succeeded to the throne after his predecessor had died. 'Mine is not only alive, but very much so.' He thought it better for the Duke to proceed to Paris at once.

That afternoon the Duke called for the second time on Hore-Belisha, who managed without great difficulty to persuade him that he would do better to take up his appointment in Paris without delay. The Duke asked whether his brother the Duke of Gloucester was being paid and Hore-Belisha sent for the Military Secretary. The Duke then explained that he had come back to offer his services and he did not want to be paid, and he would like this to be announced in the Press; whereupon the Military Secretary replied that the Duke of Gloucester was not being paid and that no member of the Royal Family ever accepted payment for services in the Army.

[The Duke] then raised the question of his Hon. Colonelcy in the Welsh Guards. He had ascertained that they wanted him back again, and said he would like this. I told him that I did not appoint Honorary Colonels of the Regiments and asked if he had spoken to the King about it. I then said that if the Duke was asking my advice, the best advice I could give him was to get back into the Army as a Major-General. He asked if he could wear his decorations on his battle-dress and I replied 'Yes'.

Hore-Belisha also records that the Duke of Windsor at this interview asked for Major Metcalfe to be appointed as his Equerry.

After the Duke of Windsor had left, Hore-Belisha telephoned to Major Hardinge at the Palace to let him know that the interview had gone off satisfactorily.[2]

It is usually taken for granted that the Duke of Windsor's job with the British Military Mission was created in order to get him out of England and give him the illusion of usefulness, and that it carried no responsibility and no influence. This may be so, but it was not uninteresting, and, in the despatches the Duke wrote, after inspecting different sectors of the front line and the Maginot Line, he showed an alert observation, familiarity with his subject and confidence in reporting on it that suggests that here he was in a sphere in which he felt at home and could exercise a natural ability. The first of his tours took place between 6 and 8 October and was a visit of inspection to the French First Army. Writing later to the War Office, Major-General Howard Vyse said:

He [the Duke of Windsor] has produced a valuable report on the defence, of which three copies are coming over today;
The more important points may be summarised as follows:
(a) There is little or no attempt at concealment.
(b) The revetment of the anti-tank ditches is weak. Other anti-tank obstacles do not seem to be adequate.
(c) Wiring, against infantry, coincides in location with anti-tank obstacles, so that the same bombardment would destroy both.
(d) Anti-tank crews seem to be insufficiently trained.
(e) Work does not seem to be carried on intensively and very few troops were seen.
It will be realized that to give the French any sort of inkling of the source of this information would compromise the value of any missions which I may ask HRH to undertake subsequently.[3]

Some authorities have also credited the Duke of Windsor with a report of far greater importance in which he is said to have been one of the first to express doubts about the French High Command. No trace of this report can be found at the Ministry of Defence, but it is not impossible that he wrote something of the kind, because it would be in accordance with views he expressed elsewhere. (See reported conversation with the American Ambassador to Spain, p. 364.)

Major Metcalfe accompanied the Duke of Windsor to France as ADC and the War Office also appointed Captain Purvis to the Duke's staff. A party consisting of the Duke and Duchess, Metcalfe and Captain Purvis crossed to France at the end of September. Major Metcalfe, who throughout this period in Paris stayed at the Ritz Hotel, immediately resumed his letters to his wife. Since the Duke's life in Paris will be seen so much through his eyes, certain observations are necessary.

It should never be forgotten that his letters were written to his wife: nor, since they inevitably give a onesided view, that for many years he had been closer to the Duke than any other man and had a good deal of influence over him. He had a strong, attractive personality, he was unconventional and easy-going and he invariably said what he felt to the Duke. This was a relationship which many wives might from time to time have resented. However, he was devoted to HRH and completely loyal to him. Often 'fed up', he is sometimes critical but never ungenerous or slow to feel pleasure when his friend was happy or successful. It is because of this last quality, as well as for his humour and wit and the liveliness of his descriptions of people and events, that his letters will once more be quoted at length and at risk of giving only one half of the picture.

Something must also be said about the letters themselves. Here only those parts directly concerning the Duke of Windsor are quoted and they follow one upon another. This gives a false idea of the actual letters which are full of news of the Metcalfes' innumerable friends who pass through Paris, of messages to his children and friends at home, and of a topic which was common to almost all the husbands and wives who were separated by the war – how to get letters and parcels back and forth across the Channel. 'Gray will bring you *one* parcel,' Metcalfe writes on one occasion, and: 'Please do expedite the things I've asked for – also please order Selfridges to send me 300 more cigarettes & please ask Nancy Tree why in Hell Reboux have sent me a black fur hat addressed to her.'

The first letter was written on 30 September, reports a bad crossing and says that the Duke and Duchess of Windsor were worn out and had gone to Versailles together for a day or two. Then:

I am delighted to get a day or two without the Windsors. Mrs Corrigan claimed me as almost a prisoner-of-war. I shall escape, believe me.

Then on 3 October he writes:

I've had a few interesting talks with Mr B (of wedding fame).* He is like a – will-o-wisp – He is never in the same place, town or *country* for more than 6 hours at a time. I can't make him out. He knows *too* much.

Wednesday, 4 October
I am afraid it is going to be extremely difficult to work. HRH is, I see, getting gradually more & more dug in at Suchet. The latest is that Marcel & one other

* Charles Bedaux.

[servant] are being sent from Croë, the idea being to open up a piece of the house. I gather this but am not sure (as who can be when dealing with them). They will have a few important people to dinner. PERHAPS it is a sound idea – but I do not like it. ... HRH is utterly impossible to deal with – if one has anything important to tell him & he is at Suchet, we'll say, he goes on suddenly getting up to notice a door has jammed & does not properly open or shut, or that the water does not run hot, or that Mrs Bedford is to pay a bill for $7\frac{1}{2}$ yds of linoleum for the back stairs. I find it trying at times. ... Last night I fixed a dinner in a private room here [the Ritz] for Charles B[edaux] to meet them. He Charles had much to say. He knows too much – about *every* country in Europe & also our Colonies. It is *terrifying* & he is right a great deal. He has left at dawn for an unknown destination this morning. He hinted at Berlin being one of the places – He beats me *but* he is my pal.!! I have seen him continually. This meeting I arranged was the *first* time they had all met since the disaster of the 'Battle of Germany' & 'the USA' in 1937 – It was very funny in a way. ...

Ritz, 4 Oct.

Today *very* interesting lunch with Gamelin, his right-hand man called Petit-Bon, also Marshal Jamet. HRH was wonderful at lunch got everything going well and everyone talking & laughing, etc. He is really 1st class at something like this. ... Coming back in the car as we were talking about going 'somewhere interesting' on Friday for 3 or 4 days *he* kept on saying how essential it was to be *really comfortable etcetc* & then I'm d——d if he didn't say 'Oh Fruity if you can do without your man it leaves us more room. You see there will be my man and Purvis's.' I said 'What on earth can we put in two motor cars? (His own car plus a 5 seater French car with driver.) I said surely the 3 of us will be in one car with some luggage behind & the 3 servants & luggage in the other. He said: 'Oh if Thomas doesn't go I'll have more room for some of my little extra things.'* He said 'Purvis's man can look after you.' I said I won't ask Purvis's man or any other man to look after me. If you order me not to take my servant of course he won't come, but if not I take him as I see no reason why he shouldn't come and look after me. *Imagine it!* All the heads of the French Divisions & HQ of a sector dining with them etc & being in the limelight & I have to try & clean my own belts & buttons etc. ... At times, Babs I see a *very vivid red*.

Hotel Ritz
Monday, 9 October

I got back here after a most interesting tour of investigation during which we saw a very great deal. ...

Reports visiting a sector of the French front (on the left of the British sector).

On the Friday we inspected various big fortifications, saw their anti-tank defences and met all the various Generals of divisions. All of whom *that* day impressed us as first class.

Later we passed into Br. Sector & went to our GHQ and there met Gort and his chief-of-staff also the Duke of Gloucester. Everyone there was delighted to see

---

* Among HRH's 'little things' was a kettle with which he made tea – usually referred to as 'Kettly'.

HRH & the visit could not have gone better. It was very important to HRH as you can well imagine. ...

We returned very late last night Sunday. We covered about 800 miles. HRH was all through absolutely delightful company. No one could have been a more interesting or amusing companion. How we laughed at many incidents & at some of the French Generals I'm afraid ... but all through he was in splendid form. The only few minutes I hated & when he went all wrong was when I had to get the hotel bills & get them paid. Then he was *frightful*.

W. I saw for a second at Suchet. ... You say in your letter 'Is your position secure or groggy?' *When* I see W I wouldn't know anything! She is like a kaleidoscope – different every time you look. All I know is I feel sure I am doing him absolutely the best and that no one could do him better or nearly as well – so there. But I wouldn't know what she would make him believe or do – I know nothing of Gray Phillips coming out to join HRH's staff, it is complete news to me ... They are now arranging to get their Chef sent to them as for his *Mess*. This is a joke. The Chef had been mobilized & sent to some unit in the S of France – but they've been upsetting the whole ruddy army to get him and today when I saw HRH for a few seconds he also looked a bit sour & unsteady & said there had been some stupid misunderstanding with the French about the Chef & he must go to the Mission to put it straight. It was not a Major-General's job but if people under that rank couldn't do certain things he as a Major-General would have to do it personally. (They say that the Germans are bombing the Maginot Line and that the French are replying. Losses are taking place on both sides but the battle of HRH's Chef is making more noise than all that shelling.)

11 Oct.

I hear Gray Phillips is arriving any day. I got this from Mrs Bedford. A room is being prepared for him, I gather, at Suchet. I don't know what capacity he comes in.

HRH is still being a very small, little soldier. He is getting in coal, as there is a likelihood of a shortage – also we are having difficulty in obtaining *the* proper cook for the 'Suchet mess'. He still fingers bills in Restaurants for *such* a long time, debating & deciding on the remuneration to the waiters, etc.

22 Oct.

I can't figger things out. She & he know every d——n thing. She will know whom I dined or lunched with or have spoken to & *even seen*. I believe she has spies out & they work well. Anyhow it's terrifying. ... Also he (HRH) said: 'I was *very much surprised* that when I was away (for 1 night) you never bothered to ring up & see if W wanted anything, etc., etc. I was staggered. I said 'Good God I thought W was much too occupied & busy to be bothered with me. I would *naturally rather* have dined with her than with old Mottiscombe & George Lloyd. Anyhow it is all very worrying & I don't like it. I'm fed up with Paris & this war – whichever you like. I don't like my job (anyhow today) & I never feel secure & safe when working for HRH.

On 28 October Metcalfe writes that he feels 'fed up' but 'Gray seems very happy' and on 30 October that he has just got back from a most interesting trip.

We had left these parts on Thursday 26th at 10 a.m. We covered 900 miles. . . . Saturday we motored for 14 hours (of course we broke off to see things & lunch etc.). . . . We started off HRH, De Salis & myself (Purvis is still convalescing he will be working this week I believe).* The atmosphere was chilly. *We* are under suspicion & must be made to feel it. But by slow degrees as we progress further & further from Paris & the environs of Suchet we *begin* to thaw gradually, slowly as another mile is put between us & Suchet! It is extraordinary. By the afternoon we become *NORMAL* & eventually again become a really delightful companion one with whom one would go anywhere. (Slight lapses when a bill has to be paid!). . . .

3 November

I am well but fed up as I always am when stuck in this infernal town. Saw the Windsors (the couple) yesterday afternoon. He now knits woollen mufflers, etc, for her 'bags for soldiers'. It is her *only* thing now. She's running it very successfully as you can imagine, collecting money etc from everyone (she made me give her Frs. 200). . . . Re HRH's funny methods of doing things – We do this last tour. He then, with de Salis who is the expert in the language, makes out his report for the CGS. I would naturally love to read it & hear what he did say, but *oh no*. I'm told nothing. Again when we start off one of these tours instructions come from French HQ a day or so ahead. Do you think I ever am told one word where we go or what the programme is. Certainly not. It is very disappointing & also lessens one's efficiency re ordering cars, being ready for meeting Generals, etc.

And on Sunday, 5 November:

I'm afraid I'm in a foul humour. Nothing seems to go. One seems to be always competing against some d——n thing. The latest here is that I am told by one of the fellows at the Mission who arranges about pay etc that the WO have got *no authority* to pay me at all as Purvis is the only one *officially* on HRH's staff. He says in his letter 'Perhaps you can get this done if it is not already in course of being so.' I dined last night with HRH. I showed him the letter & the *little tiny man* said —— Nothing —— He then looked at me & said 'Didn't they tell you at the W.O. that you wouldn't get any pay.' I said 'Good God, no.' He looked just fishey. . . . What beats me is that HRH is quite prepared to do nothing for me at all. I really think I can't stay on with him without *any authority* or *pay*. In lots of ways I won't be sorry.

It is not, of course, clear that HRH had done nothing in this matter. It is quite certain that he told Hore-Belisha he wished to have Metcalfe as ADC when he first saw him at the War Office, and it must have been a great humiliation to him that, even in this small and personal matter, his wishes were not met: indeed it is more likely that his willingness to hurt his friends was in exact proportion to his own loss of power and damaged pride. In England at about this time Oliver Harvey† was writing in his diary:

* After a motor accident.
† Then at the Foreign Office. Now Lord Harvey of Tasburgh.

Charles Peake tells me the Duke of Windsor has sent a message to Monckton from France to say he is flying over during the weekend in a private aeroplane and wants to see Winston but that the King is not to know! Monckton, after taking Charles's advice, has warned Winston, who is saying that he has to visit fleet over this weekend and is telling Hardinge about it. He is also telling Belisha and will ring up the Duke tonight to tell him he cannot come.

And he adds: 'The Duke of Windsor has some nebulous job at Gamelin's H.Q.'[4]

In Paris the slight difficulties between Metcalfe and the Windsors seem from now on to diminish (although on 7 November Metcalfe writes to his wife: 'Re my remark which you say you don't understand "we have re turned under the spell" surely it's as obvious as the nose on my face – Wallis is the spell, influence or anything you like to call her.') In any case on Monday, 20 November, he records:

I dined at Suchet last night. The Bedauxs were there – It went very easily & I *seem* to be in very good books. I was welcomed as a sheep returning to the fold. I take it all with a couple of pinches of salt.... HRH appears *now* to realise that he has no power here & is *not* to have any. It is a bitter blow but he's taking it.

20.1.40.
I dined at Suchet last night. They were in splendid form – I've never seen either of them better – I enjoyed myself a lot.... Gray is still in great spirits & charming as ever.

Then on 1 February he wrote a letter in which there occurs one of the most revealing sentences in this whole correspondence. 'HRH,' he says, 'came back from England in great shape, seemingly everything went as he wished. It was really delightful to see how pleased he & W. were to get together again. It is *very true* & deep stuff.'

The spontaneous use of the plural in the second sentence has a significance which cannot be overestimated. In all the literature about this couple this is almost the only time we are told without equivocation that after her own fashion the Duchess loved her husband. The letter tells us, too, something about this correspondent, who, however 'fed up' he is from time to time, never fails to react with pleasure to the success or happiness of his friend.

On 3 February he writes: 'W. in great form. Gray looks old. HRH very busy bee doing God knows what.' And on 5 February:

HRH told me that he goes at end of this week up to GHQ to stay for several days – He was *very* nice about it & said he'd take Purvis as he (Purvis) hadn't been 'au front' at all yet – also I think he'd have to take Purvis as he (Purvis) is his official staff officer. HRH is very pleased over it. It is – he says – 'the thin edge of the wedge'. I am glad for him I also think something better will come fairly soon for HRH – Then I disappear I guess.

Nothing better did appear for HRH, however, nor was there any 'thin edge to the wedge'. It was a little absurd to think that there would be. In 1939 there was no room in a professional war for completely untrained officers who owed their position to their birth, except that which in peace and war is the duty of the Royal Family, to appear and put heart into their subjects. But HRH was only uneasily accepted even in this role. The Duchess of Windsor tells us that on one of his visits to the British Expeditionary Force he encountered his brother, the Duke of Gloucester, who was on Lord Gort's staff. Walking slightly ahead of his brother the Duke automatically returned the salute of a company guard turned out to render the honours due to the general officers. Some days later he was notified that he had violated military etiquette by taking a salute intended for his brother. The Duchess writes: 'We had two wars to deal with – the big and still leisurely war, in which everybody was caught up, and the little war with the Palace, in which no quarter was given.' And she says that it seemed to her tragic that the Duke's gift for dealing with the troops was never used 'out of fear, I judged, that it might once more shine brightly, too brightly'.[5]

Nor did Fruity disappear. His letters cease after the end of February and certainly in April he was in England, possibly convalescing from an illness. But when the long cold winter ended and the real war began, both he and the Duke of Windsor were in Paris. On 15 or 16 May the Duchess of Windsor left Paris and travelled south to a hotel in Biarritz, the Duke accompanying her on the journey but returning then to the Mission in Paris. Metcalfe was with him there, and, as the debacle grew more and more obvious and the Germans turned from the coast towards Paris, these two continued to visit different sectors of the front together.

At the end of every day they would make plans together for the next day – sometimes a definite arrangement, sometimes simply an understanding that Metcalfe would telephone for orders the following morning. One evening towards the end of May the two parted in the evening without any precise plan. 'Good-night, Sir,' Metcalfe said, 'see you tomorrow.' The following morning at 8.30 he telephoned to the Boulevard Suchet and was answered by a servant. He asked to be put through to His Royal Highness and he received the reply 'His Royal Highness left for Biarritz at 6.30 this morning.'

Metcalfe, who was on nobody's pay roll, attached to no military mission, who had served the Duke all these months as an unpaid and unacknowledged aide, slowly took in the news that he had been left without a word to find his way back to England as best he could. It is uncertain whether the Howard Vyse Mission had been better informed.

30

ENCOUNTER WITH THE GERMANS

The Duke of Windsor left Paris on 28 May and, driven by Ladbroke, went straight to join the Duchess in Biarritz. The next morning their whole party drove to La Croë where they stayed uneasily until the middle of June. In the intervening period Major Gray Phillips joined them, having hitch-hiked from Paris on military lorries and ambulances. His exhausted appearance did nothing to reassure them.

The Windsors received their news like everyone else on the radio, and they became conscious of the dangers of their situation when Italy entered the war. Major Phillips called on some friends, Captain and Mrs Wood, and on his return seriously urged the Windsors to leave France. The Duke then telephoned to the British Consul at Nice, Major Dodds, and received the same advice. Major Dodds said that he and his colleague at Menton had received instructions to burn their papers and evacuate their posts, and that they had a permit from the Spanish Consul allowing them to cross the border into Spain. He told the Duke that, travelling in convoy, they would pass La Croë at noon the next day and strongly advised him to join them. The following day, therefore, once more driven by Ladbroke, accompanied by Major Phillips and the Duchess's maid, with their luggage in a trailer hooked on to the car, and joined by the Woods also with a trailer on their car, the Windsors attached themselves to the consular convoy headed for the Spanish frontier.

All went well until they passed Arles, but after this they were delayed at every major town by barricades across the road at which they had to pro-duce credentials. The Windsors had no permits but, correctly believing they might remember him, the Duke called out to the French veterans who manned the barriers: 'Je suis le Prince de Galles. Laissez moi passer, s'il vous plait.'¹ And each time they let him pass. When they arrived at Perpignan he learned from the concierge at the hotel that it was necessary to secure visas in that town and then cross the border at a small place called Port Bou. He set off with George Wood to the Spanish consulate.

For a few hours he suffered the experiences of any ordinary refugee who requires papers, standing in queues, and meeting with a brisk, inhuman shortage of attention or consideration. He was refused a visa on the grounds that he might become a charge on the Spanish government. However, eventually a telephone call to the Spanish Ambassador to France, Joseph Lequerica, produced the necessary authorization and the whole party crossed into Spain. Arrived at Barcelona, they rested for two days and then went on to Madrid.

In England, Winston Churchill had become aware that the Duke and Duchess had crossed the border into a neutral but unfriendly country, and as soon as they arrived in Madrid, the British Ambassador, another old friend, Sir Samuel Hoare, hastened to inform them that the Prime Minister attached great urgency to their return to England and wanted them to go on immediately to Lisbon, where, on their arrival, two flying-boats of Coastal Command would be sent to take them home. He told them, too, that the Duke of Westminster had offered them the use of his house, Eaton Hall, near Chester.

However, the days of fear and chaos and unaccustomed helplessness in face of authority had done nothing to divert the Duke's mind from his major pre-occupations. He believed that with Winston Churchill as Prime Minister the atmosphere in England would be altogether more propitious, and that he might now expect what the Duchess has called 'an appropriate job'. On what must have seemed to him a good wicket, he once more decided to make conditions for his return to England and this time there was no Fruity Metcalfe to dissuade him. He announced by telegram that unless his wife was accorded equality with the wives of his brothers and until he knew what job was proposed for him, he would not leave Portugal. He understood little and he had learned nothing, but it is impossible to decide whether most to condemn his egotism at this hour of his country's history, to pity the false assumptions on which his hopes were based, or to admire the gallantry with which he made his stand after his recent experiences. In any case, in June and July 1940 a good deal of Winston Churchill's attention had to be given to the recalcitrant Duke, and for the moment he could not make him budge. It was in these circumstances that the watching Germans conceived the idea that he might be made use of.

In order to place the German plot to acquire the services of the Duke of Windsor in its proper perspective, it is necessary to recall the history of the summer months. All through June and July Hitler remained convinced that the British would seek an accommodation and withdraw from the war. The idea of a bloodless victory had always appealed to him and, although he planned in a curiously inattentive way for an invasion of

England, he never ceased to dream of a capitulation. His attitude to the conduct of the war was indecisive and on 19 July he made a speech to the Reichstag which was intended to be understood in England as an offer of peace. This was delivered in such strange and hectoring tones that it was not recognized for what it was, nor was the British reaction in the least what he had hoped for. But Hitler did not entirely abandon the idea of a negotiated peace and a reply to his speech was solicited through diplomatic channels, while the King of Sweden made an offer to act as mediator. On 9 July Lord Halifax sent a telegram to Lord Lothian (British Ambassador in Washington) in which he said that the position of the Duke of Windsor on the Continent was causing embarrassment, as 'although his loyalties are unimpeachable there is always a backwash of Nazi intrigue which seeks, now that the greater part of the Continent is in enemy hands, to make trouble about him'.

.There are personal and family difficulties about his return to this country. [Lord Halifax went on] In all the circumstances it was felt that an appointment abroad might appeal to him and the Prime Minister has with HM's cordial approval offered him the Governorship of the Bahamas.

And he added that the Duke of Windsor had accepted the appointment.[2]

Every writer who has hitherto given an account of the German attempt to make use of the Duke of Windsor has treated it as a ludicrous example of the naïveté of the Germans, the extent of their misunderstanding of the English, and the clumsiness of their tactics. It is not easy to see why. It is true that some of the reports of the German agents are highly improbable or obviously mistaken, but judging by recent books on the subject of wartime intelligence, this seems to be neither unusual nor peculiar to the Germans. At the risk of giving an impression equally naïve, or, worse still, one that is scandalous, this plot will be given serious attention here.

The Germans believed themselves at that time – not without reason – to be within an ace of conquering Britain. What more certain than that they would be on the lookout for a man who, while not the stamp of a traitor, might see his duty to his country in the light that Pétain had seen his? And what more likely prospect than the man who as King had made no bones about his admiration for the German nation and his belief that war could settle nothing in the modern world, who less than three years before had travelled through Germany with the most notorious of the Nazi leaders, reportedly giving a 'modified version' of the Nazi salute, and who had appealed directly to Hitler for peace. Everyone who knew anything of the Duke knew that he would never fail in patriotic feeling, but he had given unmistakable evidence that he might have his own ideas as to where his duty to England lay. Once he had arrived in a neutral country friendly to Germany, how could the Germans have done less than make some effort to come to terms with him? Certainly Winston Churchill did not need to be told of the danger, and he recognized the need to get the ducal pair back to England long before he could have had firm evidence of any German intentions.

One reason for the air of scorn and disbelief with which the German plot has up to the present been treated is that, when the documents relating to it were published, the Duke's lawyers bared their teeth in a statement which left little doubt that it might be dangerous to take it seriously.* But a second and very important reason is that the Germans were not content to leave the delicate task of approaching the Duke to the diplomatic staffs of Lisbon and Madrid, but sent a man named Walter Schellenberg to make a parallel attempt.

Schellenberg was a member of the SS and of the SD (the intelligence and security services set up within the SS and part of Himmler's private empire). In 1940 he was one of half a dozen men employed in the main Security Office by Reinhard Heidrich, Himmler's lieutenant, and on whom were concentrated 'all the powers of spying and intelligence, interrogation and arrest, torture and execution on which dictatorship ultimately depends.' Towards the end of his career he became the head of Hitler's Foreign Intelligence Service. In an introduction to the English edition of Schellenberg's memoirs Alan Bullock says that it would be unwise to accept him as a trustworthy witness where his evidence cannot be corroborated, but he adds that he has the two virtues of describing for the most part only events of which he has first hand knowledge, and of being comparatively free from 'that passion for tortuous self-justification which disfigure so many German memoirs of these years.'†[5]

In July 1940 Schellenberg received orders direct from the Foreign Minister (Ribbentrop), speaking in the name of the Führer, to travel to Spain and there to try to persuade the Duke of Windsor by various means to escape from 'his present environment' and to take up residence in Spain, in Switzerland, or any other neutral country providing it was not

---

* An earlier volume of the captured documents, published in 1954, also contained references to the Duke and this occasioned an outburst of protest from Winston Churchill in the House of Commons. Count Julius von Zech-Burkersroda, German Minister to the Hague, had in two despatches dated 27 January and 19 February 1940 reported that the Duke was 'not entirely satisfied with his position' and sought a field of activity in which he would have an active rather than a merely representative role (all of which was true). Zech went on to say: 'He has expressed himself in especially uncomplimentary terms about Chamberlain, whom he particularly dislikes and who, as he thinks, is responsible for his being frozen out.'[3] Winston Churchill expended some sarcasm at the expense of the editors of the published documents and said that he had thought it proper to show the passages referring to him to the Duke. 'He thought, and I agreed with him, that they could be treated with contempt.'[4]

† The authenticity of the *Schellenberg Memoirs* is not absolutely certain. The manuscript was bought by Mr André Deutsch and reached London packed in a large suitcase and in complete disorder. Mr Deutsch then did everything possible to satisfy himself that this was Schellenberg's own manuscript. In his introduction, after discussing the reasons for believing in the authenticity of the manuscript, Alan Bullock says: 'All this amounts to less than certainty, but my own belief is that Schellenberg wrote (or supplied the material for collaborators like Herr Harprecht to write) the original draft and that the translation which follows has been made from the draft.'[6]

outside the military and political influence of the German Reich. Various inducements were to be offered to the Duke, one of which was a deposit in Switzerland of fifty million Swiss francs. 'Hitler attaches the greatest importance to this operation, and has come to the conclusion after serious consideration that, if the Duke should prove hesitant, he himself would have no objection to your helping the Duke to reach the right conclusion by coercion.'[7]

There are two sources for the details of Schellenberg's part in the plot. One is the German Foreign Office Document B/15 B002635–38, which, although his name does not appear on it, is believed to have been written by Schellenberg and is a report sent to the Foreign Ministry after the Duke had left for the Bahamas: the other is *The Schellenberg Memoirs*. These differ in one important particular. In the Memoirs, written several years afterwards, Schellenberg, who clearly hated and despised Ribbentrop, claims privately to have regarded the plot with as much contempt as was later shown by English writers, at least to the extent that force was contemplated. 'Surely,' he writes that he said to Ribbentrop, 'the whole action must depend on the voluntary co-operation of the Duke.'[8] He also claims that, when in the course of time he had to reach a decision as to whether or not to use force, he arranged through the Portuguese to have the guard on the Duke strengthened by twenty men, so that he could fail in carrying out his orders without loss of face.

It is not quite clear why any suggestion of the use of force to capture the Windsors is regarded as absurd. Obviously it would have been undesirable if instead the Duke could easily be persuaded to collaborate, but in the last resort it would have been an embarrassment to the British to have him in German hands, however this was achieved. In any case, it was the measures Schellenberg did decide to take which give the whole episode the flavour of a boy's spy story. These are described both in the Memoirs and in the Foreign Policy Document B15/B002635–38, which will be quoted, and they had the design of frightening the Duke and Duchess into believing that they were in danger of a surprise attack from the *British* Intelligence Service. It would be natural to suppose that this could only undermine the more sober efforts being made at the same time by the diplomatic staffs. But even that is not true. We know from Walter Monckton (see below p. 372) that 'although it sounds fantastic' the Duke and Duchess were impressed by the story of a British plot.

Many of the German Foreign Office documents will be quoted here, but since the outlines of the episode emerge clearly only after close study, an attempt at clarification of some of the points will be made first. Above all it is important to understand who were the personalities involved.

Ribbentrop was in contact with three men. Walter Schellenberg we have already seen as a man on whose word no reliance can be placed without corroboration. The Ambassador to Madrid, von Stohrer, was an orthodox

Nazi and was in very close touch with the pro-German Spanish government. Hoynegen Huene, the Minister to the Portuguese Legation, was of a different type. He was a man of great culture and refinement and by reputation anti-Nazi. The Legation at Lisbon was believed to attract men who were anti-Nazi, since it offered the best escape route for anyone who came under suspicion for his political opinions. Huene had been well liked by the British before the war and had retained their respect. Whatever may be thought about Schellenberg and Stohrer, it is difficult to believe that Huene regularly wrote reports to the Foreign Ministry designed to please rather than to inform, although it is perfectly possible that, like everyone else relying on agents, he sometimes was mistaken. It may be that there is an element of wish-fulfilment in all intelligence reports, but that is something different from the deliberate, gross and pointless distortions of the truth of which all the Germans in Spain and Portugal were later to be accused.*

Stohrer and Huene, proceeding with more delicacy than the clowning Schellenberg, attempted to influence the Duke through the use of emissaries, or go-betweens, Spanish and Portuguese. The Spanish emissaries received their orders throughout from the Spanish Minister of the Interior, Ramon Serrano Suner, a brother-in-law of General Franco, who acted very closely with Stohrer. The 'first' Spanish emissary was Miguel Primo de Rivera, son of the old dictator and leader of the Madrid Falangists.† He is described as 'an old friend of the Duke's'. There was a second Spanish emissary who was used on at least one occasion in order not to attract too much attention to de Rivera, who was well known. The Spanish emissaries were, according to Stohrer's reports, not informed that they were acting for the Germans and received all orders from Serrano Suner. Thus it was intended that they should influence the Duke by expressing their own views and by information which came from Spanish rather than German sources. But all this seems rather absurd, because de Rivera could not possibly have believed the Germans had no interest in the matter.

The emissary employed by Huene in Portugal was the Duke's host throughout his visit there, the banker, Ricardo Espirito Santo e Silva.‡ From the evidence of the captured documents he was used once only, on the last day of the Duke's stay, but it was he who transmitted a message direct from Ribbentrop – an overt sign to the Duke that it was the Germans with whom he was dealing.

On 23 June a telegram was sent by Stohrer to the Foreign Minister in Berlin:

* Conversation with Ralph Jarvis.
† The Spanish official Fascist Party.
‡ Espirito Santo was known to the British as the Holy Ghost, as is the international bank of that name.

The Spanish Foreign Minister requests advice with regard to the treatment of the Duke and Duchess of Windsor who were to arrive in Madrid today, apparently in order to return to England by way of Lisbon. The Foreign Minister assumes ... that we might perhaps be interested in detaining the Duke of Windsor here and possibly in establishing contact with him.[9]

Ribbentrop replied:

Is it possible in the first place to detain the Duke and Duchess of Windsor for a couple of weeks in Spain before they are granted an exit visa? It would be necessary at all events to be sure that it did not appear in any way that the suggestion came from Germany.[10]

The Windsors seem to have stayed in Madrid for something over a week. At any rate there is a report of them in Madrid on 2 July. This was sent from Madrid by the American Ambassador (Weddell) to his Secretary of State, a source which by no stretch can be said to be tainted. It reads:

In a conversation last night with [member?] of the Embassy staff the Duke of Windsor declared that the most important thing now to be done was to end the war before thousands more were killed or maimed to save the faces of a few politicians.

With regard to the defeat of France he stated that stories that the French troops would not fight were not true. They had fought magnificently, but the organization behind them was totally inadequate. In the past 10 years Germany had totally reorganized the order of its society in preparation for this war. Countries which were unwilling to accept such a reorganization of society and its concomitant sacrifices should direct their policies accordingly and thereby avoid dangerous adventures. He stated that this applied not merely to Europe, but to the United States also. The Duchess put the same thing somewhat more directly be [by?] declaring that France had lost because it was internally diseased and that a country which was not in condition to fight a war should never have declared war.

These observations have their value if any as doubtless reflecting the views of an element in England, possibly a growing one who find in Windsor and his circle a group who are realists in world politics and who hope to come into their own in event of peace. Weddell.[11]

The Windsors, accompanied by Major Phillips, arrived in Lisbon at the beginning of July. On 11 July the German Minister, Huene, sent his Foreign Ministry the following telegram:

As Spaniards from among those around the Duke of Windsor have informed us confidentially on visits to the Legation the designation of the Duke as Governor of the Bahama Islands is intended to keep him far away from England, since his return would bring with it very strong encouragement to English friends of peace, so that his arrest at the instance of his opponents would certainly have to be expected. The Duke intends to postpone his departure for the Bahama Islands as long as possible, at least until the beginning of August, in hope of a turn of events favourable to him. He is convinced that if he had remained on the throne war would have been avoided, and he characterizes himself as a firm supporter of peaceful arrangement with Germany. The Duke definitely believes that continued severe bombings would make England ready for peace. Huene.[12]

From this telegram it can be seen that like almost all German diplomats Huene believed in some sort of following of the Duke's in England – a Fronde – which in fact was non-existent.* Ribbentrop sent a copy of his telegram to Stohrer, in Madrid, with a covering letter in which he stated that the Germans were especially interested in having the Duke return to Spain and that they were convinced he was surrounded by English agents who would get him away from Lisbon as soon as possible 'if necessary by force'. Haste was accordingly required and, although Ribbentrop says that he cannot decide on the method to be used – especially in connection with the existing liaison between the Spanish Minister and the Duke of Windsor – he continues:

From here it would seem best if close Spanish friends of the Duke would privately invite him, and of course his wife, for a short one or two week visit to Spain on pretexts which would appear plausible both to him, to the Portuguese and to the English agents. That would mean, therefore, that the Duke and Duchess, as well as the English and the Portuguese, must believe that Windsor in any event is going to come back there. If it does not take place in that way there is the danger, according to our information about the company of the Duke, that the real reason for the return of the Duke to Spain will become known in England and that England then would prevent it at all costs.

Ribbentrop goes on to say that once on Spanish territory the Duke and his wife would have to be persuaded or compelled to remain there, and that if the latter alternative became necessary Germany would have to reach an agreement with the Spanish government that, through the obligations of neutrality, the Duke would be interned as an English officer and a member of the British Expeditionary Force who had crossed the frontier as a military fugitive. He asks how the Spanish government would be likely to react to this and then continues:

At any rate, at a suitable occasion in Spain the Duke must be informed that Germany wants peace with the English people, that the Churchill clique stands in the way of it, and that it would be a good thing if the Duke would hold himself in readiness for further developments. Germany is determined to force England to peace by every means of power and upon this happening would be prepared to accommodate any desire expressed by the Duke, especially with a view to the assumption of the English throne by the Duke and Duchess. If the Duke should have other plans, but be prepared to co-operate in the establishment of good relations between Germany and England, we would likewise be prepared to assure him and his wife of a subsistence which would permit him, either as a private citizen or in some other position, to lead a life suitable for a king.

* So it seems did Mr Weddell, the American Ambassador.

Ribbentrop added two points for the information of the Ambassador. The first was that he had received information that Espirito Santo, the Duke's Portuguese host, was friendly to Germany. The second was as follows:

A report has reached us today from a Swiss informant who has for many years had close connections with the English Secret Service to the effect that it is the plan of the English Secret Service, by sending the Duke to the Bahamas, to get him into English power in order to do away with him at the first opportunity. There is no objection to your informing the Spanish of this entirely confidentially.[13]

When the Duke and Duchess arrived at the house in Estoril belonging to Espirito Santo, they were met by the British Ambassador, Sir Walford Selby, who had with him the captains of two flying-boats which had been sent over to take the Windsors to England the next day.*

'But David,' the Duchess tells us, 'much as he admired Winston and anxious as he was to be back in England, was not to be persuaded.' He told the Ambassador to return the flying-boats empty to England, and although he realized 'there was a danger of his being misunderstood', he said he would not return until his demands in relation to the status of his wife were met. 'Whatever I am to be I must be with you; any position I am called on to fill I can only fill with you.'[14]

Within a few days the Germans succeeded in making contact with the Duke of Windsor through Miguel Primo de Rivera. On 16 July the German Ambassador to Madrid reported to the German Foreign Ministry that the Duke of Windsor had communicated to the Spanish Foreign Minister through this emissary as follows:

His designation as Governor of the Bahamas was made known in a very cool and categorical letter from Churchill with the instruction that he should leave for his post immediately without fail. Churchill has threatened W. with arraignment before a court-martial in case he did not accept the post (this appears to have been communicated orally only to the Duke). Through the Colonial Minister the Duke then received a postponement for a month and a half (apparently because the Duke declared he must receive from his house in Paris certain effects and objects for the move).

The confidential emissary further reports that the Duke has declared that he has given up all his military offices and is now only a Governor. The Duke sees in the appointment recognition of the equal status of his wife. The attitude of the English Embassy in Lisbon, on instructions from London, is very reserved towards the Duke.[15]

On 25 July Stohrer reports that de Rivera has returned from Lisbon.

* We have been told this by the Duchess of Windsor. It is difficult to understand why two flying-boats should have been sent, but probably one to guard, or in the event of accident, replace the other.

He had two long conversations with the Duke of Windsor; at the last one the Duchess was present also. The Duke expressed himself very freely. In Portugal he felt almost like a prisoner. He was surrounded by agents, etc. Politically he was more and more distant from the King and the present English government. The Duke and Duchess have less fear of the King, who was quite foolish ('reichlicht toricht'), than of the shrewd Queen who was intriguing skilfully against the Duke and particularly the Duchess.

The Duke was considering making a public statement and thereby disavowing present English policy and breaking with his brother.[16]

And in a second telegram Stohrer went on:

The confidential emissary of the Minister of the Interior had the following to add about his interview with the Duke and Duchess:

When he gave the Duke the advice not to go to the Bahamas, but to return to Spain, since the Duke was likely yet to be called upon to play an important role in English policy and possibly to ascend the English throne, both the Duke and Duchess gave evidence of astonishment. Both appeared to be completely enmeshed in conventional ways of thinking, for they replied that according to the English constitution this would not be possible after the Abdication. When the confidential emissary then expressed his expectation that the course of the war might bring about changes even in the English constitution, the Duchess especially became very pensive.

I would emphasize that, as already reported, I said nothing to the Minister about the considerations involving the future which were contained in your telegraphic instruction No. 1023 of 11 July and that accordingly the confidential emissary, who in any event knows nothing of my own or of any German interest in the matter, discussed the question of the throne actually on his own account as an old friend of the Duke.[17]

On 24 July Stohrer reported that a second confidential emissary from the Minister of the Interior had taken the Duke a letter from the first emissary (Miguel Primo de Rivera) in which the latter refers to a message that the Minister of the Interior (Serrano Suner) wishes the Duke to receive and says that, although he has not yet heard what this is, he has the impression that it is to do with a warning of the great danger which threatens the Duke and Duchess. He urges the Duke to go to a well-known resort in the mountains near the Spanish frontier where he will meet him 'by chance' and invite him and the Duchess for a short stay on the Spanish side.[18]

Stohrer says that the Duke and Duchess had said that they very much desired to return to Spain but that the Duke feared that in Spain he would be treated as a prisoner. This fear was dispelled by the confidential emissary who assured him the Spanish government would certainly agree to permit the Duke and Duchess to take up their residence in southern Spain (which the Duke seemed to prefer) perhaps in Granada or Malaga. The Duke had then said that he had surrendered his passports to the English Legation with a request for Spanish and French visas, but the Legation

was clearly unwilling. How then could he cross the Spanish border.*
Stohrer reports that the second emissary will be sent to try to persuade the
Duke to leave Lisbon by car as if for a long excursion and cross the border
at a place arranged where the Spanish secret police will see that he crosses
safely.

A second manoeuvre to delay the Duke's departure has up to now escaped
attention.† As soon as the Windsors arrived in Madrid an exchange of
telegrams occurred between the German Ambassador to Madrid and the
Protocol Department of the Foreign Ministry, the upshot of which was
that Abetz (in Paris) was instructed to undertake unofficially and confidentially an unobtrusive observation of the Duke's residence, and, secondly,
that Ambassador von Stohrer was instructed 'to have the Duke informed
confidentially through a Spanish intermediary that the Foreign Minister is
looking out for its protection'. This telegram, which was signed Schmidt,
added 'no written statement whatever is to be made'.[19] On 16 July von
Stohrer sent the following telegram to the Foreign Minister:

> The Duke of Windsor through the confidential emissary again expressed his
> thanks for co-operation in the matter of his house in Paris and has made a request
> for a maid of the Duchess to be permitted to travel to Paris in order to pack up
> various objects there and transport them by van to Lisbon, as they were required
> by him and the Duchess for the Bahamas. Without obligation I replied immedi-
> ately that the maid could present herself at the Madrid Embassy; meanwhile I
> would consult Berlin. I recommend acceding to the ducal couple's request since
> if necessary the maid's journey to Paris and above all the return journey to
> Lisbon can be held up by us as required in order to postpone further his
> departure.[20]

In a telegram of 29 July Stohrer reported: 'The Duchess's maid has left for
Paris. On her return journey she will be held by our Frontier authorities on
the Franco–Spanish frontier until I give free passage.'[21]

At the same time as these messages were passing to and fro a parallel
exchange was taking place between the Duke of Windsor and certain
people in England – the Prime Minister, Lord Lloyd, the Colonial Minister,
and Major Gray Phillips (whom the Duke sent to London on his appointment to the Bahamas with the request that the Prime Minister should
receive him 'to explain some details'). The Prime Minister offered the
appointment in a telegram to the Duke in which he expressed the hope
that it would be accepted and ended with the sentence: 'At any rate I have
done my best.'[22] The Duke accepted the appointment without delay but
two matters exercised his mind. The first of these was that he wished to

* In a statement made on the release of these documents in 1957 the Duke particularly drew
attention to this part of the report and said that it was quite untrue that he had surrendered his
passport.

† Some of the documents were not selected for translation and publication but are available
in the Foreign Office Library in the original language.

visit the United States on his way to the Bahamas. On 18 July he telegraphed to the Prime Minister complaining that the Colonial Office had raised some objections to his sailing on an American ship on the technical grounds of his being Commander-in-Chief as well as Governor of the Bahamas. He concluded this telegram with the words:

Have been messed about quite long enough and detect in Colonial Office attitude very same hands at work as in my last job. Strongly urge you to support arrangements I have made as otherwise will have to reconsider my position.[23]

And in a later message to the Prime Minister on the same day:

Feel sure you do not know red tape we are up against as regards new appointment. Feel diffident in asking you but it would help enormously if you could see Phillips again who can explain details.[24]

To which in due course (20 July) the Prime Minister replied:

Your message of July 18 has crossed mine of same date. The Colonial Office had nothing to do with any difficulty about your sailing in American ship. It was necessary to consider American Neutrality Legislation. Indeed it was on the suggestion of Colonial Office that we are in communication with Lord Lothian to remove any such difficulty by pointing out that, although you will technically be Commander-in-Chief, appointment of Governor is of a purely civil nature. I am therefore very glad to be able to consider the last sentences of Your Royal Highness's telegram as non-existent. I gather from your latest telegram that this is what you would wish.[25]

This did not however satisfy the Duke who wished not merely to travel on an American ship but to visit America, and he therefore wired saying that as the Duchess had to go to New York as soon as possible for medical reasons he thought the additional expense of a separate journey would not be justified and it would be more convenient to 'waive Colonial Office technicalities'.[26]

The technicalities were not caused by the Colonial Office, but were due to the fact that if the Duke had visited the USA he would have had to be treated as a royal visitor and received by the President. Roosevelt faced a Presidential election the following November and would have been seriously embarrassed by a visit from a much publicized national of one of the belligerent countries. The Duke was not easily put off however and telegrams continued to fly backwards and forwards between him and England and also between the Foreign Office and Lord Lothian on this subject, while at the same time he took up another matter.

The first intimation we have of his second concern is in a telegram from Major Gray Phillips in London to the Duke of Windsor dated 17 July. In this he says: 'Please tell Duchess best available maid asks £100. Shall I engage her. FLETCHER & WEBSTER cannot be released. Am looking for another valet butler.'[27]

To this the Duke replied: 'Absolutely essential that Fletcher re-joins me here as if you can as military officer, surely he can as soldier in plain clothes.'[28] And in a second telegram: 'Have asked Prime Minister to see you who I feel sure does not know the red tape we are up against. Fletcher essential Webster less important.'[29]

On 18 July the Duke received an official communication on the subject of the soldier servant, Fletcher, from Lord Lloyd at the Colonial Office. He said:

Phillips informs me that Your Royal Highness wishes to obtain the services of two Guardsmen as chauffeur and valet. I venture to hope that I may try and send you for this purpose men over military age or otherwise unsuitable for military service. War Office represent that to take fit and efficient soldiers out of Army at this juncture would set an unfortunate precedent. Lord Athlone, who made similar request, has acquiesced in War Office view.[30]

To this the Duke replied:

Piper Alastair Fletcher, Scots Guards, has been my servant since my appointment as Major-General last September. As change of servant at this time would constitute serious handicap to me in my new appointment strongly urge War Office make an exception in Fletcher's case and he be made available to rejoin me here not later than July 27th.[31]

On 20 July the Prime Minister himself entered the fray.

I regret that there can be no question of releasing men from the Army to act as servants to Your Royal Highness. Such a step would be viewed with general disapprobation in times like these, and I should ill serve Your Royal Highness by countenancing it.[32]

However, by 24 July, the question of the servant began to appear of little importance in England compared with the necessity to get the Duke and Duchess away to the Bahamas and to prevent them landing in the USA, and compromise was reached. The Prime Minister sent the following telegram:

Arrangements have now been made for Your Royal Highness to leave by American Export vessel on 1 August for Bermuda, and proceed thence by Canadian National Steamship 'Lady Somers' on the 13th direct to Nassau. His Majesty's Government cannot agree to Your Royal Highness landing in the United States at this juncture. This decision must be accepted. It should be possible to arrange if necessary for the Duchess either to proceed from Bermuda to New York for medical reasons, or alternatively it will always be easy for her to go there from Nassau by sea or air.
Sir I have now succeeded in overcoming the War Office objection to the departure of Fletcher, who will be sent forthwith to join you.[33]

One further exchange must be recorded. On 26 July the Prime Minister received a communication from the Duke in which he said that, while agreeing to the arrangements made for his journey, he wished for confirmation that it was not the policy of His Majesty's government that 'I should not set foot on American soil during my term of office in the Bahamas.'[34] To which he received the reply once more from the Prime Minister himself that in accordance with standing Royal Instructions to Colonial Governors he would have to consult the Secretary of State before leaving the Colony 'when we should naturally do our best to suit Your Royal Highness's convenience'.[35]

To return now to Lisbon, Schellenberg arrived there in the middle of July and Huene reported liaison with him. In a long report sent from Portugal to the German Foreign Office after the Duke and Duchess had left for the Bahamas his activities are described. They were directed to inducing the Windsors to believe they were in danger from the British and included an anonymous gift of flowers to the Duchess with a greeting card containing a warning, anonymous letters, the suggestion of a Jewish peril, and the rumour of the finding of an 'infernal machine' on the ship on which they were to sail. 'Harmless breaking of the bedroom window' was omitted as likely to increase the Duchess's desire to depart.[36]

However ludicrous all this seems in retrospect, history nevertheless owes a debt to Schellenberg. It will be remembered that from the time the Prince of Wales first met Mrs Simpson there had been rumours that she had contacts with Nazi Germany and considerable anxiety that she might be a bad security risk. Secondly, because of his own indiscretions, in particular his visit to Germany in 1937, it was inevitable that speculation should arise as to the exact nature of the Duke's relationship with the Nazis. The whole of the communications between the Germans in Spain and Portugal and the Foreign Ministry tend to clear both the Duke and Duchess of any suspicion of previous close contacts with the Nazis (other than those already described) if only in a negative way. Indeed the Duchess's name is scarcely mentioned. Ribbentrop himself was conducting the correspondence from the Berlin end and Hitler was kept informed. It is quite incredible that if either the Duke or Duchess had had the smallest previous contact of an incriminating kind with anyone in their service, there should be no mention of it here. Now Schellenberg's activities, if his memoirs can be believed, were to provide more positive evidence.

Within two days I had drawn a close net of information round the Duke's residence. I had even managed to replace the Portuguese police guard with my own people. I was able to place informants among the servants, so that within five days I knew of every incident that took place in the house and every word spoken at the dinner-table. ...

Within six days I had a full picture: the Duke of Windsor no longer intended to accept the hunting invitation; he was most annoyed by the close surveillance of the British Secret Service; he did not like his appointment to Bermuda [*sic*] and would have much preferred to remain in Europe. But he obviously had no intention whatever of going to live either in a neutral or an enemy country. According to my reports the furthest he ever went in this direction was once to have said in his circle of Portuguese friends that he would rather live in any European country than go to Bermuda.[37]

On 30 July 1940 Schellenberg was responsible for the information that 'Today there arrived at the Duke's as announced the English Minister who calls himself Sir Walter Turner Monckstone, a lawyer from Kent. The Portuguese confidential agent assumes, as I do too, that a cover name is involved. It is possible that it concerns a member of the personal police of the reigning King by the name of Camerone.'[38] Walter Monckton had in fact arrived, sent by Churchill, as a final measure to get the distracting Windsors away to the Bahamas. In his account of this Walter Monckton says:

I got very worried by an effort made by the Falangists, no doubt under Axis influence. The Marqués de Estella [Miguel Primo de Rivera] a son of the old dictator, Primo de Rivera, flew over from Madrid to persuade the duke not to go to the Bahamas on the ground that he had information of a plot by the British Government to have him killed there.*

And he added the sentence already quoted: 'It sounds fantastic, but he managed to impress the Duke and Duchess.'[39]

From this it can be seen that Walter Monckton at least had no difficulty in recognizing the German interest and influence behind de Rivera's actions.

The Duke confided his fears to Monckton who, with his permission, discussed the matter with de Rivera. Monckton said that he could not without evidence endorse the decision that the Duke should not leave Lisbon but that if de Estella could produce evidence he was prepared to act on it. De Estella urged that if the Duke could be kept in Lisbon for ten days he would undertake to produce evidence. Monckton writes:

I told him that I could not do as he wished. The Duke would go by the American ship which was about to start next day, but I would stop him in Bermuda, if by the time he was due to leave that island evidence was forthcoming to justify such a step, and that I would fly back to Lisbon at a day's notice. This did not satisfy the Marques, but neither was the Duke satisfied until I had secured by telegram the attendance of a detective from Scotland Yard to accompany them and look after them.[40]

Lord Birkenhead commenting on this episode says that Monckton was much perplexed by the whole thing, agreeing with Sir Philip Game, the Commissioner of Police, that the only possible danger to the Duke was that the Germans might fake a 'British' attempt on the Duke's life, but that this danger could be met by sending a second detective to the Bahamas.

* Miguel Primo de Rivera was the second son of the old dictator and succeeded his brother Jose Antonio, founder of the Falange, as Marques de Estella in 1936 when the latter was shot by the Republicans. He was Spanish Ambassador to London from 1951 to 1957.

Monckton's biographer then goes on to say that he would have been even more astonished had he known what was really happening.

A plot to kidnap the Duke there certainly was, but it was a German and not a British one, and hallmarked at every point by the cosmic naivety of Nazi espionage. The remoteness of these people from any sense of reality, their incredible psychological miscalculations and puerile manœuvres – all were revealed when the captured German documents were published in 1957.[41]

All the same one cannot help wondering if it is true that Monckton was ignorant of everything that was going on except the attempt to persuade the Windsors that they were threatened by the British, because, if so, the Duke withheld a good deal of information from him.*

On the day after Monckton's arrival – 31 July – the confidential emissary Primo de Rivera reported that the Duke and Duchess were strongly impressed by the reports of English intrigues, no longer felt secure, and said they could not move a step without surveillance. Then he continues:

Yet the Duke declared he wanted to proceed to the Bahamas. No prospect of peace existed at the moment. Further statements of the Duke indicate that he has nevertheless already given consideration to the possibility that the role of an intermediary might fall to him. He declared that the situation in England at the moment was still by no means hopeless. Therefore, he should not now, by negotiations carried on contrary to the orders of his government, let loose against himself the propaganda of his English opponents, which might deprive him of all prestige at the period when he might possibly take action. He could, if the occasion arose, take action even from the Bahamas.

He says, too, that the Duke may be attempting to conceal from him the true date of his departure from Lisbon for the Bahamas and that in his opinion, once in the Bahamas, where the Duke would be in the power of the English government 'even if it should settle in Canada', the Duke would not be free to intervene.[42]

On receipt of this report Ribbentrop sent a long message to Huene in Portugal for strictly confidential transmission to the Duke. His message begins:

In connection with the report that the Duke of Windsor will depart for America tomorrow I request that you inform your Portuguese friend, with whom the Duke lives, for strictly confidential transmittal to the Duke the following:

Basically Germany wants peace with the English people. The Churchill clique stands in the way of this peace. Following the rejection of the Fuhrer's last appeal

---

* Monckton also withheld a good deal. His notes on the Abdication and its aftermath purport to be an account kept at the time for the benefit, it seems reasonable to assume, of future historians. But they regularly stop short of the more interesting facts and it is quite impossible to believe that in June 1940 a member of the government was sent to Lisbon either as a courtesy to the Duke of Windsor or with no particular reason beyond a general desire to speed him on his way.

to reason Germany is now determined to force England to make peace by every means of power. It would be a good thing if the Duke were to keep himself prepared for further developments. In such case Germany would be willing to co-operate most closely with the Duke and to clear the way for any desire expressed by the Duke and Duchess. The direction in which these wishes tend is quite obvious and meets with our complete understanding. Should the Duke and Duchess have other intentions, but be ready to collaborate in the establishment of a good relationship between Germany and England for the future, Germany is likewise prepared to co-operate with the Duke to arrange the future of the Ducal couple in accordance with their wishes.

Ribbentrop goes on to say that the most earnest attempts must be made to prevent the Duke's departure since 'we are convinced that the Duke will be so under surveillance there that he will never again have the chance to come to Europe, even by airplane, as he mentioned to the Portuguese confidant'. But, he adds, should he persist in going, the Portuguese confidant might still remain in contact with him and arrange some way to transmit communications verbally, whereby we can continue beyond this present contact and, if occasion arises, negotiate.[43]

However, all contacts report that the Duke is completely under the influence of Sir Walter Monckton and on 2 August Huene reports his departure for the Bahamas. Nevertheless, in this telegram Huene reports:

In accordance with the telegraphic instruction which arrived shortly before midnight, I immediately got in touch with our confidant the Duke's host, the banker Ricardo Espirito Santo Silva, who happened to be at the Ducal couple's farewell reception at a hotel here. After the end of this affair he visited me at my residence, where we discussed thoroughly possible further courses of action. I would note at this point that the person concerned is an unobjectionable individual, who has never denied his friendly attitude toward Germany. . . .

After referring to the influence of Walter Monckton, Huene goes on:

On the other hand the message which was conveyed to the Duke made the deepest impression on him and he felt appreciative of the considerate way in which his personal interests were being taken into account. In his reply which was given orally to the confidant, the Duke paid tribute to the Fuhrer's desire for peace, which was in complete agreement with his own point of view. He was firmly convinced that if he had been King it would never have come to war. To the appeal made to him to co-operate at a suitable time in the establishment of peace, he agreed gladly. However, he requested that it be understood that at the present time he must follow the official orders of his government. Disobedience would disclose his intentions prematurely, bring about a scandal, and deprive him of his prestige in England. He was also convinced that the present moment was too early for him to come forward, since there was as yet no inclination in England for an approach to Germany. However, as soon as this frame of mind changed he would be ready to return immediately. To bring this about there were two possibilities. Either England would yet call upon him, which he considered to be entirely possible, or Germany would express the desire to negotiate with him. In both cases he was prepared for any personal sacrifice and would make himself available without the slightest personal ambition. He would remain in continuing communication with his previous host and had agreed with him upon a code word, upon receiving which he would immediately come back over. He insisted that this would be possible at any time, since he had foreseen all eventualities and had already initiated the necessary arrangements.

According to this informant the Duke's statements were supported by firmness of will and included an expression of admiration and sympathy for the Fuhrer.[44]

On the following day, 3 August, Stohrer, the German Ambassador to Madrid, sent a telegram to the Foreign Ministry as follows:

For the Foreign Minister.
The Spanish Minister of the Interior just informed me that his confidential emissary had just telephoned to him from Lisbon, using phraseology which had been agreed upon, that on the day of their departure he had spent a considerable time with the Duke and Duchess. The Duke had hesitated even up to the last moment. The ship had had to delay its departure on that account. The influence of the legal adviser of the Duke, Sir Walter Turner Monckton, was again successful, however, in bringing him around to leave. The confidential emissary added that the Duke had clearly perceived that it would have been better to have remained here so as to be able to step in at the decisive moment. The Duke believed, however, that it might be possible for him to do this from the Bahamas. For this purpose an arrangement was reached concerning which the confidential agent did not wish to say anything over the telephone.[45]

So the Duke and Duchess sailed to the Bahamas and the German plot failed. There is, however, one more document concerning the Duke on the captured files of the German Foreign Ministry. On 15 August, two weeks after he had departed from Lisbon and after all the reports of failure had been sent in, Huene wired Berlin as follows:

The confidant has just received a telegram from the Duke from Bermuda, asking him to send a communication as soon as action was advisable. Should any answer be made?[46]

No answer to this telegram was found in the captured documents. By the middle of August Hitler had at last realized that the British would not capitulate. He no longer sought a King or a Gauleiter, and the long struggle to conquer her by force had begun.

The telegram is, however, the crux of the matter. Up to that point the evidence that the Duke ever contemplated succumbing to German persuasion is very slim. There is evidence, and surely it must be regarded as very strong, that in talking to neutrals, both friendly to Britain and hostile, he voiced opinions which would have been found unforgivable in England, while he continued to have dealings with the known leader of the

Falangist (Fascist) Party even after Primo de Rivera had made suggestions to him that could have been inspired only by the Germans.* In addition, he accepted the good offices of the German Embassy in allowing his wife's maid to travel to Paris.† But that is all.

Even if one selects only the most incriminating parts of the German reports, it is still clear that, although the responses he gave under pressure in Lisbon could have been those of a man who seriously considered these things, they are equally consistent with nervous evasion. We know from Walter Monckton that the Duke had lost any certainty as to who were his friends and was half prepared to believe in a plot against him by the British. Yet no one, reading his correspondence with the Prime Minister and Lord Lloyd on the subjects of his soldier servant and his desire to visit America, could believe that at this juncture he was chiefly or largely pre-occupied with the possibilities suggested to him by the emissaries of the Germans, and the evidence is very strong that his main concern was his negotiations with Britain.

The telegram is a different matter. Its meaning seems plain. It makes no commitment but it opens, or re-opens, the lines of communication with the enemies of Great Britain.

It may be argued that the authorship is in doubt. There seem to be only three possibilities: The first, that for some reason unknown and not now very obvious, Espirito Santo decided two weeks after the whole matter was closed to re-open it by means of a forged telegram: The second, that the German Minister, Huene, decided to do this: The third, that the Duke of Windsor sent it.

Few people will believe in either of the first two when it is so much more likely that on the sea voyage to Bermuda, having completely failed to get recognition for himself or his wife, having received an appointment which he regarded as petty and provincial, holding an entirely false idea of his own capacities and the genuine opinion that British policies were mistaken, the Duke became persuaded that he had too precipitately refused an opportunity to serve his country. If this view is accepted, however, it means that it must also be accepted that he decided to re-open the door by sending a telegram to a man who, when he had last seen him, had delivered a message direct from Ribbentrop – a message which even to someone of the Duke's

---

* Primo de Rivera is not regarded as a reliable witness but he could have fabricated only the Duke's replies. In the suggestions he made to the Duke which elicited these replies he was following German instructions.

† This last is incontrovertible and is discussed in the Foreign Office document FO 371.24265 4612 of 23 October 1940. The fact that when the maid reached Spain on her return journey the Duke of Windsor applied for assistance to the US authorities (who passed the message on) is discussed with some asperity as follows: 'The next step (if any) appeared to be with HRH who had carefully refrained, apparently, from approaching either Sir W. Selby or Sir S. Hoare. I was reluctant to place on the shoulders of overworked Madrid & Lisbon the search after an (at present) nameless Frenchwoman particularly when the persons principally interested had not asked for this to be done.'

limited understanding must surely have been seen to have the most sinister implications.

In the calmer atmosphere of today no one would attribute actual guilt in the sense of deliberate treachery to the Duke, but comparative guilt is easier to estimate, and there is no doubt that his actions would have earned fierce reprisals in the atmosphere of, for instance, the French Resistance.

All one can do is to repeat that he held strong opinions about the war, never changed them, never saw any reason to disguise them. Further confirmation that he kept in touch with Espirito Santo Silva is found in a telegram sent 5 August 1941, a year later, from Hoynegen Huene at the German Legation in Lisbon to the Foreign Office in Berlin, which reads:

The intermediary familiar to us from the reports at the time has received a letter from the Duke of Windsor confirming his opinion as recently stated in a published interview that Britain has virtually lost the war already and the USA would be better advised to promote peace, not war.[47]

And, in case it is thought that the Minister to Lisbon had nothing better to do in August 1941 than invent messages from the Duke of Windsor, here is an account written by Sir John Balfour of an incident which occurred during the Duke's stay in Washington in 1945.

On the third evening of his stay the Duke asked us to invite to dinner an elderly American friend of his – a railroad tycoon named Young. Both of them seemed oblivious to Nazi misdeeds and were at one in thinking that, had Hitler been differently handled, war with Germany might have been avoided in 1939.[48]

31

THE BAHAMAS

As the Duke and Duchess sailed to Bermuda, their spirits, which had for a long time been sustained by the fight for what they regarded as their rights, gradually fell. They were appalled by their treatment by the British, which seemed to them ignoble in its rejection of the Duke's special qualifications to serve his country and spiteful in the continual difficulties over small issues of a personal kind. They believed they could expect nothing but petty thwarts so long as they were at the mercy of officialdom and that they could not escape this for the duration of the war. Above all they were heartbroken to find themselves heading for exile in a group of small islands where, except during the winter holiday season, the heat was unbearable and the society provincial. Winston Churchill had sent a personal letter to the Duke by Walter Monckton in which he had set out to persuade him that, if he made a success of governing the Bahamas, this would go a long way to improving his relationship with his countrymen, in effect towards working his passage home.* But the Duke must have been aware, if only in some remote area of his consciousness, that some of the warmth had gone even from his friendship with his erstwhile champion. (Some time in the summer of 1940 Winston Churchill discussed the Ducal couple with Lord Baldwin, probably at breakfast. At this meeting he admitted to Baldwin that he had been wrong about the Abdication and said that the prospect of Mrs Simpson being Queen 'was an eventuality too horrible to contemplate'.)[1] Lord Beaverbrook also says that in a conversation with Winston Churchill the two of them had agreed that, since they always differed about everything, one of them must always have been right. 'Except once,' Lord Beaverbrook said, and mentioned the Abdication. 'Perhaps we were both wrong that time,' Churchill replied.[2]

Only one thought comforted the Duke. He believed that the wife of the

* Conversation with Sylvester Gates.

Governor of a British Colony had a settled status with which no one could interfere.

On their arrival in Bermuda a young naval lieutenant was detailed to look after the Windsors. He lived in the same house with them for a week, accompanied them wherever they went and arranged their public appearances. He wrote a very lively account of their visit from which it is plain that, whatever their private feelings or their personal shortcomings, they had no difficulty in charming those who came in their path. The young lieutenant fell mildly in love with them.

Before they arrived on the island a telegram had been received from the Secretary of State for the Colonies, Lord Lloyd, explaining how they were to be treated. The Duchess, he said, was to be addressed as Your Grace and was not entitled to any form of curtsy. The watchful Duke immediately corrected this, insisting that his wife should be addressed as 'Duchess'.* He asked whether the Governor had sent for instructions as to their treatment and seemed relieved to find they had been sent unsolicited. 'I don't know,' he said, 'whether we will be able to stick it down in Nassau if this sort of thing is going on all the time.'

The young lieutenant left an impression of the Duchess as she seemed to him at the time. Having explained that the Governor's wife endured the usual embarrassment of feeling unable to curtsy to the Duchess even though aware that it would make the Duke happy if she did, he goes on:

She [the Duchess] appears to be oblivious of all this, for she is a very clever woman &, like all clever women, contrives to hide her real feelings behind what is in her case a highly polished exterior. I have never known a woman to have so much of what the French would call 'le style'. She is not extrinsically beautiful or handsome, but she has a good complexion, regular features & a beautiful figure, for him who likes very small waists. To her, herself, though, & not to nature, goes the palm for her appearance, for it is an article whose beauty has been fashioned by human and not divine hands which confronts us. She is, of course, beautifully dressed – and this does not mean just extravagantly dressed – with a canny sense of fitness, with knowledge of how to avoid the bizarre but strike the original. The coiffure is superb and judging from the number of times she summoned the hairdresser to the house, must – and quite rightly so – be her chief pride. ... She has good legs and ankles and she moves well – not self-consciously, but with obvious attention to appearance. More than all the charm of her physical appearance, though, is her manner: she has, to an infinite degree that great gift, of making you feel that you are the very person she has been waiting all her life to meet. With old & young & clever & stupid alike she exercises this charm, and

* The whole question of how the Duke and Duchess of Windsor were addressed and spoke of each other seems subject to no ordinary rules of etiquette. In England a Duchess who is not also a Royal Highness is addressed as Your Grace only by servants, tradesmen and so on. In the same way a Duke speaking of his wife to people he treats as friends or equals says 'my wife' or uses a christian name. Even the Queen almost invariably speaks of 'my husband'. The Windsors always spoke of each other even to their friends as 'the Duke' and 'the Duchess'. Many English people resented this or found it 'non-U'.

during the week she was here, I never saw anyone who could resist the spell –
they were all delighted & intrigued. ... Without resorting to humbug or flattery,
the Duchess manages to present the same charming exterior to all, the same
attentiveness to listen readily, the same power to converse well and amusingly.
... She does not talk much unless she sees you want to talk & she is always quiet
& dignified & composed. ... She is never anything but stately, &, when she had
to wave to the crowds on her arrival & subsequently whenever we drove
through the town, she did it with an ease and charm and grace which suggested
she had been at it all her life.

The Duke, this young man tells us, was more in love with the Duchess
than the Duchess with him. Hers was a watchful and maternal devotion
and she seemed to have done much to improve the Duke since he married
her.

His famous unpunctuality, though obviously habitual and so never to be completely eradicated, has clearly been lessened by her presence. Each night before
they went to bed she would ask me what the programme for the morning was
and what time he had to be ready for his first engagement – 'For I am the alarm
clock in this family,' she would say. She is the only person who can make him
conscious of time, and she exercises over him a control of which he is well
aware. One afternoon he set out to play golf immediately after lunch, having
arranged to meet the Duchess in the town at half-past four; he had always been
late getting back from the previous golfing expeditions, dawdling on the course,
practising the same stroke over and over again, stopping on the greens to practise
his putting. Now however it was a different thing; he drove off the first tee,
positively ran up the fairway after his ball, hit it a second time, ran after it again,
and so on all the way round eighteen holes. I did not go round with him that day
but George Wood, his ADC who did, told me that he had never known what
real exhaustion was until that afternoon. ... The Duke is conscious of the fact
that she [the Duchess] rules his movements: during the course of a shopping
tour one morning the Duke inspected some bathing trunks and eventually
selected a pair saying that he had better have some of these. 'It's I who wear the
shorts in this family, you know.'

If the Duchess's love for the Duke took a maternal form, this account
goes on, his for her was just an example of adoration, pure and simple.

Directly she comes into a room where he is he has eyes for no one save her,
and when she leaves the table after dinner, he crosses over to her to have a last
word with her before she is engulfed in the femininities of the drawing-room.
... No plan could ever be made without the approval of the Duchess, for the
scheme that did not suit her automatically ceased to exist. Her advice was asked
on every point and not even a handkerchief could be bought without her help.
... He has practically renounced the claim of a will of his own where she is concerned and actually enjoys letting himself be managed by her. One night after
dinner when she was involved in a bridge four, he was sitting talking in the
drawing-room; before she had begun her bridge she had told him that he must
not sit about but must go upstairs and work on the inaugural speech that he

would have to make on his arrival at Nassau. The prospect of going off to work at ten o'clock however was too much for him and so he remained in the drawing-room indulging his favourite pastime of talking ceaselessly. Presently she held a dummy hand and appeared at the drawing-room door with a reproachful look on her face. 'Now, David, what about all that work?' 'All right, darling. I'm just going up now.' And the Duchess returned to the bridge table. Of course, the Duke did not go up and it was not until nearly twelve o'clock that he eventually said good-night. As he walked up the stairs he looked across to the bridge table on the other side of the hall, and said, perhaps a little guiltily 'Now you see, darling, I'm going to attend to my speech.' His wife made no reply, but just looked at him & her expression by no means signified divine content; she looked like a Nanny whose charge had forgotten the precepts she had taught him & had grieved rather than annoyed her.

The Duke and Duchess landed at Nassau on 17 August, in a heat which caused the Duke, dressed in heavy khaki, to sweat so much that he found it almost impossible to put his signature to the oaths of allegiance and office. They were then conducted to Government House, only recently vacated by Sir Charles Dundas,* the previous Governor, which, in spite of being full of bright tropical flowers, was immediately revealed as not up to any standard of comfort to which they were accustomed. On 24 August cables between London and the Duke once more began. The first in the series was incompletely deciphered and the words in square brackets represent what seems to be the sense of the missing words.

Many thanks for your message of welcome and good wishes on my arrival in the Bahamas. The Duchess and I have been most cordially welcomed here and we look forward to helping BAHAMIANS in their various problems and industries. A venomous departmental situation has arisen [with regard to] Government House. [Owing to the necessity to] arrive so soon after the departure of my predecessor the considerable repairs and necessary alteration [for which the] money has already been voted have not been begun. These are essential as it is impossible to occupy Government House in its present condition and it will take at least two months to make it habitable. I shall therefore have to rent another house but as there can be no official entertaining during that period and the heat is now intense I propose with your concurrence to take advantage of the hot weather season and go to my Ranch in Canada which I shall any way have to visit for business purposes sooner or later. I would appreciate an early reply to this suggestion which will be of great help and convenience to me.[3]

To which on 24 August Lord Lloyd replied:

I was delighted to learn of the loyalty and cordiality of the welcome extended to Your Royal Highness and the Duchess on arrival in the Bahamas.

I see great difficulty in Your Royal Highness's proposal to leave your post so soon after you have assumed office. Such a step would be so unusual that it would not only inevitably create a sense of disappointment but also possibly some misgiving and anxiety amongst the public as well. There is of course no reason why,

---

* Sir Charles left unwillingly in order to make a place for the Duke of Windsor.

if the Duchess feels the heat, she should not go away for a few weeks, but I hope I may persuade Your Royal Highness to abandon your project of leaving the Colony at any rate for three or four months.[4]

And on 31 August Lord Lothian was informed of this exchange in a telegram from the Foreign Office which ended: 'As Colonial Office have heard no more from His Royal Highness they hope he has accepted decision.'[5]

The Legislative Assembly had in fact voted the sum of £1,500 to be spent on repairs and decoration for Government House, and while these were being carried out the Duke and Duchess were lent a house first by Mr and Mrs Frederick Sigrist and then by Sir Harry and Lady Oakes. The Duchess of Windsor brought an interior decorator over from New York to carry out the alterations and improvements to Government House which was brought up to the standard the Duchess thought necessary. In her account of this period of her life she says that the Duke paid for the decorations, but even so the bill finally rendered to the Legislation was for about £5,000.

The Windsors have to be judged on their record in Nassau because on this they must rest all their claims to a job of world importance, many of their complaints against the Royal Family and the governments of England, the belief that they were treated with spite and jealousy because of his superior gifts and the grievance that his years of training were thrown away.

They seem usually to have given a favourable impression to guests at Government House where the Duchess's talent for entertaining was given full play and travelling Englishmen brought home reports that they were doing well. Sir John Balfour says that Brigadier Daly who visited Nassau as Inspector for the War Office of war-time defence arrangements in British Atlantic possessions told him that he had found the Duke of Windsor to be the most capable of the various Colonial Governors he visited.[6]

They worked hard and in some respects successfully. When they first arrived their presence gave an enormous fillip to the tourist trade on which the island economy depended, and when, as a result of America's entry into the war, this fell off completely the Duke sponsored schemes to replace it. He attempted, quite properly, to boost agricultural production in preparation for a food crisis, although for reasons he could not have foreseen this did not materialize; and the Economic Committee which he formed and chaired continued as the Out Island and Economic Committee presided over by the Governor until the colony achieved independence. He founded an Infant Welfare Clinic which was badly needed. The Duchess also worked hard, as President of the Red Cross, honorary President of the local branch of the Daughters of the British Empire and later in running a canteen for American servicemen.

For the rest there may be room for differences of opinion. They were popular in all those areas where their charm and hospitality operated, but it is unarguable that they gave great offence and made many enemies, while the Duke continually showed the almost unbelievable lack of judgment which had been a characteristic of his career since the Abdication. Like a games player who on an off day finds the ball running for his opponent, he seemed also to attract bad luck. He had neither the training nor any understanding of the discipline required of His Majesty's representatives in the Colonies. One of the small complaints made against him was that whereas other Governors had made it a duty to patronize 'any attempt at art' such as concerts, picture exhibitions and so on, he resolutely absented himself from this kind of thing, which bored him, while he was seen to raise his opera glasses from the front row of seats when a strip-tease act was performed.

The Duchess was the more unpopular. Her pre-occupation with her appearance, her jewellery and her clothes was unsuitable to the role of Governor's wife on a small group of islands. It may or may not be true that she visited Miami every week to have her hair done, or that while she was in Nassau her purchases from New York averaged a hundred dresses a year at an average of $250 a dress, but these things were said in the American Press and were generally believed. Worse than this she was known to lament the fate that brought her to Nassau. The historian of the Bahamas writes:

> The Duchess of Windsor has written of the sojourn in Nassau of the Duke and herself as an involuntary and somewhat distasteful exile – and in personal correspondence has even spoken in terms of Elba and St Helena. This attitude, as can be imagined, was not well received in Nassau. ... The Duke remained much more popular than his sometimes outspoken wife throughout their stay, and undoubtedly worked his hardest at the unexpected and unfamiliar role.

But the writer adds:

> Paradoxically, however, the post unprotected by Ministers of the Crown, proved to be beset by more pitfalls than the occupation of the English throne.[7]

The Duke was regarded as in many ways a likeable man, although lacking judgment and tact. He began by quarrelling with one of the most powerful men on the island, and since Sir Etienne Dupuch is the source of much of the criticism of the Duke's conduct as Governor, something must be said about him. The proprietor and editor of one of the two daily newspapers, *The Tribune*, he is a man of very high principles and, although he is not a radical, during the whole of his youth was in rebellion against the rather corrupt establishment which ran the islands. It was a matter of honour with him to expose scandals and to champion the underdog and he said what he believed to be true in *The Tribune* at any cost to himself. He was a first-class newspaper man and, in addition to his work on *The Tribune*, he was the correspondent for Bahamian affairs to the Associated Press in Miami. He is immensely opinionated, but Major Gray Phillips used a phrase in speaking about him almost identical with one Dupuch used in speaking of Phillips. Both said: 'I thought him a straight man.'* Etienne Dupuch is a great patriot and in recognition of his services to the Bahama Islands and to the War Materials Committee during the war he received the OBE in 1949 and a knighthood in 1965.†

This was the man with whom the Duke chose to engage in a running battle almost throughout his stay in the islands. The two men were not well met because the Duke had an almost pathological dislike of the Press, while Dupuch was inclined to be touchy in guarding its liberties. The Duke began by sending for Dupuch and explaining to him that in England it was not usual for the Press to criticize members of the Royal Family – to receive the reply that he was criticized not as a member of the Royal Family but as Governor of the Colony. Dupuch also accuses the Duke of abusing his powers to censor the Press for absurdly trivial reasons. Thus in 1942 he banned the Press from a memorial service held for the Duke of Kent on the grounds of security – giving the explanation that large crowds and great publicity might attract enemy bombers. Writing of this incident Dupuch asks the question 'How?' since the nearest enemy bomber was probably 3,000 miles away. The Duke also made an unsuccessful, and in his position unsuitable, attempt to get Dupuch relieved of his job as correspondent to the Associated Press in Miami.

But these were comparatively small matters. Both in conversation and in his account of the Duke of Windsor's term in the Bahamas in *Tribune Story*, Dupuch is careful to declare an interest – he did not like the Duke. He disapproved in the first place of the Abdication but he could not forgive the fact that the Duke made no secret of strong prejudices in the matter of colour. In an island where almost the entire population except American visitors and settlers was of mixed race, the Governor invariably and openly assumed the natural superiority of the whites. Dupuch is the chief witness to the bad effects of this prejudice but there is an important and impartial witness to the fact of it. Lord Mountbatten, on his return from a visit to the Bahamas, asked the Duke of Windsor if the stories circulating there that in his day coloured men were not permitted to enter through the front door were true. The Duke freely admitted it and said that it was important for the successful administration of government that coloured people should be kept in their right place when visiting Government House.

* Conversation with the author.

† In 1965 Lord Mountbatten wrote to him: 'Of the many workers for the good of the Commonwealth, few have done so much to promote this idea as you, and few could have earned a knighthood better.'[8] In 1963 Sir Etienne received an award from the Royal Society of Arts for contributions to journalism in the Commonwealth; in 1956 the Mergenthaler award from the Inter-American Press Association for breaking down racial discrimination in the Bahamas; and in 1966 a citation from the Associated Press Managing Editors' Association.

Difficulties of a serious kind arose when the American government began to build airfields on the island (although this solved the economic crisis) because of the difference in the rates paid to the American and Bahamian labour. In these circumstances it was decided that a Liaison Officer should be attached to the American contractors to deal with the Bahamians. There was an obvious candidate for the job, a man named Harry Glinton, the largest building contractor on the islands, who was known and used by London firms seeking valuations. His name was at once proposed. Here is Etienne Dupuch's account of what happened next.

' "We can't have a coloured man for this job," the Duke declared without hesitation. "We must have a white man." All the members of the committee looked in my direction but the Duke seemed completely oblivious to his indiscretion. The job was given to Mr Karl Claridge, and soon after this Nassau had its first riot.'[9]

In the riots in Nassau thousands of angry men descended on Bay Street and broke windows and looted shops. The Company of Cameron Highlanders then in the garrison was called out, the Riot Act read and martial law declared. The dispersal of the crowds and the maintenance of order over the next two days resulted in two deaths and twenty-five people injured. Subdued but sullen the men returned to work and two weeks later their pay was raised by five shillings a day. As Governor, the Duke of Windsor was officially responsible for these things. Unofficially he was blamed, because it was believed that if Harry Glinton had been in contact with the men, it would not have come to rioting. And once more he exacerbated independent opinion by imposing a censorship on the news of these riots, so that it did not reach the outside world for many years. It was characteristic however that he won back a good deal of lost prestige because when a fire broke out a few days after the rioting he worked 'like a slave in a chain to empty the shelves of the Island Shop'.[10]

He learned nothing from these events, however, and continued to show an equal lack of judgment or even ordinary courtesy in the matter of colour. A shortage of water had occurred as a result of the extra wartime population and the Economic Committee wished to build water catchments at Oakes Field. Etienne Dupuch ran into a man who was a highly qualified water engineer by chance and made an appointment with the Governor to tell him this.

I was so pleased with my find that, when I saw the Duke, instead of going right to the point I tried to play cute. 'I have just the man to build the water catchments for the Committee,' I said beamingly. 'We can't have a coloured man to do this work,' the Duke declared, without waiting to hear anything further from me. 'It is not a coloured man,' I said. 'Then we can't have a Bahamian white man,' he declared, once more jumping to conclusions without stopping to think. 'No Bahamian white man would be qualified.' 'It is not a coloured man, nor is it a Bahamian white man, it is a highly qualified Scotsman,' I said, laying the engineer's card on the table before me. 'Oh! that's different,' he said looking at the card.

But he must have seen by the expression on my face that the matter was closed as far as I was concerned. I took up the card, bade him good day without further comment, and left the office. When the engineer came to see me I told him I was sorry he could not help.[11]

The most sensational and also the silliest mistake the Duke made however was in connection with the trial for the murder of Sir Harry Oakes.

Sir Harry Oakes was an immensely rich, tough and overbearing man who had succeeded, after fourteen years of unsuccessful prospecting, in finding the second richest gold mine in the western hemisphere. In the 1930s he met a man called Harold Christie, a pioneer of land development in the Bahamas, and in 1934, resenting the tax he had to pay in Canada (born American he had become a Canadian citizen in 1924) he transferred his enormous fortune to the Bahamas. He also bought a house in London and Tottingworth Park in Sussex, and became a baronet in 1939 after giving large sums to charity, including £50,000 to St George's Hospital. It was he who lent a house, Westbourne, to the Windsors while they were waiting for Government House, and it was in this house that he was murdered in the early morning of 8 July 1943. He was found by his friend Harold Christie who had spent the night in the house, with four deep holes in his head which might have been made by a four-pronged instrument, while an attempt had been made to burn his body by setting light to a petroleum-based liquid which had been poured on to the bed. Areas of blistering indicated that some of the burning had taken place while Sir Harry was still alive.

The Governor was informed immediately of what had happened and he reacted to the news by applying his power of censorship to all news leaving the islands. He was already too late because Oakes had invited the Press to accompany himself and Christie on a visit to his sheep farms on the morning of the murder, and Etienne Dupuch, arriving before the heat of the day, had been told the news and cabled it to Press agencies all round the world. People leaving the islands by aeroplane also carried the news to Miami.

For several days the censorship remained, however, and on 9 July *The Tribune* reproduced an article from *The Miami Herald* by Jeanne Bellamy, introducing it with the words: 'Our readers will be interested to learn from American sources some of the facts they could not learn from sources in Nassau – as well as some of the incorrect reports that could have been avoided by prudent handling of the situation.' Miss Bellamy had been sent to Nassau because London newspapers, unable to get news directly, were telephoning to the news services in the US to inquire about the censorship. The *Daily Express* sent a telegram to *The Tribune* saying 'Puzzled your statement censorship operating Oakes case. Explain why in purely civil case.'[12]

One of the facts that Miss Bellamy revealed was that two Miami police officers specializing in homicides had been called to Nassau. In the ordinary course of events the Governor of the Islands would have been expected to make one of three decisions. He could have relied on the local police forces to investigate the murder: he could have called in the services of the CID: and it seems to have been generally accepted that he might also have requested the help of the FBI. The Duke of Windsor did none of these things. Instead he asked for the help of two detectives who had been assigned to look after him on his trips to Miami. Captain E.W.Melchen, homicide investigator, and Captain James Barker, identification expert of the Miami police force, arrived in Nassau on the day after the murder.

The next day Alfred de Marigny, son-in-law of the dead man, and a titular French Count, born in Mauritius, was arrested and charged with the murder of his father-in-law. Sir Harry Oakes had quarrelled with his son-in-law because he had married Nancy Oakes when she was seventeen without the permission or knowledge of her parents, secondly because she had become pregnant while still ill from the after-effects of typhoid fever, thirdly because he was a bad-tempered and autocratic man.

The murder trial lasted for months and a great many witnesses were called both by the prosecution and the defence but the only really telling evidence against de Marigny was circumstantial, and rested on a finger-print put in evidence by Captain Barker. This purported to have been 'lifted' from a screen in the room where the body had been found (in which, owing to his quarrel with his father-in-law, de Marigny had no legitimate business). It was three months before the Counsel for the Defence cross-examined Captain Barker but, when he did so, he virtually forced the admission that the finger-print was a forgery. The procedure of lifting rather than photographing the print *in situ* was in itself unsatisfactory and difficult to explain, and, although the lift was supposed to have come from a part of the screen which had a strong background pattern, yet the print did not show it. The defence questioned Barker for a long time, attacking the same point from different angles. Here is an example of the cross-examination.

Q. Don't you think it's a coincidence that you can find no lifted area corresponding to that print?
A. No.
Q. You say you cut down the rubber lift after you lifted the print?
A. Yes.
Q. Why did you cut it down?
A. Because it was long.
Q. But had you not cut it wouldn't it have shown background?
A. No, not necessarily.
Q. What size was it before you cut it down?

A. About 1 × 3 inches.

Q. And it would have lifted an area, 1 × 3, including the scroll pattern?

A. If all this area were powdered.

Q. And wouldn't a 1 × 3 lift show background no matter where you got it from in that portion of the screen?

A. Not necessarily.

Counsel: Show me where it would have come from.

(A piece of paper 1 × 3 was cut and Captain Barker was asked to place it on the screen without it touching any of the surrounding scroll pattern.)

Captain Barker tried it and said it could not be done without a portion of the lift being extended beyond the panel.

Q. Wouldn't it have been much simpler to have extended your tape and lifted part of the background?

Chief Justice: What Mr Higgs wants to know is why you were so careful to exclude any of the background?

A. I did not attach any importance to it at the time.[13]

In his speech for the defence Godfrey Higgs, KC, the Defence Counsel, claimed that the finger-print did not come from the screen. 'If they accepted the evidence of Mr Conway,' he said, and Mr Conway was a Prosecution Witness, 'the lift would have to be obtained from one of four areas – and the Defence claimed that it was impossible to have obtained that lift from any one of those areas. None of the scroll work appeared on the lift. Captain Barker attempted to fit a piece of paper the size of his lift into one of those areas and failed in each instance. He finally did it but only by allowing some of the lift to overhang – and then he had to be very careful to omit the scroll.'[14]

The jury returned a verdict of Not Guilty by nine to three, but added a rider recommending that de Marigny should be deported as they considered him undesirable. This recommendation was beyond their jurisdiction but nevertheless carried out.

Captain Melchen seems to have been an ordinarily competent police officer but Captain Barker, chosen by the Duke of Windsor in preference to the local police forces, became a narcotics addict and died by the hand of his own son in a death ruled 'justifiable homicide' by the sheriff's office.

The significance of the Duke's intervention was twofold. In the first place de Marigny was on trial for his life for nearly four months before being acquitted, and in the second no attempt was made to apprehend the real murderer. Ever since there have been rumours to the effect that the murderer was known to the local population, and Colonel Lindopp, the Commissioner of Police, went so far as to tell Etienne Dupuch that he had reason to believe he could have solved the case if it had been left to him.[15]

In 1972 in a book called King's X, an American named Marshall Houts advanced the theory that Sir Harry Oakes was murdered by a lieutenant of the US gangster, Meyer Lansky's, after a row about a gambling concession to which the Duke (once more a sucker) was party. It was for this reason, according to Houts, that the Duke, 'pathetically terrorized', immediately imposed a censorship on hearing of Oakes's death.[16]

Houts relies entirely on 'an informant' and nothing he says can be checked. The Duke might well have agreed to the gambling concession but if it is a question of whether he imposed a censorship on the news because he was in some way implicated and was 'pathetically terrorized', or for no good or easily understandable reason, the whole of his career suggests that the latter is if anything more likely. He was not easily terrorized but held obstinately to the virtue of his own opinions and actions. If he had been aware that he had something to hide, he would not necessarily have hidden it, and it seems far more probable that he imposed the censorship because of a senseless and almost pathological dislike of the Press, and sent for Melchen and Barker on a general assumption, not the least uncommon to people of high birth or great wealth, that anyone known to him must be superior to the staffs of public services.

By 1944 the American troops training in the Bahamas had left and the centre of war had moved further away from the islands. The Duke of Windsor, satisfied in his own mind that he had made a success of his job and had done so willingly and uncomplainingly, felt that the time had come to draw the attention of the British government to his desire to work in a more important sphere and nearer the theatres of war. He wrote to his friends in England, among them Winston Churchill. In reply he received the offer of the Governorship of Bermuda or, as he saw it, the exchange of one military backwater for another. In her account of this event, the Duchess of Windsor makes it clear that she and her husband believed that even the all-powerful Prime Minister could not overcome the undiminished bitterness of his own family.

'It was clear now beyond all question that David's family were determined to keep him relegated to the farthermost marches of the Empire.'[17]

At about the same time she received another rebuff which must have done much to strengthen her convictions, and although this was in a purely private and family manner, one need not fear to discuss it because the Duchess herself has taken the public into her confidence. The Bishop of Nassau, the Right Reverend John Daughlish, was leaving for England, and, feeling certain that he would be received by Queen Mary, her daughter-in-law decided to send with him a letter telling the Queen of her sorrow that she should be the cause of the separation between Mother and Son and informing her that the Bishop could, if Her Majesty would allow him, give her personal news of the Duke. The letter was entirely modest and the Duchess asked nothing for herself, although she did remark that in her opinion the horrors of war and endless separations of families had stressed the importance of family ties. Presently the Bishop let the Duchess know that he had received an audience and delivered her letter. The only other mention ever made of it was in one sentence the Queen wrote in a letter to her son some weeks later. 'I send a kind message to your wife.'[18]

In all circumstances one cannot hold it very much against the Windsors that, some months before his term as Governor of the Bahamas had ended, he resigned his job and made plans to leave the islands. His last act as a public figure was as characteristic as Etienne Dupuch's response was predictable. He had arranged to go by boat to Miami but he imposed an embargo on 'War Security' grounds on all news about his movements. Dupuch, finding that he could not inform the Associated Press of the Windsors' arrival by boat, sent a telegram which passed the censor and which read: 'In reply to your query, the Duke and Duchess of Windsor will not be arriving by plane in Miami at 10 o'clock tomorrow.'[19] Since no query had been made, the message was understood, and, when the Duke and Duchess arrived by boat, the Press was there in force to meet them.

32

THE EXILE

The Duke of Windsor tendered his resignation as Governor of the Bahamas on 16 March 1945, rather before the end of the war and five months before his term was up. His resignation took effect at the end of April. He was unable to cross the Atlantic until September because of the shipping difficulties created by the continuing war in the Pacific, and he spent the summer in America. The Duke and Duchess had visited the USA regularly during their years in the Bahamas, had many friends there and were received with honour. On this visit as on earlier ones they were popular with crowds and an object of the attention of newspapermen, while, during the summer, a luncheon was given in their honour in Washington and the Duke was received by President Truman.

Then in September they returned to Paris travelling on the United States troopship, *Argentina*, which called at Plymouth on its way to Le Havre. British newspapermen who went on board to interview the Duke received answers to their questions. Would HRH, they wished to know, like eventually to live in England. 'Yes, very much.' Was there any reason why he should not do so? 'None at all. I should of course take a job.' Had he any particular job in mind? 'Several. I have always led an active life and, although I have passed the half century I believe I could still be useful.'[1]

In Paris the Windsors had been fortunate. Their house in the Boulevard Suchet had been undisturbed during the war, all their possessions were unharmed, and their caretaker even informed them that, when a pair of boots belonging to Major Gray Phillips had been taken, he had complained to the *Kommandantur* who had had them returned with apologies. At La Croë they were slightly less fortunate, although even here the Italians had quartered their troops in the garage, and only the curtains and some oil paintings had been taken. German landmines were thickly strewn along the coast and in the garden of La Croë, however, and it was not until the following spring that the house could be re-occupied. The Windsors had an option to buy the lease of their Paris house if the owner decided to sell, but they had had to make up their minds about this while they were still in Nassau. Uncertain of the future of Paris and also, one supposes, of their future, they had been reluctant to make up their minds and in consequence had lost it. They were able to remain in the house, nevertheless, until the following spring.

In October the Duke went to London where the Court Circular announced that he was staying at Marlborough House with his mother, Queen Mary. For a day or two he went everywhere with her, accompanying her to church and visiting bombed sites in the East End of London. On Sunday, 8 October, he went to Buckingham Palace to see the King. In January of the following year he repeated this visit to London, staying again with Queen Mary. He was reported as dining with Mr Churchill on 8 January, as visiting the King on 9 January, and as visiting the King in the company of the Prime Minister (Mr Attlee) on 10 January. On 12 January he returned to Paris. Twenty years later he told us himself the purpose of these visits.* On his return from the Bahamas some of his friends had come forward with the novel and interesting idea that he should become a specialist in Anglo–American relations, an ambassador-at-large, with no specific or formal responsibility for the conduct of diplomacy which would remain the province of the professional head of the Embassy.

Such a job would require my bringing American and visiting Britons together, providing a good table and a comfortable library for informal talks and helping what Winston Churchill called the 'mixing-up process' – the sort of thing I had done for many years as Prince of Wales.[2]

The Duke was in London to propose this to the British government. There was no thought in his mind, he wrote later, of encroaching on the Ambassadorial prerogative and he would undertake to make no speeches. On 12 January he returned to Paris and on 27 January, the Prime Minister stated in the House of Commons in a written reply to a question that no diplomatic or official position had been offered to the Duke of Windsor.

After that he came at fairly long intervals to visit his mother at Marlborough House, when he almost always paid a call on the King and sometimes on Mr Churchill. Occasionally the Duchess accompanied him and then they stayed either at Claridges or with friends, as when in October 1946 her jewellery was stolen while she was the guest of Lord Dudley at Ednam Lodge. Such newspaper readers as still retained an interest in the doings of the Windsors wondered about the relationship of this man with the mother and brother who were so relentless in their determination not to meet his wife.

* In a series of articles in the *New York Daily News*.

In the spring of the year (1946) the Duke and Duchess moved to the Ritz Hotel in Paris while she once more looked for a house, but they were able to move back into La Croë. They were very fond of this house, but they found the Riviera too much changed and in the spring of 1949 they gave it up. In the same year the Duchess found a house in Paris, 85 Rue de la Faisanderie, which they rented for four years. Then in 1953 they were offered a house in the Bois de Boulogne, which was the property of the City of Paris and had been occupied by General Charles de Gaulle during his first period as President, and they stayed in this house for the rest of their lives.

Paris was the city the Duchess loved best and she found in it almost everything that satisfied her instincts, but the Duke would have liked to live in the country. So presently they found an old mill, the Moulin de la Tuilerie in the valley of the Chevreuse only forty-five miles from Paris, which had been partially converted by the painter Etienne Drian, and which they were able first to rent and then to buy. The Duke kept his ranch in Canada until 1962 and they spent a considerable part of every year in America, but France had become their home.

This was a matter of choice. There is a widespread belief, which persisted throughout the Duke's life and was even spoken of in some of the obituaries as a matter for regret, that he was prevented from returning to England. This is not true.

After the war no one objected to the Duke returning to England, but he made his return absolutely conditional on his wife being received by his family and given the same rank and status as the wives of his two younger brothers. Once this had been refused, it was most unlikely that he would ever have weakened about a matter on which he felt so deeply. Soon, however, his resolve was much strengthened by the great generosity of the French government. He was given the house in the Bois de Boulogne at a nominal rent (this favour was continued for the Duchess after his death) and also a special status which meant that he paid no income tax. It would have cost him a fortune to live in England.

Another idea, which is prevalent but equally without foundation, is that the British denied the Duke all opportunity to work. It is true that they would not, when he visited London after the war or at any other time, offer him employment in any sphere which he thought suitable to his rank and talents. It may even be true, as the Duchess states, that the 'silent ban' extended to any form of public work in which the British government was concerned. Beyond this they had neither interest nor power, and the ex-King of England, with his vast fortune, his undoubted status, his unrivalled contacts, could surely have had for the asking a position at the head of half the organizations in the world – those for the relief of poverty and suffering, for the promotion of the arts or international relations, for the preservation of the environment, for the study of wild life, for all the myriad other things which occupy the minds of men and women of imagination and goodwill.

Yet the fact that he did not avail himself of these opportunities was his misfortune as well as his fault. He wanted not so much work as status, not so much to give, as to receive recognition, for himself and for his wife. All these things which were his by right of birth and which in his youth were so little regarded were now denied him, and denied he believed through the ill will of a few powerful people. So it was true, as his wife recorded, that he was left with a haunting sense of waste and that it took courage for him to take up the small burdens that were all that were left to him. Yet there was never any doubt that between him and despair or regrets there remained his complete and continuing happiness with his wife.

For many years the Windsors' lives in France followed the pattern of the pre-war years and the Duchess had the pleasure once more of the long sessions with architects and interior decorators and the afternoons spent on the Left Bank in Paris looking for furniture for her two houses. The Moulin de la Tuilerie consisted of the mill itself, which went back to the seventeenth century, a barn and several other outbuildings. This gave scope for converting the whole and for what the Duchess describes as 'endless changing and re-modelling',[3] and afterwards for decorating and furnishing. The Duke now had scope, too, for a garden. He fell in love with the place when he saw it and with the help of the famous gardener, Mr Russell Page, set about creating an English garden with borders and rock gardens and a wild garden round the stream. When the happy years of creation were over and there was nothing left but to enjoy what had been made, sitting on the terrace at the Mill watching her husband working in the garden, the Duchess could reflect that, while life had not turned out exactly as they had hoped, they had succeeded in reaching peace. Behind her in the room which led on to this terrace, a text had been painted on the wall as part of the decoration of the room and this expressed in her own very characteristic style her sense of having survived the unexpected turns of fate. These words were: 'I'm not the miller's daughter but I have been through the mill.'*

The Windsors spent a large part of every year in New York and they seemed to be forever travelling. When they boarded a boat or a train there were always reporters to record the fact and to count the luggage. They seldom travelled with less than thirty odd pieces, with valets and chauffeurs, secretaries and maids, with cairns or later with pugs. When in New York they stayed at the Waldorf Tower, probably the most luxurious block of apartments in the world. In the winter they went to Palm Beach

---

* The idea for this may have been suggested to the Duchess by her friend Lady Mendl who used to have cushions embroidered with such maxims as 'He who rides on the back of a tiger cannot descend', and 'never complain, never explain'.

and in the summer to Biarritz or to Venice or to some other place in Southern Europe. They presented to the world a fantasy of wealth and luxury and elegance, like a couple invented by *Vogue* or *Harper's Bazaar*. Reporters counted avidly how many times she went to the hairdresser, the number of dresses she bought and how many times she wore them, while she was listed in a famous newspaper column as the best-dressed woman in the world.

Some said they were too regal, insisted too much on the homage which, justified by his rank, was nevertheless inappropriate to his so-often-expressed desire to escape the princely role. But this was a little unjust because it is fairly clear that so many of the citizens of the two great republics in which they lived would not have had them otherwise. Human nature is the same all over the world and in Paris and New York the ex-King of England was the best royalty they had. The Duchess early made it clear what she would like. 'I expect to take my husband's name and rank, that is all. And I expect ordinary graciousness in human relationships, especially with those who are near me.'[4] This seemed explicit enough and also, to most people, reasonable enough. In any case, many people took a delight in bowing and curtsying, in calling him Sir and her Ma'am, in asking on the telephone for Her Royal Highness, Son Altesse Royale. These things roll off the tongue and it is absurd to blame the Windsors for their part in a pageantry so many other people enjoyed.

Then again, grandeur is comparative. It was true that the Windsors' houses were hung with banners, and ribbons and insignia of his illustrious past, that his servants were dressed in the Royal livery, that he collected mementoes of his reign and that he accepted without demur the bowing and scraping of shopkeepers and waiters. But the Duke was over fifty when the war ended and, apart from the peculiar circumstances of his birth, he had grown up in a world where in every nobleman's house the footmen wore powdered wigs and white gloves as well as the family livery; or, in houses with smaller pretensions, a button with the family crest on a plain livery. It was easy for American journalists to criticize, but HRH had never known any other way of life, and it would have required exceptional modesty or strongly held convictions for him to discard all these things. Possibly no one would have thought that he should if in his modest youth he had not expressed so much doubt about them.

It is often said of the Windsors that they moved in 'café society'. This is too sweeping a generalization to be discussed except in the broadest terms, particularly as the expression has little meaning in England today for all its class structure. It is true that they mixed largely in the international society which can be found entertaining one another all over the world, just as it is true that they were not known to what the French call 'le gratin' (the uppercrust), although at one time or another they must have met many of its members individually. Chiefly, it is true that in all the years they lived in France they kept a separate identity, never becoming in any thing specifically French, and never making any impact on the life of the country. In New York they were certainly often seen in that world which is grist to the mill of the columnist, and which their friend Elsa Maxwell personified as well as recorded. They did not naturally gravitate towards people whose interests were music or literature, politics or art, they were not found in the company which supported the Metropolitan Opera House or the New York Public Library.

As a young man the Duke's intellectual capacity had been very much over-estimated because he was so well briefed. No one who has not witnessed the difference in authority between someone who has 'the papers' and the same person without them can appreciate how much good briefing can mean. But he was intellectually incurious as well as very badly educated and in the post-war world, where his rank and riches ensured him a place, his superficial brightness wasted for lack of hard use. Marietta FitzGerald, the young American journalist with a piece to write on England (see p. 205) sitting next to him at dinner, asked him to explain to her the descent through the Electress Sophia which brought George I to the throne. He considered the point for some time and then he replied: 'I think my mother would know that. I could send her a telegram, if you wish.' Later she asked him if the Irish Republic was a member of the British Commonwealth. Again he thought for a time and then he once more replied: 'I think my mother would know that too.'

He had three interests – golf, gardening and money. All his life, after he gave up hunting, he was an ardent golfer, and although he never became very good at the game, he improved with practice. He seldom ate lunch and, retaining his passion for physical fitness, he could usually be seen on a golf course in the middle of the day. Then, once they acquired the mill outside Paris, he indulged his love of the physical labour of gardening as he had at Fort Belvedere. But probably the greatest of the three was money. Hilaire Belloc once said that it was easy enough to make money, all one had to do was to think of nothing else for twenty-four hours a day. The Duke did not think of it for twenty-four hours a day, but he spent many of what in some other man might have been the working hours of the day thinking about it. It was not merely that he studied the workings of the stock market with the greatest attention, but that he was naturally attracted by the society of men to whom money was a profession. When he played golf he played as often as not with some financial tycoon, with the result that, although he made a great fortune, many of his social contacts were of a rather limited kind. Money is absolutely essential but as a topic of conversation rather dull, and the corollary to Hilaire Belloc's remark is that those who spend their lives thinking of it have very little time for anything else.

The Duchess's tastes are well known and she differed from the Duke in that to the end of her life she could never resist a party. In this as in so many other things, his pleasure was to give her pleasure. He had never been fond of large parties and since the days of the Embassy Club had preferred evenings spent in the company of friends. As, over the years, he spent so many of the long hours of the night leaning against a piano or sitting at the table of some night club, he seemed to become more and more withdrawn and the sad cast of his features was ever more marked.

Then some time in the late forties he found a new and immensely profitable career. In 1951 *Life* magazine published a series of articles based on the ex-King's memoirs which were later to appear as *A King's Story* and which were the beginning of what became an industry, described by one American writer as 'big business', in books, newspaper articles, and magazine serials, an industry in which the Duchess presently joined him.*

Several misconceptions must be cleared up. Because of the Duke's known interest in money, it is assumed that his reason for breaking the rule of reticence which in a constitutional society is binding on Kings and Princes was that it brought him a second and once more considerable fortune. This it undoubtedly did. The American writer quoted above, [not an entirely reliable source, but one who because of his work might have had access to information on this matter], states categorically that the world sales of *A King's Story* netted £300,000 and that a further £200,000 was made out of subsidiary rights, magazine and newspaper articles, and the sale of photographs. Even if the figures were guess-work it was not an impossible guess. But, although the money he earned was a welcome byproduct of his labours, and certainly a contributory cause of the far less important *Family Album* and *The Crown and the People* (a small book written to mark the coronation of Queen Elizabeth), the Duke had a far more compelling motive for *A King's Story*. He wished to put history straight.

He believed himself to have been deprived of his ordinary rights ever since he left the throne for reasons which were completely unworthy and totally unexpected. 'I played fair in 1936,' he said to the late James Pope-Hennessy, 'but I was bloody shabbily treated.'[6] As he looked back on the long history of personal slights to himself and his wife, of reluctance to accord him the status and occupation which his birth would normally have ensured and which would have enabled him to live tax free in England, or in some other part of the British Empire, above all on the iron determination of his family not to receive his wife, how easy for him in addition to believe, as she had always believed, that he had been the victim of men who, because of his intractable independence and the influence his popularity gave him, were glad to replace him by his brother. Neither he nor the Duchess, who wrote later, were ever able to see the bold outlines of the

* Geoffrey Bocca.

plot or to explain how the trick was done; they simply felt they had been outplayed, and that honesty, chivalry, goodwill and decency in human relations had been beaten by cunning.

Because of this the Duke's book is never really explicit. But he achieves his effect by the dark tone of his musings and an overt hostility to men who, until then, had believed the negotiations at the time of the Abdication had been carried out with patience on their side and goodwill on both.

A second misconception is that he had some real talent as a writer. Just as years before he had been given too much credit for his speeches, which had been written by Captain Lascelles, now he was given too much credit for his books, which were written by Mr C.V.Murphy with, it is said, the able assistance of Mr T.Brien. However, the belief that he was an author of talent is very widespread. Mr Sacheverell Sitwell says that Arthur Waley, whom he regarded as the most learned person he had ever known, once said to him that he thought those parts of the Duke's book which he had written himself were very good. It is impossible to say now what Mr Waley meant, but certain general observations can be made both about the Duke's and the Duchess's books and about the art of ghosting. Both books are sententious and tendentious and neither reaches the highest standards in discussion of such abstracts as right and wrong or in passages recording strong emotions. But the ghost has successfully identified himself with each of his collaborators and produced in literary form the opinions and style not of himself but of the person who borrows his skill. On all counts the Duke's book must be thought the superior.

A King's Story sold hundreds of thousands of copies all over the world and in America it had not merely a great commercial success but admiring reviews in the Press. In England the reception was very much more mixed. The general tenor and style were admired, and the account of the Duke's early years in the Royal Household much praised. Purely literary reviewers like Raymond Mortimer received it uncritically, while, in a review which did more justice to the historical aspect of the book, Tom Jones contented himself with giving his own version of the facts rather than actually attacking the author's. But in the *Times Literary Supplement* an anonymous critic, having said that the book would be of interest to the young generation who only know the Duke 'as the man who leads a restless life, moving from hotels or hired houses in Paris, Cannes or Biarritz, to New York or Palm Beach, apparently with no settled home or occupation', made the apparently informed statement that at the time of the Abdication Baldwin had felt the struggle to have been 'one between himself and Mrs Simpson through the person of the King'.[6]

In the *New Statesman* Noel Annan, after remarking that the book was an honourable exception to the rule that in court memoirs 'reflections of inconceivable banality succeed descriptions of court life so bizarre that the characters seem permanently to be playing charades', goes on to say:

Yet in a sense I regret the old carefree style. For the Duke has chosen to turn phrases in a manner which permits one to be risqué without being witty, and to lift the veil while concealing everything of real value.[7]

While in the *Spectator* Wilson Harris wrote:

The hard inescapable fact – the Duke seems actually bent on its escaping no one – is that as Prince of Wales he resolved to marry another man's wife, and as King he carried the resolve into effect at the cost of his crown. ... His farewell broadcast was a justification of the decision he had just taken. But it was not that decision that needed to be justified. It was the decision taken years earlier to marry Mr Simpson's wife. On that there is no necessity to pass judgment here. But on the Duke's resolve to drag every detail of this old unhappy affair to light again when it had been well forgotten some judgment is called for. It must be unreservedly adverse.[8]

Behind the scenes the book caused unrestrained anger and concern. Those who had taken part in the events the Duke described were often astonished to read a version of them which bore no relation to their own memories. It is fair to say that, at the time of the Abdication, he had been too pre-occupied with his desire to protect Mrs Simpson to have much concern for anything else and, because by nature he was slow to anger, the goodwill of the King had probably been exaggerated. Thus Lord Hardinge really believed that the Duke's account of his emotions on reading the letter which precipitated the crisis was artificial, whereas we know from Walter Monckton that the King did feel anger and hostility towards him at the time. Consternation was in any case caused both by the decision to publish a one-sided view of the facts and because so many of the royal author's memories were based on inaccurate memories. One story, which he was fond of and repeated in a television interview years later, was of a political and unconstitutional bias shown by Baldwin in the matter of a journey to visit the coalfields of the north. In this the criticism of Baldwin was founded on an account of the matter which was untrue as to facts.

Many people would have liked to make some public protest. All were restrained from further publicity out of consideration for King George VI. The King's feelings about these revelations can be imagined and were much as they might have been if he had come in one day and found Crawfie installed on his hearth.* It is to be presumed the Duke of Windsor had counted the cost and felt that he had little to lose by the sacrifice of any further hope of being received at Court, while he seems also to have discovered a pleasure in his new profession. On the coronation of Queen Elizabeth II he produced a trite little book to mark the occasion called *The Crown and the People* and in 1960 he published *A Family Album.* This book was the result of a genuine urge to write about clothes, but, published

* Miss Marion Crawford was governess to Princess Elizabeth (Queen Elizabeth II) and Princess Margaret. Later she wrote several best sellers on the strength of her intimate knowledge of the Royal Family – *The Little Princesses*, *The Queen Mother*, and so on.

under a title which suggested further memoirs, and opening with a few pages which would have been appropriate to a book of that kind, it caused puzzlement and some amusement when the Duke began to develop and expand his real theme. 'Most space is given to clothes,' one critic complained, 'and much of this smells of the lamp in the sense that it reads as though it had been quarried out of dress manuals.'[9]

In 1956 the Duchess also took up the task with the publication of *The Heart Has Its Reasons*. Both the Windsors showed a complete disregard (or perhaps a lack of understanding) of the laws of copyright and the Duchess, by publishing part of the famous abdication letter, finally in November 1955 goaded Lord Hardinge into publishing it in *The Times* in full, together with his version of the facts. This was followed by some correspondence on the matter. The Duchess's book, even more revealing in many ways than the Duke's, was far less distinguished in style. Once more it made a great deal of money but in England it received little critical notice and such as appeared was not favourable.

The Duke emerges – Claud Cockburn wrote in the *New Statesman* – on the evidence of the Duchess as a man who ... understood almost nothing of the operations of the powerhouse in which he was, after all, an important and potentially powerful piece of machinery.[10]

While in *The Spectator* Gerald Fay wrote:

If it were not for the tremendous consequences they were leading up to, it might be said that the opening events of the book are commonplace and would not detain a busy reader for more than a few minutes. But, as it is, they fill in the past and make it seem feasible though not inevitable that the gay divorcee should in the end become the anxious Duchess – anxious to know why her husband, for all his notable public service, should forever be an outcast. Someone will have to explain it to her.[11]

In 1965 the Duke extended his activities to the film world. Directed by Le Vien a film was made of *A King's Story*, in which commentaries by the Duke of Windsor linked many reels of newsfilm and specially filmed sequences of royal ceremonial. Although this was in the main rather heavy handed and slow, some of the scenes were genuinely moving and interesting and did preserve for all time some of the quality which had made this man so much loved in his youth (see p. 69).

Probably the most astonishing of all the Windsor publications was a series of articles which appeared under the Duke's name in the *New York Daily News* in 1966, and which has already been referred to in the accounts of his telephone calls to his brother from Schloss Enzesfeld (see p. 317) and his desire for a job as roving Ambassador to America after he left the Bahamas. (See p. 392.) In these articles he speaks with an unusual lack of reticence of his alienation from his own family, says that he had good reason to believe that 'those closest to my brother were not displeased with the imposition of this freeze' by the British government, and hints at difficulties with his family over financial matters. These articles are also interesting for a pungent description of the life of a British sovereign.

Being a monarch, whether man or woman, in these egalitarian times can surely be one of the most confining, the most frustrating and, over the duller stretches, the least stimulating jobs open to an educated, independent-minded person.

There is also an account of his own state of mind in old age in which he confesses he is glad he will not survive to see the last valet forsake his calling and deplores the bad manners of the younger generation, about whom he writes in a manner strikingly reminiscent of King George v.[18]

For the world at large the Duke's decision to publish had many benefits. In the first place no other writer could have told us so much about his character and mentality as, both consciously and unconsciously, he revealed. In the second, by making a case which sooner or later others were bound to answer, he ensured that all the details of his reign were made public years before they might otherwise have been. In the twenty years after the publication of *A King's Story* everyone who had any part in the Abdication crisis had his say and one of the strangest aspects of the case is that the Windsors seem never to have understood the licence they were giving others to publish, and continued to resent any revelations or criticisms about themselves.

However, the publication which most disturbed the Duke was not one which he could have prevented or over which he had any control. When at the end of the war the allies captured the German Documents of Foreign Policy they were brought to London and the more interesting among them were selected for translation and publication by historians of England, Germany and France for the benefit of scholars. It was agreed that the editors should be free from any intervention on political grounds, and that the documents chosen should be issued as they stood, without any interpretive or corrective comment by way of footnotes. They were to be presented as a source book for the study of history. These documents, covering as they did every aspect of German Foreign policy during the war years could naturally not be shown to everyone whose name occurred in them. An exception was made, however, of the Duke of Windsor, who was told in 1957 of the coming publication of Series D, Volume X which contained the documents relating to his sojourn in Spain and Portugal in the summer of 1940. It was no secret to the Duke's advisers and those closest to him that, during the period which elapsed between his receiving this information and the publication of the documents he was an exceedingly unhappy and worried man. Probably because of representations made to them – although there is no evidence of this – the British Foreign Office took the unusual step of accompanying the publication of this volume with a statement. This read:

The Duke was subjected to heavy pressure from many quarters to stay in Europe, where the Germans hoped he would exercise his influence against the policy of His Majesty's Government. His Royal Highness never wavered in his loyalty to the British cause or in his determination to take up his official post as Governor of the Bahamas on the date agreed. The German records are necessarily a much-tainted source. The only firm evidence is of what the Germans were trying to do in this matter and how completely they failed.

Messrs Hunt's were the Duke's solicitors at this time, and they issued a statement on his behalf at the same time which read:

I have little to add to the statement made by the British Government relating to the Communications which passed between the German Foreign Ministry and the German Ambassadors in Spain and Portugal in July 1940, concerning myself. These communications comprise in part complete fabrications and in part gross distortions of the truth.

The record of our journey through France and Spain to Lisbon in June 1940 has already been fully described by the Duchess in her memoirs.

While I was in Lisbon certain people, whom I discovered to be Nazi sympathizers, did make definite efforts to persuade me to return to Spain and not to take up my appointment as Governor of the Bahamas. It was even suggested to me that there would be a personal risk to the Duchess and myself if we were to proceed to the Bahamas.

At no time did I ever entertain any thought of complying with such a suggestion which I treated with the contempt it deserved. At the earliest opportunity the Duchess and I proceeded to the Bahamas where I took up my appointment as Governor in which I served for 5 years.

All the national dailies gave much space to this story, and all of them adopted the tone set by these statements. The *Daily Telegraph* leader may be taken as representative of the general opinion.

Every aspiring Foreign Office official should be required to read the latest volume of German diplomatic documents as an object lesson in what diplomacy should not be. At least three-quarters of the messages sent back to Ribbentrop by his Ambassadors were not only inaccurate but highly misleading. They did not illuminate the world scene for the Nazi leaders, but simply confirmed them in all their illusions. The Nazis, in short, were not envoys extraordinary but ordinary deceivers reporting only what Berlin wanted to hear. ...[13]

Every one of the national dailies quoted some of the documents; only one, The *Daily Telegraph*, mentioned the telegram allegedly sent from Bermuda.* The *Telegraph* quoted it and also questioned Sir Walford Selby about it. Sir Walford said he knew nothing about any code word and

---

* One of the curious features of the affair is that the document referring to the telegram was published as a footnote to another document and could easily have been overlooked. There seems to have been no reason for this except that, since it was sent two weeks after the close of the affair, there was no obvious place for it. The documents referring to the Duke's house in Paris and the journey of the Duchess's maid were not chosen for translation and publication, so that they were not available for comment.

nothing about the Duke sending a telegram to Ricardo Espirito Santo e Silva. 'Ye Gods!' he is reported as saying. 'It would show me up to be a complete fool if there was one. I have never heard of that and I don't believe there was one.' And he added that the documents were grossly slanderous and contradictory in many places.

The *Daily Express* also interviewed Sir Walford Selby and this reporter had learned that it was Sir Walford himself who made the arrangements for the Windsors to stay with Ricardo Espirito Santo e Silva. He asked him whether he had not suspected him. To this Sir Walford replied: 'Silva I did suspect. He was certainly in touch with the Germans. I made the arrangements for the Duke's stay through an hotel; and I was surprised that Silva's villa was chosen. What passed between the hotel manager and Silva I do not know, but I was very displeased to find this trick had been played on me.'

From which one might get the impression that, if the Germans played the spy game with too much zest, the British played it with too little. And it is true that the British Embassy staff continued to use Silva's house and swimming pool for some time after this and only a year or two later put him on their black list. On the other hand, the arrangement made through an hotel manager was not so oddly casual as it sounds, because this man was also in the pay of the British and at least some of the time working for them.

The *Daily Express* also interviewed Lord Templewood who, as Sir Samuel Hoare, was Ambassador in Madrid in 1940. He treated the matter more seriously. He said that during the Duke's stay in Madrid 'telegrams were raining on me from London telling me to get him out of Spain as quickly as possible. The Germans were on the frontier and everyone expected them to occupy the country in the next few days.' Then he said: 'The Duke showed his common sense in the face of the temptations that were offered him. And I was relieved to think that by getting him out of very dangerous surroundings I had helped him out of temptation's way.'[14]

This was the end of the matter. For fifteen years, although many writers referred to these documents, they treated them always in a gingerly way and usually merely as a matter for ribaldry at the expense of the Germans.

In February 1952 when King George VI died the Duke of Windsor travelled immediately to England. At Southampton he read a prepared statement in which he spoke of his brother's outstanding qualities and said that he was sure the late King's well-known attributes would descend to the new Queen. Then he drove to London and, in the company of Queen Mary, visited Westminster Hall where the body of the late King lay in state. On 16 February, when the King was laid to rest in St George's Chapel, he took his place beside the other three Royal Dukes – Edinburgh, Gloucester, and his nephew, Kent – and, dressed in the uniform of an

Admiral of the Fleet, followed the coffin through the streets of London and Windsor.

In March 1953 he was already in London when Queen Mary's illness took a serious turn and he was able to visit her bedside until the end. Once more he took his place with the rest of the family in the ceremonial which followed her death. On both these occasions he came to England alone. In 1967, however, at the ceremony of unveiling a plaque to Queen Mary at Marlborough House the young Queen decided to extend the courtesy of an invitation, not merely to the Duke, but also to his wife. The Duke and Duchess of Windsor arrived smiling at Southampton together, to be greeted by shouts of 'Good old Teddy' from the dockers. Lord Mountbatten of Burma met them and they went to stay at his country house, Broadlands. They were cheered and clapped as they arrived in the procession from St James's Palace to Marlborough House, and after the ceremony they were seen to meet and chat with the Queen and the Queen Mother. The press of the crowd was so great that not much could be seen, but some said that the Duchess curtsied to the Queen, others that she merely bowed. On television that evening it could be seen that she merely bowed. The visit of the Windsors to London was marked by two things, the thirtieth anniversary of their wedding, which took place on board ship on the way over, and the first public recognition of the Duchess by the Sovereign of England.

Nothing now remained but to grow old gracefully, and this after their own fashion the Windsors undoubtedly did, the Duchess never scorning aids to the process. In 1964 the Duke was operated on for an aneurism of the abdominal aorta at the Methodist Hospital at Houston. Asked afterwards by reporters why he came to Texas, he replied that surgeons came from all over the world to learn from Dr Michael de Bakey and so 'I came to the maestro.' Following this operation the number of letters the Duke and Duchess received from well-wishers proved that, for all his years of exile, the Duke was not quite forgotten. In that year the Queen sent him a telegram of congratulations on his seventieth birthday and in the following year, when this time he chose London for an operation to the small retina of his right eye, many photographs appeared showing her visiting him and his wife at the London Clinic. Younger members of the royal family, Prince William of Gloucester and the Duke and Duchess of Kent and Princess Alexandra visited the Windsors at their home in Paris and in a public, if small and distant way, the Duchess was at last accepted by her husband's family.

As life began to close in, the Windsors lived in their homes in France for the greater part of the year, entertaining their friends from England and America at both. They spent the three spring months in New York, and the summer at Biarritz or somewhere else where the Duke could play golf. In her old age the Duchess became more beautiful and more refined, and, when she was recognized on her occasional visits to London, it was usually because someone's attention had been at first attracted by her exquisite elegance. To the end she dominated the Duke and to the end he adored her. 'The only thing that worries their friends,' Major Gray Phillips said, 'is if she should die before him.'* Nevertheless, although the Duke seemed content to submerge his likes and dislikes, his whole life into hers, it would be a mistake to think that this humility had any counterpart in his relations with anyone else. To the end of his life he carried about him the aura of his royal birth, he never outgrew the habits and expectations of his youth, and, to everyone but his wife, he could be formidable. Always moody, he could still make or mar a dinner party, and professional people who attempted to give him advice he did not wish to hear were made instantly aware of the royal displeasure. 'The Duchess has already said she is not interested in that,' he would say sharply, and finally.

People who served them seemed, nevertheless, to have liked and respected them. Englishmen travelling to Paris on their business were treated with kindness and hospitality, often asked to stay in the house, even to bring their wives. Everyone was impressed by the skill with which they put people at ease, and contrary to rumour, the servants seemed fond of them and proud to be in their employ. Nevertheless, if the head of the household still dominated it, it was no longer by exceptional magnetism. The wistful old face seemed not even to be the shell of the once brilliantly smiling Prince of Wales. Yet such is the modesty of human nature that to the end people found it irresistible that, amid all the luxury and grandeur, the servility of the servants and the memorabilia of the past, His Royal Highness, Son Altesse Royale, was in many ways the same as other men.

In 1970 the Windsors were persuaded to appear on television, and, in a long interview conducted at their home in the Bois de Boulogne, Mr Kenneth Harris introduced the Duchess for the first time to the British public. The interview consisted of a talk with the two together, followed by one with the Duke alone. The viewing figures proved, if proof were needed, the immense curiosity and interest aroused by the ex-King and his wife.† The interview itself was a *tour de force,* although it was not until it was published in a book with nine others, that the particular skill of the interviewer was revealed. On all the other occasions Mr Harris had been putting a professional of one sort or another through his paces, and the answers to his questions occupy long paragraphs, sometimes even pages of print. The interview with the Windsors consists almost entirely of short lines, and looks like the dialogue of a light comedy, or the transcript of a court case. When Mr Harris asked Maria Callas or Roy Jenkins, Lester Piggott or the Duke of Norfolk, a question, they each developed a theme. In the Windsor

* Conversation with author.

† This interview took place on a programme called *Tuesday Documentary* which had an average viewing of 3½–4 million. On the night of the Windsor interview this rose to 11.2 million.

interview the camera occasionally caught a hesitant look on his face as he paused to give the Ducal pair an opportunity to extend themselves before smoothly putting another question. Only when the Duke was left alone did he answer at any length, and then it was apparent that both he and Mr Harris had been studying his book and nothing new emerged. Yet the interview was very revealing, perhaps just because of its amateurishness more than ordinarily revealing.

They were both obviously and unexpectedly nervous and she seemed, at least superficially, more attractive, he less so, than history had led one to believe. As long as she was present she did most of the talking, and her sharp, rather wry humour suited the medium. Asked if they had anything they disagreed about, she replied: 'Hours', and explained that she liked to stay up late, whereas the Duke didn't like to, and she liked to get up early, but he did not. 'But that works itself out. And then we are a little late for things, and I am absolutely on the dot. Everybody says that they know I'm going to be the first to arrive at a dinner Party or something. We are a little bit late.'[15] But as she made the confession that, in spite of everything, in all these years she had completely failed to cure the Duke of his habitual un-punctuality, she smiled at him and touched him. The camera, we are told, cannot lie. Afterwards it seemed to many people that the most important thing the interview had revealed was that Fruity Metcalfe had been right all those years ago when he said that what bound these two people together was 'very true and deep stuff'.

33

THE HOMECOMING

In May 1972 the Queen of England paid a much heralded visit to France. The Press of both countries covered the event very fully in newsprint and with photographs, and the Queen and Prince Philip appeared in appropriate splendour and accompanied by President Pompidou and his wife at every stage of the five-day visit. The occasion which seemed to create most interest, however, was a private one, if anything connected with the Queen on a state visit to France can be called private. She went to the house in the Bois de Boulogne, accompanied by her husband and son, the Prince of Wales, to visit her uncle, the Duke of Windsor. The Duke was within a few days of his 78th birthday and it had been rumoured for some time that he was not well. The Moulin de la Tuilerie had been emptied and put up for sale some time before, because he could no longer enjoy the physical labour of his garden, and, although he and the Duchess had intended to be on holiday at Marbella in Spain when the royal visit took place, they had been forced to cancel their plans. In informed circles it was known that he had cancer of the throat and could not live for more than a few weeks.

On the day of the Queen's visit his doctor had said that it was out of the question for him to leave his room and the Press photographs showed the Duchess welcoming the royal visitors, alone and curtsying deeply. The Queen went up to his room to see the Duke, who was said to be delighted to see her. Both French and English newspapers showed great interest, but in England it was denied that, as sections of the French Press had reported, this was a reconciliation, because, it was said, if in fact this were needed, it had taken place long before. As this had been a week of Anglo–French reconciliation, however, it was thought appropriate to recall the generosity of the French authorities towards the Duke and Duchess of Windsor.

On 20 May the Queen returned to England and on 28 May the Duke of Windsor died. It was announced immediately that his body would be interred in the royal burial ground at Frogmore and that it would be flown to England, accompanied by the Duchess of Windsor, who at the Queen's request would stay at Buckingham Palace. The Queen expressed her heartfelt sympathy with the Duchess, and tributes were paid to the dead man by leading statesmen of the world. 'He was a man of noble spirit and high ideals,' President Nixon said, 'for whom millions of Americans felt a deep respect and affection.' And Mr Heath from Downing Street: 'For the Empire he made the monarchy a living reality in the tours he undertook in every part of the world. ... In all he did he sought to make the monarchy less remote and more in tune with the aspirations of the time.'

On Wednesday the body was flown to the RAF airfield at Benson in a VC 10 jet. The Duchess was said to be too unwell to accompany it, but it was hoped she would travel in an aeroplane of the Queen's flight on the Friday. In death the Duke received the pomp and ceremony he had foregone in life. He was met by a Royal Guard of Honour, by the Duke and Duchess of Kent, members of the government, and the French Ambassador, M Geoffrey de Courcel. As the coffin was carried from the aeroplane to the RAF Chapel, the guard of honour from the Queen's Colour Squadron of the RAF presented arms, and the Central Band played the first six bars of the National Anthem. The coffin lay overnight in the RAF chapel, where officers of the RAF kept a vigil. It bore the simple inscription:

HRH The Prince Edward Albert Christian George
Andrew Patrick David, Duke of Windsor
Born 1894.   Died 1972.
King Edward VIII
20 January – 11 December, 1936

Flowers from the Duchess of Windsor covered its whole length.

On the following morning at 7 o'clock it was taken by road to Windsor. As the hearse passed through the Henry VIII gate, the flag on the Round Tower was lowered. Flags in the town were at half mast as also those on public buildings, all over England. The coffin lay for one night in the Albert Memorial Chapel and then it was moved to St George's Chapel, where a catafalque had been built in the middle of the nave and where it would lie for two days, while members of the public filed by to pay their last tribute. In answer to criticisms that the body of the Duke should have lain in state in Westminster Hall, it was announced that some time in the 60s he had himself requested that he might be buried at Frogmore and made all the arrangements for his funeral, including the order of the service that would take place on the following Monday. It was also announced that one day the Duchess of Windsor would lie in the burial ground at Frogmore beside him.

The initial announcements of the death and homecoming of the Duke had been made comparatively quietly. As the week went on, however, it became apparent that there was taking place one of those large expressions of public opinion which occur as if by spontaneous combustion. The Press, which had not initiated this, was, nevertheless, extremely sensitive to it, and more and more columns of print and more and more photographs of the Duke and Duchess of Windsor filled the newspapers. The long obituary columns concentrated very largely on the dead man's achievements as Prince of Wales or the details of the story of the Abdication. In the *Daily Telegraph* Sir Colin Coote spoke of 'a trace of shoddiness under the shimmer' and exhorted history to remember 'the vivid lively Prince Charming' rather than 'the weary, wayward, wandering ghost', but he said this: 'One thing must be said. Think what you like of him, it was very largely due to him that his going was not cataclysmic. His determination that what he did should not be politically upsetting was as strong as his resolve to do it.'[1]

In this he voiced the most generally held belief. For, as the week went on, it became clear that the British were determined that, in death, they would honour this man. Most striking of all were the crowds that flocked to Windsor. Extra trains and buses had been put on and people arrived by thousands in car or on foot. On the first day it was said that some 30,000 people had stood in a mile long queue leading to St George's Chapel, and by the end of Saturday it was estimated that altogether 57,000 had filed past the coffin. There seem to have been three reasons for this demonstration of respect for the dead man, who had seemed so long forgotten in England, and there is no evidence by which to assess the relative weight of each. Nevertheless, in descending order of importance they probably were: first, the usual appeal of every event touching the Royal Family (eighteen months later 10,000 people were reported blocking the roads at Sandringham for a glimpse of a young girl driving to church because the Press had associated her with the Prince of Wales): second, the genuine affection older people felt for the memory of the Prince who had shown so much concern for simple folk (some of the women wept as they passed the catafalque). The third reason was more unexpected. There were hundreds of young people in the crowd as well as old and many foreign tourists, and soon there was no doubt that many of them were there to give expression to a feeling that the dead man had been badly treated.

'It is only the Duke's body they bring back,' one man said. 'It is too late for the Duke himself. Why couldn't things have been patched up sooner.'

'It is a great pity the English could not have let bygones be bygones,' an American was reported as saying, 'and let him live in his own country.'[2]

And a woman who came with her family from Hampshire gave as her reason:

'I am a monarchist. By what he did the Duke preserved the monarchy for all of us. But over the years he has been shabbily treated. That is what I, and my husband and my children feel.'[3]

On Friday the Duchess of Windsor arrived in an aeroplane of the Queen's Flight to be met at Heathrow by Admiral of the Fleet Earl Mountbatten of Burma. She was driven to Buckingham Palace where she had lunch with the Queen and Princess Anne in the Queen's private apartments. But she was described as tired and unwell and distressed, and she retired to the State suite on the first floor overlooking the Mall which she had been given for the duration of her visit. On the following day the ceremony of the Trooping the Colour for the Queen's birthday would include by Her Majesty's wish a tribute to the Duke of Windsor, but it was announced that the Duchess would not attend and would see it on television. A memorable photograph was taken as the Queen rode out to this function, showing the Duchess holding back the curtain of her window to look down at her. She looked sad and ill, but the vitality which was implicit in her curiosity was not unattractive, and round her neck she wore an entrancingly beautiful string of enormous pearls.

The Act of Remembrance took place as soon as the Queen had taken up her position on Horse Guards' Parade. A roll of drums was followed by a minute's silence and a second roll of drums. Then a lament, 'The Flowers of the Forest', was played by pipers of the Scots Guards. After the Trooping the Colour the Royal Family went to Windsor for the weekend but the Duchess stayed at Buckingham Palace. But on the Saturday evening, on what by a coincidence was the 35th anniversary of her wedding day, she drove to Windsor to see her husband lying in state, and she was escorted into the chapel by the Prince of Wales.

On Monday, 5 June, in both Houses of Parliament tributes were paid to the Duke by the leaders of all three political parties. The Prime Minister, Mr Heath, said:

There must be men and women on Tyneside, and in Liverpool and South Wales, who are remembering today the slight, rather shy figure, who came briefly into their lives, and sometimes into their homes, in those grim years. . . .

I have no doubt that the Duke by his conduct as Prince of Wales and as King had paved the way to a form of monarchy which today is more in tune with the times than would have been thought possible 50 years ago.

And he added that the House of Commons would wish to extend its profound sympathy to the Duke's widow 'who had repaid his devotion with an equal loyalty, companionship and love.' All the speakers in both Houses endorsed his remarks.

The funeral service took place at St George's Chapel at 11.15 on the same day. It was a private service at which were present the Royal Family, certain dignitaries of the Church, the Government and the Armed Forces, friends in England whose names the Duke had left on a list of those to be asked and some friends who had accompanied the Duchess from France. After the simple service, which included the hymns *The King of Love My*

Shepherd Is and *Lead Us Heavenly Father Lead Us*, Garter King of Arms, Sir Anthony Wagner, proclaimed the styles and titles of the Duke of Windsor.

Royal Knight of the Thistle, of St Patrick, Knight Grand Cross of the Bath, of the Star of India, of St Michael and St George, of the Indian Empire, of the Royal Victorian Order, of the British Empire. . . .

In the afternoon the body of the Duke of Windsor was buried in complete privacy at Frogmore near the garden where he had played as a child.

All through the week the newspapers had been full of photographs of the Duchess of Windsor with members of the Royal Family, of the Duke's coffin at its various resting places, and of the crowds which gathered to see it. The most dramatic photograph appeared on the day after the funeral and showed the Duchess boarding an aeroplane at Heathrow the afternoon before, immediately after the Duke's body had been lowered into the ground. She was given the fullest honours – the Lord Chamberlain escorting her to the airport and a member of the Queen's own household accompanying her on the flight, although even so some members of the public thought it would have been more graceful if one of the Royal Family had been there to see her off. In any case, it was not the figure of the man who stood at the bottom of the ladder which was so striking, but that of the small, black-clothed widow climbing determinedly up to the aeroplane on her way to her home in France. A fraction of a second in the Duchess's life had been immobilized by the camera, but it seemed entirely final. She would not turn again, one felt, for a last look at the land her husband had given up for her and this was the ending of an episode – an episode in the history of England and in the long life of its leading family.

APPENDIX

The Message from King Edward VIII to the two Houses of Parliament announcing his Abdication.

Members of the House of Commons [Lords]

After long and anxious consideration, I have determined to renounce the Throne to which I succeeded on the death of My father, and I am now communicating this, My final and irrevocable decision. Realizing as I do the gravity of this step, I can only hope that I shall have the understanding of My peoples in the decision I have taken and the reasons which have led Me to take it. I will not enter now into My private feelings, but I would beg that it should be remembered that the burden which constantly rests upon the shoulders of a Sovereign is so heavy that it can only be borne in circumstances different from those in which I now find Myself. I conceive that I am not overlooking the duty that rests on Me to place in the forefront the public interest, when I declare that I am conscious that I can no longer discharge this heavy task with efficiency or with satisfaction to Myself.

I have accordingly this morning executed an Instrument of Abdication in the terms following:

I, Edward VIII, of Great Britain, Ireland, and the British Dominions beyond the Seas, King, Emperor of India, do hereby declare My irrevocable determination to renounce the Throne for Myself and for My descendants, and My desire that effect should be given to this Instrument of Abdication immediately.

In token whereof I have hereunto set My hand this tenth day of December, nineteen hundred and thirty-six, in the presence of the witnesses whose signatures are subscribed.

(Signed) EDWARD R.I.

My execution of this Instrument has been witnessed by my three brothers,

Their Royal Highnesses the Duke of York, the Duke of Gloucester and the Duke of Kent.

I deeply appreciate the spirit which has actuated the appeals which have been made to Me to take a different decision, and I have, before reaching My final determination, most fully pondered over them. But My mind is made up. Moreover, further delay cannot but be most injurious to the peoples whom I have tried to serve as Prince of Wales and as King and whose future happiness and prosperity are the constant wish of My heart.

I take My leave of them in the confident hope that the course which I have thought it right to follow is that which is best for the stability of the Throne and Empire and the happiness of My peoples. I am deeply sensible of the consideration which they have always extended to Me both before and after My accession to the Throne and which I know they will extend in full measure to My successor.

I am most anxious that there should be no delay of any kind in giving effect to the instrument which I have executed and that all necessary steps should be taken immediately to secure that My lawful successor, My brother, His Royal Highness the Duke of York, should ascend the Throne.

EDWARD R.I.

Genealogical Table

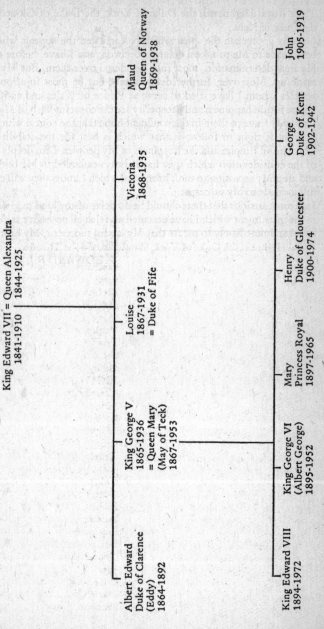

King Edward VII = Queen Alexandra
1841-1910   1844-1925

Albert Edward Duke of Clarence (Eddy) 1864-1892	King George V 1865-1936 = Queen Mary (May of Teck) 1867-1953	Louise 1867-1931 = Duke of Fife	Victoria 1868-1935	Maud Queen of Norway 1869-1938

| King Edward VIII
1894-1972 | King George VI
(Albert George)
1895-1952 | Mary
Princess Royal
1897-1965 | Henry
Duke of Gloucester
1900-1974 | George
Duke of Kent
1902-1942 | John
1905-1919 |

SOURCE
REFERENCES

I CHILDHOOD

1 *Queen Mary*, James Pope-Hennessy (George Allen & Unwin, 1959), p. 186.
2 ibid., p. 280.
3 ibid., p. 280.
4 *Diaries and Letters*, 1945–62, Harold Nicolson (Collins, 1966), p. 164.
5 *King George V, His Life and Reign*, Harold Nicolson (Constable, 1952), p. 51.
6 *King George VI*, John Wheeler-Bennett (Macmillan, 1958), pp. 14–15.
7 Pope-Hennessy, op. cit., p. 276.
8 ibid., pp. 301–2.
9 *The Times*, 25 June 1894.
10 *Parliamentary Debates*, Commons, Fourth Series, Vol. XXVI, 28 June 1894.
11 Wheeler-Bennett, op. cit., p. 17.
12 *King George V, A Personal Memoir*, John Gore (John Murray, 1941), p. 368.
13 Wheeler-Bennett, op. cit., p. 16.
14 *King Edward the Seventh*, Philip Magnus (John Murray, 1964), p. 287.
15 Gore, op. cit., p. 366.
16 ibid., p. 370.
17 *King George V*, Nicolson, p. 365.
18 *Lord Derby*, 'King of Lancashire', Randolph Churchill (Heinemann, 1959), p. 159.
19 *The Unknown Prime Minister*, Robert Blake (Eyre & Spottiswoode, 1955), p. 367.
20 Magnus, op. cit., p. 242.
21 *Diaries and Letters*, 1945–62, Nicolson, p. 137.
22 *A King's Story*, The memoirs of HRH The Duke of Windsor (Cassell, 1960), p. 1.
23 ibid., p. 26.
24 Pope-Hennessy, op. cit., p. 299.
25 ibid., p. 392.
26 ibid., p. 391.
27 Wheeler-Bennett, op. cit., note to p. 19.
28 ibid., p. 32.
29 Gore, op. cit., p. 220.
30 *Edward, Prince of Wales*, G. Ivy Saunders (Nisbet, 1921), pp. 17–18.
31 *King Edward VII*, Sir Sidney Lee, Vol. 2 (Macmillan, 1927), p. 412.
32 Pope-Hennessy, op. cit., pp. 394–395.
33 Duke of Windsor, op. cit. p. 29.
34 *Diaries and Letters*, 1945–62, Nicolson, p. 53.

35 Pope-Hennessy, op. cit., p. 413.
36 Wheeler-Bennett, op. cit., pp. 24–5.
37 *Edward VIII*, Hector Bolitho (Eyre and Spottiswoode, 1937), p. 76.
38 Saunders, op. cit., p. 24.
39 *Journals and Letters of Reginald Viscount Esher*, Vol. 2 (Nicolson and Watson, 1934), p. 53.
40 ibid., p. 139.
41 ibid., p. 140.
42 *Queen Alexandra*, Georgina Battiscombe (Constable, 1969), p. 111.
43 Magnus, op. cit., p. 72.
44 Battiscombe, op. cit., p. 81.
45 Magnus, op. cit., p. 260.
46 ibid., p. 285.
47 Battiscombe, op. cit., p. 138.
48 ibid., p. 209.

2 NAVY
1 *King George V*, Gore, pp. 247–8.
2 ibid., p. 375.
3 *King George V*, Nicolson, p. 14.
4 Gore, op. cit., p. 219.
5 ibid., p. 211.
6 Quoted in *A King's Story*, Duke of Windsor, p. 64.
7 ibid., pp. 63–4.
8 *Edward VIII*, Bolitho, p. 11.
9 *The Windsor Tapestry*, Compton Mackenzie (Rich and Cowan, 1938), p. 81.
10 Duke of Windsor, op. cit., p. 66.
11 *King Edward the Seventh*, Magnus, pp. 30–1.
12 Duke of Windsor, op. cit., p. 27.
13 *Royal Chef*, Gabriel Tschumi (William Kimber, 1954), pp. 83–4.
14 *Edward VII and His Circle*, Virginia Cowles (Hamish Hamilton, 1956), p. 359.
15 Duke of Windsor, op. cit., p. 68.
16 *King George V*, Gore, p. 237.
17 *King George V*, Nicolson, p. 154.
18 *Journals and Letters*, Esher, Vol. 3, p. 7.
19 *King George V*, Nicolson, p. 205.

20 *The Morning Post*, 23 June 1911.
21 *King George V*, Nicolson, p. 206.
22 Duke of Windsor, op. cit., p. 79.

3 OXFORD
1 *Journals and Letters*, Esher, Vol. 3, pp. 101–2.
2 *Lord Derby*, Randolph Churchill, p. 157.
3 ibid., p. 158.
4 *A King's Story*, Duke of Windsor.
5 Quoted in *A Family Album*, Duke of Windsor (Cassell, 1960), p. 61.
6 Quoted in *A Family Album*, Duke of Windsor, p. 62.
7 *The Windsor Tapestry*, Compton Mackenzie, p. 101.
8 *Journals and Letters*, Esher, Vol. 3, pp. 108–9.
9 *Another Self*, James Lees-Milne (Hamish Hamilton, 1970), p. 87.
10 *King Edward the Seventh*, Magnus, p. 214.
11 Randolph Churchill, op. cit., p. 158.
12 Quoted in *A Family Album*, Duke of Windsor, p. 24.
13 *Working for the Windsors*, Diana Hood (Allan Wingate, 1957), p. 136.
14 *Abdication*, Brian Inglis (Hodder & Stoughton, 1966), p. 11.
15 *A Family Album*, Duke of Windsor, p. 63.
16 *Oxford—1914*, J. Brett Langstaff (Vantage Press, 1965), p. 196.
17 *The Times*, 15 June 1914.
18 *The Times*, 18 November 1914.

4 FIRST WORLD WAR
1 *A King's Story*, Duke of Windsor, p. 108.
2 ibid., p. 108.
3 *Edward VIII*, Bolitho, p. 53.
4 *Journals and Letters*, Esher, Vol. 3, p. 207.
5 ibid., pp. 217–18.
6 *From Peace to War*, Lord Chandos (The Bodley Head, 1968), p. 137.

7   *The Memoirs of Lord Chandos,*
    Oliver Lyttelton, Viscount
    Chandos (The Bodley Head, 1962),
    pp. 46–7.
8   Esher, op. cit., pp. 254–5.
9   ibid., pp. 261–2.
10 ibid., p. 266.
11 *Kitchener,* Philip Magnus (John
    Murray, 1958), p. 375.
12 *Abdication,* Inglis, pp. 13–14.
13 Quoted in *A King's Story,* Duke of
    Windsor, pp. 117–18.
14 *King George V,* Nicolson, p. 254.
15 Duke of Windsor, op. cit., p. 125.
16 Bolitho, op. cit., p. 73.

    5 THE PRINCE IN LOVE
1   *Diaries 1915–18,* Lady Cynthia
    Asquith (Hutchinson, 1968), pp.
    416–17.
2   *The Heart Has Its Reasons,* Duchess
    of Windsor (Michael Joseph, 1956),
    p. 143.
3   Asquith, op. cit., p. 421.
4   *King George V,* Gore, p. 368.

    6 CANADA AND THE UNITED
    STATES OF AMERICA
1   *Diaries and Letters,* 1945–62,
    Nicolson, p. 208.
2   Quoted in *A King's Story,* Duke of
    Windsor, p. 134.
3   *The Times,* 5 May 1919.
4   *The Times,* 3 January 1919.
5   *Thatched With Gold,* The Memoirs
    of Mabell, Countess Airlie
    (Hutchinson, 1962), pp. 144–6.
6   *Coronation Commentary,* Geoffrey
    Dennis (Dodd Mead & Co., New
    York, 1937), p. 18.
7   *King George V,* Gore, pp. 153–5.
8   ibid., pp. 196–7.
9   *The Windsor Tapestry,* Compton
    Mackenzie, p. 148.
10 *The Times,* 1 September 1919.
11 *The Times,* 4 September 1919.
12 *Down Under With the Prince*
    (Everard Cotes, Methuen, 1921),
    p. 245.

13 Quoted in *A King's Story,* Duke of
    Windsor, op. cit., pp. 143–4.
14 *New York Tribune,* 19 November
    1919.
15 *New York World,* 19 November
    1919.
16 *Queen Alexandra,* Battiscombe, p.
    286.

    7 NEW ZEALAND AND AUSTRALIA
1   *The Times,* 3 March 1920.
2   *Lloyd George, A Diary,* Frances
    Stevenson. Edited by A. J. P.
    Taylor (Hutchinson, 1971), pp.
    198–9.
3   ibid., pp. 200–1
4   ibid., pp. 205–6.
5   ibid., p. 222
6   *The Times,* 26 June 1920.
7   *The Times,* 26 May 1920.
8   *The Life and Times of Lord
    Mountbatten,* John Terraine
    (Hutchinson, 1968), p. 35.
9   ibid., p. 38.
10 *A King's Story,* Duke of Windsor,
    p. 160.

    8 INDIA
1   *India Office Records: Reading
    Collection:* 238/1, 18 July 1921 and
    4 October 1921.
2   *The Times,* 10 July 1921.
3   *King George V,* Nicholson.
4   *India Office Records,* loc. cit., 238/10,
    21 April 1921.
5   ibid., 238/10, 3 June 1921.
6   ibid., 238/3, 12 August 1921,
    Letter from Lord Cromer to
    Viceroy's Secretary.
7   *The History of the Indian Tour of
    H.R.H. the Prince of Wales 1921/2.*
    L. F. Rushbrook Williams, *India
    Office Records: Reading Collection:*
    238/34.
8   Quoted in *A Family Album,* Duke
    of Windsor, p. 184.
9   Quoted in *A Family Album,* Duke
    of Windsor, p. 184.

10 Quoted in *A Family Album*, Duke of Windsor, p. 185.

11 *A King's Story*, Duke of Windsor, pp. 171–2.

12 *India Office Records*, loc. cit., 238/24, 9 January 1922.

13 ibid., 238/1, 23 February 1922.

14 ibid., 238/4, 23 February 1922.

15 ibid., 238/24, 6 March 1922.

16 ibid., 238/1, 24 November 1921.

17 ibid., 238/4, 23 February 1922.

18 *The Times*, 8 April 1922.

19 *Memoirs*, Sir Almeric Fitzroy, Vol. 2 (Hutchinson, 1926), p. 780.

20 *The Times*, 22 June 1922.

21 *Loyal to Three Kings*, Helen Hardinge (William Kimber, 1967), pp. 68–9.

22 *The Reign of Edward the Eighth*, Robert Sencourt (Anthony Gibbs and Phillips, 1962), p. 33.

9 THE PRINCE AT HOME

1 *Kenneth Harris Talking To* (Weidenfeld & Nicolson, 1971), pp. 140–1.

2 Hardinge Papers.

3 *King George VI*, Wheeler-Bennett, p. 154.

4 *Lloyd George, A Diary*, Frances Stevenson, p. 208.

5 *Whitehall Diary*, Thomas Jones (Oxford University Press, 1969). Edited by Keith Middlemas, Vol. 2, p. 162.

6 *A King's Story*, Duke of Windsor, pp. 188–9.

7 *Encounters with the Windsors*, Sir John Balfour.

8 *The Green Hat*, Michael Arlen (Heinemann, 1924), pp. 110–11.

9 *Lily Christine*, Michael Arlen (Hutchings, 1929), pp. 94–5.

10 *Exiles*, Michael Arlen (André Deutsch, 1971), pp. 70–1.

11 *Loyal to Three Kings*, Helen Hardinge, p. 71.

12 *Working Partnership*, Katherine, Duchess of Atholl (Arthur Barker, 1958), p. 129.

13 *My Life of Revolt*, David Kirkwood (Harrap, 1935), p. 260.

14 *The Crown and the Establishment*, Kingsley Martin (Hutchinson, 1962), p. 87.

15 *Memoirs of a Conservative*, J.C.C. Davidson's Memoirs & Papers, 1910–37, Robert Rhodes James (Weidenfeld & Nicolson, 1969), p. 19.

16 Helen Hardinge, op. cit., p. 68.

17 *King George V*, Nicolson, p. 121.

18 Helen Hardinge, op. cit., p. 32.

19 *Journals and Letters*, Esher, Vol. 4, p. 303.

20 *The Windsor Tapestry*, Compton Mackenzie, Author's Note, p. vii.

21 ibid., pp. 212–13.

22 *Memoirs*, Sir Almeric Fitzroy, Vol. 2, pp. 802–3.

23 *Max in Verse*, collected and annotated by J.G. Riewald (Heinemann, 1964).

24 *King George VI*, Wheeler-Bennett, p. 233.

25 ibid., p. 294.

26 Duke of Windsor, op. cit., p. 218.

27 *Edward VIII*, Hector Bolitho, p. 74.

28 Quoted in *A King's Story*, Duke of Windsor, p. 215.

10 ABROAD

1 *New York Times*, 1 September 1924.

2 *New York Herald Tribune*, 2 September 1924.

3 *New York Times*, 2 September 1924.

4 *A King's Story*, Duke of Windsor, p. 199.

5 *New York Times*, 5 September 1924.

6 *New York Times*, 7 September 1924.

7 *New York Times*, 7 September 1924.

8 *New York Herald Tribune*, 7 September 1924.

9 *New York Herald Tribune*, 11 September 1924.

10 *Chicago Tribune*, 13 September 1924.

11 *Through South Africa with the Prince*, G. Ward Price (Gill Publishing Co., 1926), p. 239.

12 *Certain People of Importance*, A. G. Gardiner (Jonathan Cape, 1926), pp. 77–9.

11 NO DOUBT OF THE YOUNG MAN'S CAPACITY FOR GOODNESS

1 *Voluntary Social Action*, Marjorie Brasnett (National Council of Social Services, 1969), p. 76.

2 *British Legion Magazine*, January 1933.

3 *Baldwin*, Middlemas and Barnes (Weidenfeld & Nicolson, 1969), p. 977.

4 ibid., p. 976.

5 *Some Memories*, Eustace Percy (Eyre & Spottiswoode, 1958), pp. 131–2.

6 *The Times*, 29 September 1928.

7 *An Unpublished Page of History*, Monica Baldwin's Diary, 1937.

8 *The Light of Common Day*, Diana Cooper (Rupert Hart-Davis, 1959), p. 161.

9 *The Heart Has Its Reasons*, Duchess of Windsor, p. 182.

10 *Double Exposure*, Gloria Vanderbilt and Thelma Lady Furness (Frederick Muller, 1959), pp. 274–275.

11 *Previous Convictions*, Cyril Connolly (Hamish Hamilton, 1963), p. 399.

12 *Nancy Astor*, Maurice Collis (Faber & Faber, 1960), pp. 176–7.

13 Duchess of Windsor, op. cit., p. 175.

12 WALLIS WARFIELD

1 *The Heart Has Its Reasons*, Duchess of Windsor, p. 243.

2 ibid., p. 20.

3 ibid., p. 21.

4 ibid., p. 27.

5 *A Paris Surgeon's Story*, Dr Charles F. Bove (Little, Brown, 1956), p. 168.

6 Duchess of Windsor, op. cit., p. 29.

7 ibid., p. 50.

8 ibid., p. 13.

9 ibid., p. 81.

10 *Edward the Eighth*, Sencourt, p. 38.

11 Duchess of Windsor, op. cit., p. 83.

12 ibid., pp. 90–91.

13 ibid., pp. 94–5.

14 ibid., p. 98.

15 ibid., p. 101.

16 ibid., pp. 108–9.

17 ibid., p. 118.

18 ibid., p. 120.

19 ibid., p. 124.

20 ibid., p. 125.

21 ibid., pp. 147–8.

22 ibid., p. 181.

23 ibid., p. 192.

24 ibid., p. 194.

13 MRS SIMPSON

1 *Chips*, The Diaries of Sir Henry Channon. Edited by Robert Rhodes James (Weidenfeld and Nicolson, 1967), p. 22.

2 *Double Exposure*, Gloria Vanderbilt and Thelma Furness, p. 274.

3 Channon, op. cit., p. 30.

4 ibid., p. 23.

5 ibid., p. 51.

6 ibid., p. 58.

7 *The Heart Has Its Reasons*, Duchess of Windsor, p. 30.

8 ibid., p. 135.

9 ibid., p. 95.

10 *A Family Album*, Duke of Windsor, p. 103.

11 *Encounters with the Windsors*, Balfour.

12 *Editorial*, Colin Coote (Eyre and Spottiswoode, 1965), p. 163.
13 *Nine Troubled Years*, Lord Templewood (Collins, 1954), p. 216.
14 *The Abdication of King Edward VIII*, Lord Beaverbrook (Hamish Hamilton, 1966), pp. 34–5.
15 Channon, op. cit., p. 51.
16 ibid., p. 33.
17 ibid., pp. 34–5.
18 ibid., p. 60.
19 ibid., p. 76.
20 *Diaries and Letters*, 1930–39, Nicolson, p. 238.
21 Channon, op. cit., p. 43.
22 ibid., p. 68.
23 ibid., p. 77.
24 ibid., p. 73.
25 ibid., p. 85.
26 *Diaries and Letters of Marie Belloc Lowndes* (Chatto and Windus, 1971), pp. 144–6.
27 ibid., p. 142.
28 ibid., p. 145.
29 ibid., p. 147.
30 *Abdication*, Inglis, p. 38.
31 *Diaries and Letters*, 1930–39, Nicolson, p. 238.
32 *Great Morning*, Osbert Sitwell (Macmillan, 1948), pp. 251–2.
33 Duchess of Windsor, op. cit., p. 201.
34 ibid., p. 202.
35 Monckton Papers.
36 ibid.
37 *Baldwin, The Unexpected Prime Minister*, H. Montgomery Hyde (Hart-Davis, MacGibbon, 1973), pp. 419–20.
38 Duchess of Windsor, op. cit., p. 211.
39 *The Light of Common Day*, Diana Cooper, pp. 161–2.
40 *Baldwin*, Middlemas and Barnes, p. 976.
41 *Thatched with Gold*, Countess of Airlie, p. 197.

14 KING EDWARD
1 *Loyal to Three Kings*, Helen Hardinge, p. 61.
2 *A Diary with Letters*, T. Jones, p. 166.
3 *As It Happened*, C. R. Attlee (Heinemann, 1954), p. 85.
4 T. Jones, op. cit., p. 166.
5 ibid., p. 162.
6 ibid., pp. 163–4.
7 ibid., pp. 167–8.
8 *Diaries and Letters*, 1930–39, Nicolson, p. 247.
9 Hardinge Papers.
10 *Chips*, The Diaries of Sir Henry Channon, p. 46.
11 ibid., p. 166.
12 'The King's Secretary', Harold Laski (*Fortnightly Review*, July–December 1942).
13 ibid.
14 Hardinge Papers.
15 *George VI*, Wheeler-Bennett, p. 273.
16 *A King's Story*, Duke of Windsor, p. 280.
17 ibid., p. 281.
18 Channon, op. cit., p. 76.
19 *The Light of Common Day*, Diana Cooper, p. 163.

15 THE KING AND NAZI GERMANY
1 *Baldwin*, Middlemas and Barnes, p. 979.
2 *Baffy*, The Diaries of Blanche Dugdale, 1936–37 (Valentine, Mitchell, 1973), p. 34.
3 *The Light of Common Day*, Diana Cooper, pp. 149–50.
4 *Documents on German Foreign Policy*, Series C, Vol. IV, 1506/E37133–35.
5 *The Morning Post*, 13 June 1935.
6 *German Documents*, loc. cit., HO 32069–70.
7 *Chips*, The Diaries of Sir Henry Channon, p. 356.
8 *Diaries and Letters*, 1930–39, Nicolson, p. 232.

9 *German Documents*, loc. cit., 7620/E544964–69.
10 ibid., 5482/E382057–78.
11 *A King's Story*, Duke of Windsor, pp. 296–7.
12 *Old Men Forget*, Duff Cooper (Rupert Hart-Davis, 1953), p. 202.
13 Channon, op. cit., p. 84.
14 *Hitler and the English*, Fritz Hesse, edited and translated by F. A. Voigt (Allen Wingate, 1954), pp. 21–3.
15 *Documents on German Foreign Policy*, Series C, Vol. V, 6710/E506679.
16 ibid., 7609/E544945.
17 ibid., 8015/E576522–4.
18 *The Ribbentrop Memoirs* (Weidenfeld and Nicolson, 1954), pp. 76–7.
19 *Documents on German Foreign Policy*, Series D, Vol. 1, FI 0339.
20 *The Fateful Years*, 1931–45, Hugh Dalton (Frederick Muller, 1937), p. 112.
21 *A Diary with Letters*, T. Jones, p. 288.

16 THE NAHLIN
1 Monckton Papers.
2 ibid.
3 ibid.
4 ibid.
5 *The Heart Has Its Reasons*, Duchess of Windsor, p. 225.
6 ibid., p. 233.
7 Monckton Papers.
8 Duchess of Windsor, op. cit., p. 230.
9 *The Light of Common Day*, Diana Cooper, p. 178.
10 Duchess of Windsor, op. cit., p. 238.
11 *Chips*, The Diaries of Sir Henry Channon, p. 79.
12 *Baldwin*, Middlemas & Barnes, p. 982.
13 Monckton Papers.

17 THE DIVORCE
1 *The Times*, 29 November 1955.

2 *A Diary with Letters*, T. Jones, p. 267.
3 ibid., p. 233.
4 *Baldwin, The Unexpected Prime Minister*, H. Montgomery Hyde, p. 447.
5 Monckton Papers.
6 *The Abdication of King Edward VIII*, Beaverbrook, p. 117.
7 ibid., p. 30.
8 ibid., pp. 32–3.
9 ibid., p. 24.
10 *An Unpublished Page of History*, Monica Baldwin.
11 *Cosmo Gordon Lang*, J. G. Lockhart (Hodder and Stoughton, 1949), p. 398.
12 ibid., p. 399.
13 *Loyal to Three Kings*, Helen Hardinge, p. 117.
14 *A King's Story*, Duke of Windsor, p. 317.
15 *Diaries and Letters*, 1930–39, Nicolson, p. 282.
16 *Parliamentary Debates*, Commons, Fifth Series, 1936–7, Vol. 318, 10 December 1936.
17 Beaverbrook, op. cit., p. 47.
18 *Abdication*, Inglis, p. 197.
19 T. Jones, op. cit., p. 277.
20 Inglis, op. cit., pp. 197–8.
21 *Geoffrey Dawson and Our Times*, John Evelyn Wrench (Hutchinson, 1955), pp. 339–42.
22 T. Jones, op. cit., p. 289.

18 THE LETTER
1 *Chips*, The Diaries of Sir Henry Channon, p. 74.
2 *Diaries and Letters*, 1930–39, Nicolson, p. 277.
3 *The Times*, 4 November 1936.
4 *Abdication*, Inglis, p. 207.
5 *Nine Troubled Years*, Templewood, pp. 218–19.
6 *The Times*, 29 November 1955.
7 *A King's Story*, Duke of Windsor, p. 327.

8 *Baldwin*, Middlemas and Barnes, p. 986.
9 *Men and Work*, Lord Citrine (Hutchinson, 1964), p. 327.
10 Middlemas and Barnes, op. cit., p. 988.
11 ibid., p. 988.
12 Buchan Papers, Queen's University Archives, Kingston, Ontario.
13 Middlemas and Barnes, op. cit., p. 991.
14 ibid., pp. 991–2.

19 'SOMETHING MUST BE DONE'
1 *A Diary with Letters*, T. Jones, p. 286.
2 *Chips*, The Diary of Sir Henry Channon, p. 80.
3 *Diaries and Letters*, 1930–39, Nicolson, p. 279.
4 Monckton Papers.
5 ibid.
6 ibid.
7 *Walter Monckton*, Lord Birkenhead (Weidenfeld and Nicolson, 1969), p. 126.
8 *Baldwin, The Unexpected Prime Minister*, H. Montgomery Hyde, p. 464.
9 *A King's Story*, Duke of Windsor, p. 329.
10 *The Heart Has Its Reasons*, Duchess of Windsor, p. 246.
11 Monckton Papers.
12 *The Abdication of King Edward VIII*, Beaverbrook, p. 38.
13 *Baldwin*, Middlemas and Barnes, p. 994.
14 *Parliamentary Debates*, Commons, Fifth Series, 1936–7, Vol. 318, 10 December 1936.
15 Middlemas and Barnes, op. cit., p. 995.
16 H. Montgomery Hyde, op. cit., p. 468.
17 Middlemas and Barnes, op. cit., p. 995.
18 Duke of Windsor, op. cit., p. 332.
19 *Queen Mary*, Pope-Hennessy, p. 575.
20 *An Unpublished Page of History*, Monica Baldwin.
21 Pope-Hennessy, op. cit., p. 573.
22 ibid., p. 582.
23 ibid., p. 576.
24 Duke of Windsor, op. cit., p. 335.
25 *An Unpublished Page of History*, Monica Baldwin.
26 *Old Men Forget*, A. Duff Cooper (Rupert Hart-Davis), p. 201.
27 Duke of Windsor, op. cit., p. 340.
28 *Parliamentary Debates*, Commons, Fifth Series, 1936–8, Vol. 318. 17 November 1936
29 *Geoffrey Dawson and Our Times*, p. 345.
30 ibid., p. 344.
31 Hardinge Papers.
32 *The Times*.
33 Channon, op. cit., p. 105.

20 THE MORGANATIC MARRIAGE PROPOSAL
1 *Baldwin, The Unexpected Prime Minister* H. Montgomery Hyde, p. 470.
2 Broadcast Review of *A History of The Times*, Beaverbrook, 25 May 1952.
3 *A King's Story*, Duke of Windsor, p. 341.
4 *An Unpublished Page of History*, Monica Baldwin.
5 *Chips*, the Diaries of Sir Henry Channon, p. 110.
6 *The Abdication of King Edward VIII*, Beaverbrook, pp. 50–1.
7 ibid., pp. 54–7.
8 *A Diary with Letters*, T. Jones, p. 288.
9 *Neville Chamberlain*, Iain Macleod (Frederick Muller, 1961), p. 197.
10 H. Montgomery Hyde, op. cit., p. 568.
11 *The Times*, 8 December 1936.

12 *Baldwin*, Middlemas and Barnes, p. 999.
13 T. Jones, op. cit., p. 288.
14 H. Montgomery Hyde, op. cit., p. 477.
15 *The Eden Memoirs, Facing the Dictators* (Cassell, 1962), p. 410.
16 *Abdication*, Inglis, p. 273.
17 H. Montgomery Hyde, op. cit., p. 478.
18 *As It Happened*, C. R. Attlee, p. 86.
19 Inglis, op. cit., p. 278.

21 THE PRESS BREAKS SILENCE
1 *Daily Telegraph*, 8 December 1936.
2 *The Heart Has Its Reasons*, Duchess of Windsor, p. 251.
3 *Baldwin*, Middlemas and Barnes, p. 1005.
4 *Baldwin, The Unexpected Prime Minister*, H. Montgomery Hyde, p. 481.
5 *Chips*, The Diaries of Sir Henry Channon, p. 77.
6 *Geoffrey Dawson and Our Times*, Wrench, p. 349.
7 *Diaries and Letters*, 1930–39, Nicolson, p. 275.
8 Middlemas and Barnes, op. cit., p. 1004.
9 *Memoirs of a Conservative*, J.C.C. Davidson, pp. 414–15.
10 Duchess of Windsor, op. cit., p. 255.
11 ibid., pp. 259–60.

22 A KING'S PARTY?
1 *A King's Story*, Duke of Windsor, p. 361.
2 *Baldwin*, G.M.Young, pp. 239–40.
3 *The Abdication of Edward VIII*, Beaverbrook, p. 71.
4 *Queen Mary*, Pope-Hennessy, p. 578.
5 Sir Edward Peacock's Notes.
6 Beaverbrook, op. cit., p. 74.

7 *Baldwin, The Unexpected Prime Minister*, H. Montgomery Hyde, p. 475.
8 Beaverbrook, op. cit., p. 42.
9 Sir Edward Peacock's Notes.
10 Monckton Papers.
11 *Diaries and Letters*, 1930–9, Nicolson, pp. 281–2.
12 *Chips*, The Diaries of Sir Henry Channon, p. 90.
13 ibid., p. 92.
14 *A Diary with Letters*, T. Jones, p.290.
15 Duke of Windsor, op. cit., p. 374.
16 *Baldwin*, Middlemas & Barnes, p. 1009.
17 ibid., p. 1007.
18 *Parliamentary Debates*, Commons Fifth Series, 1936–7, Vol. 318, 3 December 1936.
19 ibid., 4 December 1936.
20 Duke of Windsor, op. cit., p. 379.
21 H. Montgomery Hyde, op. cit., p. 489.
22 Monckton Papers.
23 Sir Edward Peacock's Notes.
24 Monckton Papers.
25 Sir Edward Peacock's Notes.
26 Baldwin Papers, cited Middlemas and Barnes, pp. 1009–10.
27 Monckton Papers, cited Birkenhead, p. 142.
28 *The Abdication of Edward VIII*, Beaverbrook, p. 77.
29 ibid., p. 78.
30 *Memoirs of a Conservative*, J.C.C. Davidson, p. 415.
31 Beaverbrook, op. cit., p. 80.

23 THE LAST DAYS
1 *Baffy*, The Diaries of Blanche Dugdale, 1936–47 (Valentine Mitchell, 1973), p. 34.
2 ibid., p. 33.
3 Monckton Papers.
4 *Baldwin, The Unexpected Prime Minister*, H. Montgomery Hyde, p. 570.
5 Monckton Papers.

6 *Baldwin*, Middlemas and Barnes, p. 1010.

7 *Neville Chamberlain*, Keith Feiling (Macmillan, 1946), p. 289.

8 *The Heart Has Its Reasons*, Duchess of Windsor, p. 273.

9 ibid., p. 273.

10 *A King's Story*, Duke of Windsor, p. 397.

11 Monckton Papers.

12 Sir Edward Peacock's Notes.

13 *An Unpublished Page of History*, Monica Baldwin.

14 Feiling, op. cit., p. 288.

15 *Baldwin*, G. M. Young, p. 243.

16 Duke of Windsor, op. cit., p. 401.

17 Sir Edward Peacock's Notes.

18 Monckton Papers.

19 ibid.

20 *George VI*, Wheeler-Bennett, p. 286.

21 Middlemas and Barnes, op. cit., p. 1013.

22 ibid., p. 1013.

23 Sir Edward Peacock's Notes.

24 Monckton Papers.

25 Wheeler-Bennett, op. cit., p. 286.

26 *Walter Monckton*, Birkenhead, p. 150.

27 *Diaries and Letters*, 1930–39, Nicolson, pp. 285–6.

28 Duke of Windsor, op. cit., p. 408.

29 Monckton Papers.

30 Sir Edward Peacock's Notes.

31 Wheeler-Bennett, op. cit., p. 287.

32 Monckton Papers.

33 Wheeler-Bennett, op. cit., p. 294.

34 ibid., p. 295.

24 AFTER THE ABDICATION

1 *Walter Monckton*, Birkenhead, p. 155.

2 *Cosmo Gordon Lang*, Lockhart, pp. 404–5.

3 *A Diary with Letters*, T. Jones, p. 309.

4 *The Heart Has Its Reasons*, Duchess of Windsor, p. 300.

5 *King Edward the Seventh*, Magnus, p. 285.

6 *Baffy*, The Diaries of Blanche Dugdale, p. 34.

7 *Editorial*, Colin Coote, p. 163.

8 Monckton Papers.

9 *The Times*, 24 December 1965.

25 SCHLOSS ENZESFELD

1 Monckton Papers.

2 *Der Mann der Feldherr Werden Wollter*, Fritz Wiedemann (Velbert, 1964), p. 152.

3 *New York Daily News*, 11 December 1966.

4 Monckton Papers.

26 THE WEDDING

1 *New Yorker*, Profile, 22 September 1945.

2 *The Heart Has Its Reasons*, Duchess of Windsor, p. 295.

3 *The Wandering Years*, Cecil Beaton Weidenfeld and Nicolson, 1961), p. 306.

4 ibid., p. 309.

5 *Baldwin*, Middlemas and Barnes, pp. 1015–16.

6 Monckton Papers.

7 *The Times*, 20 July 1972.

8 Duchess of Windsor, op. cit., p. 289.

27 THE DUKE OF WINDSOR VISITS GERMANY

1 Monckton Papers.

2 ibid.

3 *New Yorker*, Profile, 22 September 1945.

4 ibid.

5 ibid.

6 *She Might Have Been Queen*, Geoffrey Bocca (Express Books, 1955), p. 176.

7 *My Life With Göring*, Emmy Göring (David Bruce and Watson, 1972), pp. 88–9.

8 *Hitler's Interpreter*. Edited by R.H.C.Steed (Heinemann, 1951), p. 75.

9 *Forward*, 13 November 1937.

10 *New Yorker*, Profile, 22 September 1945.

28 MARRIED LIFE

1 *Diaries and Letters*, 1930–39, Harold Nicolson, pp. 351–2.

2 *Working for the Windsors*, Diana Hood, pp. 35–6.

3 ibid., p. 114.

4 *Walter Monckton*, Birkenhead, p. 166.

5 Monckton Papers.

6 ibid.

7 *Lloyd George, A Diary*, Frances Stevenson, p. 327.

8 *My Life and Times*, Octave 7, 1931–1938, Compton Mackenzie (Chatto & Windus, 1968), p. 231.

9 *Daily Express*, 9 May 1939.

10 Hood, op. cit., p. 143.

29 THE WAR

1 *Walter Monckton*, Birkenhead, p. 171.

2 *The Private Papers of Hore-Belisha*. Edited by R.J.Minney (Collins, 1960), pp. 236–9.

3 War Office, 106/1678.

4 *The Diplomatic Diaries of Oliver Harvey*, 1937–1940. Edited by John Harvey (Collins, 1970), p. 328.

5 *The Heart Has Its Reasons*, Duchess of Windsor, p. 329.

30 ENCOUNTER WITH THE GERMANS

1 *The Heart Has Its Reasons*, Duchess of Windsor, p. 335.

2 Foreign Office Series 371, 24249, Nos. 136/7.

3 German Documents on Foreign Policy, Series D, Vol. VIII, 124/122667–68.

4 *Parliamentary Debates*, Commons, Fifth Series, Vol. 533, 1953–4, cols. 215–16.

5 *Schellenberg Memoirs*, pp. 11–18.

6 ibid., p. 18.

7 ibid., pp. 129–30.

8 ibid., p. 130.

9 German Documents of Foreign Policy, Series D, Vol. X, B15/B002531.

10 ibid., 136/74207.

11 Foreign Relations of the United States 1940, Vol. III, 1939/4357, p. 41.

12 German Documents, loc. cit., B15/B002549–51.

13 ibid., B15/B002549–51.

14 Duchess of Windsor, op. cit., pp. 340–1.

15 German Documents, loc. cit., B15/B002562.

16 ibid., B15/B002582–3.

17 ibid., B15/B002588.

18 ibid., B15/B002585.

19 ibid., B15/B002536.

20 ibid., B002563.

21 ibid., B002603.

22 Foreign Office Series, loc. cit., No. 136.

23 ibid., No. 149.

24 ibid., No. 152.

25 ibid., No. 159.

26 ibid., No. 160.

27 ibid., No. 150.

28 ibid., No. 151.

29 ibid., No. 152.

30 ibid., No. 155.

31 ibid., No. 161.

32 ibid., No. 164.

33 ibid., No. 170.

34 ibid., No. 173.

35 ibid., No. 176.

36 German Documents, loc. cit., B15/B002635.

37 *Schellenberg Memoirs*, p. 138.

38 German Documents, loc. cit., B15/B002610.
39 Monckton Papers.
40 ibid., p. 180.
41 *Walter Monckton*, Birkenhead, p. 181.
42 German Documents, loc. cit., B15/B002619–20.
43 ibid., B15/B002617–8.
44 ibid., B15/B002632–3.
45 ibid., B15/B002641–2.
46 ibid., B15/B002655, published as footnote to B15/B002632–3.
47 German Documents on Foreign Policy, No. 1862, Vol. V, 8, 108869.
48 *Encounters with the Windsors*, Balfour.

31 THE BAHAMAS
1 *Baldwin*, Middlemas and Barnes, p. 1016.
2 *The Abdication of King Edward VIII*, Beaverbrook, p. 109.
3 FO 371 24249, No. 192.
4 FO 371 24249, No. 193.
5 FO 371 24249, No. 194.
6 *Encounters with the Windsors*, Balfour.
7 *A History of the Bahamas*, Michael Craton (Collins, 1962), p. 273.
8 *Tribune Story*, Sir Etienne Dupuch (Ernest Benn), 1967, p. 157.
9 ibid., p. 88.
10 Craton, op. cit., p. 275.
11 Dupuch, op. cit., p. 88.
12 *The Murder of Sir Harry Oakes Bt.* (published by the *Nassau Daily Tribune*, 1959), p. 8.

13 ibid., pp. 304–5.
14 ibid., p. 439.
15 Dupuch, op. cit., p. 87.
16 *King's X*, Marshall Houts (William Morrow, 1972), p. 71.
17 *The Heart Has Its Reasons*, Duchess of Windsor, p. 355.
18 ibid., p. 357.
19 Dupuch, op. cit., p. 93.

32 THE EXILE
1 *The Times*, 15 September 1945.
2 The *New York Daily News*, 11–16 December 1966.
3 *The Heart Has Its Reasons*, Duchess of Windsor, p. 363.
4 The *Sunday Despatch*, 12 March 1939.
5 *The Sunday Times*, 4 June 1972.
6 *The Times Literary Supplement*, 28 September 1951.
7 *New Statesman*, 29 September 1951.
8 The *Spectator*, 28 September 1951.
9 *The Times*, 13 October 1960.
10 *New Statesman*, 29 September 1956.
11 The *Spectator*, 5 October 1956.
12 The *New York Daily News*, 11–16 December 1966.
13 The *Daily Telegraph*, 1 August 1957.
14 The *Daily Express*, 1 August 1957.
15 *Kenneth Harris Talking To*, p. 128.

33 THE HOMECOMING
1 The *Daily Telegraph*, 29 May 1972.
2 ibid, 30 May 1972.
3 ibid., 30 May 1972.

INDEX

Dilke, Sir Charles—*cont.*
  advances republican views during Queen
    Victoria's retirement, 67
Dixon, Lady, 335
Dodds, Major, British Consul at Nice (1940),
  358
Dominions:
  reports from Governors-General of, go
    direct to King, 183;
  proposals on E.'s marriage submitted to,
    259, 261–2;
  Lord Beaverbrook on wording of cables to,
    267;
  'would not stand W. as Queen', 276;
  and question of title of HRH for W., 323
Drummond, Captain, of Pytchley Hunt, 75
Dubrovnik, exuberant welcome to E. and W.
  in (1936), 213
Dudley, 3rd Earl:
  (as Lord Ednam) marries Lady Rosemary
    Leveson-Gower (1919), 57;
  entertains Windsors on Riviera, 344;
  Windsors stay with, at Ednam Lodge, 392
Dudley Ward, Angela (Lady Laycock), 115,
  142, 159–60
Dudley Ward, William, M.P., Liberal Whip,
  57, 109
Dudley Ward, Mrs:
  E. and daughters of, 14, 109;
  E. and, 57–60, 61, 108–9;
  advises E. on his houses, 63, 139;
  on E. as 'very spoilt', 115;
  organizes Feathers Clubs, 134, 163;
  E. ceases to meet, 159, 160
Dugdale, Blanche, 191n;
  on Churchill's championship of E., 282;
  on unlikelihood of formation of King's
    Party, 283
Dugdale, Thomas (Lord Crathorne) 283, 288, 304
Duke of Beaufort's Hunt, 138
Duncan, Patrick, appointed Governor-
  General of South Africa, 257
Dundas, Sir Charles, Governor of Bahamas
  before E., 381
Duprès, Marcel, organist at wedding, 325
Dupuch, Sir Etienne, proprietor and editor of
  daily newspaper in Bahamas:
  E. quarrels with, 383–4;
  E. vetoes appointments suggested by,
    385–6;
  sends news of Oakes' murder to world
    press before E. imposes censorship, 386;
  dodges E.'s censorship on news of his
    departure, 390
Dyer, General, 85n

East Africa, E.'s semi-private tour in (1928),
  136–7
Easton Grey, house taken by E. for hunting,
  138
Eden, Anthony (Earl of Avon):
  as Lord Privy Seal, at Fort Belvedere, 172;
  on proposed contact between British
    Legion and Germans, 195–6);
  meets Duke of Coburg, 198n;
  as Foreign Secretary, is asked by Baldwin

'not to trouble him too much with
  foreign affairs' during Abdication crisis,
  218
Edinburgh, Prince Philip, Duke of, 403, 407
Edward VII:
  as Prince of Wales (1841–1901):
    at Oxford and Cambridge, 38;
    gives York Cottage to Duke of York
      (George v), 5;
    as parent, 9;
    his interest in clothes, 43–4;
    regrets being denied active service, 53;
    and affairs of state, 119
  as King (1901–10), 6n, 19:
    as grandparent, 15–16;
    as host, 20–1;
    and Mrs Keppel, 22–4, 33;
    at Covent Garden Opera House, 32–3;
    at centre of 'the establishment', 99;
    almost ceases to give formal audiences to
      ministers, 300;
    death and funeral of, 33–4
Edward VIII:
  as Prince Edward of York (1894–1901):
    birth and naming of, 6;
    nurse in charge of, 8
  as Prince Edward of Wales (1901–10):
    his relations with his father – as a child,
      8–12; as a schoolboy, 26–7, 30, 31, 34;
    his relations with his grandfather, 15–16,
      32–3;
    education of, 16, 18–19, 100;
    at Sandringham House, 21–2;
    at Naval Colleges, 26–9, 100;
    at death and funeral of Edward VII, 33–4;
    becomes Duke of Cornwall, 34; returns
      silver oar to Dartmouth from Duchy of
      Cornwall, 35
  as Prince of Wales (1910–36):
    given Order of the Garter, 36;
    at George v's Coronation, 35–6;
    his Investiture at Caernarvon, 36–7;
    serves as midshipman in HMS *Hindustan*,
      37;
    at Sandringham (winter 1911–12), 40;
    in Paris to learn French (1912), 40–1;
    at Oxford, 38–9, 42, 44–5, 46–8, 115;
    his relations with his father, as young
      man, 40, 46, 49, 60–1, 66–7;
    distrusts his father's friends, 43, 101;
    in Germany (1913), 45–6;
    at OTC camp (1914), 49;
    enters London social life, 49;
    pleads to go on active service, 50; in
      France, (1914–17) 50–4; (1918), 54–5;
      in Middle East (1916), 54; in Italy
      (1917–18), 54;
    and ex-servicemen, 55, 71, 122–3 (*see also*
      British Legion);
    appoints staff, and moves into York
      House (1919), 63;
    public duties of, in Britain, 64–6, 75, 84;
    as Duke of Cornwall, and landlord in
      Kennington, 64, 65;
    tours Canada (1919), 67, 69–72; in USA,
      72–3;

Edward VIII—*cont.*

    proposed in anonymous letter from
      Briton in USA, 231;

    Stanley Bruce says is only possibility, if
      E. marries W., 240–1;

    E. declares his willingness for, 246, 247,
      248;

    legal advice on, 246;

    public attitude to, 265;

    negotiations on financial terms of, 275,
      291–2;

    E. will not be party to constitutional
      crisis over, 279;

    E. formally announces his intention on,
      280, 282;

    Baldwin and others dine with E. after
      announcement, 287–9;

    announcement confirmed, 290;

    arrangements for instrument of, 290;
      Instrument signed by E., and wit-
      nessed by his brothers, 290–1;

    reactions of friends and public to, 296,
      297, 299;

    Archbishop of Canterbury broadcasts on,
      297–8;

    Windsors continually discuss, but finally
      agree not to mention, 300;

    Churchill changes his mind about, 378;

    Windsors' writings ensure publication of
      details about, 401

as Duke of Windsor (1936–72):

    question of rank and titles of, settled by
      George VI,, 293–4;

    prepares farewell broadcast; shows it to
      Churchill, 293;

    broadcasts from Windsor Castle
      (announced as HRH Prince Edward),
      294–5;

    farewells to, 295–6; leaves from
      Portsmouth, 296;

    at Schloss Enzesfeld; telephones daily to
      W., 309;

    Metcalfe's letters about, 310–16;

    masses of letters arrive for, 310, 312, 315,
      316;

    difficulties between George VI and, 316–
      317;

    choice of place for wedding, 319–20;
      cleric offers to officiate, 320–1;

    bitter about decision against title of HRH
      før W., 322–5, 335, 336, 339–40;

    wedding (4 June 1937), 325–6;

    spends summer at Wasserleonburg,
      327–8;

    visits Germany (1937), 330–2;

    decorating and furnishing of houses by
      W. and, 336–7;

    question of return of, to England, 341;

    public appearances of, 341–3;

    at La Croë, 343–4;

    at outbreak of war (1939), 346–9; ques-
      tion of appointment for, 349–51; in
      Paris, attached to army (1939–40),
      352–6;

    to Biarritz, and La Croë (1940), 357–8;

leaves in consular convoy for Spain, and
    then Portugal, 358;

makes conditions for returning to
    England, 359, 366;

German efforts to make use of, 360–8;

appointed Governor of Bahamas, 360,
    364, 402;

and his soldier servant, 369–70, 376;

in Bermuda, 379–81;

arrives in Bahamas, 381; Government
    House has to be repaired, 381, 382;
    work of, in Bahamas, 382–3, 385; and
    colour question in Bahamas, 384–5;
    imposes censorship about riots, 385;
    actions of, on Oakes' murder, 386,
    387, 388–9; resigns Governorship of
    Bahamas (1945); declines that of
    Bermuda, 390, 391;

in USA, 391;

returns to France, 391;

visits London; suggests himself as
    specialist in Anglo-American relations,
    392;

question of work for, 393–4;

golf, gardening and money, as interests
    of, 396;

takes up writing, 397;

operations on, 404;

in last illness, visited by Queen Elizabeth
    II, 407;

death of (28 May 1972), 407; funeral of,
    408–11

descriptions of:

by Lord Esher, 19–20, 34–5, 41–2, 50, 52,
    113, 114; by Sir Compton Mackenzie,
    41, 70; by fellow undergraduate, 46–7;
    by Sir Herbert Warren, 47; by Oliver
    Lyttelton, 51–2; by Rev. Tubby
    Clayton, 55, 122; by Lady Cynthia
    Asquith; 58–9; by *The Times* corre-
    spondents, 71, 76, 79, 95, 179; by
    Everard Cotes, 71; by New York
    newspapers, 73, 125–6; by Lord Louis
    Mountbatten, 81; by Lord Reading,
    93; by Lady Hardinge, 95–6, 112, 114;
    by Professor Rushbrook Williams,
    96–7; by Mrs Colin Buist, 110; by
    Duchess of Atholl, 110; by David
    Kirkwood, 110–11; by Lord Davidson,
    111; by Will Rogers, 127; by women
    readers of *Chicago Tribune*, 128; by *The
    Spectator*, 129; by A.G.Gardiner,
    129–30; by Lord Monckton, 168–9,
    216; by Lady Diana Cooper, 172–3,
    189, 213; by Sir Henry Channon, 254;
    by Stanley Baldwin, 302; by Major
    Metcalfe, 310–16, 346–7, 352–6; by
    Sir Harold Nicolson, 336; by Diana
    Wells Hood, 337–8; by naval lieutenant
    in Bermuda, 379–81

personal details about:

called David by his family, 6, 202;

physically courageous, 20, 45, 53;
    energetic, 46, 80, 138;

interested in clothes, 43, 44–5, 83 (*see also
    under* clothes);

THE LIVES OF THE GREAT COMPOSERS
VOLUME ONE

Harold C. Schonberg

Harold Schonberg traces the lives and influences of the great composers and their music with a lively and imaginative tread. Volume One begins with the early masters Bach, Handel and Mozart and covers a host of important figures including Haydn, Beethoven, Chopin, Mendelssohn and Verdi and finishes at the end of the nineteenth century with Brahms and Wolf.

'A delight to the eye, an encouragement to sustained enjoyable reading . . . the like of which we have not had for some time. It is both witty and amusing'
Punch

'It is extremely readable; it is well founded in scholarship and well written'
The Times Literary Supplement

THE LIVES OF THE GREAT COMPOSERS
VOLUME TWO

Harold C. Schonberg

Harold Schonberg traces the lives and influences of
composers and their music in the nineteenth and early
twentieth century. Volume Two begins with the lively
waltzes and polkas of Strauss and Offenbach and covers
a host of major figures including Rimsky-Korsakov,
Tchaikovsky, Grieg, Mahler, Stravinsky, and
Shostakovich, finishing in the 1940's with Schoenberg.

'Panoramic, wittily detailed . . . an important addition
to the reference and handbook library of music . . .
equally pleasing to read from end to end, to dip into
casually, or to consult in pursuit of that specific kernel
that is so much part of the music-lover's experience'
The New York Times Book Review

'Recommended as a wisely planned general history to
be read from cover to cover . . . a valuable guide to the
study of selected composers in greater depth'
The Gramophone

ARNOLD BENNETT

Margaret Drabble

'Margaret Drabble is an ideal biographer'
New Society

In the 1920s Arnold Bennett was a more celebrated
public figure than any other English novelist has been
before or since. When his weekly article on books
appeared in the *Evening Standard* on Thursdays, people
made special trips to buy the early editions of the paper.
When he lay dying in 1931 the police slowed down the
traffic outside his window and muffled the street with
straw. At the Savoy they still serve the special brand of
omelette named after him.

Margaret Drabble's sensitive biography is a brilliant
portrait of the man who rose from humble beginnings
in the Potteries to become the lion of London literary
society, and the enemy of Bloomsbury, immortalising
his native Five Towns at last in his great novels,
CLAYHANGER and THE OLD WIVES' TALE.

'A very fine biography'
The Times

'Warm and exhilarating, extremely enjoyable'
The Guardian

'Excellent'
Times Literary Supplement

MAHLER

Kurt Blaukopf

Mahler: the child prodigy who was composing at the age of four; the musician whose genius anticipated the great era of stereophonic recording; the conductor who revolutionised concert hall and opera house; the man whose symphonies inspired Thomas Mann's DEATH IN VENICE.

Kurt Blaukopf traces the story of Mahler's life and work against its background of the disintegrating Austro-Hungarian Empire, though his relationships with the three women he loved, his battle to win directorship of the Vienna Court Opera to the final breakdown and the crisis of his meeting with Freud a year before his death. An outstanding study of the man whose work is a landmark in twentieth-century music.